Dr. Christian Raetzke (ed.)

Nuclear Law in the EU and Beyond

Atomrecht in Deutschland, der EU und weltweit

Proceedings of the AIDN / INLA Regional Conference 2013 in Leipzig

Nomos

Die Deutsche Nationalbibliothek verzeichnet diese Publikation in der Deutschen Nationalbibliografie; detaillierte bibliografische Daten sind im Internet über http://dnb.d-nb.de abrufbar.

Die Deutsche Nationalbibliothek lists this publication in the Deutsche Nationalbibliografie; detailed bibliographic data is available in the Internet at http://dnb.d-nb.de.

ISBN 978-3-8487-1151-2

1. Auflage 2014

Contents / Inhaltsverzeichnis

Preface 11

Vorwort 15

Keynote Session

Nuclear Law in the EU

From Challenge to Response: Dormant Powers in Euratom Law
Jürgen Grunwald 21

Towards an Enhanced EU Regulatory Framework for Nuclear Safety – The Envisaged Commission Proposal for an Amendment of Directive 2009/71/EURATOM Establishing a Community Framework for the Nuclear Safety of Nuclear Installations
Peter Faross 39

First Working Session

Nuclear Safety and Safeguards in the EU

Chair: *Michael Micklinghoff*
Secretary: *Julian Rotter*

Comments on the Planned Revision of the Euratom Directive on Nuclear Safety
Andreas Woitecki 51

Continuous Improvement of Nuclear Safety
Rasa Ptasekaite 71

The Nuclear Safeguards System of the European Atomic Energy Community (Euratom)
Wolfgang Kilb 97

Discussion Report of the First Working Session
Julian Rotter 113

Second Working Session

Nuclear New Build

Chair: *Ian Salter*
Secretary: *Łukasz Młynarkiewicz*

Nuclear Power Programme for Poland – Establishing the Legal Framework
Tomasz R. Nowacki 121

Poland and Germany: Issues of Transboundary Consultation
Martina Palm and Markus Pfaff 167

Transportable Nuclear Power Plants – An Update on Regulatory Responses in International Nuclear Law
Rüdiger Tscherning 175

Turkey as a Newcomer in Nuclear New Build – Turkey's Development in the Field of Nuclear Energy and a Systematic View on Progress Particularly in Nuclear Legislation –
Erinç Ercan and Horst Schneider 201

Brief Update on Developments in the UK in the Nuclear New Build Arena
Ian Salter 271

Discussion Report of the Second Working Session
Łukasz Młynarkiewicz 275

Third Working Session

Nuclear Liability

Part one: Nuclear Liability in the EU

Chair: *Norbert Pelzer*
Secretary: *Sidonie Royer-Maucotel*

Activities of the EU Commission in the Field of Nuclear Liability Coverage – Some Personal Remarks
Dirk Harbrücker 281

What Can the Victims of a Nuclear Incident Expect from the Initiative of the European Commission Related to Nuclear Liability?
Roland Dussart-Desart 287

Discussion Report of the Third Working Session, Part 1
Sidonie Royer-Maucotel 309

Part two: Nuclear Liability Worldwide

Chair: *Christian Raetzke*
Secretary: *Sidonie Royer-Maucotel*

Liability Issues at Transportation of Nuclear Materials in Absence of the Global Regime of Civil Liability for Nuclear Damage
Boris Kolesnik 313

Discussion Panel: Do We Need a Global Nuclear Liability Regime?
Stephen Burns, David Davies, Kyoji Kawasaki, Alexander Matveev, Norbert Pelzer, Els Reynaers Kini, Wolfram Tonhauser 319

Introduction by the Chairman
Christian Raetzke 321

Introductory Statement
David Davies 323

Introductory Statement: Japanese Experience in Nuclear Liability Compensation after Fukushima Incident
Kyoji Kawasaki 327

Introductory Statement: On a Global Nuclear Liability Regime
Alexander Matveev 333

Theses on a Globally Harmonised Nuclear Liability Regime
Norbert Pelzer 341

Report on the Discussion Panel: Do We Need a Global Nuclear Liability Regime?
Sidonie Royer-Maucotel 347

Fourth Working Session

Nuclear Phase-Out, Decommissioning and Waste Management

Chair: *Ulrike Feldmann*
Secretary: *Simon Mayer*

Phase-Out in Germany: History and Outlook
Michael Micklinghoff 359

Phase-Out and Long Term Operation Legislation in Switzerland
David Erni 373

Decommissioning and Final Repositories in Germany
Bruno Thomauske 383

Discussion Report of the Fourth Session
Simon Mayer 385

Fünfte Arbeitssitzung

Fragen des deutschen Atomrechts

Vorsitz: *Manfred Rebentisch*
Sekretär: *Julius F. W. Weitzdörfer*

Anwendungsbereich und Schutzniveau des § 7d AtG
Thomas Fetzer 391

Unabhängigkeit der Atomaufsicht
Axel Vorwerk 407

Nukleartransportrecht und Universalhafenprinzip im Spannungsverhältnis: Das Bremer Hafenrecht
Christoph Moench 419

Die Urteile des Hessischen Verwaltungsgerichtshofs vom 27. Februar 2013 zu den Betriebseinstellungsverfügungen gegen Biblis A und Biblis B im Rahmen des deutschen Moratoriums nach den Ereignissen in Fukushima-Daiichi vom März 2011
Stefan Kochanski 447

Diskussionsbericht zur Fünften Arbeitssitzung
Ulrike Feldmann und Julius F. W. Weitzdörfer 463

List of participants / Teilnehmerverzeichnis 467

Preface

This volume contains the proceedings of the 13th Regional Conference of the German Branch of the Association Internationale du Droit Nucléaire / International Nuclear Law Association (AIDN/INLA). The conference took place on 6 and 7 June 2013 in Leipzig, Germany.

The German Branch of AIDN/INLA has a rich history which is inseparably linked to the name of Norbert Pelzer. Dr. Pelzer, then President of AIDN/INLA, caused its establishment in 1984 in preparation of the 1985 Nuclear Inter Jura conference in Constance. Dr. Pelzer remained chairman of the German Branch for 26 years and organised twelve biannual regional conferences between 1986 and 2009 – a tremendous and admirable achievement. When he resigned in 2010 after having staged the 2009 conference in Berlin, the general assembly, by universal acclamation, elected Dr. Pelzer Honorary Chairman of the German Branch of AIDN/INLA.

Dr. Pelzer's successor, Dr. Horst Schneider, organised what was planned to be the 13th conference of our association, focussing on the topic of long-term operation of nuclear power plants, for the end of March 2011. Then, not quite three weeks before that date, the Fukushima accident occurred and it was decided to cancel the conference. So when I was elected chairman in 2012, I assumed the task of making a new attempt at organising a conference in 2013. In doing this, I was resolved to continue, as far as I could, the great tradition founded by Norbert Pelzer.

The regional conferences of the German Branch have always been attended by German and non-German experts alike. This time, foreign participation reached a new peak with about half of the participants coming from outside Germany (and altogether from 20 countries). The President of AIDN/INLA, Prof. Rafael Manóvil from Argentina, was present and delivered a welcome address, mainly inviting attendants to come to Buenos Aires for the next Nuclear Inter Jura congress in October 2014.

This truly international attendance gives me and my fellow board members great delight. At the same time, a practical problem arose when it became apparent that financial constraints would prevent us from providing for the simultaneous translation which had been a feature of our previous conferences. Thus, the decision was taken to establish English as sole conference language which would be mandatory for all speakers, including the German ones. The exception was the very last session which, again following an established tradition, was devoted to intricate questions of German nuclear law; this last session was inevitably held in German language. In my introductory address at the conference I apologised to the non-German-speaking colleagues that this effectively barred them from participating in the last session (eventually quite a number of foreign colleagues revealed a certain acquaintance with German by staying for this last session....). For any non-German-speaking reader of this volume, however, this new approach results in the advantage that for the first time the papers are in English throughout (with the aforementioned exception).

The programme was designed to allow the broadest range of topics of nuclear law possible to be presented and discussed. The rationale was to cover the remarkable developments currently going on in international, EU and German nuclear law. There was a certain focus on EU issues, marked by the two distinguished keynote speakers, but this did not at all exclude worldwide or national aspects.

On the international level, the Fukushima incident has justly triggered new endeavours towards enhancement of nuclear safety and increased effectiveness of nuclear regulation. Besides, it has given new impetus to the quest for a global nuclear liability regime (one of the sessions of the conference, however, investigated the question whether such a global regime is really achievable or even necessary...).

Both nuclear safety and nuclear liability are also the subject of initiatives for EU legislation taken by the European Commission. As usual in such a context, discussion not only focuses on nuclear law, but additionally encompasses the competence of the EU, the effectiveness of EU action and the choice of instruments to be used.

In Germany, the four years since the last regional conference in Berlin 2009 have seen remarkable events in German nuclear law, especially the spectacular turnaround in nuclear policy in the wake of Fukushima. In the main English part of this volume, a presentation explains the twists and turns of the phase-out legislation and the general context of nuclear in Germany. Two other papers outline the German federal regulator's position towards the draft revised EU Nuclear Safety Directive and address practical issues of German participation in Poland's transboundary consultation on the new build programme. All these are certainly aspects of German nuclear law which are relevant for international discussion.

* * *

It is both my duty and my particular pleasure to express my thanks to a number of colleagues who have been instrumental in making the conference possible. I am grateful to my fellow board members of the German AIDN/INLA: Dr. Malte Schmans, the deputy chairman, our treasurer Dirk Harbrücker, who dealt with all accountancy issues in his usual understated but highly effective way, and Ms. Ulrike Feldmann. I am particularly grateful to Ulrike for giving me great support especially in designing the programme and in acquiring speakers, and for inspiring me with confidence and cheer if necessary. My two predecessors as chairmen, Dr. Norbert Pelzer and Dr. Horst Schneider, have contributed extensive and valuable advice. I want to emphasise Norbert Pelzer's unfailing readiness to open the treasure chest filled with his unparalleled experience of so many conferences and to share its riches with me. Annette Kaiser from the secretariat of the Deutsche Kernreaktor-Versicherungsgemeinschaft provided invaluable assistance and support in all issues of organisation. I cannot think of all these contributions without a vivid feeling of gratitude.

Dr. Axel Vorwerk and his colleagues of the German Federal Ministry for the Environment gave me valuable advice and support in designing the programme. Besides, the Ministry, continuing a tradition established for the previous conferences, again took over the costs of publishing this volume. I am very grateful for this multiple and effective support.

I also greatly appreciate the toil and trouble of all presenters, who readily followed the invitation of the German AIDN/INLA and who gave presentations and wrote papers even though everyone nowadays is overloaded with work. The same goes for the session secretaries who accepted the difficult task of summarising the discussions which were often vivid.

Some companies of the German nuclear industry gave donations which greatly helped to establish, in a critical early stage of preparation, confidence in the ultimate financial viability of the conference. In the current difficult situation for the industry, such support cannot be taken for granted and I deeply thank the colleagues who were involved in this.

I am indebted to Nomos publishing house, particularly to Dr. Stefan Grote who saw this book through publication and was an always accomodating and amiable partner.

Last not least, I fondly remember the relaxed and pleasant atmosphere of the conference, to which the international participants greatly contributed. I hope many of them will keep this in their memories as an interesting event to which the city of Leipzig, where I live, provided a beautiful and inspiring backdrop.

Leipzig, December 2013 *Christian Raetzke*

Vorwort

Am 6. und 7. Juni 2013 fand in Leipzig in der Alten Börse die 13. Regionaltagung der Deutschen Landesgruppe der AIDN/INLA e.V statt. Als dreizehnte Tagung ihrer Art bedeutete die Veranstaltung offensichtlich die Fortsetzung einer langen Tradition. Dennoch gibt es einige Änderungen, die vielleicht ebenso der Erklärung bedürfen wie der ungewohnt lange zeitliche Abstand zur vorhergehenden zwölften Regionaltagung 2009 in Berlin. Dieser Band trägt einen neuen Herausgebernamen und erstmals ist Englisch die fast durchgehend verwendete Sprache.

Die bisherigen Tagungen der Deutschen Landesgruppe sind untrennbar mit dem Namen Norbert Pelzer verknüpft. Dr. Pelzer ist der maßgebliche Gründungsvater der Landesgruppe. Er war von Anfang an, seit 1984, ihr Vorsitzender und organisierte und leitete alle ihre zwölf Tagungen bis 2009. Die stattliche Reihe der Tagungsbände, sämtlich im Nomos Verlag unter der Herausgeberschaft von Herrn Dr. Pelzer erschienen, ist ein nachdrückliches Zeugnis dieses bewundernswerten Wirkens. Nach der Berliner Tagung 2009 faßte Herr Dr. Pelzer den Entschluß, den Vorsitz in jüngere Hände zu legen, und stellte sich auf der Mitgliederversammlung des Jahres 2010 nicht mehr zur Wiederwahl zur Verfügung. Die Mitglieder wählten ihn daraufhin per Akklamation zum Ehrenvorsitzenden.

Den Vereinsvorsitz übernahm Dr. Horst Schneider. Er organisierte für Ende März 2011, dem bewährten zweijährigen Turnus folgend, eine eintägige Konferenz in Bonn, die unter dem Thema »Langzeitbetrieb von Kernkraftwerken« stehen sollte. Das Reaktorunglück von Fukushima am 11. März 2011 und die dadurch ausgelösten Entwicklungen in Deutschland und Europa führten bedauerlicherweise zur Absage der bereits vollständig vorbereiteten Veranstaltung.

Nach meiner Wahl zum Vorsitzenden 2012 war es mir ein Anliegen, bei der Vorbereitung der Leipziger Tagung die von Herrn Dr. Pelzer begründete Tradition fortzuführen, die eine so reiche wissenschaftliche Ernte erbracht hat. Die Tagung fand in der Alten Börse statt, einem Barockbau im Herzen der Leipziger Innenstadt, der von den Teilnehmern als stimmungsvoller und vorzüglich geeigneter Schauplatz empfunden wurde. An der Tagung nahmen knapp 100 Personen teil; davon kam fast die Hälfte aus dem Ausland; über 20 Länder waren vertreten. Der Präsident der AIDN/INLA, Prof. Rafael Manóvil aus Argentinien, sprach ein Grußwort, in dem er zur Teilnahme an der nächsten Tagung der AIDN/INLA im Oktober 2014 in Buenos Aires einlud.

Anders als bisher auf den Landesgruppentagungen üblich, konnte dieses Mal aus finanziellen Gründen keine Simultanübersetzung bereitgestellt werden. Deshalb stand schon früh fest, daß erstmals Englisch die einheitliche Tagungssprache sein würde. Eine Ausnahme bildete nur die letzte Sitzung, die, ebenfalls in Fortführung einer bewährten Tradition, Themen des deutschen Atomrechts gewidmet war; über diesen Bereich, der von ebenso reizvollen wie komplizierten dogmatischen Fragestellungen und von der Auslegung der Gesetze geprägt ist, kann man schlecht in einer Fremdsprache reden und schreiben. In allen anderen Sitzungen aber wurden alle Vorträge, auch diejenigen, die von deutschen Autoren stammen, auf Englisch gehalten und sind hier auch auf Englisch abgedruckt.

Diese Entscheidung fiel uns nicht leicht, denn Deutsch als Sprache der Wissenschaft ist mir und den Kollegen im Vorstand lieb und teuer. Dennoch war sie unvermeidlich, soll die Tätigkeit der deutschen Landesgruppe auch weiterhin in enger Verbindung zur AIDN/INLA und zu der Gemeinschaft der internationalen Atomrechtsexperten stehen. Ich hoffe, dies trägt auch zu einer weiten internationalen Verbreitung des Tagungsbandes bei. Gleichzeitig soll es ein Signal ans Ausland setzen, daß in Deutschland unverändert Atomrecht auf hohem Niveau betrieben wird und daß die deutschen Atomrechtsexperten weiterhin den Anspruch haben, europäische und globale Entwicklungen ihres Fachs mitzugestalten.

* * *

In diesem Sinne entfaltet das Programm der Tagung, und damit der Inhalt dieses Tagungsbandes, ein breites Panorama an aktuellen Themen des deutschen, europäischen und internationalen Atomrechts, angefangen mit nuklearer Sicherheit und Safeguards, fortschreitend über den Neubau von Kernkraftwerken, die Nuklearhaftung, Ausstieg, Stillegung und Abfallbeseitigung bis hin zu aktuellen Themen spezifisch des deutschen Atomrechts. Ein gewisser Schwerpunkt, der sich auch in den beiden Eingangsvorträgen zeigte, waren Entwicklungen im EU-Recht.

Wie die Vorträge zu den unterschiedlichsten Themen beweisen, ist das Atomrecht so lebendig wie jemals. International und auf der Ebene der EU wird nach Fukushima um eine Weiterentwicklung des Rechts der nuklearen Sicherheit gerungen. Im Bereich der Nuklearhaftung strebt das internationale Atomrecht mit erneuertem Schwung nach dem hehren Ziel eines globalen Haftungsregimes; ob dies allerdings überhaupt erreichbar ist, das war das Thema einer Sitzung dieser Tagung. Die EU-Kommission hat ihrerseits eine Tätigkeit entfaltet, die eine Vereinheitlichung der Nuklearhaftung innerhalb der EU zum Ziel hat, deren konkrete Schritte und deren Beziehung zu den weltweiten Bemühungen sich aber noch nicht deutlich abzeichnen und noch viel Stoff für Diskussionen bieten werden.

Manche Länder wollen Neubauprogramme durchführen und sehen sich vor die Notwendigkeit gestellt, einen entsprechenden Rechtsrahmen auszuarbeiten, der sowohl die erforderliche nukleare Sicherheit gewährleistet als auch einen tatsächlichen Neubau durch private oder staatliche Akteure ermöglicht. Andere Länder, vornehmlich natürlich Deutschland, steigen aus der Nutzung der Kernenergie aus. Gemeinsam ist allen Ländern die Herausforderung, Regelungen für den langfristigen Umgang mit abgebrannten Brennelementen und radioaktivem Abfall zu treffen. Abgesehen von der Entscheidung für oder gegen die Kernenergie, die bekanntlich im Ermessen der EU-Mitgliedstaaten steht, ist die EU in allen diesen Bereichen in den letzten Jahren gesetzgeberisch aktiv geworden.

Was das deutsche Atomrecht angeht, hat es seit der letzten Landesgruppentagung 2009 einschneidende Veränderungen und heftige Umschwünge gegeben. Die Laufzeiten der Kernkraftwerke wurden erst gesetzlich verlängert und wenige Monate später, nach dem Reaktorunglück von Fukushima, wieder gekürzt und an feste Kalenderdaten gekoppelt, was für acht Anlagen – in Verbindung mit dem unmittelbar nach Fukushima verkündeten sog. »Moratorium« – die zugleich kurzfristige und endgültige Abschaltung bedeutete. Die juristische Bewältigung aller dieser Vorgänge ist noch nicht abgeschlossen. Auch auf anderen Gebieten ist das deutsche Atomrecht weiterhin in voller Bewegung; das gilt vor allem für die Endlagersuche und für die Diskussion um die Notwendigkeit einer Anpassung der Struktur der deutschen Atomaufsicht an EU-Vorgaben. Insofern wird es auch im deutschen Atomrecht noch reichlich Stoff für künftige Tagungen geben.

* * *

Die erfolgreiche Durchführung der Tagung wäre nicht möglich gewesen ohne die Mitwirkung vieler Personen. Mein Dank gilt meinen Kollegen im Vorstand der Landesgruppe: dem Stellvertretenden Vorsitzenden Dr. Malte Schmans, dem Schatzmeister Dirk Harbrücker, der das Rechnungswesen für die Tagung gewohnt souverän durchführte, und Frau Ulrike Feldmann, Beisitzerin im Vorstand der Deutschen Landesgruppe und zugleich Mitglied des Vorstands der AIDN/INLA. Ulrike Feldmann möchte ich ganz besonders danken, sie hat vor allem bei der Gestaltung des wissenschaftlichen Programms, aber auch in allen anderen Dingen wertvollste Beiträge geleistet und mir, wenn erforderlich, Optimismus und Zuversicht eingeflößt. Meine Vorgänger, Dr. Norbert Pelzer und Dr. Horst Schneider, haben mir viele wertvolle Ratschläge gegeben; insbesondere Herr Dr. Pelzer hat für mich jederzeit bereitwillig und freigebig aus der überquellenden Schatztruhe seiner unvergleichlichen Erfahrung mit den bisherigen Tagungen geschöpft. Ein besonderer Dank geht schließlich an Frau Annette Kaiser vom Sekretariat der Deutschen Kernreaktor-Versicherungsgemeinschaft, die mir bei der Organisation der Tagung eine große und unentbehrliche Hilfe war.

Eine Tagung steht und fällt mit dem Niveau der Beiträge. Insofern bin ich froh und dankbar, daß eine illustre Riege in- und ausländischer Kollegen unserer Einladung gefolgt ist und trotz der Belastung durch das Alltagsgeschäft Vorträge gehalten und für diesen Tagungsband schriftlich ausgearbeitet hat. Dank verdienen auch die Sitzungssekretäre, denen die anspruchsvolle Aufgabe zufiel, die teils lebhaften Diskussionen für diesen Band zusammenzufassen.

Das Bundesministerium für Umwelt, Naturschutz und Reaktorsicherheit, Abteilung RS, hat wertvollste Hilfe bei der Programmgestaltung geleistet. Darüber hinaus hat das Ministerium, wie für die bisherigen Tagungen auch, das Erscheinen dieses Tagungsbandes mit einem Druckkostenzuschuß ermöglicht. Für diese Unterstützung auf mehreren Ebenen möchte ich Herrn Ministerialdirigent Dr. Axel Vorwerk und seinen Kollegen sehr herzlich danken.

Die Finanzierung der Tagung erfolgte letztlich weitgehend durch die Teilnahmegebühren. Wichtig aber waren auch frühe Spendenzusagen einiger Firmen der deutschen Nuklearindustrie, die das finanzielle Risiko überschaubarer machten und eine am Ende noch bestehende Lücke auszugleichen halfen. Angesichts der gegenwärtigen Lage in der Branche sind solche Zuwendungen nicht selbstverständlich und ich danke den hierbei beteiligten Kollegen auf das Verbindlichste.

Dank gebührt schließlich dem Nomos Verlag, insbesondere Herrn Dr. Stefan Grote, der erneut in bewährter Weise, stets verständnisvoll und entgegenkommend, die verlegerische Betreuung dieses Tagungsbandes übernommen hat.

Leipzig, im Dezember 2013 *Christian Raetzke*

Keynote Session

»Nuclear Law in the EU«

From Challenge to Response: Dormant Powers in Euratom Law[1]

Prof. Dr. Jürgen Grunwald M.C.L.

I. Introduction

The subject of this conference is »Nuclear Law in the EU and beyond – Nuclear Safety, New Build and Phase-out«. It is the right theme at the right time and – I may add – at the right place, given Leipzig's contribution to science, law and culture in general. The challenges are evident, it suffices to look at the range of subjects to be dealt with in 5 sessions today and tomorrow. And yet, in strictly legal terms, there is something missing in the title of this conference: it is a reference to the European Atomic Energy Community and the Treaty governing it. Of course I know that by implication the reference to the EU is meant to cover also Euratom but in law they are different legal persons,[2] pursue different objectives[3] and follow – at least in part – different legal procedures.[4] Even conflicts between the two are not excluded.[5]

As lawyers specialized in nuclear law you will know that arguing in defence of the Euratom Treaty means a constant uphill struggle. In the light of the opposition and sometimes even outright obstruction which the Treaty has encountered throughout its history,[6] it is almost an understatement to say that the Treaty has few friends. And yet, ironically, it is precisely its

1 This article is dedicated to the memory of Donald W. Allen and Thomas F. Cusack.

2 See Article 184 of the Euratom Treaty (»The Community shall have legal personality.«) and Article 47 of the Treaty on European Union - TEU (»The Union shall have legal personality.«).

3 See Thomas F. Cusack, A Tale of Two Treaties: An Assessment of the Euratom Treaty in Relation to the EC Treaty, CMLR 2003, p. 117.

4 This applies in particular to the role of the European Parliament in the legislative process. See Jürgen Grunwald, Neuere Entwicklungen des Euratom-Rechts, ZEuS 2010, p. 407 (409 et seq.).

5 In particular in the field of state aids.

6 See Jürgen Grunwald, Euratom Treaty History and the Way Forward, in: Nuclear Inter Jura 2007, Proceedings, Brussels 2008, p. 1075.

controversial nature which has guaranteed its stability in the past and which is likely to do so also in the foreseeable future: Unless all Member States agree on scrapping the Treaty or on amending it or on replacing it by another Treaty, the Treaty will remain in force as it stands.[7] Its Article 208 provides: »This Treaty is concluded for an unlimited period«. Thus, in all likelihood, the future of the Treaty will still be long. But since the Treaty is there to stay, it may be legitimate to ask what we can still expect of it in the future.

II Challenge and response

So what I propose to you this morning is to list a number of pressing challenges to the nuclear sector and to see what response the Treaty may provide over and above what has been done already. In doing so, I shall be addressing 8 points, presented in the order of the Treaty chapters concerned.

1. Establishment of an institution of university status

In commenting on the Commission's proposal for a Council Directive setting up a Community framework for nuclear safety, the European Economic and Social Committee (EESC) expressed the following concerns:[8]

> »The EESC is particularly interested in the question of building, maintaining and developing skills in the Member States, particularly those which have little or no experience with nuclear energy. These Member States must address this question without delay, in particular by developing the necessary training opportunities. In addition, the EESC suggests that consideration be given to European certification of competence in the field of nuclear power, and that training relates to the technical management as well as to the health aspects of nuclear accidents.«[9]

No doubt, the Committee is right, but the task of building, maintaining and developing nuclear skills is not only one for the Member States, but also one for the Community itself. Article 9 of the Treaty provides: »An institution of university status shall be established; the way in which it will function shall be determined by the Council, acting by a qualified majority

7 Ibid, p. 1083.
8 OJ C 306, 16.12.2009, p. 56.
9 Ibid, point 1.7.

on a proposal by the Commission.« Pursuant to Article 216 the Commission had to submit its proposal within only one year of the entry into force of the Treaty – that is, in the year 1958. As we all know, a University has never been established, despite the clear legal obligation set out in the Treaty. Already back in 1983 my former Director, Donald Allen, rightly remarked: pacta sunt servanda – why not this one?[10] There is no point here and now in pondering over the question why the institutions failed to act in 1958. What is more important is to note the Community's continued responsibility for nuclear training at all levels and in all areas apprehended by the Treaty. Article 9 is explicit when it speaks of »training of specialists, particularly in the fields of prospecting for minerals, the production of high-purity nuclear materials, the processing of irradiated fuels, nuclear engineering, health and safety and the production and use of isotopes«.

Both phase-out and new-build present new and difficult technical challenges for the Member States concerned. Now each one of them has to invent its own wheel, while a Euratom University could centralise all relevant knowledge and best practices, could disseminate them Europe-wide on a non-discriminatory basis[11] and, in doing so, could guarantee the highest technical and academic standards. Moreover, this European University could issue European diplomas in its teaching activities and act as an interface between industry and the research community, following the model of the MIT in the US. No powers of equal or similar scope exist under the EU-Treaties,[12] and the rather limited remit of the European Institute of Technology[13] bears witness to this.

---

10 Donald Allen, The Euratom Treaty, Chapter VI: New Hope or False Dawn?, CMLR 1983, p. 473.

11 See Case C-115/08 Land Oberösterreich v ČEZ as (2009) ECR I - 10265 in which the Court of Justice held that the principle of prohibition of any discrimination on grounds of nationality laid down in Article 12 EC Treaty (now Article 18 TFEU) is a general principle which is also applicable under the Euratom Treaty.

12 See Articles 165 and 166 TFEU on »Education, Vocational Training, Youth and Sport« and Article 173 TFEU on »Industry«.

13 See Regulation (EC) No 294/2008 of the European Parliament and of the Council of 11 March 2008 establishing the European Institute of Innovation and Technology, OJ L 97, 9.4.2008, p. 1.

2. Creation of a Euratom Knowledge Community

You will know that there is an entire chapter in the Treaty which, since the beginning, has led a life which one may only describe as a shadow existence: Chapter 2 bears the title »Dissemination of Information« and is designed to establish a Community of knowledge,[14] with the Commission acting as a hub and clearinghouse for the dissemination of technical information. Information over which the Community has power of disposal by virtue of its own research activities or which it is entitled to make free use of must be disseminated pursuant to Articles 12 and 13 of the Treaty. For any other information Article 15 provides that: »The Commission shall establish a procedure by which Member States, persons or undertakings may use it (i.e. the Commission) as an intermediary for exchanging provisional or final results of their research«. Here too, Member States which opt for new build or phase-out could benefit from knowledge already acquired by others, provided they know that it exists and that they may get access to it under Chapter 2.

3. Establishment of uniform safety standards for nuclear installations

In its interim-report on the stress tests after the Fukushima accident[15] the Commission stated in November 2011, that »at present, there are no common safety standards or criteria for nuclear power plants in the EU«.[16] The European Economic and Social Committee, on its part, found in October

14 It is to be noted that it took the EEC/EC/EU Treaties more than 50 years to make provisions for a »European research area in which researchers, scientific knowledge and technology circulate freely« (see Article 179 (1) TFEU). If and when the EU decides to »establish measures necessary for the implementation of the European research area« (see Article 182 (5) TFEU), Chapter 2 of the Euratom Treaty may serve as a model for rules on the dissemination of knowledge. See also on this subject: Jürgen Grunwald, Neuere Entwicklungen des EU-Forschungsrechts, ZEuS 2011, p. 607 (637 to 642).

15 Communication from the Commission to the Council and the European Parliament on the interim report on the comprehensive risk and safety assessments (»stress tests«) of nuclear power plants in the European Union, COM(2011) 784 final, 24.11.2011. See also the final report: Communication from the Commission to the Council and the European Parliament on the comprehensive risk and safety assessments (»stress tests«) of nuclear power plants in the European Union and related activities, COM(2012) 571 final, 4.10.2012.

16 Ibid, point 3.2.1., p. 9.

2012[17] that »there is no common approach to nuclear safety regulation among the Member States« and recommended that the Nuclear Safety Directive »harmonise these aspects«.[18]

In a Community of 27 – soon to be 28 – whose task it is, in the words of the 4th recital to the Treaty, »to create the conditions of safety necessary to eliminate hazards to the life and health of the public«, these findings are highly disconcerting: all the more so inasmuch as Article 2 (b) of the Treaty requires the Community to »establish uniform safety standards to protect the health of workers and of the general public and ensure that they are applied«.

Now it is true that the traditional view on health and safety and the basic standards within the meaning of Article 30 of the Treaty has been a medical and man-related one and not a plant- or nuclear source-related one.[19]

However, this narrow view is no longer valid. The reason for this can be found in Article 32 of the Treaty which allows the Community legislator to revise or supplement the basic standards if so requested by the Commission or by a Member State. The significance of this article becomes apparent when it is seen in the context of Articles 76, 85 and 90 of the Treaty. These three articles empower the Council to »adapt« or »adjust« the provisions of Chapters 6 (Supply), 7 (Safeguards) and 8 (Property ownership) of the Treaty, »where new circumstances so require«. This so-called simplified amendment procedure[20] under which the Council has to act unanimously requires neither an Intergovernmental Conference, nor a ratification by Member States' parliaments. The existence of these simplified amendment procedures can be explained by the largely experi-

17 Opinion of the European Economic and Social Committee on the »Communication from the Commission to the Council and the European Parliament on the comprehensive risk and safety assessments (»stress tests«) of nuclear power plants in the European Union and related activities«, OJ C 44, 15.2.2013, p. 140.

18 Ibid, point 1.4., p. 140.

19 This may be due to the definition in Article 30 according to which the expression »basic standards« means:
»(a) maximum permissible doses compatible with adequate safety;
(b) maximum permissible levels of exposure and contamination;
(c) the fundamental principles governing the health surveillance of workers.«
Likewise, the Article 31 Group of scientific experts advising the Commission on health and safety legislation under Article 31 shall be composed »in particular (of) public health experts.«

20 The Euratom simplified amendment procedure has provided the model for the »simplified revision procedures« set out in Article 48 (6) and (7) TEU.

mental character of the Treaty and the need for the Community to be able to react rapidly to new and unforeseen situations without lengthy intergovernmental conferences and time consuming ratification procedures.

Rapid as these simplified amendment procedures may be, they may still be too slow to react to new and pressing challenges in order to protect the »public against the dangers arising from ionising radiations«.[21] Thus, instead of foreseeing the intermediate step of a simplified amendment procedure, Chapter 3, in particular Article 32, empowers the Community legislator directly to take the necessary measures by way of supplementing the basic standards by qualified majority only. In doing so, the Treaty also removes both the need and the legal possibility for applying Article 203, a provision which – if applicable – would also require unanimity in the Council.[22]

Following the logic of Article 32, the Community legislator has gradually improved and expanded its legislative arsenal, by moving its protective measures more and more up-stream from man to the source of ionising radiation, knowing that man is best protected when radiation is kept at bay already at its source.[23] The Court of Justice endorsed this approach by holding that »it is not appropriate, in order to define the Community's competences, to draw an artificial distinction between the protection of the health of the general public and the safety of sources of ionising radiation.«[24]

With regard to the construction and operation of nuclear installations, the Court considered:

> »Even though the Euratom Treaty does not grant the Community competence to authorise the construction or operation of nuclear installations, under Articles 30 to 32 of the Euratom Treaty the Community possesses legislative competence to establish, for the purpose of health protection, an authorisation system which must

21 See Article 30.

22 Article 203 provides: »If action by the Community should prove necessary to attain one of the objectives of the Community and this Treaty has not provided the necessary powers, the Council shall, acting unanimously on a proposal from the Commission and after consulting the European Parliament, take the appropriate measures.« See also Article 352 TFEU.

23 For references see Jürgen Grunwald, Das Energierecht der Europäischen Gemeinschaften, EGKS-EURATOM-EG, Grundlagen-Geschichte-Geltende Regelungen, Berlin 2003, p. 209 to 219, and by the same author, Neuere Entwicklungen des Euratom-Rechts, ZEuS 2010, p. 407 (415 et seq.).

24 Case C-29/99 Commission v Council (2002) ECR I-11221, paragraph 82.

be applied by the Member States. Such a legislative act constitutes a measure supplementing the basic standards referred to in that article.«[25]

On the basis of Article 32 Euratom thus has the power to adopt an authorisation system requiring the Member States to apply uniform safety standards to be defined by the Community legislator for the siting, construction and operation of nuclear plants.[26]

From a procedural point of view the preparation of such legislation would call for appropriate technical expertise within the Article 31 Group which has been traditionally dominated by the medical profession. Now construction and engineering expertise will be needed. This in turn will necessitate further reflection on the role and composition of the Scientific and Technical Committee which appoints the members of the Article 31 Group. I will come back to this point later on.[27]

If the Commission is not prepared to propose appropriate legislation on common substantive safety standards for the siting, construction and operation of nuclear plants because it considers them not to be necessary or for fear of failure in the Council, there is nevertheless a second-best solution which makes it possible to arrive at least at a certain degree of harmonisation. This solution lies in Article 33 of the Treaty.

While by virtue of this article it is for the Member States to adopt the appropriate provisions to give effect to the basic standards and supplementing measures,[28] it is for the Commission to harmonise the national rules. Article 33, second paragraph, provides: »The Commission shall make appropriate recommendations for harmonising the provisions applicable in this field in the Member States.«

Thus, if the Commission is willing to accept the diversity of national safety standards, which we noted in the beginning, by refraining from proposing legislation on common standards, it can still make recommenda-

25 Ibid, paragraph 89.

26 Such a true Community system would go considerably beyond the present requirements imposed on national systems by Council Directive 2009/71/Euratom of 25 June 2009 establishing a Community framework for the nuclear safety of nuclear installations, OJ L 172, 2.7.2009, p. 18, and also those proposed by the Commission in its recent draft proposal for a Council Directive amending Directive 2009/71/Euratom, COM(2013) 343 final, 13.6.2013.

27 See point 8 below.

28 Article 33, first paragraph, reads as follows: »Each Member State shall lay down the appropriate provisions, whether by legislation, regulation or administrative action, to ensure compliance with the basic standards which have been established and shall take the necessary measures with regard to teaching, education and vocational training.«

tions for harmonising the different national provisions in this field. Although recommendations are not binding in law[29] and cannot be challenged in court,[30] they are nonetheless legally not irrelevant, since they may guide the interpretation of legal provisions.[31]

4. Access to and safety controls in nuclear installations

The Commission's right of access to nuclear installations is expressly foreseen in Article 81 of the Treaty for the Commission's safeguards inspectors.[32] Likewise, under Article 35 the Commission has the right of access to national facilities monitoring the level of radioactivity in the air, water and soil and may verify their operation and efficiency.[33]

Articles 81 and 35, however, are not the only provisions in the Treaty which enable the Commission to carry out on-site checks in the nuclear domain. Article 187 reads as follows:

> »The Commission may, within the limits and under the conditions laid down by the Council in accordance with the provisions of this Treaty, collect any infor-

29 See Article 106a (1) of the Euratom Treaty in conjunction with Article 288, fifth paragraph, TFEU.

30 See Article 106a (1) of the Euratom Treaty in conjunction with Article 263, first paragraph, TFEU.

31 See Case C-322/88 Grimaldi v Fonds des maladies professionnelles (1989) ECR 4416.

32 Article 81, paragraph 2, provides: »On presentation of a document establishing their authority, inspectors shall at all times have access to all places and data and to all persons who, by reason of their occupation, deal with materials, equipment or installations subject to the safeguards provided for in this Chapter, to the extent necessary in order to apply such safeguards to ores, source materials and special fissile materials and to ensure compliance with the provisions of Article 77. Should the State concerned so request, inspectors appointed by the Commission shall be accompanied by representatives of the authorities of that State; however, the inspectors shall not thereby be delayed or otherwise impeded in the performance of their duties.«

33 Article 35 provides: »Each Member State shall establish the facilities necessary to carry out continuous monitoring of the level of radioactivity in the air, water and soil and to ensure compliance with the basic standards.
The Commission shall have the right of access to such facilities; it may verify their operation and efficiency.«
See also the Communication from the Commission: »Verification of environmental radioactivity monitoring facilities under the terms of Article 35 of the Euratom Treaty - Practical arrangements for the conduct of verification visits in Member States,« OJ C 155, 4.7.2006, p. 2.

> mation and carry out any checks required for the performance of the tasks entrusted to it.«

All that is required to activate these checks is thus a Council Regulation setting out their modalities.[34] The only necessary condition for such a regulation in the present context would be that safety controls on-site are required for the performance of the tasks entrusted to the Commission by Chapter 3. This chapter is designed to give effect to the fourth recital of the Treaty, namely »to create the conditions of safety necessary to eliminate hazards to the life and health of the public.« To this end the Community must, pursuant to Article 2 (b), not only »establish uniform safety standards to protect the health of workers and of the general public« but also »ensure that they are applied.«

Now let me ask a couple of rhetorical questions: How can the Community ensure that the necessary safety criteria are applied when the nuclear installations where they must be applied remain an inaccessible black box to the Commission? How can the Commission ever apply Article 38 paragraph 2 of the Treaty when it has no direct knowledge of the situation on the ground? Let us recall the mandate given by this provision:

> »In cases of urgency, the Commission shall issue a directive requiring the Member State concerned to take, within a period laid down by the Commission, all necessary measures to prevent infringement of the basic standards and to ensure compliance with regulations.«

In no other field of Community and EU Law does the Commission have a greater responsibility than under this provision and Chapter 3.

34 Before the Lisbon Treaty the Council could adopt such regulations by simple majority: Article 118 (1) of the Euratom Treaty (repealed by the Lisbon Treaty) provided: »Save as otherwise provided in this Treaty, the Council shall act by a majority of its members.« Before the Lisbon Treaty the same rule applied under the EEC/EC Treaties (see Article 205 EC Treaty), and in particular to regulations under Article 284 of the EC Treaty which was the parallel provision to Article 187 of the Euratom Treaty on the EC side. Apparently due to a clerical oversight in the drafting of the Lisbon Treaty, the parallelism of procedures governing the same subject matter was broken: Whereas the reference in Article 106a (1) of the Euratom Treaty to Article 16 (3) TEU (»The Council shall act by a qualified majority except where the Treaties provide otherwise.«) now requires a qualified majority for applying Article 187 of the Euratom Treaty, Article 337 TFEU (ex-Article 284 of the EC Treaty), in conjunction with Article 238 (1) TFEU, expressly maintained the simple majority (»... the Council acting by a simple majority ...«). This obvious and legally unjustified discrepancy of procedures governing the same subject matter should be corrected as soon as possible. Unfortunately even the latest consolidated version of the Euratom Treaty (see OJ C 327, 26.10.2012, p. 1 (46)) still shows an uncorrected wording of Article 187.

Now you may ask: Is it really for the Commission to check every nut and bolt in each of more than 140 nuclear installations in the Community? The answer is: Of course not. By virtue of Article 33 this is the responsibility of the Member States and their national authorities which are to give effect to the basic standards and supplementing measures. But it is for the Commission to control and supervise the Member States in the execution of their tasks and, if necessary, to take appropriate action against them.[35] In order to do so, the Commission needs not only to be informed of all relevant national provisions (which must be communicated to it under Article 33),[36] but must also be able to check the effect of these national provisions against reality on the ground. Let me illustrate this point by giving you an example. It is not for the school-inspector to teach the children. This is the teacher's task. But in order to assess whether the teacher does his job properly, the school-inspector will need to visit the classroom from time to time to see the teacher and his pupils interacting. And just as the school-inspector's access to a classroom should not depend on voluntary offers made by teachers and pupils, the Commission should not need to rely on the good will of private parties when executing its public law mandate at Community level.

It is only where a clear-cut obligation to grant access exists that equally clear-cut sanctions can be applied in cases of infringement. Denial of access in violation of a Council Regulation could give rise to sanctions under Article 145 of the Treaty,[37] unless the Council in its Regulation wished

35 In the absence of an urgency within the meaning of Article 38, paragraph 2, the Commission may launch infringement procedures pursuant to Article 106a (1) of the Euratom Treaty in conjunction with Article 258 TFEU. The same procedure is open, pursuant to Article 259 TFEU, to Member States aggrieved by another Member State (»A Member State which considers that another Member State has failed to fulfil an obligation under the Treaties may bring the matter before the Court of Justice of the European Union.«). To the extent that Community law provides for judicial redress, no other judicial review may be sought (see Case C-459/03 Commission v Ireland (2006) ECR I-4635).

36 By virtue of Article 33 the Member States have to communicate to the Commission all draft provisions intended to ensure compliance with the basic standards and with supplementing measures. The Commission may then issue recommendations with regard to such draft provisions within a period of three months after their communication.

37 Article 145 provides: »If the Commission considers that a person or undertaking has committed an infringement of this Treaty to which the provisions of Article 83 do not apply, it shall call upon the Member State having jurisdiction over that person or undertaking to cause sanctions to be imposed in respect of the infringement in accordance with its national law.

to copy the stricter model set by the rules on the enforcement of access and sanctions under Chapter 7.[38]

5. Introduction of a formalised information and coordination procedure for phase-out and new build

When after the Fukushima accident Germany decided within a few days to phase out nuclear energy, this was meant, reported and perceived as a sovereign national decision. No account was taken and no mention was made of the Euratom Treaty and the fact that Germany was part of a Nuclear Energy Community governed by common rules, based on common long-term perspectives. Seen against the background of Article 194 TFEU this may seem perfectly legitimate, since according to this provision EU measures in the field of energy »shall not affect a Member State's right to determine the conditions for exploiting its energy sources, its choice between different energy sources and the general structure of its energy supply.« The abrupt decision, however, to phase out nuclear energy is not primarily a matter for the EU, but first and foremost one for Euratom.[39] Article 40 of the Treaty provides:

> »In order to stimulate action by persons and undertakings and to facilitate coordinated development of their investment in the nuclear field, the Commission shall periodically publish illustrative programmes indicating in particular nuclear energy production targets and all the types of investment required for their attainment.«

It must be clear that an abrupt decision on the phasing-out of nuclear energy taken by a major Member State will have negative repercussions on nuclear production targets for the Community as a whole and the investment made for the attainment of these targets. In order to enable the Commission to »facilitate coordinated development of investment in the nuclear field,« as required by Article 40, it is necessary for Member States first to inform the Commission about their intention in relation to the fu-

If the State concerned does not comply with such a request within the period laid down by the Commission, the latter may bring an action before the Court of Justice of the European Union to have the infringement of which the person or undertaking is accused established.«

38 See Article 81 paragraphs 3 to 5 and Article 83 of the Euratom Treaty.

39 See also Article 106a (3) of the Euratom Treaty: »The provisions of the Treaty on European Union and of the Treaty on the Functioning of the European Union shall not derogate from the provisions of this Treaty.«

ture development of their domestic nuclear sector – be it positive, in favour of new build or expansion, or negative, towards a complete phase-out or a substantial reduction. In addition to informing the Commission, Member States should also be ready to discuss their respective intentions with the Commission in order to arrive at a common understanding of the short-, medium- and long-term repercussions on Community policies, such as supply, safeguards and external relations. In this context it should be recalled that pursuant to Article 192 of the Treaty, the Member States have a general legal obligation »to facilitate the achievement of the Community's tasks.«

Although Chapter 4 on investments does not make any explicit provision for such information and consultation, it seems to me that it is not only implied in the logic of this chapter but that in a Community of 27 and soon 28 it should also be formalised and structured by way of a recommendation setting out the procedure to be followed.[40]

6. Establishment of Euratom waste disposal facilities

In July 2011 the Council adopted the Directive establishing a Community framework for the responsible and safe management of spent fuel and radioactive waste.[41] According to Article 4, this Directive is based on the general principle that »each Member State shall have ultimate responsibility for management of the spent fuel and radioactive waste generated in it« and that therefore »radioactive waste shall be disposed of in the Member State in which it was generated.«[42]

No doubt, this principle is entirely in line with the general rule set out in Article 191 (2) TFEU according to which »the polluter should pay«. It is also entirely in line with Chapter 8 of the Euratom Treaty according to which the Community's right of ownership of special fissile material

40 Prior to the Lisbon Treaty, Article 124, second indent, of the Euratom Treaty empowered the Commission to »formulate recommendations ... in the fields covered by this Treaty, if the Treaty expressly so provides or if the Commission considers it necessary.« This provision, however, was repealed by the Lisbon Treaty and replaced by Article 106a (1) of the Euratom Treaty in conjunction with Article 292 TFEU (»The Commission ... shall adopt recommendations.«).

41 Council Directive 2011/70/Euratom of July 2011 establishing a Community framework for the responsible and safe management of spent fuel and radioactive waste, OJ L 199, 2.8.2011, p. 48.

42 Ibid, Article 4 (4).

ceases to exist when this material, having been conditioned as waste, is no longer subject to safeguards.[43]

And yet, one may ask whether an approach which leaves each Member State to its own devices when it comes to tackling the most important and controversial problem of the nuclear sector really does justice to a Treaty which seeks to establish a Community based on joint efforts and common policies – I am almost tempted to add: for better or worse.

Yes, it is true that the Treaty does not make any specific provisions for the disposal of radioactive waste or for the solution of other downstream problems of the nuclear sector.[44] But it is equally true that the Treaty is concluded for an unlimited period[45] in which the problem of nuclear waste is bound to emerge. A reading of the Treaty shows that the Community method is based on »joint effort(s)« (second recital), the discouragement of »unnecessary duplication« (Article 5), a »coordinated development« (Article 40), »joint undertakings« (Chapter 5), »a common supply policy« (Chapter 6), etc.

Pursuant to Article 45 of the Treaty »Undertakings which are of fundamental importance to the development of the nuclear industry in the Community may be established as Joint Undertakings.« Nobody will deny that the most pressing problem of the nuclear industry consists in the yet unresolved problem of creating a safe and permanent repository for highly radioactive nuclear waste, ideally including its retrievability. As a matter of fundamental importance to the further development of the nuclear industry, this problem clearly falls within the ambit of Chapter 5. A Joint Undertaking responsible for the management of spent fuel and radioactive waste, running one or more Euratom waste repositories, would combine the advantages of economies of scale and those offered by Annex III to the

43 See Article 86, paragraph 2: »The Community‘s right of ownership shall extend to all special fissile materials which are produced or imported by a Member State, a person or an undertaking and are subject to the safeguards provided for in Chapter 7.« By virtue of Article 91, »(t)he system of ownership applicable to all objects, materials and assets which are not vested in the Community under this Chapter shall be determined by the law of each Member State.«

44 With the exception of Article 4 (2) in conjunction with Annex I, point IV.5 (»Concentration and storage of useless radioactive waste«). Contrary to the terms used in the EN version of Article 37 (»disposal of radioactive waste«), this provision is not about the disposal of radioactive waste properly so called. As the DE version (»Ableitung radioaktiver Stoffe«) and the FR version (»rejet d‘effluents radioactifs«) show, a correct EN version should use the terms »radioactive emissions«.

45 See Article 208.

Treaty.[46] The siting of the repository could be based on a geographical exploration area which covers not only the European territories of Member States but also the non-European territories under their jurisdiction, as defined by Article 198 of the Treaty. Such an undertaking would provide a European quality label and relieve Member States of difficult, disputed and dilatory domestic choices,[47] while guaranteeing the best possible geographical location also for those Member States whose geological conditions are less adequate for the purpose. A lot more could be said about this point but unfortunately time is short.

7. Euratom rules to facilitate the insurance of nuclear risks

Here I can be brief, since this item already seems to be part of your agenda.

Article 98 of the Treaty empowers and indeed instructs the Council to issue directives obliging Member States to »take all measures necessary to facilitate the conclusion of insurance contracts covering nuclear risks.«

This mandate is twofold, as the use of the plural »directives« may already suggest: First, as its place in Chapter 9 on »The Nuclear Common Market« indicates, the provision is meant to open and liberalise the insurance market for the benefit of the nuclear industry, and this at a higher pace than that foreseen for the slower liberalisation of the general insurance market under the rules on »services« in what used to be Articles 59 to 66 of the former EEC-Treaty.[48] The second mandate, implied by the term »facilitate« goes beyond a mere liberalisation of the insurance market, and seems to call for special advantages for nuclear insurance schemes.

Meanwhile, the first mandate has essentially been fulfilled under EEC-, EC- and EU-Law.

46 By virtue of Article 48 the Council may »make applicable to each Joint Undertaking any or all of the advantages listed in Annex III to this Treaty; each Member State shall for its part ensure that these advantages are conferred.« The advantages listed in Annex III include, inter alia, the recognition of »public interest status«, »compulsory acquisition on the grounds of public interest«, »exemption from all duties and charges« as well as from »direct taxes«.

47 The protracted debate in Germany on an »Endlagersuchgesetz« may illustrate this point.

48 Pursuant to Article 8 (1) of the original EEC Treaty the common market was to be »progressively established during a transitional period of twelve years.«

As regards the second mandate, however, Euratom logic should apply. Here it may be useful to note that Euratom measures facilitating the conclusion of insurance contracts covering nuclear risks may override relevant EU-rules, such as those on state aids, since, by virtue of its Article 106a (3), the Euratom Treaty takes precedence over the EU Treaties. It also needs to be stressed that Article 98 is only about insurance and not about liability, although these concepts may be closely linked, as in the hypothesis of no-fault liability.

Legislative history shows that to this day no directives have been adopted on the basis of Article 98. Based on this provision the Commission has only issued two recommendations to the Member States, in 1965 and 1966, on the harmonisation of legislation applying the Paris Convention.[49]

It is difficult to say more about Article 98 at the present stage, since the development of its potential largely depends on the liability regime upstream which defines the risks, amounts and persons to be insured. I will therefore now pass on to my last point.

8. A reinforced role for the Scientific and Technical Committee

The Treaty envisages four different types of advisory bodies to assist the Commission in the achievement of its tasks. First, there is the European Economic and Social Committee,[50] which also comes first in terms of the number of articles requiring its consultation. Second, there is the Scientific and Technical Committee (STC), established by Article 134 of the Treaty, which is to be consulted under Articles 4 and 7.[51] Third, there is its off-

49 65/42/Euratom: Commission Recommendation of 28 October 1965 to the Member States on the harmonization of legislation applying the Paris Convention of 29 July 1960 and the Brussels Supplementary Convention of 31 January 1963, OJ 196, 18.11.1965, p. 2995 (DE, FR, IT, NL); 66/22/Euratom: Second Commission Recommendation to the Member States on the harmonization of legislation applying the Paris Convention of 29 July 1960, OJ 136, 25.7.1966, p. 2553 (DE, FR, IT, NL).

50 See Article 106a (1) of the Euratom Treaty in conjunction with Article 13 (4) TEU and Articles 301 to 304 TFEU.

51 Those articles are about the promotion of research, the fields of which are listed in Annex I. Pursuant to Article 4 (2), this list may be amended by the Council, acting on a proposal by the Commission, which shall consult the STC. Article 7 provides that Community research and training programmes shall be determined

shoot, the Article 31 Group, which also has to deliver opinions pursuant to Article 37,[52] and finally there are consultative ad-hoc groups which may be established or mandated under Article 135.[53]

While the Article 31 Group plays a quasi-institutional role in the legislative process under Article 31 and in shaping the numerous Commission opinions under Article 37, thus enjoying continued visibility, the STC itself has not been assigned any statutory advisory function in Chapter 3 policies. Its role in Article 4 of the Treaty has never been exercised, since Annex I to the Treaty on the field of research has never been amended, and its contribution under Article 7 is requested only when Community research and training programmes need to be adopted – again a relatively rare event.[54] Thus, the statement in Article 134 that the »Committee must be consulted where this Treaty so provides« may sound impressive but, in reality, does not describe a degree of involvement commensurate with the high-level expertise and standing of the 41 STC members and to their appointment by the Council itself.[55]

Article 134, however, also provides that the »Committee may be consulted in all cases in which the Commission considers this appropriate«. In my view, this avenue to independent high-level expertise should be explored, especially since, pursuant to Article 134, the Members of the STC

---

by the Council, acting on a proposal by the Commission, which shall consult the STC.

52 Article 37 provides: »Each Member State shall provide the Commission with such general data relating to any plan for the disposal of radioactive waste in whatever form as will make it possible to determine whether the implementation of such plan is liable to result in the radioactive contamination of the water, soil or airspace of another Member State.
The Commission shall deliver its opinion within six months, after consulting the group of experts referred to in Article 31.«
See also Commission Recommendation 2010/635/Euratom of 11 October 2010 on the application of Article 37 of the Euratom Treaty, OJ L 279, 23.10.2010, p. 36.

53 By virtue of Article 135 the »Commission may undertake any consultation and establish any study groups necessary to the performance of its tasks.« Based on Article 135 the Commission adopted its Decision 2007/530/Euratom of 17 July 2007 on establishing the European High Level Group on Nuclear Safety and Waste Management, OJ L 195, 27.7.2007, p. 44.

54 Pursuant to Article 7 Euratom research and training programmes may cover a period of up to five years.

55 For the present composition of the STC see: Council Decision of 13 November 2012 appointing the members of the Scientific and Technical Committee, OJ C 360, 22.11.2012, p. 2.

»shall not be bound by any mandatory instructions«. Given the right composition of the STC, its role could go far beyond its traditional domain of »research« to cover fields such as nuclear safety in the broadest sense and also nuclear waste disposal, including its geological and engineering aspects.

III. Conclusion

We have now completed our survey of dormant powers in the Treaty[56] (and I hope the subject has not made you sleepy). The challenges are numerous but so are the responses which the Treaty is able to provide.[57] If the Fukushima accident has taught us one thing, it is not that men and technology can fail – that we knew before – but that an entire state can fail, and can do so at all levels of responsibility. The wisdom of Euratom is that the Treaty has from the outset warded against this potential for failure on the part of individual Member States by creating a supranational Community based on legal discipline and common control systems which are binding on Member States. These systems are open to further development, as new situations may require. In the field of nuclear safety they may and indeed should provide an additional level of redundancy to detect and correct failures in the national safety and control systems – if you wish, a supranational back-up system run by the Commission on behalf of the Community, in the interest of the Member States, neighbouring States, European citizens and international partners. The powers are there, the

56 The present survey, however, does not exhaust the subject. In particular, the potential of Articles 29 and 104 of the Treaty in the fields of export controls and the exchange of scientific and industrial knowledge may be further developed. The same is true of the potential of Article 43 which requires the Commission to »discuss with the persons or undertakings all aspects of investment projects which relate to the objectives of this Treaty.« Given that nuclear safety is one of the aspects which relate to the objectives of the Treaty, the Commission has a clear mandate to discuss all nuclear safety aspects with the persons or undertakings concerned already »before the first contracts are concluded« or the »work begins« (see Article 42) and to »communicate its views to the Member State concerned« (see Article 43).

57 Thus, the opinion expressed in the media after Fukushima that Europe is powerless in the field of nuclear safety (see Die Welt, 1.10.2012, p. 1 »Europäische Ohnmacht«) is unfounded in law. Legal powers and the political willingness to exercise them should therefore not be confused.

lawyers may defend them, but in the end it is for politicians to act. They, however, must be aware of their responsibilities.

Towards an Enhanced EU Regulatory Framework for Nuclear Safety – The Envisaged Commission Proposal for an Amendment of Directive 2009/71/EURATOM Establishing a Community Framework for the Nuclear Safety of Nuclear Installations

Peter Faross[*], *European Commission*

Ladies and Gentlemen, I would have liked to present to you today in detail the new Nuclear Safety Directive. This is impossible as adoption time by the College is only scheduled around the eleventh of June. Nevertheless I will try to give you an insight and develop the background.

- We all remember the terrible events on 11 March 2011, when a magnitude 9.0 earthquake struck some 80 km off Japan's Tohoku coast. The ensuing tsunami set off by the earthquake devastated communities along the Japanese coast, killing some 16000 people. The natural disaster also triggered the shutdown and subsequent meltdown of three reactors at the Fukushima Daiichi Nuclear Power Plant (NPP). Some 100000 people had to be evacuated because of radioactive contamination, and the total costs of the accident have been estimated as high as $250 billion.
- History has shown that each major nuclear accident (Three Mile Island [TMI] [USA, 1979], Chernobyl [Soviet Union, 1986]) has caused a re-examination of the risks of nuclear power leading to more stringent safety requirements. In Fukushima's aftermath came a vigorous reassessment of the safe use of nuclear energy in Europe and worldwide, firstly because it is a severe accident, and secondly because it occurred in a nation that was assumed to have a high standard of safety and technical expertise.
- Although the technical challenges are different with each accident, the analysis of the Fukushima nuclear accident reveals quite substantial,

* Peter Faross is Director of Nuclear Safety and Fuel Cycle and acting Deputy Director-General at the DG Energy.

well-known and recurring technical issues: faulty design, insufficient backup systems, human error, inadequate contingency plans, and poor communications.

- **What has been shown clearly by the Fukushima accident is, that well-known lessons learned from accidents decades ago have not been taken up voluntarily by parts of the industry and have not sufficiently been enforced by regulators, even in a nation that was previously assumed to have a high standard of safety.**
- This conclusion also concerns us in the EU where nuclear energy currently generates close to 30% of all electricity in the EU.
- Also here in Europe the costs of a nuclear accident could be so large, that they would be potentially ruinous to national economies. **It is therefore essential for society and the economy to avoid the occurrence of any nuclear accident in a Member State of the European Union by ensuring the highest possible quality of regulatory oversight and standards of nuclear safety.**

In this way the Fukushima nuclear accident has renewed political attention on the measures needed to minimise risk and guarantee the most robust levels of nuclear safety.

- Under this perspective, based upon a clear mandate from the European Council at its meeting of 24-25 March 2011, the European Commission, together with the European Nuclear Safety Regulators Group (ENSREG), launched an EU-wide comprehensive risk & safety assessments of NPPs (the so called »Stress Tests«). These tests highlighted a high safety level in the EU, but also identified a large number of shortcomings in nuclear safety approaches and industry practices in the participating countries.
- In addition to the Stress Tests process, the mandate from the European Council included the request to the Commission to »review the existing legal and regulatory framework for the safety of nuclear installations« and to »propose by the end of 2011 any improvements that may be necessary«.

At the same time also the European Parliament has called for an urgent revision of the Nuclear Safety Directive with a view to its strengthening, namely by taking into account the results of the Stress Tests implemented in the aftermath of the Fukushima accident.

The areas identified for revising the current Nuclear Safety Directive are described in more detail in the »Communication from the Commission to the Council and the European Parliament on the comprehensive risk and safety assessments (›stress-tests‹) of nuclear power plants in the EU and related activities« of 4 October 2012.

- To get a comprehensive picture of the situation and possible ways to improve nuclear safety within the EU, the Commission has organised with ENSREG several conferences and public debates in Brussels together with a wide range of stakeholders, including NGOs, on the process, the intermediate and final results of as well as the conclusions from the Stress Tests: the 1st European Nuclear Safety Conference on 28-29 June 2011, a Stakeholders Conference on Peer Reviews on 17 January 2012, and a Public Debate on Stress Tests and Peer Review Results on 8 May 2012. This will now be followed up by the 2nd European Nuclear Safety Conference, which will take place next week on 11/12 June 2013 in Brussels.

Key areas for improvement of nuclear safety have been identified. These problem areas concern technical issues (in particular plant siting and design), the regulatory oversight, aspects related to nuclear safety governance (regulatory independence and transparency) as well as the issue of emergency preparedness and response.

* * *

From all these discussions the following main objectives of the envisaged enhancement of the existing nuclear safety legislation were defined. The proposed amendments aim at enhancing the regulatory framework for nuclear safety in the EU, in particular by:

- Defining a new nuclear safety objective;
- Strengthening the role and effective independence of the national regulatory authorities;
- Enhancing transparency on nuclear safety matters;
- Strengthening existing principles, and introducing new safety requirements, addressing specific technical issues across the entire lifecycle of nuclear installations, particularly NPPs;
- Reinforcing monitoring and exchange of experiences, by establishing a European system of topical peer reviews;

- Establishing a mechanism for developing EU-wide harmonised nuclear safety guidelines.

* * *

As one possible way to achieve these objectives an enhancement of international cooperation in particular in the framework of the IAEA has to be considered.

Following the events at Fukushima, all IAEA Member States generally acknowledge the need to enhance the effectiveness, governance and enforceability of the international legal framework for nuclear safety. At international level, safety principles and standards governing nuclear safety have been developed and agreed. Through the IAEA, the main instruments governing nuclear safety are recommended IAEA safety »standards« and international Conventions. However, these safety »standards« are legally non-binding, while the international Conventions are legally binding but not enforceable. Thus, for example, the Convention on Nuclear Safety (CNS) does not provide sanctions, penalties or other types of coercive implementation mechanisms in case the Contracting Parties do not comply with its requirements. The CNS provides for a dispute-settlement mechanism which relies solely on consultations between Contracting Parties in case of a disagreement on the interpretation or application of the Convention. On the other hand, the Euratom legislation benefits from clear and strong mechanisms for sanction for its proper transposition and implementation.

Also, we have to acknowledge, that any revision of the international Conventions can be expected to take considerably longer than the possible Euratom legislative amendment process, due to the complex procedures in place, requiring consensus or the condition of attaining a certain quorum of the Contracting Parties' votes. Therefore we have to improve our own legislations and cannot wait for amendments of the Convention on Nuclear Safety.

Moreover, the rules agreed at international level have a more general character, as they need to be applied worldwide, while Euratom legislation would be tailored to the specific needs and situations existing in the Member States.

When assessing the cited objectives against the existing legislative framework, the weaknesses of the current Euratom nuclear safety legislation, in particular of the Nuclear Safety Directive become obvious. This Directive sets up a legally binding Euratom framework based upon internationally recognised principles and obligations, underlying a nuclear safety legislative, administrative and organisational system.

Taking into account that the scope of this Directive is limited to overall principles, it can by no means address the technical issues identified as key risk contributors in the Fukushima nuclear accident and the Stress Tests, nor take account of initiatives from various expert groups and international developments in this area, as those matters are simply not covered by the scope of the current Directive.

Therefore is very clear, that without new or revised Euratom legislation, the problem areas described will continue to exist and will show little prospect of improvement.

* * *

However, from a lawyer's view before all political considerations to legislate, the question rises about Euratom competence and the principle of subsidiarity.

- The **competence** of Euratom to regulate in the field of the health protection against ionising radiation is explicitly recognised by the Euratom Treaty. In the Treaty's Preamble, the Member States declare themselves *»anxious to create conditions of safety necessary to eliminate hazards to the life and health of the public«.* Pursuant to Article 2(b) of the Treaty, the Community is mandated to *»establish uniform safety standards to protect the health of workers and of the general public and ensure that they are applied.«* Title II, Chapter 3 »Health and Safety«, sets up a number of detailed provisions intended to establish, give effect and apply the basic safety standards mentioned in Article 2(b) of the Euratom Treaty. Article 30(1) of the Euratom Treaty establishes that *»basic standards shall be laid down within the Community for the protection of the health of workers and the general public against the dangers arising from ionizing radiations.«*
- Article 31 sets out the procedure for establishing the basic standards, while Article 32 provides that the basic standards may be revised or supplemented.
- The ruling of the Court of Justice of the EU in the Case C29/99 acknowledged that *»it is not appropriate, in order to define the Community's competences, to draw an artificial distinction between the protection of the health of the general public and the safety of sources of ionising radiation«.* The basic safety standards aiming mainly at the protection of the health of the workers and the general public against

the dangers arising from ionising radiation can be thus »supplemented«, in the sense of the Euratom Treaty, with safety requirements. Consequently, the legal basis for regulating nuclear safety on Community level is defined by Articles 31 and 32 Euratom Treaty. Therefore the Nuclear Safety Directive is legally based on Articles 31 and 32 Euratom Treaty. For this reason, any legislative amendment of the Safety Directive in the scope of the »basic standards« as defined in Article 30 Euratom Treaty has to be based on the same Treaty provisions.

- Having regard to the **principle of subsidiarity** the **cross-border consequences of a nuclear incident** and particularly the public need for information, an EU wide approach on transparency issues is essential. This can ensure that, irrespective of state borders, the public is properly informed on all relevant nuclear safety matters to ensure uniform level of transparency and information throughout the EU.

It is evident that the effects of nuclear accidents do not stop at state borders and can entail potential harmful consequences for the health of workers and citizens but also wide-ranging economic implications. In Europe, the Stress Tests have confirmed that there are not only continued differences between the EU Member States in ensuring comprehensive and transparent identification and management of key safety issues, but that also significant gaps remain. Therefore, a strengthened Euratom legislation could include a set of technical provisions at an appropriate level of detail for a framework legal instrument. These provisions should ensure a common EU approach to nuclear safety, taking into account the progress towards harmonisation reflecting the consensus reached by the Member States in fora such as the IAEA or WENRA.

A flexible mechanism of developing EU-wide technical criteria or guidelines with special regard to the principle of proportionality should be envisaged in which the knowledge and practical experience of the experts from the Member States is fully used.

The experience from the Fukushima accident and the valuable insights coming from the Stress Tests have clearly shown that a strong and transparent monitoring system (including in particular peer-reviews) is an essential element to ensure the effective and continuous implementation of any safety regime. Competent regulatory authorities coordinating in the context of expert groups such as ENSREG, could contribute with their expertise to identifying the relevant safety topics and in carrying out these peer reviews.

* * *

What would be the preferred legislative policy options under Euratom law to achieve these objectives?

Intensive discussions within ENSREG and the Article 31 Euratom Treaty group of experts resulted in the following picture:

The legislative revision should build upon and enhance the approach of the current Nuclear Safety Directive.

A first step would be to amend the Nuclear Safety Directive by strengthening existing general Principles and Requirements (e.g. role and independence of the national regulatory authorities; transparency) and adding new general Principles and Requirements (e.g. on-site emergency preparedness and response; siting, design & construction, and operation [e.g. periodic safety assessments] of nuclear installations).

At the same time, the existing mechanism of cooperation between the European Commission and the Member States on the implementation of the measures arising from the Stress Test process, through entities such as ENSREG, should be used to develop more specific nuclear criteria, or better to be called **specific safety guidelines** to define the established Principles and Requirements more in detail.

Mainly 3 different possible ways to formalize this process could be considered:

- The specific nuclear safety guidelines would be developed in close cooperation between expert working groups such as ENSREG and WENRA, and Commission experts. Subsequently, these nuclear safety guidelines would be adopted as the Commission's »implementing acts« according to Article 291 TFEU and using the relevant »comitology« procedure laid down in Regulation 182/2011. For this purpose, a »comitology« committee, composed of representatives of all Member States, would be created by the legislative proposal to assist the Commission.
- The specific nuclear safety guidelines would be developed in close cooperation between expert working groups such as ENSREG and WENRA, and Commission experts. Subsequently, these nuclear safety guidelines would become the content of Commission Recommendations issued under Article 33 paragraph 2 Euratom Treaty.
- The specific nuclear safety guidelines would be developed in close cooperation between expert working groups such as ENSREG and WENRA, on the basis of the outcome of the peer reviews, jointly by

the Member States, with the support of the competent regulatory bodies.

Offering a more flexible approach for the Member States with regard to the application of the most recent developments to be taken into account in a dynamic and innovative way, the last option would allow for a swift adoption of the criteria and their update in the future. Discussions within ENSREG have also shown that this option apparently finds the highest political acceptance amongst the relevant safety authorities in the Member States. Following a step-wise approach, it would also be possible, learning from the experience gained from the application of such guidelines.

Summarising, the preferred legislative option would therefore be the following:

- To amend the existing Council Directive 2009/71/Euratom establishing a Community framework for the nuclear safety of nuclear installations by strengthening existing and introducing new general nuclear safety objectives and requirements.
- These would be complemented by harmonised Euratom nuclear safety guidelines.
- It would establish procedures to carry out topical peer reviews to monitor their implementation at national level.
- It would also provide for greater independence of the regulators and increased public transparency about the performance of the industry and the regulators.
- While some of the underlying measures of the preferred option can be implemented without delay, others require technical development work with input from Member States to enable or complete their implementation by implementing guidelines.

* * *

At the end, for reasons of completeness I would like to add some additional remarks on our other two related projects related to nuclear safety which are however still in a preliminary phase: emergency preparedness and response and the Commission initiative on nuclear third party liability insurance.

In the course of the stress tests, the analysis of **emergency preparedness and response** arrangements (or severe accident management) was limited to the nuclear power plant sites, which is also the area falling strictly under the responsibility of the operator and the national nuclear safety regulator.

However, in light of the messages received during public meetings and the lessons learned from the Fukushima accident, the importance of ensuring appropriate off-site emergency preparedness and response arrangements has clearly been acknowledged as an important additional activity to improve citizens' safety.

In the EU, specific actions and decisions in the area of emergency preparedness and response in case of a nuclear emergency are taken mainly at national level.

A range of relevant EU legislative instruments are already in place, on the basis of which several mechanisms such as the ECURIE (European Community Urgent Radiological Information Exchange), EURDEP (EUropean Radiological Data Exchange Platform) or MIC (Monitoring and Information Centre of the Community Civil Protection Mechanism) could be activated in case of a nuclear emergency.

ENSREG and the Commission have agreed that the analysis needs to be extended to off-site emergency preparedness and response arrangements. As a first step, the Commission launched a study on the »Review of Current Off-Site Nuclear Emergency Preparedness and Response Arrangements in EU Member States and Neighbouring Countries«.

The main objectives of this study contract are:

- to review the existing arrangements in EU Member States and neighbouring countries with regard to off-site nuclear emergency preparedness and response capabilities,
- to identify inconsistencies and gaps, including cross-border arrangements, and
- to develop on this basis proposals for areas of possible improvements.

Based on the findings and recommendations of the study, a Communication on Emergency preparedness and response is planned for October/November 2013. This Communication will aim at putting forward ideas to make emergency preparedness and response arrangements in the EU and its neighbourhood more effective, to optimise resources and avoid duplications, nationally and in particular across borders.

And finally I would like to make some remarks on the **Commission initiative on nuclear third party liability insurance**.

Summarizing, one can say that in the EU, the nuclear liability regimes of Member States (MS) are governed by national laws. In 22 out of 27

MS, the main principles of these regimes have however been shaped by two international conventions: either by the Paris Convention under the auspices of the Organisation for Economic Co-operation and Development (OECD) or by the Vienna Convention under the auspices of the International Atomic Energy Agency (IAEA). In addition, 5 MS (AT, CY, IE, LU and MT) are not party to any convention.

The coexistence of these different legal regimes has led to a situation in which nuclear liability in the EU as a whole is currently **inadequately defined**.

Any initiative of the Commission should therefore aim at increasing legal coherence in the EU, in order to: 1) tackle the impact on the functioning of the internal energy market and 2) to improve victim compensation, in particular in the event of an accident with cross-border effects.

I believe that these three important initiatives of the European Commission will contribute to enhance further the level of nuclear safety throughout the EU and could serve as a good example to neighboring countries, and even worldwide, how effectively to improve the protection of the population against possible radiological risks stemming from the operation of nuclear facilities.

First Working Session

»Nuclear Safety and Safeguards in the EU«

Chair: *Dr. Michael Micklinghoff,* Senior Advisor, formerly E.ON Kernkraft, Hannover

Secretary: *Julian Rotter,* Lazarski University, Warsaw, Poland

Comments on the Planned Revision of the Euratom Directive on Nuclear Safety

Andreas Woitecki[1]

I. Introduction

The adoption of the Nuclear Safety Directive[2] in 2009 put a preliminary end to several years of intensive discussions between Member States and the European Commission which had started in 2002 with the proposal by the Commission for a nuclear package. For the first time in the history of the European Communities binding legislation on nuclear safety was available at Community level. While in the field of radiation protection several legal instruments had been developed,[3] Community action in the field of nuclear safety was until 2009 merely restricted to non-binding acts and informal cooperation.[4]

---

1 LL.M. (Edinburgh); German Federal Ministry for the Environment, Nature Protection and Nuclear Safety, Division for Nuclear Legislation. The views expressed here are those of the author and may not necessarily represent the views of, and should not be attributed to, the Federal Ministry for the Environment, Nature Conservation and Nuclear Safety. The author would like to thank Isabell Koch, Dr. Norbert Pelzer and Dr. Siegbert Schneider for their valuable comments and suggestions.

2 Council Directive 2009/71/Euratom of 25 June 2009 establishing a Community framework for the nuclear safety of nuclear installation, OJ 2009 L 172/18, hereinafter referred to as 2009 Directive.

3 See overview at W Kilb, »The European Atomic Energy Community and its Primary and Secondary Law« in *International Nuclear Law: History, Evolution and Outlook – 10th Anniversary of the International School of Nuclear Law*, OECD Nuclear Energy Agency 2010, 43, 59.

4 M Garribba, A Chirteş, M Naduzaite, »The Directive Establishing a Community Framework for the Nuclear Safety of Nuclear Installations: The EU Approach to Nuclear Safety« *(2009) Nuclear Law Bulletin No. 84*, 23, 26; T Derek, »The proposals of the European Commission for Council Directives on Nuclear Safety« in H-J Koch, A Roßnagel (eds.), *12. Deutsches Atomrechtssymposium 2003* (Nomos Verlagsgesellschaft Baden-Baden 2003), 25, 28 et seq.; G Hermes, »Die europäische Regulierung des Atomsektors und Gemeinschaftsrecht« in H-J Koch, A Roßnagel (eds.), *12. Deutsches Atomrechtssymposium 2003* (Nomos Verlagsgesellschaft Baden-Baden 2003), 37, 44; see also Council Resolution of 22

The deadline for implementation of the Nuclear Safety Directive ended in June 2011, the first report on its implementation under Article 9(1) is due in July 2014. The 2009 Directive is a framework directive whose contents are based primarily on the Convention on Nuclear Safety (CNS)[5] and on the Safety Fundamentals of the International Atomic Energy Agency (IAEA).[6] It contains certain basic principles and requirements such as the establishment of a national framework and of a competent regulatory authority, the prime responsibility of the licence holder and obligations with regard to expertise and skills in nuclear safety and with regard to transparency. Its adoption has been described by some authors as a major step in the history of the European Union which makes the EU an »example for the rest of the world«[7] and by others as the opening of Pandora's box »which the Member States had kept close for a long period of time«.[8] In any case, it is understandable that Member States are careful when for the first time responsibilities are transferred in a political sensitive domain such as nuclear safety.[9]

July 1975 on the technological problems of nuclear safety, OJ No. C 185/1 of 14 August 1975, and Council Resolution of 18 June 1992 on the technological problems of nuclear safety, OJ No. C 172/2 of 8 July 1992.

5 IAEA Doc. INFCIRC/449.

6 IAEA Safety Fundamentals: Fundamental Safety Principles, IAEA Safety Standard Series No. SF-1 (2006).

7 Garribba et al., *supra* note 4, 33; W Kilb, *supra* note 3, 86; a similar judgement has been made regarding the adoption of the Radioactive Waste Directive (Council Directive 2011/70/Euratom of 19 July 2011 establishing a Community framework for the responsible and safe management of spent fuel and radioactive waste (OJ L 199 of 2 August 2011, 48), see U Blohm-Hieber, »The Radioactive Waste Directive: a Necessary Step in the Management of Spent Fuel and Radioactive Waste in the European Union« in *(2011) Nuclear Law Bulletin No. 88*, 21, 35.

8 Y Pouleur, P Krs, »The Momentum of the European Directive on Nuclear Safety – From the Complexity of Nuclear Safety to Key Messages Addressed to European Citizens«, *(2010) Nuclear Law Bulletin No. 85*, 5, 7.

9 This conclusion is not shared by every author: a harsh critique of the 2009 Directive as a »skeleton of a legal framework« can be found at M S Ferro, »Directive 2009/71/Euratom: the losing battle against discrimination and protection of sovereignty« in *(2009) International Journal of Nuclear Law, Vol. 2, No. 4*, 295 *et seq*.

II. Fukushima and the call for a revision?

Already prior to the deadline for national implementation of the Nuclear Safety Directive in March 2011 the Fukushima accident occurred. As a reaction the European Council asked the Commission in March 2011 »to review the existing legal and regulatory framework for the safety of nuclear installations« and to propose »any improvements that may be necessary«.[10] Furthermore, the Council called in March and again in December 2011 for the »full implementation« of the 2009 Directive.[11] In neither conclusion the European Council explicitly called for the revision of the Nuclear Safety Directive.

III. The DG Energy Draft and the reaction of ENSREG

In December 2012 the Directorate Energy of the European Commission sent a draft proposal for a revised Nuclear Safety Directive[12] to the European Nuclear Safety Regulators Group (ENSREG) for consultation. ENSREG is a body set up by a decision of the Commission based on Article 135 of the Euratom Treaty.[13] It is not mandatory for the Commission under the Euratom Treaty to consult ENSREG in the legislative process based on Article 30 *et seq.* of the Euratom Treaty. The Commission is only required to obtain the opinion of the Group of Experts referred to in Article 31 of the Euratom Treaty and of the Economic and Social Committee (ECOSOC).[14]

10 Conclusions of the European Council of 24/25 March 2011 (EUCO 10/1/11 REV 1), para. 31.

11 *Ibid.*; see also Conclusions of the European Council of 9 December 2011 (EUCO 139/1/11 REV 1), para. 9.

12 See Draft proposal for a Council Directive amending Directive 2009/71/EURATOM establishing a Community framework for the nuclear safety of nuclear installations (version 28 December 2012), available at http://ec.europa.eu/energy/nuclear/radiation_protection/doc/art31/2013_04_draft_nuclear_safety_directive.pdf, hereinafter after referred to as DG Energy Draft.

13 Commission Decision of 17 July 2007 on establishing the European High Level Group on Nuclear Safety and Waste Management (2007/530/Euratom), OJ L 195/44.

14 Article 31(1) of the Euratom Treaty; the Article 31-Group has delivered its opinion in March 2013, see Opinion of the Group of Experts referred to in Article 31 of the Euratom Treaty on the Draft proposal for a Council Directive amending Directive 2009/71/EURATOM establishing a Community framework for the nuclear safety of nuclear installations (version 28 December 2012), available at

The DG Energy Draft includes a number of significant changes and amendments compared to the 2009 Directive. It introduces in particular new requirements regarding the competent regulatory authority.[15] Moreover, the draft introduces new and detailed obligations regarding information to the public both for the regulator and for the licence holder.[16] At the core of the draft are several specific obligations on siting, design and construction, operation and on-site emergency preparedness and response.[17] The 2009 Directive as a framework directive does not contain any such provisions. Furthermore, pursuant to Article 13 of the DG Energy Draft, Community nuclear safety criteria shall be developed by the Commission with the advice and assistance by experts from Member States. Finally, the draft contains a new verification mechanism which would give the Commission under certain conditions the power to carry out a »verification mission« to a Member State.[18]

The DG Energy Draft has been subject to much debate within ENSREG. Many members of ENSREG have deemed it premature to revise the Nuclear Safety Directive even before the first reports on its implementation have been submitted and evaluated.[19] The regulators in ENSREG decided not only to establish a position regarding the draft directive but also to propose alternative text for a revised directive. On 11 April 2013 ENSREG adopted a position paper and an alternative draft for a revised Nuclear Safety Directive.[20] It is highly remarkable that within only few months the regulators within ENSREG, which represent very diverse views and interests regarding the peaceful use of nuclear energy, have agreed unanimously on a full alternative text of a revised Nuclear Safety Directive.

---

http://ec.europa.eu/energy/nuclear/radiation_protection/doc/art31/2013_04_opinion_nuclear_safety.pdf.

15 Article 5 of the DG Energy Draft, *supra* note 12.

16 Article 8 of the DG Energy Draft, *supra* note 12.

17 Articles 9-12 of the DG Energy Draft, *supra* note 12.

18 Article 16 of the DG Energy Draft, *supra* note 12.

19 See ENSREG, Explanatory Note on Draft Euratom Nuclear Safety Directive (11 April 2013), available at http://www.ensreg.eu/sites/default/files/ 4%20ENSREG%20Explanatory%20note%2005042013%20ver%20final_1.pdf, 1.

20 ENSREG, Technical Input into a revised Nuclear Safety Directive and supporting documents, 11 April 2013, available at http://www.ensreg.eu/node/1323, hereinafter referred to as ENSREG Draft.

IV. Commission Proposal of 13 June 2013

On 13 June 2013 Commissioner Oettinger presented the draft proposal of the European Commission for an amended Nuclear Safety Directive.[21] Technically speaking this draft is not yet the proposal of the Commission presented to the Council but the draft presented under Article 31 of the Euratom Treaty for the opinion of the European Economic and Social Committee (ECOSOC). However, on the basis of the Commission Draft the Atomic Question Group of the Council has initiated its negotiations under Irish Presidency on 25 June 2013. The ECOSOC is expected to deliver its opinion in September 2013. Subsequently, the Commission will adopt the proposal and send it to the Council. The Commission Proposal includes some proposals of the ENSREG Draft. Not surprisingly, the Commission has also retained some of the elements of the DG Energy Draft.[22]

All three drafts – the DG Energy Draft, the ENSREG Draft and the Commission Proposal – differ from each other and from the 2009 Directive. Nevertheless there are some main topics which can be identified that are addressed in each draft. These main topics include obligations on the competent regulatory authority as well as obligations on transparency, safety of nuclear installations and the establishment of a verification mechanism. In the following it shall be examined how these topics are dealt with in the different drafts.[23] Although with the publication of the Commission Proposal in June 2013 the DG Energy Draft and the ENSREG Draft seem to be outdated, reference will also be made to their contents. This is first because the Commission Proposal can best be understood with the other drafts as a background which each illustrates a different approach to the main topics set out below. And secondly because it is not unlikely that some elements of the DG Energy Draft and the ENSREG Draft will be picked up again in the course of negotiations which have started in June 2013. But before dealing with the main topics in detail, the question of legislative competence shall be addressed.

---

21 COM(2013) 343 final (June 2013), hereinafter referred to as Commission Proposal; see also Press Release of the European Commission: »EU Nuclear Stress Tests: Legally binding reviews every six years«, of 13 June 2013, available at http://ec.europa.eu/energy/nuclear/safety/safety_en.htm.

22 See in detail *infra* part VI.

23 *Ibid.*

V. Competence of the Euratom Community?

Does the Euratom Community have legislative competence in the field of nuclear safety? One might answer that this question has been positively and comprehensively answered by the European Court of Justice (ECJ) in its decision C-29/99[24], and certainly this is the view of the European Commission.[25] Yet a closer look at the decision shows that things are slightly more complicated.

Without any doubt, in decision C-29/99 the ECJ has ruled that the Euratom Community has wide competences in the field of nuclear safety on the basis of the Euratom Treaty. The court based its finding in particular on the competence of the Community in Article 2(b) of the Euratom Treaty to »establish uniform safety standards to protect the health of workers and of the general public and [to] ensure that they are applied« and found that it was »apparent that such protection cannot be achieved without controlling the sources of harmful radiation«.[26] By this reference the court dismissed the distinction between radiation aspects and technical aspects of nuclear safety proposed by the Advocate General.[27] The court found that it was »not appropriate, in order to define the Community's competences, to draw an artificial distinction between the protection of the health of the general public and the safety of sources of ionising radiation«.[28] Thus, it is correct that after the ruling of the ECJ in decision 29/99, when defining possible activities of the Euratom Community, one can make no distinction on the basis of the sources of ionising radiation and *a priori* exclude technical aspects of nuclear safety from the competences of the Community under the Euratom Treaty.

However, this does not answer the question what *kind* of action the community is allowed to take on the basis of the Euratom Treaty and in particular on the basis of its Title II, Chapter 3. Article 30 *et seq.* of the Euratom Treaty establish a variety of competences, in particular the competence to lay down basic safety standards (Article 30, 31), the compe-

24 Case C-29/99, *Commission v Council* of 10 December 2002 (European Court Reports 2002 p. I-11221).

25 See Commission Proposal, *supra* note 21 (Page 5 of Explanatory Memorandum as well as recital 4 of the draft directive).

26 Para. 76 of the decision, *supra* note 24.

27 Case C-29/99, *Commission v Council* of 10 December 2002, Opinion of Advocate General Jacobs delivered on 13 December 2001, para. 138 *et seq.*

28 Para. 82 of the decision, *supra* note 24.

tence to supplement these standards (Article 32 I) and the competence to make recommendations (Article 33 II).

In case 29/99 it sufficed for the court to find *any* competence of the Euratom Community with regard to the areas covered by the Convention on Nuclear Safety. This is because the decision dealt with the Council decision approving the accession of the Euratom Community to the CNS. In this particular case, it did not matter what kind of competence the Euratom Treaty confers to the Euratom Community. For example, the ECJ based its finding that the Community had competences with regard to Articles 14 (Assessment and Verification of Safety), 18 (Design and Construction) and 19 (Operation) of the CNS solely on the competence of the Euratom Community to make recommendations to the Member States according to Article 33(2) of the Euratom Treaty.[29] Yet the question which has to be answered regarding the Nuclear Safety Directive is whether the Euratom Community has the competence to legislate. Binding legislation in the field of nuclear safety can only be based on the competences to lay down and supplement basic safety standards in accordance with Articles 31, 32 of the Euratom Treaty. The competence to make recommendations (Article 33(2)) would not suffice.[30]

For example, the DG Energy draft contains provisions on design and operation which are similar to those of the CNS. Thus, the draft regulates subject matters which, in decision 29/99, the ECJ has based on the competence to make recommendations. Solely on the basis of decision 29/99 it is therefore far from clear whether the Euratom Community has legislative competence in particular with regard to design and operation of nuclear power plants.[31] It could well be argued that there is no competence to legislate in the field of design and operation and that the Community only has the competence to make recommendations on these subject matters.[32]

29 Paras. 92, 105 of the decision, *supra* note 24.

30 On the basis of similar considerations, Karpenstein is very critical regarding the legislative competence of the Community for certain provisions in the 2009 Directive, see U Karpenstein, »Vorgaben für Behörden und Betreiber aus der EURATOM-Richtlinie über die nukleare Sicherheit« (2010) *Recht der Energiewirtschaft,* 170, 174.

31 Garribba et al., *supra* note 4, 27, take the view that on the basis of Case C-29/99 the Euratom Community has wide competences to legislate in the fields of nuclear safety.

32 On the legislative competence with a view to the 2009 directive see U Karpenstein, *supra* note 30, 174; S Schneider, S Schäfer, »EU-Nuklearpaket – der richtige Weg zu mehr Sicherheit in Europa? (2004) *Zeitschrift für Europäisches Umwelt- und Planungsrecht* 197, 204; G Hermes, »Die europäische Regulierung

Let aside decision 29/99, what are the criteria to establish legislative competence on the basis of Articles 31, 32 Euratom Treaty? This question is not easy to answer. Hermes[33] has developed convincing criteria regarding the limitation of legislative competences of the Euratom Community. In his view the Community has a wide range of responsibilities concerning the causes of ionizing radiation, which include technological issues of nuclear safety. However, it has only competences to legislate in matters with a *sufficient link* to radiation protection.[34] The looser such link is and the more detailed the proposed provisions are the more do these provisions need a detailed and proper justification with a view to the objectives of the Euratom Treaty and the more is the competence to legislate restricted to general framework requirements.[35] Whether there is such link with regard to all the provisions of the revised Nuclear Safety Directive has to be assessed on the basis of the Commission proposal and continuously on the basis of the texts developed during negotiations.

VI. Main topics

1. Competent regulatory authority[36]

The three drafts for a revised directive introduce new requirements with regard to the competent regulatory authority.[37] The 2009 Directive obliges Member States to ensure that the competent regulatory authority »is functionally separate from any other body or organisation concerned with the promotion, or utilisation of nuclear energy, including electricity production, in order to ensure effective independence from undue influence in its regulatory decision making.« This approach is based on the Convention on

des Atomsektors und Gemeinschaftsrecht«, *supra* note 4, 61; W Hohlefelder, »Die EU-Richtlinie zur Kernenergie – Kompetenzen und Grenzen«, (2003) *atw - International Journal for Nuclear Power*, 164, 165; see also W Frenz, »Umweltschutz und nukleare Sicherheit in der europäischen Atompolitik« in *(2011) Umwelt und Planungsrecht,* 7.

33 G Hermes, »Die europäische Regulierung des Atomsektors und Gemeinschaftsrecht«, *supra* note 4.

34 *Ibid.*, 61 *et seq.*

35 *Ibid.*, see also S Schneider, S Schäfer, *supra* note 32, 204.

36 On this topic see in detail A Vorwerk, »Unabhängigkeit der Atomaufsicht«, published in this book, p. 407.

37 Article 5 of the DG Energy Draft, *supra* note 21.

Nuclear Safety.[38] The Radioactive Waste Directive of 2011 uses a very similar approach.[39]

The DG Energy Draft goes far beyond this standard and states in its Article 5(3):

> »Member States shall guarantee the effective independence of the competent regulatory authority, for carrying out the regulatory tasks laid out in paragraphs 4 to 6, assuring that safety judgements are not subordinated to political, economic or societal interests. For this purpose, Member States shall ensure that:
>
> (a) the competent regulatory authority is legally distinct and functionally separate from any other public or private entity;
>
> (b) [...]«

This provision would oblige Member States to establish an authority which is institutionally separate from governmental hierarchy. Role model for such an authority is the independent agency. The system of independent agencies is well known in certain Member States. For example, in France there exist more than 30 independent administrative authorities.[40] One of these agencies is the *Autorité de sûreté nucléaire (ASN)*. These *Autorités de régulation indépendantes* have a major role with regard to regulation and supervision of sectors of French Economy. A common feature of all French independent regulatory authorities is that they are formally outside of governmental structures. They are not only functional separate from their objects of regulation but institutionally separated from the government.[41] That does however not imply that they are free from any governmental influence or political control (a fact that is sometimes omitted in the discussions on the advantages of independent agencies).[42]

---

38 Article 8(2) of the CNS, *supra* note 5; see also Y Pouleur, P Krs, *supra* note 8, 19.

39 Council Directive 2011/70/Euratom of 19 July 2011 establishing a Community framework for the responsible and safe management of spent fuel and radioactive waste (OJ L 199 of 2 August 2011, 48), Article 6(2).

40 M P Gélard, »Rapport sur les Autorités Administratives Indépendantes«, Office Parlementaire d'Evaluation de la Législation, (No. 3166, Assemblée Nationale, Constitution du 4 Octobre 1958, Douzième Législature, Enregistré à la Présidence de l'Assemblée nationale le 15 juin 2006; No. 404, Sénat, Session Ordinaire de 2005-2006, Annexe au procès-verbal de la séance du 15 juin 2006), available at http://www.assemblee-nationale.fr/12/pdf/rap-off/i3166-tI.pdf.

41 Y Vilain, »Demokratische Legitimität und Verfassungsmäßigkeit unabhängiger Regulierungsbehörden« in J Masing, G Marcou, *Unabhängige Regulierungsbehörden – Organisationsrechtliche Herausforderungen in Frankreich und Deutschland* (Mohr Siebeck 2010), 11.

42 *Ibid.*, 20; see also Vorwerk, *supra* note 36.

In other Member States such as Germany the concept of independent authorities is in general unknown.[43] Traditionally the whole administration is linked to governmental responsibility, i.e. authorities are embedded in an administrative hierarchy with ministries at the top. While in France authorities independent from the government are not only a permissible but even a desirable solution in Germany they are regarded as a challenge to the principle of democracy.[44] In general, it follows from the principle of democracy as enshrined in the German Constitution[45] that all administrative authorities have to be subordinated to the government (*Verbot ministerialfreier Räume*).[46] The only exceptions are the *German Federal Bank* (*Deutsche Bundesbank*) and the *German Federal Court of Auditors (Bundesrechnungshof)*. Their autonomy is guaranteed under the German Constitution.[47]

Nevertheless, there is a growing number of EU directives where independence is understood as institutional independence meaning separation not only from the objects of regulation but also from government structures. The required degree of independence varies in the legal acts.[48] For example, the directives concerning common rules for the internal market in electricity and gas as revised in 2009 require a strict standard of independence, namely an authority which is »legally distinct and functionally

43 G Hermes, »Abhängige und unabhängige Verwaltungsbehörden – ein Überblick über die Bundesverwaltung« in J Masing, G Marcou, *supra* note 41, 53; J Hellermann, »Unabhängigkeit der Behörden als Ausfluss des Trennungsprinzips oder im Sinne von Weisungsfreiheit?« in M Burgi, *14. Deutsches Atomrechtssymposium* (Nomos Verlagsgesellschaft Baden-Baden 2013), 127, 130.

44 G Hermes, »Abhängige und unabhängige Verwaltungsbehörden – ein Überblick über die Bundesverwaltung«, *supra* note 43, 53, with further references.

45 Basic Law for the Federal Republic of Germany in the revised version published in the Federal Law Gazette Part III, classification number 100-1, as last amended by the Act of 21 July 2010 (Federal Law Gazette I p. 944), Article 28(1)/(2).

46 See Decision of the German Federal Constitutional Court of 24 May 1995, 2 BvF 1/92, BVerfGE 93, 37, 66 *et seq.*

47 Article 88 / Article 114 Abs. 2 of the German Basic Law, *supra* note 45; see also Vorwerk, *supra* note 36.

48 See, for example, Directive 2009/73/EC of the European Parliament and of the Council of 13 July 2009 concerning common rules for the internal market in natural gas and repealing Directive 2003/55/EC, Article 39; Directive 2009/72/EC of the European Parliament and of the Council of 13 July 2009 concerning common rules for the internal market in electricity and repealing Directive 2003/54/EC, Article 35; Directive 2002/21/EC of the European Parliament and of the Council of 7 March 2002 on a common regulatory framework for electronic communications networks and services (Framework Directive), Article 3(2).

independent from any other public or private entity« and which can take »autonomous decisions, independently from any political body«.[49] The provisions regarding the competent regulatory authority in the DG Energy draft are apparently inspired by and based on the relevant provisions in these directives.

These requirements raise political questions: is there any evidence that institutionally independent authorities are better equipped to regulate nuclear installations? Is *institutional* independence the decisive criterion? They also raise legal questions with a view to the principle of institutional autonomy of the Member States and the legislative competence of the Euratom Community.

The EURATOM Treaty does not contain competences regarding the organisation of Member States' administrative structures.[50] It rather provides for competences on subject matters such as the competence to lay down basic standards.[51] All provisions on institutions and the organisation of national administrative procedures therefore have to be well justified and derived from these subject matter competences.[52] They can only demand what is necessary to achieve the objectives and obligations of the directive. With regard to certain general rules on the competent regulatory authority in the 2009 Directive such justification can be based on the EURATOM Treaty. For example, it follows from the competence to lay down basic safety standards that there must be a national regulatory authority to supervise their implementation and that this authority is given certain legal powers. Yet the more detailed and specific the provisions on institutional and organisational structures are regulated in the directive the more a sound justification is necessary. Similar considerations apply with regard to the institutional autonomy of the Member States. So far, convincing justification on the basis of alleged shortcomings of the existing regulatory systems in Member States has not been presented. Such justification would have to take into account the specific and diverse tradition of administrative systems in Member States. This holds in particular true for states with a federal structure.

49 *Supra* note 48; See also G Marcou, Verwaltungsbehörden und die Einflussnahme der öffentlichen Hand auf die Wirtschaft, in J Masing, G Marcou, *supra* note 41, 114.

50 J Hellermann, *supra* note 43, 21.

51 Article 30 *et seq.* of the Euratom Treaty.

52 J Hellermann, *supra* note 43, 18.

The ENSREG Draft, similar to the 2009 Directive, focuses on the independence in the decision making as an overarching objective and on the functional separation as the decisive criterion. It states in Article 5(2):

> »Member States shall ensure the effective independence of the competent regulatory authority from undue influence in its decision making. For this purpose, Member States shall ensure that the competent regulatory authority:
>
> (a) is functionally separate from any other public or private entity concerned with the promotion, or utilisation of nuclear energy, including electricity production.
>
> (b) [...]«

The Commission Proposal of June 2013 has largely included the approach as realized in the ENSREG proposal.[53]

2. Safety Obligations

Unlike the 2009 Directive the three drafts for a revised Nuclear Safety Directive include obligations on the safety of nuclear installations. However, each of them takes a different approach.

The DG Energy Draft includes detailed provisions on siting, design and construction and operation of nuclear installations. Many of these provisions are derived from the Convention on Nuclear Safety and from IAEA Safety Standards. For example, most of the obligations under Article 11 of the DG Energy Draft are directly derived from Article 19 of the CNS. It has been argued that it would create legal certainty to transform the IAEA approach into a legally binding Community system.[54] It might well be the case that it would create legal certainty if safety standards became legally binding at Community level. However, this certainty involves certain risks. First, it would duplicate parts of the well-established process at the IAEA level where EU Member States, together with other States, cooperate to develop and constantly revise safety standards and guides. It is not unlikely that this duplication would cause discrepancies between the two systems, thereby creating legal uncertainty.[55] Secondly, the IAEA frame-

53 See Article 1(7) of the Commission Proposal, *supra* note 21.

54 Garribba, *supra* note 4, 31.

55 Pelzer, in addition, points to an »apparent tension between the incentive approach of the Convention on Nuclear Safety and the Joint Convention and the strictly binding approach of the Waste Directive and the Safety Directive«, see N Pelzer, »Safer Nuclear Energy through a Higher Degree of Internationalization? – Inter-

work, which reflects the international state of the art in in nuclear safety,[56] is flexible and dynamic in particular due to its non-binding nature. In contrast, the adoption of a directive with detailed safety provisions would freeze these provisions in time, thereby hampering its constant and dynamic development. Yet such development is essential in nuclear safety regulation. Thirdly, States are more willing to commit to ambitious safety provisions when they are not legally binding. This is particular, but not only the case in the domain of nuclear safety.[57]

The ENSREG Draft takes a very different approach. Instead of safety criteria it establishes high level safety objectives, arguing that »this would primarily complement the work of the IAEA and, on the other hand, the work of the national regulators of the Member States« [58] and thereby adding a specific European layer to nuclear safety. Furthermore, in the view of ENSREG such approach »avoids the necessity of establishing fixed technical criteria and allows following state of the art progress in nuclear safety«.[59] ENSREG proposes to introduce a general safety objective which states that »nuclear power plants and, if applicable, research reactor facilities are designed, sited, constructed, commissioned, operated and decommissioned with the objective of avoiding potential radioactive releases by practically eliminating the occurrence of all accident sequences which would lead to early or large releases.«[60] This objective is based on the work of the Western European Nuclear Regulators Association (WENRA) with regard to new reactors.[61] Accordingly, the ENSREG Draft states that this general objective applies to existing nuclear power plants to »the extent reasonably achievable«.[62] The fact that the high level objective is based on work from WENRA may be seen as signal that regulators within

national Involvement vs. National Sovereignty« in *(2013) Nuclear Law Bulletin No. 91*, 43, 81.

56 *Ibid.*, 55.

57 See T de Wright, »The 'Incentive' Concept as Developed in the Nuclear Safety Conventions and its Possible Extension to Other Sectors« in *(2007) Nuclear Law Bulletin No. 80*, 29, 38; see also Pelzer, *supra* note 55, 45 *et seq*.

58 See ENSREG Explanatory Note on Draft Euratom Nuclear Safety Directive, *supra* note 19, 1.

59 *Ibid.*

60 ENSREG Draft, *supra* note 20, Article 9(1).

61 See Western European Nuclear Regulator's Association (WENRA): »Safety Objectives for New Power Reactors – Study by WENRA Reactor Harmonization Working Group«, December 2009, available at http://www.wenra.org/media/filer_public/2012/11/05/rhwg_report_newnpp_dec2009.pdf.

62 ENSREG Draft, *supra* note 20, Article 9(2).

ENSREG would like to emphasize and foster the work done within WENRA. It could become a European think tank in the domain of nuclear safety.

The Commission Proposal has included the concept of high level safety objectives.[63] However, it has also retained some of the elements on safety obligations of the DG Energy Draft, in particular in the new Article 8c (Methodology for siting, design, construction, commissioning, operation and decommissioning of nuclear installations).[64]

3. Verification Mechanism

The question of a verification mechanism regarding the implementation of the obligations of the directive is likely to play a central role in the negotiations. Both the DG Energy Draft and – albeit to a lesser extent – the Commission Proposal establish a verification mechanism which would give the Commission a central position in the Euratom nuclear safety architecture. It would result in a significantly stronger position than it has typically – including under the 2009 Directive – in the oversight of the application and implementation of EU (and Euratom) law. Within the Euratom Community as within the European Union it is the Commission's responsibility to »oversee the application of Union law under the control of the Court of Justice of the European Union«.[65] To this end, the Commission has in particular the power to start non-compliance procedures if it considers that a Member State has failed to fulfil an obligation under the Treaties.[66]

The 2009 Directive, as many other directives,[67] contains an obligation to report on the implementation of the directive.[68] These reports are a basis for the Commission to evaluate whether Member States fully implement and apply the relevant directive and thus, whether to start non-compliance procedures.

---

63 Article 1(10) of the Commission Proposal.

64 *Ibid.*

65 Article 17(1) of the Treaty on European Union; see also the overview at W Kilb, *supra* note 3, 67 et seq.

66 Article 258 of the Treaty on the Functioning of the European Union, Article 106a(1) of the Euratom Treaty.

67 See, for example, Directive 2009/73/EC (Gas Directive, OJ L 211/94), Article 52; Directive 2000/60/EC (Water Framework Directive, OJ L 327/1), Article 15.

68 2009 Nuclear Safety Directive, *supra* note 2, Article 9(1).

The DG Energy draft however does not only oblige Member States to communicate the transposition of the directive into national law[69] and report periodically on the implementation of the directive.[70] It establishes the Commission as the central supervisor of nuclear power plants in the European Union. It obliges Member States to carry out self-assessments of the design and operational safety performance of each nuclear power plant and invite an international peer review.[71] Outcomes of the peer reviews and a plan of measures are scrutinized by the Commission.[72] If the outcome of the peer review, together with the national report of the Member State, »raise concerns about the full and effective implementation of any obligation« specified in the directive, the Commission is allowed to carry out a verification mission »to get a full picture of the situation«.[73] A very similar mechanism was part of the proposal for a Nuclear Safety Directive in 2003.[74] This rather strong position of the Commission would result in a significant shift of responsibilities from Member States to the Commission in the domain of nuclear safety.

a. Shift of responsibilities

The emphasis on the national responsibility for nuclear safety and a possible shift to the European level was one of the most controversial issues in the discussions on the nuclear package in 2003 and 2004.[75] While some Member States agreed in principle on the need for regulation of nuclear safety at the level of the European Union, including safety criteria, other Member States were more reluctant. These Member States favoured the clear allocation of the responsibility for nuclear safety regulation to the Member State, accompanied by a deepening of existing international cooperation.[76] They mainly saw the risk of »blurred lines of responsibilities«

69 DG Energy Draft, *supra* note 12, Article 18.
70 *Ibid.*, Article 15(1).
71 *Ibid.*, Article 14(2).
72 *Ibid.*, Articles 4-6.
73 *Ibid.*, Article 16.
74 Proposal for a Council Directive (Euratom) setting out basic obligations and general principles on the safety of nuclear installations, COM(2003) 32 final (January 2003), Article 12.
75 Nuclear package – Note submitted by the FIN/S/UK delegations, Council document No. 16317/03 (19 December 2013), 3.
76 *Ibid.*, 2.

between national regulators and the European level.[77] Consequently, Council Conclusions of 28 June 2004 stress that »national responsibility for the safety of nuclear installations is the fundamental principle on which the regulation of nuclear safety and of radioactive waste management has been developed by the international community (…)«.[78] The issue of transferred responsibility naturally also played a major role when ENSREG adopted a position towards possible EU legislation in the domain of nuclear safety in 2008.[79]

b. Possible approaches to a nuclear safety framework

Against this background it is not surprising that, after DG Energy had sent its draft for a revised Nuclear Safety Directive to ENSREG in December 2012, the discussion within ENSREG soon focused on a possible further transfer of responsibilities. ENSREG discussed in general three possible approaches for a revised European nuclear safety framework: a decentralised concept as realised in the 2009 Directive, a two-tier level concept as displayed in the DG Energy Draft with shared responsibility between national nuclear regulatory authorities and the Euratom Community, and a fully centralised concept with one single European nuclear regulatory authority.[80] The regulators concluded that a decentralised concept would have good potential for further use and strengthening and contribute to improve nuclear safety while having the potential for a broad consensus.[81] Thus, the ENSREG Draft is based on the decentralised concept. It leaves the development of safety standards to the national regulators cooperating in international fora such as the IAEA, the OECD Nuclear Energy Agency (NEA) and WENRA. Furthermore, instead of a verification mechanism

77 *Ibid.*, 3.

78 Nuclear Safety and Safe management of spent fuel and radioactive waste – Draft Council Conclusions, Council document No. 10823/04 (25 June 2004, adopted 28 June 2004), Annex A, 3; see also S Schneider, S Schäfer, *supra* note 32 , 202.

79 See Report of the European Nuclear Safety Regulators Group (July 2009), available at http://ec.europa.eu/energy/nuclear/ensreg/doc/ 2009_ensreg_report.pdf, 20.

80 See ENSREG Ad-hoc Working Group on EC proposal for new Nuclear Safety Directive, replacing Community framework for the nuclear safety of nuclear installations (2009/71/Euratom) – Summary Report (6 April 2013), available at http://www.ensreg.eu/sites/default/files/1%20Final%20ENSREG%20Ad%20hoc%20WG%20Summary%20Report%20280213_1.pdf, 2.

81 *Ibid.*, 2.

under the auspices of the European Commission, the ENSREG proposal introduces a topical peer review system between Member States as an inter-regulatory instrument for continuously improving nuclear safety across Europe. This peer review system is in its structure similar to the peer review process subsequent to the comprehensive risk and safety assessments (»stress tests«) undertaken by the operators under the supervision of the national regulatory authorities of nuclear power plants following the Fukushima accident in 2011.[82]

c. Topical Peer Reviews

Pursuant to Article 12(2) a) of the ENSREG Draft the system of topical peer reviews shall be conducted as follows: in a first step, Member States shall jointly and in close coordination with the Commission select one or more specific topics related to nuclear safety. Based on these topics, national assessments shall be performed and its outcomes published. Subsequently, Member States shall arrange and carry out a peer review of the outcomes of those national assessments, to which the Commission is invited as an observer. Its results shall be published. The ENSREG Draft assigns the organization of the peer reviews to the Member States »with the support of the competent regulatory authorities«.[83] Alternatively, such task could be assigned to a European Nuclear Agency which would have to be established and which could be given a supporting role in conducting the peer review process. Yet regulators could not agree on such a proposal.

The Commission Proposal has adopted the concept of topical peer reviews.[84] It does no longer include a verification mission by the Commission itself as was foreseen in the DG Energy Draft. However, it still gives the Commission a strong position in the verification of Member States' obligations. In case the Commission identifies »substantial deviations or

82 On the stress tests and peer reviews see ENSREG, »Peer review report – Stress tests performed on European nuclear power plants« of 26 April 2011, available at http://www.ensreg.eu/sites/default/files/EU%20Stress%20Test%20Peer%20Review%20Final%20Report_0.pdf; see also »Communication from the Commission to the Council and the European Parliament on the interim report on the comprehensive risk and safety assessments (›stress tests‹) of nuclear power plants in the European Union« of 24 November 2011, COM(2011) 784 final, available at http://ec.europa.eu/energy/nuclear/safety/doc/com_2011_0784.pdf.

83 ENSREG Draft, *supra* note 20, Article 12(2).

84 Commission Proposal, *supra* note 21, Article 1(11).

delays in the implementation of the technical recommendations resulting from the peer review process, the Commission shall invite the competent regulatory authorities of Member States not concerned to organise and carry out a verification mission to get a full picture of the situation and inform the Member State concerned about possible measures to remedy any identified shortcomings«.[85]

4. Transparency

All three drafts expand the obligations of both regulator and licence holder with regard to transparency.[86] However, while the DG Energy Draft contains in detail which information have to be published, the ENSREG Draft and the Commission Proposal oblige both regulators and licence holders to develop a transparency strategy, covering, inter alia, information on normal operating conditions of nuclear installations, non-mandatory consultation activities with the workers and the general public and communication in case of incidents and accidents.[87] Expanding the obligations on transparency is a particular interest of smaller non-nuclear Member States.[88]

VII. Conclusions

While the European Council after Fukushima has only called for a full and timely implementation of the Nuclear Safety Directive and asked the Commission to make improvements »that may be necessary«, the Commission has seized the moment and proposed an amended Nuclear Safety

85 *Ibid.*

86 ENSREG Draft, *supra* note 20, Article 8; DG Energy Draft, *supra* note 12, Article 8.

87 ENSREG Draft, *supra* note 20, Article 8(1) subpara. 2; Commission Proposal, *supra* note 21, Article 1(9).

88 See Press Release of the Irish Department of the Environment, Community and Local Government: »Nuclear Safety and Transparency must go hand in hand says Hogan« of 19 September 2011, available at http://www.environ.ie/en/Environment/EnvironmentalRadiation/News/MainBody,27867,en.htm; see also Press Release of the Austrian Foreign Ministry: »Spindelegger: ›Transparency is decisive for nuclear safety‹« of 22 September 2011, available at http://www.bmeia.gv.at/en/foreign-ministry/news/press-releases/2011/spindelegger-transparency-is-decisive-for-nuclear-safety.html.

Directive which is more detailed than the 2009 Directive and less of a framework character.

In the discussion on the planned revision, regulators within ENSREG emphasized that a revised directive should strive for added value for nuclear safety in the EU rather than simply duplicating selected parts of existing international nuclear safety regulation. For that purpose they have proposed to introduce high level safety objectives for nuclear power plants. These objectives have the potential to foster the continuous improvement of nuclear safety in the European Union.

Furthermore, regulators have shown their readiness to enhanced inter-regulatory cooperation. To this end, they have proposed a system of European topical peer reviews similar to the peer reviews following the stress tests in 2011. At the same time regulators emphasize the national responsibility of Member States for nuclear safety. There is – for various and very different reasons – a certain reluctance of Member States to transfer responsibilities in the domain of nuclear safety to the Euratom Community which would involve a stronger position of the European Commission. Nevertheless, discussions on the fundamental question – what should be the design of a European nuclear safety architecture? – will most likely continue, even after a possible revision of the Nuclear Safety Directive.

Continuous Improvement of Nuclear Safety

Rasa Ptasekaite, Swedish Ministry of Environment, Stockholm

Introduction

There probably is no doubt that high level of safety is one of the fundamental requirements for nuclear energy to have a future and to be accepted. However, the ways of achieving, maintaining and enhancing the highest reasonably possible standards of safety is a question that seems to be slightly in a shadow of the objective itself. The concept of continuous improvement of nuclear safety is generally known, but rarely analysed or defined. What is continuous improvement of nuclear safety – an objective, a principle or an obligation? Does continuous improvement of nuclear safety have any limits? What parties are responsible for improving safety? These are only few of the questions that need to be answered in order to fully understand the role of continuous improvement in achieving high level of nuclear safety. Therefore, the main goal of this paper is to identify and define the concept of continuous improvement of nuclear safety. Due to the limitations of the article, the actual content of the latter concept, answering the question of what and how nuclear safety can be improved, is left for another occasion. The analysis is mainly based on IAEA legal framework and the reports of the OECD/NEA Committee on Nuclear Regulatory Activities (CNRA) and the IAEA International Nuclear Safety Advisory Group (INSAG). European legislation on nuclear safety and certain examples from Swedish national legislation on the matter will be presented where relevant.

For the simplicity of terminology only two terms – »regulator« and »operator« – are used in this paper. In different sources referred to in this article the regulator is called »regulatory authority«, »regulatory body« etc., and the operator has the names of »licence holder«, »licensee«, »operating organisation« etc.

1. Concept of nuclear safety[1]

In order to understand the concept of continuous improvement of nuclear safety, it is important to understand the concept of nuclear safety itself. Due to that, the first part of this paper is devoted to short description of nuclear safety.

The fundamental safety objective is to protect people and the environment from harmful effects of ionizing radiation. The restriction of the likelihood of events that might lead to a loss of control over a nuclear reactor core, nuclear chain reaction, radioactive source or any other source of radiation is one of the measures to ensure that facilities are operated and activities conducted so as to achieve the highest standards of safety that can reasonably be achieved.[2] In other words, the »restriction of the likelihood« is the base of the nuclear safety.

Nuclear safety is commonly defined[3] as the achievement of proper operating conditions, prevention of accidents, or mitigation of accident consequences, resulting in protection of workers, the public and the environment from undue radiation hazards. This definition covers the understanding of nuclear safety as freedom from physical harm, meaning both acute and latent health effects from exposure to radiation, as well as unreasonable risk and environmental damage due to the operation of nuclear facilities.

In this context it should be mentioned that, interestingly enough, the main legal act regulating nuclear safety in the international arena – the Convention on Nuclear Safety[4] (the Safety Convention) – does not define nuclear safety. It can be agreed that defining nuclear safety is quite problematic, keeping in mind that it has so many different aspects and elements. However, certain points are worth mentioning here. Firstly, as presented earlier, certain descriptions of nuclear safety have been provided in

1 More detailed in R. Ptasekaite »The Role of the Regulator: Nuclear Safety and Nuclear Safety Culture«, Proceedings of the INLA Congress, Manchester 2012. Available on internet: http://www.burges-salmon.com/INLA_2012/10193.pdf.

2 IAEA Safety Standards for protecting people and the environment, Fundamental Safety Principles, Safety Fundamentals No SF-1, IAEA, Vienna (2006), p. 4.

3 CNRA report »The Regulatory Goal of Assuring Nuclear Safety«, OECD NEA (2008), p. 11; and IAEA Safety Glossary, Terminology Used in Nuclear Safety and Radiation Protection, 2007 Edition, p.133 IAEA Vienna (2007).

4 Convention on Nuclear Safety, Legal Series No 16, IAEA, Vienna (1994).

IAEA Safety Fundamentals[5], as well as in the CNRA and the INSAG reports, which shows that defining nuclear safety is not impossible. Secondly, the main objective of the Safety Convention is to achieve and maintain high level of nuclear safety, and the lack of, if not definition, then at least a description of what exactly the Parties are aiming to »achieve and maintain« does not actually improve the possibilities of fulfilment of the latter objective.

Finally, it is worth noticing the general perception that it is not possible to achieve absolute safety (i.e., zero risk) in nuclear activities. That implies that nuclear activity is deemed to be safe if the perceived risks are judged to be acceptable.[6] In order to minimise the risks that need to be acceptable, continuous improvement of nuclear safety is essential.

2. *Concept of continuous improvement of nuclear safety*

After short definition of nuclear safety it seems reasonable to move forward towards understanding what continuous improvement of nuclear safety is. The analysis will be started by defining the latter concept. After that, the scope, limits and the parties responsible for the continuous improvement of nuclear safety will be identified, and, finally, certain deliberation on maintaining and improving safety will be presented.

2.1 The definition

The objective of the Safety Fundamentals[7] is to establish the fundamental safety objective, safety principles and concepts that provide the basis for the IAEA's safety standards and its safety related programme. While defining the fundamental safety objective – protecting people and the environment from harmful effects of ionizing radiation – the Safety Fundamentals state that, in order »to ensure that facilities are operated and the activities conducted so as to achieve the highest standards of safety that

5 »IAEA Safety Standards for protecting people and the environment, Fundamental Safety Principles, Safety Fundamentals No. SF-1«, IAEA, Vienna (2006);

6 CNRA report »The Regulatory Goal of Assuring Nuclear Safety«, OECD NEA (2008), p. 16.

7 IAEA Safety Standards for protecting people and the environment, Fundamental Safety Principles, Safety Fundamentals, No SF-1, p.3, par. 1.8, IAEA, Vienna (2006).

can reasonably be achieved, measures have to be taken«. Certain aspects seem to be worth mentioned here.

First of all, it should be noticed that the wording *the highest standards of safety that can reasonably be achieved* is better known as the universal SAHARA principle (safety as high as reasonably achievable), which just as ALARA (as low as reasonably achievable) and ALARP (as low as reasonably practicable) express the same basic question »how safe is safe enough?«[8]. An international system of safety fundamentals, requirements and guidelines creates the legal grounds for the Global Nuclear Safety Regime[9] which provides essential framework on what should and could be the answer to the question on how safe should be considered safe enough. However, there is no straight or easy answer to this question. What is considered to be *safe* and *safe enough* has a tendency to change with time and is highly dependent not only on developments in science and technology, but also on rising safety expectations of the society – if everything else (cars, hospitals, etc.) is constantly getting safer, the same is expected from the nuclear energy sector. Furthermore, the concept of »safe enough« is also significantly influenced by the global events in the nuclear energy sector. There is probably no doubt that the seismic and tsunami hazards assessment has become much more relevant criteria for nuclear safety after the nuclear accident at the Fukushima Daiichi nuclear power plant.[10]

The relation between the fundamental safety objective and the SAHARA principle could be worth discussing as well. The latter objective clearly requires that facilities have to be operated and the activities have to be conducted under the highest reasonable level of safety. This implies that the fundamental safety objective of protecting people and environment can only be achieved if highest possible level of safety is ensured. Due to that, it could be said that the SAHARA principle is an essential element of the fundamental safety objective.

---

8 CNRA report «Improving Versus Maintaining Nuclear Safety«, p.13, OECD NEA (2002).

9 INSAG, Strengthening the Global Nuclear Safety Regime, INSAG-21, IAEA Vienna (2006).

10 Such as: IAEA Report on Protection Against Extreme Earthquakes and Tsunamis in the Light of the Accident at the Fukushima Daiichi Nuclear Power Plant, IAEA Vienna 2012; Communication from the Commission to the Council and the European Parliament on the comprehensive risk and safety assessments (»stress tests«) of nuclear power plants in the European Union and related activities, European Commission, Brussels, 4.10.2012 COM(2012) 571 final.

Furthermore, the relation between the continuous improvement of safety and the fundamental safety objective should be identified. It might seem that the fundamental safety objective does not mention the continuous improvement, as it explicitly requires only the highest level standards of safety that can reasonably be achieved. However, the concept of the *highest standards that can reasonably be achieved* plays a significant role in defining and understanding the concept of the continuous improvement of nuclear safety. Due to the timespan covered by a nuclear power plant, from its initial design stages to its eventual decommissioning and dismantling, that can be as much as fifty years or more, there will certainly be major changes in the engineering and scientific knowledge that underpins the design, construction, operation and maintenance of the plant, as well as a better understanding of the threats that are posed by and to the plant from a variety of internal and external sources.[11] This means that continuous high level of nuclear safety seems not really possible without improvements. If the continuous improvement is an essential part of the highest possible level of safety and, as it was mentioned earlier, the highest possible level of safety could be considered to be an essential element in the fundamental safety objective, all that implies the conclusion that the continuous improvement of nuclear safety is a certain element of the fundamental safety objective. In other words, continuous improvement of nuclear safety could be considered as an instrument to achieve the fundamental safety objective of protecting people and the environment and that establishes the latter concept as one of the corner-stones in nuclear safety.

There should be no doubt that the latter conclusion plays a significant role in defining the concept of continuous improvement of nuclear safety. It should be noticed, however, that par. 2.1 of the Safety Fundamentals only implies the logical connection between the fundamental safety objective and the continuous improvement of safety, rather than explicitly establishing continuous improvement of nuclear safety as a part of the fundamental safety objective.

The final question in defining continuous improvement of nuclear safety is whether the latter concept should be defined as an *objective*, a *principle* or an *obligation*. Before going deeper into this discussion, it should be noticed that there probably is no straightforward answer to the latter question and the analysis presented below represents only one possible point of view on the issue.

11 CNRA report »Improving Versus Maintaining Nuclear Safety«, p.7, OECD NEA (2002).

In par. 4.27 of the Requirement 22 in the IAEA's General Safety Requirements for Governmental, Legal and Regulatory Framework for Safety[12] it is stated that »the regulatory body shall emphasize the continuous enhancement of safety as a general objective«. Several aspects should be mentioned here.

The wording of the latter requirement seems to imply that continuous improvement is an objective. Even though it might seem that the answer to the question above is clear, it might be worth analysing the latter paragraph more thoroughly. According to the wording, continuous enhancement of safety is a general objective. However, there is no elaboration on whether it is a general objective of safety, or a general objective of stability and consistency of regulatory control, which is the title of the latter requirement. As the IAEA General Safety Requirements were established in order for the IAEA Safety Fundamentals to be applied[13] it seems reasonable to come back to the fundamental safety objective and its relation to the continuous improvement of nuclear safety that was analysed earlier. As it was established in the beginning of this chapter, continuous improvement of safety is an essential element of high level of nuclear safety, which implies the logical connection between the fundamental safety objective of protecting people and the environment and the continuous improvement of safety. In other words, the continuous improvement of nuclear safety seems to be an instrument for reaching the high level of nuclear safety and not the objective of it. Besides that, under the IAEA system of Safety Standards, it seems unlikely that general objective of safety would be established not in the Safety Fundamentals, but rather under a certain Requirement in the General Safety Requirements. Therefore, the conclusion can be drawn that the continuous enhancement of nuclear safety should not be considered as a general objective of safety. In order to answer the question whether continuous improvement of nuclear safety could be defined as an objective, a systematic analysis of the Requirement 22 on stable and consistent regulatory control is required here. Paragraph 4.26 elaborating the latter Requirement states that the stable and consistent regulatory control means that regulatory process should be a formal process

12 IAEA Safety Standards for protecting people and the environment, Governmental, Legal and Regulatory Framework for Safety, General Safety Requirements Part 1, No. GSR Part 1, par.4.27, p.22, IAEA Vienna (2010).

13 IAEA Safety Standards for protecting people and the environment, Governmental, Legal and Regulatory Framework for Safety, General Safety Requirements Part 1, No. GSR Part 1, par.1.2, p.1, IAEA Vienna (2010).

based on specified policies followed by specified procedures, justifying and basing its requirements, judgements and decisions on the objectives, principles and associated criteria for safety. The following paragraph in the content of the Requirement 22 is the paragraph 4.27 on the continuous enhancement of nuclear safety mentioned above, and the last paragraph 4.28 establishes the need of consistency in the regulatory decision making process in order for the regulatory control to be considered consistent. The systematic analysis of the disposition of the Requirement 22 allows drawing the conclusion that regulator is required to emphasize the continuous enhancement in nuclear safety in the frame of the requirement on consistent and stable regulatory control, which means that promotion of continuous improvement is an essential element of the stable and consistent regulatory control. Due to that, it seems reasonable to conclude that even though the wording of the Requirement 22 implies that continuous improvement is an objective, it could be more precisely defined as an essential element of the stabile and consistent regulatory control.

The ones not convinced with the reasoning above, might contravene that the European nuclear safety legislation, to be more specific, the Euratom Nuclear Safety Directive,[14] clearly establishes the continuous improvement of nuclear safety in its objectives in Article 1. Answering that, several aspects are worth mentioning. Firstly, Article 1 in the latter Directive establishes the objectives of the Nuclear Safety Directive, which should not be identified with the objectives of nuclear safety in general, and, secondly, the wording of the Article 1 implies that the objective is to establish the Community framework which would allow maintaining and promoting the continuous improvement of nuclear safety. The latter implies that the national framework would have an objective to maintain and promote continuous improvement. None on the mentioned above, however, allows drawing the conclusion that continuous improvement of nuclear safety could be defined as an objective. Remaining provisions in the Nuclear Safety Directive that concern continuous improvement of nuclear safety will be analysed further on in this article.

Furthermore, it should be noticed beforehand (a separate section later on in this article is devoted to the following aspect), that continuous improvement of nuclear safety is not unlimited, which means that improvements have to be reasonable and evaluated with scrutiny before they are implemented. This implies that only those continuous improvements that

14 Council Directive 2009/71/EURATOM of 25 June 2009 establishing a Community framework for the nuclear safety of nuclear installations, OJ L 172, 2.7.2009.

contribute to high level of nuclear safety should be embraced. Colligating what has been said, the concept of continuous improvement as such should not be considered to be an objective.

If the continuous improvement of nuclear safety should not be generally defined as an objective the following question is whether it could be better described as a *principle* or as an *obligation*. In order to answer that, firstly, a sketchy distinction between a principle and an obligation in nuclear legal framework should be made. Besides other things, one of the main features that separate the principle from the obligation is the lack of duty-holder. The origin of the principle is so general that it applies to all and everyone that comes into contact with it, for example, well known fundamental principle of responsibility for safety. The principle clearly states that prime responsibility for safety rests with the person or organization responsible for facilities and activities that give rise to radiation risks. The latter principle only establishes the rule and does not elaborate who has to apply it, as it has to be applied by all and everyone (the government, the regulator, the operator etc.). The obligation, on the other hand, has a direct connection to a certain duty-holder – there always seems to be a certain party/parties that are responsible for fulfilling the obligation. The description of the Safety Requirements[15] implies, even though the format and style of the requirements should be harmonised with national legal framework, they have to be met, or otherwise measures have to be taken. In addition to this, it is specifically stated that if the party is not specified in the requirements the implication should be made that the appropriate parties are responsible for fulfilling them. Due to that, concerning the continuous improvement of nuclear safety, the question that needs to be answered is whether continuous improvement of nuclear safety has a duty-holder.

Requirement 19 of the IAEA's General Safety Requirements[16] state that *management system of the regulatory body* »shall maintain the efficiency and effectiveness of the regulatory body in discharging its responsibilities and performing its functions. This includes the promotion of enhancements in safety, and the fulfilment of its obligations in an appropriate, timely and cost effective manner so as to build confidence.« Requirement

15 IAEA Safety Standards for protecting people and the environment, Governmental, Legal and Regulatory Framework for Safety, General Safety Requirements Part 1, No. GSR Part 1, IAEA Vienna (2010).

16 IAEA Safety Standards for protecting people and the environment, Governmental, Legal and Regulatory Framework for Safety, General Safety Requirements Part 1, No. GSR Part 1, par. 4.16, IAEA Vienna (2010).

12 of the Specific Safety Requirements on Commissioning and Operation[17] establishes that »[...] *the operating organization* shall implement any necessary corrective actions and reasonably practicable modifications for compliance with applicable standards aiming at enhancing the safety of the plant«. These two examples show that when requiring to continuously improve nuclear safety, the party responsible for the latter is clearly established – it is the regulator's management system and the operating organisation in the cases mentioned above. The conclusion can be drawn that it is more reasonable to define the continuous improvement of nuclear safety as a certain obligation rather than principle. The actual duty-holders of this obligation will be analysed in the later section of this paper.

2.2 The scope

The fundamental safety objective states[18] that in order to »ensure that facilities are operated and activities conducted so as to achieve the highest standards of safety that can reasonably be achieved, measures have to be taken:

a) To control the radiation exposure of people and the release of radioactive material to the environment;
b) To restrict the likelihood of events that might lead to a loss of control over a nuclear reactor core, nuclear chain reaction, radioactive source or any other source of radiation;
c) To mitigate the consequences of such events if they were to occur.«

Firstly, it seems reasonable to analyse what exactly the provision above establishes – does it identify certain types of measures that need to be taken or does it aim for something else. Analysing the logical construction of the wording above it could be stated that the model is »measures have to be taken, in order to...«. This implies that measures are not really identified in the latter provision – it is only their purpose or objective that is es-

17 IAEA Safety Standards for protecting people and the environment, Safety of Nuclear Power Plants: Commissioning and Operation, Specific Safety Requirements No. SSR-2/2, par. 4.47, IAEA Vienna (2011).

18 IAEA Safety Standards for protecting people and the environment, Fundamental Safety Principles, Safety Fundamentals No SF-1, p.4-5, IAEA, Vienna (2006).

tablished here: to control, to restrict and to mitigate. This means that in order to achieve the highest standards of safety, measures that *aim* to control, restrict and mitigate need to be taken. As the fundamental objective of safety is to protect, the question that might be asked here is, what the relation between the latter objectives, the fundamental safety objective and continuous improvement of nuclear safety is.

Whereas in order to achieve the highest standards of safety, measures that aim to control, restrict and mitigate need to be taken, it implies that the three objectives above are the elements of the high level of safety. The high level of safety is an essential condition for protecting people and environment, which means that it is essential for achieving the fundamental safety objective as well. Due to that, the objectives to control, restrict and mitigate should be considered to be the necessary elements of the fundamental safety objective. Since it has already been established that continuous improvement of nuclear safety is an instrument to achieve the fundamental safety objective, it seems reasonable to conclude that continuous improvement of nuclear safety should cover control of exposure and release, restriction of likelihood, and mitigation of consequences, in order for the high level of safety to be achieved and the fundamental safety objective to be fulfilled.

The Safety Fundamentals[19] further establish that »the fundamental safety objective applies for all facilities and activities and for all stages over the lifetime of a facility or radiation source, including planning, siting, design, manufacturing, construction, commissioning and operation, as well as decommissioning and closure. This includes the associated transport of radioactive material and management of radioactive waste«.

Since the fundamental objective of safety applies everywhere, the high level of safety must also be ensured everywhere. As it was already established that continuous improvement is an essential element of the high level of nuclear safety, the conclusion could be drawn that continuous improvement should also be required for all facilities and activities and for all stages over the lifetime: planning, siting, design, manufacturing, construction, commissioning and operation, as well as decommissioning and closure.

Systematic analysis of the IAEA Safety Standards seems to confirm the latter conclusion. Certain selective examples could be given here.

19 IAEA Safety Standards for protecting people and the environment, Fundamental Safety Principles, Safety Fundamentals No SF-1, par. 2.2, IAEA, Vienna (2006).

The Specific Safety Requirements on safety of nuclear power plant's design[20] require design organization to establish and implement a management system that, among other things, shall include the means for identifying and correcting design deficiencies, controlling design changes and assuring that safety improvements shall be in accordance with established procedures that call on appropriate engineering codes and standards. This shows that continuous improvement of nuclear safety is already required in the design phase of nuclear installation. Furthermore, prior to the authorization of the construction, the regulator should review, assess and inspect on a systematic basis, the development of the design of the installation as demonstrated in the safety documentation which may include requirements to improve safety through design optimization.[21] That implies that continuous improvement of safety ought to be taken into account in the licensing process as well. In addition to this, due to the prime responsibility for safety, the management system of the operating organisation shall, among other things, monitor and assess the performance of the operating functions and overall safety performance of the organization on a regular basis, in order to verify compliance with the objectives for safe operation and assess the effectiveness of management for safety, to reveal deviations, and to identify opportunities for improvement.[22] This means that continuous improvement of nuclear safety, in form of improvements in operating functions and the management system, is required during the operations of the nuclear facility. The following final example shows that continuous improvement of nuclear safety is also required in order to restrict the likelihood of events that might lead to a loss of control and to mitigate the consequences of such events if they were to occur. Requirement 20 on design extension conditions in the Specific Safety Requirements on safety of nuclear power plant's design establishes that a set of design extension conditions shall be derived on the basis of engineering judgement, deterministic assessments and probabilistic assessments for the purpose of further improving the safety of the nuclear power plant by en-

20 IAEA Safety Standards for protecting people and the environment, Safety of Nuclear Power Plants: Design, Specific Safety Requirements No SSR-2/1, par. 3.2 and 3.3, IAEA Vienna (2012).

21 IAEA Safety Standards for protecting people and the environment, Licensing Process for Nuclear Installations, Specific Safety Guide No SSG-12, par. 3.40, IAEA, Vienna (2010).

22 IAEA Safety Standards for protecting people and the environment, Safety of Nuclear Power Plants: Commissioning and Operation, Specific Safety Requirements No SSR-2/2, par. 3.2, IAEA, Vienna (2011).

hancing the plant's capabilities to withstand, without unacceptable radiological consequences, accidents that are either more severe than design basis accidents or that involve additional failures.

Consolidating what has been said, the scope of the continuous improvement of nuclear safety is rather vast and multi-layered – not only it covers the essential elements of high level of nuclear safety, it also should be applied to all activities and installations in all stages of their lifetime. That only confirms the continuous improvement of nuclear safety being the corner-stone of high level of nuclear safety.

2.3 The limits

The SAHARA principle predicates that the level of safety has to be as high as it can *reasonably* be achieved. The Safety Fundamentals state[23] that the safety objective »has to be achieved without unduly limiting the operation of facilities or the conduct of the activities that give rise to radiation risks«. That implies that the objective of high level of nuclear safety has a certain, so called *»reasonability« factor*. The question that might be worth analysing here is how the latter reasonability factor interacts with the concept of continuous improvement. Since it was stated earlier that the continuous improvement is an essential element of high level of safety, it seems that continuous improvement of safety should be obliged to follow the same reasonability principle as well. This statement could be confirmed by several examples. The Requirement 22 on the stability and consistency of regulatory control in the Governmental, Legal and Regulatory Framework for Safety[24] states that the regulatory body shall recognise the risks associated with making modifications to well established practises. Prospective changes in regulatory requirements shall be subject to careful scrutiny to evaluate the possible enhancements in safety that are to be achieved.

23 IAEA Safety Standards for protecting people and the environment, Fundamental Safety Principles, Safety Fundamentals, No SF-1, p.4, par. 2.1, IAEA Vienna (2006).

24 IAEA Safety Standards for protecting people and the environment, Governmental, Legal and Regulatory Framework for Safety, General Safety Requirements Part 1, No GSR Part 1 p. 22, IAEA Vienna (2010).

In addition to this, INSAG has stated[25] that disciplined approach is needed when deciding whether to adopt proposed incremental safety improvements for any nuclear plant, as it is important to avoid concentrating resources on improvements that have only marginal effects, and to recognize that a safety improvement may also affect economic or other societal factors. INSAG further states that special care is needed to ensure that an intended safety improvement does not have detrimental effects that outweigh its benefits.

As the latter examples indicate slightly different aspects of reasonability factor in the continuous improvement of nuclear safety – Requirement 22 is addressed to the regulator while the INSAG statement is more directed to the operator – several implications could be done here. Firstly, general conclusion could be made that the improvements in order to achieve high level of nuclear safety should be reasonable. Secondly, the reasonability of continuous improvement of nuclear safety is required both from the regulator in improving the regulatory requirements and from the operator in introducing technical safety improvements in practice.

Another aspect that might be worth analysing is the content of the reasonability factor. In other words, the question on how it should be determined that a certain improvement is reasonable enough, could be asked here.

The INSAG report on Basic Safety Principles for Nuclear Power Plant[26] states that the proposer should justify each significant improvement in terms of its urgency, safety merit and implementation cost. Furthermore, the INSAG report elaborates that in seeking to obtain safety improvements to existing installations, account is taken of the balance between benefits and drawbacks (including costs). Also, account needs to be taken of the implications of changes for the usefulness of the experience gained and training developed in operating the plant in its existing configuration. Another example is that of organizational changes which can have the potential either to improve or to impair safety performance. It is important to ensure, prior to implementation, that the effect of the proposed changes will not reduce safety, either when the change has been completed or during the transitional period while it is being implemented.

In my opinion, INSAG gives a rather descent description on how the principle of *cost-benefit* evaluation works in the continuous improvement

25 INSAG, Basic Safety Principles for Nuclear Power Plant 75-INSAG-3 Rev. 1, INSAG-12, p. 2 IAEA Vienna (1999).

26 75-INSAG-3 Rev. 1, INSAG-12, p. 2 IAEA Vienna (1999).

of nuclear safety. As it is mentioned above, the main criteria for the adoption of the improvement ought to be its *urgency*, *safety merit* and *cost*. It seems reasonably to state that the latter criteria are listed in the priority order and all of them are closely connected together. The most urgent improvements ought to be the ones that are absolutely necessary for maintaining high level of safety. Due to the fact that their safety merit should be considered as high, the urgent improvements are the ones that should be done first. Balancing safety merit and costs of the improvement is another issue that seems to be worth a discussion.

It should be noticed that concept of costs in this context represents not only the financial or administrative costs that might occur in order to implement the improvement, but also, for example, cost of changes in established practices and safety culture as new adjustments need to be done or costs of improvement to the design integrity of the facility. Generally, the cost-benefit principle implies that only such improvements where the safety merit of the improvement outbalances the costs of it should be enforced. The rule seems to be quite simple, however, the implementation of the latter principle might to be rather complex. The main issue here is *how much* the merits of the safety improvement have to outweigh the costs.

As it was mentioned earlier, the General Safety Requirements, even though requiring the regulator to promote continuous improvement, clearly state that any modifications must be subject to careful scrutiny.[27] Furthermore, where innovative improvements beyond current practices have been incorporated, it has to be determined in the safety assessment whether compliance with the safety requirements has been demonstrated by an appropriate programme of research, analysis and testing complemented by a subsequent programme of monitoring during operation.[28] In the Specific Safety Requirements on design of the nuclear power plant[29] it is stated that it might not be practicable to apply all the requirements of this publication to nuclear power plants that are already in operation or under construction; in addition, it might not be feasible to modify designs that have already

27 IAEA Safety Standards for protecting people and the environment, Governmental, Legal and Regulatory Framework for Safety, General Safety Requirements Part 1, No GSR Part 1 par. 4.27, IAEA Vienna (2010).

28 IAEA Safety Standards for protecting people and the environment, Safety Assessment For Facilities And Activities, General Safety Requirements Part 4, No GSR Part 4, par.4.29, IAEA, Vienna (2009).

29 IAEA Safety Standards for protecting people and the environment, Safety of Nuclear Power Plants: Design, Specific Safety Requirements No SSR-2/1, par. 1.3, IAEA Vienna (2012).

been approved by regulatory bodies. For the safety analysis of such designs, it is expected that a comparison will be made with the current standards, for example as part of the periodic safety review for the plant, to determine whether the safe operation of the plant could be further enhanced by means of reasonably practicable safety improvements. In addition to this, INSAG has also emphasised[30] the importance to maintain the integrity of the design of a nuclear power plant over its entire lifetime in order to achieve a continuous high level of safety.

The practice shows that many events were reported during 2009-2011 involving deficiencies in the modification process. In some cases, modifications which were intended to improve plant safety resulted in degraded safety conditions because of unanticipated consequences. Modifications intended to improve safety, if not carried out with adequate design checks and acceptance controls, can inadvertently result in a reduction of safety. As even minor changes can lead to significant events, sufficient design rigor needs to be maintained during the modifications.[31]

Consolidating what has been said, the conclusion can be drawn that a modification can be called an improvement and should be implemented only if the safety merits of the modification *significantly* overweight the possible and probable costs. Furthermore any planned improvement should be analysed with scrutiny and evaluated according to its urgency, safety merits and costs. In addition to this, it seems important to have in mind that in some cases even if theoretically the safety merits of the improvements seem to be sufficient it can in practice result in decreasing the existing level of safety. Due to that, the analysis and the evaluation of the costs and benefits of every plan modification are of an essential importance in order for the modification to be improvement in nuclear safety.

2.4 Maintaining v. improving nuclear safety

Independent of any industry or societal demands to build in new levels of safety, the actual level of safety of any given plant is a constantly shifting

30 INSAG, Maintaining the Design Integrity of Nuclear Installations throughout their Operating Life, INSAG-19, IAEA, Vienna (2003).

31 Nuclear Power Plant Operating Experience, from the IAEA/NEA International Reporting System for Operating Experience 2009-2011, NEA No. 7120, OECD (2012).

condition and never is a single state for any plant. There are two broad sets of reasons for this[32]:

Technical reasons:

- Physically the plant is not a constant over time. It's constantly ageing, which alters some components and performance characteristics. New and updated component parts enter the plant – e.g. valve and other manufacturers alter their products slightly over time as they seek manufacturing cost reductions or upgrades in performance.
- New knowledge changes the representation of the plant in analytic models and current »understanding«. As we know more about failure probabilities, good practice or characteristics of ageing, the plant isn't the same as in its prior analytical representations.

Organisational reasons:

- Organisationally there is no constant level of safety at a plant. Key organisational variables like worker attentiveness and interdepartmental trust can decay over time. Routines, worker turnover and ageing of the workforce can change the ability of the members to cope with surprise. There will be almost imperceptible shifts in standards enforcement as safety becomes taken for granted.

Under the analysis of different OECD/NEA member countries made by CNRA,[33] the conclusion has been made that the national submissions indicate that there are differences in how member countries describe their responsibilities to ensure adequate nuclear safety and about whether their regulatory approaches require licensees to continuously *improve* safety or to continuously *maintain* safety. Furthermore, CNRA has pointed out that various descriptions of whether safety has to be maintained or improved may cause confusion for the regulator's stakeholders, particularly licensees and the general public.

One of the possible solutions to decrease the confusion could be an endeavour to identify a more defined line between maintaining and improving safety. It should be noticed, however, that the analysis below is completely theoretical and does not imply anything concerning usage of the latter terms in national legislation otherwise.

---

32 CNRA report »Improving Versus Maintaining Nuclear Safety«, p.15-16, OECD NEA (2002).

33 CNRA report »Improving Versus Maintaining Nuclear Safety«, p.19, OECD NEA (2002).

Logical perception of the concept *maintaining* already implies that there must be a certain level that should be continuously kept. In nuclear safety that »level« is established by the licencing basis. The definition of licensing basis[34] is a set of regulatory requirements applicable to a nuclear installation. The licensing basis is normally established before nuclear power plant goes into operation and consists of: a detailed description of the plant and site facilities; the design safety analysis; applicable codes and standards; operational procedures, rules and limits; emergency procedures, etc. Once the licensing basis has been established, the regulatory authority requires the plant to remain in conformity with it throughout its operational life, i.e. the level of safety as defined in the licensing basis must be *maintained.*[35]

The CNRA report[36] establishes that even though the licensing basis stays the same, the scientific and engineering understanding of the various components of it may well change. Due to that, in some cases licensees have to upgrade their safety analysis following some unexpected event or when carrying out a major review, such as a Periodic Safety Review (PSR). However, according to the report, such modifications and improvements are considered to be strictly to maintain the licensing basis. In addition to this, it should be noticed that the latter CNRA report, unlike concerning the concept of maintaining, does not really define the improving of nuclear safety.

If safety analysis is a part of licencing basis and certain scientific and engineering development requires the safety analysis to be upgraded, the question is whether the licensing basis in that case stays the same. As it was mentioned earlier, licencing basis is a set of requirements that define the level of safety for the installation. Due to that, in my opinion, any modifications that need to be implemented in the nuclear power plant which might induce the change in regulatory safety requirements ought to be defined as *improvement* of nuclear safety. Other modifications that need to be done, but do not influence the licensing basis would, in that case, fall under the process of *maintaining* nuclear safety. Consequently,

34 CNRA report »The Regulatory Goal of Assuring Nuclear Safety«, OECD NEA (2008), p. 108; and IAEA Safety Glossary, Terminology Used in Nuclear Safety and Radiation Protection, 2007 Edition, p.133 IAEA Vienna (2007).

35 CNRA report »Improving Versus Maintaining Nuclear Safety«, p.9, OECD NEA (2002).

36 CNRA report »Improving Versus Maintaining Nuclear Safety«, p.9-10, OECD NEA (2002).

the criteria for identifying and separating maintenance from improvement, is the content of licensing basis.

Article 1 of the Nuclear Safety Convention[37] states that one of the objectives of the Convention is to achieve and maintain a high level of nuclear safety. On one hand, it might seem that the latter Convention establishes only the concept of maintaining mentioned above. This would imply that the international convention on nuclear safety does not have an objective to continuously improve nuclear safety. However, this does not seem to be the case due to the following reasons. Only identifying the words »maintain« and »improve« might not give a full picture on the objective of the provision. It is important to analyse *what* the provision is aiming to maintain or improve. Since one of the objectives of the Nuclear Safety Convention mentioned above is to achieve and maintain *high* level of nuclear safety and high level of safety is an essential element of the fundamental safety objective, the conclusion could be drawn that high level of safety is a certain goal and does not need to be improved. Due to that, wording »maintaining a high level of nuclear safety« includes both – maintaining and improving nuclear safety. In other words, one can maintain and improve nuclear safety, but only maintain the high level of it.

2.5 The parties responsible

After identifying continuous improvement of nuclear safety as an obligation and defining its scope and limits, it seems reasonable to analyse whose obligation the continuous improvement of nuclear safety is considered to be.

A number of examples presented earlier in the paper on the established obligation of the continuous improvement of nuclear safety might already have given out the preliminary signal that the obligation of continuously improving of nuclear safety lays on both – the regulator and the operator. Nevertheless, it might be worth analysing how the latter parties share the obligations and interact in the field of continuous improvement of nuclear safety. In order for the latter analysis to be complete, a general reference to how do these parties interact in the field of nuclear safety might be needed.

37 International Atomic Energy Agency (IAEA), Convention on Nuclear Safety, Legal Series No. 16, IAEA, Vienna (1994).

Systematic analysis of the IAEA's legal framework[38] has shown that the main role of the regulatory body in the field of nuclear safety could be described in a following way: the regulator creates »the rules of playing safe« and controls how the operator follows them, while the operator has to play by those rules and prove it to the regulator on regular basis. In other words, »the game« is played by the regulator's rules, which means that while the operator is responsible for the actual safety in nuclear installation, it is the regulator who decides what is considered to be safe.

Having roughly described the sharing of roles between the regulator and the operator in the field of nuclear safety, the analysis on how do they interact in the field of continuous improvement of nuclear safety should be done. Keeping in mind the vast scope of the continuous improvement of nuclear safety, it seems reasonable to start by identifying the regulator's and the operator's responsibilities in the latter field.

The role of the regulator in continuous improvement of nuclear safety is basically established in two paragraphs of the General Safety Requirements[39] that already have been analysed earlier. Par. 4.16 requires the regulator to promote the enhancement in safety and par. 4.27 requires the regulator to emphasise the continuous improvement of safety considering the reasonability factor which has already been analysed in the previous section. The regulator should require that the operator reports regularly on adherence to safety objectives and compliance with specified regulatory requirements, and on efforts made to enhance safety. The regulatory body should review and assess the reports and should perform inspections to confirm compliance with regulatory requirements and to confirm that the facility is able to continue in operation.[40] In addition to this, the regulator should at all times require reasonably achievable improvements to be made in the design or operating procedures of the facility with the aim of

38 The detailed analysis of the role of the regulator in the field of nuclear safety has been done in: R. Ptasekaite »The Role of the Regulator: Nuclear Safety and Nuclear Safety Culture«, Proceedings of the INLA Congress, Manchester 2012. Available on internet: http://www.burges-salmon.com/INLA_2012/10193.pdf.

39 IAEA Safety Standards for protecting people and the environment, Governmental, Legal and Regulatory Framework for Safety, General Safety Requirements Part 1, No GSR Part 1 par. 4.27, IAEA Vienna (2010).

40 IAEA Safety Standards for protecting people and the environment, Review and Assessment of Nuclear Facilities by the Regulatory Body, Safety Guide, No. GS-G-1.2, par. 2.18, IAEA, Vienna (2002).

reducing potential radiological consequences.[41] Considering the regulations and guides issued by the regulator, the regulator should require at all times reasonably practicable improvements in the safety of facilities and to this end should periodically review its regulations and guides against scientific and technological advances. The extent to which regulations and guides should be revised should depend on their level of detail. If safety goals and general guidance only are given, less frequent revision will be necessary. If legal requirements are changed, this may necessitate changes to regulations and guides.[42] Taking to the consideration mentioned above and keeping in mind that it is the regulator that decides what is considered to be safe, the conclusion can be drawn that the regulator has the same role even in the field of continuous improvement. It is the regulator that decides when and what kind of the changes in the regulatory requirements are needed to ensure the highest reasonably possible level of safety. Furthermore, it should be noticed that comparing the regulator's role in promotion aspect of nuclear safety and continuous improvement of nuclear safety respectively, the regulator's responsibility to promote continuous improvement of nuclear safety is explicitly established in the Safety Requirements, while such obligation for the regulator to promote high level of nuclear safety is lacking. Consequently, it seems reasonable to state that regulator's obligations to establish the legal framework of requirements on how the continuous improvement of nuclear safety should be exercised and to promote continuous improvement of nuclear safety as such are of a significant importance to high level of nuclear safety.

It might seem that operator's obligations in continuous improvement for nuclear safety should emerge straight from its prime responsibility for safety established in the Fundamental Safety Principles[43]. Even though an operator is responsible for ensuring high level of nuclear safety which implies that it should also have the prime responsibility to insure that necessary improvements are done in order to achieve that high level of safety, the Fundamental Safety Principles do not explicitly devote that responsibility to the operator. Under the par. 3.6 the responsibilities of the operator

41 IAEA Safety Standards for protecting people and the environment, Review and Assessment of Nuclear Facilities by the Regulatory Body, Safety Guide, No. GS-G-1.2, par. 3.50, IAEA, Vienna (2002).

42 IAEA Safety Standards for protecting people and the environment, Review and Assessment of Nuclear Facilities by the Regulatory Body, Safety Guide, No. GS-G-1.2, par. 3.29, IAEA, Vienna (2002).

43 IAEA Safety Standards for protecting people and the environment, Fundamental Safety Principles, Safety Fundamentals No SF-1, IAEA, Vienna (2006).

are listed out and the responsibility to continuously improve nuclear safety is not there. The latter paragraph only states that operator is responsible for »establishing procedures and arrangements to maintain safety under all conditions«. General Safety Requirements on safety assessment for facilities and activities establish[44] that it is the person or the organisation responsible for the activity of facility that has a responsibility to carry out the safety assessment. Putting it into the context of nuclear safety, it is a responsibility of the operator. The purpose of the safety assessment is, among other things, to determine whether an adequate level of safety has been achieved and what appropriate safety related improvements to the design and operation are needed. Under the par. 4.64 of these General Safety Requirements the safety report must include conclusions of the acceptability of the level of safety achieved and the identification of necessary improvements and additional measures. This implies that operator has to continuously control that certain level of nuclear safety is achieved and identify the measures that need to be taken in order for that level of safety to be maintained. In operational safety, the connection between the operator's prime responsibility for safety and its obligation in continuous improvement of safety is established in par. 3.2 of the Specific Safety Requirements for Safety of Nuclear Power Plants: Commissioning and Operation. Under the latter paragraph, due to the prime responsibility for safety, the management system of the operating organisation shall, among other things, monitor and assess the performance of the operating functions and overall safety performance of the organization on a regular basis, in order to verify compliance with the objectives for safe operation and assess the effectiveness of management for safety, to reveal deviations, and to identify opportunities for improvement.[45] Furthermore, the latter Specific Safety Requirements require the operator to establish and implement operational policies that give safety the highest priority. The latter policy must include a commitment to achieving enhancements in operational safety.[46] Concerning the safety policies, INSAG has concluded[47] that an

44 IAEA Safety Standards for protecting people and the environment, Safety Assessment for Facilities and Activities, General Safety Requirements Part 4 No GSR Part 4, Requirements 3 and 4, IAEA, Vienna (2009).

45 IAEA Safety Standards for protecting people and the environment, Safety of Nuclear Power Plants: Commissioning and Operation, Specific Safety Requirements No SSR-2/2, par. 3.2, IAEA, Vienna (2011).

46 IAEA Safety Standards for protecting people and the environment, Safety of Nuclear Power Plants: Commissioning and Operation, Specific Safety Requirements No SSR-2/2, par. 4.5, IAEA, Vienna (2011).

operator needs to demonstrate a commitment to achieving improvements in safety wherever it is reasonably practicable to do so as part of a continuing commitment to the achievement of excellence. The organization's improvement strategy for achieving higher safety performance and for more efficient ways to achieve existing standards will have the best chance of success if it is set out as part of a well-defined programme with clear objectives and targets against which to monitor progress. In addition to this, the operator is required to establish an adequate audit and review system to ensure that the safety policy of the operating organization is being implemented effectively and that lessons are being learned from its own experience and from the experience of others to improve safety performance.[48] According to what is mentioned above, the conclusion can be made that operator's obligation in continuous improvement of nuclear safety basically consists of controlling, assessing, reviewing and ensuring that regulator's established level of safety is maintained.

Consolidating what has been said and defining the regulator's and the operator's role in continuous improvement of nuclear safety, the conclusion could be drawn that role of each of the latter parties and the concepts of *maintaining* and *improving* safety seem to interact very closely – the regulator is responsible for determining the level of safety that should be considered to be as high as reasonably achievable which implies that the regulator is *improving* nuclear safety, and the operator concentrates on fulfilling the existing safety requirements that have been established by the regulator and that way is *maintaining* nuclear safety.

At this point it seems reasonable to look slightly deeper in to the European legislation. Article 6.2 of the Nuclear Safety Directive[49] states that Member States shall ensure that the national framework in place requires licence holders, under the supervision of the competent regulatory authority, to regularly assess and verify, and continuously improve, as far as reasonably achievable, the nuclear safety of their nuclear installations in a systematic and verifiable manner. The latter article clearly establishes that it is the operator's obligation to improve safety and the regulator only has

47 INSAG, Management of Operational Safety in Nuclear Power Plants, INSAG-13, IAEA Vienna (1999).

48 IAEA Safety Standards for protecting people and the environment, Safety of Nuclear Power Plants: Commissioning and Operation, Specific Safety Requirements No SSR-2/2, par. 4.33, IAEA, Vienna (2011).

49 Council Directive 2009/71/EURATOM of 25 June 2009 establishing a Community framework for the nuclear safety of nuclear installations, OJ L 172, 2.7.2009.

a function of supervision. In addition to this, in Article 5 on Competent Safety Authority the improvement of nuclear safety is not mentioned at all. If to look at the Article 6.2 from the perspective of the continuous improvement of nuclear safety, it might seem that Directive implies that it is the operator, and not the regulator, that is obliged »to push up the bar« of safety requirements and decides what level of safety is considered to be the high, and how safe is safe enough. Nevertheless, in this case it seems reasonable to notice that even though continuous improvement is in the wording of the article, the main focus of the latter provision is not identifying the share or responsibilities between the regulator and the operator in continuous improvement of nuclear safety, but rather establish periodical safety review as the essential responsibility of the operator that also falls under the regulator's supervision. As it has been mentioned earlier, periodical safety review (or safety assessment) allows the operator to evaluate the level of safety and identify the necessary improvements that are needed to be implemented. The wording »under the supervision of the competent regulatory authority« implies that even though it is the operator that might find certain improvement necessary it is the regulator that decides whether and how they should be enforced. Due to that, the even though the Directive does not establish it directly, the conclusion on the definition of the regulator's and the operator's role in continuous improvement of nuclear safety mentioned above seems to be applicable even on the European level. This does not, however, change the fact, that regulation on continuous improvement of nuclear safety in the Directive is not really flawless – it still lacks clear establishment that continuous improvement of nuclear safety falls under the regulator's responsibilities as well.

3. *Continuous improvement of safety in national legal framework – Sweden*

After thorough analysis on international regulation on continuous improvement of nuclear safety, it seems reasonable to do a certain descriptive analysis the national Swedish legislation on the matter.[50]

50 Due to the author's employment in the Swedish Government Offices, only the descriptive part of the analysis will be done in this chapter.

The main legal act establishing the legal framework for nuclear safety is the Act on Nuclear Activities (1984:3)[51] (the Act). The provisions of the Act that are of a relevance to this research are the following.

> **Section 4** Safety of nuclear activities shall be maintained by implementing the measures necessary in order to:
>
> 1. prevent defects in or the malfunction of equipment, improper handling, sabotage or other circumstance that could result in a radiological accident, and
>
> 2. prevent unlawful handling of nuclear material and nuclear waste.
>
> **Section 10** A party that holds a licence for nuclear activities shall be responsible for ensuring that all the necessary measures are taken for:
>
> 1. maintaining safety, taking into account the nature of the operation and the circumstances in which it is conducted, [...].

As it can be seen above, the main focus in the latter legislation is on maintaining safety of nuclear activities. However, section 9 in the regulation on Safety in Nuclear Facilities[52] issued by the Swedish Radiation Safety Authority requires the licence holder to have a documentation of safety objectives and guidelines on how safety shall be maintained and improved. The Swedish Radiation Safety Authority, being the national regulator, elaborates[53] the latter regulation as requiring the licensee to maintain and develop safety, where »develop« includes a continuous work to »hunt« for safety deficiencies in the reactor design and the quality of the safety work, and to take actions if deficiencies are discovered. This means technically improved safety, but formally safety is maintained. The Swedish Radiation Safety Authority further consolidates that they require »licensees to continuously analyse safety and take actions if deficiencies are discovered, not to continuously improve safety in an absolute sense«.

51 The English version translated by the Swedish Radiation Safety Authority can be found here: http://www.stralsakerhetsmyndigheten.se/Global/IRRS/Act%20on%20Nuclear%20Activities.pdf.

52 It is a free translation of latter regulation done by author of the article.

53 CNRA report »Improving Versus Maintaining Nuclear Safety«, p.28, OECD NEA (2002).

Conclusions

Consolidating all that has been said, the conclusions are following:

- Continuous improvement of nuclear safety being an instrument to achieve the fundamental safety objective is one of the corner stones in nuclear safety.
- Continuous improvement of nuclear safety is best defined as an obligation, rather than principle or objective.
- Continuous improvement of nuclear safety is required for all facilities and activities and for all stages over the lifetime and covers control of exposure and release, restriction of likelihood and mitigation of consequences.
- One of the criteria for separating maintenance of nuclear safety from improvement might be the licensing basis. Modifications which might induce the change in regulatory safety requirements are improving nuclear safety, while those modifications that do not influence the licensing basis are for maintaining nuclear safety. Nuclear safety can be maintained or improved, but a high level of nuclear safety can only be maintained.

The Nuclear Safeguards System of the European Atomic Energy Community (Euratom)

Wolfgang Kilb[*]

Introduction, history and overview

Based on the Treaty on European Union (TEU) for the overall »constitutional« framework and the Treaty on the Functioning of the European Union (TFEU) for procedures and policies, European law has, in the more than five decades of its existence, developed into a plethora of legislation and jurisprudence. At first sight, primary law in the field of energy consists of only one provision: Article 194 TFEU.

It is often forgotten that post-war European integration started with the Treaty establishing the European Coal and Steel Community (ECSC) of 1951 (»Paris Treaty«). The Treaty establishing the European Atomic Energy Community (EAEC or EURATOM) was signed together with the Treaty establishing the European Economic Community (EEC) in 1957 (»Treaties of Rome«). Hence, two of the three initial Communities deal with energy questions in great detail. While the ECSC expired in 2002, the EAEC still exists, although the continuing of the EURATOM Treaty as a separate primary law Treaty is sometimes ignored by mainstream EU lawyers.

The long negotiations on the European constitution, its rejection by referenda in some Member States and the entering into force of the TEU and TFEU (»Lisbon Treaty«)[1] on 1 December 2009 left the EURATOM Treaty largely unchanged. It was the Fukushima nuclear accident of March 2011 that revived public interest in its provisions with a focus on nuclear safety and security. By contrast, nuclear safeguards is an area of European law which, even for EU energy lawyers, remains largely *terra incognita.*

* Wolfgang Kilb is a senior lawyer in the European Commission's Directorate-General for Energy, Directorate Nuclear Safeguards. The views expressed are purely those of the author and may not under any circumstances be regarded as stating an official position of the European Commission.

1 Official Journal of the European Union (OJ) C 306 of 17 December 2007, page 1 et seq.

As nuclear materials such as uranium and plutonium can be used both for peaceful and military purposes, EURATOM nuclear safeguards were established as an international requirement and guarantee for the citizens to ensure that nuclear materials are only used for their declared and intended (peaceful) purposes. It was also a condition for the development of the nuclear industry in Europe in the 1950s and 1960s.

In other words, nuclear safeguards is one of the major guarantees, in addition to nuclear safety and nuclear security, that nuclear energy is used in the most safe and secure way in the EU. Independent of the wish of individual Member States to opt for nuclear power or not, a choice guaranteed under Article 194 TFEU, it is the task of the European Commission to ensure that nuclear material is not diverted.

EURATOM safeguards has four separate legal dimensions: First, the »supranational« relation with the Member States, second, the classic »international« relation with third countries outside the Community, third, the »cooperation« relation with the International Atomic Energy Agency (IAEA) in Vienna and fourth, the direct »supervision« relation with nuclear operators.

All four dimensions will be dealt with along the lines of the relevant legal instruments, starting with primary and secondary European law, followed by bi- and multilateral international agreements, then individual decisions and finally (scarce) case law.

I. The European legal framework

Unlike the TEU[2] and the TFEU[3], the »sectorial« EURATOM Treaty[4], dealing only with the peaceful use of nuclear energy, goes into much greater detail on issues like research, dissemination of information, health and safety, investment, supplies, etc. Its chapter 7 on Safeguards is very concrete with regard to rights and obligations of the European Commission, Member States and nuclear operators. Technical details are spelled out in a Commission Regulation, which in turn is interpreted by two Commission recommendations, while other legislative acts regulate other technical details.

2 OJ C 326 of 26 October 2012, page 13 et seq (consolidated version).
3 OJ C 326 of 26 October 2012, page 47 et seq (consolidated version).
4 OJ C 327 of 26 October 2012, page 1 et seq (consolidated version).

1. Primary law

a) Chapter 7 of the EURATOM Treaty is entitled »Safeguards«. It defines in Art 77 the duty of the European Commission to *»satisfy itself that (...) ores, source materials and special fissile materials are not diverted from their intended uses...«* and that *»safeguarding obligations (...) under an agreement concluded with a third State or an international organisation are complied with.«* The first obligation relates to the overall duty to ensure non-proliferation of nuclear materials to non-civil use by controlling nuclear operators, while the second refers to the international obligations of the Community vis-à-vis third states and international organisations such as the IAEA.

The chapter defines the duties of nuclear operators, which have to declare to the Commission the basic technical characteristics of their nuclear installations (Art 78) and are obliged to keep operating records to permit accounting for nuclear materials (Art 79).

b) The Commission may send inspectors into the territories of Member States. They have direct rights vis-à-vis nuclear operators as *»inspectors shall at all times have access to all places and data and to all persons (...) to the extent necessary in order to apply (...) safeguards to ores, source materials and special fissile materials...«*. In case of opposition to an inspection, an urgency procedure is foreseen which requires the President of the Court of Justice of the European Union either to decide within three days (!) or, if there is danger in delay, subsequently approve a written order issued by the Commission in form of a decision (Art 81). Both aspects, the right to directly inspect (private) parties – and not only to instruct the Member State to carry out a decision – and the extremely short delays of the Court to decide on these inspections, constitute extraordinary powers for the Commission.

Art 81 limits the right of the Commission to send inspectors to the EU Member States' only by two conditions: First, *»before sending an inspector on his first assignment (...) the Commission shall consult the State concerned; such consultation shall suffice to cover all future assignments of this inspector.«* This does not mean that the Member State has to approve the nomination of an inspector. Second, inspectors act *»on presentation of a document establishing their authority«*, i.e. by showing at least their inspector's card to the nuclear operator.

As there are no legal precedents, numerous questions can arise from this primary law framework: Is it an infringement to ask an inspector for an identity card or a passport? For how long should an inspector have to wait for access to a nuclear installation? Is it in line with his rights if he has to undergo an alcohol or drug test? Can the Member States require national authorisations of any kind or oblige the inspector to participate in safety training? The test how the President of the Court of Justice of the European Union would decide on a dispute within three days is still to be made.

c) In case of an infringement, the Commission has equally strong rights vis-à-vis the Member States: It »*may issue a directive* (in fact: a decision) *calling upon the Member State (...) to bring such [an] infringement to an end...«* Again, due to the potential danger of infringements related to nuclear material, if the Member State does not comply by the time limit set, *»the Commission or any Member State concerned may (...) refer the matter to the Court of Justice of the European Union direct.«* (Art 82). Hence, the procedure is again significantly streamlined when compared to the standard infringement procedure (delivery of a reasoned opinion by the Commission, then opportunity to submit its own case and its observations by the Member State before referral to the Court) of Art 258, 259 and 260 TFEU.

d) In the event of an infringement on the part of the nuclear operator *»the Commission may impose sanctions«*, i.e. in order of severity: a warning, the withdrawal of special benefits, the placing under administration or the *»total or partial withdrawal of source materials of special fissile materials«* (Art 83). Once more, the right to directly sanction a (private) party – without the detour via the Member State in which the party is domiciled – constitutes an extraordinary power attributed to the Commission and which has its equivalent only in very few other policy areas.

Commission »directives« in infringement procedures against Member States, based on Art 82 (3) and (4) Euratom Treaty as well as Commission decisions pronouncing sanctions against nuclear operators under Art 83 Euratom Treaty will be dealt with below.

2. Secondary law

a) The obligations of nuclear operators under chapter 7 are set out in more detail in Commission Regulation (Euratom) No 302/2005 of 8 February

2005 on the application of Euratom safeguards.[5] This Regulation, based on Art 79 Euratom Treaty, specifies the information to be declared by nuclear operators to the European Commission, and how and when these declarations must be produced. It also specifies the records that nuclear operators are obliged to produce, in order to allow the European Commission to fulfil the duties imposed by Art 77 Euratom Treaty.

b) Enacted on the basis of Art 37 of Commission Regulation 302/2005, Commission Recommendation of 15 December 2005 on guidelines for the application of Regulation (Euratom) No 302/2005 on the application of Euratom safeguards (2006/40/Euratom)[6] provides guidance to the nuclear operators on the information to be provided to the European Commission. Being a recommendation, it is of a legally non-binding nature (cf. Art 288 TFEU) while in practice it is widely recognised as »soft law«.

c) Commission Recommendation of 11 February 2009 on the implementation of a nuclear material accountancy and control system by operators of nuclear installations (2009/120/Euratom)[7] provides guidance to nuclear operators on how to implement a high quality Nuclear Material Accountancy and Control (NMAC) system, fulfilling the requirements of Regulation 302/2005. Again, this »soft law« act is not legally binding.

d) Accessorily, Regulation (Euratom) No 3[8] implements Art 24 Euratom Treaty with regard to security gradings to be applied to information disclosure, whereas Regulation (Euratom) No 9[9] defines the concentration of uranium in ores needed to qualify as *»ores«* in the sense of Art 197 (4) Euratom Treaty.

e) Finally, secondary law comes in the form of Particular Safeguard Provisions (PSP). Having their legal foundation in Art 6 of Commission Regulation 302/2005, these Commission decisions contain details of safeguards for individual nuclear installations. These are decisions directly addressed to a specific nuclear operator and therefore are not published in the Official Journal (OJ). Moreover, there are Commission decisions related to reprocessing plants. Based on Art 78(2) Euratom Treaty, these decisions approve, as far as necessary for nuclear safeguards, certain aspects of the

5 OJ L 54 of 28 February 2005, page 1 et seq.
6 OJ L 28 of 1 February 2006, page 1 et seq.
7 OJ L 41 of 12 February 2009, pages 17 et seq.
8 OJ 406/58 of 6 October 1958, pages 63 et seq.
9 OJ 482/60 of 22 February 1960, page 43.

techniques to be used for chemical processing of irradiated materials and are equally unpublished.

II. International Agreements

Art 77 b) Euratom Treaty stipulates that »the Commission shall satisfy itself that (…) any particular safeguarding obligation assumed by the Community under an agreement concluded with a third State or with an international organisation are complied with.«

Next to the classic international dimension of the 1st alternative of Art 77 b), which finds its expression in bilateral EURATOM agreements between the Community and third countries, the cooperation dimension with the other main actor in the field of nuclear safeguards is important: The 2nd alternative of Art 77 b) relates to a number of multilateral agreements between EURATOM, the IAEA and the non-nuclear weapon States (NNWS) of the Community as well as with the nuclear weapon States (NWS) United Kingdom and France.

1. Bilateral Agreements with third countries

The European Atomic Energy Community (EAEC) has concluded a number of bilateral international agreements under Art 101 Euratom Treaty. Provisions in various areas related to the civil use of nuclear energy are complemented by commitments on non-proliferation, safeguards, physical protection and export controls for nuclear materials. They were made with regard to

- **USA (1958, replaced in 1995):** Agreement for cooperation in the peaceful uses of nuclear energy between the European Atomic Energy Community and the United States of America (96/314/Euratom);[10]
- **Canada (1959, replacement expected in 2013):** Agreement between the Government of Canada and the European Atomic Energy Community (Euratom) for co-operation in the peaceful uses of Atomic Energy;[11]

10 OJ L 120 of 20 May 1996, pages 1 et seq.

11 OJ 60 of 24 November 1959, pages 1165 et seq.

- **Australia (1982, replaced in 2012):** Agreement between the Government of Australia and the European Atomic Energy Community (Euratom) for cooperation in the peaceful uses of nuclear energy;[12]
- **Uzbekistan (2004):** Agreement for cooperation in the peaceful uses of nuclear energy between the European Atomic Energy Community (Euratom) and the Government of the Republic of Uzbekistan;[13]
- **Japan (2006):** Agreement between the Government of Japan and the European Atomic Energy Community for co-operation in the peaceful uses of nuclear energy (2007/58/Euratom);[14]
- **Ukraine (2006):** Agreement between the European Atomic Energy Community and the Cabinet of Ministers of Ukraine for Co-operation in the Peaceful Uses of Nuclear Energy;[15]
- **Kazakhstan (2008):** Agreement for co-operation in the peaceful uses of nuclear energy between the European Atomic Energy Community and the Government of the Republic of Kazakhstan.[16]

An agreement with South Africa is negotiated and is expected to be signed in the course of 2013. More bilateral agreements are currently being negotiated (e.g. a revised agreement with Canada) or there are plans for such negotiations (e.g. with Russia, South Korea and possibly China).

Beyond nuclear safeguards aspects, these agreements vary widely in scope: They may include provisions on supply of nuclear material, technology transfer, transfer of equipment, procurement of equipment and devices, access to and use of equipment and facilities, management of spent fuel and radioactive waste, nuclear safety and radiation protection, use of radioisotopes and radiation in agriculture, industry and medicine, geological and geophysical exploration, etc., regulatory aspects, research and development, exchange of information and experts and other areas of mutual interest.

However, key elements of these agreements are nuclear safeguards clauses.

For example, the Euratom agreement with the Government of Canada (1959) requires in its Article IX that

12 OJ L 29 of 1 February 2012, pages 4 et seq.
13 OJ L 269 of 21 October 2003, pages 9 et seq.
14 OJ L 32 of 6 February 2007, pages 65 et seq.
15 OJ L 261 of 22 September 2006, pages 27 et seq.
16 OJ L 10 of 15 January 2009, pages 16 et seq.

> »The Government of Canada and the Community each undertakes that material or equipment … and source material or special nuclear material derived from the use of any material or equipment so obtained, shall be employed solely for … peaceful uses… and that no material or equipment … shall be transferred to unauthorized persons or beyond its control except with the prior consent in writing…«

More specifically from a legal point of view, the latest Euratom Agreement with the Government of Australia (2012) expressly stipulates in its Article VII that *»Nuclear material (...) shall be subject to (...) the Euratom safeguards pursuant to the Euratom Treaty and to the IAEA safeguards pursuant to (...) safeguards agreements...«.*

2. Multilateral Agreements between EURATOM, EU Member States and the IAEA

There are two main actors for safeguarding nuclear materials and installations in the territories of the 27 (soon 28) Member States of the European Union: The European Commission as main executive organ of the European Atomic Energy Community (Euratom headquarters in Luxembourg) and the International Atomic Energy Agency (IAEA headquarters in Vienna, Austria). Amongst the EU Member States, a distinction has to be made between, on the one hand, the vast majority of the 25 (soon 26) non-nuclear weapon States (NNWS) and, on the other hand, the two nuclear weapon States with a permanent seat in the United Nations (UN) Security Council, i.e. the United Kingdom and France.

a) Non-nuclear weapon States

The Agreement between the non-nuclear weapon States (NNWS), the European Atomic Energy Community and the International Atomic Energy Agency in implementation of Article III (1) and (4) of the Treaty on the Non-Proliferation of Nuclear Weapons (NPT) was signed in 1973 and came into force in 1978.[17] Recognising the existence of a Community-wide system of EURATOM safeguards, it contains a main text with the general principles of cooperation between the partners and details for nuclear safeguards arrangements such as inspections, design information,

17 OJ L 51 of 22 February 1978, pages 1 et seq. (also published by the IAEA as Information Circular INFCIRC/193).

records and reports systems. It also comprises a Protocol amplifying certain provisions of the Agreement, especially the means to avoid unnecessary duplication of the Community's safeguards activities and the ways for the coordination of EURATOM and IAEA safeguards activities.

Art 23 of the Agreement provides for the accession to the Agreement of all non-nuclear weapon States that become Member States of the EU and EURATOM, e.g. Croatia in 2013.

An Additional Protocol (AP) to the Safeguards Agreement was signed in 1998 and came into force in 2004.[18] It contains provisions to further enhance non-proliferation by strengthening the effectiveness and improving the efficiency of the IAEA's safeguards system. Both the IAEA and the Community have an interest in deepening their cooperation in order to free resources on the side of the IAEA for its activities outside Europe (e.g. Iran, North Korea). Hence, the AP foresees an increased cooperation through the provision of information by Member States, designation of inspectors, communication systems and protection of confidential information. It especially provides the IAEA with the means to enhance their capabilities to detect undeclared activities.

Both organisations cooperate on the basis of a partnership approach agreed in 1992.[19] Such cooperation relates, for example, to common development of instruments and techniques, common training, or common inspection approaches and procedures. However, it also comprises the possibility of performing certain inspection activities by only one party (European Commission or the IAEA) and the full use of the results of these activities by the other. This is based on the general principle that each party can fulfil its objectives and draw its conclusions independently. The European Commission and the IAEA are currently reflecting on further enhancement of this cooperation.

b) Nuclear weapon States

Both the United Kingdom (UK) and France as nuclear weapon States are in a different position compared to the NNWS of the European Union: they are legitimate holders of nuclear weapons in terms of the NPT.

18 OJ L 67 of 13 March 1999, pages 1 et seq. (also published by the IAEA as INFCIRC/193/Add8).

19 IAEA GOV/INF/654 of 13 May 1992 at http://www.iaea.org/About/Policy/GC/GC37/GC37Documents/English/gc37-1073_en.pdf (no 19-22).

Moreover, the Euratom Treaty in general does not apply to military use of nuclear energy, a principle which for nuclear safeguards is expressly stipulated in Art 84 (3).

However, both the UK[20] and France[21] have voluntarily concluded separate Agreements with the European Atomic Energy Community and the IAEA in 1976 and 1978. Both Agreements contain, as above, a main text and a Protocol, amplifying certain provisions of the Agreements. The respective Additional Protocols (AP) to both Agreements were signed in 1998.[22] [23]

Whereas EURATOM safeguards activities relate to all nuclear material in peaceful use in the UK and in France, IAEA safeguards is only applied in a relatively small number of nuclear installations in these two Member States.

III. Individual decisions

Compared to the standard infringement procedures against Member States only (Articles 258, 260 TFEU), the EURATOM Treaty gives the European Commission extraordinary powers: Both the Article 82 »directives« against Member States and the Article 83 decisions against nuclear operators take into account the potential danger and hence the need for urgency action in case of non-compliance.

1. Art 82 (3) »directive« against Member States

The infringement procedure of Art 82 (3) Euratom Treaty is directed against a Member State failing to fulfil its safeguards obligations. Although the wording speaks of »directive«, this is not a directive in the sense of Art 288 (3) TFEU *(»... binding, as to the result achieved upon each Member State to which it is addressed, but (...) leav[ing] the national authorities the choice of form and methods.«)*. Technically it is a decision in the sense of Art 288 (4) TFEU, which is *»binding in its entirety... to whom it is addressed...«*

20 INFCIRC/263.

21 INFCIRC/290.

22 INFCIRC/263/Add1.

23 INFCIRC/290/Add1.

This can be the case if a Member State itself acts as a nuclear operator or, in any other way, infringes safeguards obligations. In this context, the general duty of cooperation enshrined in Art 192 Euratom Treaty obliges the Member States to

> »take all appropriate measures ... to ensure fulfilment of the obligations arising out of this Treaty or resulting from action taken by the institutions of the Community. They shall facilitate the achievement of the Community's task. They shall abstain from any measure which could jeopardize the attainment of the objectives of this Treaty.«

Example: Sellafield pond B30 (BNFL)

Sellafield (formerly Windscale) is one of the largest nuclear centres in the EU and was previously owned by British Nuclear Fuels plc (BNFL). Irradiated Magnox fuel elements (consisting of uranium and plutonium) stored in underwater ponds (pond B30) awaiting reprocessing were left there longer than planned. This led to oxidation and subsequent decay of the elements, making a further handling impossible, while moreover access to the pond was limited because of significant radiation.

The Commission adopted a Directive addressed to the UK on 30 March 2004 because BNFL has infringed Articles 79 and 81 Euratom Treaty by not producing and keeping appropriate operating records in order to permit accounting for all nuclear material present in pond B30 at Sellafield. Moreover, Commission inspectors were not enabled to verify all nuclear material stored in pond B30, due to radiation protection constraints. The Directive imposed on the United Kingdom the obligation to submit a comprehensive plan in order to bring these infringements to an end.[24]

The work is currently on-going.

24 See press release no IP/4/419 at http://europa.eu/rapid/press-release_IP-04-419_en.htm?locale=en and the answer by the Commissioner in charge of Energy to written parliamentary question P -1038/04 in OJ C 88 E of 8 April 2004, page 276.

2. Art 83 (1) decisions against nuclear operators

Art 83 (1) Euratom Treaty foresees that

> »in the event of an infringement on the part of persons or undertakings of the obligations imposed on them ..., the Commission may impose sanctions... These sanctions shall be in order of severity: (a) a warning, (b) the withdrawal of special benefits..., (c) the placing ... under ... administration and (d) total or partial withdrawal of source materials or special fissile materials.«

Whereas sanctions as the withdrawal of special benefits or of nuclear materials have, so far, never been imposed, a number of nuclear operators were subject to warnings for various breaches of safeguards obligations.[25] In one case, a nuclear operator was even placed under administration (see below Case C-308/90).[26]

Example: Jenson Tungsten Ltd[27]

A British engineering firm was operating from premises previously occupied by other firms who carried our machining operations on depleted uranium. When the firm began operating, it took possession of a residual stock of depleted uranium from earlier operations and thus became the owner of this material. Following a first inspection by EURATOM, it was established that there was no accountancy system for nuclear material which satisfied the Commission Regulation in place, that it was not possible to carry out a satisfactory inventory verification due to unsatisfactory and incomplete records of the material on stock and that

25 *UKAEA Dounreay (UK)*, Commission decision of 4 March 1992 (92/194/Euratom), OJ L 88 of 3 April 1992, pages 54 et seq.; *Escuela Técnica Superior de Ingenieros Industriales de la Universidad Politécnica de Madrid (ES)*, Commission decision of 21 December 1994 (94/955/Euratom), OJ L 371 of 31 December 1994, pages 16 et seq.; *Enusa Juzbado (ES)*, Commission decision of 12 December 1997 (97/873/Euratom), OJ L 354 of 30 December 1997, pages 30 et seq.; *Sellafield (UK), THORP Fuel Reprocessing Plant*, Commission decision C(2006)412 of 15 February 2006, repealed by Commission decision C(2009)6055 of 3 August 2009, OJ C 16 of 22 January 2010, pages 17 et seq.

26 Overview in Sebastian Wolf: Euratom Before the Court: A Political Theory of Legal Non-Integration, in: European Integration online Papers (EIoP), vol. 15, Article 10 at http://eiop.or.at/eiop/texte/2011-010a.htm.

27 *Jenson Tungsten Ltd.*, Hemel Hempstead (UK), Commission decision of 13 November 1996 (96/671/Euratom), OJ L 313 of 3 December 1996, pages 20 et seq.

many of the submitted reports were either incorrect, missing or revealing inconsistencies. Following several requests and reminders, the firm subsequently acted and finally established a stock figure. However, a second inspection three years later revealed a discrepancy of 1466 tonnes (!) depleted uranium and 7.5 kilograms natural uranium, which was not satisfactorily explained or justified.

The Commission in its decision established several infringements: (1) the breach of Art 79 Euratom Treaty and of the duty to keep operating records under the predecessor of Commission Regulation 302/2005; (2) the incompatibility of the accounting system with the requirements derived from Art 81 and 82 Euratom Treaty in that it was impossible to verify the materials and the accounting and (3) breach of the duty to communicate to the Commission dispatches and receipts of nuclear material.

In the choice of the sanction, the objective element consists of the breach of essential elements of Community law in the field of safeguards, while the material in question had a low strategic value. From a subjective point of view, although the firm did not establish a nuclear materials accounting system for a long time despite several requests and reminders, it is not carrying out any activity involving nuclear material and is only holding its predecessor's material awaiting disposal.

As a consequence, a warning was issued under Art 83(1)(a) Euratom Treaty with the understanding that the established shortcomings are to be rectified within a certain deadline.

IV. Cases decided by the Court of Justice of the European Union

Only few cases in the field of the Euratom Treaty have reached the Court of Justice of the European Union (formerly »Court of Justice«) or the General Court (formerly »Court of First Instance«). Those that did (around 30) mostly concerned other areas of the Euratom Treaty. However, two decisions are worth mentioning because they are of specific interest to nuclear safeguards:

1. Case C-61/03 (Commission v United Kingdom – »Jason reactor«), 2005

In this action against the United Kingdom, the Commission tried to extend the scope of Euratom law to security and defence policy. The Commission argued that Euratom secondary law applies to the decommissioning of a military nuclear reactor and to the safety risks arising from a damaged nuclear-powered submarine. Although only a few provisions of the Euratom Treaty deal explicitly with security and defence policy (e.g. Art 24 – 28), the Court ruled that Euratom law generally does not apply to military installations and activities: *»It is necessary ... to emphasise the fact that the Treaty in not applicable to uses of nuclear energy for military purposes...«*[28]

This confirms the literal interpretation of Art 84 that *»The safeguards may not extend to materials intended to meet defence requirements...«*

2. Case C-308/90 (Advanced Nuclear Fuels GmbH v Commission – »ANF Lingen«), 1993

In this action against the Commission, a nuclear company *Advanced Nuclear Fuels GmbH* (ANF) unsuccessfully challenged the sanction imposed by the Commission under Art 83 (1).[29] The facts of the case merit to be presented as they are an example of the (human) risks involved in nuclear operations and the necessity of a robust nuclear safeguards regime:

A loading pallet with two containers, each containing two boxes, was moved from the storage area at the nuclear site of the applicant to the material entry lock at the plant for the purpose of removing the box containing uranium pellets enriched to 3.3 %. Once this operation had been completed the pallet was mistakenly placed outside, close to the storage area for empty containers, and forgotten about. The two containers on the pallet now only contained three boxes with nuclear material. The pallet was loaded by mistake on to a lorry belonging to a normal goods transport company.

The employee in charge believed the containers (standing in the area for empty containers) to be empty and removed the labels indicating the pres-

28 Judgment of 12 April 2005, in: ECR I-2477, section 44.

29 ANF Lingen (DE), Commission decision of 1 August 1990 (90/413/Euratom), OJ L 209 of 8 August 1990, pages 27 et seq.

ence of nuclear materials, replacing them with ones indicating that the containers were empty. The lorry was unloaded at Luxembourg airport and the containers transported to the USA. The recipient in the USA, after carrying out a routine dosimetric check had established the presence of nuclear materials in the containers that were supposed to be empty. An examination of the seals revealed that no material could have been removed from the boxes.

The nuclear operator notified the European Commission's safeguards Directorate and the Euratom Supply Agency (ESA) of this occurrence.

In its sanctioning decision, the Commission placed the operator under administration for a period of four months. Although from a subjective point of view there was no intention behind the actions and that these should not be seen as a form of diversion, the objective facts breached essential elements of safeguards rules, especially with regard to the control of export of nuclear materials outside the EU. Moreover, the seriousness of the case was reinforced by the fact that it involved a significant quantity of material.

Although the operator himself notified Euratom authorities of his errors, the Court held that neither a continuation of the infringement (which had ended) was necessary to uphold the Commission's sanctioning decision nor that the sanction itself was disproportionate. The application of ANF was therefore dismissed in its entirety.[30]

V. Conclusion

Before the International Atomic Energy Agency established its own safeguards system in 1961 and before the Non-proliferation Treaty was signed in 1968, the Euratom Treaty had already established a regional system to guarantee the intended and declared peaceful use of nuclear material. Although not all cases of non-conformity could be prevented, it contributes to the global safeguards system and allows the IAEA to focus on more dangerous countries outside Europe.

Therefore, mutual trust needs to be maintained by enhanced cooperation between the two organisations. Only if the provisions of the Euratom Treaty's chapter 7 are perceived as efficient, the IAEA, third countries, Member States and, last but not least EU citizens can feel assured of its effectiveness and efficiency.

30 Judgment of 21 January 1993, in: ECR-I-349.

Discussion Report of the First Working Session

Julian Rotter, Lazarski University, Warsaw, Poland

The Chairman of the panel, *Mr. Micklinghoff*, suggested that discussions should immediately follow each presentation since the presentations covered quite different topics.

Following the presentation of *Andreas Woitecki*, the first question was raised by *Mr. Tannion* concerning the introduction of European peer reviews. He wondered whether the draft directive would foresee interfaces with other international peer reviews such as OSART or IRRS missions of the IAEA. Mr. Woitecki explained that the idea of ENSREG was clearly to introduce an additional system of European topical peer reviews. Within this system, Members States should first conduct a national assessment on a specific topic selected by ENSREG and write a national report. Subsequently, this report should be peer reviewed by regulators from other Member States and conclusions be implemented. This design would differ very much from other international peer review systems offered by the IAEA. For example, the IRRS would focus on the regulatory system whereas the European peer reviews would focus on specific nuclear safety topics.

The discussion was continued by *Dr. Micklinghoff* who asked Mr. Woitecki about the independence of the regulator. He made reference to the fact that the speaker had criticized the approach of the DG Energy which – according to the speaker – would require the regulator to be an independent and separate legal institution in order to avoid undue influence. Mr. Micklinghoff pointed to the fact that it was generally assumed that undue influence came from the institutions which were supervised by the regulators. However, undue influence might also originate in the political sphere. He was interested how this phenomenon should be addressed. Mr. Woitecki answered that, in his view, the key objective should be the independence in regulatory decision making in safety matters, also from the political sphere. However, he emphasized that in order to achieve this objective, the establishment of an institutionally separate regulator was only one solution. According to Mr. Woitecki, there might be other ways how a member State could achieve this objective, for example through provisions regarding the personnel of the regulator which would safeguard independent advice and decisions.

Dr. Pelzer addressed the issue of possible conflicts between the obligations under the Nuclear Safety Convention (NSC) on the one hand, and the obligations under the EU Nuclear Safety Directive, on the other hand. EU Member States that are party to the NSC are in parallel also subjected to the obligations under the Directive. While the NSC is a so-called »incentive« convention, which does not establish enforceable obligations but solves disputes on the application and the interpretation of the NSC by a agreement at a meeting of the parties, the Directive sets up a mandatory regime which may be enforced, if necessary by a decision of the European Court of Justice. Within the EU, Member States are part of a mandatory system, and at the same time, vis-à-vis the parties to the NSC (which may include other EU Members), they are bound by an »incentive« international convention without enforceable obligations. This seems to describe a conflict situation. He stressed that he never had heard a convincing answer on how this possible conflict, if any, can be solved.

The Chairman proposed *Mr. Faross* to take a position on this question. According to Mr. Faross, there is no disarray because Member States under the Convention on Nuclear Safety made a political commitment. The convention is legally binding but not enforceable. With the revision of the directive the Commission would only take Member States by their word and turn some of the obligations of the CNS into enforceable Euratom law. Moreover, Mr. Faross added a comment that in his view it was pointless to still reflect on the competence of the Euratom Community to legislate. He pointed out that 27 Member States had adopted legislation on nuclear safety, namely the Nuclear Safety Directive, with the opinion of the EU Parliament with more than 500 MEPs. Moreover, he referred to the well-known judgment of the European Court of Justice 29/99 from 2002 concerning the accession of the Euratom Community to the Convention on Nuclear Safety, where the Court had established the competency of the Community in the domain of nuclear safety.

The last comment to the presentation was made by *Prof. Bohne* who pointed out that the concept of independent regulatory agencies originated in Anglo-Saxon law and was established long ago in reaction to corruption and conflicts of interest with state-owned industries. According to Prof. Bohne there is no evidence that a regulatory body organized as an independent agency is more effective than a regulatory body based on the Ministry principle as is the tradition in Germany. The impact assessment of the EU on the revision of the directive, according to him, is based on theoretical concepts and assumptions. He did not see that in Germany and other States there was today an analogous situation to that experienced in the US long time ago.

Finally, *Mr. Woitecki* responded to Mr. Faross' remark concerning the competence of the Euratom Community in the domain of nuclear safety. He said that he would not put into question the competency of the Euratom Community in the domain of nuclear safety in general. However, the question of how far this competence would go and whether the Euratom Community had legislative competence was not as easy to answer as sometimes presented. He reiterated that the European Court of Justice in its decision 29/99 had based its findings concerning the safety of operation and design only on the competence of the Euratom Community to make recommendations. As a consequence, the issue of legislative competence would return on the agenda as the directive is likely to shift from a framework directive to a more prescriptive directive.

After the second speaker, *Rasa Ptasekaite*, made her presentation on »Continuous Improvement of Nuclear Safety«, the chairman remarked that he was impressed that a lawyer talked about nuclear safety regulation aspects in such a detailed way.

The discussion was commenced by *Mr. Davies*. He wondered if there is a universal way to evaluate cost-benefits of the modification. In other words he wanted to know how significantly the benefits of the safety improvement should overweight the costs. Ms. Ptasekaite answered that there is no universal way to assess how significant the safety improvement must be in order for it to be significant enough to overweigh the costs. It has to be evaluated and decided on case by case basis. She added that the regulator plays a very important role in latter evaluation of the significance of the safety improvement.

Mr. Faross followed up on this issue by asking how to avoid subordinating safety to costs. He gave an example from the US concerning the installation of a specific filter to upgrade reactor safety. The regulator was confronted by the industry with arguments that it was far too expensive and there were cheaper solutions. Ms. Ptasekaite responded that there are two different aspects that might be important in the latter question. Firstly, she stated that it should not be forgotten that nuclear energy sector is still an industry sector which means that it has to be profitable. This implies that there will always be a question of costs. She elaborated that if costs are very high and the significance of the improvement is very little the implementation of such improvement becomes questionable. She also added that nowadays the technology development is so fast that if to implement every new modification that has a theoretical chance of improving safety, the nuclear energy sector might just not survive. Secondly, she pointed out, that, as it was mentioned earlier, the role of the regulator in evaluating the cost-benefits of the improvement is very important – it is the regulator who decides about safety requirements and due to that it should be the regulator that has the knowledge and capability to evaluate industry's arguments on the cost-and-benefits proportion of a certain improvement. The regulator should have the competence to know whether the industry's arguments on cost are reasonable or not.

The chairman, *Dr. Micklinghoff*, appreciated the question as well as the answer. He contributed to the discussion by stating that the continuous improvement of safety might be easier to understand than to define in strict legal terms. The chairman also added that continuous improvement of safety is a field where both – the regulator and the operator – have their roles to play, in order to achieve and maintain high level of nuclear safety.

The chairman also commented that the legal system in the US is quite different from the one in most European countries. In the US, the safety requirements are more static and the legal position of a license holder is very strong. The regulator is bound to formal rules when he asks for further improvements and backfitting, the criteria »proportionality« and »appropriateness« being very important. At first sight the situation in most European countries seems to be different. The regulation is more dynamic and – from the legal point – it is easier for the regulator to ask for backfitting measures. However, according to Dr. Micklinghoff every dynamic system is bound to rely on proportionality by nature. Thus the principles of proportionality and appropriateness (what is reasonable?) govern the regulation in Europe to a similar extent as in the US.

The chairman added that most people think that the dynamic system leads to higher safety, whereas this was not true in his view. Sometimes static requirements are established which in a dynamic system are seen as not appropriate. Vice versa, in a dynamic system sometimes »formal deficiencies« are tolerated because corrective measures are not possible or seen as not reasonable. Experience shows that plants are easier and more often shut down for regulatory reasons when there are high static requirements.

Dr. Raetzke agreed with Dr. Micklinghoff and added that in legal terms it is generally difficult to impose an obligation of »continuous improvement« on someone, as this seems to be rather uncertain and ill-defined and a »shifting target«. Normally, legal obligations in safety aim at a determined level of safety which is clearly defined as being »safe enough« and which allows for unambiguous evaluation of compliance.

Ms. Ptasekaite answered that »continuous improvement« is indeed an obligation but it is sufficiently clear for the operator since the regulator is responsible for determining the level of safety that should be considered to be as high as reasonably achievable at any given time. The operator concentrates on fulfilling the existing safety requirements that have been established by the regulator.

Following the presentation of *Wolfgang Kilb*, there were no questions.

Second Working Session

»Nuclear New Build«

Chair: *Ian Salter,* Burges Salmon, Bristol, UK
Secretary: *Łukasz Młynarkiewicz,* Phd C., Nicolaus Copernicus University, Toruń, Poland

Nuclear Power Programme for Poland – Establishing the Legal Framework

Tomasz R. Nowacki, Head of Unit for Strategy, Legal and International Relations, Nuclear Energy Department, Polish Ministry of Economy, Warsaw

1. Introduction

In 2009 Poland decided to launch the nuclear power implementation programme. It is expected that the Council of Ministers will approve the final version of the governmental programme as regards the development of the nuclear power at the turn of the year.

So far a Government Commissioner for the Polish Nuclear Power together with a supporting body in the form of Nuclear Energy Department within the Ministry of Economy have been established.

The company responsible for the construction of nuclear power plants – PGE Polska Grupa Energetyczna S.A. – has established a special purpose company tasked solely with the preparation and construction of nuclear power plants in Poland. In meantime, significant amendments to existing legislation were introduced thus creating virtually complete legal framework for the planned investments.

2. First Polish nuclear power programme

2.1 General

Poland has used nuclear technologies since the fifties. In 1958 the first research reactor »Ewa« was commissioned. The first strategic governmental document in the scope of atomic questions, covering also nuclear power, envisaged the construction of the first nuclear power plant with approx. 200 MWe of installed capacity by 1965, as well as further intense development of nuclear power throughout the seventies.[1]

1 See the Long-term plan in the scope of nuclear power development in Poland of 1957, in: Supplement to Postępy Techniki Jądrowej (Progresses of Nuclear Technology) no. 302-303(1982/1-2), p. XVI (in Polish).

In 1971 a preliminary decision to build the first nuclear power plant in Poland was taken,[2] while in 1972 the location of the prospective power plant was determined as Pomeranian county of Żarnowiec.[3] Then, an updated nuclear power programme was adopted,[4] which envisaged the construction of nuclear power plants with 8,5 GWe of total installed capacity by 1990.[5] In the framework of this programme a decision was taken in 1982 to commence the construction of the first Polish nuclear power plant in Żarnowiec,[6] which was to be equipped with two, and ultimately four, VVER-440-type reactors of Soviet design. Meanwhile the necessity of nuclear power implementation had been confirmed by the Government[7] and the Sejm (the lower chamber of the Polish Parliament).[8]

After the political transition in 1989 the construction of Żarnowiec Power Plant although completed in more than 50% was suspended[9] to be eventually abandoned in connection with the goals of the new Polish Energy Policy for the period 1990-2010.[10] Officially, the reasons behind the withdrawal from the investment were purely economic. However, the government's position was in fact strongly influenced by numerous protest campaigns linked to the still fresh, despite the technological differences between VVER and RBMK-type reactors, memories of the Chernobyl nu-

2 Decision no. 113/71 of the Government's Presidium of 12 August, 1971 on the commencement of the construction of the first Polish nuclear Power plant equipped with power units with WWER-440-type reactors and on pre-construction activities (unpublished).

3 Decision of the Planning Commission by the Council of Minister of 19 December 1972 (unpublished).

4 Decision no. 20/75 of the Government's Presidium of 14 February 1975 on the possible applications of nuclear power in the national economy until 1990 (unpublished).

5 By 2000 the programme envisaged the construction of power plants with total capacity of 35 GWe (sic!).

6 Resolution no. 10/82 of the Council of Ministers of 18 January 1982 on the construction of the Żarnowiec power plant (unpublished).

7 Resolution of the Council of Ministers of 11 March 1985 on nuclear power development in Poland until 2030 (unpublished).

8 Resolution of the Sejm of the Polish People's Republic of 21 March 1985 on activities towards securing fuel and energy deliveries for national economy until 2000 (Official Journal of 1985, No. 6, item 41).

9 Resolution of the Council of Ministers of 4 September on suspension of the construction of the Nuclear Power Plant Żarnowiec (unpublished).

10 Resolution no. 204 of the Council of Ministers of 17 December 1990 on putting into liquidation of investment – »Żarnowiec« Nuclear Power Plant under construction (Official Journal of 1990, No. 49, item 373 as amended).

clear accident, as well as general lack of trust in everything coming from the Soviet Union.

2.2. Legal dimension

The need for a legal framework covering various applications of nuclear energy was already signalled at an early stage, by domestic jurisprudence[11] as well as within programme documents[12].

At the moment when the construction of Żarnowiec Power Plant was commenced no comprehensive nuclear legislation existed in Poland. Nuclear provisions in force at the time were dispersed among several universally binding legal acts (laws and regulations)[13] as well as in a number of governmental internal acts, i.e. resolutions and orders issued by the Council of Ministers and their subordinate bodies.[14] In addition, existing regulation was virtually limited to the questions of radiation protection of workers and patients. The regulation of the nuclear installations' licensing process was only rudimentary.

In view of the planned and eventually commenced construction of the Żarnowiec Power Plant, the need for a comprehensive legal framework governing such investments, in particular as regards nuclear safety, became clear, which was also articulated in literature.[15] As a result, on 10th

11 See the oldest Polish source of literature on nuclear law (limited, however, to medical applications) – C. Pawłowski, *Rules on protection measures for physicians, auxiliary workers and patients during application of X rays for diagnostic and therapeutic purposes and conditions of work of physicians and auxiliary workers in radiological institutes*, Warszawa 1947 (in Polish).

12 See footnote 1.

13 Polish nuclear regulations of that time (in Polish, English, German and French) are reproduced in: G. Zieger, G. Strauch (eds.), *Göttinger Atomrechtskatalog 1969. Teil L: Rechtsvorschriften, Verträge – Laws and Regulations, Treaties - Dispositions juridiques, traités. Bd. 18: Nicaragua-Poland*, Göttingen 1969. On Polish nuclear law at the turn of 50's and 60's see also H. Drück, *Atomrecht von Polen*, WGO-MfOR 1961, pp. 134-141; H. Drück, G. Liebsch, *Das Atomrecht in Osteuropa: internationale Abkommen und Gesetzgebung*, WGO-MfOR 1962, pp. 186-194.

14 Prime Minister, Ministers, Government Commissioner for the Nuclear Power Utilization, State Council for the Peaceful Nuclear Power Utilization, President of the National Atomic Energy Agency (PAA President) and others.

15 See e.g.: S. Chwaszczewski, T. Kazimierski, A. Strupczewski, A. Wierusz, A. Witort, W. Dąbek, *The role of nuclear power and actions determining its proper*

April 1986 (only two weeks before Chernobyl accident) the Sejm adopted the Atomic Law,[16] which constituted the first comprehensive legal act regulating the entirety of peaceful uses of nuclear energy.[17] The Act addressed all areas of nuclear energy utilization, namely: nuclear installations, nuclear materials, radioactive sources, radioactive waste, transportation, radiation protection, civil liability for nuclear damage as well as the system of supervision in the field of nuclear safety. Included were also penal provisions. In addition, its secondary legislation as well as the still binding preceding legislation covered the questions of radiation protection, emergency planning, emergency procedures and nuclear security.[18]

---

development in Poland, Postępy Techniki Jądrowej Vol. 25(1981), pp. 558, 560 (in Polish).

16 Journal of Laws of 1986, no. 12, item 70 as amended. For unofficial English translation of the 1986 Atomic Law along with accompanying secondary legislation see: Polish People's Republic National Atomic Energy Agency National Nuclear Safety and Radiological Protection Surveillance, *National Regulations of Polish People's Republic in atomic energy domain*, Warszawa 1989. Unofficial English translation of the Law is also reproduced in: Supplement to Nuclear Law Bulletin no. 43(1988/1). Short description of the Law in: Nuclear Law Bulletin no. 40(1987/2), pp. 16-18. On amendments in English see: Nuclear Law Bulletin no. 60(1997/2), pp. 89-90.

17 The construction license was issued by the nuclear regulator (PAA President) 6 months earlier (11.11.1985) on the basis of the Act of 27 February 1982 establishing the National Atomic Energy Agency (Journal of Laws of 1982, No. 7, item 6). However, construction works regarding the reactor building were carried already since 1984 without the required license – see: PAA President's Team for the nuclear power plant Żarnowiec, *Report on nuclear power plant Żarnowiec*, Warszawa 1990, p. 14 (in Polish). On the licensing process in practice of that time see M. Bernatowicz et al., *Legal status and regulatory practices in nuclear power plant licensing in Poland*, in: IAEA (eds.), *Regulatory practices and safety standards for nuclear power plants. Proceedings of an international symposium held in Munich, 7-10 November 1988*, Vienna 1989, pp. 155-163.

18 For more information on the content and elaboration of the 1986 Atomic Law see: Z. Brodecki, *Die Geburt des polnischen Atomrechts*, OstEuR 1988, no. 2, pp. 108-121; G. Strauch, *Das polnische Atomrechtsgesetz*, atw 1986, pp. 463-465; On subsequent amendments see *Poland*, in: OECD NEA Legal Affairs (eds.) *Overview of Nuclear Legislation in Central and Eastern Europe and the NIS*, Paris 2000, pp. 117-126. On Polish nuclear law in those times see also: T. Gadkowski, *Some international law elements of national nuclear regulations from the Polish point of view*, in: N. Pelzer (eds.), *Deutsches Atomenergierecht im internationalen Rahmen*, Baden-Baden 1992, pp. 83-93; E. Szkultecka, K. Guzowski, *Polish nuclear legislation: short information*, in: NEA/IAEA/EC (eds.), *Advanced Training Seminar on Nuclear Law: The Convergence of Legislation in Central and Eastern Europe with EU and International Nuclear Law. Dubrovnik, Croatia, 25-29 August 1997*, pp. 1-5.

In the meantime, Poland had ratified and implemented almost all international conventions in the scope of nuclear law existing at the time.[19] Bearing in mind the scope of nuclear power exploitation, the Polish nuclear law system of that time could be considered coherent and in compliance with the existing international standards in the field. The only identifiable weakness of the contemporary nuclear law was, without question, the lack of detailed requirements applicable throughout the subsequent phases of the nuclear installation's lifecycle. This issue was practically solved by filling in the gaps through direct application of the Soviet regulations,[20] issuing of nonbinding regulatory guidelines[21] and supplementary application of current IAEA recommendations.

It should also be noted that nuclear inspection of the time, although not formally independent in the meaning of e.g. the Convention on Nuclear Safety, displayed nevertheless a high level of safety culture and robustness with regard to the licensee, as well as governmental institutions tasked with the promotion of the construction of nuclear power plants in Poland.

3. *The current Polish nuclear power programme*

3.1. The political decision to implement nuclear power in Poland

The decision to discontinue the construction of the Żarnowiec NPP did not mean that Poland completely abandoned the plans to develop nuclear power. Even as late as in 1990 the Sejm of the Republic of Poland consid-

19 1960 Radiation Protection Convention (Journal of Laws of 1965, No. 8, item 45), 1963 Vienna Convention (Journal of Laws of 1990, No. 63, item 370), 1968 NPT (Journal of Laws of 1970, No. 8, item 60), 1979 CPPNM (Journal of laws of 1989, No. 17, item 93), 1986 Early Notification Convention (Journal of Laws of 1988, No. 31, item 216), 1986 Convention on Assistance in Case of a Nuclear Accident (Journal of Laws of 1988, No. 31, item 218).

20 Soviet provisions were incorporated into Polish law through the Ordinance no. 21 of the Minister for Mining and Power Engineering of 16 November 1983 on the rules of implementing Soviet norms and provisions to the realization of the construction of Żarnowiec nuclear power plant.

21 Guidelines of the PAA President's Commissioner for Nuclear Safety no. 1/84 of 9 September 1984 on the nuclear safety of nuclear installations and no. 2/84 of 5 October 1984 on the siting of nuclear power plants. Additionally since 1988 in force was the ordinance of PAA President of 1 June 1988 on detailed rules for creating and development of nuclear installation protection zone (Official Journal of 1988, No. 20, item 180).

ered nuclear power, based on new reactor technologies, as one of the main directions of future development of the Polish power sector.[22]

The possible construction of nuclear power plants was also considered in subsequent government's documents in the scope of energy policy,[23] as well as in the Prime Minister Jarosław Kaczyński's exposé from 2006.[24]

The breakthrough in the process came with the resolution of the Council of Ministers of 13 January 2009, adopted under Prime Minister Donald Tusk.[25] The said resolution was the first document in a long while to finally and unequivocally decide upon the necessity of the implementation of nuclear power in Poland and the commencement of concrete activities in this regard. According to § 1 of the resolution:

> »The Council of Ministers considers necessary the preparation and the implementation of the nuclear power programme for Poland.«

A Government Commissioner for the Polish Nuclear Power to be appointed pursuant to separate provisions, was tasked with the preparation of the Polish Nuclear Power Programme (further as PNP Programme), as well as the programme of legal and institutional amendments necessary to implement the PNP Programme.[26]

The Government's position regarding the advisability of the implementation of nuclear power was then confirmed with further decisions. According to the Energy Policy for Poland until 2030[27] approved by a resolution of the Council of Ministers of 10 November 2009[28] the diversification

22 Resolution of the Sejm of the Republic of Poland of 9 November 1990 on guidelines for Polish Energy Policy until 2010 (Official Journal of 1990, No. 43, item 332) – see point 3 of the resolution.

23 See e.g. 2002 Assumptions for Energy Policy for Poland until 2020, p. 6, 2005 Energy Policy for Poland until 2025 (Official Journal of 2005, No. 42, item 562), p. 34, 2006 Programme for the Power Engineering Sector, p. 20.

24 Available at: <http://www.poprzedniastrona.premier.gov.pl/archiwum/1433_18017.htm> (in Polish).

25 Resolution no. 4/2009 of the Council of Minister of 13 January 2009 on activities to be undertaken in the scope of nuclear power development (unpublished).

26 § 2 of the resolution.

27 Appendix to the announcement of the Minister of Economy of 21 December 2009 on state's energy policy until 2030 (Official Journal of 2010, No. 2, item 11), unofficial English translation under <http://www.mg.gov.pl/files/upload/8134/Polityka%20energetyczna%20ost_en.pdf>.

28 Resolution no. 202/2009 of the Council of Ministers of 10 November 2009 on the »Energy Policy of Poland until 2030« (unpublished), amended by the resolution no. 157/2010 of the Council of Ministers of 29 September 2010 amending the resolution on the »Energy Policy of Poland until 2030« (unpublished).

of power generation through the introduction of nuclear power[29] was considered one of the main energy policy objectives, which was justified i.a. as follows:

> »(...) nuclear energy has become one of the most desired energy sources. Apart from the lack of CO2 emission, it also ensures independence from typical directions from which energy resources are obtained.«[30]

Moreover, in the Long-term Development Strategy for Poland, approved by a Council of Ministers' resolution on 5th February 2013,[31] it was indicated that:

> »The nuclear power programme currently under implementation constitutes one of the best solutions ensuring at the same time long-term security and stability of power supply (...) as well as the fulfilment of climate and environmental objectives (...). In combination with economy based on coal it becomes an energy source offering additional technological possibilities contributing towards lowering of energy generation costs. Despite the investment process being long and costly (...) the afterward long-term exploitation at relatively low operational cost makes nuclear power the cheapest available energy source (...).«[32]

In addition to strategic political decisions adopted by the Council of Ministers by way of resolutions[33] the Council of Ministers' regulation dated of 12 May 2009 establishing the Government's Commissioner for the Polish Nuclear Power[34] is another example of an important legal instrument. The regulation, according to its title, created a special authority[35] in the rank of Undersecretary of State in the Ministry of Economy,[36] tasked exclusively with the implementation and development of nuclear power in Poland.[37] The Government Commissioner for the Polish Nuclear Power is in partic-

29 Point 4, p. 16 of the Energy Policy of Poland until 2030.

30 Ibidem.

31 Resolution no. 16 of the Council of Ministers of 5 February 2013 on approval of the Long-term Country's Development Strategy Poland 2030. Third Wave of Modernity (Official Journal of 2013, item 121).

32 p. 113 of the Strategy.

33 See also Country's Development Strategy 2020 (p. 91) approved by the resolution no. 157 of the Council of Ministers of 25 September 2012 on approval of the Country's Development Strategy 2020 (Official Journal of 2012, item 882).

34 Journal of Laws of 2009, No. 72, item 622.

35 § 1(1) of the regulation.

36 § 1(2) of the regulation.

37 § 2(1) of the regulation. Government Commissioner for the Polish Nuclear Power along with supporting Nuclear energy Department of the Ministry of Economy can be regarded as nuclear energy programme implementing organization (NEPIO) as indicated in documents of the IAEA.

ular responsible for the elaboration of the draft PNP Programme[38] and its submission to the Council of Ministers. Among the Commissioner's responsibilities the regulation explicitly mentions tasks in the area of legislation, namely: elaboration and submission to the Council of Ministers of the draft programme as regards legislative and institutional amendments,[39] initiating and elaboration of draft laws[40] and giving opinions on draft laws as well as other governmental documents linked to the implementation and development of nuclear power.[41]

The above-mentioned resolutions of the Council of Ministers adopted over these few years, as well as the regulation establishing Government Commissioner for the Polish Nuclear Power tells unequivocally of the existence of a consistent political will for the implementation of nuclear power in Poland.[42] This will in the end be confirmed by the adoption of the PNP Programme by the Council of Ministers.[43] Although formally it will be no difference from any other document confirming the hitherto policy direction, it will be in fact the main act determining the ways of implementing nuclear power in Poland as an already fixed policy direction. The PNP Programme shall in particular determine the time frame for actions to be undertaken by the governmental administration, as well as resources in this regard.

3.2. Main objectives of PNP Programme

PNP Programme envisages the construction of nuclear power plants with approx. 6000 MW of total installed capacity until 2030, based on III or III + generation of reactor design and in compliance with the highest

38 § 2(2)(1) of the regulation. It is a repetition of the Commissioner's obligation derived from the above mentioned resolution of the Council of Ministers no. 4/2009 and from the Energy Policy for Poland until 2030.

39 § 2(2)(2). Again this obligation derives also from the Council of Ministers no. 4/2009 and from the Energy Policy for Poland until 2030.

40 § 2(2)(3) of the regulation. Obligation derives also from the Energy Policy for Poland until 2030.

41 § 2(2)(7) of the regulation.

42 It is worth mentioning that similar, favourable attitude towards nuclear energy as presented by the ruling coalition (PO-PSL) is also presented by the biggest and most important party of the opposition (PiS). Moreover the »nuclear package« – laws enabling the implementation of nuclear power – has been approved by the parliament in 2011 with only one (1) opposite vote.

43 Expected at the turn of 2013 and 2014.

standards of nuclear safety. Introduction of nuclear power into the power system is to contribute to:

- Securing energy supplies through diversification of the fuel mix;
- Securing the affordable electricity costs in the long run;
- Replacement of old generation sources;
- Making the power sector more environmental friendly through reductions of CO_2, SO_2, NOx and fumes emissions (thereby achieving the EU commitments in this regard);
- Increase in electricity generation efficiency;
- Economical and scientific development of the country in general.

4. Establishing new nuclear legislation

4.1. Starting point

At the time when the resolution on the nuclear power implementation was adopted in 2009 the main legal act in the nuclear field was the Atomic Law of 29 November 2000,[44] successor of the above-mentioned Atomic Law of 1986, together with numerous secondary legislation in the form of commonly binding regulations, as well as internally binding orders. In addition, Poland was party to virtually all international conventions existing at the time in the scope of nuclear law[45] having also implemented into domestic legal order the entirety of Euratom *acquis communautaire* (until 2009), having joined the Community on 1st May 2004.

As in the case of the Atomic Law of 1986, in 2009 Poland still did not have any specific requirements applicable to nuclear installations.[46] It was

44 Journal of Laws of 2001, No. 3, item 18 as amended. For the unofficial English translation see: Supplement to Nuclear Law Bulletin no. 68 (2001/2), pp. 21-74, available also on OECD NEA's website: <http://www.oecd-nea.org/law/nlb/nlb-68/Poland.pdf>. Brief description of the Law in: Nuclear Law Bulletin no. 67 (2001/1), pp. 47-52. On amendments of 2001 and 2004 see respectively: Nuclear Law Bulletin no. 69 (2002/1), pp. 86-87 (along with some secondary legislation) and Nuclear Law Bulletin no. 74 (2004/2), pp. 55-56.

45 With exception of the 1997 Protocol to Amend the 1963 Vienna Convention and 1997 CSC. Being party of the Vienna liability regime Poland obviously has never been party to the legal instruments of the Paris-Brussels regime.

46 What is not surprising given the fact that Poland has only four nuclear installations: two research reactors (one in decommissioning) and two storage facilities. Moreover until 2009 no new investments in this regard have been planned.

also necessary to enhance the *de iure* independence of the nuclear regulatory body.

What is more, Poland did not have any specific regulation as regards the realisation of strategic infrastructure investments that would respond to the needs of such difficulty and complexity as in the case of the construction of nuclear power plants together with technical facilities and all associated infrastructure.

It was therefore necessary to adapt Polish legal framework to the needs of nuclear power investments. As regards nuclear law in the strict sense – that is pertaining to nuclear safety related issues – the envisaged amendments were aimed above all at creating a comprehensive legal framework covering safety requirements with regard to all the subsequent phases of nuclear installations lifecycle, providing a framework for radioactive waste management and decommissioning of nuclear facilities, as well as increasing the independence of nuclear regulator. By that time it was also necessary to implement Council Directive 2009/71/Euratom of 25 June 2009 establishing a Community framework for the nuclear safety of nuclear installations.[47] In addition, a decision was taken to ratify and implement the 1997 Protocol to Amend the 1963 Vienna Convention on Civil Liability for Nuclear Damage.[48] Moreover, it was deemed useful to establish appropriate legislation in the scope of spatial development/planning as well as investment and construction process in order to facilitate the realization of planned investments.

4.2. Brief introduction to the Polish legal system – sources of law

Any analysis of subsequent amendments to Polish nuclear law should be preceded with some introductory remarks, in particular as regards the system of sources of law in Poland.

47 OJ L 172, 2.7.2009, p. 18 and OJ L 260, 3.10.2009, p. 40, further in text as »nuclear safety directive«.

48 INFCIRC 566; Journal of Laws of 2011, No. 4, item 9.

4.2.1. Commonly binding legal framework

According to the Polish Constitution[49] the Polish commonly binding legal framework consists of: the Constitution,[50] ratified international conventions, other international agreements binding upon Poland and customary international law,[51] laws (acts of the Parliament),[52] regulations[53] and acts of law adopted by local self-government units.[54]

Regulations may only be issued by bodies indicated in the Constitution, on the basis and within the limit of a specific statutory authorization and with the aim of implementation thereof.[55] The so-called local law is also adopted on the basis and within the limit of an explicit statutory authorization, although bodies competent for their adoption are local self-government units, while the applicability of such acts is limited to territory of their competence.[56]

Commonly binding nuclear law provisions are mainly contained in laws and regulations, however, self-executing international agreements as well as regulations adopted by the Council and the European Commission on the basis of the Euratom Treaty,[57] in view of the Polish membership in the Euratom Community, are also commonly binding. International law binding upon Poland takes precedence over laws, regulations and acts of law issued by local self-government units.[58]

4.2.2. Internally binding acts of law

In the legal system, apart from the above mentioned legal instruments, there are also legal acts binding only upon a limited number of addressees.

---

49 The Constitution of the Republic of Poland of 2 April 1997 (Journal of Laws of 1997, No. 78, item 483 as amended). Unofficial English translation available under <http://www.sejm.gov.pl/prawo/konst/angielski/ kon1.htm>.

50 Art. 87(1) of the Constitution.

51 Art. 9, art. 87(1), art. 88(3), art. 90, art. 91 of the Constitution.

52 Art. 87, art. 88 of the Constitution.

53 Art. 87(1), art. 88(1), art. 92 of the Constitution.

54 Art. 87(2), art. 88(1), art. 94 of the Constitution.

55 Art. 92 of the Constitution.

56 Art. 94 of the Constitution.

57 OJ C 326, 26.10.2012, p. 1; Journal of Laws of 2009, No. 203, item 1569.

58 As a result of the interpretation of art. 9 of the Constitution. See in this regard e.g.: B. Banaszak [et al.], *Constitutional Law in Poland*, Wolters Kluwer International, Alphen aan den Rijn 2012.

Here the Constitution enumerates resolutions of the Council of Ministers and orders applicable only to entities that are organisationally subordinate to authorities issuing them.[59]

In a resolution the Council of Ministers may impose obligations upon their subordinate entities, including ministers and heads of central authorities (e.g. Chief of the nuclear regulatory body – PAA President[60]). All strategic national policy documents, also in the field of energy policy, are approved by the Council of Ministers by way of resolutions. As regards realisation of particular policies, said resolutions oblige relevant authorities and institutions to undertake certain actions, and are, in this regard, binding upon their addressees. For example, the Minister of Economy, the Government Commissioner for the Polish Nuclear Power or the PAA President may be obliged to undertake certain actions in a manner and within means prescribed.

Orders may be issued by the Prime Minister, ministers and heads of central authorities, including the PAA President as the head of nuclear regulatory body. Orders are issued on the basis of statutory provisions and, similarly to Council of Ministers' resolutions, may not constitute legal basis for decisions addressed to individuals or legal entities nor any other subjects of law.[61] For example according to provisions of the Atomic Law, by way of an order the Minister of Environment provides the PAA with a statute determining its internal organization,[62] while the PAA President provides PAA with organizational regulations determining in detail the structure, procedures and competencies of its organizational units.[63] On the other hand, the Minister of Economy provides a statute for the Waste Management Plant,[64] while Ministers of National Defence and Internal Affairs respectively issue orders determining the way of implementing provisions of the Atomic Law in their subordinate entities.[65]

Contrary to appearances all the above mentioned orders play a significant role. Although they do not impose obligations upon physical and le-

59 Art. 93 of the Constitution.

60 PAA President is the central organ of the governmental administration, competent for nuclear safety and radiological protection (as follows from current art. 109(1) of the Atomic Law). PAA stands for »Państwowa Agencja Atomistyki« – »National Atomic Energy Agency«.

61 Art. 93(2) of the Constitution.

62 Art. 113(1) of the Atomic Law.

63 Art. 113(2) of the Atomic Law.

64 Art. 121(3) of the Atomic Law.

65 Art. 132 of the Atomic Law.

gal persons nor any other subjects of law, they indirectly influence these entities by determining the functioning of institutions that are key for the safe use of nuclear energy in Poland. Resolutions and orders may not conflict any commonly binding provisions, which is subject to control.[66]

Administrative decisions, issued on the basis of statutory law, constitute another type of acts imposing obligations upon their addressees. The most important administrative decision within nuclear law is the licence for activities related to the use of nuclear energy, including those in relation to nuclear installations.[67] Each license issued by the PAA President, unless successfully challenged in court, constitutes a source of obligations to be fulfilled under administrative penalty.[68] Other administrative decisions, e.g. orders and bans issued by nuclear inspectors or the PAA President,[69] as well as other actions of sovereign nature performed by them e.g. in the form of suspension or revoking of a licence etc. are also binding upon the licensee.

4.2.3. Non-binding instruments

Technical and organisational guidelines in the scope of nuclear safety and radiation protection issued by the PAA President on the basis of art. 110(3) of the Atomic Law are the main non-binding instruments of nuclear law in Poland.

Despite their non-binding character and, thus, lack of legal effect in the form of obligations imposed upon their addressees, they play an important interpretational role in the process of application of the binding legislation. In particular, recommendations outline optimal means of implementation of the requirements contained in laws, regulations and licence conditions. In this sense their role consists in facilitating communication between the nuclear inspection and the licensee thus simplifying the licensing process.

Apart from the »regular« PAA President's recommendations, in individual cases the so called *ad hoc* recommendations may be issued as a result of an inspection. In the scope of nuclear security recommendations of this sort may be issued by Internal Security Agency (ABW) officers,[70]

66 Art. 93(3) of the Constitution.

67 Licences for all activities with ionising radiation are being issued on the general basis of art. 4(1) of the Atomic Law.

68 Art. 123 of the Atomic Law.

69 Art. 37(6), art. 37b(1), art. 37c(3), art. 38d(7), art. 68b of the Atomic Law.

70 Art. 41m(5)(7) of the Atomic Law.

while recommendations as regards nuclear safety and radiation protection are issued by the nuclear inspectors, however, only upon condition that situations having negative influence on the level of nuclear safety do not constitute violation of laws or the licence conditions.[71] In all the other cases nuclear inspectors issue binding administrative decisions.

4.3. Legislative procedure in Poland

According to constitutional provisions the right to introduce legislation belongs to deputies, the Senate,[72] the President of the Republic, the Council of Ministers or 100.000 citizens.[73] The vast majority of acts is adopted on a proposal from the Council of Ministers. Same applies in the scope of nuclear law. All draft laws (including amending laws) pertaining to the use of nuclear energy were submitted to Sejm by the Council of Ministers.

Legislative procedure within the Council of Ministers is very complex and time-consuming and normally consists of two main phases – the first of which consists in the preparation of a pre-draft by the relevant minister. A pre-draft is a kind of proposal within the council of Ministers and constitutes a description of the draft law's objectives together with the indication of areas that should be regulated, proposed ways of regulation and a justification of a proposal.[74] Phase two consists in drafting the law in question. By approving the pre-draft the Council of Ministers considers the law to be drafted as expedient. It is when the Government Legislation Center converts the descriptive pre-draft into a strictly legal document edited according to the Principles of the legislative technique[75] and divided into sectioning levels appropriate for a legal text, i.e. articles, paragraphs, points, etc. (draft law). Draft law finally approved by the Council of Min-

71 Art. 68a of the Atomic Law.

72 The higher chamber of the Polish parliament.

73 Art. 118 of the Constitution.

74 In exceptional circumstances an exemption from this obligation can be obtained by the authority obliged to prepare a pre-draft. This is the case of the implementation of the Council Directive 2011/70/Euratom of 19 July 2011 establishing a Community framework for the responsible and safe management of spent fuel and radioactive waste (OJ L 199, 2.8.2011, p. 48), further in text as »nuclear waste directive«. The Minister of Economy has been entitled by the Council of Ministers to start the procedure already with the draft law.

75 Established by the regulation of the President of the Council of Ministers (Prime Minister) of 20 June 2002 on the »Rules of legislative techniques« (Journal of Laws of 2002, No. 100, item 908).

isters is then submitted to Sejm where it is taken further on the parliamentary track.

During each phase of the legislative process it is necessary to conduct numerous consultations both within the Council of Ministers as well as with the representatives of the public, including obligatory consultations with trade unions, employers associations and local government.[76] Preparation of a pre-draft may take even up to approx. 160 days within standard procedure, exclusive of time necessary to draft the substantive content of the document. Same applies to the preparation of the draft law. Once the pre-draft is converted into the draft law (within up to 90 days), consultations need to be repeated (as a subject of the proposed document could have changed), which may take up to another 160 days. In addition, at this stage also time necessary for the notification of the draft law to the European Commission needs to be considered,[77] which may take up to 90 days.

The draft law is then submitted to the Parliament – first of all to the Sejm, then, in the form of an already adopted law, it is transferred to the Senate in order to make possible corrections thereof. Parliamentary works, according to internal regulations of Sejm[78] and Senate[79] respectively, may take under normal conditions up to even 150 days.

Once the parliamentary phase is completed, the law is submitted to the President, acting as the Head of State, for signing, which, according to the Constitution, takes place within 21 days.[80] One also has to consider time

76 Specified by the resolution no. 49 of the Council of Ministers of 19 March 2002 – Working regulation of the Council of Ministers (Official Journal of 2004, No. 13 item 221 as amended), the law of 23 May 1991 on worker unions (Journal of Laws of 1991, No. 55, item 234 as amended) and the law of 23 May 1991 on employer's organisations (Journal of Laws of 1991, No. 55, item 235 as amended).

77 Based on both art. 33 Euratom Treaty and eventually also on provisions of the Directive 98/34/EC of the European Parliament and of the Council of 22 June 1998 laying down a procedure for the provision of information in the field of technical standards and regulations and of rules on Information Society services (OJ L 204, 21.7.98., p. 37 as amended by the directive 98/48/EC, OJ L 217, 5.8.98., p. 18).

78 Resolution of the Sejm of the Republic of Poland of 30 July 1992 – Working regulation of the Sejm of the republic of Poland (Official Journal of 2012, item 32).

79 Resolution of the Senate of the Republic of Poland of 23 November 1992. Working regulation of the Senate (Official Journal of 2010, No. 39, item 542).

80 Art. 122(2) of the Constitution, however in accordance with art. 122(3) the President may refer the law to the Constitutional Tribunal for an adjudication upon its conformity to the Constitution or according to art. 122(5) he may refer the bill,

necessary for the publication of the act in the Journal of Laws as well as the *vacatio legis* period, that is up to another 21 days.[81]

The entirety of procedures related to the preparation, adoption and entry into force of an act may even take up to approx. 700 days. Notwithstanding the above, the legislative process also includes time necessary for the preparation, consultation and adoption of the accompanying secondary legislation, i.e. another 150 days as regards a single regulation.

Situations when the legislative procedure exceeds the time frame described above are very rare and take place mostly as a result of a difficult and complex legislative plan. In most cases the whole procedure takes in fact much less time than the above-mentioned maximum periods as a result of drafters' increased efforts to push the draft forward. In the case of amendments to the Atomic Law the entire process took approx. two years until their entry into force as of July the 1st 2011. In addition, about 20, often very detailed, acts of secondary legislation were prepared and entered into force one by one. Considering that the last regulation will enter into force by the end of 2013, it means that establishing a complete legal framework for nuclear power will take about 4,5 years in total, which is in compliance with the initial estimates.

4.4. Public consultations

Public consultations constitute the most sensitive, however, extremely important point of the governmental legislative procedure. This is because the use of nuclear power quite naturally raises emotions and concerns. Therefore, the Government takes great care over public consultations as means of proper communication with the public.

---

with reasons given, to the Sejm for its reconsideration. Both cases further lengthen the procedure. The adjudication of the law on conformity to the Constitution takes under normal circumstances at least 3 months (fast track).

81 According to the art. 4(1) of the Law of 20 July 2000 on announcement of legal acts (Journal of Laws of 2011, No. 197, item 1172 as amended) the regular minimum time limit for *vacatio legis* is 14 days. Without determining the cause the *vacatio legis* can be longer but any remission of the prescribed 14 days limit is strictly reserved to extraordinary situations and requires a proper justification.

4.4.1. Legal requirements

In Poland, everybody may register their interest in a pre-draft law, draft law or regulation.[82] The use of the term »everybody« means that the group of entities entitled to participation in public consultations is not limited to Polish citizens. Also foreign individuals and legal entities may, upon own request, take part in the public consultations. Interest in a particular legislative process may be registered as soon as the given document (may be pre-draft, draft law, draft regulation) is published within the legislative work index of a relevant Minister or the Council of Ministers.[83]

Notwithstanding the above, the governmental authority carrying a given legislative process may decide upon referring the pre-draft in question to other governmental authorities, as well as non-governmental organizations and other entities or institutions for an opinion.[84] This means that it is entirely up to the author of the draft to decide upon whether and where to refer the draft for an opinion. Decision of this sort may be taken during all stages of governmental legislative works, i.e. drafting of the pre-draft law, draft law and regulations. In practice, although the procedure is optional, each of the above stages is subject to consultations with the representatives of the public.

As departure from the optional general nature of the consultations, governmental administration is under obligation to refer draft laws for opinion to the management of trade unions and employers' associations[85] as well as to the Joint Commission of Government and Self-Government – in the case of draft laws covering issues touching upon local self-government units.[86]

For each stage of the legislative process (i.e. pre-draft, draft law, draft regulation) the term for public consultations may not be shorter than 14 days.[87] However, considering that the statutory term for consultations with

82 Art. 7(1) of the Law of 7 July 2005 on lobbying in the legislative process (Journal of Laws of 2005, No. 169, item 1414 as amended).

83 Art. 7(1) in connection with art. 3 and art. 4 of the Law on lobbying in the legislative process.

84 § 12(5) of the Working regulation of the Council of Ministers.

85 Art. 19(2) of the Law on worker unions and art. 16(2) of the Law on employer's organisations.

86 Art. 3(5) of the Law of 6 May 2005 on Joint Commission of the Government and Self-government (Journal of Laws of 2005, No. 90, item 759), § 6(3a) of the Working regulation of the Council of Ministers.

87 § 13(2) of the Working regulation of the Council of Ministers. However in exceptional cases, after special justification the term can be limited to less than 14

trade unions and employers' associations is set as 30 days,[88] in practice the 30-day period is applied to all types of consultations. Also, since statutory terms are in practice being considered as minimum terms,[89] if the statutory term for consultations proves to be insufficient for a given entity, the authority carrying consultations may extend the consultation deadline, which is a common practice.

Consultations usually consist in submitting written opinions, comments, proposals or proposed modifications of drafts together with their substantive analysis. They may also take the form of a direct exchange of views during bilateral and multilateral meetings (consensus conferences).

Since consultations are repeated at each stage of the legislative process interested entities may in fact take part in consultations of a single matter even up to three times, i.e. as regards the pre-draft, draft law and draft regulation. Independently from the governmental stage of the legislative process interested parties may further influence the final shape of the provisions in question during parliamentary works, however, the latter possibility is obviously limited to draft laws only.[90]

4.4.2. Public consultations in practice based on the example of legislative process in the field of nuclear law

The so-called »Nuclear package« consisted in two draft laws: draft law amending the Atomic Law and the draft law on the preparation and implementation of nuclear power facility investment and associated investment (further as draft investment law). In addition, the amended Atomic Law was to be accompanied by approx. 20 regulations. In each legislative process drafts together with all accompanying documentation were sent to approx. 150 different entities, both at the pre-draft and draft law stages. Interested entities were thus invited to give opinion on the same legal matter twice.

---

days for laws and less than 7 days for other types of documents (here mostly regulations).

88 Art. 19(2) of the Law on worker unions and art. 16(2) of the Law on employer's organisations.

89 Regardless of the provision saying that the public consultation should not exceed time limit of 30 days – § 13(2) of the Working regulation of the Council of Ministers.

90 As the Constitution gives both chambers of parliament no power to issue regulations.

The public turned out to be extremely passive. The right to register interest in the above legislative works was exercised only by two entities, namely EDF Polska and PGE. Draft laws and regulations were sent to approx. 25 environmental organizations, both worldwide (like WWF and Greenpeace) as well as small ones active only locally. None of them did express any interest in the received drafts. The majority of comments was sent by research institutes and local self-government units, however, they usually referred to the draft investment law, while the draft Atomic Law was subject to comments to a much lesser extent. A substantial part of the comments was sent by the energy industry, however, only a small number thereof was eventually acknowledged.

Little interest in the process was expressed by the representatives of the public nor at the stage of parliamentary works, with the participation of some research institutes, EDF Polska, PGE and the Polish Chamber of Insurance only. During the entire consultations drafts of all legal acts together with all of their subsequent versions were made available on the internet by all institutions engaged in the legislative process.[91] In addition, all submitted comments and opinions together with the Government's standpoint, including justifications for not considering public proposals, were also made available on an ongoing basis. Submitted comments, even if considered by the Government, had no significant impact on the final shape of the enacted legislation, however, in same cases, they allowed for the refining of particular provisions.

91 Ministry of Economy, PAA, Ministry of State Treasure, Government's Legislation Centre, Sejm and Senate.

4.5. Main changes introduced into Atomic Law[92]

4.5.1. Detailed requirements for lifecycle stages of nuclear installations[93]

Introducing detailed requirements as regards nuclear safety and radiation protection applicable throughout all the stages of nuclear installation's life-cycle, namely siting, design, commissioning, operation and decommissioning, together with detailed requirements for performing the safety analysis and the initial safety report, as well as periodic safety assessments of nuclear installations, was the main, if not the most important change in the Polish nuclear law. Until then no detailed provisions in this scope existed, which called into question the possibility to build nuclear power plants. Certainly, building nuclear installations in Poland, including nuclear power plants, was never prohibited, however, the lack of detailed and – most importantly – written-in-law safety requirements effectively constituted a considerable obstacle to the implementation of nuclear power investments.

The above-mentioned requirements are outlined in regulations issued on the basis of the Atomic Law. Their substance is based on numerous sources, the most important of which being the IAEA Safety Standards and WENRA Requirements. Notwithstanding the above, said regulations are also based to some extend on EUR and URD requirements and foreign legislations, as well as external expertise provided by independent technicians and engineers with experience in nuclear safety. Moreover, alongside the Atomic Law amendments, an obligation to take into account the IAEA Safety Standards and WENRA Requirements while elaborating the

92 For a brief overview of the 2011 Amendment of the Atomic Law in English see: the homepage of the PAA (regulatory body): <http://www.paa.gov.pl/en/node/254>, Nuclear Law Bulletin no. 88 (2011/2), pp. 89-90 and Nuclear Law Bulletin no. 89 (2012/1), pp. 127-128. Unofficial English translation of the consolidated text of the Law is available under <http://www.paa.gov.pl/sites/ default/files/Specjalistyczne/!Atomic_Law.pdf>.

93 The 2011 Atomic Law amendment introduced also the new definition of »nuclear installation«. According to the current wording of the art. 3(17) of the Atomic Law a nuclear installation is a nuclear power plant, research reactor, enrichment plant, nuclear fuel fabrication plant, reprocessing plant, spent fuel storage facility and storage facility for radioactive waste that is on the same site and is directly related to other nuclear installation. Thus this definition is in practice identical with the one contained in art. 3(1) of the nuclear safety directive.

above-mentioned regulations was introduced.[94] The above obligation does not necessarily mean that the authority issuing a regulation is required to apply, nor, all the more, thoroughly implement the IAEA and WENRA documents. Obligation to take the latter into account requires that the legislator becomes fully familiar with the said documentation in terms of their possible implementation into regulations to be issued.

The requirements take into account the state of the art with respect to nuclear safety of nuclear installations, including experience derived from the Fukushima accident and stress tests performed within the EU. Regulations will be accompanied by technical recommendations issued by the PAA President (regulatory guidelines) aimed at facilitating the implementation of provisions contained in the Atomic Law and its secondary legislation by the applicant (see above).

The above-mentioned requirements are specified in following Regulations of the Council of Ministers:[95]

- Regulation of 10 August 2012 on detailed scope of **assessment with regard to land** intended for the site of a nuclear installation, cases excluding land to be considered eligible for the site of a nuclear installation and on requirements concerning **site report** for a nuclear installation;[96]
- Regulation of 31 August 2012 on nuclear safety and radiological protection requirements which must be fulfilled by a nuclear installation **design**;[97]
- Regulation of 11 February 2013 on requirements for the **commissioning and operation** of nuclear installation;[98]
- Regulation of 11 February 2013 on nuclear safety and radiological protection requirements for the stage of **decommissioning** of nuclear installations and the content of a report on decommissioning of a nuclear installation;[99]
- Regulation of 31 August 2012 on the scope and method for the performance of **safety analyses** prior to the submission of an application

94 See: art. 35b(4), art. 36c(3), art. 36d(3), art. 37e(11), art. 38, art. 38c(3) of the Atomic Law.

95 For unofficial English translations of all enlisted regulations see: <http://www.paa.gov.pl/en/node/287>.

96 Journal of Laws of 2012, item 1025.

97 Journal of Laws of 2012, item 1048.

98 Journal of Laws of 2013, item 281.

99 Journal of Laws of 2013, item 270.

requesting the issue of a license for the construction of a nuclear installation and the scope of the preliminary safety report for a nuclear installation;[100]

- Regulation of 27 December 2011 on **periodical safety assessment** of a nuclear installation.[101]

4.5.2. Changes in the licensing process

4.5.2.1. New structure of the licensing process

According to the new regulations it is necessary to obtain a separate licence for each of the main phases of the nuclear installation life cycle, namely the construction, commissioning, operation and decommissioning.[102] There are no separate licences for the design and siting of nuclear installation. Both aspects are considered within the proceedings aimed at the issuing of a construction licence.

Prior to obtaining a licence for each stage of the nuclear installation lifecycle a number of requirements must be met. For instance, application for the construction licence must include such important documents as the nuclear installation design, the siting report,[103] the preliminary safety report,[104] documentation pertaining to the safety classification,[105] documentation outlining the integrated management system,[106] a decommissioning programme for the nuclear installation,[107] opinion of the European Commission issued pursuant to Article 43 of the Euratom Treaty,[108] the decision on environmental impact of investment (environmental decision) as well as documentation confirming the possession or the ability to raise capital sufficient for ensuring nuclear safety and radiation protection until the construction is completed.[109]

100 Journal of Laws of 2012, item 1043.
101 Journal of Laws of 2012, item 556.
102 Art. 4(1)(2) of the Atomic Law.
103 Art. 35b of the Atomic Law.
104 Art. 36d of the Atomic Law.
105 Art. 36j of the Atomic Law.
106 Art. 36k of the Atomic Law.
107 Art. 38b of the Atomic Law.
108 Art. 39i of the Atomic Law.
109 Art. 38g(1) of the Atomic Law.

In order to obtain subsequent licences the precedent stage of the nuclear installation lifecycle must be successfully completed. In addition to issuing licences nuclear regulatory authorities deal with approving a number of documents as well as issue authorizations to perform a number of actions necessary to obtain a licence or to continue a given activity. The Atomic Law provides the following deadlines for the issuance of a licence by the nuclear regulatory body: 24 months in the case of a construction licence, 9 months in the case of a commissioning licence, 6 months in the case of the operation licence and 9 months in the case of the decommissioning licence – from the date of submission of the application together with any required documents.[110]

Towards this time limits, according to general rules of administrative proceedings, shall not be calculated time foreseen in other provisions of law for the performance of actions, periods of stay of the proceedings, periods of delay caused by party's fault or for reasons not attributable to the issuing authority.[111]

In addition to licences issued for different stages of the nuclear installation lifecycle, it is necessary to obtain a PAA President's written consent prior to carrying any upgrade of a system or element of the structure of a nuclear installation that is significant for nuclear safety and radiation protection, as well as each start-up of a reactor after a break to load nuclear fuel or perform an upgrade.[112]

In addition to licences issued for different stages of the nuclear installation lifecycle there are also positions and activities holding or performance of which requires separate permissions issued by the nuclear regulatory body. This applies to positions related to operating research reactors (e.g. operator, dosimetrist, senior dosimetrist, shift manager, manager, deputy director for nuclear safety and radiological protection), specialist for nuclear material accountancy and operator of spent nuclear fuel storage facility.[113] Activities for which an authorization from the regulatory body is required are connected directly with operation of NPPs: general management of a NPP, management of commissioning and operations of a NPP,

110 Art. 39a of the Atomic Law.

111 Art. 35 § 5 of the Law of 14 June 1960 Code of Administrative Proceedings (Journal of Laws of 2000, No. 98, item 1071 as amended).

112 Art. 37d(1) of the Atomic Law.

113 See Regulation of the Council of Ministers of 10 August 2012 on positions important for nuclear safety and radiological protection and radiological protection inspectors (Journal of Laws of 2012, item 1022). Unofficial English translation under <http://www.paa.gov.pl/en/node/287>.

operating supervision, control of nuclear reactor and nuclear power unit and performance of operations with nuclear fuel in a nuclear reactor and in re-load fuel pool.[114]

4.5.2.2. Pre-licensing elements

Recent amendments of the Atomic Law also included elements of pre-licensing aimed at reducing the regulatory risk for investors. For the first time a possibility was created to request opinions from the regulatory body prior to the formal submission of the application for a licence. Also, other solutions were introduced aiming at facilitating the communication between the licensee and the regulatory body.

There are two major steps in pre-licensing phase. The applicant can request the regulatory body to issue the preliminary, general assessment of the planned organizational and technical solutions.[115] The same applies to the site – the investor can apply to the regulatory body for a preliminary assessment of the site of a future nuclear installation.[116]

General assessment of the planned organizational and technical solutions

Prior to obtaining the licence (for construction, commissioning, operation or decommissioning) the investor can make an application to the PAA President for issuing the general opinion on the planned organizational and technical solutions to be used in the course of future activities and draft documents to be filed together with the licence application.

The above provision provides the future applicant with broad possibilities as regards applying for regulator's opinion. In practice, the applicant may submit questions regarding any topic of interest. As regards the technical aspects, the applicant may ask for the regulator's opinion on elements of the structure and equipment of the planned nuclear installation, as well as the reactor design or even the design of the entire nuclear installation. Thus, the above provision may in some respect be considered as the

114 See Regulation of the Council of Ministers of 10 August 2012 on activities important for nuclear safety and radiological protection in an organizational unit conducting activity which consists in commissioning, operations or decommissioning of a nuclear power plant (Journal of laws of 2012, item 1024). Unofficial English translation under <http://www.paa.gov.pl/en/node/287>.

115 Art. 39b of the Atomic Law.

116 Article 36a of the Atomic Law. The same possibility exists in case of a nuclear waste repository – see art. 55a(3) of the Atomic Law.

equivalent of the British Generic Design Assessment or the US Standard Design Certification. As regards the organizational aspects the future applicant may ask for the regulator's opinion e.g. as regards the management of the nuclear installation, possible upgrading and maintenance, emergency preparedness and response or permissions that should be vested with the employees. In addition, the application may concern draft documents to be attached to the licence, thus allowing the future applicant to determine their content at this early stage, which eliminates the risk of delays in the licencing process due to the fact that the documentation submitted does not fulfil the regulator's requirements.

The application for a general opinion on the planned organisational and technical solutions may be submitted at any time prior to the submission of the application for the licence. Application for a general opinion may be submitted several times according to the needs of the future applicant for the licence.

It should be noted, however, that the nuclear inspection's opinion is non-binding. This means that nuclear inspection may theoretically issue decisions within the licensing process that contradict the previously issued general opinion. It may seem, however, that the latter should only occur in exceptional cases related to the need to ensure nuclear safety and radiation protection, e.g. as a result of a significant change of the legal requirements or state of the art in the scope of nuclear safety and radiation protection.

The standard term for issuing a general opinion is 6 months from the date of the application and may be extended up to 9 months in exceptionally complex cases. Applying for a general opinion is in principle optional, however, in practice it is only optional in the case of research reactors. As regards other nuclear installations it constitutes an obligation. Such obligatory character does not stem, however, from the provisions of the Atomic Law but is written in the investment law, which requires that the general opinion is submitted together with the application for the decision in principle as regards any nuclear power facility.[117]

117 Art. 23(2) of the Law of 29 June 2011 on preparing and implementing an investment in a nuclear power facility and associated investments (Journal of Laws of 2011, No. 135, items 789, 951) – in text of this article as »investment law«. On the investment law and »nuclear power facilities« see below.

Preliminary siting assessment

Assessment in this regard may be requested prior to the submission of the application for the construction licence. Such assessment, although non-binding upon the issuing authority, significantly reduces the investment risk by settling the siting issues at an early stage. While assessing the application for the nuclear installation construction the PAA President may decide upon the siting differently than in their previous assessment. However as in the case of the general opinion on the planned organizational and technical solutions the latter should only occur in exceptional cases related to the need to ensure nuclear safety and radiation protection, e.g. as a result of a significant change in law or state of the art in the scope of nuclear safety and radiation protection or change in the factual circumstances at the assessed site. Preliminary siting assessment and the above-mentioned general opinion are also similar in terms of their optional character exclusively as regards research reactors. The investment law requires the investor of a nuclear power facility (constituting in the same time a nuclear installation as defined in Atomic Law) to attach the preliminary siting assessment to the application for the decision on the siting of the investment (in terms of land use and planning).[118] The PAA President issues the above-mentioned opinion/assessment within 3 months from the date of the application.

Submission of comments as regards the draft licence

In addition to requesting the above mentioned preliminary opinions the applicant may also submit comments to the draft licence.[119] Although not part of the pre-licensing process in the strict sense, it is aimed at facilitating the communication between the regulator and the applicant and may eventually contribute to improving the licencee's situation if the licence is amended according to his comments.

The PAA President is under obligation to present the applicant with the draft licence within 1 month from the date on which the regulator's advisory body – Council for Nuclear Safety and Radiation Protection issues its (non-binding) opinion on the draft. The deadline for submitting comments to the draft licence is 1 month from the date on which the applicant receives the draft.

118 Art. 5(1)(7) of the investment law.

119 Art. 39f (4) of the Atomic Law.

Regulatory guidelines

Apart from the above instruments the 2011 amendment to the Atomic Law also introduced the above-mentioned[120] technical and organisational guidelines in the area of nuclear safety and radiation protection. The guidelines are aimed at facilitating communication with the nuclear inspection and fulfilling requirements written in laws, regulations, licence conditions by the applicant and/or licence holder.

4.5.3. Strengthening the independence of the regulatory body

Notwithstanding the 2011 amendments to the Atomic Law, the Polish Constitution as well as already existing provisions guaranteed and still guarantee the high degree of independence of the nuclear regulatory body (PAA President). First of all the supervision over the PAA President's activities is vested in the Minister of Environment,[121] while the regulator's employees enjoy the constitutional guarantees of impartiality and political neutrality stemming from their status as civil servants.[122] In addition, the supervision of the Minister of Environment does not consist in providing the PAA President with instructions as regards the settlement of administrative proceedings in the scope of licensing, supervision, inspection etc.[123] The supervision over the PAA President is limited to adjusting the general directions of PAA activities to the general policy line of the state as well as representing the PAA President within the Council of Ministers, e.g. by submitting draft laws and other governmental documents elaborated within the PAA according to its competence. In addition, the PAA President enjoys the budgetary autonomy.

The 2011 amendment introduced, however, a number of provisions strengthening the independence of the regulator. First of all, it is now explicitly prohibited that the PAA President should engage in the promotion of the uses of nuclear energy, in particular the promotion of nuclear pow-

120 See. point 4.2.3. of this article.

121 Art. 28(3) of the Law of 4 September 1997 on the branches of governmental administration (Journal of Laws of 2007, No. 65, item 437 as amended).

122 Art. 153 of the Constitution.

123 Art. 34a(2) of the Law of 8 August 1996 on the Council of Ministers (Journal of Laws of 2012, item 392).

er,[124] while his tasks are exclusively limited to the area of nuclear safety, including security and safeguards according to IAEA's »3S« concept.[125]

In addition, the amendment transferred the competence to allocate grants for the national nuclear safety improvement to the Minister of Economy.[126] The previous framework in this regard contradicted the principle of independence causing a permanent conflict of interests, in which the regulator allocated grants for improving safety of e.g. research reactors and, at the same time, supervised their safety. Also, a legal requirement to ensure impartiality of the TSO was introduced.[127]

Changes were also introduced as regards the PAA President's advisory body. The hitherto Council of Atomic Sciences was replaced by the Council for Nuclear Safety and Radiation Protection.[128] As opposed to the Council of Atomic Sciences the latter does not deal with the entirety of atomic questions in the broad sense, including the promotion of different uses of nuclear energy and nuclear power. Its competences are limited to giving opinions on draft licences for nuclear installations, draft legal acts and recommendations/guidelines issued by the PAA President, as well as bringing forward own initiatives aimed at streamlining the supervision performed by the PAA President.[129] In addition, the PAA President is no longer responsible for the matters pertaining to Polish membership in international organizations unrelated to the questions of nuclear safety and radiation protection. The above responsibilities were transferred to the Ministry of Science (as regards CERN[130] and JINR[131] membership) and the Ministry of Foreign Affairs (as regards the CTBTO[132] membership).

Despite a number of changes the legal framework aimed at guaranteeing the regulator's independence is still missing the principle of retirement by rotation of the PAA President. Currently the PAA President is still appointed for an indefinite time period and can be removed at the discretion of the Prime Minister, thus potentially enabling the latter to influence regulatory decisions by removing and appointing desired candidates. It is ex-

124 Art. 110(6) of the Atomic Law.
125 Art. 110 of the Atomic Law.
126 See current wording of the art. 33(1) of the Atomic Law.
127 Art. 66a of the Atomic Law.
128 Art. 112(2) of the Atomic Law.
129 Art. 112(8) of the Atomic Law.
130 European Organization for Nuclear Research based in Geneva (Switzerland).
131 Joint Institute for Nuclear Research based in Dubna (Russia).
132 Comprehensive Test Ban Treaty Organization (actually the Preparatory Commission for CTBTO) based in Vienna (Austria).

pected that the above situation will eventually change in the future together with the name of the institution and authority (currently: PAA – National Atomic Energy Agency and PAA President) into names that would unequivocally indicate that their competencies are limited to the questions of nuclear safety and radiation protection.[133]

4.5.4. Financial arrangements for waste management and decommissioning of NPPs

In order to materialize the »polluter pays« principle the provisions of the amended Atomic Law oblige the operator to establish a dedicated fund in order to accumulate capital to cover any costs related to the financing of the final handling of spent nuclear fuel and radioactive waste, as well as costs of decommissioning of the nuclear power plant.[134] The so called »decommissioning fund« constitutes an operator's internal fund in the form of a separate bank account, in which the operator makes payments on a quarterly basis for each megawatt hour of electricity generated by the nuclear power plant.[135]

It seems that the above solution, despite its construction, is not contrary to the EC Recommendation 2006/851/Euratom,[136] notwithstanding the non-binding character of the latter. Although the Polish language version of the Recommendation (section 5(9)) explicitly refers to »separated external« funds other language versions refer only to the obligation to establish »separate« funds without any directly visible externality requirement.[137]

133 E.g. »UDJ« – Urząd Dozoru Jądrowego (Office for Nuclear Safety) or »UDJiOR« – Urząd Dozoru Jądrowego i Ochrony Radiologicznej (Office for Nuclear Safety and Radiation Protection) and as a consequence »UDJ President« or »UDJiOR President«.

134 Art. 38d of the Atomic Law. This rule does not apply to other nuclear installations.

135 Art. 38d(1-2) of the Atomic Law.

136 Commission recommendation 2006/851/Euratom of 24 October 2006 on the management of financial resources for the decommissioning of nuclear installations, spent fuel and radioactive waste (OJ L 330, 28.11.2006, p. 31).

137 See other language versions: English – »separated«, German – »getrennte«, Spanish – »separados«, French – »séparés«, Italian – »separati«, Dutch – »gescheiden«, Slovak – »oddelené«.

Since all language versions of European Law instruments are considered authentic the Polish legislator may as well read and interpret the said recommendation according to language versions other than Polish.

Meanwhile, the Polish solution provided for in the Atomic Law is consistent with the definition of »separation«. Although the fund belongs to the operator, it is established, in the form of a dedicated and separate bank account, while funds accumulated in it are allocated exclusively to cover the costs related to the financing of the final handling of spent nuclear fuel and radioactive waste, as well as costs of a nuclear power plant decommissioning.[138] Any withdrawal of the assets from the decommissioning fund requires obtaining a positive opinion of the PAA President.[139] The NPP operator is also charged with some reporting obligations with regard to the PAA President,[140] while failure to make payments into the fund may result even in a suspension of the NPP operation.[141]

4.5.5. Public information

The amended Atomic Law provides for general obligations as regards public information, which lie upon the operators of all nuclear installations, specific duties imposed upon operators of nuclear power facilities, powers the public enjoys with regards to such facilities, as well as information obligations upon the PAA President.

4.5.5.1. General requirements for all nuclear installations

According to general rules of the Atomic Law everyone has the right to obtain from the operator of a nuclear installation (during commissioning, operation and decommissioning phase), information on the nuclear safety and radiation protection status of the installation, its impact on human health and the environment and on the magnitude and isotopic composition of any releases of radioactive substances. Such information should be published on the operator's website at least once every 12 months. Moreover the operator shall inform the PAA President and other authorities

138 Art. 38d(4) of the Atomic Law.
139 Art. 38d(5) of the Atomic Law.
140 Art. 38d(6) of the Atomic Law.
141 Art. 38d(7) of the Atomic Law.

(voivode – provincial governor, county and municipality authorities where the nuclear installation is located and the authorities of the neighbouring municipalities) of any occurrences at the nuclear installation that may lead or actually lead to a danger. Information on all such occurrences in the last 12 months should be published on operator's website. All sensitive information (on physical protection, safeguards and business secrets) shall not be disclosed.[142]

4.5.5.2. Specific requirements for nuclear power facilities

Apart from the above-mentioned duties imposed on the operators of all nuclear installations there are also duties that lay upon operators of nuclear installations constituting nuclear power facilities in the meaning of art. 391 point 1 of the Atomic Law (i.e. all nuclear installations with the exception of research reactors). The investor of such facilities is obliged to create a Local Information Center (LCI) prior to the commencement of the construction works and to ensure its functioning until the decommissioning of the facility is completed.

The main duties of LCI include: collecting and providing updated information on the operation of the nuclear power facility and on the status of nuclear safety and radiological protection in the surrounding area. LCI shall also cooperate with other bodies and entities on activities related to public communication, education, popularization and distribution of scientific, technical and legal information concerning nuclear power engineering, nuclear safety and radiation protection of nuclear power facilities. All information should be available on the LCI's website and in the information bulletin issued by the LCI.[143]

In addition to obligations imposed on the operators the Atomic Law also provides the public with special powers to obtain information, monitor the implementation of the investment project and the operations of nuclear power facilities as well as adopt own information policy. The local community[144] may set up a Local Information Committee (LIC), tasked i.a.

142 Art. 35a of the Atomic Law.

143 Art. 39m of the Atomic Law.

144 The term »local community« according to art. 391(2) of the Atomic Law states for the inhabitants of municipalities where the nuclear power facility is or will be located and of municipalities with administrative boundaries within less than 15 km distance from the area.

with: providing community supervision over the nuclear power facility from the start of its construction to its decommissioning, informing the local community on the activities of the nuclear power facilities, representing the local community in relations with the investor and operator. To perform their duties, LIC members (in the maximum number of 5 and in the presence of an appointed investor's/operator's employee) can enter the facility and are entitled to obtain information and documents on its construction and functioning.[145]

The LCI are not as developed and institutionalised as for example their French counterparts. In principle, they are intended as an independent representation of the local community and are aimed at the promotion of citizen engagement without the limitations due to the excessive regulation.

The LCI composition is decided upon by citizens themselves since, in order to obtain LCI membership it is sufficient for an adult member of the local community enjoying full civil rights to file an application to take part in the LCI activities. Applicant fulfilling the above conditions cannot be refused membership, especially as there is no upper limit as regards the number of LCI members. The number of official representatives is, however, limited to one person per municipality within the territory of which the nuclear power facility is located in whole or in part.

LCI adopts resolutions in simple majority voting and may invite external experts to take part in their meetings to give opinion on the issues discussed. The financing of LCI activities is not upon the local residents, but is ensured by the municipality within the territory of which nuclear power facility is located in the largest part.[146]

Notwithstanding the above it is possible that the local government of the municipality within the territory of which nuclear power facility is located, or the investment in this regard is envisaged or implemented, may decide to adopt own information policy, independent of the operator's or LCI activities. That is why the Atomic Law provides for the possibility to establish Community Information Points.[147]

145 Art. 39n of the Atomic Law.

146 Art. 39n of the Atomic Law. On detailed rules of functioning of the LIC see the regulation of the Minister of Economy of 23 July 2012 on detailed rules of formation and activities of the Local Information Committees and on co-operation in the area of nuclear power facilities (Journal of Laws of 2012, item 861).

147 Art. 39o of the Atomic Law.

4.5.5.3. New obligations as regards public information lying upon the PAA President

Providing information on nuclear safety and radiation protection to the society is one of the general tasks of the PAA President. It includes performing activities such as public communication, education, popularization, as well as the scientific, technical and legal information including the information on ionizing radiation and its impact on human health and the environment, and on feasible measures to be implemented in the event of radiation emergency.[148]

As to nuclear installations PAA President is obliged to inform about: their nuclear safety and radiation protection level, impact on human health and the natural environment, magnitude and isotopic composition of the releases, occurrences which may lead to a danger, licences related to the nuclear installations and annual assessments of their security and safety status.[149] PAA President shall also immediately publish the construction licence application with an abbreviated safety report along with information on: the initiation of proceedings, the right to make submissions or observations, how and where the submissions or observations are to be made (within 21-day deadline) and how and where the administrative proceedings take place. All those informations are to be published on the PAA website (in the Public Information Bulletin) and in press available in the municipality within whose boundaries the site referred to in the application is located, and in the neighbouring municipalities.[150]

4.5.6. Liability

The hitherto provisions of the Atomic Law pertaining to civil liability for the nuclear damage have not been subject to any substantial amendments. As a result of the ratification of the Protocol amending the Vienna Convention the liability limit of the operator as well as the minimum coverage per incident were increased to 300 mln SDR (from 150 mln SDR).[151]

148 Art. 110(6) of the Atomic Law.
149 Art. 35a of the Atomic Law.
150 Art. 39d of the Atomic Law.
151 Art. 102(1) and art. 103(6) of the Atomic Law.

Also, a separate obligation to conclude insurance agreement covering damages caused in transport was explicitly provided.[152] In addition, the Atomic Law provides preferential terms of insurance as regards research reactors and nuclear installations used to store nuclear material originating from research reactors.[153] The minimum coverage in this regard may not be lower than 400 thousand SDR nor higher that 5 mln SDR. The latter also applies in the case of transportation of nuclear material originating from such nuclear installations.[154]

4.6. Law on investment in nuclear power facilities

In addition to regulating nuclear safety and radiation protection of nuclear facilities, in order to successfully implement a nuclear power programme it is also necessary to appropriately regulate the investment and construction process. The existing gap in this regard within the Polish legal framework was filled by the above mentioned investment law.

4.6.1. Investment law as *lex specialis* in relation to the general provisions regulating the investment and construction process

The investment law provides for a dedicated framework for the implementation of nuclear power investments and constitutes an exception from the general regulation of spatial development and construction process existing in Poland by establishing a privileged path for nuclear projects, and, thus, reducing the associated investment risks.

This is achieved through the establishment of new types of decisions streamlining the investment process, the shortening of deadlines, simplifi-

152 Art. 103(2) of the Atomic Law.

153 What in practice means transferring the previously existing provisions from the secondary legislation (regulation) to a level of a law.

154 Art. 103(7) of the Atomic Law. However if any nuclear material originating from nuclear installations other than research reactors and nuclear installations used to store nuclear material originating from research reactors is kept, stored or transported jointly with the nuclear material originating from research reactors the general rule of art. 103(6) of the atomic Law finds its application and thus the minimal guaranteed amount of the insurance shall be equivalent to SDR 300 million – see art. 103(8) of the Atomic Law. In any case the state guarantees the payment of compensation up to SDR 300 million.

cation of environmental and public procurement procedures, a dedicated regulation as regards acquiring legal title to estate and incentives for local communities. Adopting laws envisaged as *lex specialis* in relation to general provisions regulating the investment and construction process is common in relation to large infrastructure projects important in view of national economic interests. Polish legal framework already includes 10 other laws establishing comprehensive and privileged frameworks for the investment and construction process, dedicated to specific types of investments,[155] or even specific individual undertakings.[156] The need for such dedicated frameworks is due to the fact that the general investment framework is rather complex and fragmented within a number of different laws. What is more, the Polish legal framework is lacking a single and comprehensive legal act that would encompass both spatial development and construction law.

Similar dedicated frameworks are in force in other EU Member States. In Finland there is a dedicated law, in force since 1928(!), on the expropriation for the purpose of power plants construction, according to which the real estate owner is obliged to renounce the ownership of his property for the purpose of a power plant construction, which is considered an important public good.[157] Similar framework is provided by the Lithuanian Law on Nuclear Power Plant,[158] while, according to the Bulgarian Law on the territorial development the construction of a nuclear power plant may be deemed as a strategic investment, which reduces deadlines for the issuance of decisions in the scope of spatial development and construction law.[159]

155 Development of railroad's, airport's, road's, highway's, telecommunication's and flood protection's infrastructure as well as reconstructions after natural disaster and investments connected with the preparation of UEFA EURO 2012 Championship.

156 Construction of LNG-Terminal in Świnoujście.

157 Act 168/1928 on Expropriation for Electricity Plant, see K. Talus, A. Guimaraes-Purokoski, A. Rajala, L. Huomo, P. Vesa, T. Kaijalainen, L. Salminen, *Energy Law in Finnland*, Kluwer Law International 2010, p. 152, 153.

158 Art. 13 of the Law No. X-1231 of 28 June 2007 on the Nuclear Power Plant (The Official Gazette of 10 July 2007, as amended). Text reproduced in: Nuclear Law Bulletin no. 80 (2007/2), pp. 93-101, as well as a brief description, pp. 75-76. On 2008 Amendment see: Nuclear Law Bulletin no. 81 (2008/1), p. 108.

159 The Law on the territorial development (State Gazette No. 1 of 2 January 2001, as amended). By the decision No. 259 of 8 April 2005 Bulgarian government granted the status of a strategic investment to the construction of the Belene nuclear power plant.

4.6.2. Scope of the law

The law is applicable to two types of investments, namely: direct investments in nuclear power facilities, which could be referred to as principal investments, and to the so called associated investments.[160]

The law defines »nuclear power facilities« as facilities operating for the purpose of serving the needs of nuclear power generation, i.e. for generating power in the process of nuclear fission. Apart from nuclear power plants the said definition also encompasses isotopic enrichment facilities, nuclear fuel production facilities, spent nuclear fuel reprocessing facilities, spent nuclear fuel repositories, radioactive waste repositories, as well as uranium and thorium ore mining and preliminary processing facilities.[161] Thus, the definition does not cover such important installations as research reactors, but at the same time guarantees a privileged treatment of uranium and thorium ore mines, which do not even constitute nuclear installations.

According to the investment law »associated investments« are investments in the scope of construction or extension of transmission power lines necessary to take off power generated at the nuclear power plant or other investments necessary to build and ensure proper operations of the nuclear power plant.[162] It was the intention of the legislator to extend the privileged legal regime onto additional investments, the implementation of which conditions the eventual success of the principle investment (e.g. construction of a NPP). Associated investments can benefit from the investment facilitations to a lesser extent than nuclear power facilities. For instance, the investor implementing the associated investment may not apply for a decision designating the site for investment nor the permission to enter the premises to carry the preparatory works. Neither does he enjoy the privileged treatment as regards public procurement procedures.[163]

---

160 Art. 1 of the investment law.

161 Art. 2(2) of the investment law. This definition differs therefore from the definition of nuclear power facility created for the purpose of Chapter 4a of the Atomic Law (on public information obligation of the investor/operator and rights of the local community in this regard) encompassed in the art. 39l(1) of the Atomic Law, see point 4.5.5.2. of this article.

162 Art. 2(1) of the investment law.

163 Art. 53 of the investment law.

4.6.3. Facilitations for nuclear power investments

4.6.3.1. Decision on siting the investment in a nuclear power facility (siting decision)

The autonomous siting decision issued independently from the spatial development provisions constitutes one of the major elements of the investment law.[164] Simple notification on the commencement of proceedings aiming at siting an investment in a nuclear power facility is enough to trigger a number of consequences as far reaching as a suspension of the ongoing proceedings in the scope of spatial development and the investment process within real estates under motion. Also, a final siting decision is binding upon relevant authorities as regards spatial development. This means that spatial development must take into consideration nuclear power investments, irrespective of the position of the local self-government in this regard. The same applies to decisions issued on the basis of the existing local zoning plans – the ongoing proceedings are extinguished, while in the case of new motions the relevant authorities are obliged to refuse the issuance of decisions.[165]

The siting decision is also important as it enables securing the real estate for the purposes of the construction and operation of nuclear power facilities. On the date the decision on siting the investment in a nuclear power facility has become final listed real estates necessary to implement the investment by law become the property of the State Treasury by means of expropriation for compensation. Then, the investor, having obtained the decision in principle may submit a request to create the perpetual usufruct of such land.[166] However, the investor may as well decide to build the nuclear power facility on its own real estate, therefore, the expropriation option is only intended as a remedy in the case when acquiring the real estate through other means (e.g. through acquisition) proved impossible.[167]

164 Art. 4 of the investment law.

165 Art. 6, art. 8 and art. 9 of the investment law.

166 Art. 24, art. 30 of the investment law.

167 E.g. due to »antinuclear« attitude of the owners.

4.6.3.2. Decision indicating the site for the nuclear power facility investment (indication decision)

The application for the construction licence as well as the siting decision submitted to the regulatory body must include a siting report.[168] The report also needs to be drawn in order to perform a number of examinations that require entering the premises of the potential location. If the premises do not constitute the investor's property, their owner may refuse access. In such case it would appear that the only solution for the investor would be to buy the real estate in question.[169] However, after the site surveys are completed it may turn out that the acquired site does not fulfil the conditions for the siting of nuclear facilities, thus creating a financial loss and postponing the whole undertaking. The optional decision designating the investment site is intended to reduce such risk, at the same time without preordaining the final location of the nuclear power facility. Obtaining such a decision simply enables entering the necessary site and carrying the necessary surveys (upon obtaining separate permits) even without the permission of the estate owner. Having finished surveys the investor must however return the real estate to its original state or pay the damages.[170] What is as much important is that the area upon the decision has been issued although not owned by the investor is excluded from other purposes than nuclear facility construction up to five years.[171] Reception of the notification informing on the commencement of the proceedings has similar effect to the reception of the notification informing on the commencement of the proceedings to issue the siting decision.[172]

4.6.3.3. Permission to enter the premisses

Since the issuance of the far-reaching indication decision may not be necessary for the success of the investment the law also provides for a possi-

168 According to the requirements of art. 35b(3) of the Atomic Law and art. 5(1)(7) of the investment law.

169 Although even in such a case there is no certainty whether the property's owner would not refuse to sell it regardless of the price because of e.g. ideological reasons.

170 Art. 11 and following articles of the investment law.

171 Art. 13(1) of the investment law.

172 Art. 12(4) of the investment law.

bility to apply for the permission to enter the premises.[173] Performing land surveys on the basis of such permission will be much less burdensome for the owner (similarly the user, the lessee, or the land lessee) of the property. Contrary to the indication decision the permission to enter the premises does not result in the suspension of the ongoing proceedings. The duration of the permission is also shorter than in the case of the indication decision (i.e. maximum 3 years instead of 5 years).[174] Also, the investment law does not provide for mechanisms securing the durability of the permission as it is in the case of the indication decision. It is thus possible to issue other permissions enabling entering the premises or indication decisions with regard to the same property while the permission in question is in force. As in the case of the indication decision, having finished surveys the investor must return the real estate to its original state.[175] Also, similarly to the indication decision obtaining the permission to enter the premises is optional and does not preordain the final location of the nuclear power facility.

4.6.3.4. Decision in principle

Prior to obtaining the construction permit or permission to conduct preparatory works the investor is obliged to obtain a decision in principle issued by the minister competent for economic questions.[176] The said decision is a form of direct control of the government over the investment process in the scope of nuclear power infrastructure, which stems from the fact that nuclear investments are considered as strategic in terms of national security. This is linked both to the necessity to ensure energy security, as well as the existence of certain risks pertaining exclusively to the use of nuclear technologies. Apart from the standard operational risk there is also the risk of a potential terrorist attack or proliferation of nuclear materials together with their consequences. It is also important to consider that building even a single plant equipped with a single nuclear reactor automatically results in the state's engagement in the nuclear power programme for the next decades, that is next few generations of citizens. The capital-intensive character of the investment is also a factor, which is es-

173 Art. 11(1)(2) of the investment law.
174 Art. 13(3) of the investment law.
175 Art. 14 of the investment law.
176 Art. 22 of the investment law. As for now it is the Minister of Economy.

pecially important in the case of state's financial engagement, e.g. in the form of state guarantees or implementing investments by companies wholly or partially owned by the State Treasury. Finally, nuclear investments, especially in the case of states that have not developed own reactor technologies, may significantly influence their foreign policy through increased bonds with the vendor's state. In view of the above, it appears justified that issuing a decision allowing for the implementation of nuclear investments should be vested within the highest possible levels of decision makers capable of considering the entire economic and political situation of the state.

Apart from ensuring state control over the operation of nuclear power facilities the decision in principle also ensures a greater stability of the implemented investment since its issuance is a sign of an explicit approval by the Polish government for the construction of a particular nuclear power facility.

4.6.3.5. Permission for preparatory works

In order to reduce the time necessary to implement the investment the investment law provides for the possibility to obtain another optional decision in the form of a separate permission for conducting preparatory works within the area subject to the decision on the siting of the investment in the scope of the construction of the nuclear power facility.[177]

After obtaining the decision on siting of the investment and the decision in principle and prior to obtaining the construction permit the investor may apply for a permission to conduct preparatory works covering land levelling, land development including construction of temporary buildings, connection to the technical infrastructure for the purpose of construction and other work not requiring the drafting of architectural and construction design, demolition of existing buildings, as well as removal of trees or shrubs located on the property covered by the decision on siting of the nuclear power facility investment.[178]

177 Before the investment law went into force preparatory works were allowed only on the premises for the construction permit has been already issued according to art. 41(3) of the Construction Law of 7 July 1994 (Journal of Laws of 2010, No. 243, item 1623 as amended).

178 Art. 17 of the investment law.

Since preparatory works may be conducted prior to obtaining the construction permit,[179] once the permit is obtained the investor may move straight to the implementation of the principle investment. On the one hand the above solution saves a lot of precious time, on the other, it creates risk for the investor, who, despite having covered the costs of preparatory works eventually may not receive the construction licence (in the scope of nuclear safety and radiation protection – based on Atomic Law) or the construction permit (based on the provisions of the Construction Law) or have difficulty obtaining them.

4.6.3.6. Distribution of profits

Investment law also provides for an innovative solution in the scope of tax provisions. Although it is not part of the investment process in the strict sense, it may have a positive influence on the implementation of the investment. However it does not apply to all nuclear power facilities but is limited to nuclear power plants only. The law obliges the municipality, on a territory of which the investment in a nuclear power plant is to be sited at least in part, to pay to the neighbouring municipalities a fee of 50% of property tax obtained from the nuclear power plant. Such fee constitutes an income of the neighbouring communes, which also become beneficiaries of the NPP's location.

The above solution helps to obtain support for the investment within the neighbouring municipalities. Such effect could also be achieved through establishing a separate fee payable by the operator directly to the neighbouring municipalities, however, such construction would adversely affect the profitability of the investment. At the same time, the expected income that remains after distribution in the possession of the municipality on a territory of which the nuclear power plant is sited is sufficiently high to secure its development. The fee is shared in equal parts between all the neighbouring municipalities, with the exception of those on which the nuclear power plant or part thereof is sited.

179 The »construction permit« should however be distinguished from the »construction licence«. The construction permit constitutes the last decision determining the start of the construction and is being issued by the construction administration authorities (art. 28 of the Construction Law). Before the application for a construction permit the investor should already possess a valid construction licence issued by the nuclear regulator – PAA President.

4.6.3.7. Facilitations within environmental procedures

The investment law also simplified environmental procedures for the purpose of the construction of nuclear power facilities. First of all the number of environmental decisions necessary at different stages of the investment process was reduced. According to the previous framework it was necessary to obtain environmental decisions at the following stages of the investment: decision on the siting of the facility, construction licence (»nuclear« licence) and the construction permit (according to the provisions of the Construction Law). Currently the environmental decision obtained prior to the issuance of the siting decision remains valid until the construction licence is issued. In addition, the durability of environmental decisions for investments in nuclear power facilities was extended up to 10 years,[180] while the deadline for their issuance was reduced to 45 days.[181]

Investment law also introduces more stringent conditions as regards the participation of environmental organizations in the investment process by allowing environmental organizations to take part in the environmental proceedings on the condition that they were entered into the relevant register at least 1 year prior to their initiation.[182] This is aimed at the elimination of *ad hoc* environmental organizations established only for the purpose of blocking the investment from the process.

4.6.3.8. Other facilitations

The law also introduces other facilitations to the investment process. As regards acquiring the legal title to the land it provides that limited property rights (usufruct, servitudes, pledge, cooperative member's ownership right to residential premises, mortgage), encumbering real estates expropriated

180 Art. 62 of the investment law amending the Law of 3 October 2008 on access to information on the environment, its protection, public involvement in environment protection and on environmental impact assessments (Journal of Laws of 2008, No. 199, item 1227 as amended).

181 Art. 20(3) of the investment law. In practice the proceeding will last longer as according to art. 20(4) the limit of 45 days does not include the time limits provided by law to execute certain activities, particularly in context of the transboundary environmental impact assessment, periods of suspension of proceedings and periods of delays caused by the fault of the party or for reasons beyond the authority.

182 Art. 20(2) of the investment law.

in favour of the State Treasury as well as right of perpetual usufruct, permanent administration as well as lease, land lease, use or other obligations, expire, for compensation, on the date the siting decision has become final.[183]

There is also the possibility to restrict the use of land property in order to assure proper implementation of the investment. Upon investor's application the voivod is under obligation to issue a permission to enter the premises for placing installations and equipment needed for construction works.[184] In addition, in order to pass through the area of public roads, railroad tracks or water flows, the investor is entitled to occupy such areas for the duration of the investment and operation.[185] The law also reduces the terms within administrative proceedings and provides for pecuniary penalties to be imposed on the administration authorities in the case of delays in settling administrative proceedings as well as restrictions as regards appealing administrative decisions.[186] Also, public procurement procedures as regards the investment implementation were simplified to some extent.[187] It is also important to note that decisions aiming at the delivery of the investment were transferred to higher rank authorities. The majority of decisions is issued by voivods (with appeals to be submitted to the relevant ministers), ministers or central authorities, which is aimed at accelerating the investment process through engagement of more competent authorities that display greater experience and predictability in the field.

4.7. What should be done next?

Besides the currently running legislative works regarding implementation of the next acts of the Euratom secondary legislation (nuclear waste directive, expected new BSS directive and the amendment of the nuclear safety directive) there are three main areas requiring further legislative actions. As to the development of nuclear power most challenging task is the creation of mechanisms for support of long-term and capital intensive investments in nuclear power plants in order to assure their predictability in the long perspective. The main task of the Euratom Community is the

183 Art. 24 and following articles of the investment law.
184 Art. 28 of the investment law.
185 Art. 29 of the investment law.
186 Art. 35 and the following articles of the investment law.
187 Art. 41 and the following articles of the investment law.

promotion of nuclear power[188] so all supporting schemes devoted to nuclear power plants would seem to have a treaty based justification. However other aspects should be taken into account as well i.e. common market principles and state aid rules (even assuming the existence of some favourable distinctions for the nuclear industry resulting from the provisions of the Euratom Treaty). This all makes this task complex and challenging.

In the area covered by the regulation of the Atomic Law competences of the PAA President and Internal Security Agency regarding nuclear security should be further specified in order to avoid their eventual overlapping. The responsibilities regarding elaborating the Design Basis Threat document also require proper assignment and direct placement in legal provisions. Further actions should be also undertaken in order to fully assure the independence of the regulatory body – PAA President. As first action in this regard the fixed term appointment should be introduced along with the specification of condition for dismissal of the PAA President. The name of the function as well as of the supporting office (PAA) should be changed to be perceived as responsible exclusively for nuclear safety and radiation protection (according to the actual legal situation) and not necessarily for the whole atomics in Poland together with the promotion of nuclear energy applications. Thus together with many guarantees already present in the Polish legal system the highest possible degree of (*de iure*) independence of the nuclear regulatory body as stated in the international conventions, Euratom directives and non-binding IAEA recommendations will be reached.

5. *Conclusions*

Although the Żarnowiec Nuclear Power Plant project was abandoned Poland has never given up its nuclear plans, as demonstrated by following strategic governmental documents in the area of energy policy. Currently a strong political will exits towards the implementation of the nuclear pro-

188 So is the conclusion derived from the content of art. 1, art. 2(c) and paragraph 3 of the preamble of the Euratom Treaty. According to this provisions main task of the Euratom Community is the creation of conditions necessary for the speedy establishment and growth of nuclear industries mainly through facilitation of investment and ensuring the establishment of the basic installations (i.e. mainly nuclear power plants) necessary for the development of nuclear energy. This goal should be reached particularly by encouraging ventures on the part of undertakings.

gramme finding its acknowledgement in internal legal acts of government and in political consensus between main Polish political parties having its origins also in the support of public opinion.[189] The final governmental document in this regard determining the ways and directions of the nuclear power implementation will be the PNP Programme. Its endorsement is being expected at the turn of the year.

Regarding establishing the Polish legal system for nuclear power implementation a huge legislative work has been done during last few years. The tasks designated for the public administration have been fulfilled through creation of a complex nuclear legislation comprising both nuclear safety (with radiation protection, nuclear security and safeguards) and facilitation of the investment and construction process. While working on new legislation actual technical and scientific knowledge has been used as well as modern international standards and nuclear legislations of advanced nuclear states. It is a remarkable achievement for a non-nuclear power state such as Poland even in spite of some its traditions and experience in the nuclear domain.[190]

During preparation of the draft documents a number of IAEA Safety Standards and other non-binding instruments have turned out to be very useful as well as examples of nuclear legislation from experienced nuclear countries. However all known documents had to be verified and adapted to the specific local conditions as legal system and legal tradition of Poland. Crucial element in this process was also a permanent co-operation of lawyers and engineers/technicans/nuclear safety experts (also external) in order to prepare a comprehensive system of provisions satisfying both the practical and legal requirements.

Most problems experienced by drafters during the legislative process have been implied by the detailed and arduous legislative procedure. The reasons for the length of the process have been among other things questions of public involvement and broad consultations of drafts. Despite many possibilities to take part in this consultations (part of them being ob-

189 According to last public opinion poll 56% of Polish population is favoring nuclear power plants construction in Poland. Surprisingly the rate is even higher in some of the potential sites of the first nuclear power plant, most probably as a result of good memories connected with the construction of Żarnowiec NPP in the same region during 80'.

190 Complexity of the established legal framework and extensive public consultations both of the draft PNP Programme and of the proposed legislation have been indicated as good practices while preparing nuclear programme by the 2013 IAEA INIR mission to Poland.

ligatory and other part organised voluntarily by the government) the public has been rather passive. Particularly disappointing has been the attitude of the environmental organisations and anti-nuclear groups. Although every piece of draft-legislation has been sent to all of them identified in Poland no single reply has been given.

Regardless of the above mentioned the public nuclear administration in Poland is fully aware of the fact that the new nuclear law will require testing in practice. Most probably respective changes will turn out to be necessary in order to react flexibly to the surrounding environment. Besides the questions of nuclear safety and investment and construction process the key role in implementing nuclear power successfully in Poland will have the creation of appropriate supporting mechanisms for the construction and functioning of nuclear power plants being capital intensive and long-term investments pursuing the EU strategy to tackle climate change and securing energy supply among EU Member States.

Poland and Germany: Issues of Transboundary Consultation

Dr. Martina Palm and Markus Pfaff, German Federal Ministry for the Environment, Nature Conservation and Nuclear Safety

Following the nuclear accident in Fukushima, Germany embarked on a course that other countries have looked upon with great interest. As part of a transformation of our energy system, Germany will gradually phase out the peaceful use of nuclear power by 2022.

In line with this sovereign right based on European and international law, other countries, whether worldwide or in the European Union, pursue different approaches. The Republic of Poland for instance plans to introduce nuclear power into its energy mix.

Parts of the German public, however, are quite concerned about the continued use of nuclear power especially in neighbour countries. Therefore, the development of nuclear power abroad is being critically monitored. The peaceful use of nuclear energy as such is called into question. When our neighbours plan nuclear power related measures, parts of the German public voice concern as they see a conflict with our general political approach phasing out the use of nuclear power.

For projects, plans or programmes in the nuclear sector instruments of environmental assessment are vital cornerstones. To mention are the Strategic Environmental Assessment, the so called SEA, and the Environmental Impact Assessment, the so called EIA.

An EIA, - namely a transboundary EIA- was carried out by the Czech Republic for the enlargement of the Temelin plant.

With Poland, a transboundary SEA in line with the Polish Environmental Information Act is currently ongoing. The Federal Ministry for the Environment together with 10 Länder – namely Brandenburg, Mecklenburg-Western Pomerania, Saxony, Saxony-Anhalt, Berlin, Bremen, Hamburg, Rhineland-Palatinate, North Rhine-Westphalia and Saarland – are taking part in this assessment.

The German public participated in the assessments with great interest. These examples therefore demonstrate the importance of and the need for transboundary assessments for the improvement of environmental protection in cooperation with local residents and local authorities.

Basic principles

Germany and in particular the Federal Ministry for the Environment has been given the task of protecting German interests against those of a neighbouring state, where a particular project, programme or plan may significantly impact Germany's environment. Both examples which have been mentioned – Czech Republic and Poland – have demonstrated that two instruments for precautionary environmental protection are available and in particular are necessary to ensure that environmental implications of decisions are taken into account before decisions are made.

The primary aim of both instruments is to identify and evaluate, using regulated assessment procedures, the direct and indirect impacts of certain projects on the environment (nature, society, economy) prior to allowing the project to be undertaken.

In order to facilitate assessment at the early stages of a project, the strategic environmental assessment has been introduced in the interest of precautionary environmental protection. The SEA takes place prior to the environmental impact assessment. The scope of the SEA includes plans and programmes. It is already on-going long before a decision is made about a concrete individual project. In the case of plans or programmes that may impact on the environment of neighbouring countries, the public and authorities of those countries affected are given the opportunity to participate in the assessment (a so called transboundary SEA).

Unlike the SEA, the environmental impact assessment deals with concrete projects or project areas that have already been specified. The EIA comes into effect in the later stages of a project whether it is a non-transboundary or a transboundary EIA.

The basic requirement for both instruments is that the country of origin assesses that the project, programme or plan may have significant impacts on the environment outside of the country of origin. Of course, opinions can differ on this crucial question. E.g. it may well be that the state of origin expects no transboundary effects, but the neighbouring state is quite convinced that its territory might be affected.

If no consensus can be reached on the issue of whether significant adverse transboundary impacts are probable, this question can ultimately be presented to an inquiry commission in accordance with the Espoo-Convention.[1] All parties to the convention are entitled to do so.

1 Appendix IV of the Espoo Convention (Article 3 (7) of the Espoo Convention)

An example is the British nuclear power plant project at the Hinkley Point site. UK is planning to build an EPR which, according to the manufacturer, will limit adverse effects to a 25 km zone. UK carried out an EIA at national level. According to Annex I of the European EIA Directive nuclear power stations are considered as having significant effects on the environment and require an EIA mandatorily. Concerning a transboundary EIA, Article 3 of the Espoo Convention requires notifying other parties in case that the activity is likely to cause a significant adverse transboundary impact. UK does not expect such impacts on other countries and therefore did not carry out a transboundary EIA whereas Austria assumes possible impacts of its territory. Such a controversial question for instance could be brought to the Espoo inquiry commission.

In both procedures, whether the SEA or EIA, the competent body responsible for drawing up a programme, plan or project will evaluate the information or objections resulting from the assessment. The information and opinions of the public and authorities will be taken into account in the further drawing up of the programme, plan or project.

What often proves to be a problem are the expectations of the public connected with the environmental procedures. False assumptions are often made regarding how much influence transboundary environmental instruments can have on political decisions whether the origin state will be using nuclear power or not.

It is the country of origin's responsibility to tackle objections raised. However, the results of the SEA or EIA only need to be taken into account in an appropriate manner when adopting a programme, plan or project. There is no need to follow the arguments made by the objector. Finally, it would hardly be possible to prevent a nuclear project using the SEA or EIA having in mind the goals of such instruments which are to guarantee public participation and information, as well as to contribute to avoid and decrease adverse environmental impacts.

Addressing the Polish nuclear energy draft programme, the question of interest is, how was the SEA procedure structured?

Poland intends their nuclear energy draft programme to serve as the foundation for introducing the independent use of nuclear power. The Polish nuclear programme presents both the scope and structure of measures needed for the introduction of nuclear power in Poland in order to ensure the safe and productive operation of nuclear power plants, their decommissioning and the safe use of nuclear fuels and radioactive wastes.

The draft programme firstly plans for the construction of two nuclear power plants. A final decision has not yet been reached on the specific type of reactor. The first nuclear power plant is planned to be up and running by 2023.

Poland has laid down criteria, according to which the various locations have been prioritised. For this, the entire Polish territory was taken into consideration.

Due to the fact that no specific location had been determined, the Federal Ministry for the Environment was the competent body to lead the consultations on the German side, of course with the extensive support of the Länder concerned. This is an exception because normally, the German Länder are the competent bodies, and not the Federal level.

This follows from the German Act on the Assessment of Environmental Impacts in conjunction with the German Atomic Energy Act.

According to the Act on the Assessment of Environmental Impacts, in the case of an ongoing environmental impact assessment abroad, responsibility is generally given to the authorities who would carry out a parallel assessment in Germany (for example in case of nuclear licensing procedures: Section 9b German Act on the Assessment of Environmental Impacts in conjunction with Section 7, 24 of the Atomic Energy Act).

In general, this also applies for plans and programmes in the framework of transboundary SEA procedures[2] as long as they are not applicable to the entire state and therefore would not have a direct equivalent regulation in German law. This, however, is the case with Poland.

Legal foundations

Poland decided to notify Germany, among others, of their nuclear energy draft programme and to forward a copy and environmental report. This was done in accordance with Article 10 of the protocol on strategic environmental assessment from the Espoo Convention and also pursuant to Article 7 of the SEA Directive from 2011.[3] Both Poland and Germany ratified the Espoo Convention and as EU member states are obliged to transpose the EU-Directives into their domestic regulatory framework.

2 Article 14j (3) in conjunction with Article 9b of the German Act on the Assessment of Environmental Impacts.

3 Article 10 of the protocol on strategic environmental assessment from the convention on environmental impact assessment in a transboundary context (Espoo Convention) and also pursuant to Article 7 of the European Parliament and Council directive (2001/42/EG) from 27 June 2001 on the assessment of the effects of certain plans and programmes (SEA Directive)

German Participation

Once the notification was received, Germany informed Poland of its interest in participation. The German public and authorities were thus given the opportunity to view and evaluate the procedural notification documents received.

Public participation was carried out in Germany during the period from October 2011 to January 2012. The presentation period was not subject to German law as it is always determined by the provisions of the country of origin. Germany submitted its statement on 3 January 2012.

In its statement Germany recognises Poland's right to freely choose its energy mix, but also promotes the upholding of internationally recognised high safety standards and the use of the most modern reactor units – generation III or III^{+} – under the supervision of independently appointed authorities.

Most of the Länder used this opportunity to issue a statement as well. A total of 35,000 German petitions were submitted directly to the Polish side by this time.

Amendment to SEA documentation

In January 2012 Germany was informed by Poland of an amendment to the Polish nuclear energy draft programme. This amendment to the nuclear power programme was made in order to newly include the site Gaski, previously not considered in the programme.

The Federal Ministry for the Environment regarded this amendment as significant and, in agreement with the participating Länder, applied to Poland for an extension of the deadline for public consultation in Germany by 21 days. Once this extension was granted, the German public had once again the chance to send their petitions directly to the competent body in Poland.

Following the principle of equal treatment the Ministry for the Environment thus ensured that the German public had the same consideration as the Polish public.[4]

4 The Federal Ministry for the Environment and participating Länder uploaded the documentation received from Poland onto their websites so that the public was given access to the project information available. The documents themselves were also made available in the above mentioned time frame. Also at that time,

The amendment made to the nuclear power draft programme did not call for another statement from the Federal Government however; as it was limited to the addition of a new site and the Federal Government's statement on energy policy from 3 January 2012 had not explicitly addressed individual sites at all.

Consultation date

At the end of November 2012, a comprehensive consultation took place in Warsaw. Participants from Germany were the Ministry for the Environment with the Länder that are particularly affected namely Brandenburg, Mecklenburg-Western Pomerania, Saxony and Berlin. The other Länder which are taking part in the transboundary SEA decided not to join.

Germany presented its concerns in relation to various points in the draft programme. It was noted that there is a particular need for more detailed discussions and reworking on the documentation for instance in the areas of

- emergency preparedness and management
- in relation to specifying the list of criteria, evaluation methods and detailed analysis of data for other sites
- monitoring measures during normal operation or incidents
- regulations for limited use zones within a 3km radius of nuclear power plants.

Moreover, the review of alternative energy supply paths and forecast of energy demand was a significant part of the consultation.

As the SEA procedure is carried out in the earlier stages of a project, its particular purpose is to ensure a comprehensive review of alternatives. Against this background Germany stressed the need for verifying other options and offered to share experience in the area of renewable energies with Poland.

the Federal Ministry for the Environment and the participating Länder issued a press release to inform the public of the possibility of submitting statements. In addition, the Federal Ministry for the Environment submitted an official notice to the Federal Gazette.

Outlook

The final revised version of the Polish nuclear power programme is due to be finished by summer 2013. Poland will officially notify Germany of the final version of the nuclear power programme once it has been adopted by the Polish ministerial council. The notification will also contain a summarised declaration of the SEA results, which will conclude the transboundary SEA procedure. This concluding statement must also take German petitions into consideration in adequate measure.

Once the SEA has been concluded, Poland has to carry out an environmental impact assessment. This second step will be assessing a specific site and it has to be implemented in a transboundary context as well.

In case of introducing nuclear energy in the Polish energy mix, Germany would prefer if the assessment at EIA stage already included a specific type of reactor. Thus, important nuclear safety aspects could be addressed within the EIA framework and its objectives.

This request seems to be not relevant in transboundary procedures where national legislation determines that EIA procedures are an integral part of the licensing process. This is the case in Germany, not however, in the Republic of Poland. In Poland the EIA is independent of the licensing process. Therefore, a so called »black-box« procedure is possible, which means that during the transboundary EIA process no reactor specification is necessary and only potential environmental impacts are part of the consultations. Actually, in such cases participating states do not have a legal basis to call for specification at this stage of procedure.

If the reactor type is not included in the EIA, these aspects can only be dealt with at environmental assessment stage in a so called monitoring procedure. However, there is no monitoring procedure available with clearly defined rules, but rather a procedure that is to a certain extent freely negotiable (Article 12 SEA protocol from the Convention on transboundary EIA).

Another issue is the extent of relevant information. According to the legal basis of environmental assessment instruments, the country of origin is obligated to submit a defined minimum of relevant information. Whether this defined minimum of information is sufficient for a comprehensive environmental assessment or not, is open to interpretation and is often influenced by the different interests of stakeholders.

Just these two examples show that several practical questions have to be solved during transboundary procedures. In order to accelerate and to ease transnational procedures, Germany and Poland have signed an agreement on the implementation of the Espoo Convention in 2006.[5] Such an implementation agreement concerning transboundary SEA procedures is in preparation.

Independently of these agreements, Germany expects for on-going and upcoming procedures that not only the defined minimum of information will be processed and translated into German. Furthermore, Germany expects that a decision on the reactor type will be taken in the transboundary EIA. Only in this case the German public and authorities will have a sound basis to assess the transboundary environmental impacts of a Polish nuclear power plant project.

If Polish procedures do not allow such an approach, Germany however, counts on Poland's readiness to agree on a monitoring procedure. The bilateral agreement between Germany and Poland on information exchange in nuclear matters could be an appropriate framework for such a monitoring process.

5 Agreement between the Government of the Federal Republic of Germany and the Government of the Republic of Poland on the Implementation of the Convention on Environmental Impact Assessment in a Transboundary Context signed 11 April 2006, Neuhardenberg (Land Brandenburg).

Transportable Nuclear Power Plants – An Update on Regulatory Responses in International Nuclear Law

*Rüdiger Tscherning**

Russia's Nuclear Energy State Company is progressing with a new programme of nuclear power plants installed on floating barges, so-called transportable nuclear power plants, with the first such installation launched in 2010 and now expected to be commercially operable by end of 2019. The programme of transportable nuclear power plants was launched to meet the increasing focus on natural resources extraction in the Arctic region, in particular energy and heat for exploitation projects and to supply ancillary settlements with electricity. In order to increase the export potential of these power plants, Russia has also undertaken a concerted effort to market the technology for the use in desalination projects, in addition to acting as temporary energy supply units for mega-infrastructure projects.

Transportable nuclear power plants have evolved within a pre-existing and comprehensive legal and institutional framework that is designed for the regulation of classic permanently installed nuclear plants in a single jurisdiction, with the only international element consisting of the shipment of nuclear fuel and waste. As this paper will discuss, transportable plants, by contrast, involve a »double international element« (the plants are transported from the supplier country to the host State and back to the supplier country) and can be considered, within the existing regime, as both nuclear installations, a nuclear activity and to involve the transportation of nuclear materials including spent fuel. They require not only legal responses from the supplier and recipient States, but also involve any number of ancillary third party coastal) transit States. Those transit States may, in turn, invoke arguments of non-innocent passage of the nuclear plants, based on pre-emptive and precautionary environmental and national security considerations.

The objective of this paper is to submit this existing nuclear regulatory regime and its applicability to transportable nuclear plants, in particular the regulation of environmental, proliferation and security concerns, to a rigorous assessment in order to identify the potential components for a future convention on small and medium sized mobile nuclear reactors. Such a convention should be advanced, as argued in this paper, by the IAEA, not only to create legal certainty for the transportable plant programme but also to serve as a modernisation tool of general international nuclear law, a trend that is already emerging by way of the inclusion of »impairment of the environment« as a head of damages within the 1997 Protocol to Amend the 1963 Vienna Convention on Civil Liability for Nuclear Damage.

1. Introduction

The proposal by Russia's Nuclear Energy State Company Rosatom to construct and to operate a fleet of low-capacity nuclear power plants mounted on barges, so-called transportable nuclear power plants (»TNPP«), is an innovative development of Russia's technical expertise in the field of nuclear energy, in particular her pioneering fleet of nuclear-powered icebreakers for operation in the Arctic. Also called »floating nuclear power plants« or »transportable nuclear installations«,[1] the development of the technology has received wider global interest not for its initially intended purpose, to supply remote settlements in the Arctic with electricity and heat, but as this paper will argue, for its role in supplying energy to natural resources extraction projects in the Arctic. In parallel, TNPPs are also designed to power medium capacity desalination infrastructure.[2]

In a challenging climate such as the Arctic, their application could, in part, reduce traditional and costly maritime supply routes of fuel, kept open by a fleet of nuclear powered icebreakers. This, in turn, is opening

---

* Director, Center for Energy and Sustainability Law, Qatar University College of Law, Doha, Solicitor (England & Wales) specialising in energy, climate and environmental law. A prior version of this paper, *Transportable Nuclear Power Plants for Natural Resources Extraction in the Arctic – International Environmental, Proliferation and Security Concerns,* was published in the OGEL Journal – Special Issue on the Arctic Region, Volume 10(2), February 2012 www.ogel.org. The author would like to reiterate his special appreciation to Mr. Patrick Reyners for his helpful comments on the earlier paper but as usual, all errors remain those of the author.

1 International Project on Innovative Nuclear Reactors and Fuel Cycles (INPRO), 2009 Progress Report, at 34; see http://www.iaea.org/NuclearPower/Downloads/INPRO/Files/INPRO-ProgressReport-2009.pdf.

2 Ignatenko, E., *et al., A buoyant new market? Floating nuclear power plants for remote regions*, Nuclear Engineering International (1997) 28-31, at 28.

up a new dimension of energy generation for the Arctic with associated climate benefits of reduced emissions from fewer shipments of imported fuel and from using nuclear instead of fossil fuel as a source of energy. Although in 2000 the IAEA predicted that nuclear desalination would be the most likely area of commercial development opportunities for the TNPP technology,[3] it is apparent that today, we have moved away from this position. This is in part due to the fact that retreating ice fields in the Arctic will in future allow easier access to the Arctic's vast natural resources,[4] thus fuelling the drive towards the Arctic.

As TNPPs are designed to be installed in a relatively fast and flexible manner, it is no surprise that the developments are watched very closely by the natural resources industry.[5] Flexible transportation and non-permanent installation of TNPPs also introduce a novel element to long-term extraction projects. In short, the technology has the potential to mark a shift away from traditional resource extraction projects dependent on imported fossil fuels or the at-source consumption of extracted resources.

The development of the technology also serves Russia's commercial ambitions to re-activate its somewhat stagnant nuclear export markets, with TNPPs considered »*a viable commercial concept and an important part of its domestic and international strategy regarding nuclear power*«.[6] Thus, the TNPP technology is also intended for the use in desalination infrastructure (discussions have circulated about a potential export orientated »build-own-operated« model with interest from countries as varied as Indonesia, China and Namibia)[7] or to act as temporary power installations

3 »Implementation of the Project for the construction and operation of a nuclear heat and power plant on the basis of a floating power unit with KLT-40C Reactors«, in *Small power and heat generation systems on the basis of propulsion and innovative reactor technologies*, IAEA-TECDOC-1172 (2000), at 53.

4 *Floating Nuclear Power Plants and Associated Technologies in the Northern Areas,* Norwegian Radiation Protection Authority, Strålevern Rapport: 2008(15), Østerås (2008), at 6 available for download at http://www.nrpa.no/dav/0e1f312fc9.pdf (last visited 12 May 2010).

5 Bellona, »Floating Nuclear power plants attracting interest of the oil industry«, 12 February 2008, http://www.bellona.org/articles/articles_2008/floatingNPPs_oil (last visited 4 May 2010).

6 *Floating Nuclear Power Plants and Associated Technologies in the Northern Areas,* at 16.

7 Bellona, »Russian floating nuclear plant builder Sevmash diverting cash to other projects«, http://www.bellona.org/articles/articles_2008/fnpp_sinking (last visited 29 April 2010).

to support mega-infrastructure projects in remote and inaccessible locations.

Though initial trials of the civilian use of barge mounted nuclear technology took place in the late 1960s in the United States of America,[8] the programme was not progressed further on a commercial scale. Since the commencement of a development and construction period in Russia in 2007,[9] the technology gained wider public attention. The latest status is that the official launch of the first of a fleet of TNPPs, the *Academik Lomonosov*, took place in St. Petersburg on 27 August 2010[10] and that on 27 September 2013, the first two reactors were installed in the reactor compartment. As a result of a number of set-backs in the project, the IAEA now predicts that the first commercial operability of the technology will be end 2019, with the IAEA's International Project on Innovative Nuclear Reactors and Fuel Cycles[11] (»INPRO«) having dedicated extensive time and resources to study the legal issues related to TNPPs, in particular within the environmental and safety, liability and international proliferation context.

2. Design and Technical Characteristics of Transportable Nuclear Power Plants

Based on available information, it is understood that TNPPs will have a potential capacity of 70MW of electricity output, capable of supplying energy to a settlement of 200,000. Crucially for any discussion of the potential regulatory responses to TNPPs, the IAEA has described TNPPs as *»physically transportable, but not designed to produce energy during transportation nor provide energy for the transportation itself«.*[12]

---

8 Kindt, J.W., *Floating nuclear power plants – US and international regulations*, Marine Policy (1983) 90-100, at 90.

9 *Floating Nuclear Power Plants and Associated Technologies in the Northern Areas,* at 9.

10 »*Russia Launches Floating Nuclear Power Plant*«, 27 August 2010, http://spectrum.ieee.org/energywise/energy/nuclear/russia-launches-floating-nuclear-power-plant (last visited 30 August 2010).

11 See generally the website of the IAEA INPRO section, http://www.iaea.org/INPRO/ (last visited 26 April 2010).

12 International Project on Innovative Nuclear Reactors and Fuel Cycles (INPRO), INPRO Dialogue Forum on Multilateral Approaches,TC INT/4/142 Workshop, October 2010, presentation by Peter J. Gowin, at 22,

Thus, TNPPs will be towed to their semi-permanent locations by barges, where they will be supported by pontoons or barriers to protect them against ice floes, general collision or marine based terrorist attacks.[13] As a starting position, this design and operational characteristic make TNPPs fundamentally different to typical nuclear fuel shipments, let alone classic permanently installed plants.

In terms of the potential grade of nuclear fuel, available information suggests that the modified version of the KLT-40 reactor (developed and extensively used in Russia's fleet of Arctic ice-breakers with fuel enriched to 90 per cent U235)[14], the KLT-40S reactor, would require a fuel enrichment level of below 20 per cent U235.[15] There are, however, efforts undertaken to improve existing reactor designs, so as to utilise fuel enrichment of less than 20 per cent[16] and to require off-site refuelling at 10-yearly intervals only, thus also significantly increasing commerciality and the proliferation resistance of TNPPs.[17]

3. Legal Regimes Applicable to Transportable Nuclear Power Plants

Three distinct but inter-related sets of legal regimes apply to TNPPs. Firstly, the national laws and corresponding international obligations of the Supplier State; secondly, the national laws and international obligations of the Recipient State of the TNPPs; and thirdly, the laws governing the international transport of nuclear materials within the bi- and multi-lateral context. Thus, TNPPs not only involve the regimes of the supplier and recipient State, but ancillary coastal/transport States who may raise arguments on environmental/preventive/pre-emptive grounds and seek to curtail the principle of 'freedom of navigation' enshrined within public inter-

---

http://iaea.org/INPRO/2nd_Dialogue_Forum/INPRO_DF_2010_09_30(Gowin).pdf.

13 Status of Small Reactor Designs Without on-Site Refuelling, IAEA-TECDOC-1536 (2007), Annex VI, at 297.

14 *Floating Nuclear Power Plants and Associated Technologies in the Northern Areas*, at 24.

15 Standring, W.J.F., Dowdall, M., Amundsen, I., and Strand, P., *Floating nuclear power plants: Potential implications for radioactive pollution of the northern marine environment*, 58 Marine Pollution Bulletin (2009) 174-178, at 175.

16 Status of Small Reactor Designs Without on-Site Refuelling, IAEA-TECDOC-1536 (2007), Annex VI, at 269.

17 *ibid.*, at 283.

national law, namely to declare the passage of TNPPs as non-innocent and correspondingly to deny passage to the nuclear shipment.

For the purposes of this paper, the national law context will not be examined. Suffice to say that a major potential exists to harmonise and to coordinate the regulation of design and construction of TNPPs in one supplier country with the end-user regulatory regime and requirements of the recipient State, from the outset of development. This will reduce potential overlaps, modifications and delays and act as an overall expedient of TNPP technology and operations. In instances where the recipient country is presently a non-nuclear energy State or adequately equipped to regulate any nuclear activity, that country should establish a domestic nuclear law regime compliant with the provisions and standards of the IAEA and to enlist the necessary assistance from the IAEA.

4. Environmental Risks of Transportable Nuclear Power Plants

The Transportation Stage of Operations – General Considerations

Like any nuclear shipment, the proposal to operate a fleet of TNPPs has the potential to pose considerable environmental risks during the entire cycle of operations. Firstly, risks arise during the initial fuelling stage at base (not examined further due to the essentially domestic regulation of this stage), secondly during the transportation of the TNPP to its intended location, thirdly during the day-to-day operations of the installations and fourthly, during the refuelling stage as a result of an accident.[18]

In addition to the risks of »*collisions ... groundings, fire and explosions ... and the result of hostile action*«,[19] the highest risk of environmental contamination is considered to occur during the transportation and refuelling phases[20] of TNPPs. The prospect of increased nuclear marine traffic,

18 *Floating Nuclear Power Plants and Associated Technologies in the Northern Areas*, at 39.

19 Request for Provisional Measures by Ireland, *MOX Plant* case (Ireland v United Kingdom), International Tribunal for the Law of the Sea, 9 November 2001, Page 18, para. 34 http://www.itlos.org/case_documents/2001/document_en_191.pdf.

20 The events at Chazhma Bay near Vladivostok of August 1985 involved the refuelling of the submarine K-431 which was subsequently destroyed as a result of the resulting criticality also leading to the death of a number of its crew, see Standring, W.J.F. *et al.*, *Floating nuclear power plants*, at 176.

especially in sensitive environments such as the Arctic, has also raised considerable concerns.[21]

The inclusion of a new head of damages for »impairment of the environment« in the *1997 Protocol to Amend the 1963 Vienna Convention on Civil Liability for Nuclear Damage*[22] (to which the Russian Federation is not yet a signatory) is consistent with wider developments in international environmental law to extend liability for environmental degradation arising from a failure to contain it and marks a general move towards the inclusion of explicit references to environmental considerations in nuclear law.

In addition, an assessment of the general regulatory regime for the transportation of nuclear material has revealed that the regime makes extensive direct and indirect references to the protection of the environment in the maritime transportation context, for example in the following legal texts:

Safety of Nuclear Vessels

Maritime transportation of dangerous goods is governed, in principle, by Chapter VII of the *International Convention for Safety of Life at Sea* (»SOLAS«) and the *International Maritime Dangerous Goods Code* (»IMDG«), which became mandatory as a result of amendments to the SOLAS Convention in 2004. In light of the general provisions of SOLAS and the absence of specific references to the transportation of radioactive materials, a separate code was prepared by the International Maritime Organisation in 1999. This specific code governs the *Safe Carriage of Packaged Irradiated Nuclear Fuel, Plutonium and High-Level Radioactive Wastes on Boards Ships*[23] and is generally referred to as the INF Code (»INF«).

The INF relates to the transportation of nuclear cargo. This is defined to include packaged irradiated nuclear fuel, plutonium and high-level radioactive waste, carried »as cargo« aboard an INF ship. The first difficulty in

21 *Ibid.*, at 176.

22 Protocol to Amend the 1963 Vienna Convention on Civil Liability for Nuclear Damage, Vienna, 12 September 1997, Article I(k), http://www.iaea.org/ Publications/Documents/Conventions/protamend_annex.html.

23 International Code for the Safe Carriage of Packaged Irradiated Nuclear Fuel, Plutonium and High-Level Radioactive Wastes on Boards Ships, International Maritime Organization, London, 2000.

the context of TNPPs is therefore, whether a TNPP, owing to its design, would qualify as an »INF ship«.

It would appear difficult to include TNPPs within the INF as a result of this narrow definition, especially if one also takes the definition of »cargo« into consideration. As the fuel in the reactor core of the TNPP is not designed to be taken off the TNPP at its place of installation it would not constitute »cargo«. A potential argument could, however, be made that on the TNPP's return to its refuelling base, the spent fuel in the irradiated core could constitute »cargo«, in light of the fact that the material is technically unloaded and replaced.

Based on a restrictive interpretation of the INF, however, the only realistic contribution the INF will make to a future regulatory framework governing TNPPs is the definition of »incident«, which constitutes loss of container integrity, and the definition of »release«, which is the escape of INF cargo from its containment during transport.

Packaging and Safety of Nuclear Material in Transportation

The IAEA's *Regulations for the Safe Transport of Radioactive Material*[24] (»TS-R-1«) are the cornerstone of protecting the public and the environment from the effects of radiation of nuclear material during transportation, based as they are on IAEA's *Basic Safety Standards for Radiation Protection*. The key principle is that the protection comes from the design of the packaging.[25] A review of TS-R-1 suggests that the definition of »vessel«, namely *»any seagoing vessel or inland waterway craft used for carrying cargo«*[26] could, potentially, include TNPPs, although this may require a liberal interpretation of the regulations. In any case, the reference to »carrying cargo« in the regulation opens up the same difficulties as the reference to »cargo« in the INF and as such, the same considerations may also apply in this instance.

24 Regulations for the Safe Transport of Radioactive Material, 2005 Edition, TS-R-1,Vienna, IAEA, http://www-pub.iaea.org/mtcd/publications/pdf/pub1225_web.pdf.

25 World Nuclear Association, Transportation of Radioactive Material, January 2010 http://www.world-nuclear.org/info/inf20.html (last visited 26 April 2010).

26 Regulations for the Safe Transport of Radioactive Materials, 2005 ed., Section II. Additional requirements relating to the transport of nuclear material by vessels are set out in Section V.

The Transportation of Nuclear Waste and Spent Fuel

The Russian Federation ratified the *Joint Convention on the Safety of Spent Fuel Management and on the Safety of Radioactive Wastes Management 1997*[27] in August 2006. The objective of the convention, as set out in Article 1, is the achievement and maintenance of high levels of safety worldwide in spent fuel and radioactive waste management.[28]

The definition of »nuclear facility« under the convention, which refers to »*a civilian facility and its associated land, buildings and equipment in which radioactive materials are ... processed, used ... stored or disposed of*« would very likely encompass TNPPs, in any case, once the spent fuel is processed and stored aboard the TNPP for ultimate disposal at a »spent fuel management facility«, as prescribed by the convention.

In addition, the provisions of Chapter Three of the convention, in particular Article 11, require that »*at all stages of radioactive waste management individuals, society and the environment are adequately protected against radiological and other hazards*«.[29] This is particularly relevant in the context of TNPPs. For example, a report on TNPPs by the Norwegian Radiation Protection Authority concluded that »*accidents during refuelling ... probably present the greatest risk due to the fact that the reactor is ... exposed to the environment due to necessary opening of the containment vessel*«.[30]

The Operational Phase – Environmental Risks, Nuclear Safety and Physical Protection

Many aspects of the environmental regulatory regime for nuclear installations, examined above, and the considerations related to maritime terrorism, security and nuclear proliferation considerations examined in more

27 Joint Convention on the Safety of Spent Fuel Management and on the Safety of Radioactive Waste Management, IAEA INFCIRC/546, Vienna, 24 December 1997, http://www.iaea.org/Publications/Documents/Infcircs/1997/ infcirc546.pdf.

28 Summary Report of the Third Review Meeting of the convention, May 2009, at 2 http://www-ns.iaea.org/downloads/rw/conventions/third-review-meeting/final-report-english.pdf (last visited 27 April 2010).

29 *ibid.*, Article 11.

30 Standring, W.J.F. *et al.*, *Floating Nuclear Power Plants and Associated Technologies in the Northern Areas*, Norwegian Radiation Protection Authority (2008), at 4.

details below also apply to the operational phase of TNPPs (therefore, reference to the operational phase will be correspondingly short at this juncture). This is partly due to the fact that the prevention of a breach of radiation integrity is equally relevant during the transportation and operational phases of TNPPs. The extensive body of rules and regulations related to the safety and security of nuclear installations has evolved with time and part of this corpus is specifically designed to protect both the employees operating the installation and the surrounding environment against radiation release.[31]

An argument can therefore be made that the ultimate, »ancillary«, beneficiary of the combined nuclear law regime is the environment. This is due to the fact that any regulatory regime encompassing the transportation, safety, security, liability anti-terrorism and anti-proliferation aspects of nuclear operations will be motivated by a desire to prevent the release of radioactive material into the environment, namely by restricting access to it. This key motivation is also reflected in the provisions of the Nuclear Safety Convention, which will briefly be examined below.

The Nuclear Safety Convention

The Convention on Nuclear Safety 1994,[32] to which the Russian Federation made a declaration of acceptance (pursuant to the convention) on 12 July 1996, imposes a high level of safety standards on signatories with regard to the operation of »nuclear installations«. The definition of nuclear installations under the convention is quite limited, given that it applies only to »land-based civil nuclear power«.[33] It is questionable whether TNPPs are covered by this definition, given that they are not, technically speaking, outright »land-based installations«. Nevertheless, an argument could be made that as TNPPs are intended to be attached to the ocean floor and supported by land-based infrastructure, moored in close proximity to the shore, they are, at the very least, »quasi land-based installations«. If one follows this line of argument, TNPPs could be included within the scope

31 Sarkisov, A., *et al.*, *Expected Radiological and Radioecological Consequences of Operating Floating Nuclear Heath and Power Plants*, Atomic Energy Vol. 104, No.3 (2008) 237-249, at 239.

32 Convention on Nuclear Safety, IAEA INFCIRC/449, Vienna, 5 July 1994 http://www.iaea.org/Publications/Documents/Infcircs/Others/inf449.shtml (last visited 28 April 2010).

33 *ibid.*, Article 2(i).

of the convention, especially as they would be operating for the generation of civilian nuclear power.

5. Maritime Terrorism, Security and Proliferations Issues

Terrorism and Security

The prospect of marine terrorism, consistent with wider geo-political security trends, may increase considerably in the foreseeable future.[34] On this basis, it is essential to assess the TNPP fuel cycle and operations in the context of the existing regime on terrorism and proliferation prevention.

Whilst a comparison can be drawn with the marine shipment of hazardous nuclear material aboard INF ships, for example aboard the fleet of Pacific Nuclear Transport Limited, it should be recalled that the quantity and quality of nuclear fuel aboard a TNPPs differs considerably from the large, MOX-style shipments. Nevertheless, when one considers the »tug-and-barge style« of proposed TNPP shipments, the most likely instances of marine terrorism could arise in the following circumstances:

- A malevolent attack on the reactor during transport[35] or seizure of the TNPP from its installed location;
- Seizure and removal of nuclear material from the reactor aboard the TNPP during the transportation/operational phase;
- Use of the TNPP as a terrorist weapon after seizure either during transport or operation, for example by detaching the TNPP from its tug-boat during transport; and
- Commission of an assault upon the TNPP, for example by using a fast vessel either during transport or during the operational phases.

Drawing on the experience of INF shipments, distance from land and speed of the vessel are two key defences against maritime-based attack.[36] For TNPP shipments, however, this raises the first critical difficulty. As the transportation of TNPPs is by way of tug-boats and requires naviga-

34 Smith, R., *Terrorism and the Marine Shipment of Nuclear Material*, University of Waikato, New Zealand, September 2006, at 5, http://www.pntl.co.uk/pdf/ Terrorism_Nuclear_Cargo.PDF (last visited 10 May 2010).

35 Beatty, Randy, International Project on Innovative Nuclear Reactors and Fuel Cycles (INPRO), at 11.

36 *ibid.*

tion close to the shore for logistical reasons, it is correspondingly slow. Previous attacks on vessels such as the *USS Cole* or *MV Limburg* have demonstrated that vessels are particularly vulnerable whilst navigating inside harbours or close to the shoreline.[37]

But even in the context of INF shipments, Jane's Intelligence has noted that INF ships are »capable of repelling only a light armed attack« and therefore require the support of an armed frigate.[38] This vulnerability has lead to the established practice of INF ships travelling in tandem and with specialist armed security personnel aboard. It can safely be assumed that these security measures would also be applied to TNPPs, despite the considerably reduced quantities of nuclear material being transported. This would potentially detract marine based attacks on TNPP, but would also involve a significant and costly security operation.

Security During Transport – The Physical Protection of Nuclear Material

The IAEA has consistently stated that nuclear material is the most vulnerable during the transportation stage of the nuclear cycle, a security concern that is addressed by both the *Convention on the Physical Protection of Nuclear Material 1980*[39] (»CPPNM«) and the IAEA's *INFCIRC/225/Rev. 4* document on »The Physical Protection of the Nuclear Material and Nuclear Facilities«.[40]

The CPPNM specifies the security requirements that are compulsory for three types of classes of nuclear material during international transport, with the Norwegian Radiation Protection Agency concluding that the classes most relevant to TNPPs are Classes I and II.[41] In addition, the convention requires signatory States to take appropriate steps to ensure that dur-

37 *ibid.*

38 Jane's Information Group Foreign Report, May 1999, as quoted in Request for Provisional Measures by Ireland in the *MOX Plant* case, para. 35.

39 Convention on the Physical Protection of Nuclear Material, IAEA INFCIRC/274/Rev.1,Vienna, 26 October 1979, http://www.iaea.org/Publications/Documents/Infcircs/Others/inf274r1.shtml.

40 The Physical Protection of the Nuclear Material and Nuclear Facilities, IAEA INFCIRC/225/Rev.4, Vienna, June 1999, http://www.iaea.org/Publications/ Documents/Infcircs/1999/infcirc225r4c.pdf.

41 *Floating Nuclear Power Plants and Associated Technologies in the Northern Areas*, at 53.

ing the international transport of nuclear materials, nuclear material in its territory or on board a ship under its flag is adequately safeguarded.[42]

In addition, two issues directly relevant to TNPPs arise from the *Amendment to the Convention on the Physical Protection of Nuclear Material 2005.*[43] Firstly, Fundamental Principle B of the 2005 amendment provides that *»the responsibility of a State for ensuring that nuclear material is adequately protected extends to the international transport thereof, until that responsibility is properly transferred to another State«.*[44] This clarifies the obligation on physical protection of nuclear material aboard a TNPP in the international context but leaves open the question of how the »in-transit« transportation of TNPPs between base and the intended location of operation, within the same country, will be regulated. This is neither a purely domestic question, nor a wholly international question, but instead a hybrid of both regimes, in addition to an international element. To a great extent, an analogy can be made to the regulatory body applicable to the general shipment by sea, land or air of nuclear fuel, material and equipment.

Despite the fact that Article 2 of the CPPNM confirms that the convention applies also to domestic use, storage and transport of nuclear materials, the 2005 amendment of paragraph 3 of Article 14 of the CPPNM suggests that where an offence involving nuclear material in domestic transport has occurred and both the offender and the nuclear material *»remain in the territory of the State Party in which the offence was committed«*, the State Party is under no obligation to provide information concerning criminal proceedings arising from such an offence. This would suggest that in a purely domestic context, the CPPNM would not apply to TNPPs.

Security During Operational Phases of TNPP

The operating phase of a TNPP will be governed by the provisions of the domestic Russian regulatory regime or the regulatory regime of the Host State of the TNPP. It is thus a pre-requisite for the export of TNPPs to

---

42 Convention on the Physical Protection of Nuclear Material 1979, Art. 3.

43 Amendment to the Convention on the Physical Protection of Nuclear Material, Final Act, GOV/INF/2005/10-GC(49)/INF/6, Vienna, 6 September 2005, http://www.iaea.org/About/Policy/GC/GC49/Documents/gc49inf-6.pdf.

44 *ibid.*

third countries that the applicable domestic regime contains adequate provisions to safeguard the TNPP operational stage, against breaches of nuclear security. As a starting position, any domestic regime will have to comply with the core provisions of the international nuclear regime on nuclear operations and these provisions are examined next.

Risk of Nuclear Terrorism during the Operational Phase

United Nations Security Council Resolution 1540 of 2004[45] and *the International Convention for the Suppression of Terrorist Bombings of 1997*[46] set out the reactive elements[47] of the universal legal framework in International Law to nuclear terrorism.

This framework prescribes that domestic legal regimes must contain mechanisms that bring perpetrators of nuclear terrorism to justice or alternatively, to extradite accordingly. *The Convention for the Suppression of Unlawful Acts Against the Safety of Maritime Navigation 1988*[48] reflects this reactive element and, by virtue of its 2005 Protocol, criminalises »*uses against or on a ship or discharging from a ship any explosive, radioactive material or ... nuclear ... weapon*«.[49] The commission of the preceding acts imposes an obligation on the State party to »extradite or prosecute« the perpetrator. As discussed in the context of the Nuclear Safety Convention above, the concept of »permanency« also remains a contentious issue for TNPPs in the nuclear terrorism debate. Thus, Article 1 of the 1988 Convention requires a »ship« not to be permanently attached to the seabed, making the question of TNPPs, their characteristics and their definition all the more relevant.

45 United Nations Security Council, Resolution 1540 (2004) On the Non-Proliferation of Weapons of Mass Destruction, 28 April 2004, http://daccess-dds-ny.un.org/doc/UNDOC/GEN/N04/328/43/PDF/N0432843.pdf?OpenElement.

46 United Nations General Assembly, International Convention for the Suppression of Terrorist Bombings, 15 December 1997, http://treaties.un.org/doc/db/Terrorism/english-18-9.pdf.

47 Gehr, W., *The Universal Legal Framework Against Nuclear Terrorism*, 79 Nuclear Law Bulletin (2007) 5-15, at 5.

48 Convention for the Suppression of Unlawful Acts Against the Safety of Maritime Navigation 1988, Rome, 10 March 1988, http://www.admiraltylawguide.com/conven/suppression1988.html.

49 *ibid.,* Article 10.

The »extradite or prosecute« regime is also to be found in the provisions of *the International Convention for the Suppression of Acts of Nuclear Terrorism 2005*[50], which makes it an offence to possess nuclear material with the intent to cause death or injury to persons or substantial damage to property or the environment. Upon taking possession of the nuclear material, the State party to the convention must take steps to render harmless the nuclear material, store it appropriately and to return the material to the State party to which it belongs. The definition of »nuclear facility« in the 2005 Convention includes *»any nuclear reactor, including reactors installed on vessels ... for use as an energy source in order to propel such vessel ... or for any other purpose«*. Again, uncertainty exists as to the extension of the 2005 Convention to TNPPs, in light of the restrictive definition of »nuclear facility«.

6. Transportable Nuclear Power Plants and the Nuclear Liability Regime

An interim conclusion of the above study of environmental, proliferation and security considerations raised by TNPPs is that the novel design, technical aspects and operational features of the installations raise a number of uncertainties in international nuclear law. No study of TNPPs would be complete without brief reference to the ancillary topic of nuclear liability, which this section seeks to examine.

For simplicity, this regime consists of the *1960 Paris Convention on Third Party Liability in the Field of Nuclear Energy*[51] and the *1963 Vienna Convention on Civil Liability for Nuclear Damage*[52]. To recall established principles of the regime, absolute liability is channelled to the operator of a nuclear installation in the event of a nuclear accident, limited in time and financially capped. Since the TNPP technology is presently being developed in the Russian Federation, an examination of the nuclear liability regime will be restricted to the provisions of the 1963 Vienna Conven-

50 International Convention for the Suppression of Acts of Nuclear Terrorism 2005, New York, 13 April 2005, http://untreaty.un.org/cod/avl/pdf/ha/icsant/ icsant_e.pdf.

51 Convention on Third Party Liability in the Field of Nuclear Energy, Paris, 29 July 1960, http://www.nea.fr/law/nlparis_conv.html.

52 The Vienna Convention on Civil Liability for Nuclear Damage, Vienna, 21 May 1963, IAEA INFCIRC/500, http://www.iaea.org/Publications/Documents/Infcircs/1996/inf500.shtml.

tion, to which the Russian Federation has been a signatory since 13 August 2005. The nuclear liability regime as set out in the Vienna Convention counted 39 parties as of April 2013.[53]

It is beyond argument that the above study of the international nuclear law regime and the unique features of TNPP operations will challenge the *status quo* of what can be termed the classic nuclear installations. Within the context of the international nuclear liability regime, two stages of TNPPs are of most relevance, namely the crossing of international liability boundaries and the operating phases.[54] That is not to say that the issue should be more complicated than necessary. There is a well established body of laws and regulations related to the liability regime for the shipment of nuclear materials. For TNPPs, however, the first hurdle of the international nuclear liability regime is the definition of »nuclear installation« in Article I.1.j of the Vienna Convention. Can TNPPs, in light of their design and operational features, even constitute a *»nuclear reactor other than one with which a means of sea or air transport is equipped for use as a source of power, whether for propulsion thereof or for any other purpose«*[55]?

What is apparent from this definition is that »nuclear installation« would appear to exclude nuclear propulsion from its scope. This, in itself, does not pose an issue for TNPPs, given their characteristics of being transported to their operational locations by tug boat and that they do not rely on any means of self-propulsion. If, however, a restrictive interpretation of the Vienna Convention definition is taken and the emphasis is placed on the *»source of power ... for any other purpose«* part of the definition, then the TNPP must be viewed as a single-unit of operation. As a result, it would be difficult to differentiate the nuclear reactor from the TNPP barge upon which it is placed, meaning that TNPPs would fail to constitute a »nuclear installation« under the convention, making them fall outside the well established and complex nuclear liability regimes as applied internationally.

---

53 IAEA, International Convention on Civil Liability for Nuclear Damage, Latest Status, April 2013 http://www.iaea.org/Publications/Documents/ Conventions/liability_status.pdf.

54 Fourth GIF-INPRO Interface Meeting IAEA HQs, Vienna. 1-3 March, 2010, presentation by Hussam Khartabil, http://www.iaea.org/INPRO/cooperation/ 4th_GIF_Meeting/09-4-Khartabil_Innovation_ProgrStatus.pdf.

55 The Vienna Convention on Civil Liability for Nuclear Damage, Vienna, 21 May 1963, IAEA INFCIRC/500, Article I.1.j, http://www.iaea.org/Publications/ Documents/Infcircs/1996/inf500.shtml.

An alternative broader interpretation would disregard the single unit of operation, separating the nuclear reactor from its transportation element entirely. Instead, this interpretation places a greater emphasis on the operational phase of TNPPs. This broader interpretation gains in strength considering that the exclusion in the definition of »nuclear installation« of Article I.1.j is very closely connected to the »transportation« element of the nuclear reactors only. The fact that the TNPP's reactor is placed on a barge and transported to its place of temporary installation by sea should be a secondary factor only, particularly if one considers that TNPPs are not self-propelled and are connected to the seabed and the shore by way of land-based supporting infrastructure. Furthermore, in the context of an overall operating cycle of five to ten years, the transportation phase is disproportionately short.

A second issue raised by the international operations of TNPPs is what can be termed the »export« scenario, that is where the TNPP is exported to a third party Host Country from Russia. As the international nuclear liability regime clearly has to address the transfer of nuclear material across borders in such instances, the special liability rules of the Vienna regime should be reflected in the regime for TNPPs as these rules are designed to ensure that at any one point in the chain of liability, only one operator is liable. Where there are two operators, the parties are able to determine the transfer of liability by way of contract. Alternatively, Article II of the Vienna Convention specifies that the receiving operator assumes responsibility at the point of taking charge of the nuclear material.

7. *Maritime Transport of Nuclear Material: Freedom of Navigation in International Law*

As examined above, the concept of TNPPs highlights a number of uncertainties and regulatory gaps within the established international nuclear law regime of classic, permanently installed nuclear power plants. TNPPs also raise a number of questions within the context of maritime shipment of nuclear fuel and materials, a fact that is compounded by Russia's ambitions to exploit lucrative export markets for its TNPP technology. Thus, potentially any number of States may be involved in the TNPP chain, correspondingly increasing the likelihood of vociferous objections being raised to the non-innocent passage through territorial waters and adjacent maritime jurisdictions.

To recall, TNPPs, using the Russian Arctic as an example, will require shipment from their base at St. Petersburg along a shipping route through the Baltic and past the Norwegian coast before installation in the Barents or Kara Seas of the Arctic. In addition to an adequate regulatory regime safeguarding their transportation and operations, TNPPs will also depend upon a supporting international regime based on political negotiations and diplomatic relations.

Since the early 1990's, a number of coastal States have sought to curtail the right to »innocent passage of ships«, as enshrined in the *United Nations Convention on the Law of the Sea 1982*[56], by denying innocent passage through their territorial seas and exclusive economic zone (»EEZ«) when vessels are carrying ultra-hazardous nuclear cargo. The usually applied argument is one of the precautionary principle, against the risk of potential nuclear maritime pollution.[57]

For the purposes of this paper, the most high profile of these incidents is the decision by the United States of America, following extensive international protest, to abandon its plan to transport by sea the 770-tonne decommissioned *San Onofre* nuclear power plant from Southern California to South Carolina around the southern tip of the American continent.[58] The *San Onofre* proposal faced considerable legal and diplomatic resistance, including the passing of the Law for Nuclear Safety by Chile in 2002, which requires prior notification and authorisation of any transport of nuclear substances through Chile's EEZ, together with a court case in Argentina in January 2004 prohibiting outright the passage of the barge through Argentina's EEZ.[59]

The maritime transportation of large volumes of highly radioactive and radiotoxic nuclear cargo continues to face international opposition and give rise to diplomatic incidents. Other notable examples include the

56 United Nations Convention on the Law of the Sea, 10 December 1982, see in particular Part II Section 3, in particular Art. 17, 19, 23 and 26 http://www.un.org/Depts/los/convention_agreements/texts/unclos/unclos_e.pdf.

57 Beaufoy, M., *Is the Law of the Sea Ready for Nuclear Leasing,* 3 MqJICEL (2006) 91-117, at 96. See also Van Dyke, J.M., *The Legal Regime Governing Sea Transport of Ultrahazardous Radioactive Materials*, 33 Ocean Development & International Law (2002) 77-108.

58 Van Dyke. J.M., *Balancing Navigational Freedom with Environmental and Security Concerns*, 15 Colo. J. Int'l Envtl. L. & Pol'y 19-28 (2004), at 19.

59 Currie, D. E. J., and Van Duke, J. M., *Recent Developments in the International Law Governing Shipments of Nuclear Materials and Wastes and their Implications for SIDS*, 14(2) RECIEL 117-124 (2005), at 120.

shipment of plutonium from France to Japan aboard the *Akatsuki Maru* or South Africa's diplomatic request for the *Pacific Pintail*, carrying nuclear fuel elements from France to Japan, to stay out of South Africa's territorial waters and EEZ.[60]

The International Tribunal for the Law of the Sea *MOX Plant Case*[61] has illustrated, during the Provisional Measure proceedings, that coastal States will not refrain from attempting to prevent the transportation of nuclear material by sea through the mechanisms of public international law. In the proceedings, the Republic of Ireland failed to secure provisional relief from the Tribunal. The Republic had sought to stop the development of a MOX Plant at Sellafield on the western coast of the United Kingdom and to secure the cessation of maritime shipments of nuclear material on the Irish Sea associated with the plant. The Republic of Ireland argued that the predicted increase of MOX shipments on the Irish Sea would pose an additional threat to its environmental security.[62]

While the above examples all involved marine transport of large quantities of highly radioactive cargo, quantities and levels of radioactivity that will arguably not be carried aboard a single TNPP shipment, the issues highlighted are nevertheless directly applicable to TNPPs. This is especially so given that TNPPs are required to travel within or close to coastal States' territorial waters, for safety and operational reasons. In order to ensure that Russia's TNPP technology can become a successful export product, the legal and diplomatic positions relating to proposed maritime passages under international law must be urgently clarified. Such agreements must include provisions on the requirement of prior notification for consent to the transportation of hazardous waste at sea. As a starting position, the *IAEA Code of Practice on the International Transboundary Movement of Radioactive Waste*[63] requires such notification and therefore, at a minimum, Russia must secure bilateral agreements safeguarding free passage along the Baltic Sea and, for example, the Norwegian coast so as to ensure that shipments to and from the Barents Sea are possible.

60 Van Dyke, J.M., *The Legal Regime Governing Sea Transport of Ultrahazardous Radioactive Materials*, at 78.

61 *MOX Plant Case*, Ireland v. United Kingdom, International Tribunal for the Law of the Sea, Request for Provisional Measures by Ireland, 9 November 2001, http://www.itlos.org/case_documents/2001/document_en_191.pdf.

62 *ibid.*, para. 27.

63 Code of Practice on the International Transboundary Movement of Radioactive Waste, IAEA INFCIRC/386, Vienna, 13 November 1990, http://www.iaea.org/Publications/Documents/Infcircs/Others/inf386.shtml.

Proliferation Issues – Geo-Political Implications

The discussions in this paper have been premised on the understanding that any commercial operation of TNPPs would be operated on a »double international« regulatory regime, whereby both the supplier and recipient State would regulate TNPPs, in addition, as set out above, the international element.

Whereas initial discussions and proposals did include the prospect of Rosatom operation TNPPs on a »build-own-operated« model basis, the most recent information available from the INPRO study, as of October 2011, concludes that this type of operational model has *»no basis in the current and previous legal and institutional practices«*.[64] Still, this type of operational model had previously been identified by the IAEA as the model to best safeguard non-proliferation of nuclear materials, due to the fact that the entire cycle of energy production would be controlled by Russia, with Russian security personnel securing the installation continuously and throughout all phases of international deployment.

For the international community, it can be assumed that this closed-fuel cycle of operations would have been the preferred one, not least due to the fact that Russia, as a signatory to the *Treaty on the Non-Proliferation of Nuclear Weapons of 1968*[65], is bound by the international regime relating to the non-proliferation of nuclear materials.

8. *Concluding Remarks*

The provisions of the international nuclear regime, which this paper has sought to examine, reveal that in most part, the environmental, security and proliferation risks of TNPPs are addressed. In the limited instances where provisions are explicitly restricted to the classic definition of installed nuclear power plants, a more flexible interpretation may be neces-

64 INPRO, Major Findings of IAEA/INPRO Activity on Legal and Institutional Issues on Transportable Nuclear Power Plants, PowerPoint Presentation by Vladimir Kuznetsov, Technical Meeting, Vienna 3-6 October 2011, Slide 9, http://www.iaea.org/NuclearPower/Downloadable/Meetings/2011/2011-10-03-10-06-TM-NPTD/2-Tuesday/8_IAEA_INPRO_TNPP_Kuznetsov_TM3-4Oct2011.pdf.

65 Treaty on the Non-Proliferation of Nuclear Weapons, New York, 12 June 1968, IAEA INFCIRC/140, http://www.iaea.org/Publications/Documents/Infcircs/ Others/infcirc140.pdf.

sary or, more likely, requisite amendments to the legal texts undertaken. An effort to coordinate the extensive web of laws, regulations, codes and guidelines that touch upon TNPPs should thus be undertaken, especially when one considers the multiplicity of interpretations that arise from the categorisation of TNPPs as both a nuclear installation, a nuclear activity and nuclear material. Are TNPPs »ships« during their transport phase and »installations« during their operating phases? Even the IAEA's own definition illustrates the confusion, describing a TNPP with KLT-20 reactor as a »non-self-propelled flat-deck vessel classified as a harbour ship«.[66]

In the public international law context, Russia needs to secure and safeguard her long-term export strategy and ensure that a global network of friendly coastal states will continue to tolerate the innocent passage of TNPPs throughout the entire cycle of TNPP deployment and the duration of the TNPP project. Bi-lateral agreements are the minimum requirement for this.

With their relative mobility, TNPPs could significantly contribute to addressing global shortages of energy supply, contribute to the generation of energy for the extraction of natural resources or power smaller scale desalination projects. A disjointed and incomplete legal regime, however, reduces confidence in the international regulation of TNPPs and in turn, deters both investment in the technology and reduces Russia's export opportunities. An agreement which codifies the complexities of the existing regulatory regime, and which would address the legal uncertainties or lack of clear regulation which this paper has sought to identify, is urgently required. To this effect, the late Professor Van Dyke's proposal for a »Protocol on the Prevention of Pollution by Sea Transport of Radioactive Materials«,[67] devised in the more general context of pollution prevention measures for maritime transport of hazardous nuclear materials, may serve as an appropriate starting point for a first draft legal text.

On this occasion, it is strongly argued that the IAEA should coordinate and promote the global effort towards a comprehensive convention on small and medium sized mobile nuclear reactors. Not only would the IAEA efforts on a convention strengthen the legitimacy of the TNPP programme and create legal certainty, but these efforts would also underline

66 *Status of Small Reactor Designs Without on-Site Refuelling*, IAEA-TECDOC-1536 (2007), at 295.

67 Van Dyke, J.M., *The Legal Regime Governing Sea Transport of Ultrahazardous Radioactive Materials*, *Appendix I*, 33 Ocean Development & International Law (2002) at 103.

an emerging trend within international nuclear law to include elements of what I would term »environmental maturing«, for example akin to the inclusion of »impairment of the environment« as a head of damages within the *1997 Protocol to Amend the 1963 Vienna Convention on Civil Liability for Nuclear Damage.*

Bibliography

International Conventions and Codes

Code of Practice on the International Transboundary Movement of Radioactive Waste, IAEA INFCIRC/386, Vienna, 13 November 1990, http://www.iaea.org/Publications/Documents/Infcircs/Others/inf386.shtml

Convention for the Suppression of Unlawful Acts Against the Safety of Maritime Navigation 1988, Rome, 10 March 1988, http://www.admiralty lawguide.com/conven/suppression1988.html

Convention on Nuclear Safety 1994, Vienna, 5 July 2004, http://www.iaea.org/Publications/Documents/Infcircs/Others/inf449.shtml

Convention on the Physical Protection of Nuclear Material, IAEA INFCIRC/274/Rev.1,Vienna, 26 October 1979, http://www.iaea.org/Publications/Documents/Infcircs/Others/inf274r1.shtml

Amendment to the Convention on the Physical Protection of Nuclear Material, Final Act, GOV/INF/2005/10-GC(49)/INF/6, Vienna, 6 September 2005, http://www.iaea.org/About/Policy/GC/GC49/Documents/gc49inf-6.pdf

Convention on Third Party Liability in the Field of Nuclear Energy, Paris, 29 July 1960, http://www.nea.fr/law/nlparis_conv.html

IAEA Code of Practice on International Transboundary Movement of Radioactive Waste, IAEA INFCIRC/386 (November 1990) http://www.iaea.org/Publications/Documents/Infcircs/Others/inf386.shtml

IAEA Safety Standards, Regulations for the Safe Transport of Radioactive Materials, 2005 edition, http://www-pub.iaea.org/mtcd/publications/pdf/pub1225_web.pdf

International Code for the Safe Carriage of Packaged Irradiated Nuclear Fuel, Plutonium and High-Level Radioactive Wastes on Board Ships (INF Code), International Maritime Organisation, 2000 ed.

International Convention for the Safety of Life at Sea 1974 (SOLAS), http://treaties.un.org/doc/Publication/UNTS/Volume%201184/volume-1184-I-18961-English.pdf

International Convention for the Suppression of Acts of Nuclear Terrorism 2005, New York, 13 April 2005, http://untreaty.un.org/cod/avl/pdf/ha/ icsant/icsant_e.pdf

International Convention for the Suppression of Terrorist Bombings 1997 http://www.un.org/en/sc/ctc/docs/conventions/Conv11.pdf

International Maritime Dangerous Goods Code, IMO Publications, London

Joint Convention on the Safety of Spent Fuel Management and on the Safety of Radioactive Waste Management, IAEA INFCIRC/546, Vienna, 24 December 1997, http://www.iaea.org/Publications/Documents/Inf circs/1997/infcirc546.pdf

Regulations for the Safe Transport of Radioactive Material, 2005 Edition, TS-R-1, Vienna, IAEA, http://www-pub.iaea.org/mtcd/publications/pdf/pub1225_web.pdf

Treaty on the Non-Proliferation of Nuclear Weapons, New York, 12 June 1968, IAEA INFCIRC/140, http://www.iaea.org/Publications/Documents/Infcircs/Others/infcirc 140.pdf

The Vienna Convention on Civil Liability for Nuclear Damage, Vienna, 21 May 1963, IAEA INFCIRC/500, http://www.iaea.org/Publications/Documents/Infcircs/ 1996/inf500.shtml

Protocol to Amend the 1963 Vienna Convention on Civil Liability for Nuclear Damage, Vienna, 12 September 1997, http://www.iaea.org/Publications/Documents/ Conventions/protamend_annex.html

United Nations Convention on the Law of the Sea, 10 December 1982, http://www.un.org/Depts/los/convention_agreements/texts/unclos/unclos_e.pdf

Judicial Proceedings and International Legal Materials

International Tribunal for the Law of the Sea, Request for Provisional Measures by Ireland, *The MOX Plant case* (Ireland v United Kingdom), 9 November 2001, http:// www.itlos.org/fileadmin/itlos/documents/cases/case_no_10/request_ireland_e.pdf

United Nations Security Council, Resolution 1540 (2004) On the Non-Proliferation of Weapons of Mass Destruction, 28 April 2004, http://daccess-dds-ny.un.org/ doc/UNDOC/GEN/N04/328/43/PDF/ N0432843.pdf?OpenElement

United Nations General Assembly, International Convention for the Suppression of Terrorist Bombings, 15 December 1997, http://treaties.un.org/doc/db/Terrorism/ english-18-9.pdf

Articles

Beaufoy, M., Is the Law of the Sea Ready for Nuclear Leasing?, 3 MqJICEL (2006) 91-117

Currie, D. E. J., and Van Duke, J. M., *Recent Developments in the International Law Governing Shipments of Nuclear Materials and Wastes and their Implications for SIDS*, 14(2) RECIEL (2005) 117-124

Gehr, W., *The Universal Legal Framework Against Nuclear Terrorism*, Nuclear, 79 Nuclear Law Bulletin (2007) 5-15

Ignatenko, E., *et al.*, *A buoyant new market? Floating nuclear plants for remote regions*, 28 Nuclear Engineering International (1997) 28-31

Kindt, K. W., *Offshore Siting of Nuclear Power Plants*, 8 Ocean Development & International Law (1980) 57-103

Kindt, K. W., Floating nuclear power plants: US and international regulations, Marine Policy (April 1983) 90-100

Sarkisov, A., *et al.*, *Expected Radiological and Riodioecological Consequences of Operating Floating Nuclear Heath and Power Plants*, Atomic Energy Vol. 104, No.3 (2008) 237-249

Smith, R., *Terrorism and the Marine Shipment of Nuclear Material*, University of Waikato, New Zealand (September 2006), available for download at http://www.pntl.co.uk

Standring, W.J.F., Dowdall, M., Amundsen, I., and Strand, P., *Floating nuclear power plants: Potential implications for radioactive pollution of the northern marine environment*, 58 Marine Pollution Bulletin (2009) 174-178

Suaraz, A. S., *Post September 11 Security Challenges to the Legal Regime of the Maritime Carriage of Nuclear and Radioactive Materials*, 18 Int'l J. Marine & Coastal L. (2003) 423-440

Van Dyke. J.M., *Sea Shipment of Japanese Plutonium Under International Law*, 24 Ocean Development & International Law (1993) 399-430

Van Dyke. J.M., *Applying the Precautionary Principle to Ocean Shipments of Radioactive Materials*, 27 Ocean Development & International Law (1996) 379-397

Van Dyke, J.M., *The Legal Regime Governing Sea Transport of Ultrahazardous Radioactive Materials*, 33 Ocean Development & International Law (2002) 77-108

Van Dyke. J.M., *Balancing Navigational Freedom with Environmental and Security Concerns*, 15 Colorado Journal of International Environmental Law and Policy (2004) 19-28

Reports

Economics of Nuclear Desalination: New Developments and Site Specific Studies, IAEA-TECDOC-1561 (2007) http://www-pub.iaea.org/MTCD/publications/PDF/te_1561_web.pdf

Floating Nuclear Power Plants and Associated Technologies in the Northern Areas, Norwegian Radiation Protection Authority (2008) http://www.nrpa.no/dav/0e1f312fc9.pdf

Fourth GIF-INPRO Interface Meeting IAEA HQs, Vienna. 1-3 March, 2010, presentation by Hussam Khartabil, http://www.iaea.org/INPRO/cooperation/4th_GIF_Meeting/09-4-Khartabil_Innovation_ProgrStatus.pdf

Implementation of the project for the construction and operation of a nuclear heat and power plant on the basis of a floating power unit with KLT-40C reactors, IAEA-TECDOC-1172 (1998) http://www.iaea.org/inisnkm/nkm/aws/fnss/fulltext/1172.pdf

International Project on Innovative Nuclear Reactors and Fuel Cycles (INPRO), INPRO Dialogue Forum on Multilateral Approaches,TC INT/4/142 Workshop, October 2010, presentation by Peter J. Gowin, http://iaea.org/INPRO/2nd_Dialogue_Forum/INPRO_DF_2010_09_30(Gowin).pdf

International Project on Innovative Nuclear Reactors and Fuel Cycles (INPRO), IAEA Programs on SMRs with specific update on Transportable Nuclear Power Plants (TNPP), March 2011, presentation by Randy Beatty, at 11, http://www.nrc.gov/public-involve/conference-symposia/ric/past/2011/docs/abstracts/beattyr-h.pdf

Kimball,L. A., *International Ocean Governance: Using International Law and Organizations to Manage Marine Resources Sustainably* (Gland, Switzerland and Cambridge, United Kingdom, IUCN- The World Conservation Unit, 2001)

Status of Advanced Light Water Reactor Design, IAEA-TECDOC-1391(2004) http://www-pub.iaea.org/MTCD/publications/PDF/te_1391_web.pdf

Status of Design Concepts of Nuclear Desalination Plants, IAEA-TECDOC-1326 (2002) http://www-pub.iaea.org/MTCD/publications/PDF/te_1326_web.pdf

Status of Nuclear Desalination in IAEA Member States, IAEA-TECDOC-1524 (2007) http://www-pub.iaea.org/mtcd/publications/pdf/te_1524_web.pdf

Status of Small Reactor Designs Without on-Site Refuelling, IAEA-TECDOC-1536 (2007) http://www-pub.iaea.org/MTCD/publications/ PubDetails.asp?pubId=7772

Summary Report of the Third Review Meeting of the Joint Convention, May 2009 http://www-ns.iaea.org/downloads/rw/conventions/third-review-meeting/final-report-english.pdf

Other Sources

Bellona, »Floating Nuclear power plants attracting interest of the oil industry«, 12 February 2008 http://www.bellona.org/articles/articles_2008/floatingNPPs_oil

Bellona, »Russian floating nuclear plant builder Sevmash diverting cash to other projects«, 8 July 2008 http://www.bellona.org/articles/articles_2008/fnpp_sinking

Spectrum.ieee.org, »Russia Launches Floating Nuclear Power Plant«, 27 August 2010, http://spectrum.ieee.org/energywise/energy/nuclear/russia-launches-floating-nuclear-power-plant

World Nuclear Association, Transportation of Radioactive Material, January 2010 http://www.world-nuclear.org/info/inf20.html

Turkey as a Newcomer in Nuclear New Build – Turkey's Development in the Field of Nuclear Energy and a Systematic View on Progress Particularly in Nuclear Legislation –

Erinç Ercan, Lawyer, Hamburg, and *Horst Schneider,* Bonn

»Bir mum diğer bir mumu tutuşturmakla ışığından birşey kaybetmez.«
Mevlana Celaleddin Rumi*

Abstract

Turkey is an economically rapidly developing country. The growing need of energy may not be guaranteed by more energy imports. In order to diminish the dependence of foreign energy sources and imports the Government of the Republic of Turkey stresses the opportunities of nuclear energy. Government's conviction of the need of nuclear energy within an energy mix comprising a growing part of renewable energy results in the ambitious political goal of 20% of electricity production from nuclear power plants (NPPs) by 2023. This can only be reached on the basis of comprehensive technical knowledge and experienced staff and lastly after establishment of a substantial and detailed nuclear legal framework. Parallel to constant progress in concrete projects for NPPs in Turkey nuclear laws, decrees, regulations, directives and guides are getting more and more numerous. Nevertheless compared with standards of the International Atomic Energy Agency (IAEA), the Nuclear Energy Agency of the Organization of Economic Cooperation and Development (OECD-NEA) and the norms of the European Atomic Community (EURATOM) a general and fundamental nuclear law is missing as well as a clearer structure in the existing legal norms particularly for the upcoming licensing processes of siting, construction and commissioning for several NPPs should be estab-

* It means in English: »A candle doesn't lose its light by enlightening another candle.« See ingilizce delisi at http://ingilizcedelisi.com/mevlananin-sozleri-turkce-ingilizce/ (accessed 24/04/2013).

lished. Moreover, particularly Environmental Impact Assessment should be executed in a legally more credible manner. Finally a generally high degree of transparency of political decisions together with national administrative acts and international cooperation could be improved. Some international conventions should be ratified soon.

Introduction

The economic growth of Turkey in 2012 with its still increasing population of round about 76 million people was accordingly to the annual gross domestic product of 9.2% at current prices and of 2.2% at constant prices.[1] Deputy Prime Minister Ali Babacan recently announced the expected economic growth for 2013 at 4 % and for 2014 at 5 %.[2] Corresponding to the economic growth the net consumption of electricity increased from 172 050,6 GWh in 2010 to 186 099,6 GWh in 2011.[3] The Turkish Minister for Energy and Natural Resources, Taner Yıldız, estimates the development until 2023 at about 90 % higher consumption of primary energy.[4] At the same time he strikes the necessity of diminishing the dependence of energy imports.[5] Therefore the Government of the Republic of Turkey is con-

1 See for the annual gross domestic product TURKISH STATISTICAL INSTITUTE, available at http://www.turkstat.gov.tr/ PreHaberBultenleri.do?id=13471 (accessed 23/04/2013), and for the population statistics TURKISH STATISTICAL INSTITUTE of 28 January 2013, The population of Turkey became 75 627 384 on December 31, 2012, available at http://www.turkstat.gov.tr/ PreHaberBultenleri.do?id=13425 (accessed 03/05/2013).

2 See (only Turkish) at http://www.trthaber.com/haber/ekonomi/buyume-hedefini-acikladi-82017.html. The European Commission announced on 3 May 2013 for Turkey an annual economic growth in 2013 and 2014 of 3.2 respectively of 4 per cent – see TRT HABER of 3 May 2013, available (only Turkish) at http://www.trthaber.com/haber/gundem/abden-turkiyeye-iyi-haber-84711.html (accessed 03/05/2013).

3 See TURKISH STATISTICAL INSTITUTE, Annual Electricity, Gas and Water Statistics, Power installed of power plants, gross generation and net consumption of electricity, available at http://www.turkstat.gov.tr/VeriBilgi.do?alt_id=11 (accessed 23/04/2013).

4 See Republic of Turkey Ministry for Energy and Natural Resources, Budget Presentation for the Year 2013 by Minister Taner Yıldız at the Turkish Grand National Assembly (TGNA) on 15 December 2012, p. 6, available (only Turkish) at http://www.enerji.gov.tr/yayinlar_raporlar/2013_Genel_Kurul_Konusmasi.pdf (accessed 23/04/2013).

5 See Taner Yıldız (footnote 4), p. 8; for his appeals of 14 December 2012 and of 29 April 2013 on saving energy in private households which could save until

vinced of positive energy economics and environmental effects by including the peaceful use of nuclear energy to the national energy mix.[6]

The primarily competent authority for nuclear energy is the Turkish Atomic Energy Authority (TAEK) which has to execute the necessary enforcement and the control for ensuring nuclear safety and radiation protec-

2023 up to 20 % of electricity consumption see (only Turkish) TRT HABER at http://www.trthaber.com/haber/ekonomi/taner-yildizdan-enerjide-tasarruf-vurgusu-67096.html (accessed 26/04/2013) and http://www.trthaber.com/haber/ekonomi/ev-hanimlari-yilda-4-milyar-tl-tasarruf-saglayabilir-84220.html (accessed 29/04/2013). In the same manner Economy Minister Zafer Çağlayan underlined on 4 April 2013 the goal of diminishing the dependence of Turkey with regard to energy imports – see (only Turkish) http://www.trthaber.com/haber/ekonomi/turkiyeye-dev-yatirim-81059.html (accessed 04/04/2013). Moreover Taner Yıldız expressed on 24 April 2013 in the same direction the preference for local energy production; see (only Turkish) HABERLER.COM at http://www.haberler.com/icci-2013-19-uluslararasi-enerji-ve-cevre-fuari-ve-4558342-haberi/ (accessed 24/04/2013). With regard to financial speculations see for the aspect of diminishing the dependence of foreign energy supply SETA of 17 June 2013, *»Faiz Lobisi ve Marifetleri«* (*»Bu nedenle makroekonomik göstergelerdeki iyileşmelerle daha daha geniş manevra alanı elde eden politika yapıcılar bu yapısal sorunun çözümü için nükleer enerji santralleri kurulması kararını almışlardır.«*) and *»Faiz Lobisi Nedir?«* (*»Ekonomide en önemli yapısal sorun olan cari açığı düşürecek ve Türkiye'nin enerjide dışa bağımlılığını azaltacak olan nükleer enerji santrallerinin kurulması kararı bu lobiyi endişelendirmiştir.«*), available (only Turkish) at http://setav.org/tr/faiz-lobisi-ve-marifetleri/yorum/6820 and at http://setav.org/ tr/faiz-lobisi-nedir/yorum/6819 (accessed 25/06/2013).

6 See Circular 2012/8 of Prime Minister Recep Tayyip Erdoğan, first paragraph, published (only Turkish) in the Official Gazette No. 28240 of 21 March 2012, and Taner Yıldız (footnote 4), pp. 8 and 27, further the 10th Development Plan for Turkey (2014-2018), submitted by the Prime Minister on 13 June 2013 to the Turkish Grand National Assembly, p. 117 no. 781 and 784, available at http://pbk.tbmm.gov.tr/dokumanlar/10-kalkinma_plani.pdf (accessed 26/06/2013). The biggest Turkish opposition party, Cumhuriyet Halk Partisi, is not in favour of the concrete nuclear projects of the Turkish government (in the light of the facts the NPP projects to be constructed in Akkuyu and Sinop serve neither for peoples' advantages nor for the public), but would prefer energy economics with nuclear energy on the basis of fourth generation reactors and advanced waste management technology (CHP Enerji Komisyonu, (2012), AKP'nın Nükleer Macerasına Hayır!, Kasım 2012, p. 4 paragraph 2 and p. 35 last paragraph, available (only Turkish) at http://www.chp.org.tr/wp-content/uploads/2012/11/ nukleer_enerji_raporu_kasim_2012_myk.pdf – accessed 03/06/2013); that attitude seems to follow a »wait and see« strategy.

tion.[7] For licensing and control of the envisaged projects, particularly at the site of Mersin-Akkuyu, the administrative acts and activities are based on national and international legislation which is quite developed.[8]

Nuclear law is not a new matter in Turkey. First regulations date from 1956, particularly Law No. 6821 establishing the Atomic Energy Commission was accepted in the Turkish Grand National Assembly on 27 August 1956, but the Atomic Energy Commission was restructured in 1982 by Law No. 2690 establishing the Turkish Atomic Energy Authority.[9] The Decree on Licensing of Nuclear Installations which is still in force without having been amended dates from 1983.[10] After several unsuccessful steps to plan and construct NPPs in Turkey first 2007 concrete important and decisive progress was reached also with regard to nuclear law: One law and many regulations, a directive and many guides were published in the years 2007 – 2013; the licensing of siting and construction accordingly to the decree of 1983, actually relevant for the NPP projects in Mersin-Akkuyu (construction) and Sinop-İnceburun (siting), was detailed by several regulations, directives and guides. [11] Nevertheless the structure of the

7 See Taner Yıldız (footnote 4), p. 52. With regard to the abbreviation for the Turkish Atomic Energy Authority it is preferred to use the Turkish TAEK (for Türk Atom Enerjisi Kurumu) instead of the not widespread English TAEA.

8 See Taner Yıldız (footnote 4), p. 53.

9 Law No. 6821 was published in the Official Gazette No. 9398 of 4 September 1956. See Turkish Atomic Energy Authority, History: »*In 1956, General Secretariat of Atomic Energy Commission was established in Ankara by the law numbered 6821, as an organization affiliated to the Prime Ministry. In 1982, the Commission was restructured as Turkish Atomic Energy Authority affiliated to the Prime Ministry by the law numbered 2690.*«, available at http://www.taek.gov.tr/en/institutional/history.html (accessed 23/04/2013). Law No. 2690 on Turkish Atomic Energy Authority of 9 July 1982 was published in the Official Gazette No. 17753 of 13 July 1982; an English version is available at http://www.taek.gov.tr/en/belgeler-formlar/documents/law/ (accessed 17/04/2013). See for Law No. 2690 and today's function of the Atomic Energy Commission chapter 3.3.2 below. Instead of Turkish Grand National Assembly sometimes Grand National Assembly of Turkey is used in publications of the Turkish government.

10 Decree on Licensing of Nuclear Installations, published in the Official Gazette No. 18256 of 19 December 1983; unofficial translation available at http://www.taek.gov.tr/en/belgeler-formlar/documents/Regulations/nuclear-safety/ (accessed 23/04/2013).

11 See chapters 2.1 and 3 below and already Ercan, E., Schneider, H. (2012), »Turkey's way to nuclear energy – An example for a newcomer's new build«, *International Journal for Nuclear Power,* atw 57. Jg. (2012) Heft 10 / Oktober, chapters 2 and 3, pp. 585–588, available as pdf document at http://www.kernener

legislation has to be proved in depth in order to evaluate the existing nuclear legislation in Turkey which was criticized particularly as regards the lack of a framework nuclear law by the European Commission in autumn 2012[12] by verifying the conformity with IAEA, NEA and EURATOM standards. A systematic description and on this basis a scientific appraisal and assessment has to focus on the organizational structure settling the permission principle, control principle, transparency principle as well as on the norms which contain the requirements for safety, security, safeguards, compensation (nuclear liability) and radiation protection of nuclear power plants including procedural measures (for example licensing procedures) and the possibility of judicial review by administrative courts.[13] Moreover legal regulations parallel to nuclear law must be taken into account as well, particularly Environmental Impact Assessment (EIA) and some aspects of energy economics.

The following analysis lays stress on the legal basis for the realization of commercial NPPs in Turkey. Having done this a brief evaluation may be drawn on, whether Turkish nuclear legislation is consistent particularly with the Convention on Nuclear Safety of 17 June 1994 (CNS) entered in-

gie.de/kernenergie-en/service/fachzeitschrift-atw/hefte-themen/2012/oct/index.php (accessed 24/04/2013).

12 European Commission (10.10.2012), »2012 TURKEY PROGRESS REPORT«, Document SWD(2012) 336 final, Chapter 15: Energy, p. 62 (»No development can be reported on the adoption of a framework nuclear law, which would ensure a level of nuclear safety in full compliance with EU standards; existing applicable national legislation mainly covers protection against ionizing radiation and the licensing of nuclear installations.«). The document is available at http://ec.europa.eu/enlargement/pdf/key_documents/2012/package/tr_rapport_2012_en.pdf (accessed 24/04/2013).

13 See Pelzer, N., (2009) »Legal Issues Associated with Preparing for a Nuclear Energy Programme«, in *International Ministerial Conference on Nuclear Energy in the 21st Century, Beijing, 20-22 April 2009,* pp. 2–4, http://www-pub.iaea.org/MTCD/Meetings/PDFplus/2009/cn169/Beijing_TS/TS3/3%20Pelzer%20newtext.pdf (accessed 24/04/2013), and Pelzer, N., (2009) »Nuclear New Build – New Nuclear Law?«, *Nuclear Law Bulletin,* No. 84 (Volume 2009/2), pp. 5 et seq. (footnotes 11–13). See further Vasmant, A., (2009) »International Legal Instruments Promoting Synergies in Nuclear Safety, Security and Safeguards: A Myth or Reality?«, *Nuclear Law Bulletin,* No. 84 (Volume 2009/2), pp. 81–102, Kuş, S., (2011) »International nuclear law in the 25 years between Chernobyl and Fukushima and beyond…«, *Nuclear Law Bulletin,* No. 87 (Volume 2011/1), pp. 7 et seq. The articles in the Nuclear Law Bulletin are available at http://www.oecd-nea.org/law/nlb/ (accessed 28/05/2013).

to force in Turkey on 24 October 1996[14] and the Council Directive 2009/71/EURATOM of 25 June 2009 establishing a Community framework for the nuclear safety of nuclear installations[15] which Turkey has to transpose as acquis communautaire in the course of the EU accession process. Thus the method of this article is not »top-down« in the sense of reviewing the pyramid »International Law/National legislation« but presents for better comprehension the historical development of national legislation taking into consideration international aspects and finally the status reached at present. This approach is elaborated on the background of Turkish Prime Minister's Circular of 2012 focusing as a general instruction on the Akkuyu NPP project and demanding all public administrative bodies to fulfill rather quickly all tasks with regard to the Turkish-Russian Agreement of 12 May 2010.[16]

---

14 Ratification by Turkey on 14 January 1995 and deposit on 8 March 1995, see IAEA INFCIRC 449 of 5 July 1994 and http://www.iaea.org/ Publications/Documents/Conventions/nuclearsafety_status.pdf (accessed 24/04/2013). Up to now Turkey did not publish the National Reports to the Review Meetings or to the Extraordinary Meetings; see IAEA, Nuclear Safety & Security, Convention on Nuclear Safety, available at http://www-ns.iaea.org/conventions/nuclear-safety.asp?s=6&l=41#1 (accessed 31/05/2013).

15 Official Journal of the European Union L 172/18 of 2 July 2009. See Kuş, S., Emmerechts, S., (2009) »A legislative framework for the safety of nuclear installations in the European Union«, *NEA updates, NEA News 2009* – No. 27.2, pp. 20 et seq.; Kilb, W., (2010) »The European Atomic Energy Community and its Primary and Secondary Law«, in OECD, *International Nuclear Law: History, Evolution and Outlook, 10th Anniversary of the International School of Nuclear Law,* OECD, pp. 43 et seq., particularly pp. 61-63; Garribba, M., Chirteş, A., Nauduzaite, M., (2009) »The Directive Establishing a Community Framework for the Nuclear Safety of Nuclear Installations: The EU Approach to Nuclear Safety«, *Nuclear Law Bulletin,* No. 84 (Volume 2009/2), pp. 23 et seq. See for the aspect of nuclear new build in a newcomer state World Nuclear Association, WNA Report (2011), Emerging Nuclear Energy Countries, WNA, London, p. 46 (*»Several barriers to entry must be overcome for a nuclear energy program to succeed. Before nuclear plants can be built, governments need to take a number of measures, including setting up professional and independent regulatory regimes, implementing policies on nuclear waste management and decommissioning, as well as establishing international non-proliferation measures and insurance arrangements for third party damage.«*) and pp. 20-21 (on Turkey's way to nuclear energy).

16 See footnote 6.

1 A brief view over history of nuclear energy in Turkey

The history of nuclear energy[17] started in the middle of the nineteen-fifties. Formally, »In 1956, General Secretariat of Atomic Energy Commission was established in Ankara by the law numbered 6821, as an organization affiliated to the Prime Ministry.«[18] In 1957 Turkey joined the International Nuclear Energy Agency (IAEA) as one of the first 27 members.[19] Already in 1962 and 1967 research and training centers were created (Çekmece Nuclear Research and Training Centre, CNAEM, Ankara Research and Training Center, ANAEM) and a research reactor started operation in 1962 (TR-1 Research Reactor);[20] for the first time commercial electricity production by a NPP in Turkey was subject of studies in

17 On the history of nuclear energy in Turkey see Turkish Atomic Energy Authority (TAEK), Institutional History, available at http://www.taek.gov.tr/en/ institutional/history.html (accessed 26/04/2013); IAEA, Country Nuclear Power Profiles, 2012 Edition, TURKEY (Updated 2012), available at http://www-pub.iaea.org/ MTCD/Publications/PDF/CNPP2012_CD/countryprofiles/Turkey/Turkey.htm (accessed 26/04/2013); NEA, Nuclear legislation in OECD countries: Turkey, available at http://www.oecd-nea.org/law/legislation/turkey.pdf (accessed 26/04/2013), and Country profile: Turkey, available at http://www.oecd-nea.org/general/profiles/turkey.html (accessed 26/04/2013); World Nuclear Association (WNN), Nuclear Power in Turkey (Updated 9 April 2013), available at http://www.world-nuclear.org/info/Country-Profiles/Countries-T-Z/Turkey/#.UXrzf0qQg1c (accessed 26/04/2013); Gürbüz, M., (2012) »AN EVALUATION OF TURKEY'S NUCLEAR ENERGY JOURNEY IN LIGHT OF THE DISCUSSIONS REGARDING NUCLEAR REACTORS' SAFETY IN THE WORLD«, *Enerji Hukuku Dergisi,* Volume 2012/2, pp. 109-129, 121–124. In Turkish only see the detailed description in the Nuclear Energy Report of THE UNION OF CHAMBERS OF TURKISH ENGINEERS AND ARCHITECTS: TMMOB FİZİK MÜHENDİSLERİ ODASI, (2011) NÜKLEER ENERJİ RAPORU 2011, Aralık 2011 Ankara, pp. 123–138, available at FMO_Nuk_Enr_Rap_2011_aralik_son as DOC (accessed 27/04/2013).

18 See TAEK (footnotes 9 and 17).

19 IAEA, Member States of the IAEA, available at http://www.iaea.org/About/Policy/MemberStates/ (accessed 26/04/2013).

20 See TAEK (footnotes 9 and 17) and TAEK, Çekmece Nuclear Research and Training Center, available at http://www.taek.gov.tr/en/institutional/affiliates/cekmece-nuclear-research-and-training-center.html (accessed 26/04/2013), and Ankara Nuclear Research and Training Center, available at http://www.taek.gov.tr/en/institutional/affiliates/ankara-nuclear-research-and-training-center.html (accessed 26/04/2013). Only in 2005 Saraköy Nuclear Research and Training Center (SANAEM) was created – see TAEK (footnotes 9 and 17) and TAEK, Saraköy Nuclear Research and Training Center, available at http://www.taek.gov.tr/en/institutional/affiliates/saraykoy-nuclear-research-and-training-center.html (accessed 26/04/2013).

1967 – 1970.[21] First specific and detailed nuclear legislation on licensing and radiation protection was established in the nineteen-eighties.[22] Nevertheless several tenders for the creation of NPPs in Turkey failed and only after the reorganization in 2002 (TAEK was transferred to the Ministry of Energy and Natural Resources by approval of the Presidency of the Republic of Turkey) Law No. 5710 of 2007 with concrete steps for the realization of NPPs in Turkey was the starting point for today's status.[23] Notwithstanding Law No. 5710 lays down the procedure for tender on selection of and contracts with the future constructor and operator of NPPs in Turkey, the choice of the project company for the Mersin-Akkuyu site was terminated by a Turkish-Russian agreement and was decided for the site of Sinop-İnceburun also by a bilateral international agreement with the engaged state, namely between Turkey and Japan.[24] Even a third site situated

21 Gürbüz, M. (footnote 17), p. 121. Even at that period for NPPs in Turkey sites were envisaged at Mersin-Akkuyu, Sinop-İnceburun and Kırklareli-İğneada, see ntvmsnbc, »Nükleer enerjinin Türkiye'deki tarihçesi«, available (only Turkish) at http://www.ntvmsnbc.com/id/25022241/ (accessed 28/04/2013); for details see chapters 2.2–2.4 below.

22 TAEK (footnotes 9 and 17).

23 Gürbüz, M. (footnote 17), pp. 122-124, Ercan, E., Schneider, H. (footnote 11), pp. 585, 588. Details on Law No. 2690 and Law No. 5710 can be found in chapter 3.3 below.

24 See for Akkuyu the AGREEMENT BETWEEN THE GOVERNMENT OF THE REPUBLIC OF TURKEY AND THE GOVERNMENT OF THE RUSSIAN FEDERATION ON COOPERATION IN RELATION TO THE CONSTRUCTION AND OPERATION OF A NUCLEAR POWER PLANT AT THE AKKUYU SITE IN THE REPUBLIC OF TURKEY, published (also with an English version) in the Official Gazette No. 27721 of 6 October 2010 (decision of the Council of Ministers of 27 August 2010 referring to Law No. 6007 of 15 July 2010 by which accordingly to Article 90 paragraph 1 of the Constitution of the Republic of Turkey the Turkish Grand National Assembly had approved the ratification, published in the Official Gazette No. 27648 of 21 July 2010); on 6 August 2009 Turkey and Russia had concluded the »Agreement between the Government of the Republic of Turkey and the Government of the Russian Federation for Cooperation in the Use of Nuclear Energy for Peaceful Purposes« (Official Gazette No. 27844 of 12 February 2011), available at http://www.taek.gov.tr/en/international/agreements.html (accessed 26/04/2013). As regards Law No. 5710 and the Turkish-Russian Agreement see Özdemir, H. E. (2012), *Nükleer Güç Santrallarının Kurulmasına İlişkin Hukuki Esaslar,* (not yet published as book), pp. 78-79. For Sinop see Taner Yıldız on 24 April 2013 at the 19. ICCI 2013, HABERLER.COM, available (only Turkish) at http://www.haberler.com/icci-2013-19-uluslararasi-enerji-ve-cevre-fuari-ve-58342-haberi/ (accessed 24/04/2013) and the declarations of 3 May 2013 (footnote 40).

in the north-western part of Turkey (Thrace) is actually concretely envisaged.[25]

2. Actual Status of the Projects in Mersin-Akkuyu and Sinop-İnceburun as well as Perspectives for a Third Site in Thrace

2.1 Strategic remarks on nuclear new build in Turkey

Turkey's importance in energy matters is repeatedly mentioned by the Turkish government with regard to the transport of gas from Russia and Central Asia states to Europe.[26] The eminent strategic and economic role of Russia for Turkey is obvious.[27] Therefore it was not surprising that by decision of the Turkish government Russia was chosen for the first NPP. Recently Russia underlined the role of cooperation in the energy sector with Turkey and mentioned especially the Akkuyu NPP project.[28] For the second site in Sinop-İnceburun the decision on the construction and opera-

25 Taner Yıldız at GAZETE TRAKYA, available (only Turkish) at http://www.gazetetrakya.com/Haber-Bakan_Yildiz_acikladi__3__nukleer _santralin_yeri_icin_igneada_adaylardan_biri-986952.gazetetrakya (accessed 26/04/2013), while the 10th Development Plan for Turkey (footnote 6), p. 119 no. 790, where 5.000 MWe are announced for this NPP, remains vague.

26 See Taner Yıldız (footnote 4), p. 8 (using the advantages of our geopolitical situation), and Efe, H., (2011) »TURKEY'S ROLE AS AN ENERGY CORRIDOR AND ITS IMPACT ON STABILITY IN SOUTH CAUCASUS«, *OAKA,* Volume 6, No. 12, pp. 118–147, available at http://www.usak.org.tr/dosyalar/dergi/rHs1uy5VFvZZz5RQBgHvskJVOFU8cR.pdf (accessed 30/04/2013).

27 See the reports published by the Akkuyu NGS A.Ş. project company on the meetings of Turkish Minister of Energy and Natural Resources with Russian authorities and with Russian Minister of Energy on 2 December 2012 (available at http://www.akkunpp.com/in-istanbul-a-meeting-between-the-general-director-of-the-russian-state-corporation-rosatom-sergei-kirienko-and-the-turkish-minister-of-energy-and-natural-resources-taner-yildiz-was-held/update and at http://www.akkunpp.com/in-istanbul-a-meeting-between-the-russian-minister-of-energy-aleksandr-novak-and-the-turkish-minister-of-energy-and-natural-resour-ces-taner-yildiz-was-held-recently/update – accessed 29/04/2013) and of Prime Minister Erdoğan with Russian President Putin on 4 December 2012 (available at http://www.akkunpp.com/in-istanbul-negotiations-between-russian-president-vladimir-putin-and-prime-minister-of-the-republic-of-turkey-recep-erdogan-were-held/update – accessed 27/04/2013) and the declarations of Russian Foreign Minister Lavrov on 16 April 2013, available (only Turkish) at http://www.trthaber.com/haber/dunya/rusyadan-turkiye-iliskileri-ile-ilgili-onemli-aciklama-82644.html (accessed 27/04/2013).

28 See Russian Foreign Minister Lavrov (footnote 27).

tion company was expected to be taken probably also for strategic reasons.[29] Anyhow, for each project all kinds of safety measures have priority and thus any concern of the public with regard to the accidents of Chernobyl and Fukushima shall be avoided, Turkish Minister for Energy and Natural Resources (ETK Minister) Taner Yıldız underlined on 26 April 2013.[30]

2.2 The Mersin-Akkuyu site

As place for a NPP the Mersin-Akkuyu site in the south of Turkey at the coast of the Mediterranean Sea was envisaged already in the late sixties and examined in depth by the Turkish Energy Commission's Nuclear Plants' Office starting in 1974 taking into account particularly aspects of earthquake, meteorology and oceanography; a site license was granted on the basis of a report submitted to the Atomic Energy Commission in 1976; whether this license was already or has still to be transferred to Akkuyu NGS as the construction and operation company is not known nor the procedure to be realized for such a transfer;[31] however, Article 13 paragraph 1

29 See Taner Yıldız for example on 4 April 2013, available (only Turkish) at http://www.trthaber.com/haber/ekonomi/sinop-nukleer-santralini-japon-fransiz-ortakligi-yapacak-81022.html (accessed 04/04/2013), and on 24 April 2013 (at this occasion Minister Yıldız considered possible a public-private-partnership for the Sinop NPP), available (only Turkish) at HABERLER.COM: http://www.haberler.com/icci-2013-19-uluslararasi-enerji-ve-cevre-fuari-ve-4558342-haberi/ (accessed 24/04/2013). For the final political decision see chapter 2.3 below.

30 See (only Turkish) TRT TÜRK at http://www.trtturk.com.tr/haber/yildiz-akkuyu-ve-sinopta-yapilacak-nukleer-santraller-icin-her-turlu-tedbiri-alacagiz.html (accessed 26/04/2013) and oda TV at http://www.odatv.com/n.php?n=bakan-yildizakkuyu-turkiyenin-en-guvenli-ve-saglam-yapisi-olacak-2604131200 (accessed 26/04/2013). The Ministry of Energy and Natural Resources is abbreviated in Turkish ETKB (Enerji ve Tabii Kaynaklar Bakanlığı).

31 For the site license of 11 June 1976 see for example (only Turkish), SİNOP NÜKLEER TEKNOLOJİ MERKEZİ, 12 Şubat 2008, slide 11 (and for the site works slides 17-39), available at http://www.taek.gov.tr/belgeler-formlar/mevzuat/yonerge-kilavuzlar/genelge-yonerge/taek-olcutleri/Sinop-N%C3%BCkleer-Teknoloji-Merkezi/ (accessed 26/06/2013), ntvmsbc, »Nükleer enerjinin Türkiye'deki tarihçesi« (footnote 21), TÜRKİYE'DE NÜKLEER ENERJİNİN TARİHÇESİ, available at http://www.nukleer.web.tr/cgi-bin/showhtml.cgi?turkiye/tarihce (accessed 27/04/2013), Adalıoğlu, U., (2002) »TÜRKİYE'DE NÜKLEER ENERJİNİN TARİHÇESİ VE GELİŞİMİ«, available (only Turkish) at http://www.nukte.org/node/122 (accessed 27/04/2013), Aslan, S., (2011) »Ak-

of the Decree on Licensing of Nuclear Installations of 1983 requires that the applicant for the construction license has obtained a site license.

After several failures of tenders, finally based on Law No. 5710 in 2009 the Mersin-Akkuyu site was definitely determined by the Turkish-Russian Agreement of 12 May 2010.[32] This agreement implies especially construc-

---

kuyu'da Nükleer Maceranın Tarihçesi«, available (only Turkish) at http://www.kaldiracdergi.com/index.php?option=com_content&view=article&id=195:akkuyuda-nuekleer-macerann-tarihcesi-sabahat-aslan&catid=22:ariv-mart-2011-119say&Itemid=10 (accessed 27/04/2013), and TMMOB (footnote 17), p. 125. The sources cited are not clear with regard to the institution which granted the license; on the one hand the Turkish Energy Authority (abbreviation in Turkish TEK) is mentioned as competent institution for the site license, on the other hand the Atomic Energy Commission (abbreviation in Turkish AEK) is referred to, especially in SİNOP NÜKLEER TEKNOLOJİ MERKEZİ, slide 11. For Law No. 1312 of 15 July 1970 establishing TEK see Official Gazette No. 13559 of 25 July 1970. The AEK based on Law No. 6821 (footnote 9) was competent for all scientific and technical subjects related to nuclear energy (Article 2 lit. a of Law No. 6821), competent also for site investigations and moreover in principle for the coordination of administrative activities (Article 1 of Law No. 6821). TEK based on Law No. 1312 had to construct and operate electricity production facilities and plants or to arrange the construction or operation of such facilities and plants (Article 3 lit. b and c of Law No. 1312). For the site see (only Turkish) TAEK, Akkuyu Nükleer Santral Sahası, available at http://www.taek.gov.tr/nukleer-guvenlik/nukleer-enerji-ve-reaktorler/165-akkuyu-nukleer-guc-santrali/431-akkuyu-nukleer-santrali-sahasi.html (accessed 29/04/2013). As regards the subject of transfer of the site license (of which it is not known to whom it was accorded) to Akkuyu NGS in practice the site license's scientific and factual data possibly could be actualized in the framework of the construction licensing process within the Preliminary Safety Analysis Report accordingly to Article 14 no. 1 of the Decree on Licensing of Nuclear Installations of 1983 (see footnote 9) which reads as follows: *»The Preliminary Safety Analysis Report must include the following information: 1. New information related to site and its environment acquired after the issuance of site report.»*

32 See footnote 24 and 10th Development Plan for Turkey (footnote 6), p. 117 no. 781. Turkish Constitutional Court's ruling of 1 June 2012 upholds conformity of Law No. 6007 of 15 July 2010 (Agreement of 12 May 2010) with the Constitution (as of 18 June 2013 the ruling is not yet published in the Official Gazette and a date for the publication cannot be given; by the way, the Commission of the Turkish Grand National Assembly for a new Constitution consented on 17 June 2013 that rulings of the Turkish Constitutional Court should be published only after the reasons for the judgement are finalized – *»yüksek mahkemenin kararları kesin olacak ve bu kararlar, gerekçesi yazılmadan hiçbir surette açıklanamayacak«* –, see TRT HABER at http://www.trthaber.com/haber/gundem/anayasa-mahkemesiyle-ilgili-uzlasma-89822.html – accessed 25/06/2013). For further steps following the agreement see AKKUYU NGS AŞ, Project History, available

tion and operation of a Russian type of reactor – third-generation standardised VVER-1200 (V-392M and V-491) reactor of 1200 MWe gross and 3200 MWt like in the AES-2006 plant at Novovoronezh –, the BOO (build operate own) model accomplished by a company under Turkish legislation for construction, operation and decommissioning including that spent fuel is taken back by Russia, future ownership of the Akkuyu NGS project company, price calculation for produced electricity and references to obligations on non-proliferation, physical protection and nuclear liability.[33] Article 8 paragraph 1 clearly states that *»The NPP shall be licensed and inspected in accordance with the laws and regulations of the Republic of Turkey in terms of nuclear safety and radiation protection.«* Therefore the next steps required to be undertaken by the Akkuyu Project Company are the application for the construction license and, if necessary, the submission of a report for Environmental Impact Assessment (EIA), further-

at http://www.akkunpp.com/project-history-2 (accessed 29/04/2013). For the last tender see Gürbüz, M. (footnote 17), p. 18.

33 Articles 3, 5, 10, 12, 15 and 16 of the Agreement. See on this agreement and the BOO model particularly Kuzeyli, K. (2012), *The Akkuyu Nuclear Power Plant Project – Risks and Obligations Under Nuclear Law,* unpublished thesis (Master of Laws in International and Comparative Nuclear Energy Law and Policy) at the University of Dundee of August 2012, pp. 16 – 21, Gürbüz, M. (footnote 17), pp. 126-127, TMMOB (footnote 17), p. 131, TAEK – Akkyuyu Nuclear Power Plant (available at http://www.taek.gov.tr/en/institutional/akkuyu-nuclear-power-plant.html – accessed 20/04/2013), Centre for Economics and Foreign Policy Studies (2011), *The Turkish Model for Transition to Nuclear Power,* Istanbul, pp. 91 et seq. and pp. 126 et seq., available at http://www.edam.org.tr/EDAMNukleer/edamreport.pdf (accessed 20/05/2013), Ercan, E., Schneider, H. (footnote 11), p. 588 right column with footnote 65. Details on the project company are presented by AKKUYU NGS AŞ, Akkuyu NPP JSC, available at http://www.akkunpp.com/akkuyu-npp-jsc (accessed 29/04/2013). For the Russian VVER-1200 reactor type see World Nuclear Association, Advanced Nuclear Power Reactors, available at http://www.world-nuclear.org/info/Nuclear-Fuel-Cycle/Power-Reactors/Advanced-Nuclear-Power-Reactors/#.UY1LIkqQg1c (accessed 10/05/2013), and AKKUYU NGS AŞ, NPP, GENERAL INFORMATION ABOUT AKKUYU NPP, available at http://www.akkunpp.com/npp-2 (accessed 31/05/2013). By the way, in the United States a comparable BOO model would perhaps not be accepted, because license could not be granted if the operating company belongs exclusively to a foreign owner (on 30 August 2012 the judges of the Atomic Safety and Licensing Board of the US Nuclear Regulatory Commission [NRC] ruled this decision in an arbitration against which could be appealed to the five NRC Commissioners; see Nuklearforum Schweiz of 17 September 2012).

more to continue working on physical protection measures.[34] TAEK for its part has to provide technical support capacities for the construction licensing process, although international experts appraised technical works at the site.[35] As announced by the Akkuyu Project Company the construction

34 For construction license see Articles 13–21 of the Decree on Licensing of Nuclear Installations of 1983 (footnote 10; for details see chapter 3.3.4 below) and TAEK, Akkuyu Nuclear Power Plant: *»APC started site investigations in Akkuyu for updating the site characteristics and parameters according to the national procedures laid out in the Decree on Licensing of Nuclear Installations«,* available at http://www.taek.gov.tr/en/institutional/akkuyu-nuclear-power-plant.html (accessed 29/04/2013), and TAEK, Akkuyu Nükleer Güç Santrali – Gelişmeler, on the updated site report and the evaluation by TAEK in May and June 2012, available (only Turkish) at http://www.taek.gov.tr/nukleer-guvenlik/nukleer-enerji-ve-reaktorler/165-akkuyu-nukleer-guc-santrali/432-akkuyu-ngs-gelismeler .html (accessed 26/06 /2013), finally AKKUYU NGS AŞ (2012), *Project History, »06.2012 Transfer of the Updated Akkuyu NPP Site Report to TAEK«,* available at http://www.akkunpp.com/project-history-2 (accessed 29/04/2013); with regard to EIA see TAEK, (2013) »2012 Yılı Faaliyet Raporu«, Ankara, p. 45, available since 30/04/2013 (only Turkish) at http://www.taek.gov.tr/belgeler-formlar/sgm/faaliyet_raporlari/TAEK-2012-Y%C4%B1l%C4%B1-Faaliyet-Raporu/ (accessed 30/04/2013), AKKUYU NGS Elektrik Üretim Anonim Şirketi (2011), *AKKUYU NÜKLEER GÜÇ SANTRALI PROJESİ, ÇEVRESEL ETKİ DEĞERLENDİRMESİ BAŞVURU DOSYASI,* Ankara, available (only Turkish) at http://www.csb.gov.tr/dosyalar/images/file/akkuyungscbd.pdf (accessed 28/04/2013), p. 3, and Dünya Enerji Konseyi (World Energy Council) Türk Milli Komitesi, Enerji Raporu 2012, Aralık 2012, Ankara, p. 195, available (only Turkish) at http://www.dektmk.org.tr/upresimler/enerjirapor2012.pdf (accessed 29/04/2013): EIA report was submitted on 2 December 2011 to the competent Ministry of Environment and City Planning and was presented from 23 February 2012 on to the public with which was held a meeting on 29 March 2012; for details on EIA legislation relevant for NPPs see chapter 4.1 below. Lastly the ruling of the Council of State of 13 February 2012 bringing to a stop the execution of the environmental arrangement plan for the Mersin-Karaman planning area in which is situated the Mersin-Akkuyu NPPs' site has to be mentioned (T.C. Danıştay Altıncı Daire Esas No: 2011/6066) as well as the Council of State's ruling of 1 April 2013 and the afterwards recently published new regulation on exemptions from EIA (see chapter 4.1 below). For activities on physical protection see TAEK, (2013) »2012 Yılı Faaliyet Raporu«, Ankara, p. 47.

35 TAEK's tenders for technical support were not yet successful; the third »Tender for Procurement of Technical Support Services During Review and Assessment of Construction License Application for Akkuyu Nuclear Power Plant« No: 2012/190420 was cancelled on 22 March 2013; the announcement of TAEK is available at http://www.taek.gov.tr/en/latest-news/1042-announcement-of-cancellation-of-tender-no-2012-190420.html (accessed 28/04/2013). TAEK started a new tentative by announcing on 12 June 2013 the invitation to an *»Informative Meeting on Procurement for Akkuyu NPP Technical Support«* on 25 June 2013, the outcome of this meeting was published on 28 June 2013 (Bidders Meeting

license shall be granted in 2014, construction will start in 2015 and operation of the first reactor is envisaged to start in 2020.[36] The total capacity of the NPP at the site will be 4800 MWe.

2.3 The Sinop-İnceburun site

At this site situated in the north of Turkey at the coast of the Black Sea in 2008 a center for nuclear power engeneering was established.[37] The nega-

Presentation), available at http://www.taek.gov.tr/en/news-flash/1077-informative-meeting-on-procurement-for-akkuyu-npp-technical-support-2.html (accessed 23/06/2013) respectively at http://www.taek.gov.tr/en/latest-news/1080-bidders-meeting-presentation.html (accessed 01/07/2013). By the way, the President of the Republic could request the State Supervisory Council to conduct an inquiry, inspection or investigation of TAEK's tender procedures (Article 108 paragraph 1 of the Constitution – see footnote 47). – See for international appraisal of technical works at the site Akkuyu NPP news, available at http:// www.akkunpp.com/akkuyu-npp-news-2 (accessed 08/05/2013), 27.08.2012 *»IAEA experts highly appraised engineering surveys on Akkuyu NPP site«*. In the framework of assistance to the Turkish Atomic Energy Agency (TAEK) the IAEA's representatives visited the Akkuyu NPP site last August (General Designer – Atomenergoproject OJSC, Moscow) to make a peer review of the nuclear power plant siting and become familiar with the conducted engineering surveys; see further Akkuyu NGS haberleri, available (only Turkish) at http://www.akkunpp.com/akkuyu-ngs-haberleri (accessed 08/05/2013), 05.09. 2012 *»Akkuyu santralına uzmanlardan tam not«*: Uluslararası Atom Enerjisi Kurumu (UAEK) uzmanları, Mersin'in Gülnar İlçesi'ne bağlı Büyükeceli Beldesi'nde yapılacak Akkuyu Nükleer Santrali sahasındaki çalışmaları inceledi.

36 See for the establishment of the project company Akkuyu Electricity Generation JSC on 13 December 2010 and for TAEK recognizing on 7 February 2011 the project company as the owner according to Article 6 of the Decree on Licensing of Nuclear Installations TAEK, Akkuyu Nuclear Power Plant, available at http://www.taek.gov.tr/en/institutional/akkuyu-nuclear-power-plant.html (accessed 31/05/2013) and AKKUYU NGS AŞ, Project History, available at http://www.akkunpp.com/project-history-2 (accessed 31/05/2013); for licensing, construction and operation dates see AKKUYU NGS AŞ, Project implementation, available at http://www.akkunpp.com/project-implementation (accessed 29/04/2013), and Akkuyu NGS haberleri, available (only Turkish) at http://www.akkunpp.com/akkuyu-ngs-haberleri (accessed 08/05/2013): 03.04. 2013 Akkuyu'da İnşaat 2015 Sonunda Başlayacak, TMMOB (footnote 17), p. 104 (construction will start in 2013), Dünya Enerji Konseyi (World Energy Council) Türk Milli Komitesi, Enerji Raporu 2012 (footnote 34), p. 195, and 10th Development Plan for Turkey (footnote 6), p. 118 no. 790.

tive experiences on tenders in order to select and appoint a company for construction and operation of a NPP at the site of Mersin-Akkuyu seem to have determined the Turkish government as regards the Sinop-İnceburun site not to procede on the basis of Law No. 5710 of 2009 by a tender but to negotiate directly with interested partner companies respectively the origin states of the interested companies.[38] On 24 April 2013 ETK Minister Taner Yıldız informed that Japan and China are the last two applicants for the NPP at the Sinop-İnceburun site, while on 2 May 2013 he proved true a report of a Japanese newspaper that a Japanese-French consortium had won the battle for the Sinop-İnceburun site and that in an agreement a two years period for site investigations will be fixed in order to confirm the site's appropriateness.[39] On 3 May 2013 already the Prime Ministers of Turkey and Japan signed two agreements, one on construction and operation of four reactors of type ATMEA1 by a French-Japanese joint venture at the Sinop-İnceburun site, time of beginning operation is ten years later in 2023, if possible earlier, and one on cooperation in the use of nuclear energy for peaceful purposes.[40] The final total capacity of the NPP at Sinop-İnceburun will be about 4480 MWe.

37 See Sinop Nükleer Teknoloji Merkezi (12 Şubat 2008), available (only Turkish) at http://www.taek.gov.tr/belgeler-formlar/func-directinfo/97/; the site characteristics are shown on slides 5-7.

38 Dünya Enerji Konseyi (World Energy Council) Türk Milli Komitesi, Enerji Raporu 2012 (footnote 34), p. 196.

39 At the 19. ICCI 2013 (footnote 24) and at TRT HABER of 2 May 2013, available (only Turkish) at http://www.trthaber.com/haber/ekonomi/sinop-nukleer-santrali-japon-fransiz-ortakliginin-84567.html (accessed 02/05/2013). See further Prime Minister Erdoğan of 2 May 2013: »Sinop'taki nükleer santrali Japonya yapacak«, ZAMAN at http://www.zaman.com.tr/_erdogan-sinoptaki-nukleer-santrali-japonya-yapacak_2085049.html (accessed 03/05/2013).

40 See TRT HABER, »2. nükleer santral için rakam netleşti«, 3 Mayıs 2013, available (only Turkish) at http://www.trthaber.com/haber/gundem/2-nukleer-santral-icin-rakam-netlesti-84720.html (accessed 03/05/2013), ZAMAN, »Erdoğan: Sinop'taki nükleer santrali Japonya yapacak«, available (only Turkish) at http://www.zaman.com.tr/_erdogan-sinoptaki-nukleer-santrali-japonya-yapacak_2085049.html (accessed 03/05/2013), and 10th Development Plan for Turkey (footnote 6), p. 117 no. 781 and pp. 118-119 no. 790. See also Le Monde.fr, M Économie du 2 mai 2013, Le duo Mitsubishi-Areva va construire quatre réacteurs nucléaires en Turquie, available at http://www.lemonde.fr/economie/article/2013/05/02/le-duo-mitsubishi-areva-va-construire-quatre-reacteurs-nucleaires-en-turquie_3169790_3234.html (accessed 03/05/2013), and wnn world nuclear news, »WNN First Selection of Atmea1 nuclear reactor« of 3 May 2013, available at http://www.world-nuclear-news.org/NN_First_selection_of_Atmea1_nuclear_reactor_0305132.html (accessed 15/05/2013). For ATMEA1 see World Nu-

Meanwhile TAEK is preparing administrative capacities for the licensing phase, the start of operation is intended for 2023, whereas the partition of parts of the operation company and the role of Turkish Energy Electricity Generation Corporation (EÜAŞ) is not yet decided.[41] Nevertheless it has to be stated that the selection procedure of the company for construction and operation of the NPP was postponed several times.[42] Moreover,

---

clear Association, Advanced Nuclear Power Reactors, available at http://www.world-nuclear.org/info/Nuclear-Fuel-Cycle/Power-Reactors/Advanced-Nuclear-Power-Reactors/#.UY1LIkqQg1c (accessed 10/05/2013), and ATMEA available at http://www.atmea-sas.com/scripts/ATMEA/publigen/content/templates/ Show.asp?P=57&L=EN (accessed 15/05/2013). An anticipated start for operation required the Turkish Prime Minister on 3 May 2013, see TÜRKİYE CUMHURİYETİ BAŞBAKANLIK, »Nükleer santral, Türk mühendislik tecrübesinin, deneyiminin ve ekonomik girişiminin de adımı olacak«, available (only Turkish) at http://www.basbakanlik.gov.tr/Forms/pActuelDetail.aspx (accessed 03/05/2013). Turkey signed bilateral agreements on nuclear cooperation with France on 21 September 1999 (Agreement Between the Government French Republic and The Government of the Republic of Turkey for Co-operation in the Peaceful Uses of Nuclear Energy, ratified on 18 May 2011), and with Japan on 3 May 2013 (Agreement between the Government of the Republic of Turkey and the Government of Japan for Cooperation in the Use of Nuclear Energy for Peaceful Purposes, ratification is outstanding), see TAEK, Anlaşmalar Tablosu, available (Turkish and English) at http://www.taek.gov.tr/kurumsal/uluslararasi/anlasmalar-tablosu.html (accessed 11/06/2013).

41 TAEK, (2013) »2012 Yılı Faaliyet Raporu«, Ankara, p. 46, available since 30/04/2013 (only Turkish) at http://www.taek.gov.tr/belgeler-formlar/sgm/faaliyet_raporlari/TAEK-2012-Y%C4%B1l%C4%B1-Faaliyet-Raporu/ (accessed 30/04/2013), T.C. ENERJİ VE TABİİ KAYNAKLAR BAKANLIĞI, NÜKLEER SANTRALLER VE ÜLKEMİZDE KURULACAK NÜKLEER SANTRALE İLİŞKİN BİLGİLER, p. 29, available (only Turkish) at http://www.enerji.gov.tr/yayinlar_raporlar/Nukleer_Santraller_ve_Ulkemizde_Kurulacak_Nukleer_Santrale_Iliskin_Bilgiler.pdf (accessed 29/04/2013). For the possible participation of state owned Turkish EÜAŞ in the operation company see T.C. Enerji ve Tabii Kaynaklar Bakanlığı, Bakanlık Haberleri, Bakan Yıldız Basın Mensuplarıyla Bir Araya Geldi. [06/05/2013], available (only Turkish) at http://www.enerji.gov.tr/index.php (accessed 07/05/2013).

42 On 20 October 2012 ETK Minister Taner Yıldız told the selection process with four competing countries is still ongoing, see TRT HABER at http://www.trthaber.com/haber/ekonomi/4-ulkeden-birini-secegegiz-60284.html (accessed 29/04/2013). On 22 January 2013 he announced that the tender process has reached the end, see TRT HABER at http://www.trthaber.com/haber/ekonomi/nukleer-santral-ihalesinde-sona-gelindi-71881.html (accessed 30/04/2013). At the 19th ICCI he declared on 24 April 2013 that only China and Japan are still competing after Canada and South Korea having dropped out of the process (see footnote 24).

the declaration with regard to nuclear safety of NPPs of ETK Minister Taner Yıldız that a NPP was desired which spent more money for safety[43] seems to be ambiguous. But it could be evaluated positively in the light of his declarations on nuclear safety of NPPs at the Mersin-Akkuyu and the Sinop-İnceburun sites he made on 26 April 2013 when he strongly assured that all kind of measures will be taken and thus no concerns should remain in the public.[44]

2.4 Third site for NPPs in Turkey in the north-western part (Thrace) at Kırklareli-İğneada, also situated at the coast of the Black Sea

After having been selected already in the nineteen seventies the site of Kırklareli-İğneada as third site for a NPP in Turkey is after concrete developments at the sites of Mersin-Akkuyu and Sinop-İnceburun more and more confirmed; specific plans and detailed preparative works for choosing the project company and starting administrative steps (site investigations, EIA, siting license) are not yet known while Turkish Prime Minister announced on 3 May 2013 a cooperation with Japan could be realised, Turkish ETK Minister adding that the works should be finished within two years and that finally the reactors at this site will be Turkish-designed, the latter confirmed by Prime Minister Erdoğan on 9 May 2013.[45] It could

43 »Taner Yıldız, nükleer santrallerin güvenliği için ›güvenliğe daha çok para harcanan bir santral istiyoruz.‹ diye konuştu.«, see (only Turkish) TRT HABER at http://www.trthaber.com/haber/ekonomi/4-ulkeden-birini-sececegiz-60284.html (accessed 29/04/2013).

44 See footnote 30.

45 Dünya Enerji Konseyi (World Energy Council) Türk Milli Komitesi, Enerji Raporu 2012 (footnote 34), p. 196. For the cooperation with Japan on site investigations see (only Turkish) ZAMAN, »Erdoğan: Sinop'taki nükleer santrali Japonya yapacak«, available (only Turkish) at http://www.zaman.com.tr/_erdogan-sinoptaki-nukleer-santrali-japonya-yapacak_2085049.html (accessed 03/05/2013). For duration of site works and for the goal of Turkish-designed reactors at the third site in Turkey see for example TRT HABER, »Hedef yerli nükleer - Yıldız: Yerli nükleer santraller hedefimizi büyük ihtimalle hayata geçireceğiz«, available (only Turkish) at http://www.trthaber.com/haber/gundem/hedef-yerli-nukleer-84960.html (accessed 06/05/2013), and Prime Minister Erdoğan: »Biz üçüncü nükleer santrali yaparız«, TRT HABER, available (only Turkish) at http://www.trthaber.com/haber/ekonomi/biz-ucuncu-nukleer-santrali-yapariz-85458.html (accessed 09/05/2013), and 10th Development Plan for Turkey (footnote 6), p. 119 no. 790, where 5.000 MWe are announced for this NPP.

be deemed probable that future activities depend on progress at the Mersin-Akkuyu and Sinop-İnceburun sites and projects.

3. *Nuclear legislation in Turkey*

3.1 General Remarks on the subjects and on the legal hierarchy of Turkish nuclear legislation

The main fields which nuclear legislation covers are nuclear safety and security, safeguards, radiological protection (radiation safety), nuclear third party liability for NPPs, other facilities or nuclear activities as for example enrichment plants, transport, import and export of nuclear material, storage and final disposal. Legal instruments result from international law, i.e. multilateral conventions or bilateral treaties as well as international recommendations and guidelines, and in principle from national legislation. On the national level the legal hierarchy constitutes of the constitution, laws including the transposed international conventions and agreements, decrees and regulations as binding legislation.[46] These binding norms are complemented by directives and guides, issued by administrative bodies as instruments of further detailing regulations to which they may not create contradictions; thus they constitute more than a self-commitment of the administration and consequently are binding somehow also external bodies; all these norms as administrative activities as well as the administrative acts on the basis of those norms can be reported to the competent courts for judicial review.[47]

46 Articles 115 and 124 together with Articles 2, 8 and 123 of the Constitution of the Republic of Turkey (see footnote 47). Turkish legislation comprises two kinds of binding norms subordinated to laws: In the field of nuclear legislation TAEK translates *»tüzük«* by decree, *»yönetmelik«* by regulation (details see chapter 3.3 below). For the terminology see also footnotes 49 and 50.

47 Article 125 (as amended on 7 May 2010) of the Constitution of the Republic of Turkey (voted as Law No. 2709 on 7 November 1982 and published in the Official Gazette No. 17874 of 20 November 1982), available in English at http://www.byegm.gov.tr/content.aspx?s=tcotrot (accessed 21/05/2013) or at http://www.constitution.org/cons/turkey/turk_cons.htm (accessed 07/06/2013). See for the character of directives and guides and their judicial review Kuluçlu, E., (2008) »TÜRK HUKUK SİSTEMİNDE NORMLAR HİYERARŞİSİ VE SAYIŞTAY DENETİMİNE ETKİLERİ«, *SAYIŞTAY DERGİSİ,* Sayı (Volume) 71, pp. 7 and 17. For details of the judicial review as regards licenses for NPPs see Özdemir, H. E. (footnote 24), pp. 179-182.

3.2. The Constitution of the Republic of Turkey and its importance for the existing Turkish nuclear legislation

The Constitution[48] is relevant for the use of nuclear energy in Turkey in many aspects. Firstly stands the obligation of guaranteeing health of people, also in a healthy and balanced environment (Article 56 paragraph 1 and 2); in matters of working conditions Article 50 together with Article 49 paragraph 2 (state obligation of protecting workers by improving general conditions of labour) has to be observed. The coasts of Turkey are mentioned in Article 43 with regard to special use for the community. Organizational rules exist in Articles 90 and 104 concerning international conventions, Articles 88 and 91 aiming at laws and decrees having the force of law, Article 115 with regard to issue regulations[49] and Article 124 with regard to issue by-laws[50] , finally Article 123 paragraphs 1 and 3 stating the necessity to regulate the administrative organization by law and Article 125 enabling the recourse to judicial review. Since Article 124 states that by-laws shall *»ensure the application of ... regulations«* the prior-ranking of regulations (TAEK: decrees) compared with by-laws (TAEK: regulations) is obvious. Recently the individual recourse to the Constitutional Court was introduced.[51] Consequently the aspect of judicial

48 See footnote 47.

49 See footnote 46, but the terminology used in the English version of the Constitution (see footnote 47) does not accord to the translations of nuclear legislation published by the Turkish Nuclear Energy Authority, Documents (English) Law Regulations (available at http://www.taek.gov.tr/en/belgeler-formlar/documents/ – accessed 01/05/2013). Article 115 paragraph 1 of the Constitution reads as follows: *»The Council of Ministers may issue regulations governing the mode of implementation of laws or designating matters ordered by law, provided that they do not conflict with existing laws and are examined by the Council of State.«*

50 See footnote 49. Article 124 paragraph 1 of the Constitution reads as follows: *»The Prime Ministry, the ministries, and public corporate bodies may issue by-laws in order to ensure the application of laws and regulations relating to their particular fields of operation, provided that they are not contrary to these laws and regulations.«* This makes clear that the »tüzük« (regulation respectively [so TAEK] decree) mentioned in Article 115 of the Constitution is superior to the »yönetmelik« (by-law respectively [so TAEK] regulation) as referred to in Article 124 of the Constitution.

51 See (only Turkish) T.C. ANAYASA MAHKEMESİ, Ekinci, H., Sağlam, M., (2012) 66 Soruda Anayasa Mahkemesine Bireysel Başvuru, Ankara, p. 7: *»Anayasa Mahkemesine bireysel başvuru, 7.5.2010 günlü, 5982 sayılı Türkiye Cumhuriyeti Anayasasının Bazı Maddelerinde Değişiklik Yapılması Hakkında Kanun'un 12 Eylül 2010 tarihinde yapılan referandumla kabul edilmesiyle hukuk sistemimize girmiş yeni bir hak arama yoludur.«*, available (only Turkish) at

review is rather important and significant for the consistency and the substance of legislation on the one hand as well as for executing administrative acts on the other hand.

3.3 Turkish nuclear legislation – concrete approach, development up to now, particular legal instruments in the main fields, perspectives

3.3.1 The approach of detailed and comprehensive Turkish nuclear legislation

After initial steps since 1956 in 1982 the Turkish Atomic Energy Authority (TAEK) was established and provided with competences in the field of nuclear science and technique as well as for the scope of nuclear legislation.[52] An important practical step was realised in 1983 by putting into force the Decree on Licensing of Nuclear Installations[53] which was never changed and is still in force and thus builds the basis for the outstanding licensing procedures for the planned NPPs at the sites of Mersin-Akkuyu and Sinop-İnceburun. In 1985 the Radiation Safety Decree[54] and in 1991 respectively in 2000 the Regulation on Radiation Safety, changed in 2004 and 2010, were put into force.[55]

---

http://www.ankarabarosu.org.tr/Siteler/2012yayin/2011sonrasikitap/66-Soruda-Anayasa-Mahkemesine-Bireysel-Basvuru.pdf (accessed 22/06/2013).

52 Details in chapter 3.3.2 below. For the *»Mission of TAEK«* see http://www.taek.gov.tr/en/institutional/mission-of-taek.html (accessed 17/04/2013).

53 Published in the Official Gazette No. 18256 of 19 December 1983; unofficial translation available at http://www.taek.gov.tr/en/belgeler-formlar/documents/Regulations/nuclear-safety/ (accessed 04/05/2013).

54 Official Gazette No. 18861 of 7 September 1985; an English version is available at http://www.taek.gov.tr/en/belgeler-formlar/documents/Regulations/radiation-safety/Radiation-Safety-Decree/ (accessed 17/04/2013). The basis of this decree are Articles 4 and 10 of Law No. 2690 of 1982 (Article 26 of the Decree): *»Environmental Protection Article 10- The secretariat measures to be taken for public health and radiation protection, during the implementation of the duties stated in Article 4 of this Law shall be determined by a decree to be prepared by the Turkish Atomic Energy Authority.«*

55 See Official Gazette No. 20983 of 6 September 1991, abolished nine years later by a new regulation in 2000 (Article 77 of this regulation), Official Gazette No. 23999 of 24 March 2000, changed for the last time by regulation of 2010, Official Gazette No. 27600 of 3 June 2010. An English version is available at http://www.taek.gov.tr/en/belgeler-formlar/documents/Regulations/radiation-safety/ (accessed 01/05/2013). The Regulation is based on Article 4 lit. d of Law No.

As a major step in Turkish nuclear legislation is evaluated the Law No. 5710 on *»Construction and Operation of Nuclear Power Plants and Energy Sale«* of 9 November 2007.[56] The previous version of this law, voted in the Turkish Grand National Assembly (TGNA) as Law No. 5654 of 8 May 2007, was sent back to the TGNA for revision by the President of the Republic of Turkey with notice of 24 May 2007 because of inconsistency with Articles 89 and 104 of the Constitution.[57] Law No. 5710 deals particularly with nuclear technology and energy economics: *»The aim of this law is to provide, in accordance with the energy plan and policy, the procedures and principles for the construction and operation of nuclear power plants and the sale of energy from those plants«* (Article 1). It seems not to be clear whether this law is only applied in the case of a tender for the construction and the operation of a NPP or has to be observed for all NPPs' activities, even if no tender had been accomplished, particularly in the context of licensing.[58] Law No. 5710 was nevertheless the signal for elaboration and putting into force of several regulations on nuclear safety issues in 2007 - 2009.[59] Following the failure of tenders for the Akkuyu

---

2690 of 1982 and *»The provisions of this Regulation shall be executed by the Prime Minister.«* (Article 79), what may be deemed to underline the importance contributed to radiation safety by the Prime Ministry, see Article 124 paragraph 1 of the Constitution of the Republic of Turkey (see footnote 50).

56 Official Gazette No. 26707 of 21 November 2007; unofficial translations in English and French are available at Nuclear Law Bulletin No. 80 2/2007, pp. 105 et seq.; remarks on the draft by Ercan, E., (2007) »Die Energiepolitik der Türkei mit besonderem Augenmerk auf die Kernenergie«, *International Journal for Nuclear Power,* January 2007 – atw 52. Jg. (2007) Heft 1 – Januar, pp. 18, 19. For the evaluation of this law see for example Kuzeyli, K. (footnote 33), pp. 2 et seq., Gürbüz, M. (footnote 17), pp. 17 – 21, Centre for Economics and Foreign Policy Studies (footnote 33), p. 126, and Özdemir, H. E. (footnote 24), pp. 12-62 and 78-79.

57 See (only Turkish) *TBMM Dönem: 23 Yasama Yılı: 2 (S. Sayısı: 45)* including the report of the Turkish Grand National Assembly's Commission on Industry, Commerce, Energy, Natural Resources, Knowledge and Technology of 24 October 2007 finalizing the version of Law No. 5710.

58 This aspect is discussed in chapter 5.1 below.

59 See Regulation on the Basic Quality Management Requirements for Safety in Nuclear Facilities, published in the Official Gazette No. 26642 of 13 September 2007 (unofficial translation available at http://www.taek.gov.tr/en/component/remository/documents/Regulations/nuclear-safety/orderby,2/page,2/ – accessed 01/05/2013), changed by regulation of 2009 (Official Gazette No. 27144 of 17 February 2009), Regulation on Specific Principles for Safety of Nuclear Power Plants, published in the Official Gazette No. 27027 of 17 October 2008 (unofficial translation available at http://www.taek.gov.tr/en/component/remository/documents/Regulations/nuclear-safety/orderby,2/page,2/ – accessed 01/05/2013),

NPP[60] and in consequence of negative rulings of the Constitutional Court of 6 March 2008[61] and the Council of State as a supreme administrative court of 16 September 2009 and of 4 March 2011[62] the Turkish government started early in 2010 bilateral negotiations with Russia because the only interested company in the tender process came from Russia; on 12 May 2010 the Turkish-Russian agreement was signed.[63] Afterwards further regulations, directives and guides especially aiming at ensuring nuclear safety were published.[64]

Regulation on Design Principles for Safety of Nuclear Power Plants, published in the Official Gazette No. 27027 of 17 October 2008 (unofficial translation available at http://www.taek.gov.tr/en/component/remository/documents/Regulations/nuclear-safety/orderby,2/page,1/ – accessed 01/05/2013), Regulation on Nuclear Power Plant Sites, published in the Official Gazette No. 27176 of 21 March 2009 (unofficial translation available at http://www.taek.gov.tr/en/component/remosi tory/documents/Regulations/nuclear-safety/ord erby,2/page,1/ – accessed 01/05/2013). For details see chapter 3.3.5 below.

60 See Kuzeyli, K. (footnote 33), pp. 5–8.

61 Published (only Turkish) in the Official Gazette No. 27173 of 18 March 2009.

62 See (only Turkish) T.C. DANIŞTAY İDARİ DAVA DAİRELERİ KURULU YD. İtiraz No. 2009/722 and T.C. DANIŞTAY ONÜÇÜNCÜ DAİRE Esas No: 2009/333 Karar No: 2011/876, further Kuzeyli, K. (footnote 33), p. 5.

63 See Kuzeyli, K. (footnote 33), pp. 5–8. For the Turkish-Russian agreement see footnote 24.

64 Directive on Determination of Licensing Basis Regulations, Guides and Standards and Reference Plant for Nuclear Power Plants, available at http://www.taek.gov.tr/en/component/remository/documents/Regulations/nuclear -safety/orderby,2/page,1/ (accessed 01/05/2013); the directive repealed the *»Directive on Principles of Licensing of Nuclear power Plants, approved by the Atomic Energy Commission at its meeting No. 113/4, dated 24/05/2010«,* Article 8- (1); Guide on Specific Design Principles, available at http://www.taek.gov.tr/en/component/remository/documents/Regulations/nuclear-safety/orde rby,2/page,1/ (accessed 01/05/2013). See for details of the directive Özdemir, H. E. (footnote 24), pp. 154-162, further together with details of the directive and the guide chapter 3.3.7 below. Further should be mentioned the Regulation of Nuclear Safety Inspections and Enforcement (published in the Official Gazette No. 26642 of 13 September 2007, unofficial translation available at http://www.taek.gov.tr/en/component/remository/documents/Regulations/nuclear-safe ty/orderby,2/page,2/ – accessed 01/05/2013, changed by regulation of 2008, published in the Official Gazette No. 27034 of 24 October 2008), the Directive on the Granting of Functions to Inspectors for Nuclear Safety (NÜKLEER GÜVENLİK DENETÇİSİ YETKİLENDİRİLMESİNE İLİŞKİN YÖNERGE, was formerly available – only Turkish – since 2 March 2012 at http://www.taek.gov.tr/belgeler-formlar/func-directinfo/739/) and the Regulation on Physical Protection of Nuclear Materials and Nuclear Facilities (Nükleer Tesislerin ve Nükleer Maddelerin Fiziksel Korunması Yönetmeliği), published in the Official

The activities in 2007 and the following two and a half years until the signing of the agreement with Russia on 12 May 2010 aimed at legally fixing basic requirements for safety in order to direct the tender process to safe NPP offers and to promote the safety legislation in Turkey step by step. The strategy for regulating nuclear safety following the agreement of 2010 seems having been changed: According to Article 6 paragraph 2 of the Directive on Determination of Licensing Basis Regulations, Guides and Standards and Reference Plant for Nuclear Power Plants[65] the legal safety approach aims at a step-by-step norm hierarchy for site selection, construction and operation of NPPs with *»a) regulations of the Republic of Turkey, b) IAEA Nuclear Safety Series documents under the categories of ›safety fundamentals‹ and ›safety requirements‹«,* c) if necessary *»nuclear regulations in the Vendor Country«* and d) if necessary *»a third country regulation conforming to relevant IAEA safety guides or to the design of the plant, for which the license application has been made«*. The execution of such a legal hierarchy in legislation seems to be not yet experienced and therefore comprises and implies high risks of failure in the case of judicial review.[66]

3.3.2 The development of systematic Turkish nuclear legislation and regulatory infrastructure

In today's view Law No. 2690 of 1982[67] establishing TAEK as regulatory body has to be deemed crucial for the understanding of Turkish nuclear law in force, particularly with regard to NPPs' site, construction and operation licenses. In accordance with Article 123 paragraphs 1 and 3 of the Constitution[68] TAEK is established as state authority and provided with clearly defined competences by a law voted by the Turkish Grand National Assembly. Following the objective of Article 1 of Law No. 2690 *»to*

Gazette No. 28300 of 22 May 2012, available (only Turkish) at http://www.taek.gov.tr/component/remository/mevzuat/yonetmelikler/nukleer-guvenlik/orderby,2/page,2/ – accessed 01/05/2013 (being translated at http://www.taek. gov.tr/en/component/remository/documents/Regulations/nuclear-safety/orderby,2/page,2/ – accessed 01/05/2013). For details see chapters 3.3.5 – 3.3.7 below.

65 See footnote 64.

66 See chapter 3.2 (at the end) above.

67 See footnote 9. In Article 4 lit. e the word *»instruction«* correctly reads *»construction«*.

68 See for the Constitution of the Republic of Turkey footnote 47.

render the peaceful use of atomic energy in Turkey for the benefits of state« and therefore *»to determine and recommend the basic principles and policies, to implement, organize, support, coordinate and control the scientific, technical and administrative studies and affairs«* Article 4 specifies these duties by implementing the duty of taking into account also *»the State's ... economic development«* (lit. a), further by the tasks

> »to determine the general principles to be complied with all kinds of ... special fissionable material ... used in nuclear fields and to make recommendations ... hereon« (lit. b),
>
> »to establish ... research and training centers, units, laboratories, test centers and pilot plants ... to direct the national industry towards the nuclear technology« (lit. c),
>
> »to determine the guiding principles and provisions for the protection against the damages of the ionizing radiation in the activities done using ... special fissionable materials ... and to determine the limits of legal liability« (lit. d),
>
> particularly »to give approval, permission and license related to the site selection, instruction [construction], operation and environmental protection of nuclear power and research reactors and nuclear fuel cycle facilities; to do necessary studies and controls, to limit (restrict) the operating authority in case of noncompliance with the permission or license; to cancel permanently or temporarily the permission or license given and to make recommendations to the Prime Minister for the shutdown of those installations; to prepare the necessary technical guides, decrees and regulations for those purposes« (lit. e),
>
> »to take the necessary measures or have them taken for the safe process, transport, permanent or temporary storage of the radioactive wastes of the nuclear facilities ...« (lit. f),
>
> »to train the personal who will work in the nuclear field or to assist their training when necessary ...« (lit. h), »to collect, disseminate and introduce the necessary information ... related to the application of atomic energy; to announce the necessary information to public; to enlighten the public in nuclear matters« (lit. i),
>
> »to carry out studies related to national and international law in the nuclear field and to propose the necessary regulatory arrangements« (lit. j) and
>
> »to prepare and implement the decrees and regulations determining the basis related to the protection of nuclear materials and facilities and to control the subjects related to those and to give comments about the regulations to be prepared by other institutions related to this subject« (lit. k).

Article 18 paragraph 2 provides that *»The regulations prepared by the Turkish Atomic Energy Authority shall enter into force after the approval of the Prime Minister.«*

In the light of the tasks, duties and competences of TAEK its function and role for the development of the nuclear legislation in Turkey and the execution of the detailed prescriptions and norms at the level below laws are evident. In particular the number of regulations published in the recent years is a strong proof hereon.[69] Moreover Law No. 2690 regulates the establishment of the Atomic Energy Commission (Article 6)[70] and the Advisory Council (Article 7).[71] These institutions as well as the Advisory Committee on Nuclear Safety[72] are assigned and attached to the President of TAEK[73] and their working systems are arranged by regulations (Article 6 lit. c paragraph 2 and Article 7 paragraph 4).[74]

- The Atomic Energy Commission (AEC) »meets at least four times a year« (Article 6 lit. c paragraph 1), is chaired by TAEK President, particularly »consists of the Vice Presidents, one member from each of the Ministries of National Defense, Foreign Affairs, Energy and Natural Resources ...« and »The Prime Minister, presides the Atomic Energy Commission's meetings whenever he deems necessary« (Article 6 lit. a paragraph 1 sentence one and paragraph 2) which underlines the importance of the AEC. The main duties of the AEC are »1) To fix the working principles and programs of the Turkish Atomic Energy Authority ... 2) To prepare and submit the draft bills and decrees related to nuclear field to the Prime Minister and to accept the regulations related to the Turkish Atomic Energy Authority« (Article 6 lit. b). An important role of AEC consists in deciding in substance on the site license, the limited work permit, the construction license, the full power operating permit and the operation license (Article 3, Article 12 paragraph 1, Article 17 paragraph 1, Articles 20 and 31 of the Decree on Licensing of Nuclear Installations of 1983).

---

69 See footnotes 59 and 64, for details chapter 3.3.5 below.

70 Details available at http://www.taek.gov.tr/en/institutional/atomic-energy-commission.html (accessed 17/04/2013).

71 Details available at http://www.taek.gov.tr/en/institutional/advisory-council.html (accessed 17/04/2013).

72 Details available at http://www.taek.gov.tr/en/institutional/advisory-committee-on-nuclear-safety.html (accessed 02/05/2013).

73 See *»TAEK Organization Chart«* at http://www.taek.gov.tr/en/institutional/taek-organization-chart.html (accessed 17/04/2013).

74 See Regulation on Working Procedures of Atomic Energy Commission, published in the Official Gazette No. 17927 of 13 January 1983, Regulation on Organization and Working Procedures of Advisory Council, published in the Official Gazette No. 19312 of 15 December 1986 and Regulation on the Establishment and Working Procedures of Advisory Committee on Nuclear Safety, published in the Official Gazette No. 23106 of 10 September 1997.

- The Advisory Council (AC) »studying the subject given by the Atomic Energy Commission submits its results and proposals to the Atomic Energy Commission. Turkish or foreign experts can be invited to the Advisory Council, can be consulted.« (Article 7 paragraphs 2 and 3).
- Advisory Committee on Nuclear Safety: The »Advisory Committee on Nuclear Safety performs the duties specified in the Decree on Licensing of Nuclear Installations. The Committee also comments on the work submitted by the Presidency.«[75] The Advisory Committee on Nuclear Safety assumes important functions within the licensing procedures, particularly by giving advice on reports submitted with the license application or by recommendations (Articles 5, 10, 15, 23, 29, 35, 54 and 55 of the Decree on Licensing of Nuclear Installations of 1983).
- Although the TAEK's Ethics Commission does not specifically refer to nuclear topics it should be mentioned for its tasks particularly related to the correct exercise of the tasks and to the fight against corruption.[76]

Law No. 2690 abolished Law No. 6821 of 1956[77] and thus transformed the Atomic Energy Commission into TAEK's system: »In 1956, General Secretariat of Atomic Energy Commission was established in Ankara by the law numbered 6821, as an organization affiliated to the Prime Ministry. In 1982, the Commission was restructured as Turkish Atomic Energy Authority affiliated to the Prime Ministry by the law numbered 2690.«[78] Finally it has to be noted that Law No. 5710 of 2007[79] states in Temporary Article 1: »TAEK shall carry out its duty … until a new institution which will execute the duty of regulating and inspection of nuclear activities is founded.« Notwithstanding this Temporary Article 1 it is not clear whether Law No. 5710 has to be observed hereafter in all activities for the construction and operation of NPPs.[80] Moreover, Temporary Article 1 creates

75 See at http://www.taek.gov.tr/en/institutional/advisory-committee-on-nuclear-safety.html (accessed 17/04/2013). For the duties within the licensing process see chapter 3.3.4.1 below.

76 Details (only Turkish) available at http://www.taek.gov.tr/kurumsal/taek-etik-komisyonu.html (accessed 20/04/2013).

77 See footnote 9.

78 See Article 19, particularly lit. a of Law No. 2690, and http://www.TAEA.gov.tr/en/institutional/history.html (accessed 17/04/2013).

79 See footnote 56.

80 For detailed deliberations see chapter 5.1 below.

uncertainties with regard to the organizational structure of the competent authority in the future and thus a possible inconvenience during the licensing process.[81] Nevertheless, TAEK is up to now very active in the field of nuclear legislation[82] in conformity to Article 4 lit. j) of Law No. 2690.

3.3.3 Laws as legislation instruments – international conventions and agreements, national laws

International multilateral conventions and bilateral agreements are in Turkey legally at the level of national laws, but in case of contradiction they are prior-ranking.[83] Turkey is member of several conventions on nuclear and radiation safety as well as security, safeguards and third party liability, particularly the Paris Convention on Third Party Liability in the Field of Nuclear Energy, the Treaty on the Non-proliferation of Nuclear Weapons (NPT), the Convention on the Physical Protection of Nuclear Material (but not the Amendment to the Convention of 8 July 2005), the Convention on Early Notification of a Nuclear Accident, the Convention on Assistance in the Case of a Nuclear Accident or Radiological Emergency, the Joint Pro-

81 See Ercan, E., Schneider, H. (footnote 11), p. 589 (chapter 5. with footnote [81]), furthermore chapter 5.1.4 (with footnote 184) below.

82 See TAEK, »New Regulation of TAEK«, recently referring for example to the publications accomplished on 18 and 19 March 2013 of the Regulation on Radioactive Waste Management respectively the Regulation on Clearance in Nuclear Facilities and Removal of Site from Regulatory Control (both regulations published in the Official Gazette No. 25852 of 9 March 2013) at TAEK's homepage, available at http://www.taek.gov.tr/en/home.html (accessed 03/05/2013).

83 See Article 90 paragraph 5 of the Constitution (see footnote 47): (sentence 1) »*International agreements duly put into effect bear the force of law.*«, changed on 7 May 2004 by annexing a new sentence to paragraph 5: (sentence 3) »*In the case of a conflict between international agreements in the area of fundamental rights and freedoms duly put into effect and the domestic laws due to differences in provisions on the same matter, the provisions of international agreements shall prevail.*« See on the constitutional change Belgin, D., (2008) »Anayasa'nın 90. Maddesinde (7 Mayıs 2004) Yapılan Değişikliğin Getirdiği Sorunlar ve Çözüm Önerileri«, *Ankara Barosu Dergisi*, Yıl (Volume): 66, Sayı (Issue): 4, Güz 2008, pp. 110–113 (available – only Turkish – at http://www.ankarabarosu.org.tr/siteler/ankarabarosu/tekmakale/2008-4/10.pdf – accessed 10/05/2013) and uludağ sözlük, anayasa madde 90, available (only Turkish) at http://www.uludagsozluk.com/k/anayasa-madde-90/ (»*anayasamızda yer alan en önemli maddelerden birisidir. özünde : eğer uluslar arası antlaşma ile ülke içinde ki yazılı kanunlar arasında bir çelişki varsa, uluslar arası antlaşma geçerlidir.*«) – accessed 10/05/2013.

tocol Relating to the Application of the Vienna Convention and the Paris Convention, the Convention on Nuclear Safety and the International Convention for the Suppression of Acts of Nuclear Terrorism,[84] and concluded many agreements with other states especially on cooperation in the field of nuclear science and research as well as nuclear energy, the newest ones with Finland, China and Japan, dating of 20 September 2011, 9 April 2012 and 3 May 2013.[85]

After the Law No. 2690 of 1982 establishing TAEK[86] the Law No. 3154 of 19 February 1985 constituting the competences of the Turkish Ministry of Energy and National Resources (ETKB)[87] has to be mentioned. ETKB being in administrative hierarchy the responsible ministry for TAEK – consequently TAEK being subordinated to ETKB – has the task with regard to energy supply to investigate the country's short- and long-term energy needs, to support an appropriate energy supply policy and to take the necessary measures, especially in the areas of research, implementation, development, evaluation, control and protection, and to found and establish the appropriate institutions (Article 2 lit. a-c, f, g). In the recent years the most important task of ETKB's appropriate institu-

84 See TAEK (Türkiye Atom Enerjisi Kurumu), Anlaşmalar Tablosu 1-, available (bilingual Turkish and English) at http://www.taek.gov.tr/kurumsal/ uluslararasi/anlasmalar-tablosu.html or (in English only – Arrangements) at http://www.taek.gov.tr/en/international/agreements.html (accessed 03/05/2013). For the text of the conventions see IAEA, International Conventions and Agreements, available at http://www.iaea.org/Publications/Documents/Conventions/index.html (accessed 27/05/2013), and for the International Convention for the Suppression of Acts of Nuclear Terrorism see UN, available at http://www.un.org/en/sc/ctc/docs/conventions/Conv13.pdf (accessed 10/06/ 2013).

85 See TAEK (Türkiye Atom Enerjisi Kurumu), Anlaşmalar Tablosu 2- and 3-, available (bilingual Turkish and English) at http://www.taek.gov.tr/kurumsal/uluslararasi/anlasmalar-tablosu.html or (in English only – Arrangements) at http://www.taek.gov.tr/en/international/agreements.html (accessed 03/05/2013); Arrangement for Cooperation between the Radiation and Nuclear Safety Authority of Finland and the Turkish Atomic Energy Authority of 20 September 2011 and Agreement between The Government of the People's Republic of China and The Government of the Republic of Turkey for Cooperation in the Peaceful Uses of Nuclear Energy of 9 April 2012 (not yet approved); for the Agreement between the Government of the Republic of Turkey and the Government of Japan for Cooperation in the Use of Nuclear Energy for Peaceful Purposes of 3 May 2013 see footnote 40.

86 See chapter 3.3.2 above.

87 Law No. 3154 on the Establishment and Organization and the Tasks of the Ministry of Economics and Natural Resources of 19 February 1985, published (only Turkish) in the Official Gazette No. 18681 of 1 March 1985.

tions was the privatization of the energy market in Turkey.[88] Nuclear energy's development is underlined by the importance for Turkey to diminish the dependence of energy imports.[89]

Finally Law No. 5710 of 9 November 2007[90] seemed to constitute a crucial basis for the progress of Turkey's way to nuclear energy, but actually has no importance, since in the same way as on 12 May 2010 for the Mersin-Akkuyu site the instrument of international bilateral agreement was used on 3 May 2013 for the Sinop-İnceburun site and thus between Turkey and Japan an agreement was signed without having organized nor followed through a tender before.[91]

3.3.4 Decrees as legislation instruments

Decrees are voted and issued by the Council of Ministers; decrees govern »the mode of implementation of laws or designating matters ordered by law, provided that they do not conflict with existing laws and are examined by the Council of State« (Article 115 of the Constitution).

88 See Taner Yıldız (footnote 4), p. 8 bullet point 4 (»*Serbest piyasa koşullarına tam işlerlik kazandırmak ve yatırım ortamının iyileşmesini sağlamak*«) and pp. 28-30.

89 See Taner Yıldız (footnotes 4 and 5).

90 See footnote 56 and furthermore as instruments completing Law No. 5710 the »Criteria to be Met by Investors Who Will Construct and Operate Nuclear Power Plants« of 19 December 2007 (available at http://www.taek.gov.tr/belgeler-formlar/func-directinfo/94/ – accessed 05/05/2013) and the Regulation on Procedures and Principles with regard to Law No. 5710 (only Turkish) *»NÜKLEER GÜÇ SANTRALLARININ KURULMASI VE İŞLETİLMESİ İLE ENERJİ SATIŞINA İLİŞKİN KANUN KAPSAMINDA YAPILACAK YARIŞMA VE SÖZLEŞMEYE İLİŞKİN USUL VE ESASLAR İLE TEŞVİKLER HAKKINDA YÖNETMELİK«,* voted by the Council of Ministers on 10 March 2008 and published in the Official Gazette No. 26821 of 19 March 2008 (this regulation does not deal with nuclear safety topics); the Criteria and the Regulation are mentioned in Article 3 paragraph 3 of Law No. 5710.

91 See chapter 2.3 above.

3.3.4.1 Licensing of nuclear installations

For NPPs producing commercially electricity the Decree on Licensing of Nuclear Installations of 1983[92] remains unchanged until today, is still in force and therefore the fundamental legal basis for enabling by licensing the phases of siting, construction and operation of NPPs in Turkey (Articles 1 and 2 sentence 2 no. 7 and Article 8). Article 6 sentence 1 states that *»in order to construct and operate a nuclear installation, it is compulsory that a license is to be obtained from the Authority«* (TAEK); the wording could be understood as a general prescription meaning that all activities for achieving electricity production in a NPP are subject to previous licensing according to Articles 8-43, but in practice TAEK seems to be determined to accord a separate and precedent license to each company which intends to build and operate a NPP in Turkey, performed already for the Akkuyu NGS AŞ in 2011.[93]

92 Published in the Official Gazette No. 18256 of 19 December 1983; unofficial translation available at http://www.taek.gov.tr/en/belgeler-formlar/documents/Regulations/nuclear-safety/ (accessed 04/05/2013). See for details Özdemir, H. E. (footnote 24), pp. 142-173.

93 Özdemir, H. E. (footnote 24), pp. 159 and 161 evaluates the license required under Article 6 as the determination of the applicant (owner) and refers to Article 6 paragraph 6 of the Directive on Determination of Licensing Basis Regulations, Guides and Standards and Reference Plant for Nuclear Power Plants: *»The Owner shall be notified ..., upon recognition as the Owner in accordance with Article 6 of the Decree.«* (footnote 64). The wording taken in a general sense as the necessity of prior licensing Turkey fulfills by Article 6 of the Decree the requirement of Article 7 No. 2. lit. ii. of the Convention on Nuclear Safety of 17 June 1994 (IAEA INFCIRC 449 of 5 July 1994. Ratification by Turkey on 14 January 1995 and deposit on 8 March 1995, see http://www.iaea.org/Publications/Documents/Conventions/nuclearsafety_status.pdf - accessed 04/05/2013) and the requirement of Article 4 no.1 sentence 2 lit. (b) of the Council Directive 2009/71/EURATOM of 25 June 2009 establishing a Community framework for the nuclear safety of nuclear installations, published in the Official Journal of the European Union L 172/18 of 2.7.2009. Accordingly Article 174 paragraph 1 of the Criminal Code of the Republic of Turkey (*»Türk Ceza Kanunu«,* Law No. 5237 of 26 September 2004, published in the Official Gazette No. 25611 of 12 October 2004), deals with handling of dangerous nuclear materials without permit or license, available in Turkish at http://www.mevzuat.gov.tr/Metin.Aspx?MevzuatKod=1.5.5237&sourceXmlSearch=&MevzuatIliski=0 (accessed 23/05/2013) and in English at http://legislationline.org/documents/action/popup/id/6872/preview (accessed 23/05/2013). For the practice of TAEK to license the project company see footnote 36; comparable to Article 6 of the Decree on Licensing of Nuclear Installations Article 5 paragraph 1 of Law No. 5710 (see footnote 56) reads: *»The enterprise is obliged to obtain all kinds of permis-*

Since Article 6 sentence 2 features requirements for the applicant of the license who *»has to submit an application ... with enclosing documents describing the nature of the installation to be constructed and describing his technical and financial abilities«,* a license as practiced by TAEK seems legally to be conceivable, particularly as regards the objective conditions of technical and financial abilities. However, the requirements for the site license, the construction license and the operation license preceding permits comprise the aspect of technical abilities (Article 9 no. 2 for the site license, Article 14 no. 9 for the construction license and Article 23 paragraph 1 no. 5 for the commissioning permit and Article 26 paragraph 1 no. 3 for the fuel loading and pre-operational tests permit), moreover with Article 34 paragraph 1 *»it is compulsory that the applicant should provide a regular and periodical training for his licensed operating staff«* what may be evaluated as a requirement for technical abilities, thus only the »financial abilities« of the applicant are solely evaluated under Article 6. On the other hand Article 6 being taken as a general norm on the necessity of licensing may require to evaluate the *»financial abilities«* of the applicant at each step of the licensing phases; that would be more appropriate, because the circumstances of this requirement may develop during the licensing phases and consequently are still or even more important when according the definitive operating license. Finally it seems not to be clear, whether Article 35 on *»Revoking the license«* is applicable for the license approved accordingly to Article 6, because the wording *»technical and financial abilities«* of Article 6 is not reflected in Article 35. Furthermore the wording of Article 8 within part one section three of the decree underlines the view of not taking Article 6 as a requirement for the applicant to obtain a separate license. Thus the *»financial«* requirements of the CNS and the EURATOM directive of 2009 could be deemed to be widely accomplished. A provisional overall evaluation therefore results in the statement, that in either case the obligations under the Convention on Nuclear Safety (Article 11 in connection with Article 8 lit. iv) and the pre-

sions, approvals and licences required by this law and the other legislation.«, while Article 3 paragraph 5 of this law dealing with a license to be granted by the Energy Market Regulatory Authority (EPDK) to the enterprise selected in the framework of the tender process seems to substitute this license to that one required in Article 6 of the Decree on Licensing of Nuclear Installations. Finally it may be stated that Articles 5 (PROJECT COMPANY), 6 (IMPLEMENTATION OF THE PROJECT) and 8 (LICENSING; APPROVALS AND REGULATIONS) of the Turkish-Russian Agreement on Akkuyu of 12 May 2010 (see footnote 24) do not shed light on the matter.

scriptions of Article 6 no. 5 together with Article 5 no. 3 of the Council Directive 2009/71/EURATOM of 25 June 2009 establishing a Community framework for the nuclear safety of nuclear installations are not completely met. By the way, no requirement for licenses or permits refers to the reliability of the applicant as a subjective aspect, such as Article 24 of the Swiss Atomic Energy Act or Section 7 paragraph 2 no. 1 of the German Atomic Energy Act.

The licensing process starts with the site license (Article 8 no. 1, Articles 9–12). The following construction license (Article 8 no. 2, Articles 13–21) is separated in the limited work permit and the construction license (Article 13). The final operating license (Article 8 no. 3, Articles 22–35) is in a first step the commissioning permit, afterwards the fuel loading and pre-operational test permit and at least the full power operating permit and the operating license (Article 22). Moreover Article 33 allows for a permit to operate at reduced power. Each licensing procedure is dependant from an application in which the applicant has to demonstrate by means of *»documents describing the nature of the installation to be constructed and describing his technical and financial abilities«* (Article 6 sentence 2) that particularly nuclear safety will be ensured in conformity with the requirements of the decree (primarily in Articles 12, 17/18, 20/21, 24, 27, 28 and 31/32) as well as other pertinent nuclear legislation[94] and to submit therefore the relevant documents and reports to the licensing authority TAEK (Articles 6, 9, 14, 23, 26, 29). As regards nuclear third party liability the applicant shall provide insurance or other financial guarantees according to the provisions of the Paris Convention (Article 7). The contents of the Site Report, the Preliminary Safety Analysis Report and the documents for the Commissioning Permit are listed in detail in Articles 9, 14 and 23.

The licensing process for NPPs is conducted by the Vice President for Nuclear Power and Safety of TAEK (afterwards cited as Vice President), the Advisory Committee on Nuclear Safety and TAEK's Department of Nuclear Safety (Article 4 sentence 1). The documents and reports submitted by the applicant to TAEK are forwarded to the Advisory Committee on Nuclear Safety for its advice (Article 10 sentence 1, Article 15 paragraph 1 sentences 1 and 2, Article 23 paragraph 2 sentence 2, Article 26 paragraph 2 sentence 2, Article 29 paragraph 2 sentence 2). In the case of deficiencies in the documents and in the reports the applicant is notified

94 See details in chapter 3.3.5 and 3.3.7 below. Whether other pertinent legislation not directly related to nuclear subjects (see chapter 4.2 below) has to be observed within the nuclear licensing process is not evident, but should be recommended.

about this, and he *»has to complete and correct these deficiencies and to submit them to the Authority as soon as possible«* (Article 10 sentences 2 and 3; see also Article 15 paragraph 1 sentence 3 and paragraph 2). After the accomplishment of necessary studies, inspections, assessments and tests required by the relevant articles of the decree the Nuclear Safety Department of TAEK prepares an evaluation report in which the views of the Advisory Committee on Nuclear Safety are included; subsequently the Vice President *»submits a report to The President of the Authority indicating the results of the [evaluation] report and work realized«* (Article 11). The President of TAEK takes the evaluation report as well as the report prepared by the Vice President to the Atomic Energy Commission (AEC) which has to determine whether the evaluation report is adequate or not; in the latter case the report is sent back for reevaluation or the AEC consults experts and then issues the decision released to the applicant by TAEK (Articles 11/12 paragraph 1 sentence 1-3, see also Articles 16/17, 19/20, 30/31 and with more simple procedures Articles 24, 27 and 28).

Conditions of the site license are given as an appendix to the license (Article 12 paragraph 2). Conditions for a permit or a license are regulated in detail in Article 18 for the Limited Work Permit, in Article 21 for the Construction License and in Article 32 for the Full Power Permit and the Operating License. If changes are required due to safety as regards the Limited Work Permit or the Construction License, the permit respectively the Construction License may be modified accordingly and the applicant is obligated to perform these changes (Article 18 no. 3 and Article 21 no. 2 and 3). In the same sense Article 32 (Conditions for a Full Power Permit and Operating License) no. 3 states: *»No modifications can be made in nuclear reactor facility, in the operating limits and conditions, and operating instructions and procedures without having obtained the permission of the Authority.«* However, notwithstanding the regulations in Article 18 no. 4 and Article 21 no. 2-4 on new findings respectively experiences gained after a license was accorded and on the necessity of an approval by the Authority the procedure for the permit mentioned in Article 32 is not outlined in detail in the decree.

The requirements for revoking of the license either temporarily or permanently are regulated in Article 35; the administrative procedure invo lves TAEK Department of Nuclear Safety, the Advisory Committee on Nuclear Safety, TAEK Vice President of Nuclear Safety, TAEK President and the Atomic Energy Commission as the decision maker, but *»If it is found necessary to prohibit the facility from operation then the Commis* *sion with its decision on this line forwards the matter to the Prime Minister«* (Commission means the AEC). Inspections are regulated in Articles 51 - 53, the Permission to Re-Start Operation when the operation license was temporarily revoked is dealt with in Article 54 and the permission by TAEK for Modifications at the Installation appears in Article 55.

This decree on licensing does not arrange for the involvement of the public which is up to now formally regulated only in the framework of the environmental impact assessment process. Apart from Article 21 no. 2 referring to modifications of the conditions of the construction license *»in a later date«* and Article 32 no. 3 as regards modifications of the conditions of the operation license the decree comprises no basic and general regulation on the necessity of licensing modifications of the site, construction and operation licenses after being issued but before being carried out by the licensee; the extent of and the procedure for a permission of the Authority mentioned in Article 32 no. 3 are not obvious. This may create difficulties within the whole licensing process also since the decree does not provide for the involvement of the public when changing a license or a permit. Finally, periodical safety review is not an operation license condition nor is regulated in other Turkish nuclear legislation at this stage.

The decree on licensing, entered into force with its promulgation in the Official Gazette on 19 December 1983 (Article 58), does not regulate the validity of licenses issued before the enforcement date of this decree.[95] Therefore it seems not undoubted that the site license of 1976 for the Akkuyu site is legally still valuable. Finally it should be noticed that Article 59 rules the execution of this decree by the Council of Ministers; that means the Council of Ministers in accordance with Article 115 of the Constitution decided on and issued this decree. Even if the AEC decides on licenses in substance (for example Article 20 for the construction license and Article 31 for the operating license; TAEK is only the body which releases the decision to the applicant) the Prime Minister according to Article 112 of the Constitution may be deemed politically as the highest competent executive body,[96] moreover the Prime Minister presides AEC's meetings *»whenever he deems necessary«* (Article 6 lit. a paragraph 1 sentence 1 and paragraph 2 of Law No. 2690).

95 In contrast the Radiation Safety Decree (see footnote 54) deals with this topic in Article 25 Provisional article (see footnote 103).

96 See Özbudun, E. (1996), »Constitutional Law«, in Ansay, T., Wallace, D. (Editors), *INTRODUCTION TO TURKISH LAW,* The Hague London Boston, Kluwer Law International, p. 40.

Another concern arises from several regulations, a directive and several guides adopted in 2007 and the following years and dealing especially with safety related matters referred to in the Decree on Licensing of Nuclear Installations of 1983, as for example the Regulation on Specific Principles for Safety of Nuclear Power Plants (2008), the Regulation on Design Principles for Safety of Nuclear Power Plants (2008), the Regulation on Nuclear Power Plant Sites (2009), the Directive on Determination of Licensing Basis Regulations, Guides and Standards and Reference Plant for Nuclear Power Plants (2012) and the Guide on Specific Design Principles (2012); the Regulations are based on Law No. 2690 as the Decree on Licensing of Nuclear Installations does as well. [97] Therefore the question raises whether the principle of *»lex posterior derogat legi priori«* is valuable and if so, what the legal and practical consequences for the licensing procedure will be. It has to be stated that the reference in the Decree on Licensing of Nuclear Installations as well as in the regulations aims only at Article 4 lit. (e) of Law No. 2690 describing the duty of TAEK *»to give approval, permission and license related to the site selection, instruction [construction], operation ... of nuclear power ... reactors ...; to prepare the necessary technical guides, decrees and regulations for those purposes«* and not at Article 4 lit. (j) which gives the duty to TAEK *»to carry out studies related to national and international law in nuclear field and to propose the necessary regulatory arrangements«*. Although Article 9 no. 12 of the Decree on Licensing of Nuclear Installations (the applicant has to submit a site report comprising *»12. Other information which may be requested in the light of developments and new practices in nuclear safety«;* the same wording is used in Article 14 no. 11, Article 23 no. 8 and Article 26 no. 9) constitutes a gateway for *»developments and new practices«* the interaction between the different legal texts has legally to be clarified otherwise the risk of courts' interventions seems to be given, particularly since the clause *»which may be requested«* seems to be very open for interpretation. Nevertheless, the nuclear legislation following the entry into force of the Decree on Licensing of Nuclear Installations may not be neglected when deciding on and issuing a license.

97 See for details of the regulations, the directive and the guide chapters 3.3.5 and 3.3.7 below. For the legal basis of the Decree on Licensing of Nuclear Installations and the regulations see Article 58 of the Decree on Licensing of Nuclear Installations of 1983 on the one hand and for example Article 3 of the Regulation on Specific Principles for Safety of Nuclear Power Plants (2008) on the other hand which both refer to Article 4 lit. e of Law No. 2690.

Finally permits and particularly licenses as administrative acts must be conform to the basic requirements of administrative law; mainly permits and licenses must be justified in written form; in this context it is important to know whether the administrative acts have to be executed with administrative discretion, but the Decree on Licensing of Nuclear Installations is not obvious on this point. [98]

3.3.4.2 Radiation Safety

The Radiation Safety Decree of 1985[99] deals with ionizing radioactive sources (Article 1 paragraph 1) which are in general all radioactive materials and equipments (Article 2 paragraphs D, E and F).[100] The decree is based on Articles 4 and 10 of Law No. 2690 and *»shall be executed by the Council of Ministers«* (Articles 26 and 27). *»The keeping, using, producing, import and export, acquiring, selling, transporting, storing of the radiation sources and working with sources within the scope of this Decree are dependent on the license issued by the Authority«* (TAEK) (Article 7)[101] and therefore the licenses required under the Decree on Licensing

98 See for some principles of administrative acts in Turkish law for example (only Turkish) Akyazan, A. E., (2009) »MADDÎ AÇIDAN İDARİ İŞLEMLER«, *TBB Dergisi,* Sayı (No.) 85, 2009, pp. 220-240; Kanlıgöz, C., (1988) »İDARİ İŞLEMLERİNDE YAZILI BİLDİRİM«, available at http://auhf.ankara.edu.tr/dergiler/auhfd-arsiv/AUHF-1988-40-01-04/AUHF-1988-40-01-04-Kanligoz.pdf (accessed 14/06/2013); Kırışık, F., Aydın, N., (2002) »İDARİ İŞLEMİN UNSURLARINDA TAKDİR YETKİSİNİN VARLIĞI SORUNU«, *Süleyman Demirel Üniversitesi İktisadi ve İdari Bilimler Fakültesi,* Y.2002, C.7, S.2, pp. 331-344; Yılmaz, Y., (2006) »İDARE HUKUKUNDA SEBEP UNSURU VE SEBEP İKAMESİ«, *Askeri Yüksek İdari Mahkemesi Dergisi,* 21 NUMARALI DERGİ (2006), available at http://www.msb.gov.tr/ayim/Ayim_makale_detay.asp?IDNO=72 (accessed 14/06/2013); and Çağlayan, R., (2000) »İDARİ İŞLEMİN GERİ ALINMASI ÜZERİNE«, *AÜEHFD,* C.IV, S.1-2, 2000, available at http://www.erzincan.edu.tr/birim/HukukDergi/makale/2000_1_4.pdf (accessed 14/06/2013).

99 See footnote 54.

100 *»D - Radiation source; the radioactive materials which emit ionizing radiation and equipments which produce or emit ionizing radiation. E - Radioactive materials; materials containing an isotope, the nucleus of which has been disintegrated spontaneously by emitting one or more ionizing radiation, as alloy mixture, solvent or composite. F - Radiation emitting equipments; equipments containing radioactive materials and manufactured in order to emit one or more ionizing radiation within certain safety measures and under control.«*

101 Authority means TAEK (Article 2 paragraph N).

of Nuclear Installations of 1983 are accompanied by a license under the Radiation Safety Decree.[102] But it seems not to be evident to which category of license the operation of a NPP with nuclear fuel has to be assigned (license for the use or for the place); Article 8 *»Types of Licenses«* states in paragraphs B and C: *»B - Licenses issued for the radiation sources, 1- ... 2- Licenses issued for the radiation sources used for industrial or other purposes. C - Licenses issued for the places where the radiation sources are used, stored, manufactured and places where the radioactive wastes are disposed and other similar places.«* The validity of a license is five years (Article 11 paragraph A). *»Transportation, transit passage, entry and exit in or from the country of the radioactive sources depends on the written permission of the Authority«* (TAEK); a license under the decree *»does not remove the obligation for taking written permission«* (Article 14). Inspections are regulated in Articles 18 and 19. Article 20 states an *»Obligation for keeping records«,* Article 21 deals with *»Theft and loss of radioactive sources«* and thus can also be situated in the area of nuclear security, Article 22 regulates obligations in the case of *»Radiation Accidents«* and therefore refers to emergency issues. A provisional article regulates the validity of licenses issued before the entrance into force of the decree: *»The licenses issued before enforcement date of this Decree, are valid for a period of 5 years beginning from their date of issuance. For the renewal process of expired licenses, it is necessary to make an application to Authority [TAEK] within the period of two years beginning from the enforcement date of this Decree.«*[103] General information on radiation safety is published by TAEK.[104]

102 Limoncuoğlu, S. A., (2012) »The Missing Part of Nuclear Power Plant Regulations in Turkey: Occupational Health and Safety«, *Mediterranean Journal of Social Sciences,* Vol. 3 No. 6, March 2012, pp. 123-128 (chapter 3.2 second paragraph third sentence).

103 Paragraph 2 of Article 25.

104 See TAEK, Radyasyon Güvenliği ile İlgili Genel Bilgi, available (only Turkish) at http://www.taek.gov.tr/radyasyon-guvenligi/radyasyonguvenligi/480-atik-guvenligi.html (accessed 05/05/2013). For the whole system of radiation protection in Turkey see for example Turkey/EU (2006), »SCREENING CHAPTER 15 ENERGY, AGENDA ITEM: NUCLEAR ENERGY, Radiation Protection«, Country Session: The Republic of TURKEY, 14 – 15 June 2006, available at http://www.abgs.gov.tr/tarama/tarama_files/15/SC15DET_Radiation%20Protection.pdf (accessed 23/05/2013).

3.3.5 Regulations as legislation instruments for matters of nuclear safety, radiation safety, nuclear security, physical protection and safeguards

In accordance with Article 124 of the Constitution »The Prime Ministry, the ministries, and public corporate bodies may issue by-laws in order to ensure the application of laws and regulations relating to their particular fields of operation, provided that they are not contrary to these laws and regulations. The law shall designate which by-laws are to be published in the Official Gazette.« TAEK's terminology being different from the English version of the Constitution (Article 115 »regulation« respectively Article 124 »by-law«) refers to »decree« and »regulation«.

3.3.5.1 Regulations aiming at ensuring nuclear safety including radiation safety

It could be made a distinction between regulations in order to ensure safety by technical means and those with reference to organization, management and personal. The regulations more or less oriented at technical requirements are

- Regulation on Specific Principles for Safety of Nuclear Power Plants[105] which is based on Article 4 lit. e) of Law No. 2690 (Article 3) and is dealing especially with technical matters but also with organizational aspects.[106]
- Regulation on Design Principles for Safety of Nuclear Power Plants[107] which is based on Article 4 lit. e) of Law No. 2690 (Article 3) and is dealing especially with General Design Specifications for Nuclear

105 Published in the Official Gazette No. 27027 of 17 October 2008, unofficial translation available at http://www.taek.gov.tr/en/belgeler-formlar/func-startdown/776/ (accessed 07/05/2013). For all safety matters important is the Regulation on Nuclear Definitions with a catalogue of definitions for nuclear topics, voted already in 1991 (Nükleer Tanımlar Yönetmeliği, published in the Official Gazette No. 20986 of 9 September 1991), available (only Turkish) at http://www.taek.gov.tr/belgeler-formlar/func-startdown/48/ (accessed 31/05/ 2013).

106 See Ercan, E., Schneider, H. (footnote 11), p. 587.

107 Published in the Official Gazette No. 27027 of 17 October 2008, unofficial translation available at http://www.taek.gov.tr/en/belgeler-formlar/func-startdown/766/ (accessed 07/05/2013).

Power Plants (Articles 5 – 11) and Specific Design Features of Power Plants (Articles 12 – 25) the latter being specified in the Guide on Specific Design Principles.[108]

- Regulation on Nuclear Power Plant Sites which is based on Article 4 lit. f) of Law No. 2690 (Article 3) and on the one hand is laying down as main subjects for a site of a NPP the effects of external events, site and site area characteristics possibly influencing transport of radioactive material and population distribution and intensity and on the other hand is stating that »*the site shall be deemed unsuitable*« if deficiencies identified cannot be compensated (Article 5); as regards siting two guides are to be taken into consideration.[109]
- Regulation on Radioactive Waste Management[110] which is based on Article 4 lit. e) of Law No. 2690 (Article 3) and focuses in Section Two on Requirements and Principles of Radioactive Waste Management (particularly Responsibility, Control of Radioactive Waste Generation, Management System, Safety Management, Safety Culture, Human Factor and Transparency), in Section Three on Radioactive

108 The Guide on Specific Design Principles is available (only Turkish »*Özel Tasarım İlkeler Kılavuzu*«) at http://www.taek.gov.tr/en/component/remository/mevzuat/yonerge-kilavuzlar/kilavuzlar/orderby,2/page,3/ (accessed 12/06/2013); see also chapter 3.3.7 below. For the importance of design for new nuclear reactor types see Raetzke, C., Micklinghoff, M. (2012), »Regulatory challenges in the licensing of new nuclear power plant – From CORDEL to ERDA –«, *International Journal for Nuclear Power,* atw 57. Jg. (2012) Heft 12 I Dezember, pp. 720-724. Design is especially dealt with by IAEA, (2012) Safety of Nuclear Power Plants: Design Specific Safety Requirements IAEA Safety Standards Series No. SSR-2/1 – Published 20 February 2012, available at http://www-ns.iaea.org/standards/documents/pubdoc-list.asp?s=11&l=96 (accessed 31/05/2013), and IAEA, (2007) Nuclear Power Plant Design Characteristics, IAEA-TECDOC-1544, March 2007.

109 Published in the Official Gazette No. 27176 of 21 March 2009, unofficial translation available at http://www.taek.gov.tr/en/belgeler-formlar/func-startdown/769/ (accessed 07/05/2013). The guides are available only in Turkish at http://www.taek.gov.tr/en/belgeler-formlar/mevzuat/yonerge-kilavuzlar/ kilavuzlar - accessed 26/05/2013 (NÜKLEER TESİSLERE YER LİSANSI VE SINIRLI ÇALIŞMA İZNİNİN VERİLMESİNDE ARANACAK DEPREMLE İLGİLİ KONULAR HAKKINDA KILAVUZ of 1989 and Nükleer Güç Tesisi Sahalarının Gözlem, Değerlendirme ve Onaylanması için Kalite Temini Programı Kapsamında Kullanılan Doküman Örnekleri, Prosedürler veya İş Talimatları için Kılavuz); see also chapter 3.3.7 below.

110 Published in the Official Gazette No. 28582 of 9 March 2013, unofficial translation available at http://www.taek.gov.tr/en/belgeler-formlar/func-startdown/830/ (accessed 07/05/2013).

Waste Management Steps, in Section Four on Release of Radioactive Wastes to the Environment, in Sections Five and Six on General Principles and General Safety Principles in Radioactive Waste Facilities, in Section Seven on Radioactive Waste Management in Nuclear and Radiation Facilities and in Section Eight on Inspections and Sanctions.

- Regulation on Clearance in Nuclear Facilities and Release of Site from Regulatory Control[111] which is based on Article 8 lit. a) of Law No. 2690 (Article 3) and comprises Clearance Principles (Article 5) and Clearance Limits (Articles 6 – 8), Measurements (Article 9) and especially the Removal of Site from Regulatory Control (Chapter 3, Articles 14 - 15).

Regulations dealing with quality management requirements are

- Regulation on The Basic Quality Management Requirements for Safety in Nuclear Facilities[112] aiming at establishing *»the statutory basic principles and requirements for quality management in order to enhance the safety of nuclear facilities«* (Article 1). This regulation is based on Article 4 lit. e) of Law No. 2690 and the Decree on Licensing of Nuclear Installations of 1983 (Article 3). The principle of Priority of Safety in Article 13 is implemented in the quality management system's improvement. Many Safety Guides for Quality Management Systems are based on the regulation.[113]

Documentation being a substantial element of quality management is not subject of a regulation.[114] The importance of documentation is acknowledged by Akkuyu NPP.[115]

111 Published in the Official Gazette No. 28582 of 9 March 2013, unofficial translation available at http://www.taek.gov.tr/en/belgeler-formlar/func-startdown/835/ (accessed 07/05/2013).

112 Published in the Official Gazette No. 26642 of 13 September 2007, changed by regulation of 2009, published in the Official Gazette No. 27144 of 17 February 2009, unofficial translation available at http://www.taek.gov.tr/en/belgeler-formlar/func-startdown/783/ (accessed 09/05/2013).

113 See chapter 3.3.7 below.

114 But guides on site report's format and content as well as on management of document control and records do exist (see chapter 3.3.7 below).

115 See (only Turkish) Akkuyu NGS haberleri, 29.11.2012 Atomenergoproekt şirketi, Akkuyu NGS'nin proje dokümantasyonunu hazırlamak için yürüttüğü etüt çalışmalarını tamamladı, available at http://www.akkunpp.com/akkuyu-ngs-haberleri (accessed 08/05/2013).

Regulation on emergency topics presents the

- National Application Regulation on Nuclear and Radiological Emergency.[116] This regulation is based on Article 4 of Law No. 2690 and *»Article 4 of Radiation Safety Statute put into force with the Cabinet Decision dd. 24.07.1985 and no. 85/9727«* (Article 3). It *»describes the responsibilities of relevant ministry, institutions and affiliates and governorships relating to accident or dangerous situation before and after any nuclear and radiological accident or danger«* (Article 1). *»Informing the public«* is task of TAEK (Article 10). Article 12 states the execution of this regulation *»by the Prime Minister«.*

Several regulations are thematically supplemented by directives and guide(line)s.[117]
Radiation safety[118] is subject primarily of the

- Regulation on Radiation Safety,[119] which after the changes of 2010 clearly comprises the three Basic Principles of Dose Limitation System: Necessity of Applications, Optimization and Dose Limitation (Article 7) and contains Dose limits (Articles 8 – 14) and therefore actually might be in keeping with EURATOM basic standards and the IAEA Radiation Protection Basic Safety Standards.[120] The regulation is based on Article 4 lit. d) of Law No. 2690 (Article 3), but does not comprise NPPs (Article 2 Scope, paragraph 2: *»This Regulation does not cover the activities regarding nuclear facilities, nuclear fuels, re-*

116 Published in the Official Gazette No. 23934 of 15 January 2000, changed in 2009, published in the Official Gazette No. 27144 of 17 February 2009, available at http://www.taek.gov.tr/en/belgeler-formlar/func-startdown/843/ (accessed 10/05/2013).

117 Directive on Determination of Licensing Basis Regulations, Guides and Standards and Reference Plant for Nuclear Power Plants, Guide on Specific Design Principles, further guides on especially management, quality assurance and documentation; for details see chapter 3.3.7 below.

118 TAEK, Radiation Safety, available at http://www.taek.gov.tr/en/belgeler-formlar/documents/Regulations/radiation-safety/ (accessed 11/05/2013).

119 See footnote 55.

120 See IAEA Safety Standards (2011), »Radiation Protection and Safety of Radiation Sources: International Basic Safety Standards«, IAEA, General Safety Requirements Part 3, No. GSR Part 3 (Interim), Vienna, 2011, available at http://www-pub.iaea.org/MTCD/Publications/PDF/p1531interim_web.pdf (accessed 26/05/2013), and Ercan, E., Schneider, H. (footnote 11), p. 588.

sultant radioactive wastes arise from nuclear facilities and nuclear substances.«).[121]

Recently published was the

- Regulation on Protection of Outside Workers from Risks of Ionizing Radiation in Controlled Areas which aims at providing *»protection against ionizing radiation for outside workers«* (Article 1) and which has been issued on the legal basis of Article 4 lit. d) of Law No. 2690 and *»in parallel with European Union Council Directive 90/641/EURATOM of 4/12/1990«* (Article 3); Article 5 lays down the *»Responsibilities of authorized persons and outside undertaking«,* Article 6 deals with *»Outside worker's obligations«;* the regulation does not solve the problems and concerns raised on workers inside NPPs.[122]

TAEK assigns to Radiation Safety among other things also the following regulations having importance for NPPs' construction and operation:[123]

121 This is due to a change of the regulation in 2010, see also Limoncuoğlu, S. A. (footnote 102), chapter 3.2 fifth paragraph. Therefore the RADYASYON GÜVENLİĞİ KOMİTELERİ ÇALIŞMA USUL VE ESASLARI are not relevant for NPPs, because this document refers particularly to Articles 71 - 73 of the regulation (Article 1 paragraph 2), available (only Turkish) since 13/01/2010 at http://www.taek.gov.tr/en/belgeler-formlar/func-startdown/293/ (accessed 26/05/ 2013).

122 Published in the Official Gazette No. 27698 of 18 June 2011, unofficial translation available at http://www.taek.gov.tr/en/belgeler-formlar/func-startdown/757/ - (accessed 07/05/2013). For the subject of workers inside NPPs see Limoncuoğlu, S. A. (footnote 102). The recent Law No. 6331 of 20 June 2012 (Occupational Health and Safety Law), published in the Official Gazette No. 28339 of 30 June 2012, available in English at http://www.ilo.org/wcmsp5/groups/public/---ed_protect/---protrav/---ilo_aids/documents/legaldocument/wcms_202369.pdf (accessed 09/06/2013), is valid also for workers inside NPPs; see also the three regulations published in order to ensure the application of Law No. 6331 (only Turkish, published in the Official Gazette No. 28512 of 29 December 2012: İŞ GÜVENLİĞİ UZMANLARININ GÖREV, YETKİ, SORUMLULUK VE EĞİTİMLERİ HAKKINDA YÖNETMELİK; İŞ SAĞLIĞI VE GÜVENLİĞİ HİZMETLERİ YÖNETMELİĞİ; İŞ SAĞLIĞI VE GÜVENLİĞİ RİSK DEĞERLENDİRMESİ YÖNETMELİĞİ).

123 See http://www.taek.gov.tr/en/belgeler-formlar/documents/Regulations/radiation-safety/ (accessed 07/05/2013).

- Regulation on Safe Transportation of Radioactive Materials;[124] the regulation is based on Article 4 lit. d) of Law No. 2690 (Article 3).
- Regulation on Wastes from the Use of Radioactive Materials;[125] the regulation is based on Law No. 2690 and Radiation Safety Statute (Article 3) and repeals the *»Regulation on Radioactive Wastes those do not need Special Processes issued in Official Gazette dd. 15/1/2000 and no. 23934«* (Article 20). *»The purpose of this regulation is to determine the conditions of discharge of wastes from the use of radioactive to the environment, by not giving damage to public, workers and environment.«* (Article 1).

3.3.5.2 Regulations aiming at ensuring security and physical protection

The only issued regulation is the

- Regulation on Physical Protection of Nuclear Materials and Nuclear Facilities.[126] This regulation is based on Article 4 lit. b) and k), Article

124 Published in the Official Gazette No. 25869 of 8 July 2005, unofficial translation available at http://www.taek.gov.tr/en/belgeler-formlar/func-startdown/775/ (accessed 07/05/2013).

125 Published in the Official Gazette No. 25571 of 2 September 2004, unofficial translation available at http://www.taek.gov.tr/en/belgeler-formlar/func-startdown/779/ (accessed 11/05/2013).

126 Published in the Official Gazette No. 28300 of 22 May 2012, available (only Turkish, English translation being under way) at http://www.taek.gov.tr/belgeler-formlar/mevzuat/yonetmelikler/nukleer-guvenlik/N%C3%BCkleer-Tesislerin-ve-N%C3%BCkleer-Maddelerin-Fiziksel-Korunmas%C4%B1-Y%C3%B6netmeli%C4%9Fi/ (accessed 09/05/2013); the Regulation on Physical Protection Measures for Special Nuclear Materials (published in the Official Gazette No. 16702 of 20 July 1979) was replaced (Article 42). Turkey ratified the Convention on the Physical Protection of Nuclear Material (INFCIRC/274/Rev.1) in 1985, available at http://www.iaea.org/Publications/Documents/Conventions/cppnm_status.pdf (accessed 01/06/2013). See for matters of physical protection and security Stoiber, C. (2010), »Nuclear Security: Legal Aspects of Physical Protection, Combating Illicit Trafficking and Nuclear Terrorism«, in OECD, *International Nuclear Law: History, Evolution and Outlook (10th Anniversary of the International School of Nuclear Law),* OECD, pp. 219 et seq., Nuclear Energy Agency (NEA), (2008) NUCLEAR ENERGY OUTLOOK, NEA No. 6348, Chapter 9 *»Non-proliferation and Security«,* pp. 272 et seq., IAEA, (2012) Nuclear Security Achievements 2002 – 2011, Working to build a global response to a global threat, available at http://www.iaea.org/Publications/Booklets/ (accessed 01/06/2013). The text of the International Convention for the Suppression of Acts of

8 lit. a) and Article 11 of Law No. 2690 and on Articles 13, 14, 25, 35, 39, 45 and 50 of the Decree on Licensing of Nuclear Installations of 1983 (Article 3). It outlines particularly nuclear physical protection culture (Article 5), nuclear physical protection and nuclear safety (Article 6), goals of nuclear physical protection (Article 7), responsibility (Article 8) and physical protection system and program (Articles 10-11). The special measures of physical protection including theft and sabotage are dealt with in Articles 18-35.

3.3.5.3 Regulations aiming at ensuring safeguards

Regulations are

- Regulation on Accounting for and Control of Nuclear Materials[127] which is based on Article 4 lit. b) of Law No. 2690, the Non-Proliferation Treaty, an Agreement between Turkey and IAEA on Safeguards Control and a Supplementary Protocol (Article 3).
- Regulation on Issuing Documents Base to Export Permission for Nuclear and Nuclear Dual Use Items[128] which is based on Article 4 of Law No. 2690 (Article 3).

Nuclear Terrorism (Nükleer Terörizmin Önlenmesine İlişkin Uluslararası Sözleşme) is available at http://www.taek.gov.tr/anasayfa/218-uluslararasi/uluslararasi-cok-tarafli-anlasmalar-sozlesmeler/999-nukleer-terorizmin-onlenmesine-iliskin-uluslararasi-sozlesme.html (accessed 11/05/2013). See for the issue of nuclear terrorism Demerici, S. (2012), »NÜKLEER TERÖRİZM VE TEHDİT BOYUTLARINA YÖNELİK ÇIKARIMLAR«, *ESAM (Ege Üniversitesi Araştırmalar Merkezi) Dergisi,* Ocak 2012 Sayısı, CİLT (Volume) 3, Sayı (No.) 1, pp. 59-84, abstract available (only Turkish) at http://esam.ege.edu.tr/ocak-2012.html (accessed 31/05/2013).

127 Published in the Official Gazette No. 28308 of 30 May 2012, available (only Turkish – the regulation is being translated by TAEK) at http://www.taek.gov.tr/en/belgeler-formlar/mevzuat/yonetmelikler/nukleer-guvenlik/N%C3%BCkleer-Maddelerin-Say%C4%B1m-ve-Kontrol%C3%BC-Y%C3%B6netmeli%C4%9Fi/ (accessed 10/05/2013); the regulation replaces the regulation of 1997 (Article 40) which was published in the Official Gazette No. 23106 of 10 September 1997.

128 Published in the Official Gazette No. 26642 of 13 September 2007, unofficial translation available at http://www.taek.gov.tr/en/belgeler-formlar/documents/Regulations/nuclear-safety/Regulation-on-Issuing-Documents-Base-to-Export-Permission-for-Nuclear-and-Nuclear-Dual-Use-Items/ (accessed 11/05/2013).

A Seminar on »*Peaceful Use Of Nuclear Energy And Nuclear Nonproliferation*« was arranged on 19-20 February 2013 in Ankara.[129]

3.3.6 Regulations on matters of administrative activities and acts

Regulations are

- Regulation of Nuclear Safety Inspections and Enforcement[130] which is based on Article 4 lit. e) of Law No. 2690 and the Decree on Licensing of Nuclear Installations of 1983 (Article 3). This regulation is completed by the Directive on the Granting of Functions to Inspectors for Nuclear Safety.[131]
- Regulation on Radiation Safety Inspections and Enforcements.[132] This regulation is based on Article 4 lit. d) of Law No. 2690 and Article 19 of the Radiation Safety Decree of 1985 (Article 3). Although the Radiation Safety Decree of 1985 is applicable to NPPs the aforementioned regulation is not applicable to NPPs (Article 2).

TAEK needs experts' support for technical examination and evaluation particularly within the outstanding construction licensing process for the Akkuyu NPP. External experts shall be consulted in a formally organized manner. But the existing nuclear legislation of Turkey does not establish a system for Technical Support Organisations (TSO) inspite of the possibility of the Atomic Energy Commission (AEC) to consult with experts before issuing the site license, to seek the opinions of experts before granting the construction license or to ask for expert recommendations before

129 Available at http://www.taek.gov.tr/haberler/1046-peaceful-use-of-nuclear-energy-and-nuclear-nonproliferation-konulu-seminer-19-20-subat-2013-tarihlerinde-ankara-da-jw-marriott-otelde-gerceklestirildi.html (accessed 20/04/2013). See for Non-Proliferation also (in Turkish) TMMOB (footnote 17), pp. 108–112 (»Nükleer Silahsızlanma«).

130 Published in the Official Gazette No. 26642 of 13 September 2007, changed by regulation of 2008, published in the Official Gazette No. 27034 of 24 October 2008, unofficial translation available at http://www.taek.gov.tr/en/belgeler-formlar/documents/Regulations/nuclear-safety/The-Regulation-of-Nuclear-Safety-Inspections-and-Enforcement/ (accessed 09/05/2013).

131 See footnote 64 and chapter 3.3.7 below.

132 Published in the Official Gazette No. 27658 of 31 July 2010, available at http://www.taek.gov.tr/en/belgeler-formlar/func-startdown/774/ (accessed 09/05/2013).

granting the full power operating permit and the operating license (Article 12 paragraph 1 sentence 2, Article 20 sentence 2 and Article 31 sentence 3 of the Decree on Licensing of Nuclear Installations of 1983). In general the AEC may invite experts to participate in their meetings (Article 6 paragraph 2 of the Regulation of Working Procedures of the Atomic Energy Commission of 1983). However, TAEK aiming at ensuring procurement of technical support services for the construction license procedure published tenders for prequalification which were cancelled three times yet; although the tender documents provided some criteria for experts' qualification and experience no binding legislation on these items is in force actually; generally the role of TAEK as regulatory body in Turkey is criticized on the one hand with a view to the separation principle and on the other hand aimed at the staff.[133] Finally, as regards TAEK's activities there is no obligation to formally involve the public, especially not in the licensing procedure for NPPs siting, construction and operation.

133 As regards the tenders see footnote 35. For the separation principle see Article 8 paragraph 2 CNS (footnote 14) and Article 5 no. 2 EURATOM directive on nuclear safety of 2009 (footnote 15) and Centre for Economics and Foreign Policy Studies, 2012, »The Turkish Model for Transition to Nuclear Energy II«, Istanbul, pp. 125–151, available at http://edam.org.tr/eng/EDAMNuclear/ Nuclear%20Report%202012/edamreport2012big.pdf (accessed 01/05/2013), and Gürbüz, M. (footnote 17), pp. 122-124, Kuzeyli, K. (footnote 33), pp. 39–44. On the subjects of separation and independence see Kuş, S., (2004) Erweiterte Unabhängigkeit im atomrechtlichen Gesetzesvollzug, Nomos, Baden-Baden, and MacKenzie, B. (2010), »The Independence of the Nuclear Regulator«, *Nuclear Law Bulletin,* No. 85 (Volume 2010/1), pp. 35-63, available at http://www.oecd-nea.org/law/nlb/NLB-85-E.pdf#page=35 (accessed 26/05/2013). On staff shortage see also TAEK, (2013) »2012 Yılı Faaliyet Raporu« (footnote 41), p. 143 (chapter B fifth bullet point – *»Vasıflı personel temininde güçlükler«* – and sixth bullet point – *»Verilen hizmet yoğunluğuna rağmen personel sayısının yetersiz olması«*). The importance of the regulatory body in nuclear newcomer states underlines World Nuclear Association, WNA Report (footnote 15), p. 46. The relation between TAEK, particularly the Department of Nuclear Safety and Technical Support Organizations (TSO) is not regulated expressively; see Ercan, E., Schneider, H. (footnote 11), p. 588 with footnote [57]. For TSO items see already Ercan, E., Schneider, H. (footnote 11), p. 588 (chapter 3 with footnote [57]) and p. 589 (chapter 5 with footnote [84] referring particularly to Sellner, D., Hennenhöfer, G., Schaefer, A., Sailer, M., (2007) Expert's Report The Role of the Independent Expert Organisation and the Risks Related to Changing the Supervision Process, Verlag VdTÜV, Berlin).

3.3.7 Directives and Guides

3.3.7.1 Directives

The Directive on Determination of Licensing Basis Regulations, Guides and Standards and Reference Plant for Nuclear Power Plants, the Guide on Specific Design Principles and the Directive on the Granting of Functions to Inspectors for Nuclear Safety[134] engross in substance the corresponding regulations.

The Directive on Determination of Licensing Basis Regulations, Guides and Standards and Reference Plant for Nuclear Power Plants has been prepared in accordance with Article 4 lit. e) and Article 6 lit. b) subparagraph 1 of Law No. 2690 and the Decree on Licensing of Nuclear Installations of 1983 (Article 3). In order to reach the objective of the directive *»to identify principles and processes for determination of regulations, guides and standards as well as selection of a reference plant for the licensing of«* NPPs (Article 1) Article 5 requires that a *»complete list of regulations, guides and standards forming the licensing basis for the plant shall be determined at the beginning of the licensing process«* and Article 6 lays down the *»order of priority of the regulations to form the licensing basis«*: *»a) Regulations of The Republic of Turkey, b) IAEA Nuclear Safety Series documents under the categories of ›safety fundamentals‹ and ›safety requirements,‹ c) In the areas deemed not adequately covered by subparagraphs (a) and (b), nuclear safety regulations in the Vendor Country, in force as of a date approved by the Authority.«* (TAEK). Moreover it is required for *»safety related issues deemed not adequately covered by regulations mentioned in subparagraphs (a), (b), and (c), a third country regulation conforming to relevant IAEA safety guides or to the design of the plant, for which the license application has been made.«*[135] Finally shall be mentioned the procedure of proposing a refer-

134 See footnote 64.

135 See already the similar Criteria to be Met by Investors Who Will Construct and Operate Nuclear Power Plants of 19 December 2007 accordingly to Article 3 of Law No. 5710 (footnote 90): *»2) Licensing: The nuclear power plant shall comply with the up-to-date nuclear safety regulation effective in the designer's country, except for site-related requirements and conditions. A licensed power plant, currently under operation and representing the most recent example of the same technology, shall be presented as a reference plant. In case there is no operational reference, a representative of the same technology that has been approved or authorized for construction by a regulatory body shall be presented as the reference. Turkish legislation related to licensing, and conditions that will be re-*

ence plant (Article 7 paragraph 1). The order of priority reflects the approach of TAEK to ensure safety of NPPs and is crucial for the licensing process (Article 6 paragraph 2: »licensing basis«) as well as for the support to TAEK by external experts.[136]

3.3.7.2 Guides

The guides serve primarily to transpose IAEA Safety Standards into Turkish non binding nuclear legislation. The guide which is obviously the most important for nuclear safety in NPPs is the Guide on Specific Design Principles; this guide requires Levels of Defense in Depth, Plant States and Objectives, Independence Between All Levels, Safety and Security Interface, Radiation Protection and Waste Management and External Events – Earthquakes and Aircraft Crash (Articles 4-10), while a series of further

---

quested by the national nuclear regulatory body are reserved. Explanations:
a) By compliance with up-to-date regulations of designer's country in addition to national regulations and the International Atomic Energy Authority regulations at the licensing phase, ensuring both home country licensibility and up-to-date technological features is aimed. Compliance of the power plant with the regulations of the designer's country, except site related requirements and conditions, is required to be demonstrated via supporting information and documentation.
b) The aim by the reference plant consideration is to make a comparison between the proposed power plant and the presented reference power plant during licensing. In case there is no reference, a representative one with design approval (certificate) or at the stage of construction may be accepted.
c) The requirements of national legislation and conditions that may be requested by TAEK are reserved and it is emphasized that TAEK is the final authority for any decision regarding licensing. Regulations related to nuclear safety, which will form part of the basis for TAEK's decisions during licensing, in order of priority, are national regulations and the International Atomic Energy Agency regulations given in ›Fundamentals‹ and ›Requirements‹ of Safety Standards Series.«

136 See the structure of the list provided for tender no. 190420 of 26 December 2012, available at http://www.taek.gov.tr/en/belgeler-formlar/documents/ans-tso-tender/New-Tender-Documentation-With-Addendum/ (accessed 11/05/2013) as pdf-document 2012_190420_3_App_III_Licensing_Basis.pdf *(»Licensing Basis for Akkuyu Nuclear Power Plant (Approved) Revision 1«)*; this tender was cancelled on 22 March 2013 (see *»Announcement of Cancellation of Tender No: 2012/190420«*, available at http://www.taek.gov.tr/en/latest-news/1042-announcement-of-cancellation-of-tender-no-2012-190420.html – accessed 11/05/2013). Law No. 5710 of 2007 (see footnote 56) is not registered in this licensing basis list nor are the criteria and the regulation mentioned in Article 3 paragraph 3 of this law (see footnote 90).

guides deal with management issues[137] and quality assurance (programmes).[138] Finally other guides aim at the form of the Site Report for NPPs, at Inspection and Testing, at Safety of Fire Protection, at man-made external events to be taken into consideration in the design of NPPs, at documentation of NPP site activities, at NPPs' earthquake design and sufficiency and at earthquake subjects as regards site license and limited work permit.[139]

137 For the Guide on Specific Design Principles see footnote 108; furthermore see Guide on Management of Non-Conformance Control and Corrective Actions for Safety in Nuclear Installations / GK-KYS-02, 10.12.2009; Guide on Management of Document Control and Records for Safety in Nuclear Installations / GK-KYS-03, 10.12.2009; all these guides are available (only Turkish) at http://www.taek.gov.tr/belgeler-formlar/mevzuat/yonerge-kilavuzlar/kilavuzlar/ (accessed 26/05/2013).

138 See Guide on Establishing and Implementing a Quality Assurance Programme for Safety in Nuclear Installations / GK-KYS-01, 10.12.2009; Guide on Assessment of the Implementation of the Quality Assurance Programme for Safety in Nuclear Installations, GK-KYS-05, 24.05.2010; Guide on Quality Assurance in Procurement of Items and Services for Safety in Nuclear Installations / GK-KYS-06, 24.05.2010; Guide on Quality Assurance in Manufacturing for Safety in Nuclear Installations / GK-KYS-07, 31.05.2011; Guide on Quality Assurance in Research and Development for Safety in Nuclear Installations / GK-KYS-08, 31.05.2011; Guide on Establishing and Implementing a Quality Assurance Programme in Siting for Safety of Nuclear Installations / GK-KYS-09, 24.05.2010; Guide on Quality Assurance in Design for Safety of Nuclear Installations / GK-KYS-10, 29.09.2011; Guide on Quality Assurance in Construction for Safety of Nuclear Installations / GK-KYS-11, 29.09.2011; Guide on Quality Assurance in Commissioning for Safety of Nuclear Installations / GK-KYS-12, 29.09.2011; Guide on Quality Assurance in Operation for Safety of Nuclear Installations / GK-KYS-13, 29.09.2011; Guide on Quality Assurance in Decommissioning for Safety of Nuclear Installations / GK-KYS-14, 29.09.2011; all these guides are available (only Turkish) at http://www.taek.gov.tr/belgeler-formlar/mevzuat/yonerge-kilavuzlar/kilavuzlar/ (accessed 26/05/2013).

139 Guide on Format and Content of Site Report for Nuclear Power Plants / GK-GR-01, 10.12.2009, available (only Turkish »Nükleer Güç Santralleri için Yer Raporu Biçim ve İçeriği Kılavuzu«) at http://www.taek.gov.tr/en/belgeler-formlar/func-startdown/607/ (accessed 11/05/2013). Guide on Inspection and Testing for Acceptance for Safety in Nuclear Installations / GK-KYS-04, 10.12.2009; NÜKLEER GÜÇ SANTRALLARINDA YANGINDAN KORUNMA GÜVENLİK KILAVUZU; NÜKLEER GÜÇ SANTRALLARININ TASARIMINDA İNSAN KAYNAKLI DIŞ OLAYLAR ÜZERİNE GÜVENLİK KILAVUZU; NÜKLEER GÜÇ TESİSİ SAHALARININ GÖZLEM, DEĞERLENDIRME VE ONAYLANMASI İÇİN KALİTE TEMİNİ PROGRAMI KAPSAMINDA KULLANILAN DOKÜMAN ÖRNEKLERİ, PROSEDÜRLER VEYA İŞ TALİMATLARI İÇİN KILAVUZ; NÜKLEER SANTRAL TESİSLERİNİN DEPREM TASARIMI VE YETERLİLİĞİ KILAVUZU;

3.3.8 Nuclear third party liability

Turkey has ratified the Paris Convention on Third Party Liability in the Field of Nuclear Energy of 29 July 1960, the Protocol to Amend the Convention on Third Party Liability in the Field of Nuclear Energy of 28 January 1964, the Protocol to Amend the Convention on Third Party Liability in the Field of Nuclear Energy of 29 July 1960, as Amended by the Additional Protocol of 28 January 1964 (1982)[140] and the Joint Protocol Relating to the Application of the Vienna Convention and the Paris Convention (1988)[141], but neither the Brussels Supplementary Convention on Nuclear Third Party Liability and the 2004 Protocol to amend the Brussels Supplementary Convention,[142] nor the Convention on Supplementary Compensation for Nuclear Damage of 12 September 1997[143] or the Protocol to Amend the Convention on Third Party Liability in the Field of Nuclear Energy of 29 July 1960, as Amended by the Additional Protocol of 28 January 1964 and by the Protocol of 16 November 1982 (2004); moreover Turkey did not sign nor ratify the International Convention on the Liabil-

NÜKLEER TESİSLERE YER LİSANSI VE SINIRLI ÇALIŞMA İZNİNİN VERİLMESİNDE ARANACAK DEPREMLE İLGİLİ KONULAR HAKKINDA KILAVUZ (1989); all these guides are available (only Turkish) at http://www.taek.gov.tr/belgeler-formlar/mevzuat/yonerge-kilavuzlar/kilavuzlar/ (accessed 26/05/2013).

140 See NEA, Legal instruments and related documents, Nuclear liability conventions and protocols, available at http://www.oecd-nea.org/law/legal-documents.html#agreements (accessed 26/05/2013).

141 INFCIRC/402, May 1992, available at http://www.iaea.org/Publications/ Documents/Infcircs/Others/inf402.shtml (accessed 12/05/2013).

142 See footnote 140. Turkey has not even signed these two instruments; Önal, Y., Cihan Alat, D., (2011) NÜKLEER SANTRAL İŞLETİMİNDEN DOĞAN SORUMLULUĞA İLİŞKİN ULUSLARARASI SÖZLEŞMELER, slideshow (only Turkish), December 2011, explain the system of the Brussels Supplementary Convention on Nuclear Third Party Liability of 1963 as well as the 2004 Protocol to amend the Brussels Supplementary Convention (slides 2, 9, 10, 11), but do not indicate why Turkey did not sign nor ratify these instruments and do not mention whether the Turkish government intends to do so in the future, while Smirnov, I. (2012), »Liability for Nuclear Damage«, slideshow presented at Istanbul, Turkey, on April 27, 2012, does not at all mention the Brussels Supplementary Convention on Nuclear Third Party Liability.

143 See INFCIRC/567 of 22 July 1998, available at http://www.iaea.org/Publications/Documents/Infcircs/1998/infcirc567.shtml (accessed 12/05/2013), and Önal, Y., Cihan Alat, D. (footnote 142), slide 18.

ity of Operators of Nuclear Ships of 15 May 1962.[144] A specific national legislation regulating details of nuclear third party liability in order to complete the international regulations as regards subjects left for national law and to adapt the international regulations to the national legal framework has not yet been elaborated,[145] thus the Paris Convention is applica-

144 See footnote 140 and TAEK, Arrangements (footnote 84). A general presentation (PPP) on the international conventions and agreements with regard to nuclear liability resulting from operation of NPP in Turkish was given by Önal, Y., Cihan Alat, D. (footnote 142) who even mention (slide 19) the International Convention on the Liability of Operators of Nuclear Ships of 15 May 1962 (UNITED NATIONS JURIDICAL YEARBOOK 1962, Part Two, Chapter IV, pp. 209 et seq., available at http://untreaty.un.org/cod/UNJuridicalYearbook/ pdfs/english/ By-Chapter/chpIV/1962/chpIV.pdf – accessed 07/06/2013; see for this convention Colliard, C.-A., (1962) »La Convention de Bruxelles relative à la responsabilité des exploitants de navires nucléaires«, in *Annuaire français de droit international,* volume 8, 1962, pp. 41-64, available at http://www.persee.fr/ web/revues/home/prescript/article/afdi_0066-3085_1962 _num_8_1_957 - accessed 08/06/2013). A comprehensive composition in Turkish was published by Kocaoğlu, N. K. (2010), »Nükleer Tesis İşletenin Hukuki Sorumluluğu: Karşılaştırılmalı ve Uluslararası Özel Hukuk Analizi«, *Ankara Barosu Dergisi,* Yıl: 68, Sayı: 2010/2, pp. 33-112 (international conventions are dealt with on pp. 55-56 and 72-82); the most recent books are Aydoğdu, M., (2009) Sivil Amaçlı Nükleer Santral İşletenin ve Nükleer Madde Taşıyanın Hukuki Sorumluluğu, Ankara, Adalet Yayınevi, and Korkmaz, M. H. (2012), NÜKLEER SANTRAL İŞLETMENİN HUKUKİ SORUMLULUĞU, İstanbul, Beta. New articles were published in 2011 and 2012, Özdamar, M. (2011) »Tesislerin İşletilmesinden Doğan Hukuki Sorumluluk«, *ICCI 2011 Proceedings Book,* available at http://www.butekom.com/docs/ICCI2011BK.pdf (accessed 12/05/2013), Özdamar, M., (2012) »NÜKLEER TESİSLERİN İŞLETİLMESİNDEN DOĞAN HUKUKİ SORUMLULUK«, *Enerji Hukuku Araştırma Enstitüsü Dergisi,* Sayı: 2012/1, pp. 119-135, and Aydoğdu, M., (2012) »SİVİL AMAÇLI NÜKLEER SANTRAL İŞLETENİN VE NÜKLEER MADDE TAŞIYANIN HUKUKİ SORUMLULUĞUNUN KOŞULLARI«, *Enerji Hukuku Araştırma Enstitüsü Dergisi,* Sayı: 2012/2, pp. 1-83. See also Antalya, O. G., (2013) Borçlar Hukuku Genel Hükümler, CİLT I (Volume I), 2. Baskı (2nd edition), İstanbul, Beta, pp. 718-728. Lastly should be mentioned the publication of Güneysu, G. (1989-1990), »NÜKLEER REAKTÖRLERİN YOL AÇTIĞI ZARARLARDAN DOĞAN HUKUKİ SORUMLULUK«, *Ankara Üniversitesi Hukuk Fakültesi,* pp. 207-223, available at http://auhf.ankara.edu.tr/dergiler/auhfd-arsiv/AUHF-1989-1990-41-01-04/AUHF-1989-1990-41-01-04-Guneysu.pdf (accessed 13/05/2013).

145 See Centre for Economics and Foreign Policy Studies, (2011) The Turkish Model for Transition to Nuclear Power (footnote 33), pp. 97-98, Korkmaz, M.H. (footnote 144), p. 65, Smirnov, I. (footnote 142), slide 20, Gürbüz, M. (footnote 17), pp. 124-125.

ble directly in Turkish legislation.[146] Possibly the liability regime of Turkish Civil Code is deemed applicable.[147]

However, already in October 1986 a Predraft of a Bill on Legal Liability in the Sector of Nuclear Energy was completed; this predraft was based on the regulations of the Paris Convention and some national legislation especially in Switzerland, but was not finalized nor submitted to the Turkish Grand National Assembly and accordingly an actual conclusion states: *»Besides, the preparation of a special legislation in order to identify the legal liability of the nuclear facility operators is still in progress in our country.«*[148] At the end of the nineteen nineties another draft was submitted to the Turkish Grand National Assembly, but was also not voted definitely.[149] The establishment of Turkish national nuclear liability legislation is intended for the near future as well as the creation of a Nuclear Insurance Pool in Turkey;[150] such a national legislation has to take into account the national insurance legislation which is regulated in the Turkish Commercial Code (Law No. 6102 of 2011, amended in 2012).

Actually in national nuclear legislation Article 7 of the Decree on Licensing of Nuclear Installations of 1983 requires insurance or other financial guarantees for third party liability to be provided by the applicant,[151] Law No. 5710 (Article 5 paragraph 4 sentence 1) obliges to obtain an investment insurance in order to cover any damage from the outset of the creation of the plant and (paragraph 5) regulates the application of the Paris Convention for transports and accidents within the NPP,[152] finally the Turkish-Russian Agreement of 12 May 2010 refers to nuclear third party liability in its Article 16.[153]

146 See Aydoğdu, M. (footnote 144), pp. 40-42.

147 Korkmaz, M. H. (footnote 144), p. 67, Aydoğdu, M. (footnote 144), p. 42.

148 See Özdamar, M. (footnote 144), p. 190 no. 3 and p. 194.

149 See Kocaoğlu, N. K. (footnote 144), pp. 57-59.

150 See Smirnov, I. (footnote 145), slides 20 and 22.

151 See for the Decree footnote 53. Correctly Smirnov, I. (footnote 145), slide 18, states: *»The founder shall provide insurance or other financial guaranties according to the Paris Convention – a precondition to issuing the operating license«,* but does not quote an article of the decree.

152 See Smirnov, I. (footnote 145), slide 18, and Kocaoğlu, N. K. (footnote 144), p. 63. Concerns about the validity of Law No. 5710 for construction and operation of NPPs in Turkey are indicated in chapter 3.3.3. above and chapter 5.1.2. below.

153 See Centre for Economics and Foreign Policy Studies (footnote 33 and 145), p. 98, and Kocaoğlu, N. K. (footnote 144), p. 65. For the Turkish-Russian Agreement see footnote 24; Article 16 NUCLEAR LIABILITY reads as follows:

Since in Turkey a nuclear insurer pool has not been established up to now the nuclear insurance company has not the possibility to follow the licensing process already for the construction license.[154] Moreover the future nuclear insurance pool in Turkey has to implement as soon as possible a comprehensive regulatory system for dealing with damages and their compensation.[155]

3.4 Perspectives of nuclear legislation in Turkey

A fundamental nuclear framework law does not yet exist in Turkey, although it was announced in 2009.[156] Such a comprehensive law was reminded by the European Commission in the Progress Report 2012 for Turkey.[157] Whether the enhanced EU-Turkey energy cooperation includ-

»Third party liability for nuclear damage, which may arise in connection with cooperation under this Agreement will be regulated in compliance with the international agreements and instruments to which the Republic of Turkey is or will be a party and national laws and regulations of the Turkish Party.«

154 See International Guidelines for Nuclear Safety · Operation · Third-Party Liability at Nuclear Power Plants, (2010) Published on behalf of the Nuclear Pool's Forum, 1 July 2010, p. 30 chapter 3.5.1 first bullet point, available at http://www.nuclearpools.com/downloads/procedures/NSO_TPL_GUIDELINES.pdf (accessed 13/05/2013). Further information provided by the NUCLEAR POOLS, for example on guidelines for fire protection, machinery breakdown, is available at http://www.nuclearpools.com/home.asp (accessed 13/05/2013).

155 See NUCLEAR ACCIDENT COMPENSATION, *INSURANCE & CLAIMS HANDLING FROM THE NUCLEAR INSURANCE POOLS,* available at http://www.nuclearpools.com/downloads/liability/2013-03-01-DRAFT_CM_handbook.pdf (accessed 13/05/2013).

156 See for example Kocaoğlu, N. K. (footnote 144), p. 54 *(»Türkiye'de genel bir nükleer enerji yasası bulunmamaktadır.«*). For the announcement of the elaboration of a nuclear law see NEA Nuclear Law Bulletin No. 2/2009, page 109, paragraph 2: *»Recently, the Turkish Atomic Energy Authority (TAEK) issued a draft nuclear law which is being revised according to stakeholders' input. It is expected to enter into force in 2010. The current Law on the Turkish Atomic Energy Authority (Law No. 2690) will become void when the new nuclear law is enacted. [Issues under the objective of the new law are listed in lit. a) – d).] ... The scope of the draft nuclear law will extend to all activities relating to nuclear and radiation facilities, devices and materials excluding those involving non-ionizing radiation.«*

157 TURKEY 2012 PROGRESS REPORT, Chapter 4.15., p. 62: *»No development can be reported on the adoption of a framework nuclear law, which would ensure a level of nuclear safety in full compliance with EU standards; existing applicable national legislation mainly covers protection against ionizing radiation and*

ing nuclear safety and radiation protection, agreed on 14 June 2012,[158] will accelerate the process for a framework nuclear law, is not yet proven; IAEA and OECD-NEA provide vast advice for nuclear legislation and regulation, but at present no concrete activities in Turkey in the direction of a framework nuclear law are known.[159] The United Arabic Emirates (UAE) as a newcomer in nuclear build put into force a nuclear framework law in 2009.[160]

---

the licensing of nuclear installations.«, available at http://ec.europa.eu/enlargement/pdf/key_documents/2012/package/tr_rapport_2012_en.pdf (accessed 13/05/2013). For nuclear framework legislation see for example Switzerland (Kernenergiegesetz – KEG – of 21 March 2003 together with the Kernenergieverordnung – KEV – of 10 December 2004), France (Loi n° 2006-686 du 13 juin 2006 relative à la transparence et à la sécurité en matière nucléaire) and Germany (Atomgesetz [German Atomic Energy Act – Act on the Peaceful Utilization of Atomic Energy and the Protection against its Hazards] of December 23, 1959).

158 See *European Commission,* Memo of 14 June 2012, Enhanced EU-Turkey energy cooperation, No. 5. (*»Nuclear safety and radiation protection«*). Whether this initiative will contribute to the development of adequate legal standards and an appropriate administrative framework with regard to nuclear safety in Turkey, will be proved in the future after special meetings EU-Turkey on these subjects. However, Turkey participated in the stress tests carried out by the European Commission by submitting a report comprising information on the future NPP at Mersin-Akkuyu as regards nuclear safety characteristics and earthquake resistance; see the joint declaration of the Commission and EU neighbouring countries at the high level meeting of 23 June 2011, available at http://ec.europa.eu/energy/nuclear/safety/doc/20110623_stress_test_joint_declaration_eu_neighbouring_countries.pdf (accessed 26/05/2013), and the Communication from the Commission to the Council and the Parliament on the comprehensive risk and safety assessments (»stress tests«) of nuclear power plants in the European Union and related activities, COM(2012)571 final, available at: http://ec.europa.eu/energy/nuclear/safety/doc/com_2012_0571_en.pdf (accessed 26/05/2013).

159 See the recommendations of IAEA (Handbook on Nuclear Law, Publication 1160 of 2003, Implementing Legislation, Publication 1456 of 2010) and NEA (Improving Nuclear Regulation, NEA No. 6275 of 2009) and IAEA's legal as well as technical assistance programmes (IAEA, available at http://www-ns.iaea.org/ Our Work Services for Member States – accessed 13/05/2013; NEA, available at http://www.oecd-nea.org/nsd/ Work Areas Nuclear safety and regulation and http://www.oecd-nea.org/law/ Work Areas Nuclear Law – both accessed 13/05/2013). However, the 10th Development Plan for Turkey (footnote 6), p. 119 no. 791, notes as a goal the strengthening of the legal and organizational infrastructure.

160 See A FEDERAL LAW BY DECREE NO. 6 OF 2009 CONCERNING THE PEACEFUL USES OF NUCLEAR ENERGY, unofficial translation available at http://www.fanr.gov.ae/SiteAssets/PDF/20101024_nuclear-law-scan-eng.pdf (ac-

The lack of a basic nuclear law at the top of the nuclear legislation hierarchy along with the existing compilation of two decrees on licensing nuclear installations and on radiation safety and several regulations could cause difficulties in the enforcement process and later on in the supervision, inspection and enforcement. In the same way the hierarchy of safety requirements being reflected in decrees, regulations, directives and guides is at least not evident for the public which moreover is not formally involved in the licensing procedure for nuclear power plants. Beyond that judicial review may not be conveniently achieved. Finally the Russian influence arising from the construction of a Russian-designed nuclear reactor on administrative procedures must not be underestimated; for example the clear and comprehensible translation of all Russian documents for the reference NPP seems to be a difficult action especially in matters of legal certainty. Thus particularly the judicial review by administrative courts could at the end of the day result in risks for the state authorities' licenses' reliability.

In order to diminish these regulatory risks intensive and transparent international cooperation could be rather helpful to establish *»best practice«* in Turkish nuclear legislation and execution by administrative acts and activities; in that sense the meeting of TAEK with OECD-NEA members (11 and 12 February 2013) on cooperation and support during the licensing process for nuclear power plants, to which involved Russian participants of the Russian regulatory body as well as Rosatom and the Akkuyu Project Company were invited, has to be evaluated positively, because exchange of information and knowledge transfer between regulatory bodies on the one hand and briefing on the planned Russian-type reactor as reference plant including possible differences to the reference plant's design on the other hand are certainly valuable in order to strengthen the capabilities of staff and administrative management so as to carry out particularly the licensing process in a convenient manner.[161]

cessed 13/05/2013), Federal Authority for Nuclear Safety, *»Nuclear Safety, Licences for Nuclear Power Plants«,* available at http://www.fanr.gov.ae/En/AboutFANR/OurWork/Pages/Nuclear-Safety.aspx (accessed 13/05/2013).

161 See for the meeting of TAEK with OECD-NEA on 11 and 12 February 2013, TAEK, *»TAEK, OECD/NEA ve Rusya Federasyonu'ndan İlgili Kuruluşların Katılımıyla Nükleer Tesislerin Lisanslanması Sürecinde İşbirliği ve Destek Konulu Toplantı 11-12 Şubat 2013 Tarihlerinde ANKARA'da Yapıldı«,* available (only Turkish) at http://www.taek.gov.tr/haberler/1045-taek-oecd-nea-ve-rusya-federasyonu-ndan-ilgili-kuruluslarin-katilimiyla-nukleer-tesislerin-lisanslanmasi-surecinde-isbirligi-ve-destek-konulu-toplanti-11-12-subat-2013-tarihlerinde-ankara-da-yapildi.html – accessed 20/04/2013. – As regards the involvement of the

4. Other legislation particularly relevant for siting, construction and operation of NPPs in Turkey

4.1 Environmental Impact Assessment

Environmental Impact Assessment (EIA) legislation in Turkey on the basis of the Environmental Law and particularly the Regulation on Environmental Impact Assessment[162] covers in principle NPPs[163] in the way

public during the licensing procedures the German Constitutional Court (Bundesverfassungsgericht) already in 1979 ruled that formal public participation in decision-making for nuclear power plants is guaranteed by the fundamental right of life and health (Article 2 paragraph 2 sentence 1 of the Constitution), see the official collection of rulings of the German Constitutional Court (BVerfGE), volume 53, pp. 30 et seq., pp. 59 et. seq., pp. 65-66; whether in Turkish constitutional law the similar Article 56 paragraph 1 and 2 of the Turkish Constitution (see footnote 47) would be interpreted in the same way is not predictable (Article 56 paragraph 1 and 2 reads as follows: *»Everyone has the right to live in a healthy, balanced environment. It is the duty of the state and citizens to improve the natural environment, and to prevent environmental pollution.«*).

162 Environmental Law No. 2872 (Çevre Kanunu), published in the Official Gazette No. 18132 of 11 August 1983, changed for the last time in 2006 (Law No. 5491 of 26 April 2006 »ÇEVRE KANUNUNDA DEĞİŞİKLİK YAPILMASINA DAİR KANUN«, published in the Official Gazette No. 26167 of 13 May 2006); Regulation on Environmental Impact Assessment (Çevresel Etki Değerlendirmesi Yönetmeliği), of which the first regulation was published in the Official Gazette No. 21489 of 7 February 1993, the actual regulation was published in the Official Gazette No. 26939 of 17 July 2008, changed for the last time in 2011 (ÇEVRESEL ETKİ DEĞERLENDİRMESİ YÖNETMELİĞİNDE DEĞİŞİKLİK YAPILMASINA DAİR YÖNETMELİK, published in the Official Gazette No. 27905 of 14 April 2011; for the NPP at the Mersin-Akkuyu site the change of the preliminary Article 3 seemed to be relevant: The change states that projects are exempted until 17 July 2015) and in 2013 after the Council of State having ruled on 1 April 2013 the cancellation of parts of the 2011 regulation (ÇEVRESEL ETKİ DEĞERLENDİRMESİ YÖNETMELİĞİNDE DEĞİŞİKLİK YAPILMASINA DAİR YÖNETMELİK, published in the Official Gazette No. 28609 of 5 April 2013); the Regulation on Environmental Control (Çevre Denetimi Yönetmeliği, published in the Official Gazette No. 27061 of 21 November 2008) is not applicable to NPPs (Article 2 paragraph 2; paragraph 3 however envisages a coordinated control if a protocol is elaborated between TAEK and the competent Ministry of Environment and City Planning). Likewise the Regulation on Environmental Permits and Licenses to be taken in Accordance with Environmental Law (Çevre Kanunu'nca Alınması Gereken İzin ve Lisanslar Hakkında Yönetmelik), published in the Official Gazette No. 27214 of 29 April 2009, is not relevant for NPPs nuclear matters (they do not figure in the annexes 1 and 2); for

that EIA procedure must be terminated before the first license is granted, even investment or tenders may not be accomplished (Article 10 paragraph 2 of the Environmental Law). For a NPP the site license (Articles 9-12 of the Decree on Licensing of Nuclear Installations of 1983) is the first nuclear license. An EIA application file or an EIA application report, for a project of minor importance a project description file has to be submitted (Article 6 of the Regulation on Environmental Impact Assessment) to the competent Ministry of Environment and City Planning or in special cases to the competent province governorship. The decision to be taken is either a positive EIA or a negative EIA or the statement that EIA is not necessary (Article 5 of the Regulation on Environmental Impact Assessment).[164] The Ministry of Environment and City Planning is competent in principle for the protection of the environment, the prevention of environmental pollution and the remedy of environmental problems, but the topics which are subject of Law No. 2690 are executed by TAEK (Article 3 lit. j) of the Environmental Law). The public participation in the framework of the EIA process is regulated in Article 9 of the Regulation on Environmental Impact Assessment; in preparing a public meeting information on the project has to be published and the opinions and proposals of the public have to be received by a Commission established by the Ministry of Environment and City Planning.[165]

---

the importance of non-nuclear pollution aspects see chapter 4.2 below. Since the regulation concerning the competent persons and the environmental experts' firms (ÇEVRE GÖREVLİSİ VE ÇEVRE DANIŞMANLIK FİRMALARI HAKKINDA YÖNETMELİK, published in the Official Gazette No. 27757 of 12 November 2010) depends on the two aforementioned regulations, it too is not applicable to NPPs.

163 NPPs figure in the catalogue of projects for which EIA is necessary, i.e. No. 2-b) in Annex I (EK-I Listesi) of the Regulation of Environmental Assessment (see footnote 162). See (only Turkish) T.C. Çevre Orman Bakanlığı, (2006) Çevresel Etki Değerlendirmesi Özel Sektörel Rehberleri, ÇED Rehberi - Nükleer Enerji Santralları, 2006, available at http://www.csb.gov.tr/gm/dosyalar/belgeler/belge387/Sektorel_rehber_nukleer.pdf (accessed 16/05/2013), and Ünver, Ö. (2012), »LICENSING AND ENVIRONMENTAL IMPACT ASSESSMENT (EIA) FOR NPP's IN TURKEY«, slideshow presented at the Technical Meeting on Environmental Issues in Nuclear Power Programmes, Vienna/Austria, 20-23 March 2012.

164 See (in Turkish) Alıca, S. S. (2011), »ÇEVRESEL ETKİ DEĞERLENDİRMESİNİN YARGI KARARLARI ÇERÇEVESİNDE İRDELENMESİ«, *Gazi Üniversitesi Hukuk Fakültesi Dergisi,* Cilt (volume) XV, Yıl (year) 2011, Sayı 3, pp. 111-112.

165 See for the public participation (in Turkish) Alıca, S. S. (footnote 164), pp. 110-111.

For the Mersin-Akkuyu site a nuclear site license was issued in 1976 before the entry into force of the Environmental Law of 1983 and the first Regulation on Environmental Impact Assessment of 1993. The problem of projects underlying an EIA but for which a license was already accorded was regulated in provisional articles and after a negative decision of the Council of State of 7 October 2010 with regard to NPPs the application of the Regulation on Environmental Impact Assessment perhaps would have been not applicable until 17 July 2015; but that regulation was also cancelled by a ruling of the Council of State on 1 April 2013. After that the competent Ministry of Environment and City Planning issued only a few days later a new regulation.[166] Despite all those changes in practice an EIA must be made up as regards the NPP project at the Mersin-Akkuyu site and it seems that the competent authorities deem the EIA being finished before the second step of the nuclear licensing process, the construction license in accordance with Articles 13-21 of the Decree on Licensing of Nuclear Installations; the further development of EIA legislation and exemptions seems to be unclear at this moment. Nevertheless the Akkuyu NGS was and is ready to submit an EIA in the context of the construction license; however, notwithstanding EIA the applicant for the construction license has to submit in the Preliminary Safety Analysis Report *»New Information related to the site and its environment acquired after the issuance of site report«* (Article 14 no. 1 in connection with Article 9 of the Decree on Licensing of Nuclear Installations of 1983).[167]

166 The date of 17 July 2015 was due to the change of the Regulation on Environmental Impact Assessment in 2011 (footnote 162), see Alıca, S. S. (footnote 164), pp. 108-110. Özdemir, H. E. (footnote 24), p. 175, states that the Akkuyu NPP would not be obliged to obtain an EIA due to the regulation of 2011. The new regulation, published in the Official Gazette of 5 April 2013 (footnote 162), exempts projects which were taken to the investment programme before 23 June 1997 and had accomplished the planning phase by 5 April 2013 or for which a tender was carried out before that date. See also the critics on the new regulation expressed by the UNION OF CHAMBERS OF TURKISH ENGINEERS AND ARCHITECTS (TMMOB) on 5 April 2013, available (only Turkish) at http://www.tmmob.org.tr/genel/bizden_detay.php?kod=8963&tipi=9 (accessed 03/06/2013).

167 See Akkuyu NGS haberleri, available (only Turkish) at http://www.akkunpp.com/akkuyu-ngs-haberleri (accessed 08/05/2013), of 12.04.2013: *»Türkiye istemese de nükleere çed alırız«* and *»Akkuyu için ÇED başvuru«* and of 03.12.2012: *»Akkuyu Santrali için ÇED raporu Haziran'a hazır«*. See also Ünver, Ö. (footnote 163), slide 26. The principle that licenses accorded before the entry into force of a new regulation may keep validity is acknowledged as regards Council Directive 85/337/EEC of 27 June 1985 on the assessment of the ef-

For the Sinop-İnceburun site a positive EIA decision according to Article 5 of the Regulation on Environmental Impact Assessment is a prerequisite for the site license according to Articles 9-12 of the Decree on Licensing Nuclear Installations; moreover investments and tenders may not be started until the positive EIA is granted (Article 10 of the Environmental Law).

The fact that the Council of State ruled in several cases at the disadvantage of the competent state authorities[168] illustrates the risks of administrative failure of EIA procedures. Finally it has to be taken into consideration that changes of the project require an EIA procedure (Article 24 paragraph 1 lit. d), Article 15 paragraph 1 lit. b), Article 18 paragraph 3 and Article 19 paragraph 3 lit. b) of the Regulation on Environmental Impact Assessment).

4.2 Other important legislation for NPPs' construction and operation

With regard to NPPs the non-nuclear pollution, the protection of groundwater, surface water, the coasts and the agriculture are deemed to be prior-ranking, moreover sabotages in general are a major concern, hence the Environmental Law, the Agriculture Law, the Ground Water Law, the

fects of certain public and private projects on the environment (OJ 1985 L 175, p. 40) – EIA – also by the European Court of Justice (Judgement of 9 August 1994 – Case C-396/92, I-3744-3756, marginal number 19 at I-3753-3754), available at http://curia.europa.eu/juris/showPdf.jsf?text=&docid=98772&pageIndex=0&doc lang=en&mode=lst&dir=&occ=first&part=1&cid=3469696 (accessed 27/05/ 2013). For the updated site report see TAEK, Akkuyu Nükleer Güç Santrali – Gelişmeler (footnote 34).

168 See Alıca, S. S. (footnote 164), pp. 97-130, further Alıca, S. S., (2011) »ÇEVRENİN KORUNMASINA İLİŞKİN HUKUKİ SORUMLULUK KURALLARININ YARGITAY KARARLARI KAPSAMINDA İNCELENMESİ (AN ANALYSIS OF CIVIL LIABILITY REGARDING ENVIRONMENTAL PROTECTION IN THE FRAME OF TURKISH CASE LAW)«, *YEDİTEPE ÜNİVERSİTESİ HUKUK FAKÜLTESİ DERGİSİ (JOURNAL OF YEDITEPE UNIVERSITY FACULTY OF LAW),* Cilt (Vol.): VIII, Sayı (No.): 1, İstanbul, pp. 37-89, and Alıca, S. S., (2011) »ÇEVRE DENETİMİNDE İDARENİN SORUMLULUĞU«, *Gazi Üniversitesi Hukuk Fakültesi Dergisi,* Cilt (Vol.): XV Ekim (October)-2011, Sayı (No:) 4, pp. 87-120; whether the liability described stands back with regard to the nuclear third party liability regulations is not dealt with in these articles. Moreover the ruling of the Council of State of 13 February 2012 (footnote 34) bringing to a stop the execution of the environmental arrangement plan for the Mersin-Karaman planning area in which is situated the Mersin-Akkuyu NPPs' site is a sign of concern.

Coastal Law, the Regulation on the Protection of Groundwater Against Pollution and Degradation, the Environmental Permits and Licenses Regulation, the Regulation on Control of Pollution from Hazardous Substances in Water and its Environment, the Regulation on Implementation of Coastal Law and the Regulation on Protection Against Sabotages have to be taken into account for siting, construction and operation of NPPs.[169]

With regard to earthquakes the Regulation on Buildings to be Constructed in Earthquake Regions is not applicable to NPPs.[170] Consequently only some special norms in nuclear legislation[171] and particularly the two Guides of TAEK referring to the subject of earthquake[172] are to be taken into account when siting, constructing and operating NPPs.

169 This selection follows the list of TAEK tender of 26 December 2012, Annex III. Articles 11, 13 and 14 of the Environmental Law (see footnote 162), Agriculture Law (Tarım Kanunu), published in the Official Gazette No. 5488 of 18 April 2006, Ground Water Law (Yeraltı Suları Hakkında Kanunu), published in the Official Gazette No. 167 of 16 December 1960, Coastal Law (Kıyı Kanunu), published in the Official Gazette No. 3621 of 4 April 1990, Environmental Permits and Licences Regulation (ÇEVRE KANUNCA ALINMASI GEREKEN İZİN VE LİSANSLAR HAKKINDA YÖNETMELİK), published in the Official Gazette No. 27214 of 29 April 2009 (see also footnote 162), Regulation on the Protection of Groundwater Against Pollution and Degradation (Yeraltı Sularının Kirlenmeye Ve Bozulmaya Karşı Korunması Hakkında Yönetmelik), published in the Official Gazette No. 28257 of 7 April 2012, Regulation on Control of Pollution from Hazardous Substances in Water and its Environment (Tehlikeli Maddelerin Su ve Çevresinde Neden Olduğu Kirliliğin Kontrolü Yönetmeliği), published in the Official Gazette No. 26005 of 26 November 2005, Regulation on Implementation of Coastal Law (3621 Sayılı Kıyı Kanununun Uygulanmasına Dair Yönetmelik), published in the Official Gazette No. 20594 of 3 August 1990, Regulation on Protection Against Sabotages (Sabotajlara Karşı Koruma Yönetmeliği), published in the Official Gazette No. 20033 of 28 December 1988.

170 »DEPREM BÖLGELERİNDE YAPILACAK BİNALAR HAKKINDA YÖNETMELİK«, published in the Official Gazette No. 26511 of 6 March 2007, Annex No. 1.1.5 sentence 2 (Ek numara 1.1.5 tümce 2: »*nükleer santrallar ... bu Yönetmeliğin kapsamı dışındadır*«).

171 For example Article 9 paragraph 1 no. 4 and Article 14 no. 4 of the Decree on Licensing of Nuclear Installations (footnote 53), Articles 19 and 20 of the Regulation on Nuclear Power Plant Sites (footnote 59) and Article 8 of the Regulation on Specific Principles for Safety of Nuclear Power Plants (footnote 59).

172 See footnote 139 (Nükleer Santral Tesislerinin Deprem Tasarım ve Yeterliliği Kılavuzu and Nükleer Tesislere Yer Lisansı ve Sınırlı Çalışma İzninin Verilmesinde Aranacak Deprem ile İlgili Konular Hakkında Kılavuz).

4. 3 Informing of the public and of neighbouring and potentially affected countries

»The Espoo (EIA) Convention sets out the obligations of Parties to assess the environmental impact of certain activities at an early stage of planning. It also lays down the general obligation of States to notify and consult each other on all major projects under consideration that are likely to have a significant adverse environmental impact across boundaries. The Convention was adopted in 1991 and entered into force on 10 September 1997.«[173] Turkey has not signed the Espoo Convention.[174] Nevertheless there is interest in Germany of being informed on the NPP activities at the Mersin-Akkuyu site; Turkey offered information on a voluntary basis.[175] Furthermore, the Turkish government will certainly be confronted with the demand of informing neighbouring and potentially affected states, particularly Bulgaria, Cyprus[176] and Greece as nearby EU states as well as other neighbouring or potentially affected states in the southeast (Iraq, Lebanon, Syria) and in the Caucasus region.

With regard to NPPs in Turkey the Convention on Access to Information, Public Participation in Decision-Making and Access to Justice in Environmental Matters of 25 June 1998 (Aarhus Convention) which is not signed and thus not ratified by Turkey[177] seems to be not fully respected in

173 See UNECE, Introduction to Espoo Convention, available at http://www.unece.org/env/eia/eia.html (accessed 15/05/2013). For the Espoo Convention, the corresponding EU legislation and the transposition in German legislation see Feldmann, U., (2007) »Was bedeuten Aarhus-, Espookonvention und SEA-Protokoll für das Atomrecht?«, in Pelzer, N. (editor), *Elements of a Global Nuclear Law Regime, Proceedings of the Regional Conference of the German Branch of AIDN/INLA in Goslar 2006,* Nomos, Baden-Baden, pp. 233-257.

174 See http://treaties.un.org/Pages/ViewDetails.aspx?src=TREATY&mtdsg_no=XXVII-4&chapter=27&lang=en (accessed 15/05/2013).

175 See the answer of the Federal Government to a Written Question to the Federal Parliament (Deutscher Bundestag) in Plenarprotokoll 17/239 Deutscher Bundestag Stenographischer Bericht 239. Sitzung, 15 Mai 2013, pp. 30106-30107, Annex 6.

176 For Cyprus the state of the Republic of Cyprus has to be taken into consideration; see for the status in general Ercan, B. (2012), *Zypern, die Türkei und die EU,* Nomos, Baden-Baden.

177 See European Commission, ENVIRONMENT, The Aarhus Convention, available at http://ec.europa.eu/environment/aarhus/ (accessed 15/05/2013), and for the status of signature and ratification see United Nations Treaty Collection, available at http://treaties.un.org/Pages/ViewDetails.aspx?src=TREATY&mtdsg_no=XXVII-13&chapter=27&lang=en (accessed 16/05/2013).

substance concerning the access of the public to environmental information. Although in Turkey exists Law No. 4982 of 9 October 2003 on the Right to Information[178] and the Regulation on the Substance and the Procedures of the Law on Right to Information decided by the Council of Ministers according to Article 31 of Law No. 4982 on 19 April 2004 by decision 2004/7189[179] is available, the practical application of the right to information is deemed not to satisfy entirely the needs of the public.[180]

5. *Evaluation and outlook*

5.1 Evaluation

Turkish nuclear legislation covers most issues of nuclear matters and is still developing. Though the presentation of this legislation in detail identified some concerns as regards the overall systematic as well as several special points particularly in licensing. In order to accomplish the ambitious schedule for beginning operation of NPPs in Turkey, improvements of nuclear legislation to be achieved as soon as possible are strongly recommended.

5.1.1 International conventions and EU (EURATOM) legislation

Several international conventions should also be ratified as soon as possible. The ratification of the Protocol of 2004 to the Paris Convention, of the

178 In Turkish Bilgi Edinme Hakkı Kanunu, published in the Official Gazette No. 25269 of 24 October 2003, available in an English version at http://www.bilgiedinmehakki.org/en/index.php?option=com_content&task=view&id=7&Itemid=8 (accessed 15/05/2013).

179 Bilgi Edinme Hakkı Kanununun Uygulanmasına İlişkin Esas ve Usuller Hakkında Yönetmelik in Turkish, published in the Official Gazette No. 25445 of 27 April 2004.

180 See (only Turkish) Güney, N. A. (2010), »TÜRKİYEDE ÇEVRESEL BİLGİLENME HAKKI VE AB DİREKTİFLERİ«, slideshow presented at the AVRUPA BİRLİĞİ, ALMANYA VE TÜRKİYE ÇEVRE HUKUKU SEMPOZYUMU, TOBB Plaza Konferans Salonu, 18-20 Ekim (October) 2010, slide 27. See also for informal information TAEK, (2008) »Sinop Nükleer Teknoloji Merkezi«, slideshow dated 12 Şubat (February) 2008, available (only Turkish) at http://www.taek.gov.tr/belgeler-formlar/func-directinfo/97/ (accessed 16/05/2013), slides 40-44.

Brussels Supplementary Convention together with the Protocol of 2004, of the Joint Convention on the Safety of Spent Fuel Management and on the Safety of Radioactive Waste Management of 12 September 1997, of the Amendment to the Convention on the Physical Protection of Nuclear Material of 8 July 2005 and of the Espoo Convention as well as the Aarhus Convention promoted for all Contracting Parties the development and completion of national legislation.

Even if a complete check along the Convention on Nuclear Safety (CNS) *»Reporting article by article«* systematic is not available on the basis of Turkey's National Reports to the Review Meetings[181] it may be stated that the existing nuclear legislation in Turkey complies with many requirements of CNS. However, for reasons of transparency the national reports to the CNS review meetings should be published as soon as possible by the Turkish government. Just as for CNS it is evident with regard to EU (EURATOM) legislation that Turkish nuclear legislation is well on the way to fulfill the specifications of EU law.

Anyhow, to reach the international level of »good practice« all requirements of the CNS and the EURATOM legislation should be taken into consideration for the next steps of elaborating nuclear legislation in Turkey. This could be accomplished by examining in detail the international regulations on the one hand and existing Turkish legislation respectively the legislation to be developed on the other hand.

5.1.2 Nuclear laws

It has to be stated that up to now in Turkey no general and comprehensive framework nuclear law is in force, although framework laws for example in the field of environmental legislation exist for a long time, especially the Environmental Law of 1983. The structure of the existing voluminous nuclear legislation in Turkey therefore has to be deemed as lack of framework and consequently seems to be difficult to execute and to survey until such a framework law is put into force. Thus at the end of the day gaps and overlaps in Turkish nuclear legislation could even cause risks for the

181 For the CNS and the fact that Turkey up to now does not publish the National Reports to the Review Meetings see footnote 14, for the *»Reporting article by article«* see IAEA, (2009) Guidelines regarding National Reports under the Convention on Nuclear Safety, INFCIRc7%/"7Rev:3, Date: 28 September 2009, pp. 6-17.

legal execution when claims against administrative acts such as licenses or permits are put to courts for judicial review.

The reasons for not elaborating and putting into force such a nuclear framework law which is recommended by IAEA and demanded by the European Commission[182] are not comprehensible. Perhaps the process finally started with the Turkish-Russian Agreement in 2010 and the Agreements of 3 May 2013 between Turkey and Japan shall not be disturbed. But the uncertainties with regard to judicial review by administrative courts and finally the Constitutional Court create concerns of high risks of at least partial failure or of considerable loss of time. Law No. 5710 anyhow could not be evaluated as a general legal basis for safety and security requirements for NPPs because it is not formulated in the sense of substantial requirements for safety and security but aims at a tender process to select a construction and operation company, it was abolished in parts by court rulings and consequently was not executed for the final selection process of construction and operation companies for the Mersin-Akkuyu and Sinop-İnceburun sites: The Turkish government itself selected authorities and companies responsible for constructing and operating NPPs not according to Law No. 5710. Lastly Law No. 5710 seems to be superfluous in substance in addition to the Decree on Licensing of Nuclear Installations of 1983 together with the safety oriented regulations, directives and guides which in principle refer to all relevant safety, security and safeguards issues for new NPPs.[183] The framework nuclear law should in order to

182 See footnotes 159 (IAEA, Implementing Legislation) and 157 (EU, TURKEY 2012 PROGRESS REPORT). See further Ercan, E., Schneider, H. (footnote 11), p. 585 (chapter 2 with footnote [18] particularly referring to Raetzke, C., Micklinghoff, M. (2006), *Existing Nuclear Power Plants and New Safety Requirements – An International Survey*, Köln Berlin München, Carl Heymanns Verlag), p. 589 (chapter 5 with footnote [83] particularly referring to Hennenhöfer, G., Schneider, H. (2010), »50 Jahre Atomgesetz – Eine Zwischenbilanz«, in Dolde, K.-P., Hansmann, K., Paetow, S., Schmidt-Aßmann, E. (editors), (2010) *Verfassung – Umwelt – Wirtschaft, Festschrift für Dieter Sellner zum 75. Geburtstag*, München, Verlag C.H.Beck, pp. 347 et seq., in particular pp. 350-357).

183 For example with regard to Article 3 paragraph 2 sentence 2 and paragraph 3 of Law No. 5710 together with the *»Criteria to be Met by Investors Who Will Construct and Operate Nuclear Power Plants«* of 19 December 2007 and the Regulation of 2008 (footnote 90) see the Regulations of 2007 - 2009 (footnote 59); concerning Article 5 paragraph 1 and 3 of Law No. 5710 see the Decree on Licensing of Nuclear Installations of 1983 (footnote 53), the Regulation of 9 March 2013 (footnote 111), the directives and the guides on safety issues (for details on this legislation including directives and guides see chapter 3.3 above). By the way, TAEK does not refer to Law No. 5710 in the list of nuclear legislation, pub-

transpose the obligations of the Convention on Nuclear Safety (CNS) and the requirements of the Council Directive 2009/71/EURATOM of 25 June 2009 establishing a Community framework for the nuclear safety of nuclear installations (Safety Directive 2009) comprise inter alia the principles of license holder's prime responsibility for nuclear safety (Article 9 CNS and Article 6 no. 1 Safety Directive 2009) and of priority to nuclear safety (Article 10 CNS and Article 6 no. 4 Safety Directive 2009), public involvement during the licensing process, in an optimal way at each stage, i.e. siting, construction, operation, and clear as well as stringent regulation of periodical safety review of NPPs during their lifetime (Article 14 CNS and Article 6 no. 2 Safety Directive 2009).

5.1.3 Nuclear third party liability

Until now no specific national regulation on nuclear third party liability at the level of law does exist in Turkey. Moreover, a national insurance pool is not yet established. Consequently any necessary activities of the insurer with regard to developments during the licensing process cannot be carried out. This state could be deemed to be an obstacle for accelerated realization of NPP projects in Turkey. Beyond that the amounts of compensation are not satisfying, at least as long as the Protocols of 2004 to the Paris Convention and to the Brussels Supplementary Convention are not ratified and transposed into national Turkish law.

5.1.4 Licensing procedure

The Decree on Licensing of Nuclear Installation of 1983 is not the status quo of internationally acknowledged nuclear legislation. Although several new regulations were put into force in order to reach at an actual state, the coherence of the whole licensing system seems not very obvious. Contradictions between licensing under the Decree on Licensing of Nuclear Installation of 1983 and the Radiation Safety Decree of 1985 on the one hand and between the Decree on Licensing of Nuclear Installation of 1983 and new regulations on the other hand are highly probable. A rather critical topic as regards the licensing of the NPP at the Mersin-Akkuyu site

lished in the framework of a tender, to be observed with regard to the outstanding construction license for Akkuyu NPP (see footnote 136).

could raise from the fact that a license issued before 1983 may no longer be valid after the entry into force of the Decree on Licensing of Nuclear Installation in 1983, because in this decree no transition clause for old licenses such as in Article 25 paragraph 2 of the Radiation Safety Decree of 1985 was included. Furthermore, in nuclear legislation no involvement of the public during the licensing process is arranged. Therefore in specific regulations on licensing public involvement and participation should also be taken into account by supplementary details. Finally the competences of Atomic Energy Commission seem not in line with the internationally accepted »separation principle«, because the possibility of a final decision by the Prime Minister is given; in the same way TAEK's organisational separation in nuclear safety affairs could be clarified.[184]

5.1.5 Safety Requirements

The hierarchy of safety requirements for NPPs as laid down in the Directive on Determination of Licensing Basis Regulations, Guides and Standards and Reference Plant for Nuclear Power Plants (national/IAEA/Russian/other countries' regulations and guidelines) could be evaluated as not practicable and not transparent as well as precise enough for issuing legally reliable licenses. Moreover, this hierarchic system not evidently seems to harmonize with the Decree on Licensing of Nuclear Installations of 1983. A periodical safety review during the lifetime of NPPs is not being regulated in principle or in detail, also as regards administrative aspects and technical specifications.

The evaluation, amendment, control and revision of measures to ensure the necessary safety and security requirements deserves the establishment of an experienced network of external technical experts. In the last two years TAEK's TSO tenders failed and up to now no TSO system for support of TAEK was published. Technical efforts to be made by a skilled

184 See for the separation principle respectively the independence of the regulatory body Kuş, S. (footnote 133) and MacKenzie, B. (footnote 133). For Prime Minister's role in licensing see Article 6 of Law No. 2690 and for his role in issuing regulations by TAEK see Article 18 paragraph 2 of Law No. 2690. The 10th Development Plan for Turkey (footnote 6), p. 119 no. 791, notes the creation of an independent, efficient and competent regulatory system (*»Nükleer alandaki faaliyetlerin güvenli ve emniyetli bir şekilde yürütülmesini tespit ve teyit etmek için bağımsız, güçlü ve yetkin bir nükleer düzenleme ve denetleme sistemi oluşturacaktır.«*).

staff of a huge number of experts within the construction licensing procedure and the time needed of about one and a half year are well in mind from another nuclear newcomer's construction license.[185]

Another matter of concern may be the documentation. Probably the Akkuyu NGS will work on the basis of Russian documents for construction and operation of the Russian-designed reactor; translation into Turkish language for the licensing procedures is necessary and may create huge problems. At least, whether international cooperation with EU, NEA and IAEA brought forth concrete results, is not publicly known. Against that background a comprehensive international evaluation of Turkish legislation and the safety as well as security measures is strongly recommended in order to evaluate whether CNS and EU legislation and IAEA respectively OECD-NEA standards are in principle and to what extent complied with; the IRRS methodology[186] could serve as guideline. By that manner risks and doubts as regards lastly judicial reviews by administrative courts could be widely diminished.

5.2 Outlook

Officially planned further steps for initiatives towards new nuclear legislation, particularly for more systematically detailed legislation are not

185 The license for the construction of the United Arab Emirates' first nuclear power plant has been granted for Barakah units 1 and 2 after *»comprehensive review of the construction licence application ... carried out by more than 200 technical experts over a period of 18 months«*; see wnn of 18 July 2012, »UAE nuclear cleared for construction«, available at http://www.world-nuclear-news.org/NN-UAE_nuclear_cleared_for_construction-1807124.html (accessed 03/06/2013). Moreover it should be mentioned that no regulation on requirements for the qualification of external experts firms does exist, while in the field of environmental legislation such a regulation was put into force in 2010 (see in footnote 162 the ÇEVRE GÖREVLİSİ VE ÇEVRE DANIŞMANLIK FİRMALARI HAKKINDA YÖNETMELİK).

186 For the Integrated Regulatory Review Service (IRRS) see International Atomic Energy Agency (IAEA), Our Work, Nuclear Safety & Security, Services for Member States, available at http://www-ns.iaea.org/reviews/rs-reviews.asp?s=7&l=47 (accessed 19/05/2013). See for the recently concluded IRRS mission to Poland as a nuclear newcomer IAEA Press Release 2013/04, International Expert Team Concludes IAEA Peer Review of Poland's Regulatory Framework for Nuclear and Radiation Safety, available at http://www.iaea.org/newscenter/pressreleases/2013/prn201304.html (accessed 27/05/2013).

known. For further steps of developing nuclear legislation in Turkey it is highly recommendable

- with view to international law to ratify nuclear conventions (Paris Convention Protocol of 2004, Brussels Supplementary Convention and the Protocol of 2004 hereto and Joint Convention on Spent Fuel and Waste of 1997) and the Conventions of Espoo and Aarhus, to publish the national reports to CNS review meetings by making the reports available for the public in order to strengthen transparency and to take into consideration the EU/EURATOM legislation,
- as regards national legislation to work out a national atomic energy act as a framework nuclear law including obligatory public involvement during the licensing process, periodical safety reviews especially for NPPs during their lifetime; the role and the importance of Law No. 5710 of 2007 should be revised; the hierarchy of nuclear legislation should be arranged in order to clearly identify the content as well as the systematic relations of the provisions in laws, decrees, regulations, directives and guides. Therefore a new systematic compilation of these legal instruments should be put into force according to the missing, but urgently needed framework nuclear law in order to establish a comprehensive structure of particularly safety and security requirements and thus accomplish a reliably basis for judicial review,
- concerning adequate compensation for victims of nuclear incidents to establish specific and detailed national legislation on nuclear third party liability and a national insurance pool for nuclear liability issues of NPPs,
- to regulate radiation safety for NPPs clearly in a single decree or regulation, if possible by avoiding the necessity of a separate license on radiation safety issues parallel to licenses for siting, construction and operation of NPPs,
- to establish a regulatory body conform to the requirements of CNS and EURATOM-Safety Directive 2009 (taking into account the changes planned by the European Commission),
- to take the necessary measures to obtain sufficient technically experienced staff within the regulatory body and benefit from competent external experts by developing a TSO network being available for the regulatory body,
- to clarify the scope of EIA as well as the interplay with nuclear legislation and licensing,

- to promote and implement in binding norms public information on nuclear issues and take the necessary steps to guarantee considerably the individual right to information.

Particularly the concerns as regards the validity of the site license and potentially the process of EIA for the NPP at the Mersin-Akkuyu site may turn to serious delays in the ambitious nuclear energy plans of Turkey in the case of judicial review.

6. Conclusion

With regard to several doubts whether the system of nuclear legislation in Turkey developed and established up to now will – looking especially at judicial review at administrative and constitutional courts – approve, confirm and thus ensure the licensing of siting, construction and operation of the first NPPs in Turkey in time, the vision of the Turkish Prime Minister announced on 7 April 2013 of breaking open the bureaucracy respectively the bureaucratic oligarchy by a future presidential system[187] may be taken into consideration.

A comprehensive, systematic and transparent nuclear legislation accordingly to international »best practice« including the organisation of competent state authorities and their knowledge of nuclear technical subjects might be realized within short delay and stabilize the consequent way to start the peaceful use of nuclear energy in Turkey by 2020.

Anyway, nuclear law with the whole legal extent of administrative law including civil third party liability regulations will have significantly growing importance in Turkey in the next years.

187 See for example ANADOLU AJANSI at http://www.aa.com.tr/tr/haberler/155863--oligarsinin-belini-baskanlik-sistemi-kirar, BEYAZ GAZETE at http://www.beyazgazete.com/video/anahaber/tvnet-75/2013/04/08/erdogan-baskanlik-sistemi-burokratik-oligarsiyi-kirar-396792.html, DÜNYA BÜLTENİ at http://www.dunyabulteni.net/?aType=haber&ArticleID=254867 and ZAMAN POLITIKA at http://www.zaman.com.tr/politika_erdogan-burokratik-oligarsinin-belini-baskanlik-sistemi-daha-rahat-kirar_2075047.html (each of 7 April 2013, accessed 18/04/2013).

»İyi sözün aslını bilen derdi bu söz nerden gelir
Söz aslını anlamayan sanır bu söz benden gelir.«
Yunus Emre[188], [189]

188 Yunus Emre Hazretleri (kaddesallahu sirrahu); this wisdom means that those who know the origin of a good word, ask themselves where it is from, while those who do not recognize the origin of the word think it is from me; available (only Turkish) at http://www.yunusemresozleri.com/iyi-sozun-aslini-bilen/ (accessed 18/04/2013).

189 The text of this article was finished on 5 July 2013.

Brief Update on Developments in the UK in the Nuclear New Build Arena

Ian Salter, Burges Salmon, Bristol, UK

Ian Salter reported that over the last eight years nuclear law had developed radically to facilitate new nuclear development in the following five major areas:

- Land use planning – the UK had undertaken a major overhaul of its rules concerning major infrastructure projects which had laid the ground for (by UK standards) a rapid approval and consenting process for new nuclear development. Similarly, policy developments had greatly assisted in this process with clear Government statements of support being made for new nuclear development. That policy had been also heavily supported by Government on the ground through the Office of Nuclear Development.
- Access to sites – from an early stage Government had undertaken a Strategic Siting Assessment to identify suitable sites for development and then (where possible) facilitated the disposal of those sites where they had an interest (for instance through the sale of those sites owned by the Nuclear Decommissioning Authority).
- Nuclear licensing – a soft law development had devised (through the offices of the regulator) the generic design assessment (GDA) process which had been successfully followed in relation to the Areva EPR design. In addition the nuclear site licenses for Hinkley Point C, which was the principal development in the UK at present, had been approved.
- Long term waste disposal and funded decommissioning plans – the fourth area where the law had changed to enable nuclear development was in relation to making provision for decommissioning NPPs at the end of their life. New legislation had been passed to prescribe how that should be undertaken. In addition progress had been made in relation to long term waste disposal issues, although it was noted that in January 2013 this programme had suffered a setback with the withdrawal of Cumbria County Council from the volunteering process which had been originally devised by the Government's Committee

on Radioactive Waste Management. The Government, however, remain firmly committed to the policy which focussed on finding a volunteer site to host a long term geological disposal facility.
- Electricity price – at the time of the presentation reforms were being considered by the UK Government and negotiated with EDF.

Ian then went onto address where progress on the principal development in the UK – Hinkley Point C – had got to in relation to these issues. Huge progress had been made.

The GDA was completed at the end of 2012 as was the grant of the nuclear site licence. Planning approvals were given in March 2013.

Two key challenges remained. In relation to Electricity Market Reform, negotiations were currently well underway between EDF and the UK Government on the pricing of electricity from NPPs. The current issues understood to still be under negotiation were the length of time that a guaranteed price would be in place; and the actual price (known as the strike price) which would be given to EDF under a Contract for Difference.

The second issue concerned the land use planning arrangements. These had been approved under the new major infrastructure planning rules on the 19 March 2013. However, two legal challenges had been brought to the planning consent.

Legal Challenges to Development Consent Order

The two challenges had been brought independently of one another by An Taisce (the National Trust for Ireland) and Greenpeace Limited. It was very likely that those two challenges would be heard together.

It was very early days in those proceedings and whilst the grounds of challenge were known the response from the UK Government (which would no doubt be robust) had not yet been filed. The grounds of challenge were understood to be based on two grounds. The An Taisce challenge was a review of the transboundary rules which had been applied in the land use planning process. Essentially it is understood that the Irish organisation claimed that it should have been more widely consulted and was not. The Court's consideration of this point is likely to turn on the way the relevant European directive has been implemented in the UK which might potentially differ in subtle ways to the manner in which the same directive has been implemented in other European countries.

The second challenge by Greenpeace Limited is understood to focus more centrally on the Government's policy on long term waste disposal, which it argues has been not met following the withdrawal of Cumbria County Council from the volunteer process outlined above. As a result Greenpeace, it is understood, will argue that the government's policy requirement for nuclear new build which requires new build to proceed only if satisfactory arrangements are in place for long term waste disposal had not been met because of the setbacks suffered as a result of the January decision by Cumbria CC.

There are clearly, therefore, important issues to be resolved in this second half of 2013. The legal challenges to the planning consent raises potentially important issues of UK and European law. In addition, significant commercial conditions for EDF's investment in the development remain unresolved, as does the existence of a commercial partner for EDF in this enormously significant infrastructure development.

Discussion Report of the Second Working Session

Łukasz Młynarkiewicz, Phd C., Nicolaus Copernicus University, Toruń, Poland

The discussion was initiated by *Mr. Dussart-Desart* with a question addressed to Mr. Schneider whether intentions of the Turkish government were known to ratify the Brussels Supplementary Convention on Nuclear Third Party Liability or the Joint Protocol Relating to the Application of the Vienna Convention and the Paris Convention.

Horst Schneider noted that Turkey did ratify the Joint Protocol, but did not ratify the 2004 Protocol to amend the Paris Convention on Nuclear Third Party Liability. He also expressed the opinion that Turkey does not intend to ratify the Brussels Supplementary Convention. Mr. Schneider added that actually no national legislation on nuclear third party liability exists in Turkey, although in the past national legislation was drafted twice but never finished or regulated by law. He concluded that lack of a national framework in the field of nuclear third party liability should be considered as a big gap in Turkish legislation.

Mr. Kardaras raised a question regarding compliance of Turkish legislation with the transboundary consultation requirements to which Horst Schneider answered that Turkey did not sign nor ratify the Espoo Convention or the Aarhus Convention. Nevertheless, Turkey had announced and promised to inform, on a voluntary and informal basis, the EU Member States on the Akkuyu NPP project. He also pointed out that legislation as regards to public information on nuclear projects exists in Turkey, however, this legislation and the practice of the right to information seem to be rather weak. Moreover, he hinted at the deficiency of a nuclear law framework in Turkey, which had been criticized by the European Commission several times.

Subsequently, *Mr. Salter* turned to Tomasz Nowacki and Markus Pfaff with a question about whether the transboundary consultations, which are being carried out with Germany, are also being done at the same or at a lower level with countries that are not neighboring states to Poland, such as France. Mr. Nowacki noted that Poland notified ten eventually interested countries about the possibility of taking part in the procedure of transboundary consultations concerning the cross-border environmental impacts of planned nuclear power plants. Moreover, the information regarding transboundary consultations was also sent to countries that are not bordering states of Poland, however, according to Mr. Nowacki France did not figure on that list. He added that three out of ten countries, namely, Lithuania, Estonia and Latvia had informed Poland that they did not want to participate in consultations.

Markus Pfaff informed that, for instance, Austria as non-neighboring country to Poland was involved in the same consultation process as Germany. He noted that because of the Espoo Convention there is a general obligation to notify and to involve in the EIA process those states whose territory could be significantly affected by the activity of another country. Moreover, according to Mr. Pfaff, it is difficult for states of origin to really assess transboundary impacts, so in case of potential risks they should undertake transboundary consultations. He also brought up the example of the Hungarian project regarding NPP Paks Site expansion, for which Hungary decided to notify all EU member states.

Mr. Burns raised a question addressed to Rüdiger Tscherning regarding floating nuclear power plants and their legal status. He asked about the legal difference between an ordinary nuclear power plant and a floating – but potentially operational – nuclear reactor, which after being fixed in a location (e.g. tied to a dock) would be considered land based. From Mr. Burns' point of view, such differentiations sometimes create too many legal complications and he suggested that such construction should be perceived from a more traditional perspective. He added that the floating nuclear power plant has never been built in the United States, however, the design license was in a planning phase.

Mr. Tscherning replied that the key issue in this matter may be that such construction is neither preliminarily fixed nor is it just something that floats all over the time in terms of moving. As far as Mr. Tscherning is concerned, states that pose excessive concern are usually motivated by additional environmental risks and security reasons. He concluded that in terms of maritime public international law issues, the matter of fixing construction to the seabed is also something that needs to be looked at more and clarified.

Mr. Matveev agreed with Mr. Burns that sometimes the nuclear society's approach to particular definitions – such as with respect to transportable nuclear power plants – is far too complicated. He noted that mobile or movable nuclear power plants were initially designed to make things simpler. For instance, this also means simpler for producers for cost reasons. He pointed out that obviously it is the host state that regulates and licenses the TNPP. As for the status of the TNPP, Mr. Matveev suggested that it may be considered as a platform or a normal nuclear installation while being fixed to the seabed, however, it will not be a floating device anymore. He concluded that the Russian experience after finishing the first TNPP, as well as the commercial practice will provide new legal solutions and determine the future of TNPPs.

Mr. Raetzke expressed the conviction on the legal status of transportable nuclear power plants that there are practical and legal issues which necessitate differentiating TNPPs from ordinary nuclear power plants. He remarked that, for instance, floating nuclear power plants provide an opportunity to deploy nuclear power in countries which cannot or do not have time to create nuclear infrastructure. Mr. Raetzke noted that the establishment of a national nuclear regulatory infrastructure is a long-term process. Therefore, from Mr. Raetzke's point of view, it should be considered whether transportable nuclear power plants may be used in a way that does not necessitate the host country to build up an entire regulatory structure as in the case of licensing an ordinary nuclear power plant but in a way that relies to a certain extent on the authorisations and certifications given by the supplier country. This would be somewhat similar to the situation in aviation.

Third Working Session

»Nuclear Liability, Part One: Nuclear Liability in the EU«

Chair: *Dr. Norbert Pelzer,* University of Göttingen, Honorary Chairman of the German Branch of AIDN/INLA

Secretary: *Sidonie Royer-Maucotel,* CEA, Gif-sur-Yvette, France

Activities of the EU Commission in the Field of Nuclear Liability Coverage – Some Personal Remarks

Dirk Harbrücker, Deutsche Kernreaktor-Versicherungsgemeinschaft (DKVG), Cologne

The Fukushima disaster triggered two actions by the EU Commission for Energy: the first one being the stress tests for nuclear power plants, the other one was aimed at improving the third party insurance of operators. While the stress tests have been widely reported in the press, the second one was unknown to the public for a long time. The second initiative became only known, when the Commissioner for energy, Mr. Oettinger, first spoke about his intention to introduce a mandatory insurance on nuclear operators in October 2012 – I will come back to his statement later.

To prepare the grounds for Mr. Oettinger's plan a working group on nuclear liability has been established to elaborate proposals for the compensation of victims after a nuclear accident. This group started its work on April 2011 and ended its work after six meetings at the end of February 2013.

Within the EU member states there are different legal regimes in the field of nuclear third party liability in force, namely Paris and Vienna Convention states and states not party to any of those conventions. This situation is apparently contrary to the principles of unity within the European Union. The working group's task was defined to give advice on (1) insurance (i.e. claims handling), (2) amounts of insurance cover and (3) other possible areas. Three subworking groups have been established to make suggestions in this respect to be presented at plenary meetings. Art. 98 EURATOM Treaty (»Member States shall take all measures necessary to facilitate the conclusion of insurance contracts covering nuclear risks«) was quoted to be the legal basis for the Commissions' intervention. But how to impose a mandatory insurance without an underlying liability?

Members of the group have been invited from different sectors: OECD/NEA, IAEA, EESC, Operators, Suppliers, Group of European municipalities with nuclear facilities, Nuclear (Re-)Insurers=Pools, Mutual Insurance Companies owned by operators, Academics in the nuclear field. They represented a wide background. But as most of them have had a financial or economical interest in that matter and were not independent in the requested brain storming process, they could rather be considered as »lobbyists«. Representatives of the (nuclear) industry for example pleaded for maintaining the status quo or at the utmost to move up to the inevitable increase of limits already provided by the revision of the conventions, whereas insurers – apart from the mutuals – quietly would not mind to see limits be increased, as a new source for premium, however did not want to upset their clients. As from the beginning this made the work more complicated and challenged any substantial outcome.

While independent experts received a reimbursement of their travelling expenses to attend the plenary sessions, there was no compensation for their participation in the work of the subgroups. Thus, the subgroups have been recruited mainly from the industry (operators or insurers).

The sub working groups met without any logistical support from the Commission, which means that the respective chairman of such group formed his own think tank, and his secretary was the organizer of his meetings. The chairmen had to draft their (own) ideas, to distribute them for discussion and to finally earn lively criticism from the other members; a most thankless job, which only was paid back by the honour to present the (common, if ever) findings at plenary sessions. A cold comfort only as at plenary sessions criticism started again, sometimes even supported by members of the own subgroup(s).

Apart from the reports of the subgroups additional presentations have been made at plenary sessions by different experts, of which the most outstanding questioned the principle of legal channelling of operators' liability.

Sub working group 1 divided the claims handling process in three sections: (1) claims registration, (2) claims handling to be understood as decision on the acceptance of a claim, the collection of medical or expert statements, the evaluation of the claims and of the injuries of victims respectively and the decision on amounts payable and (3) the claims settlement (preliminary, partial or final pay out of compensations to victims). Academically I can understand this splitting, but in practice this is random, as all actions go hand in hand.

This first sub working group recommended in its first draft that an European wide »one stop shop« for claims registration should be established where victims could file claims in their language by using a uniform single claim form. At first glance the proposal sounds absolutely victim minded, but in my view such a registration office on EU-wide or national basis – which was the later outcome of the group – would only be another bureaucratic animal producing substantial costs to operators. The request for a uniform claims notification form is perfectly understandable, as the victims will have to be treated equally all over Europe regardless of their nationality, ethnic origin or place of residence. Nevertheless it is not realistic, as the legal systems differ from country to country: just to mention the direct action as one example or the different social systems (health insurance, workmen's compensation). Accordingly the claims notification would have to be adapted for each country. The simple publishing of a claims registration form is a pure IT-task, publishing the form in all languages spoken in the EU would provoke huge handling problems in answering if handled in one office; therefore only a diversification on a national basis will ensure an adequate processing and answering.

As well we should not limit victims by not allowing them to submit their claims in any form they want: be that by telephone, e-mail, letter or personally. You will have to keep open all ways of communication, as any infrastructure might no longer work after a severe catastrophe like Fukushima. Even the ad hoc formation of a »simple desk« would bring more administration problems than advantages and is not necessary in my eyes as the insurance industry has repeatedly proven their ability to handle large number of claims after floods, storms or earthquakes. As from the beginning you will need experienced staff with both legal and insurance background to answer all conceivable questions of victims. The compensation of victims is best done locally, also think of a »first aid« to be paid out to the victims of a nuclear catastrophe accommodated in the evacuation centres. Establishing a »one stop shop« on European level would also make it necessary to overrule national insurance acts which describe the obligations of insurers in case of a claim.

Sub working group 2 gave a detailed overview on the different existing liability schemes within the EU and outlined specific alternative solutions like the solidarity agreement in Germany or the post funding scheme in the US. The insurance markets providing capacity have been described, namely the nuclear insurance pools based on their relevant national insurance markets, of which the Nordic Pool being the only combination of two countries (Finland and Sweden). In addition (or competition) to pools operators had developed their own insurance company (mutual) ELINI and are in process of forming a reinsurance company in Luxemburg, BLUE Re, which would offer new capacity. Even the simple description of facts was discussed very controversial, as for example the question of reliability or volatility of insurance capacities after a larger catastrophe.

Insurers generally do not design the content, extent or the amount of mandatory insurance. They rather try to fulfill the demands of the legislator, but might impose exclusions or limitations on coverage. For most classes of insurance capacity is not a problem, but coverage for nuclear third party liability is somewhat delicate. The reason might be that the number of risks is very limited and premiums are low in relation to the amount covered. Therefore capacity for nuclear third party has developed rather slowly than in large steps always following the needs of the industry instead of going ahead.

Nevertheless capacity for nuclear third party liability has quite significantly increased over the last years to prepare for the higher amounts under the revised Paris Convention. Another reason for increased capacities is that in most European markets the available financial amounts for the insurance of own property could not be used in full by the pools because of the activity of industry owned mutual and therefore became available for third party liability. In other words capacities initially provided to cover so called material damages were rededicated to be used for the coverage of damages to third parties. Meanwhile limits of € 1200 million have been covered easily in Belgium and Netherlands where the limits of the revised Paris Coventions have already been installed. These amounts offered by the conventional insurance markets organised in pools might go up to € 1500 million, but not far beyond – this is my personal expectation. One would have to add another € 100 million or slightly more from the mutual.

There is a question mark whether the capacity from pools will stand under the revision of the Paris and Vienna Convention: a clear no go is the extension of the prescription period from 10 to 30 years. Whether all heads of the enlarged environmental coverage will be met by all pools is still not clear yet. The mutual serving their members will provide full coverage – no doubt.

The chairman of Sub working group 3 was more progressive in trying to look into the future. His proposal for unlimited liability provoked a »petition« from most participants for turning it down; only the German delegates saw it quite relaxed as their operators experience unlimited liability since the mid 80's. This resulted in a modest final statement recommending that all EU members are required to join the Paris or Vienna Convention in their revised versions (2004 and 1997 amendments respectively).

This was the common thread in the plenary session and as well to maintain the conventions and their basic principles, which have been developed over so many years. All participants have been most diplomatic in even not expressing the recommendation that a concentration on one convention only within EU would be desirable, nor the harmonization of the highly differing liability amounts.

Time did flow and the (EU) chairman of the working group showed his dissatisfaction as no progress was achieved. There were no trailblazing proposals made until Munich Re came up in October 2012 with a proposal of offering € 10bn for a nuclear cat(astrophe) cover in excess of underlying € 2,5bn of traditional (insurance) capacity. The Munich Re idea was published by the press in Germany on October 8, 2012 (Financial Times Germany) and followed a press statement of Mr. Oettinger four days earlier (Frankfurter Allgemeine Zeitung, October 4, 2012) pushing for mandatory insurance in Europe, when presenting the results of the European stress tests in Brussels. Obviously he had in mind to bring up limits for mandatory insurance or to harmonise the varying existing limits. Later press statements by the Commissioner made his intention clear that he wanted to go for substantial increases of the liability insurance amounts beyond limits set by the revised conventions.

Munich Re had developed new ideas after the Deepwater Horizon accident in the Gulf of Mexico in April 2010 in order to generate substantial insurance capacities for catastrophic kind of accidents and called their project »oil spill cover«. Based on the reflection that substantial financial means are available to cover large natural catastrophes (material damages) this project was developed for extraordinary environmental liability damages arising out of oil drilling platforms. According to their statement it could be made available as well for catastrophic nuclear accidents like Chernobyl or Fukushima. Munich Re would see (reinsurance) markets prepared to provide a substantial amount of money when they would know by the end of the (underwriting) year whether coverage had been incepted or not. This shows the (short tail) character of material damage cover where you know by the end of the year that your engagement remained loss free or you will have to pay (partially or in full). This proposal found the enthusiasm of the chairman as for the first time this would bring a substantial higher amount of coverage. This however would only be available for incidents classified as INES 5 or higher excluding anything which could arise out of the normal operation of a plant including personal injuries in the neighbourhood which only might become obvious after a certain period of time – and therefore not be in accordance with the conventions. Nevertheless I am personally firmly convinced that this is the only way how to generate substantial additional financial means from third parties for covering higher liability limits. However one should be aware that this coverage will not be available for free.

Having shared with you my private criticism please allow me to conclude my presentation with my personal outlook:

The whole exercise did not bring any dramatic new ideas, but the proposal of Munich Re. The Commissioner for Energy will nevertheless use the findings and conclusions of the working group as basis for a public consultation and will continue working on the mission to improve the protection of the EU citizens by looking for any solution allowing to broaden the nuclear liability and increase insurance limits respectively.

Had this not been the case before the Fukushima catastrophe, at least since then it has become popular for most European political parties to opt for substantial increases of nuclear liability limits and some of these parties are seeing their long-standing demand for higher limits dramatically justified. They will take up any offer of reliable (insurance) capacities.

What Can the Victims of a Nuclear Incident Expect from the Initiative of the European Commission Related to Nuclear Liability?

Roland Dussart-Desart, Chairman of the Nuclear Law Committee (NEA, OECD), Conseiller général, Head of the legal division of the Belgian Federal public service Economy, SMEs, Self Employed and Energy [1]

Some reminders

For more than half a century, The European Commission didn't really venture into the strange world of nuclear liability. The Euratom Treaty had however a provision in that field. Article 98 states that: *»Member States shall take all necessary measures to facilitate the conclusion of insurance contracts covering atomic risks. Within a period of two years after the date of the entry into force of this Treaty and after the Assembly has been consulted, the Council, acting by means of a qualified majority vote on a proposal of the Commission which shall previously obtain the opinion of the Economic and Social Committee, shall issue directives as to the particulars of application of this Article.«*

This article didn't find any application. The six original members of the European Union (»EU«) (with the exception of the Grand-Duchy of Luxembourg) and most new members joining the EU up to the eighties were Parties to the same Paris Convention on Nuclear Third Party Liability (»The Paris Convention«), concluded within the frame of the OECD and, for those Parties developing effectively a nuclear program, of the Brussels Supplementary Convention on Nuclear Third Party Liability (»The Brussels Convention«). There were just three discording voices, namely Austria, Grand-Duchy of Luxembourg and Ireland, which developed an anti-nuclear policy which was incompatible with the principles of legal channeling and limited liability, to name a few, which were among the founding pillars of the Paris Convention.

1 Disclaimer: these views are expressed as personal remarks; they do not represent the official position of the Belgian government

The situation changed radically with the collapse of the Berlin wall and the adhesion of former Eastern bloc States to the EU. Most of those States were or became Parties to the Vienna Convention on Civil Liability for Nuclear Damage (»The Vienna Convention«). That Convention had been »bridged« with the Paris Convention thanks to the Joint Protocol relating to the Application of the Vienna Convention and the Paris Convention (»The Joint Protocol«) adopted hastily in 1988 after the Tchernobyl accident, but Parties to the Paris Convention were less prone to ratify that text than their Viennese counterparts. Although the concerns and amounts quoted in both conventions were rather similar, the western legislators already had inscribed far higher amounts to be insured than those requested under their international commitments. Quite surprisingly, only one Party to the Vienna Convention, namely Slovenia, considered that its adhesion to the EU offered also the motive, the opportunity or the need to denounce the Vienna Convention and to adhere to the Paris/Brussels Conventions, even if Slovenia wasn't member of the OECD.

In the meantime, the Vienna Convention was revised by the 1997 Protocol but unfortunately, the original version remained opened for accession. In addition to the revision of the Vienna convention, another supplementary instrument, the Convention on Supplementary Compensation for Nuclear Damage (»the CSC«) was deemed to »top« not only the Vienna Convention, but also the Paris Convention and even legal systems coping with a number of common principles. Only one EU member State, Romania, ratified the CSC.

So, over a ten-years period, the monotonous and flat landscape of nuclear liability within the EU had become a jungle with member States in about ten different positions in terms of adhesion to international instruments, not to mention a remarkable variety of amounts to be insured and the German exception of unlimited liability.

This situation can only be detrimental to the smooth and fair indemnification of the victims of a nuclear accident with transboundary effects within the EU. It puts also to the test the competitive situation of the nuclear operators, even within the Paris/Brussels Conventions. In 2011, a Belgian operator has to provide an insurance 13 times higher than its French neighbor and competitor on the grid, both Parties to the same Paris Convention.

The European Commission decided then to charge the solicitors Gomez-Acebo y Pombo abogados to submit a detailed report on those issues. A questionnaire was sent to a number of interested stakeholders, academics, law practitioners and officers of international organizations and the exercise was followed by interviews of a selected array of experts. The questionnaire was concluded by a poll between several alternatives to either get rid of the »patchwork« situation … or to ignore it.

The by far-preferred option was to see all 27 (read now: 28) EU member States remain or become Parties to the (revised) Paris Convention.

Two other options gained the same level of support:

- the status quo and
- only 22 (23) EU member States remain or become Parties to the (revised) Paris Convention, in other words, leave the 5 non-contracting States out of the system.

The last option, namely the accession of Euratom to the Paris Convention (which would require an amendment of the latter) or the adoption of a Euratom directive had no success at all.

This rather provocative exercise was followed in June 2010 by a workshop on the prospects of a civil nuclear liability in the framework of the EU, organized jointly by the Belgian Nuclear Law Association and the European Commission.

Among the numerous interventions, one must underline three themes:

- an analysis of the powers of the EU to intervene in the field of nuclear liability, by Melchior Wathelet, a former judge of the European Court of Justice. The speaker advocated an extensive interpretation of article 98 of the Euratom Treaty, how to throw away its two-year time limit and even offered alternatives to offer a legal basis for the intervention of the EU legislator, at the cost of unanimity;
- a study about the impact of EU competition rules: can the nuclear liability systems be qualified as state aid, by Laurent Garzaniti and Andrew Renshaw. The authors were less affirmative than the former one and identified several elements putting the existing nuclear liability systems at risk, under the qualification of State aid; such fears could be prevented by
  1) the adhesion of Euratom to the Paris Convention,
  2) by EU legislation or
  3) by a block exemption for State aid for nuclear liability;
- a voice from Ireland: Una Nidhubhghaill from the office of the Attorney general, quoted the existing Conventions as inadequate and expressed the wish to oblige the Member States having nuclear installa-

tions on their soil to indemnify any damage not covered by the coverage of the operator liable.

The nuclear liability group 2011 – 2013

The European Commission finally launched a »think tank« which was convened in Luxembourg to reflect on a number of issues related to nuclear liability. By a tragic irony, the group started its work just a few weeks after the tsunami which devastated the north-eastern coast of Japan and caused the Tepco Fukushima Daïchi accident.

The group included a wide panel of profiles: stakeholders from the electric and insurance industry, officers from the IAEA and of the NEA *(the respective depositaries of the Vienna and Paris Conventions on nuclear liability)*, and several academics known for their articles in the *Nuclear law bulletin*. There was a reasonable balance between the EU member States Parties to the Paris and Vienna conventions, even if the »Paris« views were over-weighted. There were almost no public servants from the national administrations, probably because the European Commission knew they would intervene at a later stage.

Unfortunately, in spite of repeated invitations, the organizers failed to attract speakers from any of the 5 EU member States which are neither Parties to the Vienna Convention nor Parties to the Paris Convention (Austria, Cyprus, Grand-Duchy of Luxembourg, Ireland, Malta, quoted further as »the 5 non-contracting States«). There was just one exception: we give one point for Ireland which sent one representative for one meeting. However, the Irish delegate did just express general reserves and didn't really take part in the discussions.

So, straight from the beginning, one important point of view was missing around the table and, especially when the group was dealing with nuclear liability, one had to guess how the legitimate concerns and interests of those States could be dealt with.

Three sub-working groups (*WG*) were installed to deal with specific issues:

<u>WG1 had to deal with claims handing and related matters.</u> The Chairman of the nuclear liability group, Mr Garribba, expressed repeatedly doubts and concerns about the ability and preparation of the insurance pools to treat in an equitable and efficient way the claims from victims of damages suffered in other countries than the operator's one.

WG2 had to cope with insurance, pools & other financial guarantees. The capacity of the insurance market to cover nuclear liability is a long standing issue and those limits generated alternative ways to increase the amounts available; beside the State intervention as organized by the Brussels supplementary Convention and the CSC, WG2 had to explore the pooling systems and other ways to provide financial guarantees.

WG3 was charged to study the matter of nuclear liability amounts and »other areas«. The purpose of this group was quite wide, since it had to reflect on the best ways to enhance, replace or amend the present complex architecture of Conventions, to deal with the 5 non-contracting States, and to look at the soundness of the basic principles ruling nuclear liability in Europe, a.o. the channeling and the strict liability of the operator.

The three WG's had six joint meetings in Luxembourg between April, 5, 2011 and February, 28, 2013, and also had meetings of their own.

The results

WG1 (claims handling)

I don't wish to enter too deeply into the conclusions of WG1. Please find hereunder their 7 recommendations; the full text, including the objectives and the ways to implement each of them is available under ANNEX 1.

Recommendation 1 –	*Member States having nuclear installations on their territories should have a claims management system up and running.*
Recommendation 2 –	*Member States to establish a »one stop shop« for claims registration and record*
Recommendation 3 –	*Establish criteria for EU-wide claims handling communication in the case of an accident*
Recommendation 4 –	*Establish »one single desk« for claims handling (national level)*
Recommendation 5 –	*Allow for the assessment of insurers abilities by national authorities*

Recommendation 6 –	*Set up rules for advance payments on compensation*
Recommendation 7 –	*Clarify how claims management costs are borne*

Although all those principles are quite sound and reflect the best practices available, the European Commission should resist the temptation to enter into a too much stringent and detailed directive. A directive is deemed to give objectives to the member States which have to choose the best option to implement them; far too often, directives become so detailed that they sound like regulations. This might interfere with the particularities of some national legislations, such as the right of direct recourse against the insurer. It would rather be advisable to organize regular peer reviews to encourage and develop those preparations.

WG2 Insurance, pools and other financial security

I suspect the precedent speaker, who was a very active member of both WG2 and WG3, will evocate the issues studied by WG2. Please find hereunder the 4 recommendations of WG2 (full text in ANNEX 2).

> *<u>RECOMMENDATION 1</u>*
>
> *The member states must work jointly with nuclear operators and nuclear insurance providers, to put in place cover that fulfills the revised Convention requirements & ratify the applicable Convention as soon as possible.*
>
> *<u>RECOMMENDATION 2</u>*
>
> *The EU Commission is to clarify & communicate the acceptable conditions under which EU states are allowed to act, directly or indirectly, to cover nuclear third party liability risks (e.g. for the uninsurable Convention new heads of damage, limits & cover extensions).*
>
> *<u>RECOMMENDATION 3</u>*
>
> *Ensure that all financial security provided is sufficiently secure, stable & solvent to guarantee maximum protection for nuclear accident victims; also ensure that a robust & effective claims handling system is put in place.*

<u>*RECOMMENDATION 4*</u>

In the longer term the operators & financial security providers are to continue working together to investigate any additional nuclear liability capacity that might become available in future

WG2 had a hard task; to find capacity is the core business of the nuclear insurance industry and those capacities tend to vanish as soon as doubts can be raised about a particular risk. We no longer enjoy a world when we looked confidently at a perpetual climb of the capacities. Bearing in mind those facts, I would have expected more emphasis on the identification of the pre-requisite for the erection of a European pool of operators. Time might not be yet ripe for that, but I think such a move is unavoidable in the future, especially if, thanks to the work of international organizations like IAEA and NEA, all the nuclear installations reach a similar level of safety.

WG3 – Amounts and other issues – a missed opportunity

As I was requested to chair WG3, I tried to fulfill this job by a first analysis of the situation on nuclear liability within the EU – the famous patchwork described in the analysis by Gomez-Acebo y Pombo abogados. This assessment was followed by several successive proposals to achieve not only a unification of the nuclear liability system within the EU, but also an improvement of that system. Unification and standardization are no objectives in themselves. One might even pretend that unification is already is force, since for each accident, there should be (in the 1997/2004 and full adhesion to the Joint Protocol perspective) only one applicable law and only one competent court.

However, in order to keep what we already have, and more particularly the Treaty relations with the Paris and Vienna Parties which don't belong to the EU, the idea was to base the proposed EU-system on the Paris and Vienna Conventions, as amended. The Vienna States would have been asked to put the legal provisions of their respective national legislations up to the amounts requested under the Paris Convention, within a reasonable time frame. Finally, the EU would not only stress all the Parties to Paris and Vienna to ratify the amending Protocols of 1997 and 2004 (this has already been done for Paris and should happen soon for Vienna), but also to ratify the Joint Protocol: there are 4 Parties to the Paris Convention not yet

Parties to the Joint Protocol, namely Belgium, France, Spain and the United Kingdom, due to the lack of balance between the amounts offered by both systems (in the meantime, France has decided to ratify the Joint Protocol).

However, some additional elements are still deeply needed to attract the 5 non contracting States in the frame of the Conventions. In my view, this is the main challenge for the full harmonization of nuclear liability within the EU.

The main element I proposed was the generalization of unlimited liability. I don't know for how long professors will be able to teach seriously and sincerely that the limitation of liability is a fair compensation of the strict liability of the operator. I heard in Luxembourg a lone voice in the assembly saying that the limitation of liability was like a subsidy to the nuclear industry and could be assessed as an infringement against the EC competition rules. In my own personal view, I wish to underline that a system of limited liability doesn't correspond anymore to the level of protection and justice the population expect from their authorities. The level of acceptance by the public of such rules inherited from the fifties has since dropped significantly. As long as there is no accident, it would be in the interest of the operators themselves to be subjected to an unlimited liability, as it would enhance the acceptance of their activities by the public opinion. May I add that such a move would also help the setting up of an international pool of operators at the European level? If we wish that the operators show their readiness to share the risks across the borders, they should first be subjected to the same obligations.

Another element was to assure the immediate availability of additional funds through an international pool of operators. However, this was supposed to be evocated under WG2 and I was asked to rely on that group for that issue.

A final element would be a concession on the front of legal channeling. Of course, the assets of the operator are limited and that's why the 5 non contracting States also challenge the legal channeling and wish to be able to sue anyone related to a nuclear incident (the economic channeling). We know this would jeopardize the availability of insurance. Professor Pelzer (the famous lone voice) suggested then to add to the package some kind of a tolerance of economic channeling as far as it would concern victims in those non-Contracting States. I included his proposal within an interim proposal, but it failed to attract much support. With all my respect for Professor Pelzer, I fear such a construction would be quite difficult to apply to any accident with transboundary effects: it would pave the way for endless and costly recourses and judicial procedures, a perspective which won't rejoice the insurers. The claims handling costs are indeed one of their major concerns, due to the foreseeable high number of plaintiffs. More prosaically, it would request amendments to both Vienna and Paris Convention, preferably in the presence and with the participation and full agreement of the 5 non contracting States. Finally, it would be in contradiction with the principle of fair and equal treatment of all the victims within the EU; I fear this would mean the opening of Pandora's box and incur further delays for the modernization of the rules related to the nuclear liability within the EU.

Sadly enough, those few modest steps seemed to exceed the goodwill of most WG3 members. Trials to rise some emulation or to convince members that it was necessary, in an EC perspective, to fill the black hole of the 5 non contracting States, ended in failure.

On one side, most stakeholders from the nuclear industry didn't wish to enter into the world of unlimited liability, although it doesn't seem to pose many problems in Germany or Switzerland which will be soon joined on that field by Sweden and Finland.

The stakeholders from Parties to the Vienna Convention even didn't hesitate to oppose vividly the idea to upgrade their liability amounts up to those of the Paris Convention, namely 700 million EUR, although some Paris countries already have obtained insurances for up to 1,2 billion EUR (in the frame of the non-revised Paris Convention, I concede).

So, just like Evelyne Ameye from solicitors Gomez-Acebo y Pombo abogados stated it 6 years ago, there is a global reluctance from the stakeholders to amend in any way the present structure.

A few other voices were heard from academic speakers, pleading for the dismantling of all the main pillars of the nuclear liability in Europe, namely the strict liability, the legal channeling and the possibility to limit the liability amounts, just to name a few. Those views were a very small minority in WG3, but they certainly reflect a part of the public opinion and proved later to be enough to ruin any consensus.

In spite of those predictions, WG3 members were invited in Brussels before the 6th meeting of Luxembourg to write down a »*minimum minimorum*« proposal. Sadly enough, the participation was rather limited in comparison with the full WG3 group which finally agreed on the following text (this is the full text of the recommendations so they are not again reproduced in an Annex):

Working Group 3 – Nuclear Liability Amounts and other Areas

Recommendations

It is useful to state the mandate of this EU nuclear liability group as confirmed in the minutes of its first meeting on 5 April 2011:

»The purpose of the group is to explore common ground amongst the stakeholders (consensus building) who should give recommendations for a future (legislative) proposal of the European Commission under Article 98 of the Euratom Treaty«.

»The purpose of any Commission proposal would be to increase (legal) coherence in the EU, which is needed to improve, on the one hand, victim protection in different Member States, and, on the other hand, to tackle the impact on the functioning of the internal market because of diverging financial guarantee obligations of operators as well as availability of insurance, which might give rise to distortion of competition«.

With a view to fulfilling this mandate, WG3 explored a number of different issues, such as the existing conventional structure within the EU, the position and interests of the EU members without nuclear installations, unlimited liability versus limited liability, the application of the common law, economic channeling versus legal channeling and the sustainability of higher liability limits. The group tried to take into account the concerns and opinions of participants and stakeholders from different horizons. This work led to the Recommendations at the end of this document. The thorny issue of nuclear liability amounts and indeed other aspects of the nuclear liability regime remain controversial and consensus was not always easy to obtain.

To this end, the WG3 Recommendations have attempted to reconcile as far as possible a number of legitimate and occasionally contradictory concerns:

- *The desire to improve the position of victims of a nuclear accident;*
- *The objective of avoiding discrimination between victims of different EU Member States , irrespective of where an accident happened or where damage is suffered;*
- *The need to maintain existing Treaty relations with non-EU Parties to Paris Convention on Third Party Liability in the field of Nuclear Energy (PC) and to Vienna Convention on Civil Liability for Nuclear Damage (VC);*

- *The need to exploit to the highest level possible the insurance capacities available;*
- *The need to offer a fair, predictable and workable legal framework for victims, insurers & operators.*

You will find to follow the Recommendations of WG 3.

RECOMMENDATIONS

The following proposals are all subject to confirmation of EU competence under Article 98 of the Euratom Treaty, to the subsidiarity and proportionality principles, and to their compatibility with the VC (1997) and the PC (2004).

Two complementary recommendations might be considered.

RECOMMENDATION 1 – EU DECISION(S)

A1. *All EU members are required to join the VC or the PC as amended respectively in 1997 and 2004.*
OR
A2. *EU members wishing to join the VC or the PC should ratify exclusively the VC or the PC as amended respectively in 1997 and 2004.*

B. *All EU members Parties to either the VC or the PC are urged:*
i) to adhere as soon as possible to »their« respective amending Protocols of 1997 and 2004 (N.B. this sub-section (i) to be deleted if Option ***A1*** *is retained above) and,*
ii) if they have not already done so, to adhere to the Joint Protocol.

Instrument(s): decision(s)

In order to reach this goal, the Commission may provide a deadline for the fulfillment of this Recommendation. However, the Commission should take the necessary steps to lift any requirement for EU members Parties to either the VC or the PC to simultaneously deposit their ratification instruments of the amending Protocols of 1997 or 2004, as applicable (e.g. the Commission should put forward a proposal to amend the 2004/294/EC Council Decision of 8 March 2004 accordingly and/or to provide for an exemption under Council Regulation (EC) No 44/2001 of 22 December 2000).

RECOMMENDATION 2 - EU DIRECTIVE

A Directive should, in its recitals, recognize the relevance and robustness of the basic principles of the VC(1997) and PC(2004) establishing the rules of a unified regime of nuclear liability (inter alia, strict liability, legal channeling, the right to limit the operator's liability in amount and in time, the obligation of the operator to cover its liability by insurance or other financial security), and the importance of the Joint Protocol.

The provisions of the Directive would:

1) *establish amounts for nuclear third party liability and compulsory financial security up to these amounts in line with the PC(2004) provisions [Members States would have a reasonable timeframe to implement such requirement (e.g. 10 years)];*
2) *require Member States to ensure that, up to the amounts quoted under 1, compensation available under their legislation shall indemnify victims in all EU Member States without discrimination based upon nationality, domicile or residence.*

As I already quoted it, this text couldn't reach a consensus in the plenary meeting. The few voices against this text were motivated by quite different and even antagonist concerns: for some, it goes too far in imposing higher amounts on operators; for another, the solution was the replacement of legal channeling by economic channeling; a last one advocated unlimited liability but, this time, it wasn't Prof. Pelzer and I thank him for his constructive silence.

Does everyone realize how different are the victims of the XXIst century?

What can the victims hope now from this EU exercise?

The Tchernobyl accident triggered the redaction and the adoption of a number of international instruments dealing a.o. with the nuclear safety, the early notification of accidents, the interactions between the Paris and Vienna Conventions on nuclear liability and the revision of those both Conventions, even if those 1997 and 2004 Protocols didn't enter yet into force. These steps were taken in spite of the fact that the information about the circumstances and effects of the Tchernobyl accident was, at the beginning anyway, rather scarce and subject to conflicting interpretations, under-estimations and misunderstandings.

25 years later, the Tepco Fukushima Daïchi accident threw another light on the subject of nuclear liability, just when the EC started its investigations about the challenges of the nuclear liability regimes in the EU. This time, the accident happened in a country with a nuclear liability regime quite similar in many ways to the one applicable in Germany or in Switzerland. It happened also in a new era, a world of communication and information: it is no longer possible to hide or to put aside the crude realities of the effects of a nuclear accident. Fortunately, the Tepco Fukushima Daïchi accident didn't cause fatalities outside the damaged installations and one may expect that the Japanese authorities will organize an adequate sanitary follow-up of their remarkably cooperative and stoic population. In the Nuclear Law Committee, we were privileged to host three times at the Nuclear Law Committee Japanese experts led by Prof. Nomura who gave us detailed explanations about the way the victims were being indemnified, even if the total amount of the damages far exceed the amounts insured under the Japanese law or the operator's assets.

It was quite dazzling to see how differently the European governments and opinions reacted to that tragedy. It seems that for most Parties to the Vienna Convention, there is nothing new under the sky. On the contrary, in some Parties to the Paris Convention, the reactions were quite vivid: Germany accelerated its phasing out and the Belgian Parliament was able to quadruple the amount of the operator's liability up to 1,2 billion EUR within a few months, even if there was no government in full charge.

The accident reopened the speculations about the costs of nuclear accidents: the French *Institut de Radioprotection et de Sûreté Nucléaire (IRSN)* valued the damages of a major accident in France up to 1.000 billion EUR last year. The Nuclear Development Committee of the NEA will try to do its own simulations in that field in 2013-2014. No doubt these studies will be compared and of course challenged by green movements which will advocate even higher figures and alarm once again the opinion.

Do we really need those figures? What do we expect from those calculations? On the field of national policies, those results may just feed the thoughts about the phasing out. On the field of nuclear liability, they are rather useless, since we know from the start that the consequences of a major nuclear accident within a Paris or a Vienna Convention State would far exceed the amounts insured, the intervention of the Brussels supplementary Convention, or of the CSC if it ever enters into force and, of course, the assets of the operator, should the latter bear an unlimited liability.

This is a fact of life which is shared by other industries, the most dramatic industrial accident up to date being the Bhopal chemical catastrophe. And in the field of the so-called Seveso-industries, there are no international conventions about nuclear liability, no channeling, no strict liability, no minimal amount to insure or guarantee, even if accidents in such industries can have substantial transboundary effects.

Although it may be difficult to explain that to the public, the Paris and Vienna Conventions and the legislations implementing them in the national laws have certainly their merits for small or medium size accidents. Once we have to deal with a major accident, even within the frame on unlimited liability, they also offer the basic legal frame within which additional ad hoc measures can be implemented on the spot, just as the Japanese authorities are acting now.

Will the European Commission be able to write down a legislative proposal which copes with our goals and resists the crude realities of figures? How far will the proposals made by the WG1, 2 and 3 inspire those texts? Will the European Commission dare to go beyond those too conservative proposals?

At the end of each of the 6 meetings in Luxembourg, Mr Garriba, the Chairman, concluded his final speech with the same sentence »I want a directive«. Yes, nobody dared to remind him that this option was unanimously disregarded in the poll ending the famous questionnaire. Of course, a directive would be nice. It would lift or help to lift definitely the issue of State aid, and a directive should be applicable to all 27 (28) member States, including the 5 non contracting States. My own answer was always, and stands firmly: *»pacta sunt servanda, pacta Paris et Vienna non delenda sunt«*… But if those Conventions are to be kept, we should exploit their full potential and, sorry to repeat myself, look beyond the limitation of liability.

The calendar

When Mr Garriba presented his own conclusions during the last meeting in Luxembourg, he stated that it was unlikely that the Council could adopt a Nuclear liability directive during the present legislature, as the European Parliament would meet for the last time in March 2014. According article 98 of the Euratom Treaty, the Commission would also have to request an opinion from the Economic and Social Committee before the proposal could be adopted by the Council and the European Parliament. In spite of that schedule, the Commission will try to present a draft legislative proposal in October 2013. Such a proposal would be widely discussed and a further conference could be organized to further discuss the recommendations.

So, we don't know yet **if**, **when** and **to which extent** the Commission will follow the recommendations edicted by the three workgroups.

Keeping in mind my own concerns about WG3, I just hope that the amending Protocols of Paris and Vienna will have registered some more successes by October 2013. The credibility of those instruments will doubtless be questioned and be at stake.

Disclaimer: these views are expressed as personal remarks; the views do not represent the official position of the Belgian government

* * *

ANNEX 1 – WG1 recommendations

Working Group 1 - Claims handling and related matters

<u>Recommendations</u>

<u>Background documents</u>:

- *WG 1 Non-Paper, 9 November 2011*
- *In the context of drafting the present recommendations, a questionnaire was sent in 2011 to almost all nuclear insurance pools operating in the EU and Switzerland[2] and to all nuclear power plant operator pools active in the EU[3] in order to obtain their views on claims management. Of a total of 16 nuclear insurance pools and nuclear power plant operators pools, 7 responses were received.*

2 The following pools were contacted: Syndicat belge d'assurance et de réassurance des risques nucléaires (SYBAN), Czech Nuclear Insurance Pool, Nordic Nuclear Insurers, Assuratome, Deutsche Kernreaktor Versigcherungsgemeinschaft, Hungarian Atomic Pool, Nederlandse Pool voor Verzekering van Atoomrisico´s, Slovak Nuclear Insurance Pool, Nuclear Insurance and Reinsurance Pool in Slovenia, Aseguradores de Riesgos Nucleares a.i.e. (ESPANUCLEAR), Nuclear Risk Insurers Limited in the UK and Schweitzer Pool für die Versicherung von Nuklearrisiken. It proved impossible to contact the Bulgarian National Nuclear Insurance Pool and the Romanian Pool for the Insurance of Atomic Risks.

3 The German operator pool and the European operator pool ELINI.

Preliminary remarks:

1. The present recommendations address the entire process of claims management, in its three different parts: claims registration, claims handling and claims settlement.
2. The WG agreed that recommendations regarding claims management within the European Union should remain non »regime-dependant«, so that they can be applied in the same manner, in each of the 27 EU Member States, irrespective of the nuclear liability legislation/convention in force.
3. These recommendations are made irrespective of the question of the community competence in this field, which still needs to be examined.
4. These recommendations need to be assessed in the light of the subsidiarity and proportionality principles.

General »disclaimer«:

The reflexions of WG 1 and the present document lack some information which can only be provided by national authorities, which were not involved in the working group process.

Recommendation 1 – Member States having nuclear installations on their territories should have a claims management system up and running.

Objective: Remedy the fact that some entities providing financial securities in the EU do not have a claims management system.

➔ ***Implementation:***

Member States to ensure that entities providing financial securities have and maintain an appropriate claims management system.

Recommendation 2 – Member States to establish a »one stop shop« for claims registration and record

Objective: establishement, in the »Accident State«, of a system designed to:

- register any claim, irrespective of where the accident occurs or where damage is suffered and of the nationality of the victim;

- simplify claims through easy-to-understand forms in all EU languages;
- allow for victims and claims inventory and for damage assessment.

➔ ***Implementation:***

- *Member States to designate a single entity or set of entities for claims registration:*
  - *designed to register any claim;*
  - *ensuring the availability of forms in all EU languages;*
  - *compulsorily informed of any claim presented elsewhere;*
  - *recording a database of claims.*
- *The appropriate measures have to be established in advance, but the entity should remain inactive and should not be a permanent structure. Instead, it should only be set up when needed, in case of an accident.*
- *This entity would be set up in the »Accident State«, but could be duplicated in other Member States as well, if necessary.*
- *The statute of this entity should be defined by each Member State, depending on its own administrative organization.*

Recommendation 3 – Establish criteria for EU-wide claims handling communication in the case of an accident

Objective:

- ensure victims are prepared throughout the EU and know how to act in the event of a nuclear accident;
- the message to the public should be clear and easy to understand.

➔ ***Implementation:***

EU to provide communication guidelines.

Recommendation 4 – Establish »one single desk« for claims handling (national level)

Objective: establishment, in the »Accident State«, of an entity designed to ensure the following:

- coordination between the national authorities, the liable operator and the insurer;
- definition of procedures in cases where both insurers' funds and State guarantee are triggered;
- definition of criteria for paying out compensations, including the appropriate status of emergency payments (first help);
- recording of payments (on whatever basis: operator, insurer, State (emergency funds), worker compensation regime, social insurance, courts, etc.);
- simplification of the follow-up of the availability of the funds;
- simplification of medical monitoring and epidemiological surveillance;
- compensation structure over the long-term to allow for the medium and long term administration of compensation claims.

➔ ***Implementation:***

- *Member States to set up »one single desk« (at the national level) for claims handling ensuring the coordination between all stakeholders, allowing victims to enforce their right to compensation without having to bring separate proceedings according to the origin of the funds, and enabling the centralization of information regarding funds allocation.*
- *The appropriate measures have to be established in advance, but, as previousely stated, the entity does not need to be a permanent structure. It should remain inactive and should only be set up when needed, in case of an accident.*
- *This entity would necessarily be set up in the »Accident State«, but could be set up in other Member States as well, if necessary.*
- *The »one single desk« may be the same entity as the »one stop shop« set up pursuant to Recommendation 2.*
- *The statute of this entity should be defined by each Member State, depending on its own administrative organization.*

Recommendation 5 – Allow for the assessment of insurers abilities by national authorities

Objective: Ensure the technical ability of the insurers (and other financial security) providing coverage in order to guarantee the availability of adequate competence and resources for claims management.

➔ ***Implementation:***

Member States to provide for the assessment of the insurers/pools technical abilities (does not cover the assessement of financial capacities).

Recommendation 6 – Set up rules for advance payments on compensation

Objective: Allow for rapid compensation of victims, especially in case of evacuation.

➔ ***Implementation:***

EU Guidelines for the Members States to set up rules and criteria for advance payments on compensation, notwithstanding any emergency help to be provided by the States/Operators.

Recommendation 7 – Clarify how claims management costs are borne

Objective:

- clarify with whom claims-handling costs lie and the amount of these costs;
- ensure that compensation funds are not used to cover claims management costs.

➔ ***Implementation:***

- *Member States to ensure that insurers specify how claims management costs are borne and their amount in the insurance policy. The same applies to Member States regarding claims management costs when public funds are triggered.*
- *Member States to ensure and control that liability amounts are exclusively dedicated to the compensation of damage.*

ANNEX2 WG2 recommendations

Working Group 2 – Insurance, Operators' Pools and other Financial Security

Recommendations

We first recall the mandate of this EU nuclear liability group as confirmed in the minutes of its first meeting on 5 April 2011:

> »The purpose of the group is to explore common ground amongst the stakeholders (consensus building) who should give recommendations for a future (legislative) proposal of the European Commission under Article 98 of the Euratom Treaty.
>
> The purpose of any Commission proposal would be to increase (legal) coherence in the EU, which is needed to improve, on the one hand, victim protection in different Member States, and, on the other hand, to tackle the impact on the functioning of the internal market because of diverging financial guarantee obligations of operators as well as availability of insurance, which might give rise to distortion of competition.
>
> In line with the conclusions of the study published in 2009, this European initiative is not to hamper accession by Member States to any international convention improving the situation of potential victims in the European Union.«

In order to accomplish these goals, WG2 focused on several questions of importance including but not limited to the third party liability framework currently in operation within the EU, the present financial obligations of the various nuclear operators and the solutions put in place to meet such obligations throughout Europe, the possibilities of the insurance market to cover both the increased limits and the enlarged risks as per the revised Paris Convention, the other ways to cope with the financial obligations of the operators, the financial soundness of the various options and the ways to meet even larger limits.

In addition, the group took into consideration the position and interests of the EU members without nuclear installations, the various merits of economic channeling and legal channeling and the sustainability of higher liability limits.

This work led to the Recommendations at the end of this document. It is noteworthy that the definition of sustainable nuclear liability amounts andscope remains controversial and consensus was therefore somewhat lacking on this key issue. With this in mind, the WG2 Recommendations have attempted to take into account the divergent views of different stakeholders and strike a balance between their sometimes competing concerns.

The following proposals are all subject to confirmation of EU competence under Article 98 of the Euratom Treaty[4], to the subsidiary and proportionality principles, and to their compatibility with the VC (1997) and the PC (2004).

RECOMMENDATION 1

The member states must work jointly with nuclear operators and nuclear insurance providers, to put in place cover that fulfills the revised Convention requirements[5] & ratify the applicable Convention as soon as possible.

RECOMMENDATION 2

The EU Commission is to clarify & communicate the acceptable conditions under which EU states are allowed to act, directly or indirectly, to cover nuclear third party liability risks (e.g. for the uninsurable Convention new heads of damage, limits & cover extensions).

RECOMMENDATION 3

Ensure that all financial security provided is sufficiently secure, stable & solvent to guarantee maximum protection for nuclear accident victims; also ensure that a robust & effective claims handling system is put in place.

4 Article 98: »Member States shall take all necessary measures to facilitate the conclusion of insurance contracts covering atomic risks. Within a period of two years after the date of the entry into force of this Treaty and after the Assembly has been consulted, the Council, acting by means of a qualified majority vote on a proposal of the Commission which shall previously obtain the opinion of the Economic and Social Committee, shall issue directives as to the particulars of application of this Article.«

5 According to Article 7 a) of the Revised Paris Convention »Each Contracting Party shall provide under its legislation that the liability of the operator in respect of nuclear damage caused by any one nuclear incident *shall not be less than* 700 million euro«.

RECOMMENDATION 4

In the longer term the operators & financial security providers are to continue working together to investigate any additional nuclear liability capacity that might become available in future.

Discussion Report of the Third Working Session, Part 1

Sidonie Royer-Maucotel, CEA, Gif-sur-Yvette, France

This short session comprised two presentations by Dirk Harbrücker and Roland Dussart-Desart. The speakers examined the current developments in the European Union (EU) concerning third party nuclear liability. Both speakers focused on the work of the ad-hoc Expert Group on nuclear liability convened by the Commission from April 2011 to February 2013 and its recommendations.

The Chairman, *Norbert Pelzer*, introduced the topic by pointing out that for a long time the liability issue had not been a subject of discussion in the EU. Although 22 of the EU states are party to a liability convention, there are still major differences especially in liability amounts. Therefore, it would be helpful if the EU could step in and do something to harmonize the system.

Dr. Pelzer reminded participants that the Commission made an »impact assessment« including a questionnaire to all stakeholders and that an expert working group was created in April 2011. According to Dr. Pelzer, the question is whether the EU has competence in the field of nuclear liability. The only legal provision is the Article 98 of the Euratom Treaty which states that member States shall take all necessary measures to facilitate the conclusion of insurance contracts covering atomic risks and the Commission shall issue directives as to the particulars of application of this Article. The question is whether it has to be interpreted in a broad or in a narrow way. Mr. Pelzer considered that insurance cover depends on the liability law and it is not possible to harmonize the insurance cover without harmonizing the liability system.

Dirk Harbrücker in his presentation made some personal remarks on the work of the ad-hoc Expert Group on Nuclear Liability of which he was a member. He gave an account of the work of the group and its three Working Groups, dealing with claims management, insurance and other financial guarantees, and liability amounts and other topics, respectively. According to Mr. Harbrücker, the proposals of the group were not very far-reaching and this was in part due to the size and composition of the group and its subgroups. One topic which was indeed interesting is the proposal, made outside the Expert Group but subsequently discussed by it, of introducing a compulsory catastrophe cover in an unprecedented amount.

Roland Dussart-Desart, in his presentation, gave his view of the work of the same Expert Group, of which he was also a member (and chairman of WG 3). He put the group's work in a larger context, starting with the history of nuclear liability legislation and conventions in EU Member States. He focused on the work of WG 3 and particularly emphasized the importance of attracting the five non-convention Member States to either the Paris or the Vienna Convention. In this context, he pleaded for considering introduction of unlimited liability, which is allowed in both conventions.

In the discussion after the two presentations, *Ms. Ptasekaite* considered that the liability regime is related to the victims whereas State aids (under the Treaty on the Functioning of the European Union) are related to the market. She is therefore interested by the link between liability regime and state aids. Secondly, she stated having heard a rumour that a liability directive would be at discussion in the Directorate General of Justice and not for Energy.

Mr. Harbrücker emphasized that a difference between 75 million euros and 1.2 billion euros of liability within the different members States (considering the fact that the insurance premiums paid by the operators will be much higher for some as compared to others) can create big differences in competition law and the State will therefore have to step in much earlier.

Mr. Dussart-Desart stated that the fact there is a limitation in liability in almost all member States means that the State would have to intervene in the event of a large accident which could be considered as a subsidy (state aid) so there is a clear link between the two.

On the second question, Mr. Dussart-Desart answered that the Directorate General of Justice is talking about instituting a single court but he never heard that a complete directive on that subject has actually been prepared. The subject remains the one of the Directorate for Energy.

Third Working Session

»Nuclear Liability, Part Two: Nuclear Liability Worldwide«

Chair: *Dr. Christian Raetzke,* CONLAR, Leipzig, Chairman of the German Branch of AIDN/INLA

Secretary: *Sidonie Royer-Maucotel,* CEA, Gif-sur-Yvette, France

Liability Issues at Transportation of Nuclear Materials in Absence of the Global Regime of Civil Liability for Nuclear Damage

Boris Kolesnik, ARMZ Uranium Holding Co, Moscow

All of the lawyers practicing in nuclear law are surely aware of the multiplicity of nuclear liability instruments existing across the nuclear and non-nuclear European states – Paris[1] and Vienna[2] Conventions (including their revised regimes), 1988 Joint Protocol, as well as no-convention countries where the respective national rules are applicable.[3] All that traditionally labeled with a fashionable term »patchwork« of liability regimes.

So where are we, Russians, in this patchwork? Our country finally joined the Vienna Convention on civil liability for nuclear damage[4] in its initial version in 2005. According to the basic constitutional principle of preponderance of international law, the Convention has had a priority over any Russian national act adopted on this subject.

The aim of this brief overview is to focus on some selected aspects of transnational transportation that Russian companies (which are mostly sellers or consignors of the nuclear materials) used to face in absence of the global uniform regime of civil liability, and the way such transportation is consequently complicated.

1 The OECD's Paris Convention on third party liability in the field of nuclear energy 1960, amended & revised in 2004.

2 The UN's Vienna Convention on civil liability for nuclear damage 1963 amended & revised in 2007.

3 We do not consider CSC (Convention on Supplementary Compensation) for this instrument is not in effect yet.

4 So far as the subject of regulation of the Vienna Convention is the compensation of damage connected with the most active nuclear material (like fuel, waste), the Convention does not apply to natural uranium which is the basic ARMZ's staple. However we occasionally deal with the processed material of a higher degree.

Allocation of burden of nuclear liability

Both Vienna and Paris Conventions consider operators as exclusive subjects of nuclear liability. Both of them permit transferring and receiving operators to agree upon transfer of the burden of nuclear liability in a manner established by the conventions. However such liability allocation between the parties through written agreement may be possible only between the nuclear operators domiciled in countries that ratified the same convention. So far as Russia & the post-USSR republics ratified the Vienna Convention, and most of our European partners are members to the Paris one in its different revised versions, no »inter-conventional« allocation of liability can be agreed in supply contracts when the delivery of nuclear materials is taking place from Russia / Kazakhstan to Europe. Each of the parties of such contract being on opposite sides of the legal »fence« are bound by the imperative rules of the respective applied Convention and the contract as a whole shall comply with both of these imperatives.

Up to this time Russia has not yet joined the 1988 Joint Protocol linking both Conventions upon common principles and making possible this »inter-conventional« liability allocation. Therefore, for the time being, the Russian sellers on the one part and German and Swedish on the other[5] are not in a legal position to agree upon transfer of nuclear risks under their contracts. Regretful fact, as this is obvious – the Protocol had already eliminated a number of conflicts of law in international transport when cargos travel between the countries of different liability regimes.

Overlapping of liability

The operators in countries that joined different Conventions shall consider each other according to Vienna Convention art.II[6], as well as Paris Convention art.4[7] as *persons located within a territory of a non-Contracting State* accordingly.

The Russian suppliers following the Vienna Convention requirements, insure the nuclear consignment *from the moment it is handed over* from the consignor until *disembarkation moment in a port* or other place in the

5 We mean the countries that joined the 1988 Protocol.
6 Sec.1, bullets - b)iv and c)iv .
7 bullets a)iv, and b)iv .

territory[8] of the Western country-participant to the Paris Convention. At the same time, European purchaser shall be liable and insure the liability *starting the moment a vessel leaves the Russian territorial* waters *up to the moment of nuclear substances' final arrival to the consignee's facility*[9] (except for France where there is a specific approach in interpretation of the Paris Convention and the French operators are only liable within the territory but excluding neutral waters & lands)[10]. Thus, during the delivery arises an actual overlap of counterparties' liability (and theoretically, the same overlap would occur in case of deliveries vice-versa from Germany to Russia).

There's no reason to describe the given moment as some dramatic problem for an overlap of liability is not a gap of it, but so far as any liability is covered by the insurance policy, the needless costs that parties incur, make quite an unpleasant aspect for them.

COFS submission

Following the requirements of the Paris Convention, supervising bodies of its member states demand the submission of the Certificate of Financial Security (COFS) upon arrival of the nuclear material to their territory to confirm (a) the status of the operator in a Paris Convention country with respect to the transported nuclear material, and (b) to confirm the financial security. These certificates are normally issued by the European sellers or consignors and then handed to carriers for transportation, but in case the Russian supplier imports the material, the obligation on COFS issuance shall be charged only with the receiving European partner due to the fact the Russian company is not »the operator« under the Paris Convention. And very important, the certificate shall be with the carrier already by the moment of the country entry, to be exact – the border crossing. Thus, here we have some additional risk (or at least worries) of delivery frustration in

8 According to Art. II, Sec. 1b) iv) of Vienna Convention.

9 Art. 4, Sec. b) iv) of Paris Convention, and regarding Article 2: notwithstanding that Art.4 Sec. a) iv) and Sec. b) iv) PC provides (in a way similar to Vienna Convention rules) for the operator's liability staring from loading to means of transport / unloading from means of transport, Article 2 of PC establishes that PC does not apply in the territory of non-Contracting States. Therefore liability starts / ends upon crossing border of a country non-participant of PC.

10 Explanatory letter of OECD as of 02.08.2007.

case the European buyer fails to perform its duty on COFS issuance in advance of delivery.

Difference in status of the carrier. Who is the »operator«?

As a general rule, in both systems carriers are not subjects of nuclear liability. And in both systems Conventions exceptionally provide the possibility for the carriers that transport nuclear materials to be designated or recognized as operator, subject to such possibility being directly provided by the national legislation of a certain participating country to either Convention.[11] We know that such transfer of specific operator status to carriers is reality in some EU countries, including Germany, where the German Atomic Energy Act[12] provides for such option. It is not however in Russia and other post-USSR republics, in spite of the private initiatives made lately by the local business, up to this time the Russian legislation does not provide for such transfer even when the contract parties agree on that. Therefore at fulfillment of delivery from Russia to any of the mentioned countries, the carrier in transnational voyage cannot be designated as liable operator by the parties. Otherwise it would seriously simplify the liability issues for transboundary deliveries.

Let it be stressed that the latter point is hardly a matter of difference between Paris and Vienna approaches, but rather a matter of particular national conditions in this or that state where only the owners of a fixed nuclear installation may be the liable operators.

The choice of liability clauses

Due to the diversity of liability regimes that our counterparties live in, the Eastern nuclear sellers face the need to use a multiplicity of the respective clauses to settle down liability matters. Among this multiplicity any normal business can be easily lost. So, we have to choose which to use depending on the buyers' jurisdiction, including those cases where the counterparty is not the operator (the latter shall then undertake to agree on the liability with the respective operator).

11 Section »d« of Article 4 in Paris Convention; §2 of Article 2 in Vienna Convention.

12 Section 25 para. 2 of the German Atomic Energy Act.

Those are the options where

1) Seller delivers to Buyer within the Vienna Convention,
   1a) the same but actual delivery is made not to the Buyer's country, but to a consignee that is under the Paris Convention,
   1b) or in no convention country.
2) Seller under the Vienna Convention delivers to Buyer that is under the Paris Convention,
   2a) where Buyer is under the Paris Convention but is not the »operator« according to it and the delivery is made to a third party that is the Paris Convention »operator«,
   2b) where Buyer is under the Paris Convention but delivery is made to an actual consignee in the third country non-member of either convention.
3) We sell to Buyer that is in a no-convention country,
   3a) the sa me but actual delivery is made to an operator-consignee in a Paris Convention country.

And other combinations.

Insurance

Generally speaking about the insurance topic, one should take into account that even the revised liability conventions, both Paris and Vienna, leave the transport matters with significant uncertainty.

Insurers feel this uncertainty due to a rather broad nuclear damage definition provided by the revised Conventions, that in practice inevitably results in gaps in the insurance cover where the insurers on both sides are in the similar way unable to insure the new wider scope of cover. Needless to say that in this situation, in lack of an adequate insurance, or in absence of it, the liability for the revised scope of cover falls upon either the operator (consignor or consignee) or the public agency (government).

In the Russian Federation, under the applied Vienna Convention, the operator shall keep insurance or other financial security covering its liability for nuclear damage in the size, of the kind and on the terms as the Contracting State determines. The Russian law however, does not establish these parameters for the time being, but supervising bodies require insurance at transportation what is fixed in the licenses for handling of nuclear materials and is being checked during transportation of such cargos.

The *limits of the operator's liability are not established* either. The Russian operators determine by themselves a presumable size of a possible damage for purposes of setting the amount of financial security. The amount provided in Vienna Convention Art.V (about 93 million USD[13]) is used as minimally possible limit of liability of the operator, established by the state and operators apply it on a voluntary basis. The mentioned lower limit of nuclear liability will become mandatory after adoption of the respective law only, what has not occurred yet. So, the operators insure the liability using their own internal subjective risk assessment and in our opinion this is not a normal situation.

Conclusion

The present outline actually shows that rather than facing unsolvable problems at transportation, both operators and carriers suffer a number of inconveniences in this area due to the absence of a uniform regime. No doubt, as well as the Western colleagues, the nuclear business in Russia (and in the post-SU republics) is the apparent supporter of the aim to reach harmonization of nuclear liability regime. And what is important: to reach it at the global level, avoiding regional fragmentations of any kind. For that reason, in our opinion, any European initiatives to regulate the conflict matters within EU uniform legislation will not solve the problem in relation to non-EU member states. So, any regional initiatives of this kind, being of a purely local character, entail only further fragmentation.

As it was reported at the INLA Brussels nuclear liability workshop in 2010, it's practically important in the context of nuclear liability, that this issue has never been considered by any international court, the Court of Justice in Luxembourg or a national court (and as far as we're aware of the question, things haven't changed since 2010). So in the practical aspect the matter of nuclear liability enforcement remains somewhat unclear.

13 A limit of the operator's liability is established equivalent to an amount set forth in Sec.1 Art. V of the Vienna Convention, that is 5 mil. USD per any nuclear accident. It is however provided by Sec. 3 Art. V that US dollar is a legal tender to be considered equivalent to the USD value according to its »golden« parity as of April 29, 1963 (that is 35 USD for one pure gold troy ounce [http://www.cmegroup.com/]). Currently, this amount is approximately equal to 93 728 571 USD.

Discussion Panel: Do We Need a Global Nuclear Liability Regime?

Stephen Burns, Head of Legal Affairs, OECD Nuclear Energy Agency, Paris

David Davies, Chief Legal Advisor, Eskom, South Africa

Kyoji Kawasaki, Professor, Hitotsubashi University, Tokyo

Alexander Matveev, Member of the Board of AIDN/INLA, Russia

Norbert Pelzer, University of Göttingen, Honorary Chairman of the German Branch of AIDN/INLA

Els Reynaers Kini, Partner, M.V. Kini & Co., Advocates & Solicitors, Mumbai

Wolfram Tonhauser, Head of Nuclear & Treaty Law section, Office of Legal Affairs, IAEA

Note: The panel started with an introduction by the chairman Christian Raetzke and with an introductory statement by each panellist. The panellists were given the option to submit their introductory statements in writing for publication in this volume; four of the seven panellists did so. The discussion report by Sidonie Royer-Maucotel contains both a summary of all introductory statements and an account of the subsequent discussion among the panel and with the audience.

Introduction by the Chairman

Christian Raetzke

»Do we need a global nuclear liability regime?« Stressing the need for a global nuclear liability regime seems to be almost a standard element of presentations given, and papers written, by nuclear liability experts. Indeed the benefits of such a regime are quite apparent, but the means to get there are not as easily conceived and implemented. The efforts and instruments to reach a unified global regime have been manifold (which may in itself be a contradiction.....). However, it is apparent that these instruments have not yet garnered global adherence. As time is passing and the adoption of instruments such as the Joint Protocol, the Convention on Supplementary Compensation and the revised versions of the Paris and Vienna Conventions is receding (from our point of view) into a more distant past, it seems there is an increasing tendency to question these instruments as to their ability to actually lead to a unified global nuclear liability regime.

Additionally, it seems that some long-standing and seemingly universally accepted principles are back under discussion: limited liability vs. unlimited liability; channelling of liability on the operator; states as insurers of last resort – are we in fact about to lose even the global (more or less) consensus about liability principles which has united, until now, the various treaties and the legislation in most nuclear non-convention states even if there is no universal treaty link? Finally, it has become obvious that it is difficult to align the views of stakeholders with different interests: industry, potential victims, governments; established nuclear countries and newcomers; supplier and receiver states; countries with borders to other nuclear states and other countries far away from most of their nuclear peers.

Thus, the main question seems to be: should we continue the quest for such a regime or should we consider alternatives? The idea to stage a discussion with this topic was born at the AIDN/INLA congress in October 2012 in Manchester. At this congress, Norbert Pelzer gave a thought-provoking speech, concluding that a global regime is neither realistic nor necessary. For lack of time, there was no real discussion on this – which I highly regretted, given the interesting and provocative thesis which would seem to contradict the current mainstream. I also remember very well, from the same Manchester session, Stephen Burns' elegant and thoughtful keynote speech about the search for the »Holy Grail« of a global nuclear liability regime. A few weeks later I spoke to Wolfram Tonhauser who was not present in the Manchester liability session and who expressed the desire to »enter the tournament« in defence of the idea of a global regime (that's not how he expressed it but just to keep within medieval imagery...). So, the resolve was quickly taken to continue discussion in Leipzig and to explore this topic more in depth.

I am very happy to have been able to secure participation of four additional experts who will contribute their views from very dynamic and highly relevant regions of the nuclear world: Els Reynaers from India, Alexander Matveev from Russia, Kyoji Kawasaki from Japan and David Davies from South Africa. I am also happy that Sidonie Royer-Maucotel will act as a session secretary and will produce a written summary of our discussion for the conference proceedings. I am excited about having such a rich and heavyweight panel and I am looking forward to our discussion!

Introductory Statement

David Davies[*]

The first question to ponder is whether countries wish/need to join any liability conventions at all? If yes, then the question remains as to which convention and whether any of the existing conventions (or a combination thereof) can really be viewed as being able to provide a truly global regime. The reasons underpinning the existence or participation in a global regime are also varied and in the author's view don't necessarily always relate to the traditional legal »arguments« (strict liability, channelling, liability limits, jurisdiction, non-discrimination) around nuclear liability convention or global regime participation. In order to keep the discussion on the bigger question varied, this has been looked at in the context of a developing country in the international nuclear industry.

From a developing country perspective, it is generally only the Vienna Convention (VC) and Convention on Supplementary Compensation for Nuclear Damage (CSC) that are in play. As Africa comprises of developing nations almost exclusively, this is important in respect of participation in a global liability regime context as it is the author's view that for there to be any chance of a truly global nuclear liability regime, the existing major nuclear countries, of which most are advanced, will need to »buy-in« and »drive« such process. The progress and uptake by advanced countries, or any countries for that matter, in the existing nuclear liability conventions has been slow. When considering nuclear new build where most activity is taking place in developing countries, despite much good work and initiative by nuclear agencies and the like, there is not a strong legacy to follow in respect of nuclear liability convention participation or the advancement of a global nuclear liability regime.

Although as lawyers we prefer to work with words and without getting too scientific or straying from the academic discussion, as at 2012, 24 per-

* Chief Legal Advisor at Eskom Holdings SOC Ltd, the state-owned energy utility that operates the sole nuclear power station in the Republic of South Africa. This dissertation is written by the author in his personal capacity and the views expressed herein are those of the author and do not purport to represent the views of Eskom Holdings SOC Ltd or the Government of the Republic of South Africa.

cent of nuclear reactors worldwide were within »developing« countries, whilst »advanced« countries accounted for the other 76 percent. This is merely for illustrative purposes and the author has not attempted to provide a universal definition for »developing« and »advanced« countries and used the IMF's list of developing countries as the basis for classification and analysis. Factual changes to statistics since 2012 will have a negligible impact on this analysis.

In respect of the nuclear reactor construction environment, 64 nuclear reactors are under construction worldwide. Of these, developing countries account for 81 percent of nuclear reactors under construction worldwide, whilst advanced countries account for the other 19 percent.

From an analysis of the nuclear power generating countries that are party to an international nuclear liability convention[1] currently in force, 240 operating nuclear reactors are not covered by an international nuclear liability convention currently in force. The percentage of nuclear reactors of such countries not participating in an international nuclear liability convention currently in force as compared to the worldwide total of operating nuclear reactors is 55 percent. The fact that 55 percent of nuclear reactors worldwide are not covered by any international nuclear liability convention currently in force is a telling statistic.

Due to the number of reactors in India and the US, the percentage would reduce from 55 percent to 26 percent if the CSC was in force (hypothetically) with its current signatories.

In respect of the analysis that 55 percent of nuclear reactors worldwide are not covered by any international nuclear liability convention currently in force, when considering the proportion of this 55 percent of nuclear reactors *vis a vis* developing and advanced countries, developing countries only contribute to 17 percent of the reactors not covered by such an international nuclear liability convention. From this analysis in respect of current operating reactors, advanced countries hold by far the greater number or nuclear reactors (and related risk) not covered by an international nuclear liability convention.

1 For this analysis the country membership of the Paris Convention and the Vienna Convention is sufficient and excludes the CSC in that it is has not yet come into force and effect. Until such time as the CSC comes into force and effect, those signatory countries to the CSC that are not party to one of the international nuclear liability conventions currently in force but that operate nuclear reactors, have been included as part of the 240 nuclear reactors discussed above.

When the above scenario is applied to country participation[2] (of those countries with operating commercial nuclear reactors) in currently in-force international nuclear liability conventions, country participation in international nuclear liability conventions amounts to 68 percent. As liability convention participation is a »country« issue, this at least reduces and somewhat mitigates the impact of the above picture as related to nuclear reactors.

It is however interesting to note that whilst the CSC may be viewed as a promoter of developing-country participation, it is the US that has by far the greatest number of nuclear reactors and that will participate as a so-called »Annex country«. It is this advanced Annex country that, as a contracting state to the CSC, is essential to the CSC providing sufficient supplementary funding and coming into force.

Whilst the advantages of joining a nuclear liability convention or a »global regime« may be fairly compelling as opposed to relying purely on national nuclear liability laws (even to the extent they are drafted to conform as far as possible with the basic principles of international nuclear third party liability), the author is of the view that it is not these advantages (or disadvantages) that will of themselves necessarily influence or compel a country to join a convention or global regime.

The author suggests that it is rather another set of factors or drivers that further influence such decisions. These factors are *inter alia* the following:

- International nuclear industry relations and nuclear industry »citizenship«;
- Government and relevant national nuclear regulatory regimes approach to nuclear energy;
- Funding requirements;
- Country geographic location;
- Public perception of the nuclear industry per country;
- International nuclear commercial trade and contracting.

For the purposes of this note the author will not go into more detail on the above, yet it may form the subject of discussion at some point or another.

Regional regimes (and alignment between such regional regimes) are perhaps a more realistic starting point in the search for a truly global re-

2 In this scenario it is only in respect of those countries that have operating nuclear reactors and thus by implication excludes non-nuclear power states party to the CSC or other international nuclear liability conventions.

gime which is without doubt a noble cause. At least in the case of Europe and Asia there seems to be room for such an initiative, but if considering the African and specifically the South African context, due to the relative geographic remoteness and fledgling nuclear industry in most of Africa it would seem a long way off. Unfortunately, history has shown that the participation in nuclear liability conventions has left something to be desired and if a global regime is to be achieved it will require a major shift in thinking and intent by current nuclear super-powers.

Introductory Statement: Japanese Experience in Nuclear Liability Compensation after Fukushima Incident

Kyoji Kawasaki, Professor of International Law, Hitotsubashi University, Tokyo, Director of EU Studies Institute in Tokyo

Introduction

Although I am not a specialist in this subject,[1] I would like to make some contribution to today's panel discussion, by introducing you some recent developments in Japan about nuclear compensation regime now working for the redress of the victims caused by Fukushima Daiichi Incident.[2] In fact, this is our human being's first ever experience, except one unclear or hidden practice of the USSR after Chernobyl,[3] of mass and huge claims for nuclear liability compensation, actually raised and to be raised by more

1 I have been mainly working on State responsibility under international law including the legal consequences arising from a violation of obligations *erga omnes* as well as on the legal effects of *jus cogens* in international law. Among others, »Accountability of the United Nations from the perspective of international law,« in Kuyama and Fowler (eds), *Envisioning Reform: Enhancing UN Accountability in the Twenty-First Century (United Nations* University Press, 2009), pp.116-132; »International *jus cogens* in the Law of State Responsibility,« in Carlo Focarelli (a cura di) *Le nuove frontiere del diritto internazionale* (Morlacchi Editore, Perugia, 2008), pp.145-165; »A brief note on the legal effects of *jus cogens* in international law,« *Hitotsubashi Journal of Law & Politics*, vol.34 (2006), pp.27-43; »State Responsibility and Terrorist Activities,« in Andrea de Guttry (a cura di), *Oltre la reazione: Complessità e limiti nella guerra al terrorismo internazionale dopo l'11 settembre* (Edizioni ETS, Pisa, 2003), pp.65-81; »The 'Injured State' in the International Law of State Responsibility,« *Hitotsubashi Journal of Law & Politics*, Vol. 28 (2000), pp.17-31.

2 For more detail, see *Japan's Compensation System for Nuclear Damage: As Related to the TEPCO Fukushima Daiichi Nuclear Accident* (OECD, 2012). See also, Eri Osaka, »Corporate Liability, Government Liabilty, and the Fukushima Nuclear Disaster,« *Pacific Rim Law & Policy Journal*, Vol. 21 No.3 (June 2012), pp.433-459; Toyohiro NOMURA, »Japanese Law of Liability for Nuclear Damage and its Evolution after the Fukushima Accident,« http://www.burges-salmon.com/INLA_2012/10153.pdf

3 For the detailed description on the compensation practice of the Ukrain government, Ministry of Ukraine of Emergencies, »Twenty-five Years after Chornobyl Accident: Safety for the Future«, National Report of Ukraine, 2011

than 150,000 people being evacuated from contaminated areas, plus numerous companies and even public sectors suffered from the incident.

In order to cope with these claims, Japanese government already decided to provide TEPCO, through newly established »Nuclear Damage Liability Facilitation Fund,« up to 5 trillion yen, that is equivalent to 40 billion euro, for compensating Fukushima victims.[4] In addition, Prime Minister Abe recently stated that there will soon be needed considerable additional financial support for compensation and decommissioning to be made by TEPCO.

Only this fact shows us that, if a grave nuclear disaster occurred, existing nuclear liability regimes based on national legislations as well as nuclear liability conventions would be quite insufficient and a special regime must be introduced with heavy governmental involvement in institutional and financial schemes for compensation.

Comparing this Japanese special regime with already existing regimes under nuclear liability treaties, one can find, in the Japanese regime, several different measures for, or flexible approaches to, compensation in terms of both substantive and procedural aspects. Following several comments on these points, I will proceed to the international aspect of nuclear liability after Fukushima from Japanese perspective.

Substantive aspect

Nuclear damages compensation for Fukushima victims has been made in accordance with interim guidelines established by the Nuclear Damage Dispute Reconciliation Committee. First, with regard to the scope of nuclear damage, it is interesting to note that, generally speaking, compensation for moral damage plays a major role for especially individual refugee victims. This is mainly because it may serve to compensate swiftly and uniformly, without taking into account individual special circumstances of each victim. In addition, rumor-related economical damages are also extensively compensated.

Secondly, with respect to the extension in time of nuclear damage, TEPCO, last year, introduced »Comprehensive Application system« for refugee people, according to which they may receive compensation money

4 As of late November 2012, JPY 1.5 trillon (EUR 13.7 billion) has been paid in compensation for damages attributable to the accident. NEA, Fukushima Press Kit, http://www.oecd-nea.org/press/press-kits/fukushima.html

for »future« damages in advance for maximum 5 year term counting from 2012. On the other hand, »delayed« damages may be awarded when TEPCO conducted, in a case before the Dispute Settlement Center for Nuclear Disaster Compensation, with unjustified manner, making delay the process of reconciliation

Procedural aspect

Under the current Japanese compensation regime, mediation by the Dispute Resolution Center is expected to play a major role in the settlement of compensation disputes. However, it is reported that, to date, only 30 % of the total number of claims before the Center have reached an amicable settlement with average 8 months long procedures, due to the lack of human resources in the Center. Against this background, a considerable number of victims are beginning to make a (collective) recourse to domestic courts and tribunals. Since there is no specific provision on the court's jurisdiction in the Nuclear Damage Compensation Act, they are bringing their claims before several different district courts including Fukushima, Tokyo and Kyoto, etc. Some of them even make a lawsuit against the State of Japan under State Redress Act, which is, according to the prevalent view in Japan, not prohibited.

Secondly, Article 724 of the Japanese Civil Law provides that the right to demand compensation for damages shall be extinguished within 3 years from the time of knowledge on the damages and the perpetrator. Last week, Japanese Diet adopted a new Act[5] which permits the interruption of prescription if one brings his/her case to the court within one month from the date of the failure of the Dispute Resolution Center's mediation. Many lawyers assert that this new Act is too much narrow in its scope and Article 724 should not be applied to Fukushima cases.[6]

5 This act has entered into effect on 5 June 2013.

6 It is reported that the ruling LDP is planning to submit a draft Act, in the coming session of the Diet in October 2013, for extending the prescription period to 10 years in Fukushima cases. It is also reported that, among 150,000 refugee people in Fukushima prefecture, more than 11,000 victims have not yet made their main compensation claims, which are likely to be extinguished in September 2014. *Nikkiei News Paper*, 22 September 2013. As a scholarly work on this matter, MATSUMOTO Katsumi, »Atomkraftsschaden und Verjährung« (in Japanese), *Ritsumeikan Hogeku*, No.347, 2013, No.1, pp.220-243.

International aspect

First, as long as I know, there is no lawsuit outside Japan against TEPCO except one case. This is the case, before the Southern district court of California, brought in December 2012 by 8 US military servicepersons who had participated in the rescue operation after 3.11 earthquakes, which was called at that time »friendship« operation. They are asserting to be suffered health and mental damages by TEPCO's negligence of not informing them risks on the place where they were operating. The total amount of their claims is 210 million US dollars.[7] One may pose a question on why California. It is said that there is a TEPCO's branch office there and they merely brought their cases before a district court of the residence of the accused. In addition, it is reported that those who wish to join the plaintiffs are gradually increasing in its number, to 26 persons as of 12 March 2013.

Secondly, as everybody knows, Japan is not a member of any nuclear liability conventions, including Paris and Geneva conventions as well as the CSC. Following Fukushima Daiichi incident, the Japanese government has been inclined to join the CSC. In fact, last summer, the then Japanese government of Democratic Parity once decided to participate in the CSC and tried to propose related draft acts to the Japanese Diet. But this was not realized mainly due to the political turmoil, occurred soon after that, which eventually pulled down Democratic Party from the position of power. But in any event, it seems that the current LDP government is still maintaining the original position of seeking for participation in the CSC. In addition, there seems no sign on the part of the Japanese government to make an initiative for establishing a bland new regional liability regime to be applicable to east Asian countries. So the remaining question is not which international regime Japan should join, but when Japan will decide to make an accession to the CSC.

If there were a possibility of applying the CSC retrospectively to the Fukushima incident, Japan would join the CSC tomorrow. But, if not so, there still seem to remain some substantial and procedural obstacles to be overcome. With regard to the substantial aspect, some members of the Diet assert that joining the CSC, by excluding the Japanese victims of an incident occurred in neighboring countries from bringing their cases before

7 Lindsay Cooper et al. v. Tokyo Electric Power Company (U.S. District Court, Southern California) http://www.stripes.com/polopoly_fs/1.202195!/menu/standard/file/TEPCO_COMPLAINT.pdf

Japanese courts, might jeopardize the right of peaceful petition for the redress of damage recognized by Article 16 of the Japanese constitution.

Turning to the procedural matter, in spite of the fact that the Annex to the CSC seems in its nature directly applicable in contracting parties, Japan will take a way of amending all relevant clauses and articles of internal legislations. Moreover, to the extent that all recent developments after Fukushima should also be incorporated in the whole process of liability regime reconsideration in Japan, it will take considerable time to finish this amendment process in Japan.

Conclusion

In conclusion, according to one view,[8] to which I totally agree, the Japanese special regime for nuclear compensation, as a whole, seems not so much »private tort law reparation« for damages suffered in the past as »public law compensation« for the continuing intolerable situation brought about by a private company, TEPCO, which have operated nuclear power plants in accordance with a consistent State policy of promoting nuclear energy utilization for a half century in Japan.[9]

8 Hajime NAKAJIMA, *Interim Guidelines on the Determination of the Scope of Nuclear Damage* (in Japanese), 2013, pp. iv and 7.

9 As a result, it may be said that, under the current Japanese compensation regime, »unlimited« liability is not owed by TEPCO but by Japanese taxpayers, until when all the borrowing money will be reimbursed by TEPCO. However, for the reimbursement, if TEPCO raises in power rates, with boomerang effect, again the Japanese taxpayers should come to pay.
It is also interesting to note that, following Fukushima disaster, there is a movement in the Japanese Diet to introduce »limited« liability for the nuclear operator, amending Section 3 of the Act on Compensation for nuclear Damage of 1961, in order to adapt legal regime to the reality. There is also a strong opposition against that, according to which such an amendment would lead to the moral hazard on the part of nuclear operators.

Introductory Statement: On a Global Nuclear Liability Regime

Alexander Matveev, Member of the Board of AIDN/INLA

Do we need a global nuclear liability regime? At INLA Congress in Manchester, Dr. Pelzer expressed the view that »We will not achieve a global nuclear liability regime« and that »We do not need a global nuclear liability regime«.[1]

Once we start asking such questions, we understand that answers could be far from our intentions or desires. Like any social phenomenon, international law develops in the system of social relations where ideas and preferences of lawyers, industrials, consumers, ministers, and diplomats are just an element of equations, on which control could hardly be directly exercised. We should not be frustrated if the solutions that we believe evident and necessary are not achieved. We should analyze the situation of nuclear energy, understand that it will develop as an important building block of the world economy in the XXI century, that nuclear energy will continue to grow as an international business, therefore, objectively, there will be a need for international legal regulation, in which business will be interested. States will follow eventually. World economic development needs nuclear energy and legal solutions for it.

International nuclear law can develop through agreement of interested States and practice involving their companies. It can also develop within the competent international organizations willing to provide multilateral, harmonized and global solutions. Obviously, the mere fact of negotiating in international organizations does not provide any guaranty of a truly multilateral or universal solution.

For the orderly development of nuclear energy, it is essential to ensure the presence of such an order that would be compatible with modern technical and commercial realities and greatly accentuated multinational character of industrial and trade practices. Transnational nature of risks involved presupposes globalised responses conducive to the diminishment

1 On a Global Nuclear Liability Regime by Norbert Pelzer, Nuclear Inter Jura Congress, 8 – 11 October 2012, Manchester, UK, 11th October 2012.

of national and regional frameworks, the continuation of the promotion of which may become incompatible with best trade practices.

The financial and economic crisis has shown the need for greater global governance, which predicts the advent of much stronger and powerful international machinery. Despite slow reflexes and hesitations of governments still engaged to traditional State-centric thinking, the competence and executive prerogatives of international organisations keep steadily increasing, necessitated by the global nature and extreme complexity of the world economics. International organisations, being increasingly more autonomous, have to adapt themselves to a highly competitive global environment where their role is not automatically predetermined or saved.

The incident in Fukushima intensified debate on the future of nuclear power in the political circles and among the public of different countries. Following the predominant public opinion, a number of countries decided to reduce, or get out of, nuclear power. As part of the ongoing discussions, the public rightly questioned the effectiveness and adequacy of international and national legal regimes governing the development of nuclear energy. Sustainable development of the nuclear energy sector requires the strengthening and harmonization of relevant legal regimes. That may be achieved through a focused work on the codification of international law, by negotiations on a comprehensive legal instrument on nuclear law that could overcome the current fragmentation of international nuclear law.

International law of nuclear liability is highly fragmented indeed. This fragmentation has become its distinct feature and the main obstacle on the road to a global regime. Regional organizations can hardly provide global solutions. Their regional frameworks could be detrimental to global solutions. The fragmentation of legal regulation of nuclear liability affects the interests of international business, because legal uncertainty leads to increased risks and costs. However, the experience of recent decades of negotiations on nuclear liability shows that there are no reasons to expect that this fragmentation could be dealt with.

Years that have passed since the adoption of the revised Vienna Convention and the Convention on Supplementary Compensation in 1997, showed that, despite some recent progress, international community continue to shun these once-promising instruments. Moreover, the Vienna and Paris regimes have remained separate, with steps to bring them together (such as the Joint Protocol) stopping short of an actual unified regime, and still giving rise to debate. Additionally, discrepancies between the liability conventions and other international instruments regulating nuclear matters, make a ready basis for confusion and uncertainty in practical application; there are even serious collisions with instruments specialised in other fields attempting to regulate issues of nuclear responsibility.

* * *

Furtherance of nuclear safety is one of the main functions of the IAEA,[2] which has rightfully received special attention in the last decades. In some cases, the priority of nuclear safety over other objectives is expressly fixed in the IAEA instruments.[3] This is entirely justified given that, in light of past events and present public opinion, promotion of nuclear energy in science and industry is hardly possible without providing a thorough, comprehensive and constantly evolving system of nuclear security.

Many global instruments sponsored by the IAEA are devoted to achieving that goal. Examination of the entire range of nuclear safety conventions clearly demonstrates that implementation of the safety regime presents recognisable challenges in the field of nuclear liability. The 1994 Convention on Nuclear Safety actually establishes its own brand of a »nuclear liability« regime – under Article 9 all responsibility for nuclear safety should be bestowed upon the »license holder«[4] (and not the »operator« like in liability conventions). On its face an amount of uncertainty arises as to whether this norm should be preferred over the relevant provisions of nuclear liability conventions and, in particular, whether the meaning and application of the terms »licence holder« and »operator« are compatible. Therefore, it would be practical to assess the responsibility of the »license holder« under the Convention on nuclear safety while also comparing its definition of »accidents with radiological consequences« with »nuclear incident/accident« defined in other conventions.

Apart from the issue of resolving possible collisions between these instruments, there stands the question of their effective joint implementa-

2 »The Agency is authorized: ...to establish or adopt, in consultation and, where appropriate, in collaboration with the competent organs of the United Nations and with the specialized agencies concerned, standards of safety for protection of health and minimization of danger to life and property (including such standards for labour conditions)« (Article III.A.6 of the Statute of the IAEA).

3 Article 10 »Priority to safety« of the Convention on Nuclear Safety stipulates: »Each Contracting Party shall take the appropriate steps to ensure that all organizations engaged in activities directly related to nuclear installations shall establish policies that give due priority to nuclear safety«.

4 Article 9 of the CNS stipulates, »Each Contracting Party shall ensure that prime responsibility for the safety of a nuclear installation rests with the holder of the relevant licence and shall take the appropriate steps to ensure that each such licence holder meets its responsibility«.

tion. The safety and the liability conventions regulate tightly interwoven relations in the field of nuclear law. In this situation, discrepancies in approaches and details may create confusion among those who actually apply the rules. One possible example of such discrepancies can be found in the instruments' terminological basis. The definition of »nuclear accident« – a term equally critical in all fields of nuclear law – varies greatly from Article 1 of the 1986 Convention on Early Notification of a Nuclear Accident to the provisions of the liability conventions; CNS limits »nuclear facility« to »land-based civil nuclear power plant« (Article 2.i) – in contrast with definitions used in liability conventions, especially their latest reviews.

The above is also applicable to the 1979 Convention on the Physical Protection of Nuclear Material. Although it does not concern itself with civil liability, concentrating rather on criminal prosecution, its terminology is different from that used in both the safety and the liability instruments. The 2005 Amendment to this Convention shall add to the complexity of the situation, introducing, *inter alia*, the definition of »nuclear facility«[5].

Additional discrepancies can be seen in the IAEA instruments in varying references to »nuclear« and »radioactive« material, differentiated additional criteria of »significant amounts of radiation« or »consideration of safety«, lack of unanimity as to whether storage facilities are included in nuclear installation/facility.

Individual approach to every sphere of nuclear relations has certain benefits – it allows more precision and flexibility, requires less resources for developing new regulations. However, with every step that brings apart the regimes that are ultimately aimed at achieving a common goal and are daily implemented by the same personae, there is more confusion and reduced potential for constructive, unified thinking that seeks the employment of nuclear energy as a whole for the maximum benefit of humanity.

One instrument, which may have had the potential to serve as a basis for a universal nuclear liability regime, the Convention on supplementary

5 »Nuclear facility« means a facility (including associated buildings and equipment) in which nuclear material is produced, processed, used, handled, stored or disposed of, if damage to or interference with such facility could lead to the release of significant amounts of radiation or radioactive material« (GOV/INF/2005/10-GC(49)/INF/6. Attachment).

compensation for nuclear damage, in fact freezes the legal diversity and blocks real unification.

According to the Preamble of CSC, »national legislation on compensation for nuclear damage« is presumed to be »consistent with the principles of [Paris and Vienna] Conventions«. In reality, it is not so. The CSC in its provisions on internal law requirements (Annex, Article 2.1) has not upheld such universally acclaimed principles of international nuclear liability as absolute liability and exclusive liability of the operator. Instead, it offers strict liability and recourse to general tort law.

»Strict liability« is a long-standing term of municipal law, referring to a variety of regimes regulating non-contractual obligations arising from cause of harm or damage, which share a common feature of not being explicitly based on fault. It cannot be equated with absolute liability primarily because of a number of grounds for exoneration.

»Economic channelling« is also very different from the principle of exclusive liability of the operator. Suffice it to say that to enable indemnification through funds provided by the operator for damage caused by fault of third parties it is necessary to prove that these parties are liable under general tort or civil law – which more often than not includes proof of fault, thus undermining both the principles of exclusive and absolute liability.

The Annex to CSC has not carried on several improvements introduced by the newer revisions of the Paris and Vienna Conventions (such as the coverage of nuclear damage »wherever suffered« or the extension in time of the operator's liability in respect of loss of life and personal injury, among others).

All-in-all, rather than an effort of unification, CSC is a step towards fragmentation of international nuclear liability rules by creating new regimes of liability dependant on domestic law and not even sharing the basic principles recognised by the Paris and Vienna Conventions.

* * *

Every major nuclear incident drew attention to the legal principles underlying the regulation of issues related to compensation for damage to life, health, property and the environment. Absence of a single international legal regime, differences in the approaches of States did not provide the prerequisites for applying the common standards universally. That is why so many States have opted for strictly national solutions. As a result, compensation issues are addressed ad hoc, at the discretion of the government.

With this approach, the victims become dependent on the good will of the ruling circles; there is no certainty and predictability of the legal situation in the event of a nuclear incident, which undermines the foundations of the social consensus. The good will of the government to provide for compensation, in the absence of a special regime, should be transformed into its duty under relevant national and international law.

Nuclear liability was developed as an autonomous sphere, failing to reflect trends in general nuclear law. The incident in Fukushima provided additional arguments to critics of the principles underlying the regulation of liability for nuclear damage in a number of international instruments, including the possibility of limiting liability. If there is a limit of liability of the operator in national legislation, the role of the State is to be clarified as to its liability for damage in excess of limited liability. The work of the International Law Commission, *inter alia*, leads to the conclusion that there are principles in international law needed to be taken into account also in respect of nuclear liability: responsibility and liability of the State for hazardous activities under its jurisdiction or control; duty of the State to ensure the availability of compensation for nuclear damage resulting from an activity under its jurisdiction; unlimited liability for nuclear damage; the obligation of States to cooperate in safeguarding the interests of the victims.

There is a growing support to the idea of universal recognition of an institute of State responsibility for nuclear damage compensation. Suffice it to refer to the adoption by the United Nations General Assembly of Principles on the allocation of loss in the case of transboundary harm arising out of hazardous activities.[6] Principle 4 »Prompt and adequate compensation« reads:

> »1. Each State should take all necessary measures to ensure that prompt and adequate compensation is available for victims of transboundary damage caused by hazardous activities located within its territory or otherwise under its jurisdiction or control.
>
> 2. These measures should include the imposition of liability on the operator or, where appropriate, other person or entity. Such liability should not require proof of fault. Any conditions, limitations or exceptions to such liability shall be consistent with draft principle 3.

6 Resolution of the UN General Assembly 61/36 Allocation of loss in the case of transboundary harm arising out of hazardous activities (A/RES/61/36 of 18 December 2006).

> 3. These measures should also include the requirement on the operator or, where appropriate, other person or entity, to establish and maintain financial security such as insurance, bonds or other financial guarantees to cover claims of compensation.
>
> 4. In appropriate cases, these measures should include the requirement for the establishment of industry-wide funds at the national level.
>
> 5. In the event that the measures under the preceding paragraphs are insufficient to provide adequate compensation, the State of origin should also ensure that additional financial resources are made available«.

This shows that even in the absence of an applicable international convention on civil liability for nuclear damage, the host State should proceed from these principles in order to be in line with its international commitments and developing customary rules of international law.

Further expansion of a number of States-Parties to any of the conventions on civil liability for nuclear damage might encourage the resumption of debates on the recognition of State liability for nuclear damage under the general international law and specific IAEA instruments. Moreover, the existing treaty provisions on civil liability, being a fragment of solution, could hardly correspond to predominant expectations of an efficient and reliable tool for coping with nuclear damage in the interests of victims. The public might challenge the pertinence of keeping lower standards for civil liability in the nuclear industry, compared to general civil liability rules, and request consideration of proposals to set up a principle of unlimited liability for nuclear damage at the international level. A long time ago, a limitation of liability for nuclear damage was a vital element for encouraging the development of nuclear energy industry. Today, the public generally considers that the nuclear industry is strong enough, and possesses necessary financial and other capabilities to provide unrestricted compensation. Such an assessment would not imply diminishing the State's role in establishing proper legal frameworks to guarantee compensation for nuclear damage.

The above analysis shows that promoters of nuclear energy applications should be ready to the evolution of the customary international law (and its reflection in the practice of national and international courts) that would require stronger and more exhaustive remedies for victims than those contained in the nuclear liability conventions.

* * *

There are important changes in nuclear energy that will define its status tomorrow. It is becoming even more internationalized, with new powerful actors joining economic, financial, trade and innovation processes. In the past, nuclear liability development was conditioned by a limited circle of businesses at a particular point of time, where economic and political necessities played in favor of them and brought about well-known solutions where other interests of society did not play a determining role. Later, principles of nuclear liability had to adapt to growing concerns of public opinion; therefore, progressive development of this branch of law seemed to take into account the interests of society. However, according to a number of nations, this process is far from being successful and convincing.

The changing economic geography should be accompanied by new regulations reflecting the interests of new economic actors and nuclear energy nations. The absence of uniform international rules is an impediment to international development and business collaboration. New rules should be developed together with such new actors.

Sustainable development of the nuclear energy sector requires the strengthening and harmonization of legal regimes. It may be achieved through a focused work on the codification of international law, by negotiations on a comprehensive legal instrument on nuclear law that could overcome its current fragmentation. In doing so, the international community would address also the basic principles of, and cooperative approaches to, nuclear liability.

Theses on a Globally Harmonised Nuclear Liability Regime

Norbert Pelzer, University of Göttingen

1. A globally harmonised nuclear liability regime based on international treaties without any doubt is a goal to be aimed at. Such regime would be to the benefit of victims of a nuclear incident because it facilitates the bringing of claims for compensation worldwide. It would ensure legal certainty for the operator liable. Moreover, particularly due to legal channelling, it is advantageous for the supply industry. Unfortunately, international reality does not support this ideal.

2. There are two convention schemes which are apt to establish a worldwide regime: The first one is the Vienna Convention (VC) linked by the Joint Protocol (JP) to the Paris Convention (PC); the other one is the Convention on Supplementary Compensation for Nuclear Damage (CSC). The CSC may also serve as an overarching instrument to the VC scheme.

3. The CSC is the only convention which the US claims to be able to adhere to. Treaty relations with the US are desirable since the US roughly represents one quarter of the world's installed nuclear capacity. However, the so-called Grandfather Clause of Article 2 Annex CSC reserves the US the right to maintain its national nuclear liability law without any change. That means that the nuclear liability law of one quarter of the world's nuclear capacity is not included in worldwide harmonisation. Therefore, unlike stressed in its Preamble, the CSC does not substantially contribute to »establishing a worldwide liability regime«. It is true that it enhances the compensation amounts, in particular for Vienna States. Due to its »free-standing« nature it may also attract nuclear States not Party to any of the conventions (so-called Annex States). But it mainly seems to serve the US export industry by granting it legal channelling in customer countries and prevents US industry from being sued for nuclear damage before US courts.

4. In complement to the operator's compensation the CSC provides a second tier of compensation to be made available by public means of the Contracting Parties. There is no obligation of the Installation State to also provide a tier of supplemental compensation although it is responsible for

the safe operation of its nuclear installations. Such obligation exists under the Brussels Supplementary Convention (BSC), which establishes a three-tier compensation system. It is difficult to justify why under the CSC other Contracting Parties should spend tax money for compensating nuclear damage caused within the responsibility of a foreign Installation State that itself is exempt from providing a special tier of compensation.

5. The majority of European States adheres to the Vienna-Paris-Joint Protocol scheme. They are satisfied with this combination. This applies in particular to the European Paris States that are also Party to the BSC. Under the revised Paris/Brussels Conventions compensation of at least EUR 1.5 billion is ensured. The CSC ensures a minimum of approximately 600 million Special Drawings Rights (≈ EUR 691 million). For this reason alone, the CSC is not attractive for Western Europe.[1] It has, however, to be admitted that European Vienna States are not eligible for the BSC and a number of them only provide inadequately low compensation amounts.

6. Since the US insists on adhering to the CSC as the only means to establish a global nuclear liability regime and since at least the Europeans do not acknowledge the advantages of the CSC, a global regime based on the current Parties to the nuclear liability conventions cannot be achieved. The CSC currently has 4 Contracting Parties and is not yet in force. The 1963 VC has 39 Parties, the 1997 VC 11 Parties, the JP 27 Parties, the 1960 PC 16 Parties, the BSC 12 Parties and the 2004 Protocols to Amend the PC and the BSC are not yet in force. Ergo, only 59 States are Party to the basic conventions VC, PC and CSC. The majority of the States of the world are not Party to any of the conventions. A number of these States deem their national law more advantageous for domestic victims than the conventions. It will be difficult if not impossible to convince all of those States to adopt conventions, and if so, which of the two schemes should they opt for? Major nuclear States are also among non-convention States, namely Canada, China, India, Japan, Korea and South Africa. They are the main targets of the US policy to attract them to the CSC.

7. However, even if all States opt for one of the two nuclear liability schemes or for the CSC as an overarching instrument to cover all conven-

1 The French – US Joint Statement on Liability for Nuclear Damage of August 2013 (http://energy.gov/sites/prod/files/2013/08/f2/Joint%20Statement%20 Signed_0.pdf), however, seems to signal a certain extent of rapprochement between France and the USA regarding a global regime.

tions and national Annex legislations, we will not achieve a totally harmonized liability law. In certain fields the conventions grant discretion to national solutions. This applies in particular to the amount of liability. The current situation is marked by considerable differences regarding the liability amounts from country to country. Moreover, as long as nuclear liability may be limited in amount, many States will stay away from the conventions.

8. In summary: A global nuclear liability regime is an ideal. But as all ideals it cannot be achieved. It does not make sense to invest more efforts into this goal. It would be more realistic to concentrate and strengthen international endeavours to establish harmonized regional nuclear liability regimes based on the existing conventions (»regional convention clusters«). Regions are directly exposed to the nuclear risks of nuclear installations situated in the region. There is a risk community which warrants an internationally harmonised nuclear liability regime. Risk communities facilitate agreeing on high liability amounts or even unlimited liability, and they encourage and justify supplementary funding by the States of the region. At worldwide level there is no risk community. As Chernobyl and Fukushima have demonstrated, the worldwide transboundary nuclear risk is comparatively remote. It does not necessitate a global regime based on treaty relations and can be dealt with by the general rules of the laws of conflict. This applies to international transport, too, particularly since the revised Vienna and Paris Conventions compensate nuclear damage wherever occurred.

Sources

Vienna Convention

Vienna Convention on Civil Liability for Nuclear Damage of 21 May 1963 (1960 VC) (IAEA INFCIRC/500): http://www.iaea.org/Publications/Documents/Infcircs/1996/inf500.shtml

Protocol to Amend the Vienna Convention on Civil Liability for Nuclear Damage of 12 September 1997 (IAEA INFCIRC/566): http://www.iaea.org/Publications/Documents/Infcircs/1998/infcirc566.pdf

1997 Vienna Convention on Civil Liability for Nuclear Damage (Consolidated text of the Vienna Convention on Civil Liability for Nuclear Damage of 21 May 1963 as amended by the Protocol of 12 September 1997, established by the Secretariat of the IAEA) (1997 VC) (IAEA INFCIRC/566 Annex): http://www.iaea.org/Publica tions/Documents/Infcircs/1998/infcirc566.pdf

Paris Convention

Convention on Third Party Liability in the Field of Nuclear Energy of 29th July 1960, as amended by the Additional Protocol of 28th January 1964 and by the Protocol of 16th November 1982 (1960 PC): http://www.oecd-nea.org/law/nlparis_conv.html

Protocol of 12 February 2004 to Amend the Convention on Third Party Liability in the Field of Nuclear Energy of 29 July 1960, as Amended by the Additional Protocol of 28 January 1964 and by the Protocol of 16 November 1982 (2004 PC Protocol): http://www.oecd-nea.org/law/paris_convention.pdf

Convention on Third Party Liability in the Field of Nuclear Energy of 29 July 1960, as Amended by the Additional Protocol of 28 January 1964, by the Protocol of 16 November 1982, and by the Protocol of 12 February 2004. Unofficial consolidated text of the Paris Convention incorporating the three Protocols referred to above (2004 PC): http://www.oecd-nea.org/law/Unofficial%20consolidated%20Paris%20Con vention.pdf

Joint Protocol

Joint Protocol Relating to the Application of the Vienna Convention and the Paris Convention of 21 September 1988 (JP) (IAEA INFCIRC/402): http://www.iaea. org/Publications/Documents/Infcircs/Others/inf402.shtml

Convention on Supplementary Compensation for Nuclear Damage

Convention on Supplementary Compensation for Nuclear Damage of 12 September 1997 (CSC) (IAEA INFCIRC/567): http://www.iaea.org/Publications/Documents/ Infcircs/1998/infcirc567.shtml

Brussels Supplementary Convention

Convention of 31st January 1963 Supplementary to the Paris Convention of 29th July 1960, as amended by the additional Protocol of 28th January 1964 and by the Protocol of 16th November 1982 (1963 BSC): http://www.oecd-nea.org/law/nlbrus sels.html

Protocol of 12 February 2004 to Amend the Convention of 31 January 1963 Supplementary to the Paris Convention of 29 July 1960 on Third Party Liability in the Field of Nuclear Energy, as Amended by the Additional Protocol of 28 January

1964 and by the Protocol of 16 November 1982 (2004 BSC Protocol): http://www.oecd-nea.org/law/brussels_supplementary_convention.pdf

Convention of 31 January 1963 Supplementary to the Paris Convention of 29 July 1960 on Third Party Liability in the Field of Nuclear Energy, as Amended by the Additional Protocol of 28 January 1964, by the Protocol of 16 November 1982 and by the Protocol of 12 February 2004. Unofficial consolidated text of the Brussels Supplementary Convention incorporating the three amending Protocols (2004BSC): http://www.oecd-nea.org/law/Unofficial%20consolidated%20Brussels%20Supplementary%20Convention.pdf

Supplementary literature by the author on a global nuclear liability regime

On Global Treaty Relations – Hurdles on the Way towards a Universal Global Civil Nuclear Liability Regime, in: Zeitschrift für Europäisches Umwelt- und Planungsrecht (EurUP) vol. 6 (2008) pp. 268 – 280

Reflections on Establishing a Global Nuclear Liability Regime, Paper presented to the IAEA INLEX Meeting to be held from 30 May to 1 June 2012, 4 pp. (Restricted IAEA INLEX Document)

On a Global Nuclear Liability Regime, Nuclear Inter Jura Congress October 2012, Manchester, UK, 4 pp., at: http://www.burges-salmon.com/INLA_2012/10234.pdf

Report on the Discussion Panel: Do We Need a Global Nuclear Liability Regime?

Sidonie Royer-Maucotel, CEA, Gif sur Yvette, France

Introduction by the chair Christian Raetzke

Introducing the panel, Mr. Raetzke reminded participants of a working session in the 2012 Manchester Congress of AIDN/INLA. He recalled Stephen Burns' thoughtful speech saying that the search for a global nuclear liability regime is like the search for the »Holy Grail«. In the same session in Manchester, Norbert Pelzer gave a statement that a global regime is impossible to achieve and that we do not even need it. When Christian Raetzke discussed this a few weeks later in Vienna with Wolfgang Tonhauser, the latter denied that this last statement was true and emphasised that we need to strive for a global nuclear liability regime. He encouraged further discussion and so the idea to stage a panel discussion in Leipzig was born. Additional experts were invited with different perspectives from different regions. Christian Raetzke is therefore very happy to welcome a panel of experts with different perspectives, views and arguments for this discussion.

Introductory Statement by Kyoji Kawasaki

Mr. Kawasaki introduced some recent developments in Japan about nuclear compensation regime. He reminded participants that claims for nuclear liability compensation have been raised by more than 100,000 people being evacuated from contaminated areas and relocated, plus numerous companies.

In order to cope with these claims, Japanese government already decided to provide TEPCO, through established »Nuclear Damage Liability Facilitation Fund,« up to 5 trillion yen, that is equivalent to 40 billion euro, for compensating Fukushima victims. Therefore, if a grave nuclear disaster occurred, existing nuclear liability regimes based on national legislations as well as nuclear liability conventions would be quite insufficient and a special regime must be introduced with heavy governmental involvement in institutional and financial schemes for compensation.

Mr. Kawasaki stressed that if you compare this Japanese special regime with already existing regimes under nuclear liability treaties, you can find, in the Japanese regime, several different measures for compensation in terms of both substantive and procedural aspects.

On the substantive aspect, it is interesting to note that moral damage and rumor-related economic damages are extensively compensated and that there is a scheme for refugee people, according to which you may receive compensation money for »future« damages in advance for maximum 5 year term counting from 2012.

On the procedural aspect, mediation by the Dispute Resolution Center is expected to play a major role in the settlement of compensation disputes. However, it is reported that, to date, only 30 % of the total number of claims before the Center have reached an amicable settlement with average 8 months long procedures. Against this background, a considerable number of victims are beginning to make a (collective) recourse to domestic courts and tribunals.

On the international aspect, Mr. Kawasaki stressed that there is no lawsuit outside Japan against TEPCO except one case. This is the case, before Southern district court of California, brought last December by US military service persons who had participated in the rescue operation after the earthquake. The total amount of their claims is 210 million US dollars.

Mr. Kawasaki recalled the audience that Japan is not a member of any nuclear liability conventions. However, the question is not which international regime Japan should join, but when Japan will decide to make an accession to CSC. Mr. Kawasaki stated that some members of the Diet assert that joining CSC might jeopardize the right of peaceful petition for the redress of damage recognized by the Article 16 of the Japanese constitution and Japan will take a way of amending all relevant clauses and articles of internal legislations.

Mr. Kawasaki concluded that the Japanese special regime for nuclear compensation, as a whole, seems not so much »private tort law reparation« for damages suffered in the past as »public law compensation« for the continuing intolerable situation brought about by a private company, TEPCO, which have operated nuclear power plants in accordance with a consistent state policy of promoting nuclear energy utilization for a half century in Japan.

Introductory Statement by Stephen Burns

Mr. Burns stressed the fact that there is an interesting contrast between the adherence to the nuclear liability regime adopted 50-60 years ago and the adherence to the »safety regime« adopted after the Chernobyl accident (the Convention on Nuclear Safety and other »safety conventions«). In fact, contrary to the universal adherence to the Convention on Nuclear Safety (to which, among nuclear operators worldwide, only Iran is not a member), there is relatively little adherence to the liability conventions for a number of large nuclear countries (except in Europe with the Paris Convention and Vienna Convention) even with the CSC (not yet in force).

On the question whether a global nuclear liability regime is a destination or a journey, Mr. Burns stated that he became more convinced it is a journey while working for the NEA. However, despite national differences, Mr. Burns considered that there is a merit to looking toward a global regime as a goal or objective (Paris and Vienna Convention joined with the Joint Protocol and the CSC). The law suit in the California court concerning the Fukushima accident in Japan is potentially a good illustration of some of the benefits of a more global regime.

Introductory Statement by David Davies

Mr. Davies chose to expose the case of the developing nations versus the existing nuclear nations together with the question of global regime which is a noble cause.

Mr. Davies stated that the reasons underpinning the existence or participation in a global regime are also varied and, in his view, do not necessarily always relate to the traditional legal »arguments« (strict liability, channeling, jurisdiction) around nuclear liability Convention or global regime participation.

From a developing country perspective, Mr. Davies considered that the progress and uptake by advanced countries in the existing nuclear liability conventions has been slow.

In fact, 55 percent of nuclear reactors worldwide are not covered by any international nuclear liability conventions currently in force. Mr. Davies stressed that developing countries only contribute to 17 percent of the reactors not covered by such international nuclear liability conventions.

Due to the number of reactors in India and the US, the percentage would reduce from 55 percent to 26 percent if the CSC was in force (hypothetically) with its current signatories.

However, when the above scenario is applied to country participation, country participation in international nuclear liability conventions (currently in force) amounts to 68 percent.

Mr. Davies considered that the »legal« advantages (or disadvantages) of joining a nuclear liability convention or a »global regime« will not of themselves necessarily influence or compel a country to join a convention or global regime. Mr. Davies suggested that it is rather another set of factors or drivers that further influence such decisions. These factors are *inter alia* the following: international nuclear industry relations and nuclear industry »citizenship«; government and relevant national nuclear regulatory regimes approach to nuclear energy; country geographic location; public perception of the nuclear industry per country and international nuclear commercial trade and contracting.

Mr. Davies concluded that history has shown that the participation in nuclear liability conventions has left something to be desired and if a global regime is to be achieved it will require a major shift in approach and intent by current nuclear super-powers.

Introductory Statement by Ms. Els Reynaers Kini

Ms. Reynaers presented an argument in favor of proposing to use SAARC (which stands for South Asian Association for Regional Cooperation) as the relevant platform to address transboundary nuclear liability aspects. SAARC encompasses 8 countries: Afghanistan, Bangladesh, Bhutan, India, Maldives, Nepal, Pakistan and Sri Lanka. The aim is to create in this region a nuclear regional risk community and move forward within this region to find a solution to nuclear liability regime.

Ms. Reynaers reminded participants that none of these countries have ratified any nuclear liability conventions (India has signed the CSC but has not ratified it yet). There are two new countries in the nuclear field: Sri Lanka and especially Bangladesh, which has already started negotiations with the Russians to construct an NPP (50 km from the Indian border). India and Pakistan are rather ambitious about their nuclear power program. All SAARC countries are member of the 1986 Assistance Convention and the Early Notification Convention.

SAARC have 16 areas of cooperation (including energy). Interestingly, after the Indian Ocean Tsunami in 2004, SAARC countries did agree to cooperate on natural disaster management issues (including the setting up of one joint disaster management center, adopting policy guidelines, focusing on capacity building, etc.).

Ms. Reynaers concluded that the parliamentary debates in India related to the CSC show that CSC is considered to be mainly a means to raise additional funding for Western countries. Instead of the international nuclear liability treaties which show lack of interest, the regional harmonized nuclear liability mechanism might be worth considering and may be in the interest of all SAARC countries. But, for her, the question remains whether this regional cooperation actually blocks or betters the system and the international regime shall definitely more reflect these regional debates.

Introductory Statement by Norbert Pelzer

Mr. Pelzer considered that a global regime cannot be achieved considering the fact that there is a conflict between, on the one hand, the Paris and Vienna Convention system linked by the Joint Protocol, and, on the other hand, the CSC. The problem is that the United States claim to be able to adhere only to the CSC whereas other states, at least the Europeans, do not acknowledge the advantages of the CSC and would not adhere to it. Therefore, Mr. Pelzer considered that a global nuclear liability regime is an ideal. But as all ideals, it cannot be achieved.

So, the question came if we really need a global regime to cover liability for nuclear damage. The experience in Chernobyl and Fukushima showed that the major impacts of nuclear accidents happened within the regions and the worldwide transboundary risk is rather remote (which could be dealt with general rules of the laws of conflict). There is no risk community, especially as a basis for supplementary compensation, worldwide. Moreover, since the Paris and Vienna revised conventions have a new geographical scope, damages are covered and compensated wherever they occurred.

For the time being, the solution could be to have more participation at a regional scale (»regional convention clusters«) as in Europe with the Paris and Vienna Convention linked by the Joint Protocol and hopefully the European Union will improve the situation with adequate nuclear liability law.

Mr. Pelzer even wondered if the claims filed in California are not a way to attract Japan or Korea to ratify the CSC.

He concluded that we should stop aiming at a global regime that cannot be achieved right now but perhaps in 20 years time.

Introductory Statement by Wolfram Tonhauser

Mr. Tonhauser noted that the following statistics speak for themselves: There are 436 NPPs in operation worldwide, 69 are under construction and 179 of the NPPs are in 8 states which are not party to a liability regime. 8 nuclear states have not ratified any conventions (China, Canada, India, Iran, Pakistan, Republic of Korea, Japan, South Africa). The United States with 102 reactors and 3 under construction is only party to a convention that is not in force. 57 % of the world total NPPs are outside the scope of an international nuclear liability regime currently in force. Therefore, a global nuclear regime is desirable and shall be our ultimate goal.

Mr. Tonhauser reminded participants that, in June 2011, the ministerial conference at the IAEA on nuclear safety following the Fukushima accident recognized the need for a global nuclear liability regime considering the fact that all states might be affected by a nuclear damage with a view to provide a proper compensation. INLEX recommended that all member states shall strive to achieve a global nuclear liability regime. He stressed that INLEX members are not uniform (they come from Paris or Vienna convention, industries, insurance).

Mr. Tonhauser considered that a system of regional regimes will not work. First, the operation and introduction of a NPP program is not regional, the transport is not regional, the psychological effects and the effects on environment and people of a nuclear accident are not regional. Finally, even a regional regime such as in Europe faces problems such as reciprocity, entry in force or different liability limits per country. Even within the EU, the Joint Protocol has not achieved universal adherence among Vienna and Paris states and the European commission initiative for harmonization of nuclear liability has not yet reached the stage of concrete proposals.

Mr. Tonhauser concluded that it is a misconception that national law can protect industries and victims in the same way as treaty relations can do this and that liability has to be seen within the broader context of the safety and security regime. Last not least, »global« means encompassing all states, not all states minus one.

Introductory Statement by Alexander Matveev

Mr. Matveev considered that international law on nuclear liability is highly fragmented and even accession of new parties to the existing instruments would not change the nature of the global regime. As already mentioned by Mr. Kolesnik in his presentation, the interest of business and companies is to have a global regime or solid nuclear international legal foundations but preferably global.

Mr. Matveev recalled to the attention of the participants that international nuclear law has not yet been tested by the International Court of Justice.

For minor accidents with limited damage and small compensation volumes, existing liability laws and coverage concepts are sufficient. However, for catastrophic accidents such as Chernobyl or Fukushima, the solution has to involve governments and states (in case of an accident in Germany for example with compensation amounting to hundreds of billions of Euros, the German government would not remain idle and close eyes on the situation.)

Mr. Matveev concluded that, for the last 20-30 years, public international law has developed new principles and concepts (for example within the framework of environmental law) which reinforced responsibility and liability of States for hazardous activities under their jurisdiction and control. It would therefore be wise to address the issues of nuclear liability in this more general context and to strive for a new global codification which may also renegotiate some of the existing basic principles.

Discussion

Mr. Pelzer started the discussion by considering that one of the problems comes from the US which cannot adhere to any other convention than the CSC. However, for Mr. Pelzer, other parties may not be willing to adhere to the CSC which they considered as unbalanced. In fact, the CSC provides a second tier of compensation to be made available by public means of the contracting Parties but there is no obligation for the Installation state to also provide a tier of supplemental compensation although it is responsible for the safe operation of its nuclear installations. Therefore, it is difficult to justify why under the CSC other contracting parties should spend tax money for compensating nuclear damage caused within the responsibility of a foreign installation state that itself is exempt from providing a special tier of compensation.

Mr. Pelzer also commented on Mr. Matveev's remarks by cautioning that nuclear liability law belongs to the realm of private international law and should not be mixed with public international law.

Mr. Tonhauser replied that the most important is to look objectively whether the CSC is »good enough« and can provide a global regime, whether a global regime is needed and what are the alternatives, if any, to a global regime. For Mr. Tonhauser, a system of regional regimes is not a feasible alternative to a global regime, for various reasons.

He reminded participants that when IAEA provides assistance to newcomer countries, there are intense discussions on what are the benefits of being a member to a liability convention and which one is the best for each newcomer. When drafting new legislations in newcomer countries, the liability issues are in most cases resolved among the last issues, due to thorough discussion and analysis of the pros and cons of the different regimes.

In light of the complexities and interplay between the various conventions, *Mr. Davies* questioned if there would actually be a truly global regime, even if every nuclear state signed up to one or another convention.

Mr. Tonhauser added that, from the discussion at INLEX, came the subject of the benefit of non-nuclear transit countries (which are not neighbours but potentially affected states) to join any one of the regime which is a substantial discussion that should take place.

For *Ms. Reynaers*, as some of the newcomer countries in the Asian region may sign the Vienna Convention as opposed to the CSC, the regional regime was an alternative solution to harmonize the nuclear liability regime in this region.

From the audience, *Rafael Manóvil* addressed the question to Mr. Tonhauser whether, if the CSC comes into force, it will be a global regime considering the fact that some have ratified the CSC but not the Paris or the Vienna Conventions and others ratified both the CSC and one of the two conventions?

Mr. Tonhauser agreed that the situation is not very clear and that it could be very interesting for INLEX to work on it. He added that newcomer countries are looking at the Vienna Convention but keep the issue on hold for the time being, considering the question Mr. Manóvil has just mentioned.

Mr. Matveev added that when Russia joined the Vienna convention in 2005, Russia joined the Convention in its initial version (1963) as it was out of question for the Russian government to consider the 1997 protocol. And even though Russia needs, on the business point of view, to be party to the Joint Protocol 1988 (as shown in Mr. Kolesnik's presentation), the official position of the Russian ministries and governmental experts is different. The situation may change in the future with the new generation hopefully.

Mr. Burns added that the one priority is to get the 2004 Paris/Brussels protocols into force (which was anticipated by the EU Council Decision requiring simultaneous ratification of EU Member States members to the PC, if possible by 2006). It is a part of the global regime (with of course the Joint Protocol) and it is an important step towards the modernization of the regimes.

Mr. Tonhauser concluded by regretting that there is a drama about these liability conventions, which were negotiated many years ago. Some of the conventions are accused of serving only one country, others of serving the industry but the only issue should be that there is a fair and equitable compensation for the victims in case of a nuclear accident.

Fourth Working Session

»Nuclear Phase-Out, Decommissioning and Waste Management«

Chair: *Ulrike Feldmann,* Wirtschaftsverband Kernbrennstoff-kreislauf (WKK), Königswinter/Berlin

Secretary: *Dr. Simon Mayer,* Chemgineering Technology, Wiesbaden

Phase-Out in Germany: History and Outlook

Dr. Michael Micklinghoff, Senior Advisor / Executive Nuclear Consultant, Hannover

1. History

As in many countries nuclear power has always been a very controversial topic in Germany. After the last nuclear plants were commissioned in 1988 there has been a long history of negotiation and talks about the future of nuclear in Germany. The aim was always to find a broad social consensus. These discussions were therefore called »Konsensverhandlungen«. Main partners of these negotiations were the two primary political parties, the conservatives (CDU) and the socialists (SPD). Of course, industry as well as the unions have always been involved.

An important round of negotiations happened in 1993 when the conservatives were in government. The discussions were based on the awareness that the operating nuclear plants would have to be replaced after 40 years and for that the knowledgebase must be kept alive. It was foreseen that a new reactor type should be developed in Germany and *one* reactor was to be built to »bridge the knowledge gap« (accordingly called, in German, »*Fadenrissverhinderungsreaktor*«). Although some leaders in the SPD were in favor of such a concept it was not supported by the party. The draft agreement contained all aspects of energy supply such as renewables, coal, nuclear etc. Nonetheless this »Energiekonsens« eventually failed.

The next round of negotiations started after the elections in 1998, when a coalition government of the socialists (SPD) with the greens (Grüne) came to power, led by chancellor Schröder. The situation was difficult for the operators:

All transports of spent fuel to the reprocessing plants in UK and France had recently been stopped by the former conservative government because contamination had been found on some transport casks. Therefore the plants were in danger of »constipation«. In addition the red-green government planned to issue a law which would end the use of nuclear power in a short time period; this had been one of the central elements of the Green's election campaign.

On the other hand the government realised that such a law with an immediate or short-term phase-out would entail the considerable risk that the operators would successfully sue the government for compensation at the Federal Constitutional Court. The government was determined to find a solution not involving any compensation, as this would have been politically unacceptable. Therefore, in 1999 the government started negotiations with the utilities which led to the following agreement:

The lifetime of the reactors was limited to around 32 years. Before that there was no lifetime limit in the German Act on Nuclear Energy (*Atomgesetz*). According to the agreement each power plant received a calculated quota of electricity which it was allowed to produce. This was calculated to correspond to roughly 32 years of operation. In order to calculate this quota certain assumptions like presumed availability etc. were made. The allocated contingent could be transferred between the plants under certain conditions.

In addition intermediate storage facilities for spent fuel were to be built at each site in order to avoid transports. Transport of spent fuel to reprocessing in France and the UK was not allowed any more after a certain date. In recompense, the government made some concessions. The timeline of 32 years was far longer than the original draft laws had foreseen. And importantly, the government assured the undisturbed operation of the German NPPs within this agreement. It was the understanding that if the law would mirror this agreement the operators would refrain from legal action. The agreement was signed in June 2001. The corresponding phase-out law came into force in 2002.

The next government, elected in 2005, was a Grand Coalition of conservatives and socialists led by chancellor Angela Merkel. There was a stalemate within the coalition concerning the attitude towards nuclear and so nothing happened and the 2002 phase-out law was left untouched. After the next change in government in 2009, with a coalition of conservatives and liberals (FDP) under the same chancellor, and as the shut down dates of some reactors came close the government decided about a comprehensive new energy policy in September 2010. It consisted of 9 pillars: renewables, energy efficiency, grid, buildings, mobility, nuclear, coal, research etc. Some aspects of this policy were subjects in discussions between the government and the operators.

Basically the content was:

- Lifetime extension of the nuclear reactors by 12 years in average
- Operators have to pay tax on nuclear fuel absorbing part of their earnings

- Operators pay into a special fund to promote renewables and research
- Two demonstration plants for CCS (Carbon capture and storage) to be built until 2020.

2 *Turnaround in energy policy*

After the accident at »Fukushima Daiichi« the government, with the chancellor Angela Merkel in the lead, performed an abrupt U-turn in nuclear policy. The major milestones are the following:

11 March 2011 in Japan:

The seismic event and tsunami (14m) occurs, a station black-out at »Fukushima Daiichi« NPP leads to loss of cooling with ensuing core damage and hydrogen explosions in several reactors, pictures of this accident are seen around the world.

14 March 2011 in Berlin:

Chancellor Angela Merkel announces to suspend the recent legislation about the lifetime extension for the German nuclear power plants.

The Government decides to shut down 7 plants (built before 1980) plus Krümmel for 3 months (so-called Moratorium).

The German Reactor Safety Commission (RSK) is asked to perform a special safety evaluation for all 17 nuclear power plants in Germany.

17 May 2011:

The RSK submits its final report about the specific safety analysis for each plant. It states that all German reactors have a very high safety standard independent of age or type. The plants are very robust with respect to external events like earthquakes, flooding etc. – not comparable to the Fukushima reactor.

In addition to the technical safety analysis of the RSK Chancellor Merkel established an »Ethics Commission« with 17 members from research, politics, churches, industry and society.

30 May 2011:

The »Ethics Commission« submits its final report and recommends to step out of nuclear power within 10 years. »This is necessary to avoid any risks from nuclear reactors and this is possible because there are other forms for power generation with less risks«. The competiveness of the German industry should be taken account of.

6 June 2011:

The German Government (the cabinet) decides about a comprehensive body of laws regarding the future energy policy including many changes in the *Atomgesetz* (Atomgesetznovelle). This phase-out legislation determines the final closure of the 8 NPPs temporarily shut down during the Moratorium:

- Philippsburg I (EnBW)
- Neckarwestheim I (EnBW)
- Isar I (E.ON)
- Unterweser (E.ON)
- Biblis A & B (RWE)
- Brunsbüttel (Vattenfall)
- Krümmel (Vattenfall)

All plants except Krümmel were commissioned before 1980. Already the lifetime extension law from 2010 had made a difference between the plants before and after 1980. The older plants received only 8 years of additional operating time. The inclusion of Krümmel into the moratorium and the final shutdown list must be seen as purely political.

The new law also scheduled the stepwise closure of the remaining 9 plants (by the end of the year indicated, respectively):

- 2015: Grafenrheinfeld (E.ON)
- 2017: Gundremmingen B (RWE)
- 2019: Philippsburg II (EnBW)
- 2021: Brokdorf (E.ON)
- 2021: Gundremmingen C (RWE)
- 2022: Isar II (E.ON)
- 2022: Neckarwestheim II (EnBW)
- 2022: Emsland (RWE)

Although the allocated power allowance can be transferred, the remaining quota will expire at the end.

The goal to increase the share of renewable energy production to 50% by 2030 was already part of the above mentioned energy concept of September **2010**.

The Government argued that the owners and operators of the plants are now in a similar situation as 9 months before – before the lifetime extension was granted. However, according to the electricity companies which operate those plants this is not true. The main differences are:

The sudden shutdown of the plants is not comparable to a planned phase-out far ahead. Basically this is due to the uneconomical fuel burn-out and mismatched investment strategy. In the wake of the granted lifetime extension the operators had already spent money for improvements of the plants. These are stranded investment now. Also the remaining power allowance is lost, as it cannot be used as economically – if at all – as under the old regime. The quota may be irrecoverably lost. This can be demonstrated easily in the case of Vattenfall, as after immediate closure of Brunsbüttel and Krümmel they have no plant left in which the remaining contingent could be used. Also fixed shutdown dates are not compatible with allocated power contingents.

The twists and turns in summary:

- **Before 2002**: Unlimited lifetime as long as safety is assured
- **June 2002**: Lifetime of the German nuclear reactors restricted to about 32 years (by way of fixing a quota of electricity each plant is allowed to produce).
- **October 2010**: Lifetime extension by 12 years in average
- **June 2011**: U-Turn. Fixed shut-down dates. Phase-out legislation. Stranded investments...

3. German Self-Assurance / An attempt at explaining the U-turn

This very fast action is unprecedented. No other country made such a drastic move in the wake of Fukushima. Switzerland stopped new build plans but has not limited lifetime of existing installations so far. Italy voted to abandon its new build programme but has phased out its existing installations long ago.

This U-turn was supported by

- all political parties
- all the media
- and the public at large.

Why? Are the Germans different?

In contrast to other countries the Germans seem to lack a great deal of **pragmatism**. Recently I found the following description of the German Self-Assurance in literature. I quote:

> »He [a German character in the novel] was one of those hopelessly and immutably self-confident men, self-confident to the point of **martyrdom** as only Germans are, because only **Germans are self-confident on the basis of an abstract notion** — science, that is, the supposed knowledge of absolute truth.
>
> ***A Frenchman*** *is self-assured because he regards himself personally, both in mind and body, as irresistibly attractive to men and women.*
>
> ***An Englishman*** *is self-assured, as being a citizen of the best-organized state in the world, and therefore as an Englishman always knows what he should do and knows that all he does as an Englishman is undoubtedly correct.*
>
> ***An Italian*** *is self-assured because he is excitable and easily forgets himself and other people.*
>
> ***A Russian*** *is self-assured just because he knows nothing and does not want to know anything, since he does not believe that anything can be known.*
>
> **The German's self-assurance is worst of all, stronger and more repulsive than any other, because he imagines that he knows the truth — science, which he himself has invented but which is for him the absolute truth (...)**
>
> He was one of those theoreticians **who so love their theory** that they lose sight of the theory's object—its **practical** application. **In his love for theory, he hated everything practical and did not want to know about it.** He was even glad of failure, because failure, resulting from departures in practice from theory, only proved to him the correctness of his theory.«

This was written around 1868 by L. Tolstoy in »War and Peace« (Chapter X, the object of the description being the German general Pfuel).

In order to understand some of the **practical** consequences of the turnaround one has to look at the energy economics and the so-called merit order chart.

The main principle can be seen in the exemplary picture. I do not want to go into all the details. The merit order determines that the generation sources with the least marginal costs are deployed first until the demand is satisfied. As renewables are deployed first – independent of their costs – the use of other power plants depends very much on their availability. As the power production of wind and solar fluctuates very much the conventional sources are needed to compensate (shadow plants). However, they are deployed only intermittently and often only for a short time. Many of them (e.g. gas) cannot be operated economically under these conditions. From the **practical** point of view this regime makes sense only if there are power storage technologies available and installed to compensate for the fluctuation.

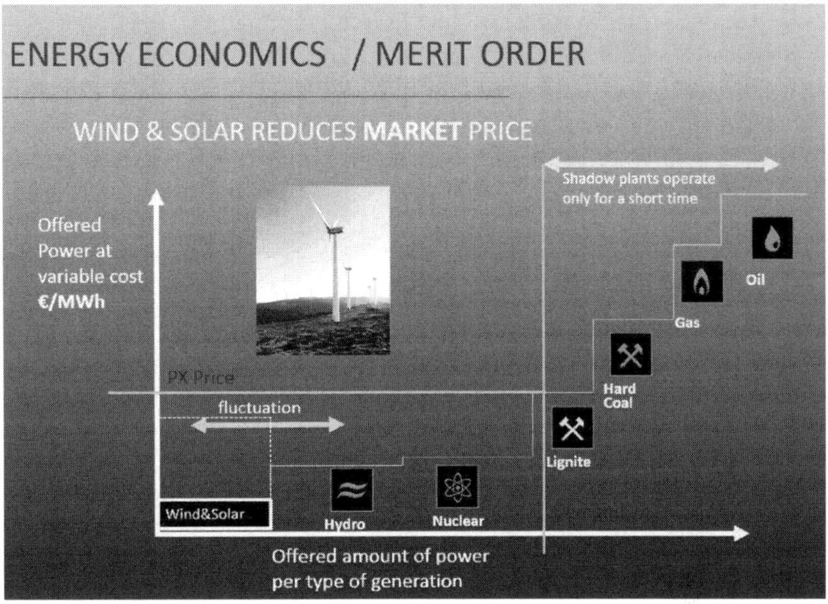

Fig. 1 Merit Order

The use of wind and solar not only affects the order of deployment, but also lowers the market price at the power exchange. This lower price in turn increases directly the subsidies for wind and solar – an absurd spiral.

In any case this power exchange price based on marginal costs does not reflect the real cost of power production including fix and system costs.

4. Legal Actions

The twists and turns of the German phase-out, and especially the last U-turn in the wake of Fukushima, have generated a number of legal actions. Without going into details, this chapter intends to give an overview of the current status.

The **original phase-out legislation in 2002** was not followed by legal actions. As explained above, German utilities had signed an agreement with the government. Government abandoned its original intention of a very rapid (if possible, immediate) phase-out in favor of the more balanced scheme with a timeline of approximately 32 years of operation, and promised to guarantee an undisturbed operation if operators complied with all requirements. In their turn, the utilities accepted the phase-out and declared they would not go to court.

The **2010 legislation** brought not only the lifetime extension, which was balanced by an obligation of utilities to contribute to a climate and renewables fund. At the same time, the government introduced a tax on nuclear fuel with the aim of absorbing part of the electricity companies' earnings and filling gaps in the general budget. The tax was expected to yield about 2.3 billion Euros per year (as long as all reactors were still in operation).

Several claims concerning the new fuel tax were filed by utilities. The status is as follows:

- Up to now there has been no final decision.
- However several provisional court decisions have been issued.
- The Financial Court in Hamburg has declared its view that the tax law is unconstitutional and has passed the issue to the Constitutional Court.
- Also the Court of Justice of the EU may have to deal with this issue to assess whether the tax is compatible with EU law.

In any case, the outcome of these lawsuits has no effect on the phase-out. It is just a question of money.

With respect to the moratorium proclaimed immediately after the Fukushima event, RWE has filed a claim at the competent administrative court concerning the temporary shutdown order for the Biblis A&B reactors in April 2011.

In February 2013 the court has decided in favor of RWE. It ruled that the shutdown order was not justified. This is the basis for punitive damage, to be claimed in a new lawsuit (media reports: 187 million Euros).

There were no claims concerning the temporary shutdown orders (Moratorium) for the remaining six NPPs which were affected. Most likely the other operators did not want to deteriorate the atmosphere for possible discussions with the government.

With respect to the phase-out legislation the operators declared they accept the political decision by parliament. However they claim that the German constitution provides compensation for such an action which can be compared to an expropriation. They expected that the government would open a round of discussions to solve this issue. As there have been no positive signs for such talks E.ON filed a suit at the Federal Constitutional Court in November 2011. RWE filed a similar suit at the same court in June 2012.

Vattenfall as a foreign company has another possibility. It claimed for compensation at the International Court of Arbitration in Washington (ICSID) in May 2012. However in addition Vattenfall filed a claim at the German constitutional court as well in June 2012.

EnBW came to the conclusion it is not allowed to go to the Federal Constitutional Court as it is owned by the public. The majority owner is the state of Baden-Württemberg. Anyway, as the state of Baden-Württemberg has a green prime minister any legal action would not be opportune.

According to some press reports the companies ask for a compensation of more than 15 billion Euros in total.

5. Decommissioning

Regardless of the pending court decisions the operators prepare for decommissioning of the shutdown plants. All operators go for immediate dismantling (no safe enclosure). However technical problems with respect to the irradiated fuel hinders immediate decommissioning at some plants. The fuel cannot be transported from some plants at the moment.

- BWR: Isar I, Brunsbüttel ..
- Defect fuel: Unterweser ..

In May 2011 E.ON submitted its application for a decommissioning license according Art. 7 para. 3 *Atomgesetz*. This application contains two reservations: The company will only use the license

- if the Constitutional Court has confirmed that the phase-out legislation complies with the constitution and
- if the final repository »Konrad« is ready to accept the waste from decommissioning in due time.

Vattenfall submitted its application for Brunsbüttel in November 2012. All applicants seem to be aligned as this application contains those reservations as well.

Krümmel is a special case. Krümmel was commissioned in 1984 (way after 1980) and there is no technical reason why this plant was included into the moratorium and the list of the final shutdown plants. Vattenfall had spent a lot of money in their backfitting program. Obviously they see Krümmel as the most likely plant they will be compensated for. Probably this is why they have not submitted an application for decommissioning.

EnBW submitted its applications for GKN 1 & KKP 1 according Art. 7 para. 3 *Atomgesetz* recently (May 2013).

The experience from the past shows that the licensing process might last 4 to 5 years. In order obtain an overview of the future decommissioning activities one has to make certain assumptions. Assuming the constitutional court decides in 2014 and the reservations in the applications do not apply the decommissioning licenses could be granted around 2016. If the dismantling takes about 14 years a rough picture of the dismantling timeline would appear as follows.

Fig. 2 Dismantling Timeline

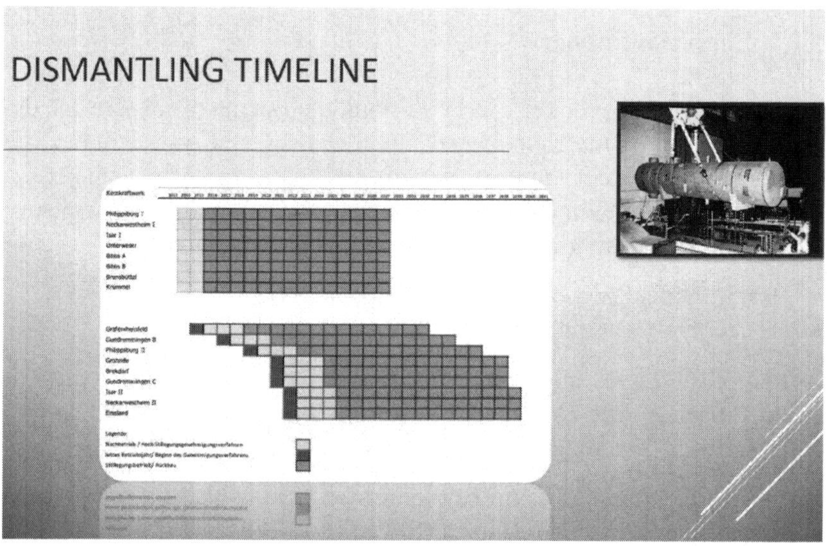

One can see that there will be many plants (up to all 17 plants) in the dismantling stage at the same time.

Considering that the available resources with respect to competent personnel, equipment, contractors and money are limited at a given point in time one can doubt that this is a realistic scenario.

6 *Outlook*

It is clear that the Constitutional Court will not decide on the claims concerning the 2011 phase-out legislation before 2014. The federal election in September 2013 will prevent any proceedings within this year.

The decision of the court is uncertain. There are mainly three possible outcomes: The court may rule that

1. the phase-out-legislation is constitutional or
2. the phase-out-legislation is declared unconstitutional and the court orders government to amend it or
3. the phase-out-legislation is nullified (cancelled by the court).

What are the consequences?

1. Phase-out-legislation is declared constitutional: In this case the operators will receive no compensation. The decommissioning licensing process will proceed as foreseen and licenses will be issued. The dismantling process will depend on the progress of the repository »Konrad« and the available resources.
2. Phase-out legislation is declared unconstitutional: A new law must be drafted respecting the reasoning of the court. A compensation regime must be developed. Negotiations between government and operators are advisable (and it is difficult to see how they can be avoided).
3. Phase-out legislation is cancelled: In theory the shut-down plants could go into operation again since the earlier legislative status would be reinstated. However, this would not be realistic because of political reasons. The operators have accepted the political phase-out decision anyway. For them it is only a question of compensation. If the phase-out legislation is cancelled the operators have a strong position in the negotiation with the government.

Perhaps there is a fourth possible outcome even before the Constitutional Court decides.

It is clear that the relation between nuclear operators and government is burdened and has suffered from the U-turn in nuclear policy. Upfront to the 2011 legislation, unlike the 2002 and 2010 legislation, there was no previous agreement between the two sides and there have been no official talks since. However, government policy is fraught with many uncertainties:

- Decisions of the Constitutional Court are uncertain.
- Liabilities for compensation might be high.
- Final decisions of the Constitutional Court and the Court of Justice of the EU about fuel tax are uncertain.
- Financial basis for the search for final repository is unclear.
- Security of supply becomes more and more endangered and very costly.

- Government plans for intermediate storage need consent with the operators.
- …

Therefore the German government might be forced into comprehensive discussion with the owners and operators of the nuclear plants.

The question is: Is there

- room,
- the need,
- the opportunity,
- a chance

for a new comprehensive agreement between government and utilities?

The huge amount of money involved (uncertain compensation liabilities) might foster those discussions. However, basically this depends very much on the progress of the so-called »Energiewende«. Will the »Energiewende« work?

In the future the power production from wind and solar in Germany will exceed the demand at certain times. At other times we need additional power from conventional sources.

The following technical difficulties will have to be overcome in due time:

- Providing enough and efficient storage capabilities to compensate partially for the fluctuation of wind and solar.
- Strengthening the grid especially to transport the power from offshore wind in the north to industrial consumers in the south.
- Having shadow plants available.

Beside those technical difficulties it is clear that all this will be very expensive. Obviously most private consumers in Germany are still willing to pay. What about industry?

Two practical examples show how we have to cope today in reality with the difficulties to secure day to day power supply – activities not much noticed by the public.

- The generators of Biblis have been modified in a way that they can be driven by external electric power. The generator is spinning without producing active electricity. It produces so-called reactive power necessary for the stability of the grid.
- The operator of the gas fired plant Irsching in Bavaria is being paid by the transmission system operator just to stay ready for production in

case of shortage from wind & solar. Otherwise the most modern and efficient gas plant in Europe would have been mothballed.

These examples stand for mending the current situation produced by the hasty introduction of the »Energiewende«. In the long term, however, we need a sound and healthy power system.

The decisive questions for the success of the »Energiewende« are:

- Will the above mentioned technical problems be solved in time in order to secure electricity supply?
- Will all this be affordable in the end?

Finally it is time to eliminate a misunderstanding: The phase-out legislation after Fukushima in 2011 does **not** represent the turnaround in energy policy (»Energiewende«). It was just a U-turn with respect to the lifetime of the nuclear plants. The »Energiewende« was established in September 2010 together with the lifetime extension. At that time all the long-term goals with respect to renewables, CO2 emissions and power production without nuclear were defined. The U-turn a few months later only shifted the timeline as nuclear power was phased out earlier (up to 14 years). **It made the already initiated »Energiewende« much more risky and more expensive, if not impossible.**

I hope the »Energiewende« will not fail. If it does, »the Germans« will probably think it was still the right decision. As L. Tolstoy wrote: »He was even glad of failure, because failure, resulting from departures in practice from theory, only proved to him the correctness of his theory«.

Phase-Out and Long Term Operation Legislation in Switzerland

David Erni, lawyer, Legal Specialist at Swiss Federal Office of Energy

1 *Nuclear Power in Switzerland*

The commercial use of nuclear power in Switzerland dates back to the end of the 1960s, when the first nuclear power unit was commissioned. Between 1969 and 1984 there have been commissioned five nuclear power units:

- Beznau-1 (KKB I) was commissioned in 1969 and is a Pressurized Water Reactor (PWR) with a net power generation of 365 megawatt electrical;
- Beznau-2 (KKB II), commissioned in 1972, is identical to Beznau-1;
- Mühleberg (KKM), 1972: Boiling Water Reactor (BWR) with 373 MWe;
- Gösgen (KKG), 1979: PWR with 970 MWe;
- Leibstadt (KKL), 1984: BWR with 1'190 MWe.

Today, Swiss nuclear power generates around 3.3 gigawatt of electricity, which corresponds to 40 % of the total Swiss electricity generation. The primary source of electricity generation in Switzerland is hydropower with around 55 % of the total production.

In 2005, more than 20 years after the last nuclear power plant (NPP) had been built, the new Nuclear Energy Act (NEA) came into force with more detailed provisions concerning the licensing procedure for construction and operation of new NPP. The Swiss Federal Council (the executive authority) stated in 2007 in its Energy Perspectives 2035 that the energy strategy should be founded on four pillars, one of them being large power plants.

It was expected that there would be a drop in electricity production around 2020, when the first NPP were to be taken out of service, resulting in a gap between supply and demand. To substitute that loss of capacity and keep up the electricity supply, there were plans for the construction of new nuclear power plants.

The current licence-holders sought to build in total three new nuclear power plants, each generating around 1'500 MWe as replacement units on the sites of the existing power plants in Beznau, Mühleberg and Gösgen. These units were supposed to be commissioned in the 2020s.

Before a new NPP can be commissioned, the Swiss NEA requires three stages of licence procedures to be passed: In order to apply for a construction and an operating licence, a potential operator has to apply for a general licence. The general licence is a political decision in principle, whether a NPP of a certain size and at a certain site is approved by the government, parliament as well as the public (optional referendum).

The applications for the new general licences were filed in 2008 and the procedures were led by the Swiss Federal Office of Energy.

In the beginning of 2011 the general licence procedures were well underway and for summer 2011, public consultations were planned.

2. Phase-Out: Energy Strategy 2050

The Fukushima Dai-ichi nuclear disaster led to a political change of direction concerning nuclear power in Switzerland. Shortly after the events in Japan, on 14 March 2011, the Federal Department of the Environment, Transport, Energy and Communications suspended the ongoing general licence procedures for the new NPP.

On 25 May 2011 the Federal Council decided to phase-out nuclear power and not to license new nuclear power plants. The National Council and the Council of the States (together constituting the Federal Assembly, the Swiss parliament) backed this decision to phase-out in June and September 2011 respectively.

Alongside with its decision to phase-out, the Federal Council assigned the Federal Office of Energy to work on a new energy strategy. The so-called Energy Strategy 2050 is designed to accommodate the loss of nuclear capacity without the construction of new nuclear power plants. In 2012, the Federal Council presented a draft of a totally revised Energy Act that allows offering optimal frame conditions for that goal.[1] The three cornerstones of the Energy Strategy 2050 are as follows:

- Increasing the energy efficiency;

1 See www.energiestrategie.ch for details (visited in July 2013).

- Extending renewable energies;
- Covering the remaining demand with fossil power production and imports.

In addition, the phase-out decision has to be adopted in the Nuclear Energy Act in order to take effect. Therefore, to legalise the phase-out of nuclear power that has been decided by the Federal Council and the Federal Assembly, the Federal Council presented a draft of an amendment of the NEA as a part of the Energy Strategy 2050.

According to that draft, new general licences for nuclear power plants shall be banned. Thus as a result, no new NPP will be built after this amendment is adopted. The existing NPPs could as well no longer apply for a general licence, meaning large alterations of existing NPPs like the installation of a new reactor pressure vessel, which require a new general licence, will no longer be possible.

Nuclear technology in general shall nonetheless not be banned. The construction and operation of new research reactors shall still be possible.

Beside the provisions to ban new general licences for NPP, the only other amendment in the draft of the NEA contains a ban on fuel reprocessing. Currently there is a moratorium on fuel reprocessing until 2016, in the future reprocessing shall no longer be allowed.

Apart from these amendments, the Federal Council drafted no other changes of the NEA. As a consequence, today and in future, all Swiss nuclear power plants shall possess operating licences for unlimited terms.[2] Although the Federal Authorities estimate an operating period of 50 years, this is just a parameter for calculations of future energy supply scenarios.

In fact there is no binding term limit and thus the Swiss NPP can be operated as long as they are safe. If the safety requirements are met, an operating term of 60 years, for example, is possible.

Between September 2012 and February 2013, there has been a public consultation on the draft of the Energy Strategy including the amendment of the NEA. On the one hand left-wing parties as well as environmental organisations welcomed the phase-out of nuclear power but criticised that the draft of the NEA didn't include a term limitation for the operation of NPP. On the other hand, right-wing parties together with economic organ-

2 A decision of the Swiss Federal Court of 28 March 2013 in the lawsuit BGE 139 II 185 granted the Mühleberg power plant the removal of the limitation in its operating licence. The KKM is the last of the Swiss NPP to obtain an unlimited operating licence.

isations were opposed to the phase-out in principle and they argued that the draft was essentially a ban on nuclear technology altogether.

But despite that criticism, the Federal Council decided to abide by its decision and to proceed with its original draft. The draft is expected to be presented to the Federal Assembly in the autumn session, starting in September 2013. It is possible that extensive discussions ensue and the parliament will come to a decision on the final provisions later than spring 2014. Subsequently, a referendum on that decision is possible with the result that the date of the coming into force of the amended NEA is currently open.

3 Phase-out Initiative of the Green Party

Aside from the Energy Strategy 2050, there have been other endeavours to achieve a phase-out of nuclear power in Switzerland. Shortly after the events in Fukushima, the Swiss Green Party launched the phase-out initiative. An initiative is a political right for everyone who collects the signatures of 100’000 citizens to bring a matter to a referendum in order to amend the Federal Constitution.

The Green Party collected more than 100’000 signatures by November 2012. The content of the phase-out initiative is very similar to several aspects of the Energy Strategy 2050.[3]

But there is one important difference: the operating term of the existing nuclear power plants shall be limited to 45 years. In effect, the three oldest Swiss units KKB I, KKB II and KKM would have to shut down shortly after the initiative were accepted by referendum. The nuclear phase-out would be accomplished in 2029, when the newest plant, KKL, would be taken out of service after 45 operating years.

The Federal Council decided its Energy Strategy 2050 shall be a counter proposal to the phase-out initiative. Meaning that the Parliament is going to debate and decide on the initiative at the same time as the Energy Strategy. It is expected that the referendum is going to take place in 2014.

3 Cf. http://www.grueneinitiativen.ch/web/grn/volksinitiative_atomausstieg/infos_atomausstieg (visited in July 2013).

4. Current Long Term Operation

As stated above, in Switzerland the operating licences are issued for unlimited periods. A nuclear power plant can be operated as long as the safety requirements are met. However, licence-holders enjoy less protection of their acquired rights than it is the case in other countries, where fixed-term licences are issued. Thus Swiss licence-holders are obliged to improve and back-fit their plants on a continuous basis.

The current legislation concerning long term operation is found in article 22, paragraph 2 NEA, where several obligations for the licence-holder are ruled. The following obligations for a licence-holder are important concerning long term operation:

- to take measures to ensure that the installation is kept in good condition;
- to carry out follow-up inspections and systematic safety and security evaluations throughout the entire service life of the installation;
- in the case of nuclear power plants, to carry out a comprehensive periodic safety review.

Although these obligations are very general, from them the Swiss Nuclear Safety Inspectorate (ENSI) has derived a couple of special obligations that are applicable for long term operation only. Long term operation according to the ENSI is the phase of operation of a nuclear power plant after 40 years of service.

In order to approve long term operation, today already the ENSI demands a proof of long term safety. That proof is not explicitly stipulated by the Nuclear Energy Act, but it arises from the obligations for the licence-holder outlined in article 22 NEA. The proof of long term safety contains several elements:

- If a licence-holder plans to operate his installation beyond 40 years of service, alongside the normal periodic safety review (which is carried out at least every 10 years), he has to prove that the design limits of the safety-relevant parts of the installation will not be exceeded during an extended operating term.
- An ageing management takes into account the safety-relevant components and structures, especially the condition of large components. These large components, which are difficult to replace, play a key role in determining the lifetime of a NPP.

- The obligation of the licence-holder to continually keep the installation in good condition binds him to take back-fitting measures in order to ensure the long term operation. The ongoing development of science and technology leads to increasing divergences between the design bases for existing and new nuclear power plants. By back-fitting an existing plant, these divergences can be reduced.

To date, the proof of long term safety has been provided by the two Beznau and the Mühleberg unit. Concerning KKB I and II the ENSI determined in 2010 that they complied with the requirements and the criteria for a provisional taking out of service would not be met in the subsequent 10 years of operation. In 2012, the ENSI also approved the proof of long term safety for KKM, but with several conditions that have to be met until 2017 in order to ensure the safety of further operation. One condition is to back-fit an additional heat sink that is independent of the Aare River.

5. Concept of Long Term Operation

Considering the current lack of specific legislation, there is some legal uncertainty concerning the enforceability of conditions set up by the ENSI. Moreover, under these circumstances the Inspectorate takes the sole responsibility in regulating the long term operation.

To alleviate this situation, in order to create more legal security for both the licence-holder as well as the Federal Authorities, the ENSI brought up the idea of a concept of long term operation.

According to this idea, a licence-holder, who plans on operating his installation beyond 40 years of service, has to set up a concept of long term operation. The ENSI then reviews that concept in order to decide on issuing a permit for long term operation.

There are several elements of such a concept of long term operation conceivable:

- Remaining years of service: The licence-holder would have to state for how long he intends on operating his plant.
- Proof of long term safety: The licence-holder would have to prove that, during the planned extended operating term, the design limits of his installation will not be reached.

- Back-fitting: The intended back-fitting measures to achieve and ensure the long term safety would have to be pointed out in a binding manner.
- Ensuring personnel and know-how: Considering the nuclear phase-out decisions in Switzerland and in Germany, it is to be expected that nuclear engineering will lose some appeal to potential employees and it will likely be more difficult to keep skilled professionals in that line of work. A licence-holder would have to show his measures to secure the required personnel and know-how on his installation during the planned operating period.

In order to achieve the most legal certainty, these and other possible provisions for such a concept should be stipulated in the Nuclear Energy Act.

6. Draft of the Federal Authorities

As pointed out above, there is a political desire for regulating long term operation. For instance the public consultation of the Energy Strategy 2050 has shown it is particularly left-wing parties that seek to limit the operation terms of NPP. Hence the Committee for the Environment, Spatial Planning and Energy CESPE of the National Council (the lower house of Swiss Parliament) has been discussing long term operation legislation during the last year.

In the context of meeting of the CESPE, three Federal Authorities, the ENSI, the Federal Office of Energy (SFOE) and the Federal Office of Justice (FOJ) have been involved. They elaborated a draft for an amendment of the Nuclear Energy Act and presented it to the committee.[4] The draft for long term operation legislation contains the following elements:

- Concept of long term operation after 40 years: According to the draft, the current unlimited operating licences would be limited to 40 years of service. If a licence-holder planned on extending the operating term of his NPP beyond 40 years, he would be obliged to elaborate a con-

4 Please note that this is a draft originating from the Federal Authorities and does not represent the opinion of the Federal Council. The Federal Council still abides by its phase-out decision made in May 2011 and has so far not commented on the draft.

cept of long term operation according to the aforementioned idea of the ENSI.

- Approval of the concept: The ENSI would have to review this concept of long term operation and to decide on issuing a permit for the planned additional operating time, which could be up to 10 years.
- Additional operating term: Although the current unlimited operating term would be converted into a limited operating term, there would still be no definite term limit. Operating terms beyond 50 years of service would still be possible. However there would be an obligation for the licence-holder to elaborate a concept of long term operation after 40 years and after that to renew and adapt his concept every 10 years, if he aimed at more than 50 years of service for his NPP.
- Compensation: One big advantage of this legislation would be in creating legal security for the operator. The operator could trust in a certain term of service as long as he abided by his concept of long term operation approved by the ENSI. In turn the Swiss Confederation would not have to compensate for any not amortised investments if the unit were shut down according to the concept of long term operation.

The issue of compensation is of great importance in the political discussion. An expertise of the FOJ showed that in some cases when a shutdown is ordered for other than safety reasons, there is a possibility that compensations are due. The lawmaker is obliged to introduce new legislation with consideration. Besides, the protection of trust emerging from the principle of good faith may also set up an obligation to compensate for some damage. This could especially be the case, when a licence-holder makes an investment in his unit while trusting in an unlimited operating term. If after that, a new legislation sets a limitation, capping the operating term in a manner that doesn't allow amortising the prior investment because the license-holder trusted in a longer operating term, then it's possible that the lawmaker has to compensate for the not amortised investments. Of course there is no compensation due if the unit is taken out of service because of safety reasons.

According to the draft of the Federal Authorities, safety reasons would still be the only reasons deciding on the duration of the plant operation. Moreover, the operating term would emerge from a proposition in the concept of long term operation by the licence-holder himself. As a consequence, the draft would help preventing compensations for not amortised investments.

7. *Current Developments Concerning Long Term Operation Legislation*

In April 2013 the CESPE discussed the draft of the Federal Authorities and decided not to adopt it. Instead, the committee adopted a so-called motion, which mandates the Federal Council to create a draft.[5]

According to this »agreement solution«, the licence-holder has to present an operation concept after 40 years of service of his unit. That concept would have to demonstrate that a safe operation for at most 10 additional years is guaranteed.

However, the Federal Council did not support this motion and stated in his answer to the motion that it abides by its phase-out decision of 2011. According to the council there should be no term limitation and a NPP should be allowed to be operated as long as it is deemed safe. Also, the Federal Council outlined that since there is a possibility the operators still have got not amortised investments at the time of shutdown, as a consequence the operators would have to be compensated for those investments made trusting in a longer operating term.

Obviously the question of compensation is a key question in the Swiss political debate. Upon receiving the Federal Council's answer, the CESPE decided to withdraw its motion in its meeting in July 2013, before the motion was discussed by the National Council. In order to make a new proposal, the CESPE decided to discuss long term operation legislation afresh and to conduct hearings with the operators as well as the ENSI.

Currently, in Parliament there are no clear political majorities for any solution concerning long term operation legislation. Therefore it is unclear, if and when long term operation legislation will be adopted in the Swiss Nuclear Energy Act and what that legislation is going to implicate.

5 Cf. 13.3284 motion of the CESPE-N (http://www.parlament.ch/d/suche/seiten/geschaefte.aspx?gesch_id=20133284, visited in July 2013)

Decommissioning and Final Repositories in Germany

Prof. Bruno Thomauske, RWTH Aachen

Prof. Thomauske decided not to submit a paper for publication in this book.

Discussion Report of the Fourth Session

Dr. Simon Mayer, Chemgineering Technology, Wiesbaden

The Chair, Ulrike Feldmann, proposed to have a first round of questions after the first two presentations by Michael Micklinghoff and David Erni, which both dealt with phase-out issues. Since the third and last presentation by Bruno Thomauske had a different scope, namely waste disposal, it was to be followed by a separate discussion.

The first discussion started with *Christian Raetzke* asking Mr. Erni how binding the final shutdown date in the decommissioning plan presented by the operator would be according to ENSI's concept? Mr. Erni replied that it will always be possible for the licensee to renew the plan and thus to change the stated date.

Tom Tannion asked Mr. Micklinghoff for his personal opinion about the following scenario: In case the energy demand of the German industry would drastically increase in the remote future, when Germany has by then lost its expertise in nuclear power, would it be thinkable that Germany buys a nuclear power plant from a (now) developing country like China? Mr. Micklinghoff expressed that even in the event of a bad economic situation, a come-back (of nuclear energy) is assumed impossible.

Alexander Matveev asked Mr. Erni on the predicted outcome of the referendum in Switzerland (on the Green's party initative) and when it will take place. Mr. Erni assumed it will take place next year. Before the events of Fukushima, the public opinion was in slight favour for nuclear, but now the supporters might have decreased. However, there is also the possibility that the Greens may retract the referendum because of the risk that there will be confusion on the different topics of »ban of nuclear« and lifetime extension.

Stanley Berger wanted to know from Mr. Micklinghoff where the nuclear waste will be stored and how the waste management is financed. The question could be formulated: What does Germany have, in this respect, on its »bank account«? As a response to the first question, Mr. Micklinghoff referred to the next presentation (Bruno Thomauske). Responding to the second question, Mr. Micklinghoff explained that internal funds have been established by the operators. However he said it may be doubted that it is the possible to simultaneously fund the decommissioning of all 17 reactors at the same time.

Julius Weitzdörfer expressed his concern based on his observation that in recent years a tendency can be observed to breach existing law in the wake of large scale events. Is it a special feature of energy and particularly nuclear law, that politics is prevailing? The personal view of Mr. Micklinghoff was that there is a general decline in the awareness of the constitution. It seems that »the goal justifies the means«. This could be observed in general and the observation is not limited to the energy sector. Ulrike Feldmann confirmed that she has also observed this tendency.

Akos Frank assumed that the phase out (of nuclear) shows that investing on base load scale will not be attractive anymore. According to Mr. Frank this will lead to a breaking point. He wanted to know the operators' view on this development and asks if Germany will be abandoned as a place for energy infrastructure investments. Mr. Micklinghoff expressed his personal view that in terms of these investments, Germany seems to be a very unstable place. It will be hard, if not impossible to find investors in this unfavourable climate. Even if the constitutional court would eventually rule for compensation for nuclear operators after the phase-out, Germany might remain unattractive for investors.

After the presentation of Bruno Thomauske a second round of questions was initiated.

Patrick Reyners wanted to know from Mr. Thomauske how the question of retrievability is taken into account? Mr. Thomauske replied that retrievability is presently a safety criterion. It has to be warranted during operation, but for the post-closure period its objective is only to assure that casks are aerosol tight for 500 years. So handling of the casks remains possible.

Christophe Depaus expressed his surprise that e.g. transmutation is considered as alternative to deep geological storage. Mr. Thomauske explained that alternatives are meant to be a reference for the evaluation of the pro and cons of deep geological storage, which should be the solution. So the alternatives are used to challenge and improve the anticipated solution. The German Act on Site Selection establishes the mandatory goal »to identify under the safety aspects the best site«. As a consequence it might be difficult to decide in case three equally safe sites are encountered at the end of the site selection process.

Christoph Moench expressed his doubts that the budget (2 BEUR) and the timescale for the site selection process are realistic. Mr. Thomauske explained that the figures given by the ministry are not based on an actual planning but rather on an estimation based on the experience with the surface investigations, which was in the order of 100 MEUR per site. For underground investigations one should calculate between 500 MEUR and 1.5 BEUR per site considering a timescale from 15 to 40/50 years. All calculations include all activities until the selection decision is taken. Moreover the maintenance costs for the Gorleben site and further investigations of the then selected site will come on top. Mrs. Feldmann added that the National Regulatory Control Council (*Nationaler Normenkontrollrat*), which is tasked not only with observing the principles of making better laws but also with validating economic considerations, has also voiced doubts in the calculations. The uncertainties currently combine to make a sound calculation impossible.

Fünfte Arbeitssitzung

»Fragen des deutschen Atomrechts«

Vorsitz: *Dr. Manfred Rebentisch,* Rechtsanwälte Clifford Chance, Düsseldorf/Mainz

Sekretär: *Julius F. W. Weitzdörfer,* LL.B., Max-Planck-Institut für ausländisches und internationales Privatrecht, Hamburg

Anwendungsbereich und Schutzniveau des § 7d AtG

*Prof. Dr. Thomas Fetzer**

I. Einleitung

Mit dem 12. Gesetz zur Änderung des Atomgesetzes ist unter der Überschrift »Weitere Vorsorge gegen Risiken« § 7d AtG eingeführt worden. Die Vorschrift war bereits im Gesetzgebungsverfahren Gegenstand von Kontroversen. Diese haben seit dem Inkrafttreten der Norm weiter zugenommen. Teilweise wird angenommen, die Norm habe einen neuen Schutzmaßstab im Atomrecht eingeführt. Zum Teil wird die Neuregelung so verstanden, dass sie zu einem Absinken des bisherigen atomrechtlichen Schutzniveaus führe. Schließlich wird sogar davon ausgegangen, die Vorschrift sei wegen einer Verletzung von Art. 2 Abs. 2 GG verfassungswidrig, da sie zu einer Unterschreitung des vom *BVerfG* in seiner Rechtsprechung entwickelten grundrechtlich determinierten Schutzniveaus für die friedliche Nutzung der Kernenergie führe. Die Kritik an § 7d AtG entzündet sich im Wesentlichen an drei Auslegungsfragen:[1] Erstens stellt sich die Frage nach dem materiellen Anwendungsbereich der Vorschrift. Hier geht es zum einen allgemein darum, gegen welche Gefahren bzw. Risiken § 7d AtG Maßnahmen der Inhaber einer atomrechtlichen Genehmigung fordert. Zum anderen stellt sich ausgehend vom Vorsorgegegenstand die Frage zum Verhältnis der Vorschrift zu § 7 II Nr. 3 AtG. Eng mit diesen beiden Aspekten zusammen hängt die zweite Auslegungsfrage des § 7d AtG: die nach dem verfahrensrechtlichen Gehalt der Norm. Schließlich ist der dritte Gesichtspunkt, der zu Unklarheiten bei der Auslegung von § 7d AtG führt, inwieweit die Norm drittschützenden Charakter hat, inwieweit also die Einhaltung der Vorschrift auch von Bürgerinnen und Bürgern – ggf. auch gerichtlich – eingefordert werden kann.

---

* Prof. Dr. Thomas Fetzer, LL.M. (Vanderbilt) ist Inhaber des Lehrstuhls für Öffentliches Recht, Regulierungsrecht und Steuerrecht an der Universität Mannheim. Der Beitrag geht zurück auf einen Vortrag, den der Verf. am 7.6.2013 bei der Jahrestagung der International Nuclear Law Association in Leipzig gehalten hat. Eine gekürzte Fassung des Beitrags ist in der NVwZ 2013, 1373 erschienen.

1 Kritisch insbesondere *Renneberg*, ZNER 2011, 106; *Roller*, NVwZ 2011, 1431; *Roßnagel/Hentschel*, ZNER 2011, 7; *Ziehm*, ZUR 2011, 3.

II. Das materielle Schutzniveau des § 7d AtG

Nach § 7d AtG hat

> »der Inhaber einer Genehmigung zum Betrieb einer Anlage zur Spaltung von Kernbrennstoffen zur gewerblichen Erzeugung von Elektrizität (...) entsprechend dem fortschreitenden Stand von Wissenschaft und Technik dafür zu sorgen, dass die Sicherheitsvorkehrungen verwirklicht werden, die jeweils entwickelt, geeignet und angemessen sind, um zusätzlich zu den Anforderungen des § 7 Absatz 2 Nummer 3 einen nicht nur geringfügigen Beitrag zur weiteren Vorsorge gegen Risiken für die Allgemeinheit zu leisten.«

Im Hinblick auf den materiellen Anwendungsbereich der Norm stellt sich davon ausgehend die Frage, gegen welche Gefahren und Risiken ein Genehmigungsinhaber weitere Vorsorgemaßnahmen zu ergreifen hat. Traditionell wird im Atomrecht seit der Kalkar-Entscheidung des *BVerfG* zwischen verschiedenen Risikobereichen unterschieden:[2] Auf der einen Seite stehen Gefahrenabwehr und Risikovorsorge; auf der anderen Seite steht das so genannte Restrisiko. Während im erstgenannten Bereich nach § 7 II Nr. 3 AtG eine atomrechtliche Genehmigung nur erteilt werden darf, sofern die nach dem Stand von Wissenschaft und Technik erforderlichen bestmöglichen Gefahrenabwehr- und Risikovorsorgemaßnahmen getroffen werden, ist der Bereich des Restrisikos, wie das *BVerfG* ausführt, »als sozialadäquate Last von allen Bürgern zu tragen«.[3] Das hinzunehmende Restrisiko hat das Gericht definiert als »Ungewissheiten jenseits der Schwelle praktischer Vernunft«, die »ihre Ursache in den Grenzen des menschlichen Erkenntnisvermögens« haben und die insofern »unentrinnbar« sind.[4]

An der grundsätzlichen Unterscheidung zwischen Gefahrenvorsorge einerseits und Restrisiko anderseits hat auch die Brunsbüttel-Entscheidung des *BVerwG* nichts geändert.[5] Entgegen teilweise in der Literatur geäußerter Auffassungen hat das Gericht nämlich gerade nicht die Unterscheidung zwischen Restrisiko einerseits und Schadensvorsorge andererseits aufgegeben.[6] Vielmehr hat das Gericht lediglich ausgeführt, dass die Abgrenzung zwischen den beiden Kategorien nicht schematisch auf Grundlage

2 *BVerfGE* 49, 89 = NJW 1979, 359.

3 *BVerfGE* 49, 89 (143) = NJW 1979, 359 (363).

4 *BVerfGE* 49, 89 (143) = NJW 1979, 359 (363).

5 *BVerwGE 131, 129* = NVwZ 2008, 1012; so auch *Müller-Dehn*, atw 2013, 30 (32 f.).

6 *Roßnagel/Hentschel*, ZNER 2011, 7 (8).

der »Sicherheitsanforderungen an Kernkraftwerke« erfolgen könne.[7] Insbesondere führt nach Auffassung des Gerichts allein die Zuordnung eines Ereignisses zur Sicherheitsebene 4 als auslegungsüberschreitendes Ereignis nicht zwangsläufig dazu, dass das Ereignis dem Bereich des Restrisikos zugerechnet werden kann.[8] Vielmehr ist jeweils im konkreten Einzelfall zu entscheiden, welche Risiken dem Restrisiko zuzuordnen sind und welche Risiken in den Bereich der Schadensvorsorge fallen, so dass alle nach dem Stand von Wissenschaft und Technik erforderlichen Maßnahmen zu ihrer Abwehr zu ergreifen sind.[9] Dies hat das *BVerwG* in seiner Entscheidung zum Zwischenlager Unterweser ausdrücklich bestätigt, wenn es darlegt, dass Drittbetroffene nur gegen solche Risiken Vorsorge verlangen können, die nicht dem Restrisiko zuzuordnen sind.[10] Weiterhin führt das Gericht in dieser Entscheidung aus, dass im Ergebnis für die Frage, ob ein Risiko dem Restrisiko zuzurechnen ist, nicht die schematische Zuordnung zu einer Sicherheitsebene entscheidend sei. Vielmehr ist demnach im Einzelfall »die Exekutive für die Risikoermittlung und -bewertung, also auch für die Entscheidung über Art und Ausmaß von Risiken, die hingenommen oder nicht hingenommen werden, allein verantwortlich«.[11] Hierbei besteht eine Einschätzungsprärogative der Behörde, so dass die gerichtliche Überprüfung dieser Entscheidung darauf beschränkt bleibt, ob die Behörde »diese Überzeugung von Rechts wegen haben durfte«[12]. Dass die Kategorie des Restrisikos durch die Brunsbüttel-Entscheidung des *BVerwG* nicht obsolet geworden ist, zeigen auch zwei Entscheidungen des *BVerfG*, die seither ergangen sind und in denen das Gericht unter ausdrücklicher Bezugnahme auf die Brunsbüttel-Entscheidung weiterhin das Restrisiko als Bereich definiert, in dem Schäden an Rechtsgütern Dritter »praktisch« ausgeschlossen sind.[13]

Geht man also davon aus, dass es grundsätzlich die beiden Kategorien Schadensvorsorge auf der einen Seite und Restrisiko auf der anderen Seite gibt, stellt sich die Frage, welche Kategorie von § 7d AtG erfasst wird

7 BMU, Sicherheitsanforderung an Kernkraftwerke vom 20. November 2012.

8 *Arndt*, RdE 2012, 81 (85).

9 I.E. so auch *Müller-Dehn*, atw 2013, 30 (32).

10 *BVerwG*, NVwZ 2012, 750 (752); s.a. *BVerwGE* 131, 129 (141, 144 ff.) = NVwZ 2008, 1012 (1015 f.).

11 *BVerwGE* 131, 129 (140) = NVwZ 2008, 1012 (1015); s.a. *BVerfG*, NVwZ 2009, 171 (176).

12 *BVerwGE* 78, 177 (180).

13 *BVerfG*, NVwZ 2009, 171 (172); *BVerfG*, NVwZ 2010, 114 (115).

bzw. ob durch die Norm möglicherweise sogar eine völlig neue Kategorie geschaffen wurde.

1. Grammatische Auslegung

Ausgangspunkt der Auslegung einer Norm ist stets ihr Wortlaut.[14] Die Auslegung einer Norm setzt somit stets die Ermittlung des Wortsinnes voraus. Der Wortsinn ergibt sich entweder aus dem allgemeinen Sprachgebrauch oder aus juristischen Fachtermini. Letzteres ist zwar aus Sicht des Bürgers (an den sich der Gesetzgeber wendet) häufig schwer verständlich. Jedoch wird hierdurch zugleich eine präzise Ausdrucksweise ermöglicht, welche zugleich keiner umständlichen Erläuterungen bedarf.[15] Der Konflikt des Gesetzgebers bei der Wahl der Sprache, wonach diese zwar einerseits präzise sein sollte, um die Auslegungsbedürftigkeit zu verringern, andererseits die Besonderheit der Rechtswissenschaft insofern berücksichtigt werden muss, als dass Verständlichkeit des Rechts eine Voraussetzung ist, damit Bürger den Alltag bewältigen können, wird verringert, indem – im Gegensatz zu anderen Wissenschaften – ein Mindestmaß an Allgemeinverständlichkeit gewahrt bleibt. Unabhängig vom Sprachgebrauch des Gesetzgebers kommt der grammatischen Auslegung insofern eine zentrale Bedeutung zu, als dass die Ermittlung des möglichen Wortsinns das Feld der weiteren Auslegung absteckt.[16]

Demnach sind die weiteren Vorsorgemaßnahmen nach § 7d AtG »zusätzlich zu den Anforderungen des § 7 Absatz 2 Nummer 3« zu leisten. Bereits der Wortlaut spricht insofern dafür, dass durch § 7d AtG ein »Mehr« an Schutz im Vergleich zum bisher nach § 7 II Nr. 3 AtG bestehenden Niveau gewährleistet werden soll.[17]

Nach bisher unbestrittener Auffassung erfasst § 7 II Nr. 3 AtG den gesamten Bereich der Schadensvorsorge.[18] Jenseits dessen kann es aber denklogisch nur noch das Restrisiko geben: Wenn sich das Restrisiko gerade dadurch definiert, dass es Ungewissheiten betrifft, die jenseits der

---

14 *Larenz,* Methodenlehre der Rechtswissenschaft, 6. Auflage 1991; *von Arnim/Brink*, Methodik der Rechtsfortbildung unter dem Grundgesetz, S. 237; *Bitter*, JuS 2009, 289 (293); *Hillgruber*, in: Maunz/Dürig, GG, Art. 97 Rn. 55 ff.

15 *Larenz*, Methodenlehre der Rechtswissenschaft, 6. Auflage 1991, S. 320.

16 *Larenz*, Methodenlehre der Rechtswissenschaft, 6. Auflage 1991, S. 324.

17 So auch *Arndt*, RdE 2012, 81 (83).

18 *BVerwGE* 72, 300 (315); *Arndt*, RdE 2012, 81 (82); *Roller*, NVwZ 2011, 1431 (1432); *Ziehm*, ZUR 2011, 1 (3 f.).

Schwelle praktischer Vernunft, also jenseits von Gefahrenabwehr und Risikovorsorge, liegen, ist alles, was an Schutz über die Schadensvorsorge hinausgehen soll, nur im Bereich des Restrisikos überhaupt möglich. Wenn § 7d AtG also zusätzlich zu dem Schutz nach § 7 II Nr. 3 AtG Maßnahmen erfordert, können sich diese nach dem Wortlaut der Norm nur auf das Restrisiko beziehen, da § 7 II Nr. 3 AtG ja bereits den gesamten Bereich der Schadensvorsorge erfasst.

Hierfür spricht auch, dass § 7d AtG ausdrücklich auf »Risiken für die Allgemeinheit« Bezug nimmt. Er adressiert also offensichtlich gerade nicht den Schutz von Individualrechtsgütern, sondern Risiken für die Allgemeinheit. In diesem Sinne versteht aber das *BVerfG* das Restrisiko, wenn es dieses als »von allen Bürgern« zu tragende Last definiert.[19]

Im Gegensatz zu teilweise in der Literatur vertretenen Auffassungen ergibt sich aus § 7d AtG nicht, dass Teile der bisher durch § 7 II Nr. 3 AtG geforderten Maßnahmen nunmehr von § 7d AtG umfasst würden.[20] Der Wortlaut der Norm liefert hierfür jedenfalls keine Anhaltspunkte. Es sei insofern nochmals betont, dass die Vorschrift von Maßnahmen »zusätzlich zu den Anforderungen des § 7 Absatz 2 Nummer 3« spricht. Dem folgend hat auch das *BVerwG* in der Entscheidung zum Zwischenlager Unterweser ausgeführt: »Sollte (...) mit der Einführung des § 7d AtG ursprünglich die Absicht verbunden gewesen sein, das erreichte Niveau der Vorsorge und des Drittschutzes zu schmälern, hat dies weder im Wortlaut noch in der Begründung Niederschlag gefunden.«[21]

2. Systematische Auslegung

Die Anzahl der durch die grammatische Auslegung ermittelnden Bedeutungsvarianten kann durch den Kontext begrenzt werden.[22] Daher ist neben dem auszulegenden Begriff oder der auszulegenden Norm zugleich das innergesetzliche Umfeld zu betrachten.

Neben der grammatikalischen Auslegung spricht auch die systematische Auslegung des § 7d AtG dafür, dass die Norm zusätzliche Vorsorgemaßnahmen im Bereich des Restrisikos und nicht im Rahmen der Scha-

19 *BVerwGE* 49, 89 (143).
20 *Renneberg*, ZNER 2011, 106 (112).
21 *BVerwG*, NVwZ 2012, 750 (752).
22 *Larenz*, Methodenlehre der Rechtswissenschaft, 6. Auflage 1991, S. 324.

densvorsorge betrifft.[23] § 7 II Nr. 3 AtG bezieht sich unmittelbar darauf, dass eine atomrechtliche Genehmigung nur erteilt werden darf, wenn die nach dem Stand von Wissenschaft und Technik erforderliche Vorsorge gegen Schäden durch die Errichtung und den Betrieb einer Anlage getroffen wird. Verändert sich seit dem Genehmigungszeitpunkt das nach dem Stand von Wissenschaft und Technik erforderliche Vorsorgemaß, können entsprechende Schutzmaßnahmen dem Inhaber einer atomrechtlichen Genehmigung durch eine nachträgliche Auflage nach § 17 I S. 3 AtG aufgegeben werden. Das *BVerfG* hat bereits im Mühlheim-Kärlich-Beschluss festgestellt, dass mit der Möglichkeit der Auferlegung nachträglicher Auflagen bei Veränderungen des Standes von Wissenschaft und Technik den Anforderungen an einen dynamischen Grundrechtsschutz genügt werde.[24] Das Atomgesetz enthielt also vor Inkrafttreten von § 7d AtG eine verfassungsrechtlich gebotene Möglichkeit, Veränderungen in Wissenschaft und Technik Rechnung zu tragen, die zu einer Neubewertung der Erforderlichkeit von Maßnahmen der Schadensvorsorge führen. Insoweit wäre eine Neuregelung in § 7d AtG, durch die Maßnahmen der Schadensvorsorge vorgegeben werden, die aufgrund eines fortschreitenden Stands von Wissenschaft und Technik erforderlich geworden sind, nicht notwendig gewesen. Verstünde man § 7d AtG so, dass er den Bereich der Schadensvorsorge umfasste, würde dies vielmehr bedeuten, dass für den Bereich der nachträglichen Auflagen nach § 7 II Nr. 3 i.V.m. § 17 I S. 3 AtG kein eigenständiger Raum mehr bliebe. Geht man davon aus, dass ein und das selbe Gesetz nicht den selben Sachverhalt zwei Mal regelt, muss § 7d AtG einen anderen Bereich betreffen, als den bereits von § 7 II Nr. 3 i.V.m. § 17 I S. 3 AtG erfassten. Umfasst § 7 II Nr. 3 AtG aber die gesamte Schadensvorsorge und gibt es jenseits dessen nur noch die Kategorie des Restrisikos, muss sich § 7d AtG auch unter systematischen Gesichtspunkten auf das Restrisiko beziehen, für das es bisher noch keine Regelung gab.

Von den Kritikern der Regelung wird hiergegen eingewendet, dass § 7d AtG bei einer solchen Auslegung keinen Sinn mehr machen könne, weil in Folge der Brunsbüttel-Entscheidung klar sei, dass Risiken, die durch Sicherheitsmaßnahmen minimiert werden könnten, grundsätzlich in den Bereich der Schadensvorsorge fallen und allenfalls die unvermeidbaren Risi-

23 A.A. *Renneberg*, ZNER 2011, 106 (112).

24 *BVerfGE* 53, 30 (58 f.) = NJW 1980, 759 (761 f.); zum Erfordernis des dynamischen Grundrechtsschutzes *BVerfGE* 49, 89 (136 f.) = NJW 1979, 359 (362 f.); S.a. *Mann*, DÖV 2013, 295 (296).

ken dem Restrisiko zugeordnet werden könnten.[25] Dies verkennt jedoch, dass sich die Beurteilung eines Ereignisses nicht danach bemessen kann, ob Maßnahmen dagegen getroffen werden können, sondern ob die Wahrscheinlichkeit seines Eintritts jenseits der praktischen Vernunft liegt.[26] Ist Letzteres der Fall, liegt das Ereignis im Bereich des Restrisikos. Dies macht auch das *BVerwG* in der Entscheidung zum Zwischenlager Unterweser deutlich, wenn es für die Frage, ob ein Fall des Restrisikos vorliegt, darauf abstellt, ob Gefahren und Risiken »praktisch ausgeschlossen seien«.[27] Noch deutlicher hat das *BVerfG* in der Entscheidung zum Zwischenlager Grafenrheinfeld ausgeführt: »Art. 2 Abs. 2 Satz 1 GG gebietet es nicht, bei der Konzeption von Standortzwischenlagern sämtliche in Betracht kommenden Sicherheitssysteme zu kombinieren. (...) Ist der Eintritt von Schäden an Rechtsgütern Dritter (...) praktisch ausgeschlossen, bedarf es von Verfassungs wegen daher nicht der weiteren Absicherung«.[28] Mit anderen Worten: Selbst wenn gegen bestimmte Risiken weitere Sicherungsmaßnahmen technisch möglich sind, verlieren sie nicht allein deshalb ihren Charakter als Restrisiko.[29]

Dass auch eine Regelung zur Erhöhung des Schutzes gegen Risiken, die dem Restrisiko in diesem Sinn zuzuordnen sind, einen eigenständigen Anwendungsbereich haben kann, vermag folgendes Beispiel zu zeigen: Der Absturz eines Meteoriten auf ein Kernkraftwerk dürfte nach allgemeiner Auffassung jenseits der praktischen Vernunft liegen – mit Worten des *BVerfG* in seiner Entscheidung zum Zwischenlager Grafenrheinfeld »praktisch ausgeschlossen«[30] – und damit dem Restrisiko zuzuordnen zu sein. Führen Fortschritte in Wissenschaft und Technik dazu, dass es Maßnahmen gibt, die zu einer nicht nur geringfügigen Vorsorge gegen Meteoritenabstürze führen, ändert dies nichts an der Einordnung von Meteoritenabstürzen als Restrisiko, allerdings sind die Maßnahmen dagegen nunmehr im Rahmen des § 7d AtG zu ergreifen. Auf Grundlage von § 7 II Nr. 3 AtG wäre ein Genehmigungsinhaber hingegen dazu nicht verpflichtet. Bei einer derartigen Auslegung haben § 7 II Nr. 3 AtG i.V.m. § 17 I S. 3 AtG einerseits und § 7d AtG andererseits jeweils eigenständige Rege-

25 *Renneberg*, ZNER 2011, 106 (106); *Roßnagel/Hentschel*, ZNER 2011, 6 (8).

26 *BVerfGE* 49, 89 (138 f.) = NJW 1979, 359 (363 f.); in diesem Sinn auch *BVerwGE* 131, 129 (135 f.) = NVwZ 2008, 1012 (1013 f.).

27 *BVerwG*, NVwZ 2012, 750 (754).

28 *BVerfG*, NVwZ 2009, 171 (175).

29 *Arndt*, RdE 2012, 81 (82 f.).

30 *BVerfG*, NVwZ 2009, 171 (175).

lungsbereiche. Zugleich führt sie insofern zu einer Erhöhung des bisher allein durch § 7 II Nr. 3 AtG i.V.m. § 17 I S. 3 AtG gewährleisteten Schutzniveaus, als sie dazu verpflichtet, im Bereich des Restrisikos ggf. Sicherheitsvorkehrungen zu ergreifen, sofern diese zu einer nicht nur geringfügigen Restrisikovorsorge führen.

3. Teleologische Auslegung

Die teleologische Auslegung sucht nach dem erkennbaren Zweck einer Norm.[31] Objektiver Zweck des Rechts ist der Ausgleich verschiedener Interessen nach dem Gebot der Gerechtigkeit. Daher kommt dem Gesichtspunkt der Gleichbehandlung maßgebliche Bedeutung zur Ermittlung des Telos zu, sofern der Gesetzgeber nicht ausdrücklich eine Ausnahmeregelung bezweckt.[32]

Neben grammatikalischer und systematischer Auslegung spricht auch die teleologische Auslegung dafür, dass § 7d AtG den Bereich des Restrisikos betrifft, wohingegen das bisher bereits bestehende Schutzniveau im Bereich der Schadensvorsorge weiterhin und uneingeschränkt über § 7 II Nr. 3 AtG fortbesteht. Die Neuregelung des § 7d AtG ist vor dem Hintergrund der seinerzeitigen Verlängerung der Laufzeiten für Kernkraftwerke zu sehen, die jedenfalls mathematisch allein aufgrund der zusätzlichen Laufzeit der Kernkraftwerke zu einer Veränderung des Restrisikos geführt hat. Vor diesem Hintergrund kann es kaum Ziel einer zusätzlichen Regelung im Atomgesetz gewesen sein, das bestehende Schutzniveau abzusenken, sondern ausschließlich das Schutzniveau zu erhöhen.[33] Eine Erhöhung des Schutzniveaus ist aber nur im Bereich des Restrisikos überhaupt möglich gewesen. Für den Bereich der Schadensvorsorge galt bereits zuvor schon das Erfordernis der bestmöglichen Vorsorge.[34] Will man also das bestehende Schutzniveau erhöhen, ist aber dieses Schutzniveau bei Schadensvorsorgemaßnahmen bereits maximal ausgestaltet, so ist eine Erhöhung ausschließlich im Bereich des Restrisikos überhaupt möglich.

31 *Larenz*, Methodenlehre der Rechtswissenschaft, 6. Auflage 1991, S. 332.

32 *Larenz*, Methodenlehre der Rechtswissenschaft, 6. Auflage 1991, S. 334.

33 So auch die Bundesregierung in ihrer Antwort auf eine entsprechende kleine Anfrage der Fraktion BÜNDNIS 90/DIE GRÜNEN, BT-Drucks. 17/3395, S. 2.

34 *BVerfG*, NVwZ 2009, 171 (172); *BVerfGE* 49, 89 (138 f.) = NJW 1979, 359 (362 f.); *BVerfGE* 53, 30 (58 f.) = NJW 1980, 759 (761 f.); *BVerwGE* 72, 300 = NVwZ 1986, 208 (212).

Dem kann auch nicht entgegengehalten werden, dass im Gegensatz zu § 7 II Nr. 3 AtG nur solche Schutzvorkehrungen ergriffen werden müssen, die jeweils entwickelt, geeignet und angemessen sind, um eine nicht nur geringfügige Risikovorsorge zu gewährleisten.[35] Tatsächlich bleibt § 7d AtG damit hinter § 7 II Nr. 3 AtG insofern zurück, als dort Schutzvorkehrungen auch dann getroffen werden müssen, wenn sie nach dem Stand von Wissenschaft und Technik erforderlich sind und auch einen nur geringfügigen Beitrag zur Erhöhung des Sicherheitsniveaus leisten.[36] Die divergierenden Vorgaben sind deshalb zwingend, weil § 7d AtG mit dem Restrisiko einen Bereich betrifft, der grundsätzlich von der Allgemeinheit zu tragen ist.[37] Sofern nunmehr Restrisikovorsorge von einem Genehmigungsinhaber – auf dessen Kosten[38] – auf Grundlage von § 7d AtG betrieben werden muss, ist es schon unter Verhältnismäßigkeitsgesichtspunkten angesichts der damit einhergehenden Belastung geboten, nur solche Maßnahmen zu fordern, deren Nutzen auch spürbar ist. Eine solche Einschränkung ist bei Maßnahmen nach § 7 II Nr. 3 AtG deshalb grundsätzlich weder geboten noch zulässig, weil § 7 II Nr. 3 AtG mit der Schadensvorsorge Bereiche erfasst, in denen Individualrechtsgüter wie Leib und Leben mit einem solch hinreichenden Maß an Wahrscheinlichkeit erfasst sind, dass bereits aus grundrechtlichen Gründen eine staatliche Verpflichtung zu einem bestmöglichen Schutz besteht.[39]

4. Historische Auslegung

Die historische Auslegung bereitet im modernen Verfassungsstaat insofern Probleme, als dass unklar ist, auf wessen Willen bei Entscheidungen durch das Parlament abzustellen ist.[40] Es liegt nämlich nicht *eine* Absicht eines Gesetzgebungsorganes vor, sondern vielmehr bestehen diverse Absichten bei verschiedensten Volksvertretern. Offensichtlich sinnlos wäre es allerdings die Vorstellungen der einzelnen Parlamentarier zu erforschen. Daher können zur rechtswissenschaftlichen Gesetzesauslegung nur solche Materialien herangezogen werden, die in den gesetzlich vorgesehenen Beratun-

35 Ausführlich dazu *Müller-Dehn*, atw 2013, 30 (34).
36 Kritisch insofern *Roßnagel/Hentschel*, ZNER 2011, 6 (9).
37 *Arndt*, RdE 2012, 81 (83).
38 So die Gesetzesbegründung BT-Drucks. 17/3052, S. 11.
39 *BVerfGE* 49, 89 (138 f.) = NJW 1979, 359 (362 f.); *BVerfGE* 53, 30 (58 f.) = NJW 1980, 759 (761 f.); *BVerwGE* 72, 300 = NVwZ 1986, 208 (212).
40 *Larenz*, Methodenlehre der Rechtswissenschaft, 6. Auflage 1991, S. 328 f.

gen ohne Widerspruch geblieben sind.[41] Die Gesetzesmaterialien setzen sich zumeist aus Begründungen der Verfasser des Gesetzestextes oder der Mitglieder beratender Ausschüsse zusammen. Zwar mögen die Beiträge der verschiedenen Personengruppen zum Entstehen eines Gesetzes durchaus erheblich sein. Dennoch ist einzig das Gesetzgebungsorgan des Parlaments zum Erlass von Gesetzen berufen und somit Gesetzgeber. Da jedoch unterstellt werden kann, dass die im Gesetzgebungsprozess kundgetanen und unwidersprochenen Äußerungen das Ziel hatten, der »gesetzgeberischen Intention« nahe zu kommen, dienen sie zwar nicht als bindende Richtschnur, können aber dennoch im Rahmen der Auslegung Berücksichtigung finden. Hierin liegt entgegen der jüngst von *Norbert Blüm* geäußerten Vermutung[42] keine Selbstüberschätzung des Rechtsanwenders, sondern die schlichte Unmöglichkeit, den Willen eines Gesetzgebungsorgans nachzuweisen, welches sich aus verschiedenen Individuen zusammensetzt. Daher ist es angesichts der verfassungsrechtlichen Stellung des Richters auch gerechtfertigt, wenn objektive Auslegungsmethoden im Kollisionsfall Vorrang genießen.

Eine Auslegung des § 7d AtG, nach der dieser den Bereich des Restrisikos umfasst, wird schließlich von der historischen Auslegung der Norm bestätigt. Ausweislich der Gesetzesmaterialien war sich der Gesetzgeber bewusst, dass § 7 II Nr. 3 AtG Maßnahmen erfordert, die alle Gefahren und Risiken nach dem Maßstab praktischer Vernunft ausschließen.[43] Zugleich ergibt sich aus den Gesetzesmaterialien, dass der Gesetzgeber über dieses vorhandene Schutzniveau hinausgehen wollte, indem er »Maßnahmen zur weiteren Risikominimierung jenseits der erforderlichen Vorsorge gegen Schäden« in § 7d AtG regelt.[44] Schließlich weisen die Gesetzesmaterialien darauf hin, dass mit § 7d AtG der Risikobereich geregelt werden soll, der nicht drittschützend ist.[45] Nicht drittschützend ist aber ausschließlich der Bereich des Restrisikos, wohingegen § 7 II Nr. 3 AtG drittschützend ist, so dass Maßnahmen der Schadensvorsorge auch von privaten Dritten subjektiv-rechtlich eingefordert werden können.[46]

41 *Larenz*, Methodenlehre der Rechtswissenschaft, 6. Auflage 1991, S. 329.
42 http://www.zeit.de/2013/27/richter-kritik-justiz
43 BT-Drucks. 17/3052, S. 13.
44 BT-Drucks. 17/3052, S. 13.
45 BT-Drucks. 17/3052, S. 13.
46 *Roller*, NVwZ 2011, 1431 (1432); *Arndt*, RdE 2012, 81 (82); *Ziehm*, ZUR 2011, 3 (3).

In der Literatur wurde aus der Gesetzesbegründung teilweise geschlossen, dass § 7d AtG eine Absenkung des bestehenden Schutzniveaus bezwecke, da terroristische Gefahren fortan dem Anwendungsbereich des § 7d AtG zuzurechnen wären. Einerseits lässt sich diese Aussage der Gesetzesbegründung kaum entnehmen[47], andererseits ließen sich solche Gesetzesmaterialien nur schwer mit den objektiven Auslegungsergebnissen, vor allem mit dem eindeutigen Wortlaut, der ja gerade von »zusätzlich[em]« Schutz spricht, in Einklang bringen.

Insofern weisen die Gesetzesmaterialien eindeutig darauf hin, dass durch die Einfügung des § 7d AtG nicht das vorhandene Schutzniveau im Bereich der Schadensvorsorge abgesenkt werden sollte, sondern vielmehr auch für den Bereich des Restrisikos eine Verpflichtung für die Inhaber einer atomrechtlichen Genehmigung statuiert werden sollte, Maßnahmen zu ergreifen, die nach dem Stand von Wissenschaft und Technik zu einer nicht nur geringfügigen (Rest-) Risikovorsorge führen.

5. Zwischenergebnis

Als Zwischenergebnis lässt sich festhalten, dass § 7d AtG nicht zu einer Absenkung des materiellen atomrechtlichen Schutzniveaus führt, sondern vielmehr zu seiner Erhöhung.[48] Während bisher nur Maßnahmen der Schadensvorsorge zu ergreifen waren, die sich nach dem jeweiligen Stand von Wissenschaft und Technik als erforderlich darstellten, besteht nunmehr auch im Bereich des Restrisikos eine grundsätzliche Pflicht, Maßnahmen zur ergreifen, die einen nicht nur geringfügigen Beitrag zur Restrisikovorsorge leisten. Da damit durch § 7d AtG ein Schutz eingefordert wird, der über das bereits bestehende hohe Schutzniveau hinausgeht, ist es gerechtfertigt, dass nicht jede Maßnahme, die zum Schutz gegen Ereignisse, die dem Restrisiko zugeordnet werden können, durch die Inhaber einer atomrechtlichen Genehmigung ergriffen werden muss, sondern nur solche

47 Begründung im Wortlaut: *»Die Maßnahmen nach § 7d können im Ergebnis auch zu einem verbesserten Schutz gegen Störmaßnahmen oder sonstige Einwirkungen Dritter führen. Dabei ist zu berücksichtigen, dass der vorhandene Schutz von Kernkraftwerken vor terroristischen Gefahren dem international Üblichen entspricht und teilweise deutlich darüber hinausgeht. Im Zusammenwirken mit den staatlichen Maßnahmen wird ein die verfassungsrechtlichen Anforderungen erfüllendes Schutzniveau erreicht.«*

48 Kritisch *Roller*, NVwZ 2011, 1431 (1434).

Maßnahmen, die zu einer nicht nur geringfügigen weiteren Schadensvorsorge im Bereich des Restrisikos führen.

III. Verfahrensrechtlicher Gehalt von § 7d AtG

Umfasst § 7d AtG also Maßnahmen im Bereich des Restrisikos, stellt sich in einem nächsten Schritt die Frage, welche verfahrensrechtlichen Implikationen sich damit verbinden. Auch zur Beantwortung dieser Frage ist zunächst einmal der Wortlaut der Norm in den Blick zu nehmen. Demnach haben Genehmigungsinhaber »dafür zu sorgen«, dass die durch § 7d AtG geforderten Sicherheitsvorkehrungen verwirklicht werden. Dies bedeutet, Genehmigungsinhaber trifft eine entsprechende Betreiberpflicht unabhängig davon, ob es eine konkretisierende Entscheidung durch die zuständige Aufsichtsbehörde gibt.[49] Anders als bei § 7 II 2 Nr. 3 AtG bedarf es auch nicht der Durchsetzung zusätzlicher Sicherheitsvorkehrungen im Rahmen einer nachträglichen Auflage nach § 17 I S. 3 AtG. Vielmehr sind Genehmigungsinhaber dazu verpflichtet, von sich aus kontinuierlich zu überprüfen, ob die Voraussetzungen des § 7d AtG vorliegen und daraus ggf. die entsprechenden Konsequenzen zu ziehen. Kommen sie dieser Pflicht nicht nach, ist ein Einschreiten der Aufsichtsbehörde nach § 19 AtG möglich.[50]

Entgegen teilweise in der Literatur vorgebrachten Stimmen handelt es sich hierbei nicht um eine reine Bemühenspflicht, die ein Genehmigungsinhaber schon dadurch erfüllt, dass er sich ernsthaft bemüht, die durch § 7d AtG gebotenen zusätzlichen Schutzvorkehrungen zu treffen, ohne dass es darauf ankäme, ob er sie denn tatsächlich jemals ergreift.[51] Ausweislich des Wortlauts der Norm haben Genehmigungsinhaber »dafür zu sorgen, dass die Sicherheitsvorkehrungen verwirklicht werden«. Die durchgängige Verwendung des Indikativs sowie des Wortes »verwirklichen«, also Wirklichkeit werden lassen, sprechen eindeutig dagegen, dass § 7d AtG nur eine Bemühenspflicht statuiert.

IV. § 7d AtG und Drittschutz

Die Hauptkritik, die § 7d AtG entgegengehalten wird und mit der teilweise sogar seine Verfassungswidrigkeit begründet wird, liegt darin, dass er

49 *Müller-Dehn*, atw 2013, 30 (35).

50 *Müller-Dehn*, atw 2013, 30 (35).

51 *Roßnagel/Hentschel*, ZNER 2011, 6 (9).

nicht drittschützend sei und damit hinter das vom *BVerfG* geforderte Schutzniveau zurückfalle.[52] Eine solche Argumentation bedeutet freilich einen Zirkelschluss: § 7d AtG erfasst den Bereich der Schadensvorsorge, der nach verfassungsgerichtlicher Rechtsprechung drittschützend ist. § 7d AtG ist – was noch zu zeigen sein wird: tatsächlich – nicht drittschützend ausgestaltet. Wenn § 7d AtG aber nicht drittschützend ist, kann er sich nicht in verfassungsgemäßer Weise auf den Bereich der Schadensvorsorge beziehen. Die Frage nach dem Anwendungsbereich einer Norm ist jedoch der Frage vorgreiflich, ob die Norm mit dem zuvor definierten Anwendungsbereich auch Drittschutz gewährt. Wenig überzeugend ist es hingegen, wenn die Reichweite einer Norm ausgehend davon bestimmt wird, ob sie drittschützend ist oder nicht.

Betrachtet man § 7d AtG aus diesem Blickwinkel ist zunächst einmal festzuhalten, dass nach hier vertretener Auffassung die Vorschrift tatbestandlich nur Maßnahmen der Restrisikominimierung betrifft. Ob § 7d AtG drittschützend ist hängt nun davon ab, ob die Norm subjektive Rechte zugunsten Dritter vermittelt. Das wiederum beurteilt sich danach, ob die Norm nicht nur dem Schutz der Allgemeinheit dient, sondern zumindest auch Rechtsgüter Einzelner zu schützen bestimmt ist.[53] Inwieweit diese Voraussetzungen vorliegen, ist durch Auslegung der Norm zu ermitteln. Auch hierbei spielt der Wortlaut der Norm wieder eine entscheidende Rolle. Finden sich im Normtext Hinweise auf bestimmte Personen oder Personengruppen, so ist dies ein starkes Indiz dafür, dass sich die genannten Personen oder Personengruppen auch auf die Norm berufen können sollen.[54] Bezieht sich der Gesetzestext hingegen auf die Allgemeinheit, ist dies ein starkes Argument dafür, dass die Norm nicht drittschützend ist, Einzelne ihre Einhaltung also nicht subjektiv-rechtlich ggf. auf dem

52 *Roßnagel/Hentschel*, ZNER 2011, 6 (10); zweifelnd insofern *Roller*, NVwZ 2011, 1431 (1432); allgemein zum Drittschutz im Atomrecht s. *Roller*, NVwZ 2010, 990.

53 *BVerwGE* 131, 129 (136 f.) = NVwZ 2008, 1012 (1014); allgemein *Kopp/Schenke*, VwGO, § 42 Rn. 78; *Erbguth*, Allgemeines Verwaltungsrecht, § 9 Rn. 4; *Detterbeck*, Allgemeines Verwaltungsrecht, Rn. 399; *Masing*, in: Hoffmann-Riehm/Schmidt-Aßmann/Voßkuhle, Grundlagen des Verwaltungsrechts, Band I, § 7 Rn. 106; *Schmidt-Kötters*, in: BeckOK, VwGO, § 42 Rn. 143; zum AtG *Wahl/Schütz*, in: Schoch/Schneider/Bier, VwGO, § 42 Rn. 177; *Wahl*, in: Schoch/Schneider/Bier, VwGO, Vorbemerkungen § 42 Abs. 2 Rn. 43 ff.

54 *Kopp/Schenke*, VwGO, § 42 Rn. 78; *Erbguth*, § 9 Rn. 4; *Schmidt-Kötters*, in: BeckOK, VwGO, § 42 Rn. 14.

Rechtsweg durchsetzen können.[55] Betrachtet man unter diesem Gesichtspunkt § 7d AtG, so fällt unmittelbar auf, dass dort von »Risiken für die Allgemeinheit« gesprochen wird, was eindeutig gegen einen drittschützenden Charakter spricht.

Bestärkt wird dieses Auslegungsergebnis durch die historische Auslegung von § 7d AtG. Ausweislich der Gesetzesmaterialien werden durch § 7d AtG weitere Maßnahmen der Risikominimierung gefordert, die dem Schutz der Allgemeinheit dienen, »also nicht drittschützend auszugestalten« sind.[56]

Schließlich spricht auch die teleologische Auslegung gegen einen drittschützenden Charakter von § 7d AtG. Bezieht sich § 7d AtG auf den Bereich des Restrisikos, so bedeutet das, dass er das Risiko betrifft, das in ständiger verfassungsgerichtlicher Rechtsprechung durch die Allgemeinheit zu tragen ist.[57] Ist aber das Risiko durch die Allgemeinheit zu tragen, so schließt dies zwingend aus, dass Maßnahmen, die zur Restrisikominimierung getroffen werden, Einzelne in einer solch individualisierten Weise schützen, dass sie auf die Durchsetzung der sich aus § 7d AtG ergebenden Betreiberpflichten einen subjektiv-rechtlichen Anspruch haben könnten.[58] Dies hat das *BVerwG* in seiner Entscheidung zum Zwischenlager Unterweser nochmals ausdrücklich bestätigt, wenn es ausführt, dass Drittschutz nicht gewährt werde, sofern ein Ereignis »dem Bereich des Restrisikos zuzuordnen ist«.[59] Der Senat verweist dabei ausdrücklich auf § 7d AtG, der an dieser Beurteilung nichts geändert habe.[60]

Ein anderes Ergebnis wird hierbei auch nicht durch die Grundrechte vorgegeben. Das *BVerwG* hat hierzu in der Brunsbüttel-Entscheidung ausgeführt: »Mehr als die erforderliche Vorsorge, die auf den praktischen Ausschluss eines sich als Grundrechtsverletzung darstellenden Schadens hinausläuft, kann ein Dritter nicht verlangen.«[61] Noch pointierter hat das *BVerfG* in seiner Entscheidung zum Schacht Konrad dargelegt: »Die Hinnahme eines nach den Grundsätzen praktischer Vernunft nicht mehr in

55 *Schmidt-Aßmann/Schenk*, in: Schoch/Schneider/Bier, VwGO, Einleitung Rn. 20; *Erbguth*, § 9 Rn. 3 f.

56 BT-Drucks. 17/3052, S. 13.

57 *BVerfGE* 49, 89 (143) = NJW 1979, 359 (363).

58 So das BVerwG allgemein auch in der Brunsbüttel-Entscheidung *BVerwGE* 131, 129 (134 ff.) = NVwZ 2008, 1012 (1013 f.).

59 *BVerwG*, NVwZ 2012, 750 (752).

60 *BVerwG*, NVwZ 2012, 750 (752).

61 *BVerwGE* 131, 129 (137) = NVwZ 2008, 1012 (1014); s.a. *BVerwGE* 72, 300 = NVwZ 1986, 208 (213).

Rechnung zu stellenden Restrisikos ist mit den Grundrechten des Bf. aus Art. 2 Abs. 2 S. 1 und Art. 14 Abs. 1 GG vereinbar. Ein grundrechtlich verbürgter Schutz auf ›Restrisikominimierung‹ besteht nicht.«[62] Das heißt aber, dass das auf Grundlage der Auslegung von § 7d AtG gefundene Ergebnis, wonach die Norm keinen Drittschutz vermittelt, nicht im Wege der verfassungskonformen Auslegung einer Korrektur bedarf.

V. Ergebnis

Mit § 7d AtG hat der Gesetzgeber eine Betreiberpflicht für Inhaber einer atomrechtlichen Genehmigung eingeführt, die sie dazu verpflichtet, Sicherheitsvorkehrungen zu ergreifen, die zu einer Restrisikominimierung in nicht nur unerheblicher Weise beitragen. Zugleich wird durch die Norm am Schutzkonzept des § 7 II Nr. 3 AtG nichts verändert, der sich wie bisher auf Maßnahmen zu einer bestmöglichen Schadensvorsorge bezieht. Insofern führt § 7d AtG nicht zu einer Absenkung des atomrechtlichen Schutzniveaus. Vielmehr wird das Schutzniveau dahingehend angehoben, dass unter bestimmten Voraussetzungen auch Restrisikominimierungsmaßnahmen durch die Betreiber zu ergreifen sind. Damit geht § 7d AtG über das verfassungsrechtlich geforderte Schutzniveau hinaus, das nach der Rechtsprechung des *BVerfG* kein Gebot zur Restrisikominimierung enthält.[63] Aus dem so definierten Anwendungsbereich von § 7d AtG ergibt sich aber zugleich, dass die Norm keinen drittschützenden Gehalt hat. Das Restrisiko ist eine grundsätzlich von der Allgemeinheit zu tragende Last. Vorschriften zu seiner Minimierung schützen daher die Allgemeinheit und nicht individualisierte Personen oder Personengruppen. Vielmehr muss § 7d AtG gegebenenfalls durch die atomrechtlichen Aufsichtsbehörden durchgesetzt werden, die insofern dann auch als Sachwalter der Allgemeinheit auftreten. Die an § 7d AtG vielfach geäußerte Kritik läuft daher ins Leere, da er weder zu einer Absenkung des atomrechtlichen Schutzniveaus noch zu einer Reduzierung des Drittschutzes führt. Beides bleibt im Rahmen von § 7 II Nr. 3 AtG bestehen, hinzu kommt nunmehr die Pflicht zur Restrisikominimierung, sofern es nicht nur um unerhebliche Maßnahmen geht.

Nicht überzeugend ist es insofern, wenn die Kritiker der Vorschrift zu ihrer Verfassungswidrigkeit kommen, weil sie den grundrechtlich gebote-

62 *BVerfG*, NVwZ 2010, 114 (115); so schon *BVerfG*, NVwZ 2009, 171 (175).
63 *Arndt*, RdE 2012, 81 (83 f.).

nen Schutzstandard unterschreite.[64] Hielte man eine solche Auslegung für § 7d AtG für möglich, wäre es geradezu geboten, eine verfassungskonforme Auslegung im hier dargelegten Sinne vorzunehmen bevor man zur Verfassungswidrigkeit der Norm kommt. Selbst wenn man also die hier vertretene Auslegung des § 7d AtG einfachgesetzlich für nicht zwingend hält, müsste man sie jedenfalls im Lichte der Grundrechte verfassungskonform in diesem Sinne vornehmen.[65]

64 *Roßnagel/Hentschel*, ZNER 2011, 6 (12), zweifelnd insoweit auch *Renneberg*, ZNER 2011, 106 (113).

65 I.E. so auch *Roller*, NVwZ 2011, 1431 (1432).

Unabhängigkeit der Atomaufsicht

Dr. Axel Vorwerk, Bundesministerium für Umwelt, Naturschutz und Reaktorsicherheit

Ausgehend von dem völker- und europarechtlich verankerten Grundsatz der Trennung der Aufgaben staatlicher Stellen für nukleare Sicherheit einerseits und für die Förderung oder Nutzung der Kernenergie andererseits ist in den vergangenen Jahren immer wieder auch das Thema einer »unabhängigen Atomaufsichtsbehörde« erörtert worden. Nach dem Reaktorunfall von Fukushima im März 2011 wird dieser Frage eine besondere Aktualität zugemessen. Dies wirft im Hinblick auf die Besonderheiten des deutschen Aufsichtssystems eine Reihe von verfassungs- und staatsorganisationsrechtlichen Fragen auf.

1. Genehmigungs- und Aufsichtsbehörden über Kernkraftwerke in Deutschland

Für den Bereich des Atomrechts regeln insbesondere Art. 87c Grundgesetz und § 24 Abs. 1 Satz 1 AtG, dass die Verwaltungsaufgaben – abgesehen von den in §§ 22 bis 23c AtG geregelten Fällen – im Auftrag des Bundes durch die Länder ausgeführt werden. Gemäß § 24 Abs. 2 AtG sind für Genehmigungen nach den §§ 7, 7a und 9 AtG sowie die Planfeststellung nach § 9b AtG die durch die Landesregierungen bestimmten obersten Landesbehörden, also ein Ministerium (bzw. eine Senatsverwaltung), zuständig. Diese Behörden üben nach § 24 Abs. 2 Satz 2 AtG auch die Aufsicht über Anlagen nach § 7 AtG (also insbesondere Kernkraftwerke) und die Verwendung von Kernbrennstoffen außerhalb dieser Anlagen aus. Das Bund/Länder-Verhältnis im Bereich der Bundesauftragsverwaltung wird unmittelbar durch die Verfassung geregelt, nämlich durch Art. 85 Grundgesetz. Insbesondere unterliegen die Länder der Bundesaufsicht im Hinblick auf die Gesetzmäßigkeit und die Zweckmäßigkeit der Ausführung, Art. 85 Abs. 4 Grundgesetz. Fragen im Zusammenhang mit der Unabhängigkeit der Atomaufsicht betreffen also in erster Linie die unmittelbar zuständigen Landesministerien, aber auch die mit der Aufsicht über diese

Behörden betraute Bundesbehörde, das Bundesministerium für Umwelt, Naturschutz und Reaktorsicherheit (BMU).

Prägend für die Atomaufsicht in Deutschland ist auch das Zusammenwirken der zuständigen Behörden mit Sachverständigen, die gemäß § 20 AtG von diesen Behörden im Genehmigungs- und Aufsichtsverfahren nach dem Atomgesetz und den auf Grund dieses Gesetzes erlassenen Rechtsverordnungen zugezogen werden können.

2. *Genehmigungs- und Aufsichtsbehörden in anderen Staaten*

Im Vergleich zu Deutschland liegt die Zuständigkeit in den meisten anderen Staaten bei einer eigenständigen Behörde bzw. Kommission. Im Folgenden wird dies – im Wesentlichen auf der Grundlage der jeweiligen Berichte im Rahmen des Übereinkommens über nukleare Sicherheit (CNS)[1] – anhand ausgewählter Beispiele dargestellt:

USA: Die US Nuclear Regulatory Commission (NRC) ist im Hinblick auf Kernkraftwerke zuständig für Genehmigungen und Aufsicht. Die Commissioner werden durch den Präsidenten ernannt. Der Präsident kann einen Commissioner lediglich aus bestimmten Gründen abberufen (z.B. »neglect of duty«). Entscheidungen der NRC können nur durch Gesetz, d.h. durch den Kongress, aufgehoben werden.

Frankreich: Die 2006 als eigenständige Behörde eingerichtete Autorité de sûreté nucléaire (ASN) ist grundsätzlich die zuständige Genehmigungs- und Aufsichtsbehörde. Allerdings werden wesentliche Einzelentscheidungen in Bezug auf kerntechnische Anlagen durch die Regierung bzw. den zuständigen Minister für nukleare Sicherheit und Strahlenschutz getroffen. Hiervon sind insbesondere die erste (Errichtungs-)Genehmigung sowie die Stilllegungsgenehmigung erfasst. Das zuständige Ministerium erlässt

1 http://www-ns.iaea.org/conventions/nuclear-safety.asp#1: The United States of America Fifth National Report for the Convention on Nuclear Safety, September 2010, S. 62; Sixth French Report under the CNS, July 2013, S. 60ff.; Convention on Nuclear Safety, The fifth Swiss report in accordance with Article 5, July 2010, S. 29ff.; National Report of The Kingdom of the Netherlands, September 2010, S. 43ff.; THE UNITED KINGDOM'S FIFTH NATIONAL REPORT ON COMPLIANCE WITH THE CONVENTION ON NUCLEAR SAFETY OBLIGATIONS, September 2010, S. 40ff.; Finnish 6th national report as referred to in Article 5 of the Convention on Nuclear Safety, August 2013, S. 24ff.

überdies generelle Vorschriften zur nuklearen Sicherheit. Die übrigen Genehmigungen erteilt ASN.

ASN ist als unabhängige Regulierungsbehörde (»autorité administrative indépendante«) ausgestaltet, von denen es in Frankreich über 30 gibt. ASN wird durch eine Kommission bestehend aus fünf Kommissaren geleitet, von denen drei durch den franz. Präsidenten und zwei durch den Präsidenten der Nationalversammlung für einen einmaligen Zeitraum von sechs Jahren ernannt werden. Die Kommissare sind weisungsfrei.

Schweiz: Die Aufsicht über Kernkraftwerke wird durch das Eidgenössische Nuklearsicherheitsinspektorat (ENSI) ausgeübt. Genehmigungen für Kernkraftwerke werden durch den Bundesrat (Regierung) bzw. das Eidgenössische Departement für Umwelt, Energie, Verkehr und Kommunikation erteilt. Das ENSI ist formell unabhängig (Art. 18 Abs. 1 ENSI-Gesetz: »Das ENSI übt seine Aufsichtstätigkeit selbstständig und unabhängig aus«).

Niederlande: Ähnlich wie in Deutschland sind in den Niederlanden die Zuständigkeiten für Genehmigung und Aufsicht auf ministerieller Ebene angesiedelt. Zwei Abteilungen im Ministerium für Bauen, Raumplanung und Umwelt (VROM) sind für Genehmigung, Rechtssetzung, Grundsatzangelegenheiten einerseits sowie für die Aufsicht in Bezug auf kerntechnische Anlagen andererseits zuständig. Es gibt allerdings offenbar derzeit Überlegungen, diese Struktur zugunsten einer eigenständigen Aufsichtsbehörde zu verändern.

Vereinigtes Königreich: Die am 1. April 2011 neu gebildete Aufsichtsbehörde (Office for Nuclear Regulation, ONR) ist eine Agentur des Health and Safety Executive (HSE), die für alle Regulierungsaufgaben im Bereich der nuklearen Sicherheit verantwortlich ist. Gemäß ihrer Homepage ist es das Ziel, das ONR zukünftig als »independent statutory corporation« auszugestalten.[2]

Finnland: Ähnlich wie in der Schweiz fallen die Zuständigkeiten für Aufsicht und Genehmigung auseinander. Die eigenständige Behörde STUK ist zuständig für die Aufsicht über die finnischen Kernkraftwerke. Genehmigungen für Kernkraftwerke erteilt jedoch – nach einer Sicherheitsbewertung durch STUK – die Regierung. STUK ist gegenwärtig eine Behörde im Geschäftsbereich des Ministeriums für Soziales und Gesundheit. Seine formelle Unabhängigkeit ist nicht gesetzlich festgelegt. Dies hatte die

2 http://www.hse.gov.uk/nuclear/about.htm

IRRS-Mission in Finnland 2012 kritisiert und eine entsprechende Empfehlung ausgesprochen.

Zusammenfassend lässt sich mit Blick auf diese Bespiele feststellen, dass die in Deutschland realisierte Organisationsform für den Regulator im Bereich der kerntechnischen Sicherheit, die Abteilung eines Ministeriums, lediglich in den Niederlanden realisiert ist, wobei dort Überlegungen für die Verlagerung in eine eigenständige Behörde angestellt werden. Allerdings existiert eine Bandbreite verschiedener Organisationsformen mit engeren und weiteren Zuständigkeiten. In mehreren Fällen liegen Genehmigungszuständigkeiten ganz oder teilweise auf der Ebene der Regierung.

3. *Trennungsgrundsatz und »Unabhängigkeit« in internationalen Verträgen*

Gemäß Art. 8 Abs. 2 des Übereinkommens über nukleare Sicherheit vom 17. Juni 1994 trifft »(j)ede Vertragspartei … die geeigneten Maßnahmen, um eine wirksame Trennung der Aufgaben der staatlichen Stellen [für nukleare Sicherheit] von denjenigen anderer Stellen oder Organisationen, die mit der Förderung oder Nutzung der Kernenergie befasst sind, zu gewährleisten.« Insbesondere geht es also um die organisatorische Trennung der Zuständigkeiten für Sicherheitsfragen von energiepolitischen oder energiewirtschaftlichen Zuständigkeiten, in Deutschland also insbesondere durch Zuweisung zu unterschiedlichen Ressorts bzw. unterschiedlichen Arbeitseinheiten innerhalb eines Ressorts.

Gemäß Art. 20 Abs. 2 des Gemeinsamen Übereinkommens über die Sicherheit der Behandlung abgebrannter Brennelemente und über die Sicherheit der Behandlung radioaktiver Abfälle vom 5. September 1997 trifft

> »(j)ede Vertragspartei … im Einklang mit ihrem Rahmen für Gesetzgebung und Vollzug die geeigneten Maßnahmen, um die tatsächliche Unabhängigkeit der staatlichen Aufgaben von anderen Aufgaben sicherzustellen, wenn Organisationen sowohl an der Behandlung abgebrannter Brennelemente oder radioaktiver Abfälle als auch an der staatlichen Aufsicht darüber beteiligt sind.«

Der Trennungsgrundsatz im Übereinkommen über nukleare Sicherheit von 1994 erfordert also eine wirksame Trennung der genannten Aufgaben, während im Gemeinsamen Übereinkommen von 1997 Maßnahmen zur Sicherstellung der »tatsächlichen Unabhängigkeit« der Management-Aufgaben von den Aufsichts-Aufgaben erfordert. In beiden Übereinkommen werden keine spezifischen Maßnahmen gefordert, so dass die Vertragsstaaten insoweit die zu ihren jeweiligen rechtlichen und staatsorganisationsrechtlichen Regelungen passenden Maßnahmen auswählen können.

4. Neue Tendenzen der EU

Die Generaldirektion Energie der Europäischen Kommission hatte Ende Dezember 2012 einen Arbeitsentwurf vorgelegt, zu dem die Leiter der europäischen Aufsichtsbehörden (European Nuclear Safety Regulators Group, ENSREG) nach intensiver Diskussion im April 2013 einen Gegenvorschlag vorgelegt haben. Im Hinblick auf das Thema »Unabhängigkeit« enthielt der Vorschlag der Generaldirektion Energie Formulierungen, die so hätten interpretiert werden können, dass in jedem Fall eine organisatorisch von anderen Stellen getrennte, eigenständige Behörde für nukleare Sicherheit eingerichtet werden muss. Dies ginge über die geltende Richtlinie zur nuklearen Sicherheit von 2009 hinaus, denn in Art. 5 Abs. 2 ist folgendes gefordert:

> »Die Mitgliedstaaten stellen sicher, dass die zuständige Regulierungsbehörde funktional von allen anderen Stellen und Organisationen getrennt ist, die mit der Förderung oder Nutzung von Kernenergie einschließlich der Elektrizitätserzeugung befasst sind, um die tatsächliche Unabhängigkeit von ungebührlicher Beeinflussung bei der regulatorischen Entscheidungsfindung sicherzustellen.«

Der Arbeitsentwurf ging sowohl im Hinblick auf das Ziel, als auch auf das Instrument der Regelung über die Richtlinie von 2009 hinaus. Die tatsächliche Unabhängigkeit bei der Entscheidungsfindung sollte nicht nur allgemein vor ungebührlicher Beeinflussung geschützt werden, sondern davor, dass Sicherheitsbewertungen politischen, wirtschaftlichen oder gesellschaftlichen Interessen untergeordnet werden. Was das zentrale Instrument zur Erreichung dieses Ziels angeht, so wies der Text über die funktionale Trennung von Stellen für die Sicherheit einerseits und die der Förderung oder Nutzung andererseits deutlich hinaus. Danach sollte die Regulierungsbehörde funktional getrennt und rechtlich eigenständig sein im Verhältnis zu jeder anderen privaten oder öffentlichen Institution.
Der Arbeitsentwurf dürfte wie folgt einzuordnen sein:

- Der Generaldirektion Energie schwebte offenbar das französische Modell einer rechtlich eigenständigen Behörde vor. Die Einbindung als Abteilung in ein Ministerium, wie dies für Deutschland sowohl auf Landes- als auf Bundesebene der Fall ist, kann schwerlich als vereinbar mit den genannten Anforderungen angesehen werden.

- Nicht nur für Deutschland waren die Formulierungen als problematisch anzusehen, sondern auch für zahlreiche andere Mitgliedstaaten. Das verwundert nur auf den ersten Blick. Wenn man sich die oben beispielhaft dargestellten differenzierten Regelungen in vielen anderen Mitgliedstaaten vor Augen führt, zeigt sich, dass es in den Mitgliedstaaten, in denen für wichtige Genehmigungen eine Entscheidung durch die Regierung vorgesehen ist, insoweit an einer rechtlich eigenständigen Behörde mit ausschließlicher Zuständigkeit für die nukleare Sicherheit fehlt.

ENSREG hat im April 2013 vorgeschlagen, auf Formulierungen zu verzichten, die die Schaffung einer eigenständigen Behörde erforderten. Der Richtlinienvorschlag der Europäischen Kommission vom 13. Juni 2013 enthält nunmehr eine Formulierung, die sicherstellen soll, dass die nationalen Regulierungsbehörden bei ihren Entscheidungen unabhängig sind und dass politische, wirtschaftliche oder gesellschaftliche Interessen keinen Vorrang vor Sicherheitszielen haben können.[3] Eine rechtliche Eigenständigkeit der Behörde wird dagegen nicht gefordert.

5. *Verfassungs- und Rechtslage in Deutschland*

a) Grundlagen

Das Grundgesetz und die grundlegenden staatsorganisatorischen Weichenstellungen sind im Hinblick auf Trennungsgrundsatz und effektive Unabhängigkeit von ungebührlicher Beeinflussung vor allem geprägt durch folgende Regelungen und Grundsätze:

- Die vollziehende Gewalt, also die Exekutive bzw. die Verwaltung, ist an Recht und Gesetz gebunden, Art. 20 Abs. 3 GG.
- Das Erfordernis einer ununterbrochenen Legitimationskette vom Volk zu den mit staatlichen Aufgaben betrauten Organen und Amtswaltern der Verwaltung, das sich aus dem Demokratieprinzip des Art. 20 Abs. 1 GG ergibt.[4]

---

3 Vgl. die Pressemitteilung der Europäischen Kommission vom 13. Juni 2013, http://europa.eu/rapid/press-release_IP-13-532_de.htm

4 *Jarass/Pieroth,* Grundgesetz für die Bundesrepublik Deutschland, 12. Aufl. München 2012, Art. 20, Rz. 9a

- Der aus diesem Erfordernis folgende staatsorganisationsrechtliche Grundsatz, dass es ministerialfreie Räume in der Verwaltung nur ausnahmsweise geben darf. Alternativ bedürfte es einer besonderen Verantwortlichkeit der Behördenleitung gegenüber dem Parlament, um die Legitimation zu sichern.[5]
- Das Remonstrationsrecht der Beamten im Hinblick auf rechtswidrige Entscheidungen, § 36 BeamtStG, § 63 BBG.

b) Ministerialfreie Behörden

Die Frage der Ministerialfreiheit soll im Folgenden näher beleuchtet werden. Ausnahmsweise sind ministerialfreie Behörden zulässig, es bedarf jedoch einer gesetzlichen oder gewohnheitsrechtlichen Grundlage und zwingender Sachgründe.[6] Die Unabhängigkeit der Deutschen Bundesbank ergibt sich aus § 12 BbankG. Die Mitglieder des Bundesrechnungshofs besitzen gemäß Art. 114 Abs. 2 Grundgesetz richterliche Unabhängigkeit. Beide nehmen erkennbar Aufgaben wahr, die mit der Atomaufsicht kaum vergleichbar sind. Daher möchte ich mich hier näher mit zwei anderen Behörden befassen, die für die Entwicklung in Deutschland, auch im Hinblick auf den Einfluss des Europarechts, von besonderer Bedeutung sind: die Datenschutzbeauftragten und die Bundesnetzagentur.

Der Bundesdatenschutzbeauftragte (seit 2006 zuständig auch für die Informationsfreiheit, BfDI) ist gemäß Bundesdatenschutzgesetz (BDSG) eine unabhängige Kontrollinstanz für die Überwachung des Datenschutzes bei öffentlichen Stellen des Bundes und bei Unternehmen, die Telekommunikations- und Postdienstleistungen anbieten. Er wird von der Bundesregierung vorgeschlagen und vom Bundestag gewählt und steht dabei in einem öffentlich-rechtlichen Amtsverhältnis, nicht jedoch in einem Beamtenverhältnis, § 22 Abs. 1 und 4 BDSG.

Die Dienststelle des Bundesbeauftragten ist beim Bundesministerium des Innern eingerichtet, gehört jedoch nicht zum nachgeordneten Geschäftsbereich, sondern nimmt verwaltungsorganisatorisch eine Sonderstellung ein, um eine datenschutzrechtliche Kontrolle von Bundesministerien zu ermöglichen. Gemäß § 22 Abs. 4 BDSG ist der BfDI in der Ausübung seines Amtes unabhängig und nur dem Gesetz unterworfen, eine Fachaufsicht besteht nicht. Allerdings untersteht er der Rechtsaufsicht der

---

5 *Jarass/Pieroth,* ebd., Art. 86, Rz. 3

6 *Jarass/Pieroth,* ebd.

Bundesregierung sowie der Dienstaufsicht des Bundesministeriums des Innern, § 22 Abs. 4 und 5 BDSG.

Bemerkenswert ist im Zusammenhang mit der Datenschutzkontrolle ein gegen Deutschland ergangenes Urteil des Europäischen Gerichtshofs (EuGH) aus dem Jahr 2010.[7] Der Europäische Gerichtshof hat sich darin mit der Vorgabe der EG-Datenschutzrichtlinie 95/46/EG befasst, wonach den Datenschutzbehörden »völlige Unabhängigkeit« gewährt wird. Gegenstand des Verfahrens war dabei nicht die Datenschutzkontrolle öffentlicher Stellen, sondern die Datenschutzkontrolle nicht-öffentlicher Stellen, d.h. insbesondere die Kontrolle über Unternehmen. Diese wurde in Deutschland von den hierfür zuständigen Ländern durch »normale«, d.h. hierarchisch strukturierte Aufsichtsbehörden, ausgeübt. Damit hat Deutschland nach Auffassung des EuGH gegen die Datenschutzrichtlinie verstoßen. Entgegen dem Votum des Generalanwaltes (!) verlangt der EuGH auch in Bezug auf die Kontrolle über den nicht-öffentlichen Bereich eine strikte Regierungsferne. Er legt dabei die entsprechende Regelung in der Datenschutzrichtlinie, wonach die Datenschutzstellen ihre Aufgaben »in völliger Unabhängigkeit« wahrnehmen, denkbar weit aus.[8] Datenschutzbehörden dürfen nach dem Urteil des EuGH weder einer Fach- noch einer Rechtsaufsicht unterliegen.[9] Die Aufsicht der Datenschutzkontrolle in Deutschland ist bzw. war entsprechend anzupassen.

Nicht vollständig ministerialfrei sind dagegen die Bundesnetzagentur und das Bundeskartellamt, beides Behörden im Geschäftsbereich des Bundesministeriums für Wirtschaft und Technologie. Die Bundesnetzagentur wird im Hinblick auf die Telekommunikation sowie der Leitungsnetze für Strom und Gas stark durch europarechtliche Vorgaben geprägt. Die Richtlinien für den Binnenmarkt für Strom und Gas von 2009 sehen die Regulierung durch unabhängige Behörden vor. Die Bundesnetzagentur ist insbesondere durch folgende Merkmale geprägt:

Das Präsidium (Präsident/in und zwei Vizepräsidenten/Vizepräsidentinnen) wird auf Vorschlag des Beirats, der aus 16 Mitgliedern des Bundestages und 16 Vertretern des Bundesrates besteht, von der Bundesregierung benannt, § 3 Abs. 3 des Gesetzes über die Bundesnetzagentur für Elektrizität, Gas, Telekommunikation, Post und Eisenbahnen

7 Urteil des Gerichtshofes (Große Kammer) vom 9. März 2010, Europäische Kommission gegen Bundesrepublik Deutschland, Rechtssache C-518/07, Sammlung der Rechtsprechung 2010 I-01885

8 Ebd., Rz. 30, 37

9 Ebd., Rz. 40ff.

(BEGTPG). Insoweit besteht ein deutlicher Unterschied im Vergleich zu den klassischen Bundesoberbehörden, bei denen eine Ernennung durch den zuständigen Minister erfolgt. Eine Sonderregelung stellt auch das öffentlich-rechtliche Amtsverhältnis für die Behördenspitze dar, § 4 BEGTPG.

Im Bereich der Telekommunikation besteht ein Weisungsrecht des Ministeriums, allerdings sind die Weisungen zu veröffentlichen, § 117 TKG. Bei Strom und Gas gilt dies, wie übrigens auch beim Bundeskartellamt, für allgemeine Weisungen, § 61 EnWG. Ob daneben Einzelweisungen zulässig sind, ist streitig.[10] Faktisch gibt es sie jedenfalls nicht, mit Blick auf das Bundeskartellamt hat der langjährige Staatsekretär im Bundesministerium für Wirtschaft Otto Schlecht bereits in den 90er Jahren von »ordnungspolitischem Gewohnheitsrecht« gesprochen.[11]

Angesichts dieser Regelungen kann jedenfalls von völliger Ministerialfreiheit bei der Bundesnetzagentur (und auch beim Bundeskartellamt) nicht die Rede sein.

c) Berücksichtigung des Föderalismus

Wichtig scheint mir noch die Berücksichtigung des Föderalismus zu sein. Die Ministerien auf Bundes- und Landesebene haben – trotz derselben Bezeichnung – deutlich unterschiedliche Aufgabenschwerpunkte. Natürlich hat auch ein Bundesministerium gegenüber einer Bundesoberbehörde im Normalfall die Fachaufsicht. Noch wichtiger ist aber die Vorbereitung der Gesetzgebung. Beim Land gibt es natürlich auch Landesgesetzgebung, die vorzubereiten ist. Der Schwerpunkt liegt aber beim Gesetzesvollzug, der in aller Regel Landessache ist und von den Ministerien beaufsichtigt oder – wie im Fall des Atomrechts – selbst durchgeführt wird. Ein Landesminister ist also vor allem der mit hoher demokratischer Legitimation ausgestattete Kopf der gesetzesgebundenen Landesverwaltung. Wer einem solchen Minister per se politische Einflussnahme auf den Gesetzesvollzug unterstellt, der trifft die deutsche Staatsorganisation ins Mark und stellt damit auch den Föderalismus in Frage. Dass der Föderalismus als solcher aufgrund Ewigkeitsklausel des Art. 79 Abs. 3 GG auch europarechtlich nicht zur Disposition stehen kann, brauche ich in diesem Kreis nicht besonders zu betonen.

10 *Stober,* Besonderes Verwaltungsrecht, 14. Aufl. Stuttgart 2007, S. 185
11 Handelsblatt v. 23.7.1996, S. 4

Im Zusammenhang mit dem Föderalismus möchte ich noch einen Blick auf Frankreich werfen, dessen »unabhängige Behörden« angesichts der zentralstaatlichen Tradition manche überraschen mögen. Nun gibt es für die Schaffung von über 30 solche Behörden sei Ende der 70er Jahre verschiedenste Gründe. Lesenswert ist insoweit eine rechtsvergleichende Studie von jeweils vier französischen und deutschen Professoren des öffentlichen Rechts von 2010 mit dem Titel »Unabhängige Regulierungsbehörden. Organisationsrechtliche Herausforderungen in Frankreich und Deutschland«[12]. Ein wesentlicher Unterschied zwischen Deutschland und Frankreich scheint mir aber die herausragende Bedeutung der großen Staatsunternehmen zu sein. Auch wenn der Staat diese teilweise privatisiert hat, was beim Stromerzeuger EdF nicht der Fall ist, so hat er doch bei allen noch einen bestimmenden Einfluss. Die Entscheidungen des Aktionärs Staat fallen in den jeweils zuständigen Ministerien. Sofern derselbe Minister bzw. ein Kollege nicht auch für die Regulierung des Staatsunternehmens (und damit ggf. auch seiner Konkurrenten) zuständig sein soll, bedarf es der Schaffung unabhängiger Behörden.

6. Europäische Regelungen zu Organisationsfragen – Chance für effektivere Strukturen oder Belastung in der Ausstiegsphase?

Es gibt also, wie wir gesehen haben, im Hinblick auf die Atomaufsicht eine Vielzahl unterschiedlicher Strukturen und Organisationsformen der zuständigen atomrechtlichen Genehmigungs- und Aufsichtsbehörden mit unterschiedlichen Graden institutionell-organisatorischer Unabhängigkeit. Festzustellen ist allerdings ein genereller Trend hin zu institutionell-organisatorisch unabhängigen atomrechtlichen Behörden (siehe die Bestrebungen in den Niederlanden, Großbritannien sowie Finnland).

Die jeweilige behördliche Struktur kann nur vor dem Hintergrund der jeweiligen allgemeinen nationalen Behörden- und Staatsorganisation verstanden und bewertet werden. So ist beispielsweise das Konzept der unabhängigen Regulierungsbehörde (autorité administrative indépendante) im zentralistischen Frankreich bekannt, anderen Rechtsordnungen jedoch eher fremd. Die deutsche Verwaltung ist beispielsweise geprägt vom grundsätzlichen Verbot ministerialfreier Räume.

12 *Masing/Marcou (Hrsg.)*, Unabhängige Regulierungsbehörden: Organisationsrechtliche Herausforderungen in Frankreich und Deutschland, Tübingen 2010

Eine völlig unabhängige Genehmigung und Aufsicht im Hinblick auf Kernkraftwerke findet in kaum einem Staat statt. Selbst in Frankreich werden bestimmte zentrale Entscheidungen im Hinblick auf kerntechnische Anlagen durch die Regierung getroffen. In der Schweiz und in Finnland werden sämtliche Genehmigungen durch die Regierung erteilt.

Die institutionell-organisatorische Trennung der Genehmigungs- und Aufsichtsbehörde von der Regierung einschließlich ihrer Weisungsfreiheit ist kein Ziel an sich, sondern kann lediglich ein Weg unter mehreren denkbaren sein, um das eigentliche Ziel der Unabhängigkeit der Entscheidungsfindung und ein ausschließlich an Recht und Gesetz orientiertes Handeln zu erreichen. Dieses Ziel kann aber auch auf anderem Wege sichergestellt werden, z.B. durch das Remonstrationsrecht der Beamten, amtsangemessene Bezahlung, angemessene finanzielle Ausstattung der Behörde etc. Schließlich dürften auch kulturelle und andere »weiche« Faktoren eine in ihrer Bedeutung kaum zu unterschätzende Rolle spielen.

Bleibt aber zum Schluss die Frage, ob die Schaffung eigenständiger, unabhängiger Atomaufsichtsbehörden in den Ländern und auf Bundesebene oder gar die Zentralisierung aller Aufsichtsaufgaben beim Bund nicht auch eine Chance ist, um angesichts der schrittweisen Abschaltung der deutschen Kernkraftwerke bis Ende 2022 dem sich abzeichnenden Problem der Erhaltung der behördlichen Fachkompetenz bis zum jeweils letzten Tag des Leistungsbetriebs (bzw. des Nachbetriebs und des Abschlusses der Stilllegungsverfahren) gerecht zu werden. Das BMU hat diese Frage bereits vor 10 Jahren unter dem Stichwort »Einführung der Bundeseigenverwaltung« gestellt, die Länder wollten damals alle an der bestehenden Struktur festhalten. Egal ob zentralisiert oder jeweils eigenständig in den Ländern und beim Bund, klar ist für mich jedenfalls, dass eine Abkehr von der Einbindung der Atomaufsicht in die Ministerien mit einer längeren Umstellungsphase verbunden wäre. Dies stünde m.E. in keinem Verhältnis zur Restlaufzeit der Kernkraftwerke und würde voraussichtlich zu einer vorübergehenden Abschwächung der eigentlichen Aufsichtstätigkeit führen. Ich glaube nicht, dass dies angesichts der bevorstehenden Phase der Kernenergienutzung in Deutschland richtig wäre. Die Einführung fester Abschaltdaten macht die Arbeit der Aufsicht nicht leichter, denn die optimale Wahrnehmung der sicherheitsrelevanten Aufgaben der Mitarbeiter in den Kraftwerken dürfte in der letzten Phase der Nutzung mit kostenbewussten Unternehmensleitungen und Schwerpunktverlagerungen in zukunftsorientierte Bereiche kollidieren. Gerade dann bedarf es einer wachsamen und kontinuierlichen Aufsicht!

Nukleartransportrecht und Universalhafenprinzip im Spannungsverhältnis: Das Bremer Hafenrecht

Prof. Dr. Christoph Moench[*], Fachanwalt für Verwaltungsrecht, Honorarprofessor an der Goethe-Universität Frankfurt a. M.

A. Einleitung

I. Bedeutung von Transport und Infrastruktur

1. Transport, Logistik und Verkehrsinfrastruktur sind als Standortfaktoren elementar. Lokal, regional, national und natürlich auch international. Das gilt gleichermaßen für alle Medien: Straße und Schiene, Luft und Wasser. **Häfen** sind das Tor zur Welt, die Voraussetzung der Globalisierung.

2. Das **tatsächlich vorhandene Netz** der Infrastruktur ist das eine. Das **gesetzliche Regelungsregime** das andere. Die Infrastruktur ist nur so gut, wie das Recht, das ihre Nutzung regelt. Jede Einschränkung hat Auswirkungen auf den Handel und die Märkte mit Konsequenzen für den Standort und die Produktion.

II. Dynamik rechtlicher Strukturen

1. Die Infrastruktur unterliegt aufgrund ihrer Einbettung in die Gesellschaft und Umwelt und als Rückgrat der Wirtschaft vielfältigem (gesellschaftlichem) Wandel und damit zugleich auch einer **rechtlichen Dynamik**.

Für den Transport und die Infrastruktur von Kernbrennstoffen sind aktuell folgende **Rechtsentwicklungen** bedeutsam:

- Die neueste Rechtsprechung des BVerwG und des BVerfG zum **Drittschutz** bei Transportvorgängen[1]. Die Routenwahl wird erschwert. Der Transport unterliegt einem Verzögerungspotential.

---

* Der Verfasser ist Partner bei Gleiss Lutz (Büro Berlin). Er dankt RA Dr. Marc Ruttloff (Gleiss Lutz Berlin) für die Mitwirkung bei der Erstellung des Manuskriptes.

- Das **Standortauswahlgesetz**[2] und die dadurch um Dekaden verlängerte Zwischenlagerung radioaktiver Abfälle werfen infolge der Befristung der Bauartzulassung der Transport- und Lagerbehälter (etwa des Castors) Fragen bei der langfristigen Nutzung dieser Behälter auf. Das Konzept von Transport, Transportbehälter und langfristiger Zwischenlagerung bedarf der Überprüfung.
- Die Änderung des **Bremer Hafenbetriebsgesetzes** (HafenbetrG): Es verhindert den Umschlag radioaktiver Stoffe – ein gefährlicher **Präzedenzfall**. Es schränkt potentiell die Ver- und Entsorgung mit radioaktiven Gütern ein.

2. Das Thema ist nur scheinbar von kleinem Zuschnitt: Es ist tatsächlich ein **Prisma** von **Grundfragen**

- verfasster föderaler Staatlichkeit und des konkreten Verhältnisses von Bundesrecht zu Landesrecht nach dem Grundgesetz,
- der Infrastruktur, der Beförderung selektiv ausgewählter Güter verbunden mit dem In- und Export,
- des gesellschaftlich sensitiven Atomrechts,
- europarechtlicher Grenzen bei der Kompetenzausübung föderaler staatlicher Hoheitsgewalt.

B. Hauptteil

I. Änderung des Bremischen Hafenbetriebsgesetzes

1. Die Bremischen Häfen – Bremerhaven und Bremen – sind der viertgrößte europäische **Universalhafen**. Ca. 115.000 Arbeitsplätze stehen mit den Häfen in Zusammenhang. Die Eigenschaft als Universalhafen beruht auf jahrhundertelanger Tradition. In Universalhäfen sind allgemein der Umschlag aller Art von Gütern und jeglicher Schiffstypen zugelassen, soweit die spezifischen gesetzlichen Beförderungsbestimmungen und der Zuschnitt der Hafenanlagen dies zulassen. Dementsprechend wurden über die Bremischen Häfen auch alle Güter umgeschlagen, die dem Bau von Kraftwerken, der Energieerzeugung, Erneuerbaren Energien oder eben

---

1 Zuletzt BVerwG, Urteil vom 14.03.2013, 7 C 34.11, ZNER 2013, 432; BVerfG NVwZ 2009, 515. Hierzu: *Leidinger/Ruttloff*, NVwZ 2013, 1369.

2 Gesetz v. 23.7.2013 – BGBl I 2013 Nr. 41 – 26.7.2013 S. 2553. Dazu BT-Drs. 17/13471.

auch der Kernenergie dienten, insbesondere etwa Kernbrennstoffe oder sonstige radioaktive Materialien.

2. Mit Wirkung zum 7. Februar 2012 wurden zwei **neue Absätze in § 2 Hafenbetriebsgesetz** eingefügt, und zwar die Absätze 2 und 3. Sie lauten:

> »(2) Die Bremischen Häfen sind als Universalhäfen gewidmet und stehen als öffentliche Einrichtungen für den Umschlag aller zulässigen Güter offen.
>
> (3) Im Interesse einer grundsätzlich auf Nachhaltigkeit und Erneuerbare Energien ausgerichteten Gesamtwirtschaft ist der Umschlag von Kernbrennstoffen im Sinne des § 2 Abs. 1 des Atomgesetzes ausgeschlossen. Der Senat kann allgemein oder im Einzelfall Ausnahmen zulassen, insbesondere für Kernbrennstoffe, die unter die Regelung in § 2 Abs. 2 Satz 2 des Atomgesetzes fallen oder nur in geringen Mengen im Umschlagsgut enthalten sind.«[3]

Dieser Gesetzesänderung ist eine längere parlamentarische Diskussion vorausgegangen, in deren Verlauf die unterschiedlichen Begründungsansätze diskutiert wurden. Die parlamentarische Mehrheit begründet den Antrag im Wesentlichen damit, das Gesetz diene der Sicherheit der Bremischen Bevölkerung durch die Beschränkung der Atomtransporte. Darüber hinaus wurde es als widersprüchlich angesehen, dass nach dem gesetzlichen Atomausstieg weiterhin Kernbrennstoffe für die Erzeugung von Kernenergie aus Deutschland exportiert werden.[4] Die Abgeordneten waren sich durchaus bewusst, dass sie mit diesem Schritt rechtliches Neuland betreten und dass die **Verfassungsmäßigkeit** dieser Regelung von Anfang an Zweifeln unterlag. Vor allem waren sie sich des **Präzedenzcharakters** bewusst. So wies ein Abgeordneter der SPD-Fraktion ausdrücklich darauf hin, dass es »ja kein Geheimnis« sei,

> »dass auch in anderen Städten wie Cuxhaven, Wilhelmshaven, Emden, Rostock und Lübeck darüber nachgedacht wird oder auch konkrete Ratsbeschlüsse vorliegen –, durch welche Möglichkeiten die Verhinderung von Transporten von Kernbrennstoffen über Häfen sichergestellt werden kann. Wir gießen das heute in einen Gesetzestext. Ich wiederhole, dass das für uns Neuland ist«.[5]

3 Gesetz vom 31. Januar 2012, Brem. GBl. S. 10.

4 Plenar-Protokoll 18/7, S. 276.

5 So der Abgeordnete Schildt, Plenar-Protokoll 18/7, 275. Demgegenüber vertrat die CDU-Fraktion der Bremischen Bürgerschaft dezidiert die Auffassung, dass das Gesetzesvorhaben verfassungswidrig sei, dazu BremBÜ-Drucks. 18 /197, 8 ff. Diese rechtlichen Bedenken haben die CDU-Fraktion veranlasst, beim Staatsgerichtshof der Freien Hansestadt Bremen einen Antrag auf Prüfung der Verfassungsmäßigkeit des Gesetzes zur Änderung des Bremischen Hafenbetriebsgesetzes nach Art. 140 Abs. 1 LV i. V. m. § 24 Staatsgerichtshofgesetz StGHG zu stellen. Das Verfahren ist unter dem Aktenzeichen St 1/12 anhängig.

Die **grundsätzliche Bedeutung** der Bremischen Gesetzgebung reicht weit über den Ausgangssachverhalt – den Umschlag von Kernbrennstoffen in den Bremischen Häfen – hinaus. Die parlamentarische Diskussion in Bremen und Stimmen anderswo haben gezeigt, dass vergleichbare Umschlagsverbote auch für **andere Waren** und Güter in der näheren Zukunft angestrebt werden. Was heute Kernbrennstoffe sind, können morgen sonstige politisch diskreditierte Güter sein, man denke etwa an genetisch veränderte Lebensmittel, Palmöl, Tropenhölzer, Tabakprodukte oder sonstige Güter, die Gegenstand politischer Diskussion sind und / oder für politische Zwecke instrumentalisiert werden. Und was heute in Bremen geschieht, kann morgen in anderen Hafenstädten geschehen. Über das Nadelöhr des Beförderungsregimes und konkret des Hafenumschlages können auf lokaler oder regionaler Ebene oder auf der Ebene eines Bundeslandes Dinge geregelt werden, die nach der verfassungsmäßigen Kompetenzordnung anderen Körperschaften oder Organen zugewiesen sind. Eine solche Regelung ist nur zulässig, wenn sie kompetenzmäßig dem Land Bremen zugewiesen ist und sie darüber hinaus auch materiell-rechtlich mit höherrangigem Recht – Verfassungsrecht, Europarecht, Völkervertragsrecht – vereinbar ist.

II. Verfassungswidrigkeit der Regelung

Die Änderung des HafenbetrG verstößt in mehrfacher Hinsicht gegen das Grundgesetz. Sie verletzt – erstens – die bundestaatliche Kompetenzordnung der Art. 70 ff. GG; die ausschließliche Gesetzgebungskompetenz für das Recht der friedlichen Nutzung der Kernenergie liegt gemäß Art. 73 Abs. 1 Nr. 14 GG beim Bund, das Land kann in diese Kompetenz nicht eingreifen. Darüber hinaus ist die Regelung – zweitens – mit dem Gebot der **Widerspruchsfreiheit** der Rechtsordnung als Kompetenzausübungsschranke unvereinbar. Und schließlich verletzt das Gesetz – drittens – den verfassungsrechtlichen Grundsatz der **Bundestreue**.

1. Verstoß gegen die ausschließliche und abschließende Bundeskompetenz gemäß Art. 73 Abs. 1 Nr. 14 GG

Der Landesgesetzgeber ist gemäß den Art. 70, 71 GG im Bereich der ausschließlichen Gesetzgebungskompetenz des Bundes **nicht** zur Gesetzgebung befugt. Er hat insoweit keine **Gesetzgebungskompetenz**. Ein ohne

Gesetzgebungskompetenz erlassenes Gesetz ist verfassungswidrig und damit nichtig.

1.1 Absolute Sperrwirkung bei ausschließlicher Gesetzgebungskompetenz des Bundes

Die Gesetzgebungskompetenz des Bundes und der Länder ist in Art. 70 ff. GG geregelt. Gemäß Art. 70 Abs. 1 GG haben die Länder das Recht der Gesetzgebung, soweit das Grundgesetz nicht dem Bund die Gesetzgebungsbefugnis verleiht. Für den Bereich der ausschließlichen Gesetzgebung des Bundes bestimmt Art. 71 GG, dass die Länder die Befugnis zur Gesetzgebung nur haben, »wenn und soweit sie hierzu in einem Bundesgesetz ausdrücklich ermächtigt werden.« Art. 71 GG begründet demnach eine **absolute Sperrwirkung** für die Materien der **ausschließlichen Bundesgesetzgebung**, ohne dass eine vollständige oder teilweise Ausübung dieser Kompetenz durch den Bund Voraussetzung wäre.[6] Die Länder haben bei diesen Materien per se keine Gesetzgebungskompetenz. Erlässt der Landesgesetzgeber dennoch Regelungen, sind sie wegen Verstoßes gegen Art. 71 GG verfassungswidrig und damit nichtig.

1.2 Ausschließliche Bundeskompetenz für die Kernenergie, Art. 73 Abs. 1 Nr. 14 GG

Art. 73 Abs. 1 Nr. 14 GG regelt, dass die **ausschließliche Gesetzgebungskompetenz** für »die Erzeugung und Nutzung der Kernenergie zu friedlichen Zwecken« beim **Bund** liegt. Dazu gehören nach dem Wortlaut dieser Bestimmung die Errichtung und der Betrieb von Anlagen, die diesen Zwecken dienen, ebenso wie der Schutz gegen Gefahren im Zusammenhang mit der Kernenergie oder ionisierenden Strahlen.[7] Der Begriff der Kernenergie – früher auch Atomenergie – wurde immer schon weit verstanden. Die Gesetzgebungskompetenz bezieht sich auf den **gesamten**

6 *Uhle*, in: Maunz/Dürig, GG, Stand: 66. EL (2012), Art. 71 Rn. 34; *Sannwald*, in: Schmidt-Bleibtreu/Hofmann/Hopfauf, GG, 12. Aufl. 2011, Art 71 Rn. 9.

7 Die ausschließliche Gesetzgebungskompetenz hat der Bundesgesetzgeber im Zuge der Föderalismusreform durch das Gesetz zur Änderung des Grundgesetzes vom 28. August 2006 erhalten, BGB I, S. 2034. Davor war dies eine Materie der konkurrierenden Gesetzgebung. Für das hier interessierende Thema spielt dies weiter keine Rolle.

Bereich des Kernenergiewesens und das gesamte Gefahrenabwehrrecht im Hinblick auf den Strahlenschutz.[8] Art. 73 Abs. 1 Nr. 14 GG enthält eine umfassende Sachkompetenz, die als **lex specialis** alle Lebensbereiche umfasst, auch soweit sie Überschneidungen mit Materien anderer Kompetenztitel hat.[9] Dazu gehören neben der Errichtung und dem Betrieb entsprechender Anlagen, alle Vorgänge im Zusammenhang mit der Beförderung, dem Transport und der Lagerung radioaktiver Stoffe. Sie sind untrennbarer Bestandteil der Nutzung der Kernenergie. Ohne Transport und die funktional damit verknüpften Vorgänge wie des Umschlages und der (Zwischen-) Lagerung radioaktiver Stoffe kann Kernenergie nicht genutzt werden.

Das bedeutet: Der Bund hat die ausschließliche Gesetzgebungskompetenz für alles, was mit der Kernenergie zu tun hat, auch für die Lagerung, Verpackung, die Beförderung, den Umschlag und den Transport insgesamt. Das gilt unabhängig von der benutzten Infrastruktur und dem Transportmittel: Ob auf der Schiene oder der Straße, zu Luft oder auf dem Schiffswege. Regelungen, die die Beförderung der Kernenergie zum Gegenstand haben, kann **nur der Bund** treffen. Sie sind dem Landesgesetzgeber entzogen.

1.3 Wahrnehmung der Gesetzgebungskompetenz durch den Bundesgesetzgeber

a) Gebrauch der Gesetzgebungskompetenz

Ich habe bereits darauf hingewiesen, dass die ausschließliche Gesetzgebungskompetenz des Bundes eine **absolute Sperrwirkung** entfaltet. Unabhängig davon gehe ich im Folgenden in aller Kürze darauf ein, dass der Bund von seiner Gesetzgebungskompetenz umfassend **Gebrauch** gemacht hat – zumindest verfassungspolitisch hätte dies den Bremischen Gesetzgeber warnen müssen. Die Nutzung der Kernenergie ist detailliert im Atomgesetz und seinen Durchführungsverordnungen geregelt. Der Bund hat in den letzten Jahren das 11., 12. und zuletzt das 13. Gesetz zur Änderung

---

8 Zur Weite des Begriffs *Fischerhof*, NJW 1992, 2095 (2096); BVerfGE 43, 25, 32; *Degenhart*, a. a. O., Art. 73 Rn. 59; *Heintzen*, in: von Mangoldt/Klein/Starck, GG, 6. Aufl. 2010, Art. 73 Rn. 136.

9 *Heintzen*, in: von Mangoldt/Klein/Starck, a. a. O. Art. 73 Rn. 34; *Degenhart*, in: Sachs, a. a. O., Art. 73 Rn. 60.

des Atomgesetzes erlassen.[10] Zur Wahrung der energiepolitischen Trias (Versorgungssicherheit, Klimaschutz und angemessene Strompreise) wurde die Brückenfunktion der Kernenergie unterstrichen.[11] Das Energiekonzept der Bundesregierung endet mit einem Bekenntnis zu einem »Mindestmaß an Kontinuität«.[12] Das umfasst auch den Anspruch auf eine verlässliche und sichere Zwischen- und Endlagerung der radioaktiven Abfälle. All dies setzt funktionell zwangsläufig den Transport und die Beförderung von Kernbrennstoffen und sonstigen radioaktiven Materialien voraus. Der Bundesgesetzgeber hat nicht nur die Anforderungen an ortsfeste Anlagen geregelt, die der Erzeugung, der Bearbeitung, der Verarbeitung, der Spaltung oder dem sonstigen Umgang mit Kernbrennstoffen dienen, insbesondere in § 7 AtG. Weitere anlagenbezogene Regelungen betreffen die Aufbewahrung, § 6 AtG, die Bearbeitung, Verarbeitung und sonstige Verwendung von Kernbrennstoffen, § 9 AtG, sowie die Verwertung und Beseitigung radioaktiver Reststoffe und Abfälle, § 9a AtG.

b) Beförderungsgenehmigung gemäß § 4 AtG

Darüber hinaus regelt das Atomgesetz des Bundes auch detailliert die gesetzlichen Rahmenbedingungen für die Beförderung und den Transport von Kernbrennstoffen gemäß § 4 AtG. Die Nutzung der Kerntechnik in ortsfesten Anlagen setzt funktionell voraus, dass die hierfür erforderlichen Kernbrennstoffe über die verfügbaren Verkehrsträger transportiert werden können. Eine sinnvolle **Regelung der Sachmaterie** »Kernenergie« ist nur möglich, wenn sie die damit zusammenhängenden **Anforderungen an eine Beförderung** in eine widerspruchsfreie Gesamtregelung einbezieht. Einschlägig ist § 4 AtG[13]. Demnach bedarf die Beförderung von Kernbrennstoffen außerhalb der entsprechenden Anlagen einer besonderen atomrechtlichen Genehmigung. Gleichzeitig werden in § 4 Abs. 2 AtG detailliert die Anforderungen normiert, die für die Erteilung einer Beförderungsgenehmigung erfüllt sein müssen. Dies betrifft insbesondere die persönliche Zuverlässigkeit der beteiligten Personen, die hinreichende persönliche Fachkunde, die Einhaltung der verkehrsrechtlichen Vorschriften,

10 Zuletzt durch Gesetz vom 31. Juli 2011, BGB I, S. 1704.
11 BT-Drucks. 17/6070, 5; ähnlich BT-Drs. 17/3051, 7.
12 BT-Drucks. 17/3049, 18.
13 Eine ähnliche Regelung enthalten die §§ 16 ff. Strahlenschutzverordnung für radioaktive Stoffe.

die Deckungsvorsorge, den Schutz vor Einwirkungen Dritter sowie die Wahrung der öffentlichen Interessen bei der Wahl des Beförderungsvorgangs (Nr. 1 bis 6). Die hierfür zuständige Verwaltungsbehörde ist gemäß § 23 Abs. 1 Nr. 3 AtG das Bundesamt für Strahlenschutz (BfS) und damit ebenfalls eine Bundesbehörde. Länderzuständigkeiten bestehen in diesem Zusammenhang grundsätzlich nicht. Die Übertragung der Verwaltungskompetenz an den Bund ist in Art. 87 c GG ausdrücklich vorgesehen.

§ 4 Abs. 1, Abs. 2 Nr. 3 AtG machen es zur Genehmigungsvoraussetzung für die Erteilung einer Beförderungsgenehmigung von Kernbrennstoffen, dass die jeweils einschlägigen **gefahrgutrechtlichen Transportvorschriften** eingehalten werden. § 4 Abs. 6 Satz 2 AtG betont zusätzlich, dass im Übrigen die für die jeweiligen Verkehrsträger geltenden Rechtsvorschriften über die Beförderung gefährlicher Güter unberührt bleiben – es handelt sich insofern um eine deklaratorische Ergänzung des § 4 Abs. 2 Nr. 3 AtG. Die verkehrsrechtlichen Anforderungen des Gefahrgutrechts sind damit auch bei der Beförderung von Kernbrennstoffen beachtlich und anzuwenden.[14] Dieser Bereich ist ebenfalls in umfassender und abschließender Weise Gegenstand bundesgesetzlicher Regelungen:

c) Gefahrgut- und Transportrecht des Bundes

Im Bereich der gefahrgutrechtlichen Transportvorschriften gelten, für den Hochseebereich, die verbindlichen internationalen Vorgaben aufgrund des International Maritime Dangerous Goods Code (IMDG-Code)[15] der International Maritime Organisation (IMO).[16] Radioaktive Stoffe und damit auch Kernbrennstoffe gehören gemäß dem international harmonisierten System zur Klassifizierung, Benennung und Kennzeichnung gefährlicher Stoffe und Gegenstände zur Gefahrklasse 7.[17] Zur Umsetzung dieser internationalen Vorgaben in nationales Recht hat der Bund mit dem **Gefahrgutbeförderungsgesetz (GGBefG)**[18] abschließend die sicherheitsrechtlichen Anforderungen an die Beförderung gefährlicher Güter gere-

14 *Büdenbender/von Heinegg/Rosin*, Energierecht I, 1999, Rn. 1178 ff.; *G. Schwarz*, atw 2012, 476 (477 ff.).

15 Zuletzt geändert durch die Entschließung MSC.294(87), in der amtlichen deutschen Übersetzung bekanntgegeben am 30. November 2010, VkBl. 2010 S. 554.

16 *Lagoni*, NordÖR 2012, 335 (337).

17 Vgl. hierzu *G. Schwarz*, atw 2012, 476 (478); *Lagoni*, NordÖR 2012, 335 (337).

18 Gefahrgutbeförderungsgesetz in der Fassung der Bekanntmachung vom 7. Juli 2009, BGBl I S. 1774, 3975.

gelt.[19] In § 3 GGBefG ist eine Ermächtigung im Sinne des Art. 80 GG zugunsten des Bundesministeriums für Verkehr, Bau und Stadtentwicklung normiert, konkretisierende Rechtsverordnungen zu erlassen.[20] Auf dieser Grundlage ist zur näheren Ausgestaltung der Beförderung und des Umschlags gefährlicher Güter – einschließlich radioaktiver Stoffe und Kernbrennstoffe – im Seeverkehr die sog. **Gefahrgutverordnung See** (GGV-See)[21] erlassen worden. Die Regelungen der GGV-See betreffen explizit auch den Umschlag von Kernbrennstoffen im Sinne der Übergabe dieses Gefahrgutes zur Beförderung auf Seeschiffen. Gemäß § 5 Abs. 1 Nr. 5 GGV-See müssen verpackte Kernbrennstoffe, Plutonium und hochradioaktive Abfälle für die Beförderung auf Seeschiffen spezifischen Anforderungen des internationalen Seerechts genügen. Gefährliche Güter der Klasse 7 gemäß IMDG-Code dürfen nur auf Seeschiffen befördert werden, die den internationalen Vorschriften des »internationalen Codes für die sichere Beförderung von verpackten, bestrahlten Kernbrennstoffen, Plutonium und hochradioaktiven Stoffen« (INF-Code)[22] entsprechen. Der INF-Code enthält ferner Stauvorschriften hinsichtlich derartiger Stoffe, die auf den entsprechenden Seeschiffen befördert werden.

Die Einzelheiten dieser spezifischen Anforderungen bedürfen an dieser Stelle keiner weiteren Vertiefung. Diese Regelungen belegen jedoch, dass auch in gefahrgutrechtlicher Hinsicht **der Bund** für den Bereich der radioaktiven Stoffe und Kernbrennstoffe **eine abschließende Regelung** vorgesehen hat.[23]

19 *Büdenbender/von Heinegg/Rosin*, Energierecht I, 1999, Rn. 1182; *Huck*, Transporte radioaktiver Stoffe, 1992, S. 168.

20 *Büdenbender/von Heinegg/Rosin*, Energierecht I, 1999, Rn. 1183.

21 Gefahrgutverordnung See in der Fassung der Bekanntmachung vom 16. Dezember 2011, BGBl I S. 2784, 2012 I S. 122, die durch Art. 4 der Verordnung vom 19. Dezember 2012, BGBl I S. 2715, geändert worden ist.

22 Internationaler Code für die sichere Beförderung von verpackten bestrahlten Kernbrennstoffen, Plutonium und hochradioaktiven Abfällen (INF-Code), BAnz. 2000 S. 23 322, zuletzt geändert durch die Entschließung MSC. 241 (83), VkBl. 2009 S. 82.

23 Die Vorstellung von der Notwendigkeit einer Regelung aus einer Hand liegt auch explizit der Arbeit der »Joint Working Group on Guidance for an Integrated Transport and Storage Safety Case for Dual Purpose Casks for Spent Nuclear Fuel« der IAEA zugrunde.

1.4 Verfassungsverstoß des § 2 Abs. 3 HafenbetrG gegen Art. 71, 73 Abs. 1 Nr. 14 GG

a) Widerspruch zur Kompetenzzuweisung der Art. 71, 73 Abs. 1 Nr. 14 GG

Der Bundesgesetzgeber hat die durch Art. 71, 73 Abs. 1 Nr. 14 GG festgelegte ausschließliche Kompetenz, die grundsätzliche Entscheidung über den rechtlichen Rahmen und den zeitlichen Horizont der Nutzung der Kernenergie im Bundesgebiet zu treffen. Damit ist die Regelung des § 2 Abs. 3 HafenBetrG unvereinbar.

Die Norm enthält **eine transportgutspezifische Regelung für Kernbrennstoffe**. Sie bewegt sich daher außerhalb der Kompetenzen des Landesgesetzgebers. Bereits der **Wortlaut des § 2 Abs. 3 HafenbetrG** gibt zu erkennen, dass dessen Regelungsintention sich diametral gegen die durch das Atomgesetz getroffene Grundsatzentscheidung des Bundesgesetzgebers für die Kernenergienutzung richtet und damit in den Anwendungsbereich des Art. 73 Abs. 1 Nr. 14 GG fällt. Nach dem Normtext »ist der Umschlag von Kernbrennstoffen im Sinne des § 2 Abs. 1 des Atomgesetzes ausgeschlossen«, wobei § 2 Abs. 3 Satz 1 HafenbetrG dies mit dem »Interesse einer grundsätzlich auf Nachhaltigkeit und erneuerbarer Energie ausgerichteten Gesamtwirtschaft« begründet. Die Regelung erfasst einen bestimmten Beförderungsweg – die Hafennutzung mit der Verschiffung – für Kernbrennstoffe; sie knüpft gezielt an diesen Energieträger an und greift damit in die Gesetzgebungskompetenz des Bundes ein. Diese Regelungsintention wird durch die in § 2 Abs. 3 Satz 2 HafenbetrG normierten Regelbeispiele bestätigt, für die die Möglichkeit der Erteilung von Ausnahmen von dem kernbrennstoffspezifischen Umschlagsverbot vorgesehen ist. Für Kernbrennstoffe, die im Zusammenhang mit der Kernenergienutzung stehen, benennen zumindest die Regelbeispiele keine ausdrücklichen Ausnahmemöglichkeiten.

Dies spiegeln auch die **Ausführungen in der Gesetzesbegründung** wider. In dieser bekennt sich der Gesetzgeber zu seinen eigenen »energiepolitischen Vorstellungen« und dem »Ausbau der erneuerbaren Energien«.[24] Mit dem »Wandel hin zu einer alternativen Energieerzeugung« sei »der Umschlag von Kernbrennstoffen in Bremischen Häfen […] nicht vereinbar«.[25] Aufgrund der »besonders auf Erneuerbaren Energien fokus-

24 BremBü-Drs. 18/96, 1.

25 BremBü-Drs. 18/96, 1.

sierten Bremischen Gesamtwirtschaft« entstünde ansonsten ein Widerspruch, der »dieser Weiterentwicklung schaden« könnte, wenn die »weiterhin gleichzeitige Nutzung der Hafenanlagen für den Umschlag von Kernbrennstoffen« zugelassen würde.[26]

Was der Bund explizit zulässt, untersagt das Land. Dieser Konflikt wird verfassungsrechtlich auf der Ebene der Kompetenzzuweisung geregelt. Der Bremer Gesetzgeber hat **keine** Kompetenz für diese Regelung.

b) Landesgesetzgeberisches ›Beeinträchtigungsverbot‹ im Bereich der Bundesgesetzgebungskompetenzen

Ein Verstoß gegen die ausschließliche Bundeskompetenz gemäß Art. 71, 73 Abs. 1 Nr. 14 GG ergibt sich noch aus einem weiteren Aspekt. Der Bremische Landesgesetzgeber verfolgt mit § 2 Abs. 3 HafenbetrG **ein eigenes energiepolitisches Konzept**, das im Widerspruch zu den Vorgaben des Gesetzgebers steht. Nach der Rechtsprechung des BVerfGs ist eine solche Beeinträchtigung der Gesetzgebungskompetenzen des Bundes unzulässig.

aa) Kompetenzielles Beeinträchtigungsverbot in der Rechtsprechung des BVerfG

Das Bundesverfassungsgericht hat bereits im Rahmen seiner Volksbefragungsurteile aus dem Jahre 1958 festgestellt, dass das Tätigwerden als Staatsorgan – gleichgültig in welcher Form und mit welcher Wirkung es geschieht – im freiheitlich-demokratischen Rechtsstaat durch Kompetenznormen verfassungsrechtlich begrenzt ist.[27] Das BVerfG sah es in dieser Entscheidung insbesondere als kompetenzwidrig an, auf den Bundesgesetzgeber durch Volksbefragungen politischen Druck auszuüben, um Sachentscheidungen zu ändern.[28]

Umso eher liegt ein verfassungswidriger Eingriff in die ausschließlichen Kompetenzen und Aufgaben des Bundes vor, wenn die Länder »ein Stück dieser Aufgabe dem Bund dadurch entziehen, dass sie selbst es

26 BremBü-Drs. 18/96, 2.
27 BVerfGE 8, 104 (LS 6).
28 BVerfGE 8, 104 (117 f.).

sachlich regeln«.[29] Wie das BVerfG betont, beginnt der verfassungswidrige Eingriff in ausschließliche Bundeskompetenzen jedoch bereits im Vorfeld einer gesetzlichen Regelung. Es erachtet bereits den in einer »amtlichen Volksbefragung liegenden politischen Druck« als hinreichend, um einen justiziablen Eingriff in die Bundeskompetenzen festzustellen. Aus dieser Entscheidung folgt der Grundsatz, dass die Länder die Zuständigkeiten des Bundes **nicht beeinträchtigen** dürfen.[30]

Dieses in der Literatur teilweise als »Ausstrahlungswirkung« bezeichnete Beeinträchtigungsverbot der durch das Grundgesetz zugewiesenen Verbandskompetenzen des Bundes einerseits und der Länder andererseits ist in der Rechtsprechung des BVerfGs auch noch in anderen Konstellationen relevant geworden. So gehört es zu den bundesverfassungsgerichtlich anerkannten Grenzen der Öffentlichkeitsarbeit, »die föderale Kompetenzaufteilung zwischen Bund und Ländern zu wahren«[31] und sich innerhalb der »zugewiesenen Aufgaben- und Zuständigkeitsbereiche zu halten«.[32] Daraus folgt, dass selbst Maßnahmen ohne rechtsverbindlichen Charakter die Grenzen der durch das Grundgesetz gezogenen **Verbandskompetenzen wahren** müssen.

bb) Beeinträchtigung der energiepolitischen Grundsatzentscheidung des Bundes

Auch zu diesen Maßstäben setzt sich das Land Bremen in Widerspruch, indem es seine **eigenen energiepolitischen Vorstellungen** dem Regelungskonzept des Bundes entgegensetzt. Es bezweckt damit, gezielt die entsprechende Zuständigkeit des Bundes zu konterkarieren. Der Bundesgesetzgeber hat sich im Atomgesetz abschließend zu einer zeitlich begrenzten Nutzung der Kernenergie bekannt. Diese energiepolitische Grundsatzentscheidung fügt sich in den Kontext des Energiekonzeptes der Bundesregierung ein, das bestätigend in dem Eckpunktepapier zur Energiewende vom 6. Juni 2011 »Der Weg zur Energie der Zukunft – sicher, bezahlbar und umweltfreundlich« in einer umfassenden Regierungserklä-

29 BVerfGE 8, 104 (LS 7, 117).

30 So im Ergebnis auch *Rengeling*, in: Isensee/Kirchhof, Handbuch des Staatsrechts VI, 3. Aufl. 2008, § 135 Rn. 84; *Kunig*, in: von Münch/Kunig, GG, 6. Aufl. 2012, Art. 71 Rn. 2; *von Komorowski*, Der Staat 37 (1998), 122 (142).

31 BVerfGE 44, 125 (149)

32 BVerfGE 63, 230 (243 f.).

rung skizziert wurde. Dieses Energiekonzept der Bundesregierung verpflichtet sich ebenfalls dem Grundgedanken der Nachhaltigkeit und dem Ausbau der erneuerbaren Energien. Insofern besteht kein grundsätzlicher Zielkonflikt. Die zeitlich begrenzte Fortführung der Nutzung der Kernenergie wird im energiepolitischen Konzept des Bundes als erforderliche »Brückentechnologie« bezeichnet. Die Kernenergie soll weiter genutzt werden, bis eine hinreichend grundlastfähige Energieversorgung aus anderen Energieträgern zur Verfügung steht. Der Bremische Landesgesetzgeber setzt seine energiepolitischen Vorstellungen diesem **bundespolitischen Gesamtkonzept entgegen**. Durch den Ausschluss des Umschlags von Kernbrennstoffen in den Bremischen Häfen maßt sich der Gesetzgeber der Freien Hansestadt Bremen nicht nur eine Regelungskompetenz an, von der der Bund im Rahmen des Atomgesetzes und – in verkehrsrechtlicher Hinsicht – durch die GGV-See erschöpfend Gebrauch gemacht hat. Er **beeinträchtigt** auch die energiepolitische Gesamtkonzeption und greift damit in den Zuständigkeits- und Kompetenzbereich des Bundes ein. Die Nutzung der Kernenergie zur Stromerzeugung setzt voraus, dass die Versorgung mit den hierfür notwendigen Brennstoffen sichergestellt ist und die Entsorgungswege beschritten werden können. Hierzu gehört auch die Nutzung der Verkehrsinfrastruktur.[33] Dem dürfen sich einzelne Länder und Kommunen nicht entgegenstellen. Könnten Länder oder Kommunen für Verkehrsträger wie Straßen, Häfen, Flughäfen etc. auf ihrem Hoheitsgebiet Transporte von Kernbrennstoffen ausschließen, würde die Gesetzgebungskompetenz des Bundes im Ergebnis konterkariert. Die ausschließliche Kompetenz besteht gerade im Interesse einer **bundesweiten** Regelung, die nicht föderal oder lokal parzelliert ist.

Mit der Regelung des § 2 Abs. 3 HafenbetrG unternimmt der Bremische Gesetzgeber letztlich den Versuch, sein Hoheitsgebiet zur »kernbrennstofffreien Zone« zu erklären. Zu vergleichbaren Konstellationen haben das BVerfG und das BVerwG[34] wiederholt entschieden, dass das Agieren von Ländern und Gemeinden auf politischen Feldern, die kompetenziell dem Bund zugewiesen sind, verfassungsrechtliche Kompetenz-Grenzen überschreitet. Diesen verfassungsrechtlichen Grenzen widerspricht der Bremische Landesgesetzgeber im Zuge des Umschlagsverbots für Kernbrennstoffe, mit dem er »das Ziel einer neuen Energie-, Umwelt-

33 *Lagoni*, NordÖR 2012, 335 (336).

34 BVerfGE 122 (136) – Volksbefragungsurteil; BVerfGE 79, 127 (146 f.); BVerwGE 87, 228 (235) – Atomwaffenfreie Zone.

und Wirtschaftspolitik«[35] verfolgt. Es besteht zwar kein absolutes Verbot, sich mit Themenbereichen zu befassen, die in die Kompetenz eines anderen Hoheitsträgers – insbesondere des Bundes – fallen. Voraussetzung ist jedoch ein konkreter örtlicher Bezug zum jeweiligen Hoheitsgebiet, der aber nicht zum Vorwand dienen darf, ein allgemeinpolitisches Mandat wahrzunehmen. An die Grenzen der verfassungsrechtlich zugewiesenen Kompetenzbereiche stoßen Länder und Gemeinden dann, wenn sie einer politischen, noch dazu normativ verfestigten Grundsatzentscheidung des Bundes aktiv entgegentreten.

2. Verstoß gegen den rechtsstaatlichen Grundsatz der Widerspruchsfreiheit der Rechtsordnung

Die Regelung des § 2 Abs. 3 Hafenbetriebsgesetz ist auch mit dem verfassungsrechtlichen Grundsatz der **Widerspruchsfreiheit der Rechtsordnung** unvereinbar.

2.1 Das Gebot der Widerspruchsfreiheit als Kompetenzausübungsschranke

Der Grundsatz der Widerspruchsfreiheit der Rechtsordnung verbietet es, Normen zu erlassen, die sich zu einem bestehenden Gesamtkonzept des Bundesgesetzgebers in Widerspruch setzen, dieses verfälschen oder in eine abweichende Richtung lenken. Ein Umschlagsverbot von Kernbrennstoffen in den Bremischen Häfen begründet einen klar konturierten inhaltlichen **Widerspruch** zu den bundesgesetzlichen Regelungen über die Beförderung und den Transport von Kernbrennstoffen und die allgemeine energiepolitische Grundsatzentscheidung des Bundes über die Kernenergienutzung.

Das BVerfG hat das Gebot der Widerspruchsfreiheit der Rechtsordnung vor allem in seiner Entscheidung zur Verpackungssteuer der Stadt Kassel entfaltet[36] und in den Urteilen zu den Landesabfallabgabengesetzen[37] und zum Bayerischen Schwangerenhilfe-Ergänzungsgesetz[38] konkretisiert. Die

35 BremBÜ-Drs. 18/96, 2.
36 BVerfGE 98, 83 ff.
37 BVerfGE 98, 106 ff.
38 BVerfGE 98, 265 ff.

verfassungsrechtliche Wurzel liegt in den Prinzipien des Bundesstaates und des Rechtsstaats.[39] Bund und Länder sind verpflichtet, ihre Regelungen inhaltlich und konzeptionell aufeinander abzustimmen. Insbesondere dem Landesgesetzgeber ist es untersagt, ein durch den Bundesgesetzgeber normiertes Regelungskonzept durch den Erlass eigener Rechtsnormen **zu konterkarieren** oder zu verfälschen. In diesem Sinne betont das BVerfG, der Landesgesetzgeber darf nur insoweit lenkend und gestaltend in den Kompetenzbereich des Gesetzgebers eingreifen, »als die Lenkung weder der Gesamtkonzeption der sachlichen Regelung noch konkreten Einzelregelungen zuwider läuft.«[40] Das Rechtsstaatsprinzip und die bundesstaatliche Kompetenzordnung verpflichten damit »alle rechtssetzenden Organe des Bundes und der Länder, die Regelungen jeweils so aufeinander abzustimmen, dass die Normadressaten nicht gegenläufige Regelungen erreichen, die die Rechtsordnung widersprüchlich machen«.[41] Diese Kompetenzausübungsschranke stellt nicht nur Anforderungen an den Bundes- und Landesgesetzgeber auf, keine Normbefehle zu erlassen, die aus der Perspektive des Normadressaten widersprüchliche Handlungsgebote oder auch nur Handlungsanreize erzeugen. Dem Landesgesetzgeber ist es bereits verwehrt, durch seine Entscheidung das Gesamtkonzept des Bundesgesetzgebers auch nur zu verfälschen[42] oder in eine abweichende Richtung zu lenken.[43]

2.2 Widerspruch des Umschlagsverbots zu den bundesgesetzlichen Vorgaben

§ 2 Abs. 3 HafenbetrG ist mit diesem Gebot unvereinbar. Der **Bundesgesetzgeber** hat im Rahmen seiner Zuständigkeit gemäß Art. 73 Abs. 1 Nr. 14 GG die Umstände für die friedliche Nutzung der Kernenergie und den darüber hinausgehenden Umgang mit Kernbrennstoffen umfassend normativ geregelt. In den bundesgesetzlichen Regelungen finden sich u. a. die wesentlichen rechtlichen Voraussetzungen über die **Beförderung** von Kernbrennstoffen. Transport und Beförderung sind unentbehrlicher Be-

39 BVerfGE 98, 106 (119); 98, 265 (301); 98, 83 (97).
40 BVerfGE 98, 106 (118 f.).
41 BVerfGE 98, 106 (119); 98, 265 (301); 98, 83 (97).
42 BVerfGE 98, 265 (301).
43 Vgl. *Sodan/Kluckert*, NVwZ 2012, 241 (243 f.); *Frenz*, DÖV 1999, 41 (43 ff.); *Weidemann*, DVBl 1999, 73 (74 ff.); *Bothe*, NJW 1998, 2333; dazu auch *Birk/Kolusa*, FR 1999, 433 (436).

standteil für die Umsetzung dieses Energiekonzepts. Gleichzeitig wird die Frage der Endlagerung und Entsorgung kernbrennstoffhaltiger Abfälle noch auf lange Sicht den Transport und die Beförderung von Kernbrennstoffen unumgänglich und erforderlich machen. Ferner ist die Nukleartechnik ein rechtlich anerkannter und zulässiger Wirtschaftsfaktor im Hochtechnologie-Land der Bundesrepublik Deutschland. Für den Im- und Export kerntechnischer Güter hat der Bundesgesetzgeber kein grundsätzliches Verbot ausgesprochen.

Das Umschlagsverbot nach § 2 Abs. 3 HafenbetrG verfolgt hingegen die offenkundige Intention, die bundespolitische Grundsatzentscheidung und deren gesetzgeberische Umsetzung über den Umgang mit der Kernenergie und die Handhabung von Kernbrennstoffen zu unterlaufen, ja, gezielt gegenzusteuern. Das gilt namentlich für den Ex- und Import. Es handelt sich um keine Regelung mit örtlich begrenzter Wirkung, die eine verkehrsträgerbezogene funktionale Regelungswirkung bezweckt. Vielmehr wird eine spezifisch transportgutbezogene Verbotswirkung statuiert, die im Widerspruch zur bundestaatlichen Rechtsordnung steht. Das übergreifende Prinzip der Widerspruchsfreiheit der Rechtsordnung wäre grundlegend verletzt, könnten Länder und Gemeinden für jeden in ihre Zuständigkeit fallenden Verkehrsträger die zulässigen Transportgüter nach freier politischer Einschätzung definieren. Die bundesstaatliche Rechts- und Wirtschaftseinheit wäre grundlegend gefährdet und bundesweite Transporte und Beförderungen maßgeblich erschwert, ohne dass es eines verfassungsrechtlich legitimen Grundes bedürfte. Dies ist mit der Konzeption des Grundgesetzes und der übergreifenden bundesstaatlichen Ordnung nicht zu vereinbaren.

3. Verstoß gegen den verfassungsrechtlichen Grundsatz der Bundestreue

Die Regelung des § 2 Abs. 3 HafenbetrG verstößt zudem gegen den verfassungsrechtlichen Grundsatz der Bundestreue.

3.1 Allgemeine Bindung des Landesgesetzgebers an den Grundsatz der Bundestreue

Im Bundesstaat bestehen zwischen den einzelnen Untergliederungen übergreifende Rücksichtnahmepflichten. Dies bedeutet zugleich ein Verbot, die bundesstaatliche Kompetenzverteilung zu umgehen oder zu konterkarieren.

Das Gebot der Bundestreue ist in der verfassungsgerichtlichen Rechtsprechung anerkannt.[44] Dieser Grundsatz wird unmittelbar aus dem Bundesstaatsprinzip als **ungeschriebener Verfassungsgrundsatz** abgeleitet.[45] Er verpflichtet den Bund und die Länder zu **wechselseitiger Rücksichtnahme** im Rahmen der bundesstaatlichen Ordnung, wie sie das Grundgesetz ausgestaltet. Diese gegenseitige Rücksichtnahmepflicht erstreckt sich auf sämtliche Bereiche staatlichen Handelns durch die Organe des Bundes und der Länder. Diese Pflicht verlangt, dass sowohl der Bund als auch die Länder bei der Wahrnehmung ihrer Kompetenzen die gebotene und ihnen zumutbare Rücksicht auf das Gesamtinteresse des Bundesstaates und auf die Belange von Bund und Ländern nehmen.[46] Die Verwaltungsbehörden, die Regierungen der Länder und die gesetzgebenden Organe unterliegen damit dem Gebot, die abstrakten Kompetenzbereiche und insbesondere bereits konkret getroffene Maßnahmen der Instanzen der jeweils anderen Ebene zu achten und widersprechende oder widersprüchliche Rechtsakte zu unterlassen. Dieses Prinzip wirkt damit vor allem als Kompetenzausübungsschranke.[47]

Letztlich lässt sich dieser Grundsatz auf den allgemeineren, die Rechtsordnung insgesamt prägenden Grundsatz des **Missbrauchsverbots** zurückführen.[48] Bund und Länder haben hiernach Rechtsakte zu unterlassen, die kompetenzgemäße Maßnahmen der jeweils anderen Ebene in ihren Rechtswirkungen konterkarieren. Dies bedeutet zugleich ein **Umgehungsverbot**. Das Missbrauchsverbot erfasst damit nicht nur Handlungsweisen, die sich unmittelbar auf dieselbe Materie beziehen oder am selben Umstand anknüpfen. Auch mittelbare Wirkungen werden erfasst. Insofern reicht der Grundsatz der Bundestreue über die bloße Abgrenzung von

44 St. Rspr. seit BVerfGE 1, 299 (315); vgl. ferner exemplarisch BVerfGE 12, 205 (254); 32, 199 (218); 43, 291 (348); 104, 249 (269 f.).

45 *Herzog/Grzeszick*, in: Maunz/Dürig, GG, Stand: 66. EL (2012), Art. 20 Rn. 118 ff.

46 BVerfGE 81, 310 (337); vgl. ferner BVerfGE 12, 205 (254); 32, 199 (218); 43, 291 (348); 104, 249 (269 f.).

47 BVerfGE 12, 205 (235); 14, 197 (215); 43, 291 (348); *Isensee*, in: Isensee/Kirchhof, Handbuch des Staatsrechts VI, 3. Aufl. 2008, § 126 Rn. 167; *Hofmann*, in: Schmidt-Bleibtreu/Hofmann/Hopfauf, GG, 12. Aufl. 2011, Art. 20 Rn. 15.

48 BVerfGE 12, 205 (239 f.); 61, 149 (205); *Degenhart*, in: Sachs, GG, 6. Aufl. 2011, Art. 70 Rn. 74; *Rengeling*, in: Isensee/Kirchhof, Handbuch des Staatsrechts VI, 3. Aufl. 2008, § 135 Rn. 15.

Kompetenzbereichen hinaus. Auch wenn nur mittelbar Anreizwirkungen einen Lebensbereich betreffen, der unter die verfassungsrechtlich zugewiesene Kompetenz eines anderen Hoheitsträgers fallen, greift das bundesstaatliche Gebot der Rücksichtnahme. Aus der Perspektive des Bürgers sollen die Rechtsakte des Bundes und der Länder sich wie Bestandteile eines in sich schlüssigen Gesamtkonzepts zusammenfügen.

3.2 Keine Kompetenzerweiterung durch das Widmungsrecht

Der Landesgesetzgeber widerspricht dem Gebot der Bundestreue, wenn er unter dem Deckmantel des Widmungsrechts in verfassungswidriger Weise die bundesstaatliche Kompetenzordnung zu umgehen versucht.

Eine Regelungskompetenz der Freien Hansestadt Bremen für das Umschlagsverbot in den Bremischen Häfen lässt sich – entgegen wiederholter Äußerungen im Rahmen des Gesetzgebungsverfahrens – **nicht** etwa aus Gesichtspunkten des Widmungsrechts ableiten. Zutreffend ist zwar, dass die Bremischen Universalhäfen als öffentliche Sachen der grundsätzlichen **Widmungskompetenz** der Gebietskörperschaft des Belegenheitsorts unterliegen. Dies sind grundsätzlich die Stadtgemeinden Bremen und Bremerhaven (Art. 143 Abs. 1, 144 BremLV), was eine einheitliche gesetzliche Widmung durch die Freie Hansestadt Bremen als Land nach dem Hafenbetriebsgesetz nicht grundsätzlich ausschließt. Allerdings unterliegt ein gesetzlicher Rechtsakt im Zusammenhang mit der Widmung einer öffentlichen Sache wie die Widmung selbst den allgemeinen verfassungsrechtlichen **Grenzen der bundesstaatlichen Kompetenzordnung**,[49] ebenso den verfassungsrechtlichen Geboten der Widerspruchsfreiheit der Rechtsordnung und der Bundestreue. Mit allen drei Geboten steht der normative Widmungsakt im Widerspruch. Der Widmungsakt widerspricht funktional den bundesrechtlichen Vorgaben. Der Landesgesetzgeber kann nicht ge-

49 Im Ergebnis in gleicher Weise, wenn man die Einschränkung der Hafennutzung nicht über eine Beschränkung der Widmung regelte, sondern diese Nutzungsregelung qualifiziert. Es spricht manches für die Auffassung, dass es hier um das »Wie« der Nutzbarkeit der Bremischen Häfen geht. Die Modalitäten der Nutzung ist jedoch der Benutzungsordnung der öffentlichen Sache vorbehalten. Dies ist vom zugrunde liegenden Widmungsakt zu unterscheiden, vgl. *Axer*, Die Widmung als Schlüsselbegriff des öffentlichen Rechts der öffentlichen Sachen, 1994, S. 184 f. Am Ergebnis ändert sich nichts. Auch die Benutzungsordnung ist in gleicher Weise wie die Widmung den verfassungsrechtlichen Grenzen der Kompetenzordnung und des bundesfreundlichen Verhaltens unterworfen.

zielt durch eine einschränkende Widmung von Verkehrsträgern bundesrechtlich zugelassene Verkehrsvorgänge ausschließen,[50] wenn jedenfalls die (neue) Widmung – ebenso wie eine möglicherweise geregelte Nutzungsbeschränkung – nicht unmittelbar sachlich-funktional, örtlich konkret begründet wird, sondern sie instrumentell eingesetzt wird, um die Entscheidung des kompetenziell zuständigen Bundesgesetzgebers zu unterlaufen oder einzuschränken. Das widerspricht der Kompetenzordnung und der bundesrechtlichen Regelung. Die Änderung des Hafenbetriebsgesetzes ist deshalb verfassungswidrig.

III. Unvereinbarkeit mit dem Recht der Europäischen Union

§ 2 Abs. 3 HafenbetrG ist mit dem Recht der Europäischen Union unvereinbar. Es verletzt die Warenverkehrsfreiheit, darüber hinaus auch die Dienstleistungsfreiheit.

1. Bindung des Landesgesetzgebers an das Unionsrecht

Die Mitgliedstaaten der Europäischen Union sind dazu verpflichtet, das **höherrangige Recht der Union** zu beachten. Das gilt für alle staatlichen Organe und Einrichtungen, unabhängig von der föderalen Struktur. Alle innerstaatlichen Rechtsakte und Vorschriften, gleich welcher Ebene und gleich welcher Behörde oder Körperschaft, müssen im Einklang mit den unionsrechtlichen Vorschriften stehen, und zwar sowohl den primären wie dem sekundären Gemeinschaftsrecht. Die unionsrechtlichen Bindungen gelten innerhalb eines Mitgliedstaates für alle föderalen (Unter-) Gliederungen und deren Rechtsakte.[51] Die innerstaatliche Bindung der Bundesländer und aller anderen rechtssetzenden (Gebiets-)Körperschaften an das Recht der Europäischen Union ergibt sich aus der Integrationsklausel des Art. 23 Abs. 1 GG, ferner aus dem verfassungsrechtlichen Gebot der Bundestreue und dem Gebot der loyalen Zusammenarbeit gemäß Art. 4 Abs. 3 EUV.

---

50 Ebenso *Schwarz*, DÖV 2012, 457 (462), der ausdrücklich von einer Verletzung des Grundsatzes der Bundestreue spricht. *Papier*, in: Erichsen/Ehlers; Allgemeines Verwaltungsrecht, 14. Aufl. 2010, § 40 Rn. 59.

51 So in st. Rspr. der EuGH, vgl. nur Rs. C-74/89, *Kommission/Belgien*, Slg. 1990, 491; Rs. C-87/02, *Kommission/Italien*, Slg. 2004, I-5975 Rn. 38.

2. Unvereinbarkeit mit der Warenverkehrsfreiheit

Das Umschlagsverbot gemäß § 2 Abs. 3 HafenbetrG ist mit der Garantie des freien Warenverkehrs, Art. 93 EAGV, Art. 34 AEUV unvereinbar.

2.1 Gleichklang der Grundfreiheiten nach dem Euratom-Vertrag (EAGV) und nach AEUV

Art. 93 EAGV enthält gegenüber Art. 34 AEUV eine spezielle Regelung der Warenverkehrsfreiheit für die in den Listen A1, A2 und B im Anhang IV zum EAGV aufgeführten Erzeugnisse. Das entspricht dem durch Art. 92 EAGV definierten Anwendungsbereich dieses speziellen Vertrages. Ob **Kernbrennstoffe** darunter fallen, ist umstritten.[52] Die in Anhang IV zum EAGV aufgeführten Erzeugnisse erwähnen Kernbrennstoffe nicht ausdrücklich, obwohl im Übrigen auch einzelne Stoffverbindungen und -legierungen sehr detailliert aufgelistet werden. Da Kernbrennstoffe in dieser detaillierten Auflistung nicht ausdrücklich genannt sind, liegt es zumindest nahe, dass sie nicht in den Anwendungsbereich des EURATOM-Vertrages fallen.[53]

Im Ergebnis ist es **unerheblich**, ob der Umschlag von Kernbrennstoffen durch die allgemeinen Bestimmungen über die Warenverkehrsfreiheit nach Art. 34 ff. AEUV oder die spezielle Normierung in Art. 93 EAGV erfasst wird. Für die **Warenverkehrsfreiheit** gelten sowohl im Anwendungsbereich des AEUV als auch des EAGV **dieselben Maßstäbe**: Mengenmäßige Beschränkungen sind ebenso wie Maßnahmen gleicher Wirkung grundsätzlich untersagt. Schließlich sieht Art. 2 lit. g) EAGV für den EURATOM-Vertrag eine Orientierung am gemeinsamen Markt vor, in dem zwangsläufig auch Maßnahmen gleicher Wirkung in den Schutzbereich der Grundfreiheiten einzubeziehen sind.[54] Dies bestätigt Art. 106a

52 Vgl. hierzu *Koenig/Müller*, EuZW 2007, 139 (141); *Everling*, RIW 1993 / Beilage 2 zu Heft 3, S. 3 f., *Epiney*, in: Ehlers, Europäische Grundrechte und Grundfreiheiten, 3. Aufl. 2009, § 8 Rn. 13; *von Komorowski*, NuR 2000, 432 (433); *Wahl/Hermes*, Nationale Kernenergiepolitik und Gemeinschaftsrecht, 1995, S. 126 ff.

53 So auch *Wahl/Hermes*, Nationale Kernenergiepolitik und Gemeinschaftsrecht, 1995, S. 126; *von Komorowski*, NuR 2000, 432 (433).

54 Vgl. hierzu *Leible/T. Streinz, in:* Grabitz/Hilf/Nettesheim, Das Recht der Europäischen Union, Stand: 48. EL (2012), Art. 34 AEUV Rn. 9; ähnlich *Schroeder*, in: Streinz, EUV/AEUV, 2. Aufl. 2012, Art. 34 AEUV Rn. 10.

Abs. 3 EAGV, wonach zwischen den Gewährleistungen des AEUV und des EAGV keine Abweichungen bestehen. Es entspricht insofern der allgemeinen Auffassung, dass die Warenverkehrsfreiheit sowohl im Anwendungsbereich des EAGV als auch des AEUV in gleicher Weise mengenmäßige Beschränkungen ebenso wie Maßnahmen gleicher Wirkung erfasst.[55] Es gelten die allgemeinen Maßstäbe der Warenverkehrsfreiheit.[56]

2.2 Schutzbereich der Warenverkehrsfreiheit

Die Warenverkehrsfreiheit ist eine der Grundlagen der Gemeinschaft[57] und von wesentlicher Bedeutung für die Verwirklichung des gemeinsamen (Binnen-)Marktes. Die Warenverkehrsfreiheit verbietet den Mitgliedstaaten, mengenmäßige Beschränkungen oder Maßnahmen mit gleicher Wirkung aufzustellen. Sie dient dem Schutz des (möglichst) ungehinderten grenzüberschreitenden Verkehrs von Waren innerhalb der Europäischen Union.[58] In Abgrenzung zu den übrigen Grundfreiheiten bezieht sich die Warenverkehrsfreiheit auf »Waren« im unionsrechtlichen Sinne. **Waren** sind Erzeugnisse, die einen Geldwert haben und daher Gegenstand von

55 Vgl. hierzu *Leible/T. Streinz, in:* Grabitz/Hilf/Nettesheim, Das Recht der Europäischen Union, Stand: 48. EL (2012), Art. 34 AEUV Rn. 9; ähnlich *Schroeder*, in: Streinz, EUV/AEUV, 2. Aufl. 2012, Art. 34 AEUV Rn. 10; *Papenkort*, Der EURATOM-Vertrag im Lichte des Vertrages über die Verfassung von Europa, 2008, S. 43 f.; *Di Fabio*, Der Ausstieg aus der wirtschaftlichen Nutzung der Kernenergie, 1999, S. 58 ff.; *Denninger*, Verfassungsrechtliche Fragen des Ausstiegs aus der Nutzung der Kernenergie zur Stromerzeugung, 2000, S. 32 ff., *Hellfahrt,* Rechtsfragen des Atomausstiegs, 2003, S. 228 ff.; *Scheuing*, EUR 2000, 1 (19)*; ders.*, in: Bayer/Huber, Rechtsfragen zum Atomausstieg, 2000, 87 (115 ff.); *Koenig/Müller*, EUZW 2007, 193 (141).

56 Legt man – entgegen der hier vertretenen Auffassung – den Schutzbereich des Art. 93 EAGV enger aus als in Art. 34 AEUV, hat dies dennoch keinen weiterreichenden Einfluss auf die Prüfungsmaßstäbe. Sollte Art. 93 EAGV keine Maßnahmen gleicher Wirkung erfassen, finden in diesem Bereich jedenfalls die subsidiären Regelungen des Art. 34 ff. AEUV zumindest ergänzende Anwendung. Vgl. hierzu *Schroeder*, in: Streinz, EUV/AEUV, 2. Aufl. 2012, Art. 34 AEUV Rn. 10; *Everling*, RIW 1993, Beilage 2 zu Heft 3, 1 (4); ebenso *Schwarz*, NordÖR 2012, 331 (333).

57 EuGH, Rs. 37/83, Slg. 1984, 1229 (LS2); *Kingreen*, in: Calliess/Ruffert, EUV/AEUV, 4. Aufl. 2011, Art. 34 bis 36 Rn. 117.

58 *Schroeder*, in: Streinz, EUV/AEUV, 2. Aufl. 2012, Art. 34 AEUV Rn. 18.

Handelsgeschäften sein können.[59] Unter den weiten Warenbegriff fallen nach der Rechtsprechung des Europäischen Gerichtshofes selbst Abfälle, unabhängig von der Frage ihrer Wiederverwertbarkeit und ob sie einen positiven oder negativen Handelswert haben.[60] Der Schutzbereich der Grundfreiheiten erfordert schließlich einen grenzüberschreitenden Bezug.[61]

Kernbrennstoffe sind **Waren** im Sinne der Warenverkehrsfreiheit. Unerheblich ist in diesem Zusammenhang, dass die Kernbrennstoffe nach Art. 86 EAGV im Eigentum der Gemeinschaft stehen. Es kommt insoweit nur auf den ›Waren‹-Charakter an und dass sie Gegenstand von Handelsgeschäften sein können. Wer dinglich Eigentümer ist, spielt in diesem Zusammenhang keine Rolle. Brennelemente, die für den Einsatz in Kernkraftwerken vorgesehen sind, sind eine grenzüberschreitend national wie international gehandelte Ware. Nichts anderes gilt für kernbrennstoffhaltige Abfälle aus der Wiederaufarbeitung. Sie werden vom Schutzbereich der Warenverkehrsfreiheit erfasst. Mit dem Umschlag in den Bremischen Häfen wird schließlich ein grenzüberschreitender Transport und Handel bezweckt.

2.3 Beeinträchtigung der Warenverkehrsfreiheit

Eine unzulässige Beeinträchtigung der Warenverkehrsfreiheit liegt bei mengenmäßigen Beschränkungen der Ein- oder Ausfuhr oder bei Maßnahmen gleicher Wirkung vor. Da die sog. **Maßnahmen gleicher Wirkung** mit den mengenmäßigen Beschränkungen **gleichbehandelt** werden, kommt es auf eine Abgrenzung nicht an, insbesondere nicht auf die Frage, ob das Nutzungsverbot des Hafens – gewissermaßen die »Nullmenge« – als mengenmäßige Beschränkung anzusehen ist. Der EUGH hat den Begriff der »Maßnahme gleicher Wirkung« in ständiger Rechtsprechung seit

59 EuGH, Rs. 7/68, *Kommission/Italien*, Slg. 1968, 633 (642); Rs. C-65/05, *Kommission/Griechenland*, Slg. 2006, I-10341 Rn. 23; *Schroeder*, in: Streinz, EUV/AEUV, 2. Aufl. 2012, Art. 34 AEUV Rn. 19.

60 EuGH, Rs. C-2/90, *Kommission/Belgien*, Slg. 1992, I-4431 Rn. 28; *Kingreen*, in: Calliess/Ruffert, EUV/AEUV, 4. Aufl. 2011, Art. 34 bis 36 AEUV, Rn. 120; EuGH, Rs. C-324/93, *Evans*, Slg. 1995, I-563 Rn. 20; *Leible/T. Streinz*, in: Grabitz/Hilf/Nettesheim, Das Recht der Europäischen Union, 48. EL (2012), Art. 34 AEUV Rn. 28.

61 *Leible/T. Streinz*, in: Grabitz/Hilf/Nettesheim, Das Recht der Europäischen Union, 48. EL (2012), Art. 34 AEUV Rn. 33.

der sog. Leitentscheidung **Dassonville** weit ausgelegt. Als Maßnahme gleicher Wirkung werden **alle** Regelungen der Mitgliedstaaten qualifiziert, die »geeignet [sind] den innergemeinschaftlichen Handel unmittelbar oder mittelbar, tatsächlich oder potentiell zu behindern«.[62] Eine spezifische Handelsregelung ist nicht erforderlich, auch eine innerstaatliche Nutzungsregelung oder ein Widmungsakt reichen aus, wenn sie geeignet sind, den Handel zu beeinträchtigen. Hinreichend ist jede **potenzielle Eignung** der Behinderung des unionsweiten Handels, ohne dass tatsächlich negative Folgen nachweislich eintreten müssen.[63] Eine hinreichende Beeinträchtigung kann auch dann vorliegen, wenn nur Teile des deutschen Staatsgebietes – wie einzelne Länder oder Gemeinden – durch eine Maßnahme gleicher Wirkung betroffen sind.[64] Es reicht eine – potentiell – **objektiv geringfügige**, geradezu marginale Beeinträchtigung aus; sie muss nicht gravierend oder spürbar sein. Bei Transportregeln oder Grenzformalitäten etwa liegt eine relevante Beeinträchtigung selbst dann vor, wenn andere Vertriebsmöglichkeiten oder Transportwege bestehen.[65]

Das Umschlagsverbot für Kernbrennstoffe gemäß § 2 Abs. 3 HafenbetrG enthält eine solche Beeinträchtigung der Warenverkehrsfreiheit. Der Umschlag in den Bremischen Häfen ist regelhaft mit der grenzüberschreitenden Verbringung von Waren verbunden. Das Umschlagsverbot für eine bestimmte Ware – wie Kernbrennstoffe – ist nicht nur eine potentielle, sondern eine unmittelbare und tatsächliche Behinderung und Beschränkung des unionsweiten freien Warenverkehrs. Denn der Unternehmer (Transporteur / Beförderer) muss sich für seine Ware einen anderen Hafen suchen, als dies sonst seinem wirtschaftlichen Kalkül oder seinen freien unternehmerischen Entscheidung entspräche. Der Warenverkehr wird gelenkt und damit beeinträchtigt.

62 EuGH, Rs. C-8/74, *Dassonville*, Slg. 1974, 837 Rn. 5; grundlegend hierzu *Dauses/Brigola*, in: Dauses, EU-Wirtschaftsrecht, Stand: 31. EL (2012), C. Rn. 90 ff.

63 *Kingreen*, in: Calliess/Ruffert, EUV/AEUV, 4. Aufl. 2011, Art. 34-36 AEUV Rn. 37; *Oppermann/Classen/Nettesheim*, Europarecht, 5. Aufl. 2011, S. 401.

64 EuGH, Rs. C-67/97, *Bluhme*, Slg. 1998, I-8033 Rn. 19 f.; verb. Rs. C-1/90 u. C-167/90, Slg. 1991, I-4151 Rn. 24; Rs. C-277/91 u.a., Slg. 1993, I-6621 Rn. 36; *Schroeder*, in: Streinz, EUV / AEUV, 2. Aufl. 2012, Art. 34 AEUV Rn. 33.

65 EuGH, Rs. 177 u. 178/82, *van de Haar*, Slg. 1984, 1797 Rn. 14; *Lux*, in: Lenz/Borchardt, EU-Verträge, 6. Aufl. 2013, Art. 34 AEUV Rn. 28.

2.4 Keine Rechtfertigung der Beeinträchtigung der Warenverkehrsfreiheit

§ 2 Abs. 3 HafenbetrG führt zu einer Beeinträchtigung der Warenverkehrsfreiheit. Diese Beeinträchtigung ist sachlich nicht gerechtfertigt. Eine sachliche Rechtfertigung ergibt sich weder aus den in Art. 36 AEUV geregelten Rechtfertigungsgründen noch aus sonstigen anzuerkennenden »zwingenden Erfordernissen«.

a) Keine Rechtfertigung nach Art. 36 AEUV

Eine sachliche Rechtfertigung auf Grundlage des Art. 36 AEUV setzt voraus, dass eines der dort **genannten Rechtsgüter** geschützt werden soll.[66] Art. 36 AEUV nennt als mögliche Rechtfertigungsgründe u. a. die öffentliche Ordnung und Sicherheit, den Schutz der Gesundheit und des Lebens von Menschen, Tieren oder Pflanzen. Keines der aufgeführten Schutzgüter ist hier einschlägig.

Der Rechtfertigungsgrund des Schutzes der **öffentlichen Ordnung** wird durch den EuGH restriktiv ausgelegt; anerkannt werden lediglich »staatliche Interessen von fundamentaler Bedeutung«.[67] Erforderlich ist darüber hinaus die tatsächliche und hinreichend schwere Gefährdung eines gesellschaftlichen Grundinteresses.[68] In engem inhaltlichen Zusammenhang mit diesem Rechtfertigungsgrund steht das Schutzgut der **öffentlichen Sicherheit**. Hierauf kann sich eine Rechtfertigung jedoch nur stützen, wenn die angeführten Gründe »wesentlich sind für die Existenz des Staates«.[69] Dies kommt nach der Rechtsprechung des EuGH in Betracht,

66 *Leible/T. Streinz*, in: Grabitz/Hilf/Nettesheim, Das Recht der Europäischen Union, Stand: 48. EL (2012), Art. 36 AEUV Rn. 1; *Kingreen*, in: Calliess/Ruffert, EUV/AEUV, 4. Aufl. 2011, Art. 34-36 AEUV Rn. 76.

67 EuGH, Rs. C-229/83, *Leclerc*, Slg. 1985, 1 Rn. 30; Rs. 177/83, *Kohl*, Slg. 1984, 3651 Rn. 19; Rs. 16/83, *Prantl*, Slg. 1984, 1299 Rn. 33; *Leible/T. Streinz*, in: Grabitz/Hilf/Nettesheim, Das Recht der Europäischen Union, Stand: 48. EL (2012), Art. 36 AEUV Rn. 20.

68 *Leible/T. Streinz*, in: Grabitz/Hilf/Nettesheim, Das Recht der Europäischen Union, Stand: 48. EL (2012), Art. 36 AEUV Rn. 20.

69 EuGH, Rs. C-72/83, *Campus Oil*, Slg. 1984, 2727 Rn. 34.

wenn das Funktionieren seiner Wirtschaft, seiner Einrichtungen, die öffentlichen Dienste oder das Leben der Bevölkerung betroffen sind.[70]

Weder der Schutz der öffentlichen Ordnung, noch der Schutz der öffentlichen Sicherheit können die Beeinträchtigungen der Warenverkehrsfreiheit durch das Umschlagsverbot für Kernbrennstoffe rechtfertigen. Durch den Umschlag von Kernbrennstoffen werden weder die Bundesrepublik Deutschland noch das Land Bremen gefährdet, ebenso wenig die dort lebenden Menschen. Die Anforderungen an die Sicherheit des Transports sind bundesgesetzlich abschließend geregelt – es gilt ein auch nach internationalen Maßstäben sehr hohes Sicherheits- und Schutzniveau. Das ist unstreitig. Auch Gefahren für das Funktionieren der Wirtschaft sind nicht ersichtlich. Insbesondere ist nicht erkennbar, welche Beeinträchtigung für den Wirtschaftszweig der Erneuerbaren Energien konkret durch den Umschlag von Kernbrennstoffen eintreten sollte, – von einer existenziellen Gefahrenlage ganz zu schweigen. Das gilt ebenso für die anderen potenziellen Schutzgüter. Es gibt keine konkrete Gefährdung irgendeines Schutzgutes.

Der EuGH räumt den Mitgliedstaaten in dieser Hinsicht zwar grundsätzlich einen weiten Beurteilungs- und Gestaltungsspielraum ein.[71] Die Mitgliedstaaten trifft aber eine »Darlegungs- und Beweislast« – sie müssen den Nachweis einer entsprechenden Gefahr führen. Bloße Vermutungen oder Behauptungen sind nicht hinreichend.[72] Grundlage müssen wissenschaftliche Erkenntnisse oder auf europäischen oder internationalen Schutzstandards beruhende konkrete Erwägungen sein.[73] Insofern gilt: Für die Gefahrenanalyse und Risikobewertung im Zusammenhang mit Kernbrennstoffen hat der **Bundesgesetzgeber** abschließende Regelungen getroffen. Für das Genehmigungsverfahren nach § 4 AtG ist das Bundesamt für Strahlenschutz zuständig. Beim Umschlag von Kernbrennstoffen in den Bremischen Häfen bestehen keine nachweisbaren tatsächlichen Gefahren, auf die sich das Umschlagsverbot stützen ließe. Es gelten allein die

---

70 EuGH, Rs. C-72/83, *Campus Oil*, Slg. 1984, 2727 Rn. 34; *Schroeder*, in: Streinz, EUV/AEUV, 2. Aufl. 2012, Art. 36 AEUV Rn. 12.

71 EuGH, Rs. C-104/75, *De Peijper*, Slg. 1976, 613 Rn. 14, 18.

72 EuGH, Rs. C-228/91, *Kommission/Italien*, Slg. 1993, I-2701 Rn. 28; *Leible/T. Streinz*, in: Grabitz/Hilf/Nettesheim, Das Recht der Europäischen Union, Stand: 48. EL (2012), Art. 36 AEUV Rn. 23.

73 EuGH, Rs. C-473/98, *Toolex Alpha*, Slg. 2000, I-561 Rn. 40 ff; Rs. C-178/84, *Kommission/Deutschland*, Slg. 1987, 1227 Rn. 44; Rs. C-17/93, *Van der Veldt*, Slg. 1994, I-3537 Rn. 17; Rs. C-420/01, *Kommission/Italien*, Slg. 2003, I-6445 Rn. 30; C-270/02, *Kommission/Italien*, Slg. 2004, I-1559 Rn. 22 ff.; *Schroeder*, in: Streinz, EUV/AEUV, 2. Aufl. 2012, Art. 36 Rn. 14.

Maßstäbe des § 4 Abs. 2 Nr. 3 AtG. Und danach liegt bei diesen Transportvorgängen keine – auch unter Berücksichtigung der gebotenen Vorsorge – Gefahr vor.

b) Keine Rechtfertigung nach den Cassis de Dijon-Grundsätzen

Schließlich ist auch keine sachliche Rechtfertigung des Umschlagsverbots für Kernbrennstoffe nach den Grundsätzen der **Cassis de Dijon-Formel** zu erkennen. Nach diesen Grundsätzen können Maßnahmen gleicher Wirkung durch **zwingende Erfordernisse** des Handelsverkehrs gerechtfertigt werden, insbesondere aufgrund von Erfordernissen einer wirksamen steuerlichen Kontrolle, des Schutzes der öffentlichen Gesundheit, der Lauterkeit des Handelsverkehrs und des Verbraucherschutzes.[74] Zu den weiteren anerkannten Gemeinwohlinteressen zählt der Umweltschutz.[75] Allerdings ist auch hierfür eine »echte Gefahr für die Umwelt« Voraussetzung.[76] Es bedarf in diesem Zusammenhang einer konkreten Nachweisführung auf Grundlage wissenschaftlicher Erkenntnisse.[77] Inhalt und Umfang der zwingenden Erfordernisse sind nicht aus der Sicht der Mitgliedstaaten, sondern aus der Unionsperspektive zu bestimmen.[78]

Zwingende Gründe dieser Art liegen hier nicht vor. Das ist evident. Allein die politische »Ächtung« des Wirtschaftsverkehrs mit Kernbrennstoffen im Allgemeinen und der Kernenergienutzung im Speziellen ist keine aus Perspektive des Unionsrechts anzuerkennende Zweckrichtung. Die Kernenergienutzung als solche und der Umgang mit Kernbrennstoffen ist in der unionsweiten Energiepolitik und im Tätigkeitsfeld des Euratom-

74 EuGH, Rs. C-120/78, *Cassis de Dijon*, Slg. 1979, 649; grundlegend hierzu auch *Dauses/Brigola*, in: Dauses, EU-Wirtschaftsrecht, Stand: 31. EL (2012), C. Rn. 109 ff.; *Leible/T. Streinz*, in: Grabitz/Hilf/Nettesheim, Das Recht der Europäischen Union, Stand: 48. EL (2012), Art. 34 AEUV Rn. 100.

75 EuGH, Rs. 302/86, *Kommission/Dänemark*, Slg. 1988, 4627 Rn. 8 f.; Rs. C-284/95, *Safety Hi-Tech*, Slg. 1998, I-4301 Rn. 64; Rs. C-341/95, *Battati*, Slg. 1998, I-4355 Rn. 62; *Leible/T. Streinz*, in: Grabitz/Hilf/Nettesheim, Das Recht der Europäischen Union, Stand: 48. EL (2012), Art. 34 AEUV Rn. 109.

76 EuGH, Rs. C-2/90, *Kommission/Belgien*, Slg. 1992, I-4431 Rn. 31; *Leible/T. Streinz*, in: Grabitz/Hilf/Nettesheim, Das Recht der Europäischen Union, Stand: 48. EL (2012), Art. 34 AEUV Rn. 110.

77 *Leible/T. Streinz*, in: Grabitz/Hilf/Nettesheim, Das Recht der Europäischen Union, Stand: 48. EL (2012), Art. 34 AEUV Rn. 110.

78 *Schwarz*, DÖV 2012, 457 (465).

Vertrages ein fester Bestandteil. Ihre Sicherheit kann nicht grundsätzlich in Frage gestellt werden.

3. Unvereinbarkeit mit der Dienstleistungsfreiheit

Das grundsätzliche Verbot des Umschlags von Kernbrennstoffen in den Bremischen Häfen gemäß § 2 Abs. 3 HafenbetrG verstößt ferner gegen die **Dienstleistungsfreiheit nach Art. 56 AEUV**. Die Dienstleistungsfreiheit ist neben der Warenverkehrsfreiheit anwendbar. Schließlich ist nicht nur die Verkehrsfähigkeit von Kernbrennstoffen innerhalb der Europäischen Union beeinträchtigt, sondern zugleich werden die grenzüberschreitenden Dienstleistungen im Zusammenhang mit den Transportvorgängen beschränkt. Dies belegt auch der Umstand, dass in diesem Kontext die Veranlasser des grenzüberschreitenden Warenverkehrs und die in den Transportvorgang eingebundenen Dienstleistungsunternehmen im Allgemeinen unterschiedliche Rechtsträger und Personen sind, die sich jeweils zum einen auf die Warenverkehrsfreiheit und zum anderen auf die Dienstleistungsfreiheit berufen können. Eine **idealkonkurrierende** Anwendbarkeit in vergleichbaren Konstellationen ist durch den EuGH bereits mehrfach anerkannt.[79] Hinsichtlich der konkreten rechtlichen Einordnung, insbesondere im Hinblick auf die fehlende Rechtfertigungsmöglichkeit – gelten die Ausführungen zur Warenverkehrsfreiheit für die Dienstleistungsfreiheit entsprechend. Gemäß Art. 62 i.V.m. Art. 52 AEUV gibt es nur enge Rechtfertigungsgründe, die hier im Ergebnis wie die Regelung des Art. 36 AEUV auszulegen sind[80]. Die energiepolitischen Erwägungen und der Wunsch nach dem Ausstieg aus der Kernenergie entsprechen diesen Anforderungen nicht. Das ist evident. Die Regelung ist unvereinbar mit der Dienstleistungsfreiheit des Art. 56 AEUV.

---

79 EuGH, Rs. C-6/01, *Anomar*, Slg. 2003, I-8621 Rn. 55 f.; Rs. C-390/99, *Canal Satélite*, Slg. 2002, I-607 Rn. 32 f.; *Randelzhofer/Forsthoff*, in: Grabitz/Hilf/Nettesheim, Das Recht der Europäischen Union, 48. EL (2012), Art. 57 Rn. 37, 39.

80 *Schwarz*, DÖV 2012, 457 (465); *Müller-Graff*, in: Streinz, EUV/AEUV, 2. Aufl. 2012, Art. 52 AEUV Rn. 7.

C. Schluss

Die Änderung des Bremer Hafenbetriebsgesetzes ist nach alldem aus einer Mehrzahl von Gründen mit dem Grundgesetz **unvereinbar** und damit **nichtig**. Es ist erstaunlich, mit welch leichtfertigen landespolitischen Überlegungen sich der Landesgesetzgeber über verfassungsrechtliche Vorgaben und Grundsätze des Bundes hinweggesetzt hat. Dies erinnert an die Schaffung atomwaffenfreier Zonen auf kommunaler Ebene. Eine solche Kirchturms-Politik widerspricht nicht nur einer sinnvollen politischen Kompetenzordnung. Sie auch mit den konkreten Regelungen der durch das Grundgesetz **verfassten Ordnung** unvereinbar. Darüber hinaus widerspricht die Bremer Regelung auch dem Recht der Europäischen Union, und zwar nicht irgendwelchen Bestimmungen, sondern den **primären Grundfreiheiten** der **Warenverkehrsfreiheit** und der **Dienstleistungsfreiheit**. All dies ist evident. Deshalb war zu erwarten, dass schon früh die Kontrollmechanismen in Gang gesetzt werden, die für die Aufhebung rechtswidriger Akte zuständig sind: Die **Gerichte**. So ist beim **Bremer Staatsgerichtshof** eine Klage anhängig, die die Verfassungswidrigkeit des Gesetzes nach der Bremer Landesverfassung geltend macht (Az. St 1/12).[81] Ferner sind beim **Bremer Verwaltungsgericht** Klagen anhängig (Az. 5 K 171/13 und 5 K 303/13), die gegen die Ablehnung von Anträgen auf Nutzung der Bremischen Hafenanlagen für den Umschlag von Kernbrennstoffen erhoben wurden. Die Klagen sind mit dem Antrag verbunden, die Verfahren gemäß **Art. 100 GG auszusetzen und dem Bundesverfassungsgericht** zur Entscheidung vorzulegen. Und schließlich ist seitens der **EU ein Vertragsverletzungsverfahren** angekündigt worden. Die EU-Kommission hat mit Schreiben vom 3. August 2012 zunächst das sog. EU-Pilotverfahren gegen die Bundesrepublik Deutschland wegen des im Bremischen Hafenbetriebsgesetz angeordneten Umschlagsverbots eingeleitet (Az. 3775/12/ENER). Der Ausgang dieser Verfahren scheint vorgezeichnet zu sein. Die Änderung des Bremischen Hafenbetriebsgesetzes wird **nicht von Dauer** sein.

81 Inzwischen hat der BremStGH die Klage mit Urteil vom 12.4.2013 als unzulässig abgewiesen: Die Kompetenzfrage sei nicht Gegenstand des Landesverfassungsrechts, mithin nicht Prüfungsmaßstab. Die Entscheidung ist 4:3 ergangen. Wir halten das Sondervotum mit der gegenteiligen Auffassung für zutreffend. Abgedruckt in NordÖR 2013, 357. Dazu auch *Ruttloff* in atw 2013 Heft 12, S. 679.

Die Urteile des Hessischen Verwaltungsgerichtshofs vom 27. Februar 2013 zu den Betriebseinstellungsverfügungen gegen Biblis A und Biblis B im Rahmen des deutschen Moratoriums nach den Ereignissen in Fukushima-Daiichi vom März 2011

Stefan Kochanski, Justiziar, RWE Power Aktiengesellschaft

1. Tatsächlicher Hintergrund der Urteile

Die Urteile des Hessischen Verwaltungsgerichtshofs vom 27. Februar 2013 sind die ersten Entscheidungen, die im Zusammenhang mit der deutschen Entscheidung ergangen sind, die friedliche Nutzung der Kernenergie für die Stromproduktion zu beenden. Sie befassen sich nicht mit dem Kern dieser politischen Entscheidung und ihrer Umsetzung in der dreizehnten Änderung des Atomgesetzes.[1] Der Hessische Verwaltungsgerichtshof hatte sich vielmehr mit dem im Vorfeld zu der dreizehnten Novelle verhängten sogenannten Moratorium zu befassen, von dem auch Block A und Block B des Kernkraftwerks Biblis betroffen waren. – Gegen die dreizehnte Änderung des Atomgesetzes sind Verfassungsbeschwerden von RWE, E.ON, Vattenfall und weiteren Betreibergesellschaften anhängig, über die noch nicht entschieden ist. – Beide Urteile[2] des Hessischen Verwaltungsgerichtshofs sind noch nicht rechtskräftig, denn gegen die Nichtzulassung der Revision hat das beklagte Land Hessen, vertreten durch das Hessische Ministerium für Umwelt, Energie, Landwirtschaft und Verbraucherschutz, Beschwerde eingelegt, der das Gericht nicht ent-

1 Dreizehntes Gesetz zur Änderung des Atomgesetzes vom 31. Juli 2011, BGBl. I S. 1704; in Kraft getreten am 6. August 2011.

2 Hess. VGH, Urteil vom 27. Februar 2013 – 6 C 824/11.T – betr. Biblis A; Hess. VGH, Urteil vom 27. Februar 2013 – 6 C 825/11.T – betr. Biblis B; beide Entscheidungen sind nahezu wortidentisch und in »Hessenrecht – Landesrechtsprechungsdatenbank – Entscheidungen der Hessischen Gerichte« abrufbar: http://www.lareda.hessenrecht.hessen.de; vgl. auch BeckRS 2013, 48797 (zu Biblis A) und BeckRS 2013, 48798 (zu Biblis B).

sprochen hat und über die das Bundesverwaltungsgericht[3] im Zeitpunkt der Abfassung dieses Beitrags noch nicht entschieden hat.

Gegenstand der Entscheidungen des Hessischen Verwaltungsgerichtshofes waren zwei auf § 19 Absatz 3 Satz 2 Nr. 3 Atomgesetz – AtG – gestützte Anordnungen des hessischen Umweltministeriums jeweils vom 18. März 2011. Mit diesen Anordnungen hatte das Ministerium der RWE Power Aktiengesellschaft als Betreiberin von Biblis die Stromproduktion in beiden Blöcken für die Dauer von drei Monaten untersagt. Biblis B war hiervon nicht mit den vollen drei Monaten betroffen, da sich der Block in einer planmäßigen Revision befunden hatte, deren Beendigung für den 22. Mai 2011 vorgesehen war.

Auslöser und Hintergrund der Anordnungen vom 18. März 2011 war das schwere Seebeben, das sich am 11. März 2011 vor der Küste Japans ereignet hatte. Der dadurch ausgelöste Tsunami hatte anschließend Teile der japanischen Ostküste schwer verwüstet. Hiervon betroffen war auch der Kernkraftwerksstandort Fukushima-Daiichi. Infolge des durch die massive Überflutung des Standortes bedingten Ausfalls der Stromversorgung war es dort zu dem schwersten Reaktorunfall seit Tschernobyl gekommen.[4]

Unter dem Eindruck dieses Reaktorunfalls kündigten Bundeskanzlerin Merkel und Bundesaußenminister Westerwelle nur wenige Tage später, am 14. März 2011, auf einer gemeinsamen Pressekonferenz eine umfassende Sicherheitsüberprüfung aller deutschen Kernkraftwerke an. Angekündigt wurde auch die Aussetzung der erst im Dezember 2010[5] beschlossenen Laufzeitverlängerung der deutschen Kernkraftwerke für einen Zeitraum von drei Monaten, das sog. Moratorium. In einer weiteren Pressekonferenz am 15. März 2011 wurde nach einem Gespräch über die Nutzung der Kernenergie in Deutschland zwischen der Bundeskanzlerin, dem Bundeswirtschaftsminister, dem Bundesumweltminister und den Ministerpräsidenten der Bundesländer, in denen Kernkraftwerke in Betrieb waren, schließlich bekannt gegeben, welche Kernkraftwerke für die Dauer der vorgesehenen Sicherheitsüberprüfung stillgelegt werden sollten. Dem Moratorium unterliegen sollten die bis Ende 1980 in Betrieb gegangenen

3 Aktenzeichen: BVerwG 7 B 18.13 und BVerwG 7 B 19.13.

4 vgl. die Darstellung des Unfallablaufs und seiner radiologischen Folgen im »Fukushima-Informationsportal« der Gesellschaft für Anlagen- und Reaktorsicherheit (GRS) mbH: http://fukushima.grs.de/.

5 Elftes Gesetz zur Änderung des Atomgesetzes vom 8. Dezember 2010, BGBl. I S. 1814; in Kraft getreten am 14. Dezember 2010.

Kernkraftwerke, die sogenannten »älteren« Kernkraftwerke. Betroffen waren damit die Anlagen Biblis A und Biblis B, Neckarwestheim I, Philippsburg I, Isar I und Unterweser. Das Kernkraftwerk Brunsbüttel war zu jener Zeit ohnehin nicht im Leistungsbetrieb.

Mit Schreiben vom 16. März 2011 an die für die genannten Kernkraftwerke zuständigen Ministerien bat das Bundesministerium für Umwelt, Naturschutz und Reaktorsicherheit (BMU) zur Gewährleistung eines einheitlichen Vollzugs darum,

> »der Anordnung der zwischen der Bundesregierung und den Ministerpräsidenten der Bundesländer mit Kernkraftwerken vereinbarten dreimonatigen Betriebseinstellung der sieben ältesten deutschen Kernkraftwerke § 19 Absatz 3 Satz 2 Nummer 3 des Atomgesetzes als Rechtsgrundlage zu Grunde zu legen und diese mit den Ausführungen unter II. zu begründen.«[6]

Ziffer II. des Schreibens lautete:

> »Für die dreimonatige Betriebseinstellung der sieben ältesten Anlagen als vorläufige aufsichtliche Maßnahme sieht das Atomgesetz § 19 Absatz 3 Satz 2 Nummer 3 des Atomgesetzes als einschlägige Rechtsgrundlage vor. Auf dieser Rechtsgrundlage kann bei Vorliegen eines Gefahrenverdachts die einstweilige Betriebseinstellung angeordnet werden. Ein derartiger Verdacht ist im Atomrecht bereits dann gegeben, wenn sich wegen begründeter Unsicherheiten im Rahmen der Risikovorsorge Schadensmöglichkeiten nicht völlig ausschließen lassen. Insbesondere für die sieben ältesten deutschen Anlagen – denen auch bereits im Rahmen einer Differenzierung der Laufzeitverlängerung eine geringere zusätzliche Elektrizitätsmenge zugewiesen wurde – ist nach den Ereignissen in Japan zu überprüfen, inwieweit bisher nicht berücksichtigte Szenarien nunmehr eine neue Bewertung erfordern. Da sich gerade bei älteren Anlagen die Frage nach den in der Auslegung berücksichtigten Szenarien in besonderer Weise stellen kann, haben sich die Bundesregierung und die Ministerpräsidenten der Bundesländer mit Kernkraftwerken dazu entschlossen, diese Anlagen für den Zeitraum der Überprüfung vom Netz zu nehmen. Dies ist Ausdruck äußerster Vorsorge, der sich die Bundesregierung und die Ministerpräsidenten zum Schutze der Bevölkerung verpflichtet sehen.«[6]

Daraufhin erließen die zuständigen Ministerien der Bundesländer Bayern, Baden-Württemberg und Niedersachsen entsprechende Anordnungen, zuletzt am 18. März 2011 auch das hessische Umweltministerium. Es gab der RWE Power auf, den Leistungsbetrieb von Biblis A für die Dauer von drei Monaten einzustellen und den Leistungsbetrieb von Biblis B vor Ab-

6 Schreiben des Bundesministeriums für Umwelt, Naturschutz und Reaktorsicherheit vom 16. März 2011 an die zuständigen Ministerien in den Bundesländern Bayern, Baden-Württemberg, Hessen, Niedersachsen und Schleswig-Holstein (nicht veröffentlicht).

lauf von drei Monaten nicht wieder aufzunehmen. Die vom BMU erbetene Begründung wurde in beide Bescheide übernommen, noch ergänzt um jeweils den Hinweis, dass von einer förmlichen Anhörung nach § 28 des Hessischen Verwaltungsverfahrensgesetzes – HVwVfG – abgesehen werden könne, weil sie im gegebenen Fall nicht geboten erscheine. Die wesentlichen Inhalte der Anordnungen seien der Betreiberin bereits bekannt, und sie habe sich diesbezüglich bereits gegenüber den Medien geäußert.

Der Betrieb von Biblis A wurde daraufhin am 18. März 2013 eingestellt; Biblis B befand sich zum genannten Zeitpunkt, wie schon erläutert, ohnehin in einer planmäßigen Revision.

Gegen die beiden Anordnungen vom 18. März 2011 hat RWE Power am 1. April 2011 jeweils Anfechtungsklage vor dem Hessischen Verwaltungsgerichtshof erhoben. Der Leistungsbetrieb von Block A konnte gleichwohl nicht wieder aufgenommen werden, weil das hessische Umweltministerium für den Fall der Ausnutzung des Suspensiveffekts der Anfechtungsklage die Anordnung der sofortigen Vollziehung ihrer Verfügung vom 18. März 2011 angedroht hatte.[7] – Die Anordnungen gegen Biblis A und gegen Biblis B sind die einzigen Anordnungen, die beklagt worden sind. Alle anderen verhängten »Moratoriums«-Anordnungen sind bestandskräftig geworden, nachdem sich die jeweiligen Betreiber entschieden hatten, keinen verwaltungsgerichtlichen Rechtsschutz in Anspruch zu nehmen.

2. *Zulässigkeit der Fortsetzungsfeststellungklagen*

Die von RWE Power gegen die »Moratoriums«-Anordnungen für Biblis erhobenen Anfechtungsklagen wurden nach Ablauf des »Moratoriums« jeweils auf eine Fortsetzungsfeststellungsklage umgestellt. Deren Zulässigkeit hatte der Hessische Verwaltungsgerichtshof bereits mit zwei Zwischenurteilen vom 4. Juli 2012 festgestellt.[8]

7 Siehe dazu Presseinformation des Hessischen Ministeriums für Umwelt, Energie, Landwirtschaft und Verbraucherschutz vom 1. April 2011: *»Statement der Ministerin zur Klage gegen die vorübergehende Stilllegung von Biblis A und B für den Zeitraum des Moratoriums: ... Wir haben RWE heute verpflichtet, uns umgehend Auskunft zu geben, wenn sie den Leistungsbetrieb vorbereiten. Für den Fall, dass RWE sich entscheidet, den Leistungsbetrieb wieder aufzunehmen, werden wir das mit dem Sofortvollzug unserer Anordnung unterbinden.«*

8 Hess. VGH, Zwischenurt. vom 04.07.2012 – 6 C 824/11.T – betr. Biblis A; Hess. VGH, Zwischenurt. vom 04.07.2012 – 6 C 825/11.T – betr. Biblis B; vgl. »Hes-

Über die Zulässigkeit der Fortsetzungsfeststellungsklagen hatte das Gericht insbesondere auch deswegen vorab durch Zwischenurteile befunden, weil die Fortsetzungsfeststellungsklagen, wie das beklagte Land vorgetragen hatte, unzulässig seien. Die von RWE Power geäußerte Absicht, auf dem Zivilrechtsweg eine Schadensersatz- und Amtshaftungsklage anhängig zu machen, könne vorliegend nicht zur Zulässigkeit der Fortsetzungsfeststellungsklagen führen. Denn der angekündigte Zivilprozess habe offensichtlich keine Aussicht auf Erfolg, weil Block A trotz der aufschiebenden Wirkung der Anfechtungsklage vom 1. April 2011 nicht wieder angefahren worden sei und weil die »Moratoriums«-Anordnung für den Stillstand von Block B nach dem Ende der planmäßigen Revision nicht ursächlich gewesen sei. Dieser Argumentation ist der Hessische Verwaltungsgerichtshof nicht gefolgt. Er hat vielmehr festgestellt, dass die von dem beklagten Land gegen den Erfolg einer Zivilklage vorgetragenen Argumente vom Zivilgericht im Rahmen der Beurteilung eines etwaigen Mitverschuldens der Klägerin zu berücksichtigen seien.

3. *Begründetheit der Fortsetzungsfeststellungsklagen*

Mit seinen (End-)Urteilen vom 27. Februar 2013 hat der Hessische Verwaltungsgerichtshof festgestellt, dass die zulässigen Fortsetzungsfeststellungsklagen auch begründet seien, denn die Anordnungen vom 18. März 2011 gegen Biblis A und gegen Biblis B seien rechtswidrig gewesen. Weder sei die nach § 28 HVwVfG gebotene vorherige Anhörung der Klägerin erfolgt, noch hätten die Tatbestandsvoraussetzungen für eine Anordnung vorgelegen. Zudem sei das gesetzlich eingeräumte Ermessen nicht ausgeübt worden, und die Anordnung der dreimonatigen Betriebseinstellung habe auch gegen das Übermaßverbot verstoßen.

Bevor er sich mit der formellen Rechtswidrigkeit der Anordnungen auseinandersetzt, stellt der Verwaltungsgerichtshof fest, dass die einschlägige Rechtsgrundlage, anders als im Bescheid zugrundegelegt, nicht § 19 Abs. 3 Satz 2 Nr. 3 AtG sei. Satz 2 Nr. 3 von § 19 Abs. 3 AtG besage lediglich, dass die Aufsichtsbehörde als Rechtsfolge insbesondere auch anordnen könne, dass der Betrieb einstweilen eingestellt wird. Dies stelle lediglich ein Regelbeispiel für eine mögliche Rechtsfolge dar. Die Voraussetzungen, unter denen die Rechtsfolge in Betracht komme, formuliere

senrecht – Landesrechtsprechungsdatenbank – Entscheidungen der Hessischen Gerichte«: http://www.lareda.hessenrecht.hessen.de; NVwZ 2012, 1350.

vielmehr § 19 Abs. 3 Satz 1 (2. Alt.) AtG. Diese Norm ermächtigt zur Beseitigung eines Zustands, »*aus dem sich durch die Wirkung ionisierender Strahlen Gefahren für Leben, Gesundheit und Sachgüter ergeben können.*« In Satz 2 schließen sich dann mit den Nummern 1 bis 3 beispielhaft (»insbesondere«) denkbare Maßnahmen an, die als Rechtsfolge ergriffen werden können.

Im Anschluss an diese Klarstellung zur zutreffenden Ermächtigungsgrundlage prüft das Gericht schulmäßig zunächst die formelle Rechtmäßigkeit.

3.1 Formelle Rechtmäßigkeit

Der Verwaltungsgerichtshof stellt zunächst fest, dass mit dem hessischen Umweltministerium die für Biblis zuständige Behörde gehandelt habe. Auf die Frage, ob sie, wie die beklagte Behörde meine, mit dem Schreiben des BMU vom 16. März 2011 bundesaufsichtlich angewiesen worden sei, kommt es nach Auffassung des Gerichts nicht an. Denn im Außenverhältnis auch gegenüber dem Betreiber sei allein die Landesbehörde für die Kontrolle der Kernkraftwerke und für den Erlass von Anordnungen zuständig. Einer Weisung komme ohnehin nur im Verhältnis zwischen den beteiligten Behörden Bindungswirkung zu, nicht im Verhältnis zum Betreiber.

Nach der anschließenden Bestätigung, dass die gesetzlichen Vorgaben zur Bestimmtheit und zur Form des Verwaltungsaktes in ausreichender Weise beachtet worden seien, setzt sich der Verwaltungsgerichtshof ausführlich mit der Frage der Notwendigkeit einer vorherigen Anhörung nach § 28 des HVwVfG auseinander.

Eine ausdrückliche Anhörung von RWE Power als Betreiberin von Biblis A und Biblis B war nicht durchgeführt worden. Aber auch in einer anderen Form, die den gesetzlichen Anforderungen entspricht, ist eine Anhörung nach der Prüfung des Gerichts nicht erfolgt oder ersetzt worden.

In diesem Zusammenhang geht der Verwaltungsgerichtshof zunächst auf einen Beweisantrag ein, den das beklagte Land in der mündlichen Verhandlung gestellt hatte. Es hatte beantragt, den seinerzeit amtierenden Bundesumweltminister Röttgen als Zeugen zur Frage der erfolgten Anhörung zu vernehmen. Aufgrund verschiedener Presseartikel, so das Land, sei davon auszugehen, dass es Gespräche mit den Betreibern, auch mit RWE, gegeben habe und dass die Betreiber in diesen Gesprächen Gelegenheit gehabt hätten, sich zu der beabsichtigten Betriebseinstellung zu äußern.

Diesen Beweisantrag hat das Gericht zurückgewiesen, weil es ihn für nicht substantiiert gehalten hat. Für eine Substantiierung wäre es erforderlich gewesen, Ort, Tag und Stunde zu konkretisieren, zu denen entsprechende Gespräche stattgefunden hätten. Das sei aber nicht erfolgt, obwohl dies ohne Weiteres hätte recherchiert werden können.

In der Sache kam es auf die unter Beweis gestellte Tatsache nach Überzeugung des Gerichts jedoch auch nicht an. Mit Recht. Denn eine Anhörung hätte durch die zuständige Behörde vorgenommen werden müssen. Die Behörde selbst, so der Verwaltungsgerichtshof, müsse dem Betroffenen Gelegenheit zur Stellungnahme zu der von ihr beabsichtigten belastenden Maßnahme geben. Es reiche nicht aus, wenn sich der Betroffene in den Medien zu der beabsichtigten Anordnung geäußert haben sollte. – Damit hatte die Anordnung selbst die Entbehrlichkeit einer Anordnung begründet. – Derartige Äußerungen könnten die gebotene Anordnung nicht ersetzen. Eine Anhörung erfordere vielmehr ein aktives Handeln der Behörde. Die Behörde müsse den Betroffenen auf die relevanten tatsächlichen und rechtlichen Umstände hinweisen, aufgrund derer sie eine ihn belastende Anhörung beabsichtige und aufgrund derer sie sich dazu befugt glaube. Dazu müsse die Behörde selbst dem Betroffenen eine angemessene Möglichkeit zur Stellungnahme einräumen. Diese Stellungnahme müsse dann von dem zur Entscheidung berufenen Bediensteten auch tatsächlich zur Kenntnis genommen und von ihm im Entscheidungsprozess berücksichtigt werden. Vor diesem Hintergrund könnten etwaige Äußerungen eines Betroffenen gegenüber der Presse keine andere den gesetzlichen Vorschriften entsprechende Anhörung darstellen.

Die Anhörung war, so die weiteren gerichtlichen Ausführungen, auch nicht im Sinne von § 28 Abs. 2 HVwVfG entbehrlich. Wenn die Voraussetzungen dieser Norm vorliegen, d.h. wenn die Anhörung nach den Umständen des Einzelfalls nicht geboten sei, dann müsse die Behörde eine Ermessensentscheidung treffen, ob von einer Anhörung abgesehen werden könne oder nicht. Ohne eine derartige Ermessensentscheidung durch die Behörde könne eine unterlassene Anhörung nicht als entbehrlich angesehen werden. Im vorliegenden Fall war keines der Regelbeispiele aus Absatz 2 gegeben. Im Übrigen hatte die Behörde auch keine Ermessensentscheidung über die Entbehrlichkeit getroffen.

Der Verwaltungsgerichtshof sieht den Anhörungsmangel auch nicht als unbedeutend an. Denn das Recht auf vorherige Anhörung sei Bestandteil des Grundsatzes auf ein faires Verfahren. Auch § 28 Abs. 1 HVwVfG bezwecke den Grundrechtsschutz durch Verfahrensgestaltung. Mit ihm solle ausgeschlossen werden, dass der Betroffene seine Rechte nicht oder nicht rechtzeitig geltend machen könne. Angesichts dessen könne der Mangel nicht als unbedeutend eingestuft werden.

Die Urteilsgründe sprechen kurz an, dass eine Anhörung nach § 28 Abs. 3 HVwVfG unterbleibe, wenn ihr ein zwingendes öffentliches Interesse entgegenstehe. Ein zwingendes öffentliches Interesse für ein Unterbleiben der Anhörung sei im konkreten Fall hingegen weder ersichtlich noch von dem beklagten Land überhaupt geltend gemacht worden.

Die Verletzung der Anhörungspflicht wird auch nicht als unbeachtlich im Sinne des § 45 Abs. 1 HVwVfG angesehen. Unbeachtlichkeit könne nur angenommen werden, wenn die erforderliche Anhörung – entsprechend Nr. 3 – nachgeholt werde. Beachtlich könne dies, so das Gericht, jedoch nur dann sein, wenn die nachgeholte Anhörung ordnungsgemäß erfolge und wenn die Funktion der Anhörung für den Entscheidungsprozess durch die Nachholung uneingeschränkt erreicht werde. Das wiederum setze voraus, dass der Betroffene nachträglich eine vollwertige Gelegenheit zur Stellungnahme erhalte und dass die Behörde die nachträglich vorgebrachten Argumente zum Anlass nehme, die ohne vorherige Anordnung getroffene Entscheidung kritisch zu überdenken. All dies ist im vorliegenden Fall zu keiner Zeit erfolgt.

Sodann stellt der Verwaltungsgerichtshof fest, dass die formelle Fehlerhaftigkeit der Anordnungen auch nicht im Sinne des § 46 HVwVfG unbeachtlich sei. Nach § 46 HVwVfG kann die Aufhebung eines – nicht nach § 44 HVwVfG nichtigen – Verwaltungsaktes nicht allein deswegen beansprucht werden, weil er unter Verletzung der Vorschriften über das Verfahren, die Form oder die örtliche Zuständigkeit zustande gekommen ist, wenn offensichtlich ist, dass die Verletzung der Formvorschrift die Entscheidung in der Sache nicht beeinflusst hat.

Im Fall Biblis wollte das Gericht nicht ausschließen, dass die Entscheidung der dreimonatigen Betriebseinstellung, politisch von vornherein festgestanden haben könnte und von den Ministerpräsidenten der involvierten Länder gemeinsam mit der Bundesregierung genau so gewollt gewesen ist. Zu begrüßen ist in diesem Zusammenhang die deutliche Feststellung, dass eine in diesem Sinne politisch vielleicht als legitim empfundene Betrachtungsweise von der juristischen Betrachtungsweise deutlich zu unterscheiden sei. § 46 HVwVfG sei auf Fallkonstellationen wie die Vorliegende nicht anwendbar sei. Dies ergebe eine sachgerechte und verfassungsrechtliche Grundsätze beachtende Auslegung von § 46 HVwVfG. Während bei gebundenen Entscheidungen die Rechtsschutzgarantie des Art. 19 Abs. 4 GG der Anwendung von § 46 HVwVfG im Regelfall nicht entgegen stehe, sei dies für Ermessensentscheidungen, bei denen das Ermessen konkret »auf Null« reduziert sei, hingegen schon zweifelhaft.

Der Verwaltungsgerichtshof hat diese Frage nicht entschieden. Denn vorliegend kam für ihn die Anwendung von § 46 HVwVfG letztlich aus zwei Gründen nicht in Betracht:

Der Ausschluss der Aufhebbarkeit rechtswidriger Verwaltungsakte komme zum Einen dann nicht zum Tragen, wenn, wie im vorliegenden Fall, Grundrechtsbeeinträchtigungen im Raum stünden. Zum Anderen finde er keine Anwendung, wenn ein Tatbestand gegeben sei, bei dem für die Behörde eine Beurteilungsermächtigung vorliege; wenn sie also unbestimmte Rechtsbegriffe anzuwenden habe, die ihr einen Beurteilungsspielraum einräumen und wenn zudem bei hypothetischer Betrachtung nicht ausgeschlossen sei, dass Informationen aus einer Anhörung Einfluss auf die von der Behörde zu treffende Entscheidung hätten haben können.

Beide Voraussetzungen sieht das Gericht im vorliegenden Fall als gegeben an: Schon bei der Frage über das Einschreiten habe die Behörde zu prüfen, ob die Umstände des Einzelfalls die Voraussetzungen der Eingriffsnorm ergeben. Das Gericht geht davon aus, dass der Behörde in Fragen des Bestehens einer Gefahrenlage ein gerichtlich nicht in allen Einzelheiten überprüfbarer Beurteilungsspielraum (exekutiver Funktionsvorbehalt) einzuräumen sei. Die Behörde habe aber nicht nur zu prüfen, ob die Voraussetzungen der Eingriffsnorm vorliegen. Sie habe darüber hinaus auch eine Ermessensentscheidung zu treffen, ob sie tätig werden wolle oder müsse. Und sie habe auch nach pflichtgemäßem Ermessen zu entscheiden, welche Maßnahme angeordnet werden soll.

Im vorliegenden Fall ergibt sich aus dem Vorbringen des beklagten Landes im Prozess, dass das hessische Umweltministerium von dem ihm zustehenden Ermessen gar keinen Gebrauch machen wollte. Es wollte allein die vom BMU erwünschte Anordnung erlassen. Würde man in dieser Situation die bewusst unterlassene Anhörung über § 46 HVwVfG als unbeachtlich ansehen – eben weil die behördliche Entscheidung von vorherein feststand – so wäre das Unterlassen, wie das Gericht ausführt, der rechtlich an sich gebotenen Anhörung folgenlos. Diese Konsequenz wäre für den Verwaltungsgerichtshof rechtlich nicht akzeptabel. Er stellt daher fest, dass § 46 HVwVfG rechtlich nicht zu dem Ergebnis führen dürfe, dass die gebotene, aber unterlassene Anhörung offensichtlich an der Entscheidung nichts geändert hätte und daher unbeachtlich sei.

In diesem Zusammenhang weist der Verwaltungsgerichtshof ausdrücklich darauf hin, dass im konkreten Fall des dreimonatigen Moratoriums vom Frühjahr 2011 gerade keine Ermessensreduzierung »auf Null« vorgelegen habe, weder auf Seiten des Bundesumweltministeriums noch auf Seiten des beklagten Landes. Das werde schon daraus deutlich, dass das Bundesumweltministerium in seinem Schreiben vom 16. März 2011 selbst bereits eine Differenzierung vorgenommen habe. So habe es ohne Feststellung von lokalen Besonderheiten, die ja für Fragen wie Erdbeben und Überflutung eigentlich durchaus bedeutsam seien, und ohne Feststellung technischer Unterschiede die Stilllegung der sieben ältesten Kraftwerke verlangt. Und auf der anderen Seite habe es für alle anderen Kraftwerke – ebenfalls ohne entsprechende Feststellungen – die Überprüfung ohne eine Stilllegung für möglich angesehen. Das Gericht konstatiert in diesem Zusammenhang, dass von alternativlosem Handeln daher keine Rede sein könne.

3.2 Materielle Rechtmäßigkeit

Die materielle Rechtswidrigkeit beruht darauf, dass die Voraussetzungen der Eingriffsnorm nicht vorgelegen haben, dass das eingeräumte Ermessen nicht sachgerecht ausgeübt worden ist und dass eine unverhältnismäßige Rechtsfolge gesetzt worden ist.

Der Hessische Verwaltungsgerichtshof stellt noch einmal ausdrücklich klar, dass die für die Aufsicht zuständige Behörde im konkreten Einzelfall den relevanten Sachverhalt zu ermitteln und aufzuklären habe und dass sie den Sachverhalt, auf den sie sich beruft, gegebenenfalls auch nachweisen müsse. Im Rahmen der verwaltungsgerichtlichen Überprüfung dürften die Ermittlung und die Bewertung von Tatsachen für die erforderliche Gefahrenprognose nicht vom Gericht anstelle der zuständigen Behörde durchgeführt werden, auch nicht mit der Hilfe von Sachverständigen. Insoweit referiert der heute beim Hessischen Verwaltungsgerichtshof zuständige 6. Senat die Entwicklung der Rechtsprechung des Bundesverwaltungsgerichts zum exekutiven Funktionsvorbehalt ebenso wie die Rechtsprechung des früher beim Verwaltungsgerichtshof zuständigen 14. Senats. Der hatte in einem Urteil vom 25. März 1997 (Az. 14 A 3083/89) darüber hinausgehend festgestellt, dass der zuständigen Behörde die sog. Einschätzungsprärogative für die Gefahrenermittlung und die Gefahrenbewertung nicht nur im Genehmigungsverfahren sondern auch im Widerrufs- bzw. Rücknahmeverfahren zustehe. Dieser Bewertung schließt sich der 6. Senat ausdrücklich an.[9]

Der vorliegende Fall gab dem 6. Senat Veranlassung dazu, im Rahmen seiner Ausführungen zu den Voraussetzungen und Randbedingungen der Ermessensregelung des § 19 Abs. 3 Satz 1 (2. Alt.) AtG mit deutlichen Worten in Erinnerung zu rufen, dass die Behörde natürlich nur dann einschreiten könne, wenn die tatbestandlichen Voraussetzungen der Norm vorlägen. Insoweit werde der Behörde Ermessen eröffnet. Dessen Ausübung sei für den betroffenen Betreiber mit erheblichen Nachteilen verbunden. Daher seien bei der Ermessensausübung die Gegebenheiten des konkreten Einzelfalls in Rechnung zu stellen, und es sei unter Berücksichtigung der, wie das Gericht es ausdrückt, »*typischen Anforderungen*« und rechtlichen Bindungen zu entscheiden: Aufklärung des Sachverhalts, Beweislast, Ermessensausübung und Beachtung des Grundsatzes der Verhältnismäßigkeit.

Die tatbestandlichen Voraussetzungen der Eingriffsnorm des § 19 Abs. 3 Satz 1 (2. Alt.) AtG haben nach den Feststellungen des Hessischen Verwaltungsgerichtshofs zu keiner Zeit vorgelegen, weder bei Biblis A noch bei Biblis B. Wörtlich heißt es in den Urteilsgründen:

> »Der Beklagte hat nicht vermocht, einen solchen gefahrauslösenden Zustand der konkreten Anlagen – hier Kernkraftwerk Biblis A – nachzuweisen. Er macht daher in der angegriffenen Anordnung im Ergebnis mangels entsprechender Nachweise zu unrecht geltend, im Zeitpunkt der behördlichen Entscheidung habe der weitere Betrieb der Anlage möglicherweise Gefahren für Leben und Gesundheit oder Sachgüter zur Folge gehabt, jedenfalls sei eine Neubestimmung der Risikosphären erforderlich gewesen. Das Vorliegen einer im Zeitpunkt des Erlasses der Anordnung bestehenden konkreten Gefahr ist zu verneinen. Eine Gefahr liegt nach der klassischen polizeilichen Begriffsdefinition, die auch im Rahmen des Atomrechts Gültigkeit beansprucht (vgl. Hess. VGH Beschluss vom 28. Juni 1989 – 8 Q 2809/88 –, ESVGH 39,262) vor, wenn eine Sachlage bei ungehindertem Ablauf des objektiv zu erwartenden Geschehens mit hinreichender Wahrscheinlichkeit zu einem Schaden bei einem polizeilich geschützten Rechtsgut führen wird. Gefordert wird eine hinreichende Wahrscheinlichkeit des Schadenseintritts, wobei dem Wahrscheinlichkeitsurteil Erfahrungssätze zugrunde liegen müssen (vgl. BVerwG, Urteil vom 13. Dezember 1967 – IV C 146.65 –, BVerwGE 28, 310; Götz, Allgemeines Polizei- und Ordnungsrecht, Rdnr. 17). Gefahren in diesem Sinne sind von dem Beklagten weder im Verwaltungsverfahren erarbeitet noch in der konkreten Anordnung oder im Gerichtsverfahren benannt worden. Sie sind aus

9 vgl. Hess. VGH, Urteile vom 27. Februar 2013, amtlicher Umdruck, jeweils Rdnr. 59.

> den vorgelegten Unterlagen der Behörde oder anderen Quellen nachträglich auch nicht erkennbar.«[10]

Auch ein Gefahrenverdacht hat, so der Verwaltungsgerichtshof, nicht vorgelegen. In Abgrenzung zum Begriff der Gefahr sei der Gefahrenverdacht dadurch gekennzeichnet, dass sich der weitere Kausalverlauf eines Zustands nicht mit einem hinreichenden Grad an Wahrscheinlichkeit prognostizieren lasse. Daher müsse in einem derartigen Fall auf die Ermittlung und Darstellung der konkreten Umstände des Einzelfalls besonderer Wert gelegt werden.

Zur Einordnung des Gefahrenverdachts in die atomrechtliche Systematik legt sich das Gericht nicht fest. Es führt jedoch aus, dass die von der beklagten Behörde vorgetragene Begründung für einen Gefahrenverdacht – unterstellt, dieser sei zu berücksichtigen – nur dann den Tatbestand von § 19 Abs. 3 Satz 1 AtG erfüllen könne, wenn sich die entsprechende behördliche Bewertung jedenfalls als willkürfrei darstelle. Unter Zugrundelegung des der Behörde bekannt gewordenen Sachverhalts müssten also hinreichende Informationen und Tatsachen vorliegen, die belegen, dass eine Gefahr möglich gewesen sei.

Wenn es im Rahmen der Anwendung des § 19 Abs. 3 Satz 1 AtG um die Berücksichtigung etwaiger neuer Erkenntnisse gehe, wie zum Beispiel aus dem Reaktorunfall in Fukushima, dann müssten, so der Hessische Verwaltungsgerichtshof, möglichst genaue Erkenntnisse der Aufsichtsbehörde dazu vorliegen, wie wahrscheinlich eine aufgrund veränderter Umstände neu als drohend empfundene oder bezeichnete Gefahr sei. Aufgrund der langjährigen Befassung mit Biblis in Genehmigungs- und Aufsichtsverfahren und aufgrund der ihr vorliegenden umfangreichen technischen Unterlagen hat das hessische Umweltministerium nach Auffassung des Gerichts umfassende und aussagekräftige Erkenntnisse zum technischen Zustand von Biblis A und von Biblis B. Es habe, wie dem Senat aus weiteren Verfahren bekannt sei, auch umfassende Erkenntnisse, die die Sicherheit der Anlage vor Gefahren betreffen, die von außen auf die Anlage einwirken könnten. Daher müsse das Ministerium in der Lage sein, fundiert darzustellen, welche Ursachen von möglichen Gefahren ihr neu bekannt geworden seien und welche Ermittlungsschritte sie unternommen habe, um eine sachgerechte Prognose abzugeben, die das bisherige Wissen und die neu hinzugetretenen Fakten einbezieht. Das mögliche Ausmaß des Schadens für das konkret oder vermeintlich als bedroht angesehene

10 Hess. VGH, a.a.O., jeweils Rdnrn. 61 ff.

Rechts- oder Schutzgut sei zu berücksichtigen. Und es sei eine möglichst umfassende Ermittlung und Bewertung des Umfangs des Schadens auf Seiten des betroffenen Kraftwerksbetreibers erforderlich.

Gemessen daran sieht das Gericht die pauschale Annahme der hessischen Behörde, es habe aufgrund der Ereignisse in Japan ein Sachverhalt vorgelegen, der zumindest eine Risikoneubestimmung rechtfertige, als – so wörtlich – »*ungenügend*«[11] an. Das folge bereits aus der Unbestimmtheit der vorgetragenen Befürchtungen. Anfangs mag dies noch, wie das Gericht einräumt, den »*unbekannten Faktoren des Unfalls in Japan geschuldet gewesen sein*«[12]. Jedoch auch in der weiteren Auseinandersetzung mit der Klägerin habe insoweit keine Konkretisierung stattgefunden. Wörtlich fassen die Urteile zusammen:

> »Allein die Vorgabe, es sei eine Neubestimmung eines Risikos oder der Annahmen, dass Risiken bestehen könnten, vorzunehmen, stellt nach den zuvor dargestellten Anforderungen keine ausreichende Grundlage für eine Anordnung nach § 19 Abs. 3 Satz 1 (2. Alt.) AtG dar.«[13]

Durchaus erwähnenswert ist in diesem Zusammenhang die Feststellung des Hessischen Verwaltungsgerichtshofs, dass das Umweltministerium im Hinblick auf die Sicherheit von Biblis A und von Biblis B gerade keine Bedenken gehabt habe. Dies würden in den Behördenakten befindliche Entwürfe von seinerzeitigen Antworten auf Fragen einer Landtagsabgeordneten belegen. Nach diesen Antworten des Ministeriums habe sich an der Sicherheit des Kernkraftwerks Biblis infolge der Ereignisse in Fukushima nichts geändert.[14]

Die Ausführungen zum Fehlen der tatsächlichen Voraussetzungen des § 19 Abs. 3 Satz 1 AtG schließen sowohl das Urteil zu Block A als auch das Urteil zu Block B mit der Zusammenfassung ab: »*Im Ergebnis ist daher festzustellen, dass mangels konkreter Nachweise einer gegenüber der ergangenen Genehmigung veränderten Sachlage (›Zustand‹) bei Erlass der streitbefangenen Anordnung weder das Vorliegen einer Gefahr noch Anhaltspunkte für eine Gefahrenverdacht bejaht werden können. Zudem bestehen auch keine Hinweise dafür, dass die Notwendigkeit einer weiteren Risikovorsorge hätte angenommen werden können und zwar unab-*

11 Hess. VGH, a.a.O., jeweils Rdnr. 72.
12 Hess. VGH, ebenda.
13 Hess. VGH, ebenda.
14 Hess. VGH, a.a.O., jeweils Rdnr. 73.

hängig davon, ob eine solche bei § 19 Abs. 3 AtG zu berücksichtigen ist.«[15]

Ein weiterer Rechtswidrigkeitsgrund liegt darin, dass das Umweltministerium das von § 19 AtG eingeräumte Ermessen nicht ausgeübt hat. Der Verwaltungsgerichtshof erinnert daran, dass die Formulierung »*kann*« in § 19 AtG nicht nur eine Ermächtigung darstelle. Vielmehr sei die zuständige Behörde »*ausdrücklich gehalten, Ermessen auszuüben, also den Zweck der Ermächtigung zu beachten und die gesetzlichen Grenzen des Ermessens einzuhalten (vgl. § 40 HVwVfG).«*[16]

Vorliegend ist demgegenüber ein vollständiger Ermessensausfall zu konstatieren. Sowohl nach dem Vorbringen im gerichtlichen Verfahren als auch nach dem Inhalt der dem Gericht vorliegenden Verwaltungsakten wollte das hessische Umweltministerium vielmehr die Bitte bzw. Vorgabe – je nach Sichtweise zur Frage der Weisung – aus dem Schreiben des BMU vom 16. März 2011 umsetzen. Es hat das Schreiben, wie es im gerichtlichen Verfahren bekundet hat, als Weisung angesehen, die befolgt werden sollte. Die Formulierung des Schreibens wie auch die Vereinbarung, die offensichtlich in dem am 15. März 2011 geführten Gespräch über die Nutzung der Kernenergie in Deutschland zwischen der Bundeskanzlerin, dem Bundeswirtschaftsminister, dem Bundesumweltminister und den Ministerpräsidenten der betroffenen Bundesländer zur Abschaltung der sog. »älteren« Kernkraftwerke erzielt worden ist, sprechen dagegen, dieses Schreiben rechtlich als Weisung zu qualifizieren. So hat denn auch der Ministerpräsident des beklagten Landes Hessen in einer Plenarsitzung des Hessischen Landtags am 28. Februar 2013 klargestellt, dass die Anordnungen vom 18. März 2011 gegen Biblis nicht auf einer Weisung, sondern auf einem gemeinsamen Vorgehen von Bund und Ländern beruhten.[17]

Der Ermessensausfall wäre, so das Gericht, nur dann unschädlich, wenn unter keinem denkbaren Gesichtspunkt eine andere als die getroffene Entscheidung rechtmäßig sein könnte. Eine derartige »Ermessensreduzierung auf Null« komme vorliegend jedoch nicht in Betracht; zum einen aus allgemeinen Erwägungen nicht und zum anderen aufgrund der Besonderheiten des Falles nicht.

15 Hess. VGH, a.a.O., jeweils Rdnr. 75.

16 Hess. VGH, a.a.O., jeweils Rdnr. 78.

17 vgl. Plenarprotokoll 18/132 der 132. Sitzung des Hessischen Landtags am 28. Februar 2013, Seite 9291 (re. Sp.): http://starweb.hessen.de/starweb/LIS/ plenarprotokolle.htm.

Der Verwaltungsgerichtshof führt aus, dass die der Aufsichtsbehörde bei Vorliegen der Eingriffsvoraussetzungen eröffneten Regelungsmöglichkeiten, wie auch die Regelbeispiele zeigten, vom Grundsatz der Verhältnismäßigkeit geprägt seien, ergänzt durch das im Atomrecht geltende Prinzip der Abwägung der Risiken. Je nach Schwere der Gefahr und in Abhängigkeit von ihrer Eintrittswahrscheinlichkeit forderten die Risiken eine Differenzierung in der behördlichen Reaktion. Der VGH stellt ausdrücklich fest, dass ein Automatismus derart, »*dass bei angenommenen oder auch nur befürchteten Fällen einer möglichen Gefahr auch gravierende Einschnitte in das durch Genehmigungsbescheid konstituierte Recht zum Betrieb einer kerntechnischen Anlage verfügt werden könnten*«,[18] verfassungsrechtlichen Zweifeln begegnen würde.

Eine vorläufige Einstellung des Leistungsbetriebs komme nur in Betracht, wenn sie verhältnismäßig sei. Das aber setze voraus, dass sämtliche Umstände des konkreten Falls in die Abwägung einbezogen werden. Dazu gehörten nicht nur die Auswirkungen der angenommenen Gefahrenlage auf die betroffenen Rechtsgüter, sondern auch die Folgen der Betriebseinstellung für den betroffenen Kraftwerksbetreiber. Im vorliegenden Fall hielt der Verwaltungsgerichtshof diese Abwägung in ganz besonderem Maße auch deswegen für geboten, weil nur wenige Monate zuvor die Sicherheit der deutschen Kernkraftwerke – auch die Sicherheit von Biblis – von der Bundesregierung so hoch eingeschätzt worden sei, dass dem vorhandenen Strommengenkontingent noch Kontingente hinzugegeben worden seien. Dass sich daran seitdem etwas geändert haben könnte, kann das Gericht weder dem Vorbringen des beklagten Landes entnehmen noch den Verwaltungsvorgängen.

Abschließend konstatiert der Verwaltungsgerichtshof, dass die Rechtsfolge der vorübergehenden Stilllegung auch nicht verhältnismäßig gewesen sei. Er betont noch einmal, dass die einstweilige Einstellung des genehmigten Betriebs die schärfste vorläufige Maßnahme ist, die gegen den Betrieb eines Kernkraftwerks ergriffen werden könne. Daher sei die Prüfung der Verhältnismäßigkeit hier von besonderer Bedeutung. Genau diese Prüfung sei jedoch nicht vorgenommen worden. Eine Abwägung der Maßnahme im Hinblick auf Geeignetheit, Erforderlichkeit und Verhältnismäßigkeit (i.e.S.) sei nicht erfolgt. Zu Recht stellt das Gericht fest, allein der Hinweis, dass durch »*die Ereignisse in Japan*« eine Neubewertung des Sicherheitskonzepts und der Auslegungsszenarien erforderlich geworden sei, genüge den gesetzlichen Anforderungen nicht. Unverhält-

18 Hess. VGH, a.a.O., jeweils Rdnr. 85.

nismäßig sei die Betriebseinstellung auch deshalb gewesen, weil das zuständige Ministerium nicht ausreichend geltend gemacht habe, dass vorrangige öffentliche Belange oder schutzwürdige berechtigte Interessen anderweitig Betroffener das private und öffentliche Interesse am Bestandsschutz der erteilten Genehmigungen ausnahmsweise überwiegen würden. Das Gericht gibt den ausdrücklichen Hinweis, dass die »*nach den Grundsätzen der Verhältnismäßigkeit und des Übermaßverbotes gebotene Abwägung*«[19] ihrer Natur nach in jedem konkreten Einzelfall erfolgen müsse und nicht in quasi allgemein gültiger Form vorgenommen werden dürfe. Es sei »*unter dem Gesichtspunkt der Gesetzmäßigkeit der zuständigen Aufsichtsbehörde nicht zu akzeptieren, wenn diese Abwägung nicht dem pflichtgemäßen Ermessen der Verwaltung überlassen bleibt, sondern pauschal und für mehrere Anlagen im Bundesgebiet ergeht.*«[20] Diese Feststellung darf wohl als deutliche Botschaft auch an das Bundesumweltministerium verstanden werden.

4. Ausblick

Die Urteile des Hessischen Verwaltungsgerichtshofs sind zum Zeitpunkt der Drucklegung noch nicht bestandskräftig gewesen. Das beklagte Land Hessen hat gegen die Nichtzulassung der Revision Beschwerde eingelegt, der der Verwaltungsgerichtshof nicht entsprochen hat. Die Entscheidung des Bundesverwaltungsgerichts steht zum Zeitpunkt der Drucklegung noch aus.

19 Hess. VGH, a.a.O., jeweils Rdnr. 91
20 Hess. VGH, a.a.O., jeweils Rdnr. 91

Diskussionsbericht zur Fünften Arbeitssitzung

Ulrike Feldmann, Justitiarin, Wirtschaftsverband Kernbrennstoff-Kreislauf und Kerntechnik e.V. / *Julius F. W. Weitzdörfer,* LL.B., Max-Planck-Institut für ausländisches und internationales Privatrecht

Im Hinblick auf die fortgeschrittene Zeit schlug der Vorsitzende der 5. Arbeitssitzung, Dr. *Rebentisch*, vor, die Diskussion zu den einzelnen Vorträgen möglichst an das Ende des letzten Vortrags zu legen.

Prof. *Kühne* nahm Bezug auf die Darstellung von Prof. *Fetzer*, wonach sich die mit § 7d AtG getroffene Regelung zur weiteren Vorsorge gegen Risiken auf den Restrisikobereich bezieht. Da das Restrisiko von der Allgemeinheit zu tragen sei, stelle sich, so Prof. *Kühne,* bei der in § 7d AtG eingeführten Betreiberpflicht die Frage, wie sich die Verfassungsmäßigkeit dieser Pflicht im Lichte des Art. 12 GG begründen lasse. Prof. *Fetzer* wies darauf hin, daß nur Maßnahmen gefordert werden können, die »geeignet« und »angemessen« sind, um einen nicht nur geringfügigen Beitrag zur weiteren Risikovorsorge zu leisten. Der Grundsatz der Verhältnismäßigkeit sei der Maßstab. Prof. *Fetzer* teilte jedoch das Bedenken von Prof. Kühne im Hinblick auf die Frage der Verfassungsmäßigkeit.

Prof. *Bohne* machte Bedenken gegenüber dem im Vortrag von Dr. *Vorwerk* angesprochenen Ansatz der EU-Kommission geltend, die nach den Erfahrungen mit Fukushima eine eigenständige, unabhängige Aufsichtsbehörde favorisiert. Die Tendenz zur »independent regulatory authority« stamme aus dem angelsächsischen Raum. Die Einrichtung einer solchen »independent regulatory authority« sei die Antwort in GB und den USA in Zeiten ineffektiver, korrupter Verwaltung gewesen. Diese Voraussetzungen lägen in Europa jedoch nicht vor. Zu fragen sei im Übrigen, ob dieser Behördentyp zu einer besseren Gesetzgebung führe. Es fehle an der empirischen Evidenz dafür. Große Behörden seien jedenfalls zu komplex und kaum noch steuerbar (Stichwort: »regulatory capture«). Dr. *Vorwerk* merkte dazu an, daß Deutschland solche Argumente in die Diskussion mit der EU-Kommission einbringen werde. Aber Hauptargument gegen den Vorschlag der Kommission müsse sein, daß es nicht sein dürfe, nur noch einen Typ von Behörde zuzulassen. Dazu bedürfe es einer besonderen Ermächtigung der EU-Kommission. Dr. *Kraß* unterstrich diese Auffassung von Dr. *Vorwerk*, bei dem jetzigen Behördensystem zu bleiben;

dies sei in Anbetracht der Probleme, die mit dem Ausstieg aus der Kernenergie bis 2022 zu regeln seien, elementar wichtig. Außerdem sei Deutschland mit der Bundesauftragsverwaltung »gut gefahren«.

Dr. *Schmans* wollte von Prof. *Moench* wissen, ob es eine Rolle bei der Frage der Verletzung der Warenverkehrsfreiheit spiele, daß Kernbrennstoffe nach dem EURATOM-Vertrag im Eigentum der EU stünden. Außerdem fragte Dr. *Schmans*, ob das Umschlagsverbot in bremischen Häfen für Kernbrennstoffe in Anbetracht der völkerrechtlich abgesicherten Rücknahmeverpflichtung nicht den Grundsatz des bundesfreundlichen Verhaltens tangiere. Die erste Frage beantwortete Prof. *Moench* dahingehend, daß es im Rahmen des Umschlagsverbots irrelevant sei, wo das zivilrechtliche Eigentum liege. Hier handele es sich um dingliche, eigentumsähnliche Nutzungsrechte der Betreiber. In Bezug auf die völkerrechtliche Vereinbarung über die Rücknahme der kernbrennstoffhaltigen Abfälle aus Großbritannien sei zu sagen, daß diese Vereinbarung allgemein gelte und nicht auf einen bestimmten Hafen bezogen sei. Eine Verletzung von Völkerrecht sei daher fraglich. Es liege jedoch, so stellte Prof. *Moench* in Beantwortung der zweiten Frage fest, eine Verletzung des Grundsatzes des bundesfreundlichen Verhaltens vor.

Dr. *Frank* erkundigte sich bei Herrn *Kochanski*, wie es nach dem Urteil des VGH Kassel vom 27.02.2013 zu dem dreimonatigen Moratorium für das KKW Biblis in 2011 nun weitergehe. Herr *Kochanski* erläuterte in seiner Antwort, daß das Verfahren vor dem VGH der Vorbereitung des Schadensersatzprozesses diene. Dieser werde vorbereitet, sobald das VGH-Verfahren rechtskräftig geworden sei.

Dr. *Micklinghoff* fragte insbesondere im Hinblick auf die einstweilige Betriebseinstellung des KKW Biblis in 2011, ob es nicht auch in Deutschland »undue influences« der Politik auf Behörden gebe. Wie werde die Unabhängigkeit von Landes- und Bundesministerien sichergestellt? Dr. *Vorwerk* betonte zunächst, daß er nicht für eine eigenständige unabhängige Behörde votiere, aber eine Diskussion darüber nicht ablehne. Er wies ferner darauf hin, daß Landes- und Bundesminister als Spitzen der Verwaltungsbehörden nicht rechtsgestaltend tätig, sondern an Recht und Gesetz gebunden seien. In jedem Behördensystem seien faktische Einflüsse jedoch nicht auszuschließen. Herr *Kochanski* erläuterte, daß das Schreiben des BMU vom 16. März 2011 an die Länder, mit denen der BMU diese aufforderte, gegenüber den Betreibern von Kernkraftwerken eine einstweilige Betriebseinstellung anzuordnen und hierbei die in dem Schreiben genannten Ausführungen zur Begründung zu verwenden, keine Weisung darstelle, aber von der Aufsichtsbehörde des Landes als solche verstanden worden sei. Die Entscheidung, das Moratorium anzuordnen, sei auf einer anderen, politischen Ebene getroffen worden.

Zu der Erläuterung von Herrn Dr. *Vorwerk*, daß vollständige Unabhängigkeit von Behörden in einer Demokratie niemals möglich sei, und zu dessen Hinweis auf einen datenschutzrechtlichen Fall (Anm. d. Red.: C-518/07), in dem der EuGH die Auffassung der Kommission bestätigt habe, Deutschland habe die Datenschutzrichtlinie 95/46/EG aufgrund unzureichender Unabhängigkeit der Behörde nicht ordnungsgemäß umgesetzt, merkte Herr *Heldt* an, bereits in den 50er Jahren habe allerdings der EuGH in der Meroni-Rechtssprechung dargelegt, daß nicht demokratisch legitimierte Organe – in diesem Fall europäische Einrichtungen – keine rechtsverbindliche Ermessensentscheidungen treffen sollten. Auf der Ebene der Mitgliedsstaaten scheine nun der EuGH aber genau dies zu fordern. Hier werde offenbar im Vergleich EU-Ebene/Mitgliedsstaaten-Ebene mit zweierlei Maß gemessen.

Mit einem Dank an die Redner, die Diskutanten und die Zuhörer schloß Dr. *Rebentisch* die Sitzung.

List of participants / Teilnehmerverzeichnis

Graham Alty
Partner
Pinsent Masons LLP
Manchester, United Kingdom

Patricia Barna
Legal Counsel
Westinghouse Electric Germany
Mannheim

Stanley Berger
Lawyer
Richmond Hill, ON, Canada

Marc Beyens
Chief Legal Officer and President
Electrabel
Brussels, Belgium

Prof. Dr. Eberhard Bohne
Universität Speyer

Khalil Bukhari
Head of Legal
International Nuclear Services
Warrington, Cheshire, UK

Stephen Burns
Head, Legal Affairs
OECD/NEA
Issy-les-Moulineaux, France

Amélie Chollet
Senior Associate, Freshfields
Bruckhaus Deringer LLP
London, UK

Markus Dapprich
F&R Services
E.ON Risk Consulting GmbH
Düsseldorf

David Davies
Chief Legal Advisor (Regulation and Legal)
Eskom Holdings SOC Limited
South Africa

Frank Deitelhoff
RWE Service GmbH
Essen

Christophe Depaus
Safety Assessor for Geological Disposal of Radioactive Waste
ONDRAF / NIRAS
Brussels, Belgium

Annette Dümmerling
E.ON Risk Consulting GmbH
Düsseldorf

Roland Dussart-Desart
Counsellor General
Belgian Ministry of the Economy
Brussels, Belgium

David Erni
Fachspezialist Recht
Bundesamt für Energie
Bern, Switzerland

Dr. Ingo Fährmann
Referent
Bundesministerium für Wirtschaft und Technologie
Berlin

Peter Faross
Director for Nuclear Safety and Fuel Cycle
European Commission
Luxembourg

Ulrike Feldmann
Justitiarin
Wirtschaftsverband Kernbrennstoff-Kreislauf e.V.
Berlin

Prof. Dr. Thomas Fetzer, LL.M. (Vanderbilt)
Lehrstuhl für Öffentliches Recht und Steuerrecht
Universität Mannheim

Dr. Akos Frank
Legal Counsel
AREVA GmbH
Erlangen

Matthias Geipel
Legal & Corporate Law Germany
Vattenfall Europe Business Services
Hamburg

Prof. Dr. Jürgen Grunwald M.C.L.
Tervuren, Belgium

Dirk Harbrücker
Managing Director
DKVG Deutsche Kernreaktor-Versicherungsgemeinschaft
Köln

Tobias Heldt
Legal Advisor and PhD Student
SCK.CEN Belgian Nuclear Research Centre
Mol, Belgium

Mark D. Herlach
Partner
Sutherland Asbill & Brennan LLP
Washington, DC, USA

Simon Hobday
Partner
Pinsent Masons LLP
London, UK

Tomoyoshi Igarashi
Japan Energy Law Institute
Tokyo, Japan

Dr. Odette Jankowitsch-Prevor
Independent Expert International & Nuclear Law
Vienna, Austria

Achim Jansen-Tersteegen
General Counsel
DKVG Deutsche Kernreaktor-Versicherungsgemeinschaft
Köln

Stefanos Kardaras
Assistant to the Director-General
EURATOM Supply Agency, EC
Luxemburg

Dr. Ulrich Karpenstein
RAe Redeker Sellner Dahs
Berlin

Kyoji Kawasaki
Prof. of International Law
Hitotsubashi University
Tokyo, Japan

Atsushi Kido
Japan Energy Law Institute
Tokyo, Japan

Wolfgang Kilb
Senior Lawyer
European Commission
Luxemburg

Stefan Kochanski
Rechtsanwalt
RWE Power AG
Essen

Boris Kolesnik
Head of Legal Department
ARMZ Uranium Holding Co.
Moscow, Russia

Dr. Guido Kraß
Rechtsanwalt, Leiter Öffentliches Recht
EnBW Systeme Infrastruktur Support GmbH
Karlsruhe

Thomas Kugler
Director, Legal Affairs & HR
Nukem Inc.
Danbury, CT, USA

Prof. Dr. Gunther Kühne
Technische Universität Clausthal
Clausthal-Zellerfeld

Stefan Kurz
Senior Consultant
E.ON Risk Consulting GmbH
Düsseldorf

Dr. Selma Kuş
Geschäftsführerin
Riskaudit IRSN / GRS International
Fontenay-aux-Roses, France

Kaan Kuzeyli
Student LLM Leiden University
Leiden, Netherlands

Maria Laguna
Underwriter
ELINI
Brussels, Belgium

Dr. Vanda Lamm
Professor
Hungarian Academy of Sciences
Institute for Legal Studies
Budapest, Hungary

Christian Lawerentz
Leiter Recht + Personal
Nukem Energy GmbH
Alzenau

Dr. Cord-Heinrich Lefhalm
RWE Power AG
Essen

Marc Léger
Head of Legal Department
CEA
Gif sur Yvette, France

Prof. Dr. Tobias Leidinger
Rechtsanwalt
Gleiss Lutz Rechtsanwälte
Düsseldorf

Rafael Mariano Manóvil
President of AIDN/INLA
M. & M. Bomchil
Buenos Aires, Argentina

Alexander Matveev
Member, Board of Management
of INLA
Geneva, Switzerland

Winfried Maus
Leiter F&R Services
E.ON Risk Consulting GmbH
Düsseldorf

Dr. Simon Mayer
Contract Manager
Chemgineering Technology GmbH
Wiesbaden

Dr. Michael Micklinghoff
Consultant
Hemmingen

Łukasz Dariusz Młynarkiewicz
PhD Candidate
Nicolaus Copernicus University
Torun, Poland

Prof. Dr. Christoph Moench
Gleiss Lutz Rechtsanwälte
Berlin

Takuya Mori
Japan Energy Law Institute
Tokyo, Japan

Dr. Christian Müller-Dehn
E.ON Kernkraft GmbH
Hannover

Hanns Näser
Justitiar
GNS Gesellschaft für
Nuklear-Service mbH
Essen

Reinhard Naß
Ltd. Reg. Dir. a. D.
Seelze

Prof. Toyohiro Nomura
Japan Energy Law Institute
Tokyo, Japan

Henny Norderyd
Manager Business Law Department
E.ON Sverige AB
Malmö, Sweden

Tomasz Nowacki
Head of Unit
Ministry of Economy
Nuclear Energy Department
Warszawa, Poland

Dr. Martina Palm
Ministerialrätin
Bundesministerium für Umwelt, Naturschutz und Reaktorsicherheit
Bonn

Dr. Norbert Pelzer
Göttingen

Markus Pfaff
Referent
Bundesministerium für Umwelt, Naturschutz und Reaktorsicherheit
Bonn

Rasa Ptasekaite
Swedish Ministry of the Environment
Stockholm, Sweden

Dr. Christian Raetzke
Rechtsanwalt
CONLAR Consulting on Nuclear Law and Regulation
Leipzig

Dr. Manfred Rebentisch
RAe CliffordChance, Düsseldorf
Mainz

Els Reynaers Kini
Partner, M. V. Kini & Co.
Advocates and Solicitors
Mumbai, India

Patrick Reyners
Consultant – INLA Scientific Coordinator
Brussels, Belgium

Marita Rickels
Niedersächsisches Ministerium für Umwelt, Energie und Klimaschutz
Hannover

Julian Rotter
Lazarski University
Warsaw, Poland

Sidonie Royer-Maucotel
In-House Lawyer
CEA
Gif sur Yvette, France

Dr. Marc Ruttloff
Gleiss Lutz Rechtsanwälte
Berlin

Ian Salter
Partner, Burges Salmon LLP
Bristol, UK

Dr. Andreas Schirra
E.ON SE
Düsseldorf

Dr. Malte Schmans
Rechtsanwalt
Hannover

Dr. Horst Schneider
former Head of Division
formerly Federal Ministry of Economics and Technology
Bonn

Dr. Holger Schramm
Prokurist
DBE
Peine

Alvin Shuttleworth
Immediate Past President, AIDN / INLA
Managing Director
Bodieco Limited
Warrington, Cheshire, UK

Risto Siilos
Senior Vice President, Deputy CEO
Teollisuuden Voima Oyj
Eurajoki, Finland

Joanne Sinar
NDA
Moor Row, Cumbria, UK

Hans Steinhauer
Geschäftsführer
Gesellschaft für Anlagen- & Reaktorsicherheit (mbH)
Köln

Dr. Daniela Stölzgen
Assistentin der Geschäftsführung
Gesellschaft für Anlagen- & Reaktorsicherheit (mbH)
Köln

Jörg Storbeck
Leiter Erzeugung Nuklear
EnBW AG
Karlsruhe

Tom Tannion
Managing Director
Overseas NEIL Ltd.
Dublin, Ireland

Prof. Dr. Bruno Thomauske
RWTH Aachen, Institut für Nuklearen Brennstoffkreislauf
Aachen

Wolfram Tonhauser
Head, Nuclear and Treaty Law Section, Office of Legal Affairs
IAEA
Vienna, Austria

Rüdiger Tscherning
Director, Center for Energy and Sustainability Law
College of Law, Qatar University
Doha, Qatar

Godelieve Vandeputte
Senior Legal Counsel
Electrabel
Brussels, Belgium

Ludo Veuchelen
Legal and Contracts Officer
SCK.CEN Belgian Nuclear Research Centre
Mol, Belgium

Dr. Axel Vorwerk
Ministerialdirigent
Bundesministerium für Umwelt, Naturschutz und Reaktorsicherheit
Bonn

Julius Friedlieb Wiesengrund Weitzdörfer
Research Associate
Max-Planck-Institut
Hamburg

Dr. Frank Winkeler
Rechtsanwalt
EnBW Systeme Infrastruktur Support GmbH
Karlsruhe

Andreas Woitecki
Bundesministerium für Umwelt, Naturschutz und Reaktorsicherheit
Bonn